to BE, or not . . .
to BOP

to BE, or not... to BOP

MEMOIRS

DIZZY GILLESPIE

with AL FRASER

Doubleday & Company, Inc.
GARDEN CITY, NEW YORK
1979

Grateful acknowledgment is made to Charlie Roisman for use of lines from his poem, *Dizzie Gillespie One Day Had to Go to Court.*

Grateful acknowledgment is made to Jon Henricks and to Henricks Music West (ASCAP) for use of the lyrics of the campaign song, "Vote Diz, Vote Diz, Vote Diz."

Except where otherwise indicated, all photos courtesy of the private collection of Dizzy Gillespie.

Library of Congress Cataloging in Publication Data

Gillespie, Dizzy, with Al Fraser
  to BE, or not . . . to BOP. Memoirs

  1. Title
ISBN: 0-385-12052-4
Library of Congress Catalog Card Number 77-76237

To my wife
LORRAINE

Her love, help, humor, and wisdom
Her unselfish and unswerving
devotion made me the man
and musician I wanted to be

Dizzy

Contents

Chronology

1939		Joins Cab Calloway Orchestra
		Records with Lionel Hampton as first modern-jazz stylist
		Jam sessions at Minton's Playhouse begin
1940	Boston, Massachusetts	Marries Lorraine Willis, May 9
	New York	Composes "Pickin' The Cabbage" and "Paradiddle"
	Chicago	Original compositions first recorded
	Kansas City, Missouri	Meets Charlie Parker
1941	New York	First recordings of modern-jazz jam session at Minton's
	Hartford, Connecticut	Separation from Cab Calloway Orchestra
	New York	Joins and separates from Ella Fitzgerald Orchestra
		Joins and separates from Coleman Hawkins Orchestra
1942		Composes "A Night In Tunisia"
		Joins and separates from Benny Carter Septet
		First performance on film sound track
		Joins and separates from Charlie Barnet Orchestra
		Joins and separates from Les Hite Orchestra
		Composes "Salt Peanuts" (Little John Special)
		Joins and separates from Lucky Millinder Orchestra
	Philadelphia	Establishes and leads his own quartet
	New York	Joins and separates from Claude Hopkins, Fess Williams, Calvin Jackson, Boyd Raeburn, and Fletcher Henderson
	Philadelphia	Joins Earl Hines Orchestra
1943	Chicago	First records with Charlie Parker
	New York	Separates from Earl Hines
		Subs with Duke Ellington Orchestra
		Becomes musical director of Billy Eckstine Orchestra
1944		Composes "Woody 'n You"
		First modern-jazz studio-recording session
		Separates from Billy Eckstine Orchestra
		Co-leader of first modern-jazz quartet/quintet
		Wins *Esquire* New Star Award
		Composes "Bebop"
1945		First recording session as bandleader
		Organizes and disbands first Dizzy Gillespie Orchestra
	Hollywood, California	First modern-jazz performance on the West Coast

1946	New York	Organizes second Dizzy Gillespie Orchestra
		Composes "Things to Come"
		First appearance on film
		Emergence of bebop cult, anti-bebop campaign
1947		First featured at Carnegie Hall Concert
		Meets Chano Pozo
1948	Paris, France	Dizzy Gillespie Orchestra tours Europe
		Composes "Manteca," "Cubana Be Cubana Bop" and "Tin Tin Deo"
		Receives diploma from Laurinburg Institute
		Chano Pozo dies
1950	Chicago	Disbands Dizzy Gillespie Orchestra
	New York	Reorganizes Dizzy Gillespie Sextet/Quintet
		Begins tours with JATP
	Paris, France	Tours Europe with small bands
1951	Detroit	Establishes Dee Gee Record Company
1953		Dee Gee Record Company closes
	New York	Trumpet bent upward in accident on January 6
	Toronto, Canada	Jazz at Massey Hall Concert
1954	Newport, Rhode Island	Performs at first Newport Jazz Festival
1955	New York	Charlie Parker dies March 12
	Lennox, Massachusetts	Opening of school of jazz
	Houston, Texas	Arrested at JATP Concert
1956	Washington, D.C.	First jazz musician appointed by U. S. Department of State to undertake cultural mission
	Overseas	Reorganizes Dizzy Gillespie Orchestra and travels to Africa, Near East, Asia, and Eastern Europe
		Travels to South America
1957	New York	Composes "Con Alma"
1959	Springfield, Massachusetts	Mother dies in November
	New York	Performs publicly for the first time with Louis Armstrong
	Cheraw, South Carolina	Performs at first integrated concert in public school
		Discovers direct link to African ancestry
1960	New Orleans	Tulane University cancels Gillespie concert because of segregation law
1962	New York	Records with quintet first U.S. album of Bossa Nova music

1964   Los Angeles   Campaigns to become President of the
                            United States of America
       New York   Soloist on soundtrack for film *The Cool
                            World*

1965   London   Composes dialogue and music for *The Hat*
                            an animated film on "World Armaments
                            Control"

1968   Memphis, Tennessee   Martin Luther King, Jr., assassinated
       Los Angeles   Accepts the Baha'i faith

1971   New York   Louis Armstrong dies, July 18

1972   New York   Awarded Handel Medallion from City of
                            New York
                            Hospitalized after heart stops beating
       Nairobi, Kenya   Guest of the government of Kenya
                            Receives Paul Robeson Award from Rutgers
                            University Institute of Jazz Studies

1976   Columbia,   Performs for and addresses Joint Session of
          South Carolina   the State Legislature of South Carolina

1977   Havana, Cuba   Visits Cuba, ending trade embargo
       Washington, D.C.   Performs at White House for President Car-
                            ter and guest, the Shah of Iran

1978   Performs "Salt Peanuts" with President Car-
                            ter at White House Jazz Concert, June 18

NEW LYRICS TO MANTECA
by Al Fraser

Georgia was a place
Tried to put down (and hang)
The human race

I'll never go back to Georgia
Never go back to Georgia

Wouldn't let us have nothin' to say (except yowzah)
Somethin' always stood in the way
Of freedom

Never go back to Georgia
Never go back to Georgia

We knew the time had come
For making earth a place of peace and love
Just
The way it was intended by our God above
Amen

Took a peaceful man whose name was King
And we changed almost everything in Georgia

Now, I love to go to Georgia
Love to go to Georgia . . .
But I'll never go back!

Preface

We began this book five years go with the aim of creating the best—the most complete, authentic, and authoritative autobiography of a jazz musician ever published. Humbled now by the many difficulties inherent in such a task, we must first thank God for our being able to complete this still imperfect and much tempered version of our originally ambitious goal.

Our title comes from an incident which occurred recently in London's Hyde Park. A little English girl was selling plaster statuettes of the great bard, William Shakespeare, the ones with the question mark hanging above his head and the famous line "To be, or not to be?" inscribed on the base. Dizzy Gillespie was walking through the park that day and stopped to talk with her. She made him a gift of a statuette. "Oh, thank you," he said, "I love it. But you should change that line on the bottom."

"To what?" she asked.

"Make it, to BE, or not . . . to BOP," he replied, just jiving. And do you know she did it? He came back the next day, and she'd changed them all to bop, hundreds of them, with countless numbers more to come from the same mold. Now the entire English-speaking world—the whole world—accepts the more modern line. And since she was the first to write it, the title belongs to her. She will probably never know it though, unless she's been educated since then.

One means of gaining knowledge is through education. However ambitious, no one, artist or otherwise, can be successful in achieving his life's goals without knowledge and education. We therefore take off our caps in gratitude to Mrs. Alice V. Wilson of Cheraw, South Carolina, an educator, who many years ago started an unruly schoolboy, John Birks (later Dizzy) Gillespie, playing jazz and educating himself in music. A huge debt is owed to the folk at Laurinburg Institute, North Carolina, who found him later at a crucial point in his life, penniless and hungry, and gratuitously fed him, pointed and pushed him toward more knowledge of himself, music, and the world around him.

Today Dizzy is of great and definite historical importance in jazz. For over forty years he has enjoyed a career as a virtuoso trumpeter and the exalted status of a musical innovator. His music, bebop, "has stood the test of time," and he has remained prominent in the public eye despite many changes in musical vogue that followed his own exceptionally durable pioneering efforts—the modern and Afro-Cuban styles he introduced during the 1940s. By noting his personal and musical transitions, we have tried to discern what happened to him, when and why? Were there any triggering incidents, any implications of his personal example that might benefit other younger musicians? Approaching the development of Dizzy Gillespie, the man and his music, from an ordered perspective, seeking truth by sketching and describing in detail his passage through different eras from early childhood to great maturity, *to BE, or not . . . to BOP* is more a history than a musicology. For this reason, Diz finally chose a historian with some musical background, whom he trusts and has known personally for twenty-five years, to write this book of memoirs.

Writing Dizzy Gillespie's personal memoirs, though interesting and challenging, was not an easy job. Preparations for writing required collecting and combing the literature, photographs, phonograph records, films, and videotapes Dizzy has accumulated. We arranged and conducted over 150 taped interviews, many of them with busy show people who were always on the move and justifiably jealous of their privacy. Dizzy's own statements were then compared and contrasted with those of other knowledgeable informants on every pertinent topic, including personal life, religion, musical development, and the impact of jazz (Dizzy's music in particular) on social life, popular culture, show business economics, national politics, and international affairs. The object of all this, especially our efforts to reveal Dizzy's aesthetic philosophy ("progressive development") and explain his religion and personal approach to life, was to get closer to the liberating truth about him—not to convince the world about anything, or anyone, else.

To BE, or not . . . to BOP focuses mainly on Dizzy but, by necessity, touches on the evolution of modern jazz, a whole beautiful and powerful body of music, the partial foundations of which were contributed by others. Support for this project, similarly, has been forthcoming from many people. Our deepest, most heartfelt thanks go out to all those who sat for interviews. For reasons of space, and to avoid needless repetition, certain interviews, regrettably, had to be shortened or entirely deleted. But all of them were great as were the relatives, friends, colleagues, and associates who selflessly shared their valuable time and printable comments.

Several important contributors to jazz and to this book, Teddy Hill, Buddy Johnson and Duke Garrett, have passed away since we began this work. Our only major regret is that they did not live to see it published. These artists who responded to us with the immense and vital enthusiasm and generosity characteristic of jazzmen have now answered the ultimate in clarion calls. God rest and bless their souls with eternal happiness.

The life and career of Dizzy Gillespie have been copiously documented over decades by many jazz writers, historians, discographers, and filmographers. We express profound appreciation for their mind-jogging assistance.

Without the skillful, dedicated, and invaluable aid of archivists, researchers, and typists—Gail Hansberry, Alexander Stewart, Joanna Williams Dovi, and Joan Ramsey—our manuscript would never have been completed on time.

The staff at Doubleday has done much to shoulder the burden of production and assisted us in making this book a fitting tribute to a wonderfully rewarding artistic career. While reading it, we modestly hope you can receive some enlightening enjoyment. Presenting it to you, finally, makes us both feel dizzily proud.

Dizzy Gillespie and Al Fraser

to BE, or not . . .
to BOP

Tan Yo' Hide

The pictures show me as a very beautiful baby, but I was the last of nine children and my arrival probably didn't excite anybody. So many people had been born at our house before. I don't think Mama felt too blessed about having nine children, unless "blessed" means "wounded" like it does in French. She probably figured someone had put the bad mouth on us.

Every Sunday morning, Papa would whip us. That's mainly how I remember him. He was usually mean; and hated to see or hear about his children misbehaving. "Wesley! John! Come on and get your whipping!" He'd tell us good morning that way, sometimes before we could wake up good, and we'd have to go on up to him and take it. Papa was big and bad, waving that strap. Sometimes, I'd holler, "But I didn't do nothing," try to duck him and hide up under the bed. As soon as I bent over and tried to get away, "Whack!" he'd hit me again; Papa never missed.

"Well, what did you do wrong?" people always ask when I tell them that my father used to beat me every Sunday. I have to explain it to them over and over again. They find it hard to believe that the whippings I got were for anything and everything that I'd done during the week because Papa was sure that I must've done something wrong in that span of time. Papa believed that a hard head made a soft behind. He treated us that way because he wanted us all to be tough and he turned me into a tough little rebel, very early, against everyone but him. He was a real man, who roared when he talked, because with so many kids around he had to be strong. I was scared of him, but after a while, I started doing some bad things to warrant all of those whippings.

Only seven of us lived long enough to get a name. Edward Leroy (Sonny) my eldest brother was born in 1900, but he died in the thirties, before I moved to Philadelphia in 1935. Sonny left home when I was only about six years old so I don't actually remember him too well.

Mattie Laura, James Penfield, Jr. (J.P.), Hattie Marie, Eugenia, and Wesley were my other brothers and sisters. My parents, James and Lottie (Powe) Gillespie, christened me John Birks soon after my birth in Cheraw, South Carolina, on October 21, 1917.

JAMES PENFIELD GILLESPIE (brother):

"Well, John was a devil all his life. I remember when he was born, for that matter. All his life. He was just a little different I suppose. I guess he had something that nobody else had. I was very young myself when I left there.

"The reason I ran away was because my father was mean. He was a real mean man. In fact, John and Wes told me he used to beat them every Sunday morning. I wasn't there, as I said, 'cause I had left. My father was wild about the girls, but he never did treat us like I think a father should treat a son. Everybody thought he was a big shot, this and that, you know.

"Once we were remodeling a house. He was a brickmason and builder, and there was a fella there who was twice as old as I, and because I couldn't carry as much mortar as this boy did, Papa told me if I didn't bring as much as this boy did, he was gonna . . . And I didn't know how. I was about twelve or fourteen years old. I couldn't even lift that bucket of mortar, but I tried like hell. I came in with half a bucket of mortar and put it down. He took one of those laths, a big piece of wood, and like to broke my neck.

"So I say, 'Next time? This is it!' That's when I stole my brother's bag and I was gonna hobo, but I got on the train and got scared and I almost jumped off in the river.

"But sometimes he was kind. Papa was a musician and he bought me a piano. It was one of those big upright pianos, and you couldn't get it in the house. They had to tear out half the side of the house to get the piano in. Because at that time he was traveling. He would be in Philadelphia and Newark, New Jersey, working. I think that piano came from Philadelphia, and he sent it home to me. I took the lessons. As a matter of fact, I was the only one in the family that took music as a child. I took private lessons, and I took music in school. I had a special tutor. Major McFarland was my music teacher. But I never followed it up or anything like that. In other words it wasn't my bag.

"Papa was a nut, that's all I can say. I used to hear him talk about his two brothers, Andrew and Nick. They'd fight crackers and did some of everything. They left Cheraw and went to Georgia. When one of 'em died, they laid him out on the porch. I heard my father say the white folks came and spit tobacco juice in his face while he was laying there 'cause they were scared to go near him when he was alive. So there musta been sumpn' mean that ran in the family. Papa was just mean. Even with all of the things that he did for me, like with the piano, he never thought about taking me to a ball game, like some fathers'll do, or taking you fishing or sumpn'. I dunno what he expected, but I knew if I stayed there and I got old enough, sumpn' would happen desperately, so I left. Diz wasn't but about four or five years old. This was in the early twenties."

Being born last into a large and poor family, my brothers and sisters used to push me around too. My sister Eugenia pushed me out of a window once in the house next door to ours in Cheraw. This was an abandoned house, and on the other side of it was a house owned by Mr. Glees, a brother of Mr. Harrington who owned the house on the opposite side of ours. These men had different names because, during slavery, one had been sold to the Glees while the other had been sold to the Harringtons. I used to always wonder why they never changed their names to show the fact that they were brothers. When I was a child, that abandoned place on the Glees side of our house was an attraction for me. I loved to play there all the time, stoop in the window and look out.

Eugenia caught me in there one day while I was stooping, sneaked up, and pushed me out of the window. I fell out on my head, hit a piece of glass, and started bleeding. When I found out how badly I was cut, it scared me. I ran home and told Mama that Eugenia had pushed me out of the window. My head was all bloody.

"You fell?" Mama asked.

"Mama, I didn't fall. Genia pushed me out of that window," I told her.

"You're sure you didn't fall?"

"No, Mama, I didn't fall. Genia pushed me," I insisted. Mama shooed me away and didn't even wipe off the blood. She wouldn't believe me. Until this day, Eugenia hasn't been punished for pushing me out of that window. Eugenia never liked me very much and she used to pinch me all the time. I can't remember her saying a kind word to me all the time that we were children.

Eugenia took care of all the other children. My first cousins and the kids in the neighborhood all loved her. She used to baby-sit a lot with them when baby-sitting was known as 'takin' care a' someone's child. Because she was good with children and would watch them and clean them, everyone loved her. But she never babied me nor Wesley. She used to say that we were too wild.

EUGENIA GILLESPIE (sister):

"John, was always mischievous. He would fight the other children. Wesley was more quiet than him. That's why, I guess, he tried to rule Wesley.

"John and Wesley and myself grew up together. My other sister, Hattie Marie, did too. He always said I put my tongue out at him all the time and made him mad. He always says that I didn't like him much. Because I used to tease and make him so mad; I guess that's why he said that.

"Pushed him out of the window in Mr. Glees's house? Well, I guess I did. My mother had a cabinet where they would put up jars preserving things where they used to keep glassware and stuff. It stood on the floor. Mama would put up preserves in these bottles. So John got on a chair—that's how mischievous he was—and climbed up on the cabinet, and it fell on him. And then Mama just *knew* he was dead. 'Oh, my God, my chile,' she said. We pulled the cabinet off him, and he's sitting on the floor with all this preserve and things on his face, *laughing*. That was too much, you know."

Paw, my grandfather, on my mother's side, was the only one of my grandparents who lived long enough for me to know. He lived down in an old house at the back of our yard. He was a very warm and funny guy and always kept a little bottle of something to nip on. Paw worked at a restaurant in town, and every weekend when he'd get paid, he and his friend, Mr. Johnson, would stand out in front of our house and put on a show.

Paw would get a little high and tell Mr. Johnson, "You know, I feel so good that I could shout."

"Don't shout," Mr. Johnson would say, "because you know what they'll do; they'll lock you up."

"I feel so good that I could shout anyway." Paw would get louder, and Mr. Johnson would pretend to try to keep him quiet.

"They're going to lock you up, now."

"I don't care what they do to me, I'm gonna shout out loud anyway!"

By then he would be screaming at the top of his voice. Mr. Johnson would get real nervous and start running away from there.

Paw would yell "WHOOOOOPEE!" but he knew how to control the sound so it would come out just above a whisper. Mr. Johnson and all of us around would go to pieces laughing. Paw kept us laughing with his great gift for comedy. That technique of "big mouthing" softly, which I still use in my act today, I learned directly from him.

Wildness never kept me from being kind though, and one old lady named Mrs. Bates and I also had a great friendship. Mrs. Bates must've been in her seventies or eighties; her hair had turned completely white, and she walked with a cane. We both used to attend Wesley Methodist Episcopal Church. From the time I reached four years old until I left Cheraw in 1933, every Sunday morning I'd stand in front of the church and wait for Mrs. Bates. She couldn't climb stairs alone, so I would wait there, open the door of her car, and help her walk up the stairs into the church. No one paid me for it. I don't know how I wound up with that gig, but Mrs. Bates and her family really appreciated my help. Even now, anytime I see someone from the Bates family, they're absolutely wild about me. Helping that old lady was my good deed on Sunday and I cried a lot when she died.

Until I was four years old, I had these curls hanging down to my shoulders like a hippie. I felt so proud of those curls that I was actually conceited. A long, long time went by before I would let them be cut. When I went out with my mother and someone looked at my long hair and said, "Oh, what a cute little boy," I'd always answer, "Oh, do you think so?" I would never say thank you or anything else to show gratitude.

My family forced me to get my first haircut. My uncle, Ernest Williams, cut it all off one night after he came from working in Mr. Charlie Robinson's barbershop. Charlie Robinson owned one of those barbershops that hired all colored barbers for help, but only a white man could go there to get a haircut. It was a hangover from slavery and Charlie Robinson became the richest black man in town. Even during the Depression, he drove four cars and had his own privately pumped water supply. Everyone else had to go to the well to draw water. Charlie Robinson's grandson owned a pony and a little cart that trailed behind it just like a little rich kid. All the children used to envy him.

We never had to worry about being spoiled by riches in our house. Papa had to work two jobs to support us. During the week he was a bricklayer, and on weekends he played piano with his band. Papa always treated Mama well, though, and whenever he had the money, bought her real expensive gifts. Sometimes Papa brought home candy for us hidden in the top pockets of his white brickmason's overalls. We kids climbed all over him, when he was acting kind like that, and searched through his pockets trying to find the candy. He'd fall apart laughing at us scrambling.

Papa kept the instruments from his band at our house during the week to prevent the other less responsible musicians from hocking them to someone. There wasn't even any pawnshop in Cheraw. People were so poor, the cat you pawned your horn to might pawn it to someone else. You'd have to go all around town looking for your horn. Papa was really a music lover, and he spent all his extra money on instruments. We had a piano, a guitar, a set of drums, a mandolin, and a big red one-stringed bass fiddle laying around our front room.

With so many instruments around, I got the chance very early to learn something about them, touch and feel them, and hear how they sounded. Papa forced all of my older brothers and sisters to take piano lessons, and he used to make them practice. If they had been musically inclined, Papa wouldn't have had to make them practice. None of them really had any eyes for playing. I was only ten when Papa died, so he never even knew about my playing the trumpet.

School Days

Next door to us lived Mrs. Amanda Harrington, a former schoolteacher. Her husband, Mr. Son Harrington, a shoemaker by trade, owned an ice cream parlor at the front of his shoe shop where my brother Wesley used to work shaving ice and making milk shakes. Her son, James ("Brother") Harrington, owned the first trumpet I ever played. I used to love to visit Mrs. Harrington because she kept an icebox full of ice cream. All day long while the men and the other kids were at work or away at school, I ran back and forth between my house and the Harringtons'. When I wasn't running, I would bang on our piano. I could hardly reach the keys and wasn't old enough to understand the meaning of music, but I knew how to play "Coon Shine Lady," a two-fingered tune I liked to fool around with, and would play that tune all day. Mrs. Amanda thought I was a bright four-year-old because she used to hear me playing. The Harringtons also had a piano, and after spending time with the lady of the house and eating ice cream, I'd drum out another half hour or so of "Coon Shine Lady."

Mrs. Amanda must've gotten tired of hearing that song, so she decided to teach me the alphabet, how to count, and how to read. She made up a kind of preschool program, like the ones they've just started recently. Her experiment with me turned out fine. By the time I was five, old enough to enter the primer grade, I knew my alphabet,

I could count to over one hundred, and could read a little. I used to show off what I knew around the house, and everybody figured my first day in school would be brilliant because I really loved learning.

They named the first school that I attended in honor of Robert Smalls, one of the black heroes. During the Civil War, Robert Smalls captured a Confederate ship and helped a whole lot of his fellow slaves to escape. When the blacks came to power in South Carolina during Reconstruction and could vote, they elected him to represent the state in Congress. He went to Washington to speak so that they could get some land. You know, the forty acres and a mule the U. S. Government promised us, but never delivered. Segregation came and turned around most of his work. The school that I attended, which was named after this great black man, never taught us three words about him. I was over forty years old before I found out. Now, that seems strange. Our teachers should have at least told us about Smalls, because they made us pay attention to everything else we were told or suffer the consequences.

A quaintly pretty little school, Robert Smalls had one little wooden building on the side of Front Street that housed the primer grades and a larger brick building that housed the first through the ninth grades. This little wooden building on the side had only one story. After you stepped off the sidewalk onto the school grounds, you'd go up these little brick stairs, and right there in front, every morning, we'd have our assembly. We'd have to stand at attention and sing, "Lift every voice and sing, 'til earth and heaven ring . . ." and then, afterward, we'd sing, "Oh, say can you see . . ." each day. I really enjoyed that part of school and couldn't wait to get into the classroom. My first teacher, Mrs. Astrada Miller, put us into a line, and we marched off to class behind her. After we had taken our seats, she began teaching us to recite the alphabet.

Naturally, that first lesson bored me, because I already knew the alphabet. I began whistling in the classroom.

Mrs. Miller believed the rules of the school were the most important thing and got very angry. She called me up to the front of the class, took a switch that she kept on her desk, and beat me on my legs. I ran out of the classroom and didn't stop running until I got home and told Mama, but she wouldn't say anything to console me.

When Papa came home and heard about it, he was burned up. He jumped up from the table and went right across the street to the principal's house, Professor Butts. I followed him part of the way then dropped off and hid around the corner listening.

"If this woman ever puts her hands on my kids again . . ." I heard Papa tell Professor Butts in a loud voice. "It's the first day of school, and he doesn't know any of the rules. He doesn't know anything, and she beat him the first day. She'd better not touch him no more!"

They'd probably call Papa an "irate parent" today, but I sure felt proud listening to him from around the corner.

After Professor Butts told Mrs. Miller not to touch me again, she became more inquisitive and serious about teaching me. The second day of school, she brought out these alphabets again, and I ran through them for her, "A B C D E F G . . ." Then she searched around and found some numbers, and I counted for her. "Where'd you learn that?" she asked, but I wouldn't answer her except to say that I already knew what she was trying to teach me. After I had spent about a month in the primer grade, they promoted me.

They pushed me up into the first grade, and I spent a lot of time getting into mischief in class and putting all sorts of stuff into the inkwells. I used to mash chewing gum into the hair of every girl that I could lay my hands on, and was so mean they thought I was going to be a gangster. The teacher, Miss Catherine Lynch, used to put me in the closet. She'd beat me until I'd threaten to tell my mother, then she'd stop whipping me and put me in a dark closet. It was only in the cloakroom where they kept the coats, but the door was closed on me, and I could have suffocated. She'd make me stay there for half-hours at a time. I was terrified of that closet and could see all sorts of things. Miss Lynch banished me to the closet regularly, but I passed the first grade without getting killed.

In the second grade I caught up with my brother, Wesley, who was two and a half years older. I imagine Wes felt pretty strange. But he didn't say anything to me about it except to ask, "What's the answer to this . . . ?" and, "What's the answer to that . . . ?" If I had put my whole soul into it, I might have caught up with Genia, but I felt satisfied to go through school with Wesley. We went all the way from second to ninth grade together.

Our teacher in second grade, Miss Emma Lowry, used to beat me with a strap. But she didn't really know how to whip. The strap would fly right back and hit her every time she'd hit me. She'd wind up whipping herself, and that made her mad because the other kids would laugh. Miss Lowry was whipping me one day, and I threatened her, "I'm gonna' tell my mama!"

"I'm going to give you something to go and tell her," she said.

All of the classrooms had potbellied wood and coal stoves, and Miss Lowry grabbed me. "I'm going to put you in that stove," she said. That red-hot stove was just crackling. When I looked at her, I could see the fire in her eyes. I thought she would really put me in that stove. I cooled out in a hurry and was good for about three days afterward. The fire in her eyes and the image of that roaring hot stove were just too convincing for me to believe that she had just been kidding. I didn't know it, but Miss Lowry and Mama had gone to school together. She was my mother's classmate, so my little threat didn't scare her at all.

I'd pick a fight over anything. All a guy had to do was come up and put out a handful of sand, and I'd flick it off. And all the time I'm flicking, I'm punching at the same time. I'd hit him and kick him both. In the third grade, I was in class with one Daniel Pegues. Everybody else, when they found out that I could really fight and would fight to the end, kept away from me. Everybody except Daniel, who also liked to do battle. We fought all through the third, fourth, fifth, and sixth grades. Throughout those years—every day—we had a standing invitation to fight. I'd whip him sometimes, and sometimes he'd get me. That old Daniel Pegues had a hard head, harder than a rock. I almost broke my fist on his head.

Daniel may have helped me a lot because all that hostility I vented on him made it easier for me to get along with my teachers. In the third and fourth grades when my fights with him began, I first started to take a real interest in school.

I developed an intelligent approach to English because I liked to conjugate verbs. I could conjugate a verb faster than anyone, especially if the teacher gave away nickels for the right answers. English became my best subject, and I was a good speller too. Most of the time, now, when I can say something, I can also spell it. I find it useful, and I surprise a lot of people when I write down names in foreign languages that I've heard but have never seen spelled. Another reason that I began taking school seriously in the third grade is that my teacher, Mrs. Alice Wilson, became my mentor and, later, the greatest early influence in my development as a musician.

Ice Cream City

In 1926, during the middle of the "Negro Renaissance," black music, jazz, raged in New York and all throughout the country. Colored America enjoyed fairly good times, better than any since Reconstruction. While the Negro remained "in vogue," more money than usual floated around. Some of it must have trickled down to Cheraw because Papa's pockets regularly had the mumps with candy, and Mama received more new gifts than ever. Papa put on a big show that summer. He decided to give Mama, my brothers, and me a long trip north to Philadelphia and New York. We should have been going to visit the moon, I became so excited about it.

"Boy, did you put your clothes in that suitcase yet?" Mama asked me.

"Yes'm," I responded. "I did that yesterday."

Mama laughed at her nine-year-old, but the idea of taking that trip made her happy too. All her friends came over the night before we left. They helped with the last-minute packing and helped my sisters prepare some fried chicken for our box lunch so we wouldn't get hungry on the train. Negroes had to carry along some good food while they traveled during those days, because the dining cars were segregated, and you'd either have to starve or eat dried-up ham sandwiches the whole way. They had a peach pie and fresh bread baking in the oven. Ice cream seemed to be the only thing missing from our travel

menu. I knew that I'd want some of it before we arrived in Philadelphia.

When the train came in the next morning, they had to pull me back
from the tracks because I stepped too close to the yellow caution line
and could have gotten mashed up under the wheels. I just couldn't
wait to get on the train and sit by the window to wave good-by to
Papa and my sisters when we pulled away. Wesley let me have the
window seat. After the train began to puff, shake, and slowly move,
we both stood up at the window waving. My sisters all laughed and
waved back at us, except Genia. She looked right at Wesley and me
and started crying. Probably she envied us and was angry because we
wouldn't be there that summer for her to boss us around. As the train
picked up speed and Cheraw lay behind us, I felt absolutely thrilled. I
had never been on anything that moved so fast. I started getting hungry and looked across the aisle at Mama to ask her for some chicken
and peach pie, but she made me wait until later.

We went to Philadelphia to visit my father's sister, Aunt Rose. Our
stay at her house really opened up things for me. Every morning before Aunt Rose left for work, she used to put fruit on the table for
Stetson and Ralph, my two cousins. Since my brother and I were
there, she left some for us too. I began to see how good you could eat
in a small family. Papa and Mama just couldn't afford to do those
kinds of things for us.

While we were visiting, they held a Horn and Hardart picnic
out at Woodside Park. Aunt Rose's husband, Uncle Henry, bought
some tickets, and the whole tribe of us took the trolley and went
to the park. That picnic really floored me; I'd never seen anything
like it. There was food for days, and everything was free. I could
never remember having enough of anything that I liked to eat, especially sweet stuff. My father would put candy in his pockets, but we
never could afford much ice cream. That day at the picnic, I ate so
much ice cream, and to top it off, white people were serving us and
smiling and I had never seen that before. All over the park that day,
colored and white kids were laughing and playing baseball together.
At first, when I saw that the guy behind the ice cream stand was
white, I only asked for a little bit of chocolate. When I saw he was
smiling, I asked for some vanilla. Then I tried another flavor and I
didn't stop sampling ice cream flavors until after I'd tasted about
twelve or thirteen different ones. I couldn't eat it all, but I just
couldn't stand to see it all there without tasting it since it was free. I
knew then that I wanted to come North again, maybe even to stay. But
we went to New York and then back to Cheraw.

Hard Times

A great depression, sudden and devastating, overwhelmed my family two years earlier than the one which closed all the banks and left people out of work and hungry in 1929. Our family was struggling hopefully at the time, with all the adolescent hands we had coming of age, thinking we might beat poverty, but this thing knocked the wind out of us.

I remember that morning well. June 1927. Wesley had gone out early to pick blackberries. He liked to go to the patch real early in the morning while it was still dark, to pick berries with the dew still on them. I got up just a little while later because of some commotion. A dog, looking glassy-eyed and frothing at the mouth, was running loose in our yard. We all suspected that it might have rabies. Mad dogs were something to be feared at that time in Cheraw, especially during the summer. They didn't vaccinate dogs then. We were searching for someone with a gun to shoot it. Papa made us run down the street, call Mr. Bert Norwood, and tell him to bring his gun. Mr. Bert came up to our house in a few minutes with a loaded .45. He stood about ten feet from the dog and put a bullet through its head. The poor animal just dropped over on its side and died. We dragged the carcass by the tail to the back yard of the empty house next door and buried it.

A short while afterward, Papa had an attack of asthma. It was a bad one, and he couldn't breathe. Mama came outside and we helped

Papa into the house and put him to bed. Then I turned around and went back outside and was surprised to find Wesley there.

Wesley had gone to pick blackberries, but he had come back before going all the way to the patch in Huckleberry. Something had told him to turn around and come back. Suddenly, I heard my mother crying in the bedroom, and no one had to tell me. I knew that my father had died. The asthma attack had killed him. I started running out of the yard and over to my Aunt Kate's on Huger Street and told her that my father had died. I turned and kept running one more block down to High Street and told Aunt Hattie and Aunt Laura. I reached Aunt Honey's house last, breathless and tired out, and told her. Then, slowly, I walked back home.

They embalmed Papa's body in the house. Mr. Marshall was the undertaker. They took out Papa's entrails and buried them outside in a hole dug up under the cedar tree. Old people used the cedar tree when they were ironing. You cut off a branch of the cedar tree and you wiped the iron clean, because the iron was coming right out of the ashes from the fireplace. The cedar wood wipes the hot iron clean, gets the ashes off, and you can go on ironing. I remember getting a strange feeling whenever I would go near that spot under the cedar tree.

At the funeral, I couldn't bring myself to cry. Everyone else was crying, especially Mama. I tried to console her, "Mama, Mama, don't cry, don't cry." I must've said it so many times. "Shut up!" she told me and went back to crying again. After the funeral, all I could do was go on back to school. Most of my classmates were sympathetic, but a guy named Buddy Sharper told me that my father had died and "gone to hell." That provoked a fight, and I almost killed him.

Poverty hit us right in the face after my father's death. We even felt poor, especially on holidays. Everyone else got new outfits for Easter, but after 1927, no one in our family received any new clothes for Easter. We were so poor that Mama didn't have enough money to buy food, much less clothes, and we started to become ashamed about not having anything. Before that time my mother never worked because my father was really a breadwinner from way back. My father left us savings. But in 1929 the president of Cheraw's bank, where my father had his money, absconded with all the money. All my father's savings that he left us were gone. Then they closed the bank; no one ever got their money back. My mother had four dependent children, with no income. You can imagine the deprivation.

Mama was taking in laundry but never got paid very much for it. There was no such thing as welfare; so year in and year out she could never afford to buy us new clothes for Easter. We'd feel too ashamed to face anyone without having new clothes to wear, and so we'd go way down into the woods, to the grape orchards, and hide. We'd pretend we were having a picnic by taking a little bit to eat and staying there all day Sunday, but all of us knew that we were ashamed to be poor. We'd work some, chopping lightwood and kindling, and bring a lot of it home so Mama would have something to burn for fuel while she was ironing.

Wesley cut so much wood that in the middle of the night he started to have nightmares. He'd see the woodman, an old ugly white man that used to sell wood. He was the ugliest soul. I don't think I've ever seen anybody as ugly as this guy. Wesley would wake up saying, "The woodman's gonna get me," and I'd have to put a lock on him and hold him in bed.

Anger got control of me after Papa died, and instead of grieving I became real mean and used to do all kinds of devilish things. I used to beat one guy, Buck Brower, down to the ground then jump on top of him and make him say his prayers, "Faddah, Faddah, I need a teacher!" Then I'd let him go. Another guy named Walt I used to tease about not being completely together upstairs. He was knock-kneed and would chase me, but he could never catch me when I ran. One day I started teasing him, "Old crazy Walt ain't got no sense . . . he ain't got no sense!" Walt had an ax in his hand. He threw it at me and missed me by about a centimeter. I never messed with him no more.

A man named Mr. Chapman threw a pitchfork at me once for making a path through his cotton patch. After he had warned me about it, I kept crossing the patch just to challenge him. I should have known Mr. Chapman was dangerous. He owned a real big white horse that was wild and mean and it would bite you or stomp you to death. Everybody in town with any sense got off the street whenever that horse came by.

I was dangerous even in playing. Once, we were playing African, using sharpened sticks for spears, and I threw my spear and stuck my cousin Clee, a real nice guy who I admired, right through his nose. We used to steal watermelons from Mr. Brown who owned this beautiful watermelon patch down near Wilsonia. We'd thump the melons to find out if they were ripe, choose the best ones, pull out the heart—the sweetest part—eat it and waste the rest. Mr. Brown had threatened to shoot Wesley, Clee, and me many times for stealing his crops, and he came out in the field one day with a loaded shotgun and caught us stealing watermelons. I don't know how we escaped. Watermelon vines are so low to the ground that you have to be as small as a doodlebug to get under them. Never try to hide your head under a watermelon vine with buckshot flying around your ass.

In school, Mrs. Butts once got so angry with me for talking loud in class that she grabbed me and started choking me. I picked up an eraser to hit her, and she quickly turned me loose. Erasers were pretty heavy in those days.

Mrs. Butts and I later became great friends though. She used to feed me. After her husband, Professor Butts, died, since they lived right across the street from me, I'd go over and offer my services, asking if there was anything that I could do to help her. Mama was only making $1.50 a week for four people to live on, so there was never enough food at home. After we'd nearly killed each other in class, Mrs. Butts ended up keeping me alive.

I tried everything I knew to help Mama. The trouble was I just didn't know very much. I could only find little odd jobs around Cheraw. Mama did washing for a white woman, Mrs. Mulloy, so whenever Mrs. Mulloy needed the grass cut, I'd mow it. When I'd finish with the whole lawn, she'd pay me something like fifteen cents. I'd say, "Thank you." She'd say, "Aren't you going to say 'ma'am'?"

I told her that I'd never seen that form in English books. She got mad and said, "Yeah, but you're going to call me ma'am." She fired me because I wouldn't call her "ma'am" and eat crap for fifteen cents.

I stood around the Lyric Theatre all day, so much that the manager saw me and asked me to watch and keep people from sneaking in. They'd let me see the movies for free. I saw Ken Maynard, Bob Steele, Tom Mix and Tony, all the Western stars of the thirties, but my main man was Yakima Canutt. He was always the second leading man, but he was bad. Sometimes he got killed, but he was a good fighter and a good gunslinger. He used to wear chaps, and when he had them on, he would always win. I used to like the serials most of all. At the end you'd see a guy hanging from a tree off a cliff and you'd think, "Gee, how is he going to get out of that?"

I saw Bill Robinson in the Shirley Temple films. I remember he didn't impress me very much. As a dancer, great, but to me Bill Robinson was living in another era. To me he was just another Uncle Remus shuffling through the film. But I knew he was a big Cotton Club star. Then I saw Duke Ellington in one of those *Big Broadcast* movies in the early thirties! Duke Ellington. They were all dressed up in white tails. I had a lot of respect for that.

One day at the Lyric a white boy sneaked in. They found him and kicked him out. He knew I had told on him and swore he would get me for it. When I ran into him again, he had six or eight other guys with him.

"Niggah! You're the one told about me going in the theater, ain't ya?"

This guy must have been about sixteen or seventeen, much bigger, older, and taller than I was. He didn't know how tough I could be. I used to fight peckerwoods all the way home. They'd call you a niggah in a minute, and I wouldn't take it. They'd tell you that you were "colored" and all that, but I never considered myself inferior to white people. No one could make me feel inferior. I would always fight it. I always knew I was something special.

I first realized a social difference between black and white people because of a little white boy at home named John Duvall. My mother used to wash for them, and we'd be out in the yard playing. I must have been seven or eight. We were tight, very, very tight. We were inseparable. The color situation never arises at that age; but the moment you hit eleven or twelve, you become aware of other things. My mama called me in the house one day and said, "Look, you gotta stop playing with that little white boy." I said, "Huh?" But there was a tacit agreement between my mother and the Mulloys that we wouldn't be tight no more. I was shocked. We were both shocked. And mad. But after that, we didn't play together any more. Years later I was playing in Miami, and this bald-headed white fella came backstage and said he wanted to talk to me because he was from South Carolina. I looked at him, and I told him he reminded me of this little white boy named John Duvall I used to play with back home. Then he handed me his card, and it was him. We had a big reunion.

But at this fight in Cheraw, Theodore Robinson and Norman Powe, two of my cousins, were with me, and if I needed it I knew I'd have some help. This cracker swung out at me, and I ducked the punch and popped him in the eye. With one eye closed, he couldn't hit me because I moved too fast. He started wading in and trying to talk me down.

"I wish I had some brass knuckles so I could kill you, niggah!"

"You ain't got none now, peckerwood."

I hit him hard, bap, one time upside the jaw, and he fell. I went to jump on top of him to beat him some more, but the other guys, his friends, started closing in when they saw that I was winning. When they pulled that stunt, I reached down and picked up two rocks, so did Theodore and Norman.

"Let's get 'em," I yelled. All those white guys tore out and left their buddy on the ground at our mercy, but we let him go free. About a week later, he caught me again. I was coming home from the white swimming pool where I had a gig as a high diver. People would throw money and I'd dive off of the high board for it, down about forty feet. Kenny McManus, a white guy, whose uncle owned that pool and the colored pool, the Buena Vista, had taught me how to do one-and-a-half gainers and swans. I had good diving form and had just picked up about $2.89 out of the deep.

"Come heah, boy," this guy who had tried to sneak into the movies called me.

"Don't do it," I said.

"I just wan' talk to ya'."

This time he had caught me alone, but I had a slingshot with me and I drew it.

"Don't come any closer," I warned him, but he kept sneaking up on me.

"I just wanna . . ."

Whap! I shot him with my slingshot, and he grabbed his forehead and fell down again. I cut out and ran all the way home from the pool. He had seen me diving, getting all the money, and he wanted to take it. He should have known better.

WESLEY GILLESPIE (brother):

"John would fight anybody. He'd fight the bigger boys, then if they'd get to be too much for him, I'd have to fight for him. He was a very bad boy when he was a kid coming up, very rough. He used to get into a lotta things, but I always bailed him out.

"He was always beating Hamp and his other smaller cousins. Once he hit Hamp in the head with a rock, and the blood was gushing out of his head. So John went and got some sand and tried to put some sand into the hole to stop it from bleeding, so that Hamp's mother wouldn't see it when he got home. We took him home and Aunt Laura said, 'Hamp, what happened . . . ?' John told her, 'Aunt Laura, a woodpecker pecked him in the head.'

"When we were kids we used to pick cotton. We'd go to the fields and have our little lunch there. John would eat all the lunch, and I wouldn't have any when time came for my lunch. Maybe I would have picked a hundred pounds of cotton, or a hundred and fifty pounds of cotton, and he would pick maybe fifteen pounds, twenty pounds, but all the lunch would be gone. We would go back home and Mama would say to him, 'Well, Wesley is picking a hundred and twenty-five pounds and you only picked fifteen pounds, and you ate all the lunch.'

"'Mama, listen,' he would say, 'I wasn't cut out for picking cotton. Someday I'm gonna be a musician; you're gonna be proud of me.'"

My brother Wesley was older. But I used to get him into trouble. With me always getting into fights, sometimes he'd be forced to jump in. Not that I needed the protection—I could fight—but sometimes there would be two or three other guys.

I always wanted to hang around with Wesley, but he would never let me follow him. He would pal around with my cousin Clee instead. Clee and I were about the same age, but he and Wesley had just started going around with girls. Whenever I wanted to go with them, they'd stop when they reached the corner and Wesley would try to run me back home. "You ain't going with us." I'd say, "Yes, I am." Then Wesley and I would get into a fight, and he'd whip me every time. I'd fight Wesley, but I could never beat him. One time I was following them, and Wesley pushed me back and then hit me in the stomach, hard. It hurt so much that I picked up a stick and threw it at him. Wesley grabbed his face, and I saw blood coming down his hand. I thought I had put out his eye, and I ran home and hid under the bed. When Mama asked me about it, I told her that Wesley had hit me first; I was glad when I found out the stick hadn't hit him in his eye. Wesley claimed I would have killed him and stuck him with a knife if I had one, but I wasn't vicious like that, just hotheaded. Mostly, I acted extremely mischievous, but it's a wonder that I didn't get killed during that time.

Horns Galore

Alice Wilson, my third-grade teacher, attracted my attention to music with her minstrel shows. Robert Smalls had a little minstrel show at the end of the year, and a line of performers would be seated on stage. On the extreme left and right sat two end men, or interlocutors, all dressed up for clowning, in blackface and top hats. In the middle, the kids wore costumes too, but no blackface. Each performer would say a speech or sing a song, then one of the end men would jump up and cut the fool and say something to top it off. "Roses are red, violets are blue. If you don't watch out, I'll come out there and get you," the end man, Robert Hammons, would say. Then he'd do a little buck dance, sit down, and wait for the audience to applaud. On the piano, Alice Wilson accompanied all of the songs.

My part in the minstrels began in about 1930. The year before that, 1929, Leonard Lynch, who had become the principal of Robert Smalls, wangled the money out of the state to buy us some musical instruments. Lynch and Mrs. Wilson walked into our fifth-grade classroom one day and asked who wanted to join the band. My hand shot up in the air. They told everyone who raised his hand to leave and report to another room downstairs.

When I entered the room, they had already started sharing out the instruments. Being the smallest and the youngest one there, by at least five years, no one figured I really warranted an instrument. They were passing out all those shiny new horns to the bigger boys. Yank Perry was standing just in front of me, and he got an E-flat clarinet. Next, they gave Bill McNeil a big brass slide trombone, and kept on passing out instruments to guys who could eat off of my head. By the time they got down to me, I had to take the last thing left in the box, another slide trombone. I was happy, though, and rushed home to start practicing. My arms were too short; I could only reach the fifth position and couldn't make the high notes in sixth and seventh position. The trombone wasn't the right instrument for me, but I was knocked out just to have some kind of horn.

I practiced hard every day and pretty soon I was gone with it. I was little, but I soon found how to make a big noise just playing the scales. The whole neighborhood knew that I was learning how to play the trombone. Though I couldn't articulate very well, I made up for that by blowing with great enthusiasm. Mrs. Wilson organized a little band at school and I surprised myself by my diligence in making rehearsals and practicing at home without any supervision. Musically, I wasn't really all that disciplined since, with all my practicing, I still played mostly by ear. Mrs. Wilson gave me my foundation in ear training but didn't teach me any music, because she couldn't read music herself. I was doing all this after the major force for discipline in my life had disappeared when my father died, mainly because I enjoyed it. Christmas of that year, I was sitting in my room pumping all of my energy into that trombone, when I heard this higher sound coming from over next door. I dropped my horn and ran over to the Harringtons'. Brother Harrington opened the door holding this big nickel-plated trumpet. His father had given it to him for Christmas, but I fell in love with it immediately.

"Boy, I sure like the way that thing sounds," I told him.

"Yeah? Let me show you what I learned already." Brother stood there and played the B-flat scale for me. He knew the fingering, and that knocked me out.

"Lemme try it once," I asked him. Brother handed me the horn and showed me how to hold it. I put the trumpet to my lips and blew a clear B-flat with all the valves open.

"You've sure got a nice tone," Brother said.

"Yeah." I smiled. Then he taught me the fingering for the B-flat scale. I spent the whole afternoon and evening over at his house listening while he practiced. Whenever he'd stop for a rest, I'd keep the trumpet warm for him, and every day after that, I'd come home from school, hurriedly put in an hour of practice on the trombone, and run over to Brother Harrington's to play the trumpet. We used to practice on that trumpet so much, double-timing it, it's a wonder we didn't wear out the horn. Mrs. Amanda would listen for a while and get tired of hearing us blow and chase us over to my house, then after a while, Mama would get tired and run us away too. Brother and I would walk out to a field somewhere, still practicing. He gave me the benefit of all of his lessons, and within nine months I became just as good as he was on the trumpet and knew how to play the trombone too. When Alice Wilson found out about it she went wild; and I felt great because being so small at twelve years old, I knew I couldn't be the best trombonist in Cheraw. This way, since I could double on trumpet and trombone, I did become unique among all the musicians in town.

ALICE V. WILSON (mentor):

"He first came to my classroom in third grade. He was always just like he is now: fidgety, and a little frisky fellow. Anything that he liked, he would stick to. He was smart. He would get his lessons, but he didn't want to study. I don't know how he did it, but he got it.

"'John, do you have your lessons?' I would say to him.

"'Yeah, I got it, I got it, Mrs. Wilson, I got it.' And when the time would come for recitations, he would know it. How? I don't know, because he wouldn't study. He didn't care about anything but music. He was always more interested in music than he was in his academic work. But he got it. He got enough to pass.

"And when he came to me later, we had just gotten a little band together. I think the principal at that time had a few instruments. We didn't have a full band, just trying to get something started. And he just went crazy! They didn't want him to have the horn at first, you know, he was so little. But he was so persistent, 'I can play it!'

"As long as he could hold that horn he was all right. And that suited me, because I taught him just the way I wanted him to play, and he would play it. And if I would teach him something, and he'd go another way, I'd say, 'That isn't what I want.' He'd say, 'Mrs. Wilson, what key is it?'

"I'd say, 'Listen to this,' and I'd hit the note on the piano. He'd, 'Dee-dee-dee, I got it! I got it!' And harmonizing it. I always believed in good harmony. He told most of his friends that I started him off in jazz. And so I told him, 'Boy, you got me now, 'cause what you play now, I don't understand.'

"There wasn't too much that I could teach them in the line of music proper, because I never played by note. I played by ear, all the time. My mother tried to give me music, and I took it a while, just to please her, but when I'd get a chance—if I'd hear anything—I'd just go right

on and play it, what I heard. So that's the way I learned music. I didn't
want to take the time to learn the notes.

"I always liked plays that were comical, and I would put music in
them because I found that the public liked that kinda thing. I had
about six or eight girls that I used as chorus girls. Whenever it came
to an intermission, I'd put a piece of music in there. And when I
would hear something somebody else played, I would learn it and
play it that way. The principal would buy sheet music for me, popular
music. I would learn the melody, and then I would change it and play
it like I wanted. And so I taught John that way.

"Annually, just before school closing, each teacher was responsible
for a play and I would always get one where I could have music in it.
And it would take everything I could do to make John listen. When
time came for practice, he'd start. I would try to give the girls instruc-
tions, and he'd play scales on his cornet. I'd say, 'Boy, listen, wait a
minute!' And they'd start, 'Make John wait! We don't hear what you
say.' Well, I'd have to call him down, you know. And he'd say, 'Mrs.
Wilson, I ain't doing nothin' . . .' And when I'd try to tell them again,
and they'd ask, 'Mrs. Wilson, how'd you say you want us to do that?'
John would be just practicing, going over the scales. He wouldn't be
doing anything connected with what I was talking about, just playing
the scale. He was so hardheaded and wouldn't listen, and I was trying
to instruct, and he just kept running the scales. And he was sitting
near me, you know, and I just kept telling him to stop, and he
wouldn't. So I knocked the horn out of his mouth, and he went, 'Uh,
uhh . . .'

"He would come to school every morning with his horn under his
arm, instead of books. His brother Wesley would have the books.
They were in the same class, but John was smarter than Wesley.

"He was a mess, but he was a loving child. All the children loved
him, and so did the teachers that had anything to do with him. In a
sense he was comical. Course we didn't call it that way then; we'd say
he was 'crazy'! Believed in fun. He was always full of fun.

"Yet he had his own individual style with everything. He was just
like that, the way he held his horn. He'd try to hold it with one hand.
Anything to show off. He's a show-off. That's the best way I can say it.
Yeah, he was a real show-off, but he was a good one."

B-flat . . .

       While the kids in the minstrel show performed their numbers, Alice Wilson used to plunk along an accompaniment on the piano, alone. She changed all that in 1930 and broadened the musical part of the program by organizing a "pit" band and a group of singers. My cousins, Cleveland Powe and Hamp McIntosh, and another guy named Fred McNeil sang in a vocal trio, barbershop style, in close harmony. In the "pit" band, Mrs. Wilson played piano; Tom Marshall, snare drum; Bill McNeil, trombone; Wes Buchanan, bass drum; and I played cornet. We provided all the music for the show: the overture, some popular songs, and accompaniments for the singers and dancers.

Having no written music we played, by ear, everything in the standard key for the blues B-flat. We created, without consciously trying to sound bluesy, a blues effect since, with Mrs. Wilson playing the piano, little else was possible. B-flat was the only key she knew how to play in. Still, on sheer exuberance, we sounded good, and the audiences loved it. I can honestly say that I've never played with a group of musicians potentially as great as some of the guys in that little pit band.

Wes Buchanan was terrific. Never since have I heard anyone beat a bass drum like him. He used to put his free hand and his knee up against the bass drum and make different tones, hambone sounds and other funky stuff. I've never heard that since and have come to realize that Wes Buchanan was actually great. Drummers today get a similar effect by using their elbow on the snare drum or tom-tom; it's the same basic idea.

Bill McNeil was fantastic, too, on trombone. He was a rough player like J. C. Higginbotham and could hit all the high notes that I would have missed, had I been playing trombone. Considering the beat-up cornet that I blew, I sounded good too. I borrowed that horn, and it was all taped up. I was blowing through tape rather than through metal. The only complaint I have, thinking back about that little minstrel band, was how much we lacked in technical ability and knowledge of reading music. For a long time, the only key I could play in was B-flat, and I depended too much on my ear to tell me what I should play. Every time we played though, we popped it to them.

We played a lot without getting paid until we had enough applause and confidence to start searching around for other jobs. We didn't have to search very far; people who had seen the minstrel shows were running around Cheraw looking for us. Our first outside gig came when the kids over at the white high school asked our band to come over and play for them at one of their dances. We felt proud and excited; it made us feel so good to know that someone actually wanted to pay to hear us play.

Because Alice Wilson played only in one key, declining to learn another, we found a new piano player for the job, Bernis Tillman. Brother Harrington loaned me his trumpet so that I would have a decent horn for the big occasion; we hired a singer, my cousin, Theodore Robinson, and added another instrument by having Clee play the bass violin. Maxy Ganzy, a clarinetist, alto saxophonist, and a student at Benedict College in Columbia, South Carolina, came home for the summer and played with us too.

Now I had found a use for that big red bass violin that had been lying around our house ever since my father died. The bass had only one string intact, the G string, but it was beautifully made, the black finger board contrasted sharply with its deep red color. Being so ignorant musically, I did a crazy thing and mutilated the instrument. I scratched a tune-up mark on the finger board where Clee could press to get the B-flat sound whenever he tightened the string. I went further and carved in spots for the other notes. I didn't know that the G string on the bass violin had to be tuned to the note G, but I called myself tuning up the instrument for him. That's how much I didn't know about music and how dumb I acted, yet people were prepared to pay to hear me play. A lot of young musicians still make the same mistake of confusing popular acclaim with demonstrating true knowledge and ability in music.

Our sense of showmanship made that first paying gig a knockout.

We played stock arrangements and little things like, "I Can't Dance, I Got Ants In My Pants," "Limehouse Blues," and other songs like "Moonglow" and the Casa Loma Orchestra's "Wild Goose Chase." Wes Buchanan was marvelous as a leader, because on top of playing the bass drum, he had such great rhythm that he would dance out in front of the band like Tiny Bradshaw. We chose Wes for our band-leader mainly because his mother had a car that we used for trans-portation to the various places where we played. Mrs. Buchanan had a little money from a government pension awarded to one of her sons who had gotten killed in World War I. She was a very kind woman, like a patron, and always laid a quarter or two on us whenever we were hungry. Our reputation spread, and we started getting other jobs at house parties, dances down at the Elks Hall, and even gigs in other little towns like Clio, Hartsville, Darlington, Florence, Chesterfield, South Carolina, and Rockingham and Hamlet in North Carolina.

In Cheraw and across the North Carolina border in Rockingham and Hamlet, the "colored" dances were all held outdoors during the summer. My older sisters' boyfriends would come by in cars to pick them up, and they'd hit the road, Bennettsville, fourteen miles away; Rockingham, twenty-three; Hamlet, twelve. In the thirties, the cars all had large bumpers on the back. I'd hide and wait until my sisters and their dates all got into the car, then sneak and jump up on the back bumper. They'd be so busy playing with each other and partying that they'd never even know that I was there. There were no paved roads, and so much of that red dust in South Carolina would fly into my face that I would look like I was white when I hopped off of the bumper at the dance. I always had some company. A lot of other people had got-ten there the same way, so I never had to worry about anyone refus-ing to dance with me because I was too dirty. When my sisters got out of the car and found out I had followed them, they'd be angry, but I wouldn't care because I knew they'd have to take me back home. I went to all the "colored" dances that way, picked up the new steps and added something of my own.

Anywhere there was a dance, I would go, with or without admission money. I used to hang around all the places in Cheraw where music was played, irrespective of color. Before I became known as a musi-cian, I built up quite a reputation among the white folks as a dancer. I used to make a little money at the "white" dances in Cheraw. They had a place called the Country Club up above the drugstore where most of the "white" dances were held. Whenever I heard music up there, I'd stick my head in the door and they'd yell for me to come in.

They'd be hollering, "Come on in, John Birch! Come on in and dance for us." The white guys I knew, my buddies, would be the first ones to throw out some quarters. My specialty was a dance called the "snake hips," and when I'd snake my way out onto the floor, the money would start falling. Sometimes, I'd make two or three dollars for just a few minutes. That was a lot of money for a young boy during the Depression to scoop up off a dance floor. Afterward, they'd let me listen to the band from the doorway of the kitchen because they knew that playing and listening to music was my thing. At one of those "white" dances, I saw for the first time in my life a band that played with their own arrangements, instead of stock arrangements. They were college boys who went on tour every summer, Neely Plumb and his Georgia Tech Ramblers.

Before we learned much music, our own little band became well known in the area. We weren't making much money but through our love for music we were gaining knowledge and experience and having a lot of fun. I became known as the best young trumpet player around Cheraw. My friends and even some people whom I didn't know started to ask me various questions regarding music. Once, a white boy, Jimmy Gainey, who had been a neighbor and a friend from early childhood, asked me for some musical advice. Jimmy played drums in a white band led by a guy named Ned Hickson, and I used to go to hear them practice. Before you knew it, I was helping them along with rhythm, which seemed to be their big shortcoming. I used to help a lot of white people back home, when I was coming up in music. I didn't know music, but I knew rhythm and I would help them with that.

Jimmy Gainey used to play the old one-two beat on the trap drum, but that sounded kind of awkward to me, so I suggested to him playing one-two-three-four. Jimmy didn't understand what I meant at first. I had to get on the drums and show it to him. Once he had heard it, boy, you couldn't imagine someone being more in love with a new sound. Jimmy got me to attend band rehearsals over at the white high school because they needed help with rhythm too. I needed to learn how to read, but they kept me so busy helping and riding high on applause that I never picked up anything. They had me thinking that I knew more than they did, when I only knew how to play in one key.

Something happened to bring me down off that cloud. This cat, Sonny Matthews, who had been up North to Philadelphia and Charlotte, North Carolina, came back home to visit his family and cut me seriously. Sonny's mother was a well-known piano teacher in Cheraw, so he had grown up reading music. From the moment that he hit town, people kept telling him about me, the bad new young trumpet player. Sonny put out the word that I should come by his house, and I was so cocky that I picked up the horn from Brother and went over to meet him. I didn't know that he had been up North playing orchestrations and things. I walked into his house, shook his hand, took out my horn, and we sat down at the piano and played this new song, "Nagasaki." I didn't know the tune, but told him that I would try it, relying on my ear. Sonny counted down and started playing in the key of C, but all I could do was fumble around because I couldn't find one note on the trumpet for "Nagasaki." "Oh, oh, I've got to learn it," I apologized, but I felt so crushed, I cried, because I was supposed to be the town's best trumpet player.

That incident with Sonny taught me that there were other keys in music besides B-flat, so I started to practice sight reading and different scales every day. Norman Powe, who had been taking lessons from Ralph Powe, started teaching me how to read. First the bass clef, then I learned the treble clef on my own.

It was funny, the other school, which was a trade school, Coulter Memorial Academy, got a band, and a bona fide instructor, a trombonist. This trombonist taught a distant cousin of mine, Ralph Powe. Ralph Powe taught my cousin Norman Powe, and Norman showed me Ralph's lessons on the trombone. So therefore I was reading in bass clef on the trumpet. I can do that now.

I worked so hard that in three or four months I became pretty good at playing in several keys, and even the guys in our little band were surprised at how much I knew.

ALICE V. WILSON:

"He started getting famous in school the year that we had a play called *The Footlight Review*. Wesley played a hick fellow from the country, and Bill McNeil who played the trombone was his son. John had the musical side of it, you know. Wesley and Bill played hicks from the country, and they showed a cabaret scene. Bill was telling Wesley, who was his 'daddy,' that he got a bargain on the street that day, a fellow had sold him the 'Empire State Building' or something like that. You know how people can do things like that. Anyway, John never was in it to learn anything in a play. He would always have the musical end, and I would put music in the play whether it belonged there or not. He did so well, and anytime I'd learn a new piece, I'd teach it to him.

"But I didn't know anything about playing in a certain key. I just played, and everything I played, I played in that same key, whatever it was. Somebody told me it was the key of B; I still don't know what it was.

"The boys kept coming in with their instruments; they wanted me to play, you know, play the piano. And I couldn't play with them because they couldn't change to my key, and I couldn't change to theirs.

"So they said, 'Mrs. Wilson, if we come up to your house every evening and show you how to play the key we're playing in, will you play with us?'

"'If you can teach me,' I said. Well, I couldn't learn. I can't play in another key. I just have to play in my same key. 'I'm sorry, I just can't play with you all,' I said. So I had to give them up and they got Bernis Tillman to play the piano. He could play whatever they wanted and the way they wanted. I hated that so bad because I wanted to play with them.

"The others who came on after that were pretty good. This fellow that wanted to try to teach me to play in another key played the clarinet. He was good too—Maxy. They were all good, but John, to my mind, was just better because he could do all kinds of foolishness with his. He'd get it and he'd just add to it, and he was the whole orchestra or a little group, whatever you wanna call it. He was just the best because anything that was needed to add to it, he'd put it there. And the others would follow. But I didn't have as much to do with them as I did with John. I started John.

"I always liked jazz music. That's why I never could bother with notes. I just didn't wanna take time. So I would play whatever I heard, just jazz it all up and play it like I wanted, and I taught him to do that. That's how he got started with it. And if he'd try to play something straight, I'd make him put that jazzing part in there. He was the only one that could do that, the only one in the little group with me that could do it whenever I'd tell him. All I had to do was just show him.

"If he was playing something correct—for instance if he was playing 'Side by Side,' one of the popular numbers—he'd be playing it just like it was written. But I wouldn't want it. I would want him to jazz it up a little bit, and he could do that. I would always have to show him by playing it myself, and he could imitate whatever I played on the piano on his horn. The others couldn't do that. Of all the students I had, John was the best. He could play it just like I wanted it played."

WESLEY GILLESPIE:

"When the white bands came to town, he would go down and they would let him come in and so forth. Nobody could go into the white dances but him. Everytime a white band would come in town, he would go to see them, and they would let him in. People were wild about him because they knew that he had talent."

Bill McNeil, our trombone player, disappeared. I hadn't seen Bill for several days. He was three years older than I, about seventeen or eighteen, and he used to go off on drinking jags, denatured alcohol, canned heat, corn, anything. None of the guys in the group thought much about him disappearing, and we thought that he had just fallen down drunk and hurt himself, when we heard that "something" had happened to him. A rumor came out that a group of white men had caught him and put him on the railroad tracks in front of a train because someone said Bill had been a "Peeping Tom" and had been caught peeping in some white person's house. No one ever found his body. Bill just vanished, and then we heard about it. The thought of Trombone Bill being murdered shook me up, and I felt it way down in my guts, his life and talent and career cut off so cruelly. We all knew that it could just as easily have happened to any of us. Our band never sounded the same again, but it made us want to improve ourselves so we could get the hell out of Cheraw. That was all we could do about it.

We hired another trombonist, my cousin, Norman Powe, and Maxy Ganzy, a saxophonist who could read music and even knew a little about writing it, became our musical director. We expanded our repertoire with new popular songs like, "Stars Fell on Alabama," and then, with Maxy's aid, we started making up our own little tunes, sanctified-like things that showed how much the church influenced us.

It's very interesting how the blacks became divided over religion in Cheraw. The top church was Second Presbyterian Church, located over at Coulter Memorial Academy, a missionary-operated private school for Negroes. Second Presbyterian was considered the highest form of worship in town. Next came my church, the Methodist church. We also had a Catholic church in Cheraw, but there were only two colored people who attended it, Miss Tempie Harrington and Miss Hattie Floyd, two old spinsters who lived together. They lived there on Huger Street right next to Catherine McKay's house, and they had a big pecan tree in their yard. Whenever pecan season came, the wind would shake the tree and we were allowed to pick up all the pecans that fell outside the fence. But if you were ever caught inside that yard, you were liable to get anything done to you. Everyone knew that law and was scared as hell of hunchbacks and hexes in that yard. Next in line among the churches came Peedee Baptist and the A.M.E. Zion church. People used to shout in both of them, but since no one visited other churches then, how much they really carried on inside was not well known. Visiting other churches was definitely not considered the thing to do, because someone might accuse you of being disloyal to your own particular kind of gospel.

Finally came the Sanctified church where everyone knew that the whole congregation shouted. That was the lowest you could go because they practiced spirit possession and speaking in tongues, which was considered too much akin to African religion. I found that people in the Sanctified church actually practiced the life of Christ better than any of the other churches because they believed in it totally. In my church they taught a lot of religion in Sunday school, and I became an inquisitive student of the catechism and the Bible. I used to ask the teacher some very hard questions. I raised so many questions about the resurrection and the virgin birth that finally my Sunday school teacher asked me, "Why don't you take over the class?" I must have been about thirteen.

Like most black musicians, much of my early inspiration, especially with rhythm and harmonies, came from the church. Not my church though. In the Methodist church there wasn't too much happening musically—mostly hymns. But the Sanctified church had a deep significance for me, musically. I first learned the meaning of rhythm there and all about how music could transport people spiritually. The Sanctified church stood down the street from us, down near the end of the street, right near the place where we used to draw water from the well. The leader of the church was named Elder Burch, and he had several sons, Willie and Johnny Burch were two of them. People used to get my name confused with Johnny's, though he was much older than I. They'd say, "John Burch, John Butts . . ." everything except John Birks.

Johnny Burch played the snare drum, and his brother Willie beat the cymbal; another one of the Burch brothers played the bass drum and the other the tambourine. They used to keep at least four different rhythms going, and as the congregation joined in, the number of rhythms would increase with foot stomping, hand clapping, and people catching the spirit and jumping up and down on the wooden floor, which also resounded like a drum. I would go down there every Sunday night and sit in the back of the church to listen, afraid to let anyone see me who might have considered it disloyal. Even white people would come and sit outside in their cars just to listen to the people getting the spirit inside. Everybody would be shouting and fainting and stomping. They used to shout awhile. The Sanctified church's rhythm got to me as it did to anyone else who came near the place. People like James Brown and Aretha Franklin owe everything to that Sanctified beat. I received my first experience with rhythm and spiritual transport going down there to the well every Sunday, and I've just followed it ever since.

Another group of religious musicians in Cheraw, the Linton Brothers, had no effect on me musically, though one of the brothers claims that he did. Fletcher Linton, a trumpet player, now a principal in Charleston, South Carolina, always tells people who go down there that he taught me how to play the trumpet. Fletcher never had any rhythm in him, couldn't blow his nose, he just came from a musical family. His brother, Charlie Linton, sang with Chick Webb when Ella Fitzgerald joined that band. A suave dark guy, Charlie had a high voice like Orlando Roberson. All the years that Chick Webb stayed on top, Charlie Linton remained the male vocalist along with Ella Fitzgerald, the female vocalist.

The Linton Brothers, Charlie, Albert, Willie and Fletcher, had a gospel quartet and sang just like James Brown and Wilson Pickett are doing today, except that they used different words. The Lintons sang about God with the gospel, while the guys today sing about how their women hurt them, but it's the same music.

Thinking back about women, I must have seemed very unromantic in Cheraw. My first girl friend, Mary, is now my cousin Theodore's wife. I used to throw rocks at her to express my affection. She looked so pretty and brown, but I acted too wild. She took up with another musician, a trombone player named Horace Sharper who went away to Benedict College and then came back home and stole Mary's heart away from me. Horace became a big Baptist minister in Newark, New Jersey. Another girl I liked named Thelma McDonald acted so shy that she could never look me in the face. I never saw her face until she up and moved to New York. I recognized her from behind one day out in Brooklyn where she lives.

In Cheraw, mischief, money-making, and music captured all of my attention. By the time I reached fifteen, I felt sure enough of my ability on the trumpet to go down and sit in with the professional colored bands that came to Cheraw to play at the Elks Hall on Market and Front streets. Many good musicians came through in bands such as Doc Pettiford, Smiling Billy Stewart, and Kelly's Jazz Hounds, from Fayetteville, North Carolina; Capitol City Aces, from Raleigh; Jimmy Gunn and Bill Davis, from Charlotte. All of these were area bands, and we never saw any groups from up North unless we drove all the way to Columbia. None of the bands from Kansas City came our way either; we only heard musicians from the East Coast.

The first time that I took a horn to the Elks', Bill Davis was playing and someone from Cheraw yelled at him, "Hey, we've got a little trumpet player here; let him sit in." I hadn't grown very tall at fifteen, so they put a little box up in front and let me stand on top of it to play. Bill counted down the tune, "China Boy," in F, and I played for two choruses. Sonny Matthews had shamed me once, but now, my ideas flowed beautifully. The dancers and all the members of the band applauded and cheered, and that night I became a big star in Cheraw. My B-flat days were over.

I didn't wait around for the dance to end; instead, I got my hat and walked over to the Harringtons'. Mrs. Amanda owned a radio and a gramophone, and next door at our house we didn't have either one. That's how jive it felt to be poor. We didn't even have a radio, and I wanted to listen to the broadcast of the band from the Savoy Ballroom in New York, Teddy Hill's Orchestra. The guy playing the lead trumpet in that band used to knock me out, but the whole band gassed me. I didn't even know their names, but, man, they used to pop it. Now I know my heroes in that band were Roy Eldridge, trumpet; Chu Berry, tenor saxophone; and Dicky Wells, trombone. That night they were terrific, and I went home with my head so full of music that I dreamed I had sat in with them. But that was a dream.

Laurinburg

In 1932, after Roosevelt came in, everybody was digging ditches to get some of that federal money from the public works program. I went on the road gang the next summer, in 1933, after I graduated from ninth grade at Robert Smalls. The boss over us looked down in the ditch at me while I was throwing up dirt, and yelled, "You over there." I looked around like he was talking to someone else. "Hey, you! You!" He hollered and pointed at me, "Gimme a shovelful and some on the handle." He meant I was supposed to give him a whole shovelful of dirt packed about six inches high, and some more on the handle. That changed my mind about common labor. I was too small and lazy for a life of hard work, so I picked up my salary and went home.

It struck me at that time how illiterate our people were. It really hurt me to see my brothers on the WPA gang walk up to the table to get their pay and have to make an X because they couldn't write their names. That made a deep impression on me. Before then, I'd never really seriously considered becoming a professional musician, but an opportunity for me to learn something and support myself by playing music fell down like a blessing out of the blue.

At the end of the summer of 1933, a neighbor of mine, Catherine McKay, a student nurse and band booster at Laurinburg Institute, in North Carolina, gave me a proposition that made me feel like kissing

Mama good-by and leaving home. She spread the word to the principal at Laurinburg that Norman and I had talent and would make
good replacements for the school's best trumpeter and trombonist who
had both left that year to go to college.

"What do I have to do?"

"Just come on up there in September and play trumpet in the band.
You know a good trombone player?"

"Yeah. Norman."

"Bring him with you then. I'll tell Mr. McDuffy y'all are coming."

"I don't have a trumpet."

She smiled. "You've got lips, don't you?"

I wasn't doing very much in Cheraw, except hanging around, so it
took me less than no time to tell Norman, convince my family, pack an
otherwise empty suitcase with a toothbrush, towel and a change of un-
derwear, and arrive at the school. I only had one shirt to my name, no
money for tuition, no really great desire to be educated, and didn't even
own a trumpet. I went to Laurinburg Technical Institute strictly on my
lips. They gave me food, tuition, room, books, and everything else I
needed, free.

During the orientation tour of the campus, Laurinburg seemed like a
complete little town. They had classrooms in McKenzie Hall, dorms
for boys and girls, a large football field and outside basketball courts,
a hospital and an administration building. The fields around there had
some of the healthiest-looking crops I'd ever seen. Laurinburg gave
lessons in agriculture and also had livestock pens for teaching animal
husbandry. I had no plans to become a farmer, but to a hungry boy
like me, the thought of all that food growing around made the place
very attractive. This was further away from home than I had ventured
in several years, but I never felt lonely that first day or had the urge to
turn around and walk the twenty-eight miles back to Cheraw. From
the moment I arrived at the school, people kept saying, "Hey, I hear
you're the new trumpet player who's going to replace Isaac Johnson."
Catherine McKay had told everybody that Norman and I were coming, and they were expecting some good music from us because Isaac
Johnson, the son of the dean, and Frank McDuffy, the principal's son,
had both made names there as excellent musicians.

They assigned Norman and me to a room in the dormitory with a
short, dark guy named Pope, from New York. I was so ragged with my
one shirt and pair of pants, and Pope was just about my size and
had some real sharp duds from New York, white suits and floppy stuff
like they're wearing again now. My eyes lit up when Pope unpacked
his bags. When we walked over to the dining hall that first day, I was
dressed better than I'd been in years. Pope, a charming and generous

guy, allowed me to wear his clothes and saw to it that I kept up a very stylish front.

Catherine McKay knew how much food I could put away. They used to serve us family style and sometimes the amount of food on the table was too skimpy for four or five people. They prayed before every meal at Laurinburg, so while they were asking for blessing, I'd reach out to fill my plate, thinking there might not be any seconds coming. That first day I looked out of the corner of my eye and noticed that the table next to ours had food piled up on it about three miles high, and a lot of great big guys sat around it with their eyes gleaming, waiting until they had finished the blessing.

"Who are those dudes over there?" I whispered to Catherine.

"They're the football players," she said. That was all I needed to know. The next day, I went out on the football field to try out for the team. I got to the locker room early and picked out all the best equipment, a helmet, shoulder pads, hip pads, shoes, and a jersey without any holes in it. I wanted to look good and make sure that my body was well protected. By the time the coach and the rest of the team arrived, I was standing there completely dressed, grinning at them as they came in. Everybody just looked at me and started grumbling, because it was my first year and I had come in and taken all the best equipment. The coach, big Ivory Smith, just looked at me, but he didn't say anything until we got out on the practice field.

"You, come over here!"

I walked over to him.

"Get down and charge," he said.

I got down and tried to charge him, but he ran over me.

"You don't know how to charge, mister," he told me and made me get down again; then he ran over me again.

"Take off that equipment!"

My jersey and shoulder pads went to John Willie, the quarterback, my hip pads to a guy who played tackle, and my shoes to a fellow who played end. Piece by piece, he undressed me and gave me the most ragged uniform on the field. Mr. Smith embarrassed the hell out of me because he didn't believe that I was serious about football. He had been a great football player at Tuskegee, the center of a championship team that had whipped ass among the southern colored colleges in 1925. He thought that stripping me out there would have discouraged me, but it had almost no effect. Every time that he took back a piece of equipment, I'd imagine three more pork chops piled up on my plate at dinner. He could make me run around the park twelve or thirteen times, I'd take my laps. Mr. Smith left me with a very funny attitude, feeling both love and fear for him. He reminded me of a tenacious bulldog, but at the same time he acted warm and kind.

By the first game, Mr. Smith and I knew a lot more about each other. After I had bumped heads with him, he found out that I really meant to make the team and gave me a good uniform. I felt something then—when I made the team—and he discovered that I could be an energetic and spirited athlete, as fast as lightning. I played right end, took over the position, and made the winning touchdown in the first game. A man my size looked smaller than average on Laurinburg's team. We had some big rough guys on our side and had to run up against some bigger and tougher ones sometimes. Cats like Sam Jones the basketball player, Wes Covington, Charlie Scott, and Jimmy Walker played there. They recruited athletes from New York. They still do steer people to Laurinburg. Grachan Moncur, the trombonist, went there. The school is still functioning and is very modern. Frank McDuffy turned out to be a great administrator. He's the president now. All that year, 1933, I played football against some very tough opponents. We never played against high schools, only junior colleges, like Fayetteville State Normal and Morristown Training School for Boys. None of the high schools wanted to play against us.

No friction between the students and the school's administration at Laurinburg was permitted. If you wanted to complain, you'd have to do it very quietly. Stool pigeons were all over the place, so if a cat was a troublemaker, they'd put him out, right quick.

It was impossible for me, with my big mouth. One night I woke up in my room in the dormitory screaming. They had chinches, bedbugs, running rampant around there in the mattresses, and they used to have a feast on my back. The chinches almost ran me crazy, and I made so much noise that the man in charge of the dorm had to come upstairs. I started to argue with him, but he shut me up quickly by starting to inspect my room. They made us keep a clean room by holding regular inspections, and if you had any complaint, they'd call impromptu inspections. He found out that our room was clean but the mattress still had chinches, and he made me take the mattress outside the next day to air it; because once outside in the sunlight, the chinches would go away. That still didn't solve my problem because the eggs were still inside. At that time, they didn't sell any products to kill the eggs. When we brought my mattress back upstairs and put it on the bed, he showed me a trick that was supposed to save me a lot of misery and sleepless nights. He lifted each post of the bed and put it in a sardine can filled with kerosene, so the chinches couldn't crawl back up the legs of the bed into the mattress. That seemed fine for the chinches we left outside and the ones on the floor, but what about the eggs in the mattress, I asked him. The houseman told me that I could either sleep on that mattress, airing it regularly to make sure that the new chinches that hatched couldn't survive, or make myself a new mattress.

I had to skip all of my classes the next day, but I was determined not to sleep with chinches any longer and spent the whole time in the shop at the school making myself a new straw mattress. After that, anyone who complained about chinches had to do the same thing, and soon we all had new straw mattresses which we made ourselves. At Laurinburg, they placed great stress on self-reliance in the Booker T. Washington tradition and on lighting candles rather than cursing the dark. It didn't pay to complain or to ask too many questions about shortcomings around there unless you were ready to do some work to change things. I learned you can get a great sense of pride from solving your own practical problems, and I know that I slept better and chinch-free on the mattress I made with my own two hands.

I learned a lot about agriculture at Laurinburg too. We practiced scientific agriculture and grew or raised everything that we ate. In agriculture, I learned about things like crop rotation, winter cover crops, and soil seepage. In the winter, you plant clover, and when spring comes, you plow that over and it rots in the soil and gives it nutrients. You plant on that richness. That's the key to raising good crops and a lesson about living a rewarding life. Plant on your own personal richness your best gifts or talent.

Strangely, because I couldn't get much help in music from anyone, I found myself becoming a musician. (Music and English were my favorite subjects at Laurinburg.) We lacked a full-time band director or music teacher, and the person in charge of the program, Mr. Barnes, a saxophone player, left after my first year. The second year, Shorty Hall, who followed him, had his hands full trying to build up a band from a group of beginners, most of whom couldn't read music. He didn't have too much time to work with me.

Musically, I had progressed much further than most of the others. I could read and in the first year had even learned a little theory. Those students who could read music spent some time helping Shorty to teach the others. Shorty gave me some pointers, but the great benefit for me in music came from the atmosphere at Laurinburg, the quiet and serenity of being in the country. Since I didn't have to study too much in other areas, I started fooling around with the piano and my ideas expanded greatly. I practiced constantly, until all times of the night, anytime I wanted. I'd practice the trumpet and then the piano for twenty-four hours straight if they didn't come around and shut me up when they checked the locks every night. I developed a very serious attitude about music, and music was the only thing I was serious about.

"G'lisspie, are you thinking about playing professional football for a career?" Shorty Hall, the bandmaster, asked me one day when I walked past him on my way to the locker room, going to practice football and be a big star again at right end.

"I'm not even thinking about that," I said. "I want to blow a horn."

"Well, suppose you get your teeth knocked out, out there? What kind of trumpet player do you think you'll make?"

"Oh, oh . . ." I said to myself. I just looked at him. And I never went near the football field again except to blow my horn in parades. After that, music became my only activity and I started to become impatient with people who didn't give a damn about the next note. We had a few uncaring guys like that in Laurinburg's band. Scurlock, the tuba player, used to get on my nerves. He must've weighed three hundred pounds and never played a right note in his life, but he acted so big and bad that nobody would fire him. Tom Blue, who played the bass drum, was unable to read and never advanced in music as I did because he never read. He started becoming jealous of me when I always corrected him. Tom was itching for a fight with me, and Scurlock egged him on.

One day at rehearsal, Tom Blue goofed. I corrected him, and he started toward me to whip me. Tom Blue must've weighed about two hundred and forty pounds; I was about a hundred pounds lighter. Before he could get from behind his drum, my knife was open. When he saw I was advancing on him, his big blue ass turned around and ran. He went out and told Mr. McDuffy that I had pulled a knife on him, and they called me into the office.

"Did you pull a knife on that boy?" Mr. McDuffy asked me.

"Yes, sir."

"Did you intend to cut him?"

"As long as I could see him," I said. "He outweighs me by over a hundred pounds and he could have hit me in my mouth and ruined my embouchure. Mr. McDuffy, I plan to go into music as a career, and I wouldn't be able to play."

Knowing that I had acted seriously and in self-defense, Mr. McDuffy didn't even whip me; he was a very understanding man.

H. N. I. C.

In the South, the elite of black society fell into this order:
1. The undertaker (everyone had to go to him)
2. The doctor (everyone who got sick)
3. The lawyer (everyone who got into trouble)
4. The schoolteacher (everyone who wasn't stupid)

Among the schoolteachers, the principal was on an elevated level, comparable in status to the undertaker, and even his children reflected that power. Mr. McDuffy, the principal at Laurinburg, knew he was a powerful man, and whenever I saw white people speak to him, they talked with respect.

He had come up to North Carolina from a little town called Snow Hill, Alabama, and started this school for poor black kids on pure balls and guts. I don't know where or whether he finished college, but he was doing a fantastic job for the people in that area. Mr. McDuffy ran Laurinburg like a family. He and the dean, Mr. I. E. Johnson, were brothers-in-law. They had married two sisters. The treasurer, Mr. H. H. Johnson, hadn't married one of the sisters, but he kept all of the money and was the brother of I. E. Johnson. It was nepotism if I ever saw it.

Mac McDuffy was the principal's eldest son. He worked and enjoyed himself around the place. We were alike in many ways, and he dug me because he could see himself, mirrorlike, in me. He knew what he might do and probably imagined me getting into the same kinds of action. One night, I sneaked outside, climbed the back bannister, and went upstairs into the girls' dormitory. I stayed up there about three hours then came on back down and returned to my room, sure that no one except the girl I had visited had seen me.

The next day, Mr. McDuffy called me into his office.

"Listen, I heard you made a little prowl last night," he said.

"What do you mean, Mr. McDuffy?" I asked, feigning innocence.

"Gillespie, are you sure there's not something you want to tell me?"

"What, Mr. McDuffy?"

"Look, do you want to take a whipping?" He didn't ask me anything else, not even who I'd been with.

Seeing that he wasn't jiving, I weakened and broke down.

"O.K., I'll take it. I was wrong, Mr. McDuffy, so let's get it on."

I took the whipping and went on about my business because I didn't want to leave school. Mr. McDuffy was such a tremendous fellow and stood for such great ideals; I wanted to be around a man of his stature. With all the deprivation, and as hard as we had it down South, he managed to uplift us and instill in us a sense of dignity. It took me a while, but I finally figured out that Mac McDuffy had gone and told his father on me because Mac considered the girls' dormitory his own private playground and didn't want me messing around in it, even for a few hours. That's how privileged the sons of our elite were.

The girls down there used to like to go out with me. One girl had me wanting to get married early, but the people down South were so narrow-minded that they turned me against her. This girl came from a good family, but there was one relative who went insane, and everybody kept asking me, "How can you hang around with that girl? You might get married and wind up having crazy children." Hell, I had a cousin in the insane asylum and was a little crazy myself.

Like a typical musician, I moved around among the women, and once, at a party, I even started trying to fool around with one of the young teachers, Miss Wilcox. They sometimes invited me to parties when one of the McDuffys or the Johnsons came home from college, and the faculty members would be there too. I found out that Miss Wilcox really liked to dance and got up the nerve to ask her to dance with me since I had always been a good dancer. They had me feeling like a member of Negro society.

Isaac Johnson whispered in my ear, "She's just being nice; you know she doesn't want to dance with you." "I'm the best dancer around," I said and took her up and started dancing. No one could tell me I wasn't one hell of a dancer, even though I didn't have any clothes. Miss Wilcox dug me, and she had a brother, Eddie, who played piano with Jimmy Lunceford's band. She became my entrée into that group. Later, when I moved to Philadelphia, Lunceford came to town and Eddie Wilcox took me up and introduced me after I told him that I knew his sister. The Wilcoxes were very nice to me, and it all started because of my dancing. A feeling for dancing was always a part of my music; to play it right, you've got to move. If a guy doesn't move properly when he's playing my music, he ain't got the feeling. Thelonious Monk, Illinois Jacquet, and all those instrumentalists who move a lot, are playing just what they're doing with their bodies.

Sometimes on weekends I'd play with Laurinburg's brass band, with guys like George Rivers, a pianist from Charleston, South Carolina, and Ezra Leaks, an alto saxophonist, but I enjoyed most coming home to play with Wes Buchanan's band. Some of the cats couldn't read, but we'd jump, man, that band jumped. We'd play house parties and dances down at the Elks Hall and hit all of the little towns around there.

BERNIS TILLMAN (piano):

"After he went to Laurinburg, he kept on playing with us, weekends; he'd bring us various riffs and things. John Birks would play, and Maxy would write them out. Some were songs that had been played already. Dizzy'd learned it and was playing it already, and would say, 'Play this.' And when the guys came in, he'd write out the trumpet part. Sometimes we'd have five or six trumpets, three or four trombones, young kids coming in because of the dough, man. We were making dough. Everybody wanted to get in on it. We went out one night with about a ten- or twelve-piece band.

"But you never heard him brag on himself. He never talked about himself. He never talked much music, just played it. You said practice, he was there. He might not stay; you might have to go get him, but he was there. If a little gal came by, you'd have to go get him. Heh, heh. He was always doing something devilish that wasn't music. He was doing something else devilish, but his music was his music.

"One particular time we played at a place on a little beach, and after the intermission, Dizzy's mouthpiece was gone. We had to take a flashlight and go out in the woods where he was with this little gal. Looked all out in the bushes and everywhere for his mouthpiece. Then after you get mad with him, curse him out, kick him around, beat him around, a little gal walks up and says, 'Here it is. . . .' She'd had his mouthpiece. Boy, he was rough on them little gals. Boy!

"He'd do something like that at every dance, except Wadesboro.

Wadesboro, he was all business there on account of the crowd. But all these other small places, if a little gal's there, Doc, and you miss him, you know where he's at.

"And whiskey. I used to carry this jar of whiskey with me—'creek' whiskey. He'd love to kid me about that; he was gonna take a drink. I'd set it behind the piano. He'd run back there, but he wouldn't take it. I mean, he would run from it. He tried it once, and it knocked him clean on his back. Clee would always drink it. Clee wouldn't make out. But Dizzy would like to play, making out he was gonna drink it, 'cause he knew somebody would tell me he was behind the piano. He'd be back there with it in his hand, but he wouldn't drink. He just wanted to be doing something. Just wanted to get into some mischief, that's all. Just a jolly guy. He's one of the greatest. If he'd fight a person, afterwards he'd be through with it. He'd be laughing the next minute. That's one thing I liked about him. He didn't carry no grudges."

We were playing once in Clio, South Carolina, and I went out in the field with this girl, Rosetta. I shouldn't have gone because I knew that her boyfriend was an old bad killer. I kept on my jacket but took off my pants, then I heard this thrashing coming through the field and picked up my pants and ran. My mouthpiece fell out of my pocket, but I couldn't go back to get it. Rosetta's boyfriend never found out who was with her, because this Croatan guy loaned me another mouthpiece so I could blow.

The Croatan's mouthpiece had cuts in it all the way around the top; everytime I'd blow, it would stick to my lips. It almost ruined my lips. I suffered until I could go out in the field after the dance and find my mouthpiece. So although I missed getting punched, I left the gig with my chops hurting anyway.

Croatans were the Indians around there, but they weren't called Indians. They weren't black, however, and the people didn't know where to put them on the social scale. They didn't go to a white school or a black school. Croatans were funny; the Ku Klux Klan tried to get smart with them once in North Carolina and got shot to pieces, but the Croatans liked niggers.

Out there in the country, the crackers always gave us a hard time. When I used to hitchhike home to Cheraw alone, I had a couple of encounters with crackers who had pistols. I stopped in this store once to get something to eat, and when I came outside, this guy pulled a gun and said, "Nigger, do you know how to dance?" I wouldn't answer him, so he shot "Bam! Bam! Bam!" down at my feet. And it made me so mad that I did a little buck dance for him. This happened between a little town called Gibson, North Carolina and Cheraw. You'd stop somewhere and get ripped off, and nobody'd ever find out what happened. I often thought about leaving the South, but there was no place better to go.

NORMAN POWE (trombone):

"We had a white booking agent booking the Laurinburg School Band, and he'd let us use his car. He was giving us only about two dollars a night, and he was taking the rest of the money. I guess he was about twenty-one years old, and we were around fifteen or so. We took the car to Cheraw from Laurinburg, and we stayed until about twelve o'clock that night. And on the way back, Dizzy said, 'I can drive,' and I said, 'O.K. . . .' And the first car he bumped into was the chief of police. That was in Cheraw. The police chief took Dizzy to jail. I brought the car on back to Laurinburg. The thing was funny. The police chief had this new car, and he just said, 'Some of them niggahs done scratched up my car.'"

I'd never driven before, and the guys asked me, "You know how to drive?" I say, "Yeah . . ." I turned that corner going across the Pee-dee River. The police saw me. Man, they tried to run me off into the water. I cut into his car. He wanted to kill me. But the other police-man knew my father. If it hadn't been for the other guy, he probably woulda sapped me up real good. I wasn't running off in that water, I'll tell you that. You'd stand a better chance hitting a police car than running off in that water. He was pushing me going down that hill. He was pushing me. If I'd gotten through that little tunnel, under the viaduct, I'd be in another county. But I couldn't get through there. He wanted to cut me off before I got across the county line. He thought we had moonshine in the car. That's what he thought, with a white man sitting up in the back seat. The white man was the insurance man, who used to book us around down there. He was sitting up in the back seat sleeping. Put my ass in jail. But the other policeman came and let me out. I thought it was a secret. When I got back home the next time, man, it was all over town. The policeman had told Wes Buchanan's brother who worked for the city as a street sweeper, "We got that little G'lisspie boy in jail." Just a coupla hours. I went to sleep on a hard bench.

Once, when King Oliver's band came to Cheraw I got an offer; Norman and I went over to play with him. But at that time, I'd just turned sixteen and was too damned scared to leave home. I'd never ever heard of King Oliver and only remember seeing him now because his eye looked funny. Cheraw only had about five thousand population, and King Oliver must have been on his way down, to play in a little town like that. I didn't know he was so famous. I wasn't hip to King Oliver and knew very little about Louis Armstrong.

NORMAN POWE:

"We were hearing Duke and Cab on the radio, and we thought they had to be wizards. We started studying classical music, man. At Laurinburg they had one of the greatest cornetists. That was Shorty Hall the music teacher. He was from Tuskegee and played all the instruments, everything. But even then I could tell he was jealous of Dizzy. I could tell that there was a little jealousy there, see. And then we would go places and listen to different professional bands all the time. And I could tell guys in them weren't any better than we were, you know. And especially Dizzy. He was so far advanced over people who were professionals at the time. Since we were kids, from about ten or eleven years old, we would slip to dance halls and listen, and as the months and years grew, I could tell that Dizzy had surpassed these people that were supposed to be so great in our eyesight. He's always been talented.

"He's a genius. We'd have old ragged instruments around the school. Pick one up if you want and take it home, nobody cared. And the trombone I finally got, man, I had to put grease on it like putting oil on a car. And the trumpet Dizzy had—this is why he's got that style now—old raggedy trumpet, broken and sticking up in the air. This is a fact.

"We'd be on the job in the school band, he'd jump down and play the piano. He'd pick up my trombone and play it. Not only trombone, bass. His daddy had a bass violin, and we sold it. We sold it for fifty dollars. You could get at least fifteen hundred for that violin now. It was an old German violin. Nobody knew the value of it.

"He wasn't ashamed. Like I'd get up and play my little solo that I had written. I'd have to close my eyes and stuff. But he was never bashful. He was outgoing. As a matter of fact, he started me off on the trombone. He was playing by ear. And, incidentally, I started to teaching him music, because I'd been taking piano lessons.

"Yeah, he had adopted a certain style. It was a very fast style.

Tonality, he didn't have a tone. He doesn't have a good tone now, but his execution outweighs all that. That's the only thing that I could say. Anybody could see it. He wasn't 'Dizzy' then, he was John Birch, rather John Birks. And to us, he was John 'Butts,' we didn't speak too clearly.

"Dizzy was the type of guy who was always good, but he didn't have any sense of responsibility. No, nothing like responsibility. Whatever happened, that's it. Well, this is a long time ago, and he has probably changed, but when we were kids, that's the way he was. If we were going someplace, Dizzy might stop suddenly, right along the street under a tree, and start reading a book, or anything, just anything. But if he likes you, he likes you. And as a matter of fact, I've seen very few people that he disliked. Dizzy doesn't care about anything but the trumpet. And he's good, he'll give you his heart, he'd do anything for you, but that's his first love. And that's it.

"When his mother came to Philly, Dizzy stayed down with me. We lived together for several months. In the meantime, we thought we were just about good enough to come East and we could come to his brother's. We didn't have a way to come, and we thought of hoboing, but I was bitten by a dog. About two weeks later, someone came, and Dizzy got a ride to Philly."

When my family moved to Philadelphia in the spring of 1935, Mama stopped off in Laurinburg to tell me good-by. I wanted to leave with them and started packing my things, but they wouldn't take me out before I'd finished high school. After Mama left, I couldn't pull my schoolwork together. I flunked one of my subjects, physics, and didn't finish high school. They wanted me to stay around another term and take physics again. All I wanted to do was get out of there. When the year ended, I was still working on the farm in Laurinburg.

I was supposed to do my share of work in the field that summer, plowing and chopping in the sun, but I was too lazy and wanted to be paid for any work I did, especially hard work. I ran away to Cheraw the first chance I got.

Over in Cheraw, I ran into this guy, Buff Long, whose brother, Tootsie, had jumped off the diving board at the pool once and didn't know how to swim. He started swallowing water, and I saved his life. I didn't know how to carry anyone, but I jumped in and dived under him. I reached up with my hands and pushed him one time. That didn't take him out, so I went under and pushed him again, and finally he grabbed ahold of something and came out. Buff had a car and was going North. He started teasing me, asking whether I wanted to ride with him.

"Just let me go and get my shirt," I told him.

"Boy, I'm not going to take you away from Miss Lottie," Buff said. "Mama's up North."

"You're a liar," he said.

I finally got him to believe me by asking Mr. Son Harrington at the shoe shop to vouch for me, and Mr. Son told Buff that Mama had moved to Philadelphia.

"Come on, let's go," Buff said. He saved me from a summer of hard work and maybe a whole lifetime of farming by giving me a free ride to the North.

On the way up North with Buff, we stopped off in Virginia to rest and slept in the car overnight. Sometimes I remember it as a peach truck, but that's how Wes came up here; on a peach truck. Compared to him, I came North in style. I got to Philadelphia, though with everything I owned in a knapsack.

It was one big surprise for Mama. One day she looked up, and there I was. Mama thought I was still down in Laurinburg, and she was so glad to see me. Everybody was working. Wesley had a job cooking in a restaurant, and my sisters, Mattie Laura, Genia, and Wesley's wife, Marjorie, were all doing piecework at a factory. What they were making, I don't know, but they were making something.

Becoming Me . . .

Before I came to Philly, my family had been telling everybody what a good musician I was and asking people to look out for me when I came up from South Carolina. They didn't realize how soon that would be, so Mama, Mattie, Genia, Wesley, his wife, and I were all living there in this one apartment. Three and a half rooms at 637 Pine Street. Bill, the barber, Mattie's husband, lived with us too. Bill was a sport. He had a Cord automobile, gold teeth, and he owned the barbershop right down the street from us. He was a hustling cat and made late hours at night, but he was really nice to me. The first week after I arrived in Philly, Bill took me up to Harry's Pawnshop and bought me one of those long trumpets. That was the first horn I ever owned. I think it was a Pan-American, and it cost him $13. He bought it on time for me, and I really appreciated that, but he didn't buy me a case for the horn, so I started carrying it around in a paper bag. For about two or three weeks, I was carrying this horn around in a paper bag. All the other musicians thought that was real funny.

Within three days after I got to Philadelphia, Johnny, an alto player who lived down the street, found a job for me playing for $8.00 a week at the Green Gate Inn at Twelfth and Bainbridge in South Philadelphia. That place was rowdy. Later on, they named it Pearl Harbor. A blind guy owned the place then, and I was playing trumpet in a trio with Fat Boy, a drummer, and a piano player whose name I can't remember.

Just coming up from down South, I didn't drink at all, but they had a kitty on the piano for the musicians to chip in and buy beer. At that time a pitcher of beer cost fifteen cents, and we were supposed to chip in a nickel to buy the beer for each set. The pitchers kept going between the drummer and the piano player, and they finally had to ask me to chip in. Fat Boy said, "Hey, it's usual for us to share the beer." I told him, "Man, I ain't buying nothing." I didn't drink. We stayed there for about four or five weeks, playing for $8.00 a week, then I got sharp. I went to Parisian Tailors, paid a dollar and a half down and bought three suits on time. Pinstripes, pegged pants, drapes, beautiful stuff, made me feel like a million wearing it. Finally, I got some clothes of my own.

Another guy offered me a job up at Twelfth and South for $12 a week, so I put in my notice at the Green Gate Inn and went out and joined the union. There was a colored union in Philadelphia at the time, and Frankie Fairfax was the secretary. I kept working at Twelfth and South for about five weeks, feeling good about making $12 a week. I used to give Mama some of that. My name started getting around, and Frankie Fairfax decided to give me a tryout for his band. Frankie Fairfax had a beautiful band then, one of the best in Philadelphia. Bill Doggett was his piano player, writer, and musical director. I was lucky to get a tryout with a big band like that so soon.

When the audition came, I didn't even feel nervous. I was used to reading stock orchestrations and could read my ass off, but I had never read any music written in pencil and with such poor notation. In music, a perfect copyist is a very important man, but these cats would take a pencil, and boom-boom-boom, make a line across, a line down, another line across the note and call it an eighth note. And the way they made an eighth rest was—boom—just one line.

Guys had gotten used to reading this bad notation, and when I got up there and they put that music up before me, I started playing eighth rests for notes, sixteenth rests for notes—everything came out wrong. It ended up with them thinking that I couldn't read music and they wouldn't give me the job. Bill Doggett was the main cause of my not getting the job. "That little dizzy cat's from down South," he said, "carries his horn around in a paper bag. You know he can't read." I must have sounded so weird playing all those rests and everything that everybody else agreed. I told them I could read, but they wouldn't believe me. The name didn't stick, but it was the first time someone had called me "dizzy."

BILL DOGGETT (piano, organ, composer):

"Dizzy had just come up from Cheraw, South Carolina. We knew him as John Birks Gillespie. He had a brother that was a swinging cat too, and we were good friends.

"When Diz came into Philadelphia, I was looking for a trumpet player, and somebody recommended him. The strange thing was we were writing music funny at the time. We were doing it for ourselves, and sometimes the stems were above the notes. When Dizzy came out of school, he had seen all of the notes written like they should be. We were making our notes peculiar; we would put the note across the line, and the stem would be above the note. When Dizzy sat down to read this music, he couldn't read it. But the real reason, truthfully, was that we had another trumpet player in the band who was playing all of the solos, and he was sort've the main influence in the band. We were much younger, and he must've seen what Dizzy's coming into the band would have done to him. And so he said, 'Well, man, I don't think we should hire this cat; this cat can't read.'

"But he could play. He could play, and it wasn't the fact that he couldn't read; it was the way we wrote our notes. But this other trumpet player was a mature musician, and he knew that if Dizzy came with the band there would go his solos. So, Dizzy didn't get the job with the band at that particular time."

They gave the job to Joe Facio, a trumpet player who played with no tops on his valves, no pearls, just spikes sticking up into his fingertips. Joe Facio was the only cat that I'd ever seen do that. He came to Philadelphia with Belton's Society Syncopators from Sanford, Florida, and he could really play. After they gave Joe Facio the job, I was heartbroken because I really wanted to play in a big band. Bill Doggett had me pretty mad with him. I told myself that I would catch him one day and really fix him. Fortunately, there were a lot of jobs for musicians around Philly then, so I could make something out of myself anyway. A lady piano player named Vy, who was well known, offered me a job out at Sixty-third and Market, and I took it. We played there for about two or three weeks, and then moved down to Tenth and Passyunk Avenue to another club.

Frankie Fairfax's whole band quit on him not long afterward in an argument about some money. It seemed that Bill Doggett and the cats

DRAWING BY LORENZ; © 1973 *The New Yorker* magazine.

My parents.

Wesley and I, Cheraw, South Carolina.

My boyhood idol, Roy Eldridge.

Lorraine in dancing costume
during the late 1930s.

That's Billy Eckstine
following my wife.

Circa 1940. With Lorraine
at Revere Beach, Massachusetts,
shortly before, or after,
we were married.

Lorraine, shortly after we were married.

1941 — Cab Calloway Orchestra in New York, (l to r) Cab Calloway; Danny Barker, guitar; Jerry Blake, clarinet, alto, baritone saxes; Keg Johnson, trombone; Hilton Jefferson, first alto saxophone; Tyree Glenn, trombone and vibes; Andy Brown, alto saxophone; Quentin "Butter" Jackson, trombone; Walter "Foots" Thomas, tenor saxophone. Standing with me in the trumpet section are Lamar Wright, Sr., and Jonah Jones. COLLECTION OF DUNCAN P. SCHIEDT.

Recording with Cab in Chicago, 1941, (l to r) Milt Hinton, bass; Cozy Cole, drums; Chu Berry, tenor sax; Andy Brown, alto saxophone; Danny Barker, guitar; Cab Calloway, leader; Jonah Jones, trumpet; Lamar Wright, trumpet; Keg Johnson, trombone; Jerry Blake, baritone sax; Diz the Wiz, trumpet; Quentin "Butter" Jackson, trombone; Walter "Foots" Thomas, tenor saxophone. FRANK DRIGGS COLLECTION.

Lorraine, in Small's Paradise chorus line, 1942; (l to r) Peggy, Alese, Louise, Lovey, Faervie, Vivian, Lorraine, and Tweety.

In high spirits after modern jazz jam session at the Village Vanguard, 1942, with (l to r) Harry Lim (organizer), Vito Musso, Billy Kyle, Cootie Williams, Charlie Shavers, and Johnny Williams. FRANK DRIGGS COLLECTION.

Don Byas, Oscar Pettiford, and I sharing some cake.

With Billie Holiday, child, and chihuahua.

Guess which one
is Harry James?

"Yardbird" and Miles
joined forces.

in the band claimed Frankie was collecting more money for jobs than he was telling his musicians, so they all mutinied on him. These cats had a meeting and all of them quit at the same time. Frankie Fairfax couldn't even keep his regular weekend date at the Strand Ballroom. Bill Doggett took the band and accepted a job in the Club Harlem down in Atlantic City. He found out, through the grapevine, that I could read music and offered me a job, but I wouldn't accept it. I told him, "I'll tell you what you can do with your job, but it's gonna hurt!"

BILL DOGGETT:

"Dizzy was living in South Philadelphia, and I was living in North Philadelphia, and I used to go by his house. At that particular time I was trying to play trumpet too. So Dizzy would play piano, while I played trumpet, and then after I got tired of playing trumpet, I'd play piano and Diz would play trumpet. That was the way we'd practice. And we'd sit around and talk music, chord changes; that was the real thing at that particular time. I knew something had to be wrong, man, because we're playing all of these things, and he's writing them, and I'm writing them, and you wonder what's happening. So he used to say about that audition, 'Man, you know what I thought? That the notes were the stems and the stems were the notes.'

"The most unique thing about Dizzy at that time was that he could really play that horn. You could see the way he played then that Dizzy was going to be something because he had a tremendous conception, a way of putting his chords, as we used to call them then, 'changes.' We used to call it, 'running them changes.'

"And there wasn't a thing Dizzy heard that he couldn't interpret on his horn. In later years he acquired the range, as he matured. His execution was always there. And with his knowledge of chords on the piano, he could play anything that he imagined in his mind. You know people said that Diz was copying Roy [Eldridge], was a carbon copy of Roy. Well, you see as you come along, everybody's influenced by somebody, until you get your thing together. And then you branch out. And that's what makes Dizzy, Dizzy Gillespie. Cause he was so far ahead of his time.

"There were several tunes that we used to play to show the virtuosity of a musician, and one of the tunes at that time was a tune called 'Liza,' where you changed chords almost every two beats. Like you'd go to a major and a diminish up to a minor seventh and then up to another diminish, and up to another major. We would try running these chords as we were playing. Running them up, running them backward,

running them upside down, and all kinds of ways. And then we would
take a tune like, 'I Can't Get Started,' which Diz made one of his great
tunes. Now this was a slow ballad, and we would try to make different
chords off of almost every note there was in the tune. We would play
the introduction, make a change there, make a change on the next
melody note. As we branched out into music, getting technical, the
third and fourth bars of 'I Can't Get Started' practically had the same
chords. But as we advanced in music, we were fooling around and we
found out that we could go from a B-minor seventh to the regular seventh, back and forth, four times. In other words, we'd make eight
chords off of this one note, and these were the type of things we were
into. And I mean we used to sit down and get together and talk about
these things. Exchange ideas. It seems as though the guys nowadays
don't have time to communicate with each other. When we were playing for a little bit of nothing around Philly at that time, we'd all meet
in this restaurant. And we would sit around talking chords and ex-
changing ideas. We were all young, and all of us were supposed to be
in before the sun came up. And we'd sit there eating bacon and eggs
and potatoes and talking, and all of a sudden, somebody would look
up and say, 'Hey, man, it's daybreak.' Then we'd all have to scatter for
home. I mean, there wasn't no staying out all night in them days. You
had to answer to somebody."

Frankie Fairfax organized another band soon afterward, and I got
the big band spot I was looking for. In the trumpet section along with
me was Palmer Davis, the first guy who ever called me "Dizzy" and
made it stick. He's known as Fats Palmer now, and his father was a
musician and the first colored captain in the Philadelphia Fire Department down on South Street. The other two trumpets were Jimmy
Hamilton and a boy named Pete Brown who looked like Joe Louis. It
was a good band that stayed together. We played the Strand Ballroom
once a week and did gigs up in the mountain resorts in Pennsylvania.

Right after New Year's, 1936, Tiny Bradshaw came through Philadelphia. He had a gig down in Charlotte, North Carolina, but didn't
have a band, so he hired Frankie's whole band. I went with him and
saved a guy's life. In the rooming house where we stayed, they had
gas heaters in all of the rooms, and one night I came in late and found
the hallway reeking with gas. I knocked on the door where the gas
smell was strongest, but nobody answered, so I walked in anyway.
Fats Palmer was in there lying across the bed knocked out; the gas
had knocked him unconscious.

Fats couldn't walk, he was totally out. He weighed about three hundred pounds, and I was a little-bitty guy, I only weighed about one forty-five, so I started pulling on him and finally managed to drag this big guy out into the hallway. When Fats woke up, he told us that he had lain across the bed for a nap.

We played a place called the Town Casino in Charlotte for about three or four weeks and then came back to Philadelphia, and Frankie started reorganizing the band. Frankie was a trombonist and had only one other trombone, Bert Clagett. The saxophonists were John Brown, Squashy Hawthorne, Tascell Richardson, and Harold Reid. Harold Reid was a very quiet alto player. He played very quietly, and never made a ripple, not one ripple in his playing; but he played a smooth ballad and could read very well.

Up until that time, I'd never really made any strong musical friendships in Philadelphia. There were several trumpet players around Philly who were supposed to be the best trumpet players in town, like "Gabriel," a guy named Jimmy Bowman who played with Jimmy Gorham, and Johnny Lynch who played with Clarence McCreary. Frankie Fairfax, Jimmy Gorham, and Clarence McCreary were the three major colored bandleaders in Philly, but there were other peripheral bands, smaller groups that played in clubs like the Harlem and the Moonglow. One trumpet player at the Moonglow named Horton, I really admired. He never made a name, but boy, this guy could play some changes, not just running the scales, beautiful, mellow, melodic changes. I used to go to listen to him and say, boy that's the kind of music I'd like to play. Horton was a little-bitty cat who must have weighed about one thirty and was smaller than I was. Sometimes I used to exchange ideas with Bowman because he lived in my neighborhood down in South Philly. But I can't think of anybody in Philly who I could really get down and study with until Frankie got his new trumpet section.

Frankie needed some trumpet players because Jimmy Hamilton and Pete Brown were leaving. Harold Reid told Frankie that two guys who had gone to school with him at Bordentown were in New York, and Frankie hired them both, Charlie Shavers and Carl Warwick. Charlie Shavers, Carl Warwick, and me—that was a powerhouse.

These two guys were like brothers and had been inseparable over the years. Carl stayed at Charlie's house in New York, and Mrs. Shavers, Charlie's mother, looked on Carl like he was her own son. Carl Warwick came from Alabama; that's why we called him "Bama." Charlie Shavers was born in New York; his father had the barbershop right under the Savoy Ballroom.

We had a beautiful relationship. At that time, I was still playing southern. I'd learned a couple of Roy Eldridge's licks and would play them and whatever else I could pick up from playing the piano. I'd get a lot of material for solos that way. Then Charlie Shavers came

along. He knew all of Roy's solos, everything. I said, "Boy, this is it
. . . looka here!" Charlie and I played solos and Bama played lead. Of
all the lead trumpet players I've played with, Bama had the most feeling. That's saying a lot because I've played in over thirty bands. Bama
could bend a note. Being from Alabama, he had that kind of soul, and
what really made it strange was that he looked like he was white.

Charlie, Bama, and I became brothers, like the Three Musketeers,
and ran around Philly together all the time. None of us had any
money, but, man, we had some fun. One time, Bama and I were walking down South Street, I think we had thirty cents between the two of
us. We saw this sign, Father Divine, chicken dinner fifteen cents, and
hesitated a little, wondering whether we should go in there, the people were so holy. We started giggling, went inside, and wound up taking care of a whole lot of delicious business for the stomach. Charlie,
Bama, and I were eating at Father Divine's all the time for a while.

I'd learned all of Roy's solos from Charlie and was playing them on
the job, so a little competition started to creep in between us. One
night on the bandstand, I sat down from playing a solo. Charlie told
me, "Say, man, why don't you play your own shit?" I told him, "Man,
I'm getting it *secondhand* now." I liked Roy's solos—both of us liked
Roy's solos—so both of us played them.

All that practice I had put in on the piano down in Laurinburg
started to come in handy. I knew from Laurinburg that your alternatives as a soloist, on any instrument, are much less limited if you know
how to play the piano. All the various combinations of notes and
chords are right there in front of you like on no other single instrument. Sometimes I would go to rehearsal early and play the piano before the other cats showed up. I'd play chord changes, inverting them
and substituting different notes trying to see how different sounds led
naturally, sometimes surprisingly, into others. I'd take them and play
them on my horn, and used to surprise people with new combinations.
When I played trumpet, they couldn't tell whether I was coming by
land or sea.

Back in Philly, before Charlie and Bama joined the band, they
named me "Dizzy." Palmer Davis walked in one day while I was playing the piano before rehearsal. It must've sounded good to him, because he just sat down in a chair and started listening. Other cats
started coming in, Norman Dibbles, the drummer, and all of them,
and everybody was listening. They were surprised that I could play
the piano. Rehearsal was about to begin because almost everybody
was there when I had finished. I got up from the piano, and Fats
Palmer looked across at my empty seat in the trumpet section, and
cracked a joke. "Where's Dizzy, man?" Everybody started laughing.
Norman Dibbles said, "Yeah, that's a good name for that cat!" My

name has been Dizzy to everybody, ever since; even my wife calls me that.

Fats Palmer considered me weird because I would get up in the trumpet section and dance sometimes. He always complimented me about my music though and swears that I was playing bebop in 1936. I appreciate that, coming from him, because he was in a position to know the technical things involved. A lot of musicians then didn't feel comfortable playing in a variety of keys, they preferred some keys to others. Without knowing how determined I was never to be embarrassed again by key changes, they used to check me out sometimes to see whether I could change keys in the middle of a solo. Playing the piano had taught me to feel comfortable any way the music went, in any key. It was totally unconscious, if I acquired my later style of playing (bebop) then. I could get over my horn faster than the average cat and had a lot of fire. Palmer used to call me "excitable," but I wouldn't go so far as to say that I had developed a unique style of my own.

"FATS" PALMER (Palmer Davis, trumpet):

"From the first day I heard him, I said to myself, man this cat is something else. And now, today, that cat is still as great as he ever was. The last time I heard him play out on Randall's Island, I was just sitting there thinking how he's still got that same fire, only now he's got more finesse.

"Dizzy used to do some of the most unthought of things. The cat had a sense of humor that was something else as a youngster. And he was, believe me, playing the same style then as later on with the modern bop when he and Charlie Parker got together. Diz was going over that horn. Boy, he was really with it.

"He was always a nice lovable cat. I'll never forget, we were playing somewhere in North Carolina, and we were living in a hotel with Tiny Bradshaw. They had gas stoves in those rooms and it was cold. I went in there and turned the gas heater on and went to sleep. If it hadn't been for Dizzy coming in and finding me . . . I was knocked out. The cat pulled me out. I should have turned off the gas heater, but I forgot it. Man, if that cat hadn't come in and pulled me out of there, I would have gotten gassed. He's a phenomenal cat.

"It was a pleasure to sit there and hear Charlie Shavers and Dizzy go over their horns. They had such finesse, and this was years before bop came out. He used to do so many crazy things. He used to get up in the section and dance. So many things that the average cat wouldn't think of, kiddish things. I said, 'Man, this cat is a dizzy cat. . . .' And I'd say 'Where's that dizzy cat at?' And the cats started calling him Dizzy.

"Diz used to be such a clown, and it was so funny because he was so great and didn't realize it. In fact, we didn't realize how great the cat was, flying over that horn. He was so unpredictable about what he was gonna play. He would never have a set thing. Like guys get a solo on a certain song and would play a certain way. You'd know just what they were gonna do. Like, for instance, 'Body and Soul,' that was supposed to be one of the hardest things. Dizzy would take 'Body and Soul' and run over it like a rabbit running over a hill. Any key, it didn't make no difference.

"In those days a cat would have his favorite key. I remember one time we were playing, and we said, we're gonna check Diz out, and started going through the keys, changing keys. That's one of the ways bop was invented. Because later, at Minton's, so many guys would come in and couldn't play their horns. So Diz and others would invert the chords and make the chords different to keep unskilled cats from getting up there. Diz was fantastic from the very beginning. Not only was he gifted for it, but he knew his foundation by playing piano. That was a hell of an asset to him in his music because he knew his chords. The other guys were just playing average; we were trying to play, man, and this cat was just going over the horn by knowing piano.

"We used to work with Frankie Fairfax's band at a place called the Rafters. We were playing 'Undecided,' different things in that vein, what we called jazz. At that time it was mostly dance music. I think the same thing that they call rock 'n' roll now was nothing but jazz. It was just a part of the repertoire. You had to play that style that people could dance by, just get one of those beats and make arrangements. In those days the band had to have arrangements.

"My father used to teach me, and Diz would occasionally take a little trumpet lesson from him. I never could compare with Diz. His technique, his execution. A million cats can play high, but going over that horn, from the bottom all the way to the top. It's just like a fighter, man, you can take some fighters who can hit, but Ray Robinson was a boxer. He had style.

"Those were some great days. We weren't making any money, but the cat had to go up because he was great, and what made it so nice was that he was just being himself, just Dizzy. When he went with Cab Calloway's band, Diz outshone all those guys who were supposed to be big stars, with his funny antics and playing his horn. He was a showman and knew his horn.

"One day we were at rehearsal up at the Strand Ballroom, and Diz was sitting down at the piano. The trumpet was his preference, but I think that if he had put in as much time on the piano, as he did on the trumpet, he would have been one of the great pianists. His mind and his style were different. He was different in those days, he was different because the average cat would take a couple of notes and play blues, but he would take his horn and run just like he was playing the scales, in any key. Sometimes, I'd just put my horn in my lap and just listen.

"He and Charlie Shavers. Charlie could go over his horn too, but still with the style they were both playing, there was a difference. Diz was excitable. Later on there were different people, Miles Davis and those guys, Fats Navarro, Clifford Brown. If a guy can play piano or guitar, that's a foundation, just like building a building. If Diz had taken saxophone, it would have been the same thing. That's something that's embedded. This is what makes the average guy less. I had an opportunity, but I never thought about it. I was just taking the trumpet. But that foundation, that chord foundation, inversions and changes of chords, on piano or guitar you have that.

"The average musician who played a wind instrument then couldn't play piano. I didn't know for quite a while that Diz could play piano, 'cause he never let it be known that he could play. I knew that he knew his chords, but when I actually heard him playing piano, then it all dawned on me. I said, 'Well, this is why this guy knows his horn.' And when he would play these changes, they would be correct. Some cats can start playing and run all off chord, but these would be correct. And he had learned to invert them so well; he could take a major chord and invert it and make it minor, and this takes a whole lot 'cause your mind's got to really be working. Now guys are doing it every day, but in those days it was a major innovation. I think a lot of musicians didn't even realize what the guys were doing. Maybe he didn't even realize it. Everybody was playing 'Body and Soul,' and they'd go into the channel* and go right back into the melody; and Diz would go into the channel and he'd run crazy. So you had to say, damn, what's with this cat, man?

"When he came to New York and was with Teddy Hill and Edgar Hayes, the cat was upsetting everybody. And if Diz had been an ofay in them days, it's no end to what he would have been, because he had said something really new in music.

"I don't care whether black, blue, or white, when he came in and put that horn up, all them cats stopped. 'Where's Diz, man?' I asked Norman Dibbles, who was a drummer. Norman said, 'Yeah, that's a good name for that cat,' because he was doing so many crazy things,

---

* Channel—A connecting passage between two statements of a jazz theme. The same as a bridge.

not to hurt or insult anyone, but just being a funny cat. You know Diz could have been a comedian."

The musicians used to have some baaad jam sessions in Philly. One night I saw Roy Eldridge, my idol, make Rex Stewart cry. Teddy Hill's band was playing at the Lincoln Theater and Duke Ellington's band was at the Nixon Grand. The session was at the Rendezvous, downstairs. Boy, that used to be a real den of iniquity. It was down under the Douglas Hotel, and the theater was right across the street, and it used to be a hangout for the people at night. When I walked in there . . . ! I imagine nightclubs look like that to real young people now, with those lights and everything, and the girls with short dresses, the waitresses. You couldn't see nothing in there. Everybody must have been out with their neighbor's wife.

The Rendezvous had a band with some real mean cats. One guy named Rufus had a mouthpiece that was straight across. That band was good. They couldn't read music, but, boy, they had some arrangements. They rehearsed regularly, big band arrangements, and not one of those cats could read music. They remind me of a big band that played later at Monroe's Uptown House in Harlem, those guys didn't read either. Charlie Parker and Max Roach were the only ones in the whole band who could read music, although George Treadwell could read a little. The rest of those guys couldn't read at all. Their arrangements weren't written. If you could read it, it wouldn't help you, no way; their arrangements were just that difficult. Those cats practiced. The jam sessions in Philly were above me; I was just an onlooker. I didn't participate. But I was in there and saw what was going on. I saw Rex Stewart and Louis Armstrong, but Roy was my man. Give me Roy, man, he was younger. It's just like right now, I can still see young guys appreciating where I come from, even though there may be two or three generations between them and me, musically. Whoever they like doesn't matter to me. If they like the younger guy better, that's fine. I just want them to understand why the guy they like plays the way he does.

If he's younger than me and playing trumpet, he's following in my footsteps.

Speaking of following, one girl in Philly used to follow me from the Strand Ballroom in the cold. She'd follow me all the way home, then turn around and go back. She was a strange girl. I never met her; she'd walk about half a block behind me, and I couldn't see her face. When I'd go in my door and look up the street, she'd turn around and cut out. At the time, I was going with another girl in Philly named

Frances, whose mother owned a restaurant on South Street. I used to eat up there a lot. Ha! Ha! I ain't no dummy. I might have been dizzy, but not stupid.

I'd never before come into contact socially with a white girl, and this white girl, Peggy, worked for a newspaper in Philadelphia, while I was working with Frankie Fairfax at a club called The Rafters. She waited for me one night with her car, and we drove off and went to a small hotel. It almost scared me to death. I don't think I even enjoyed it because I was too scared. I'd never been with a white girl before. She looked like the girl who used to sing with Paul Whiteman, "Miss Something." That's who she looked like. She had come to The Rafters a couple of times and asked me what I was doing later and whether I had a ride home. I lied and told her yes, but I didn't have any ride; I'd take the trolley car home. One night, she just waited, and when I got off she was outside. I jumped in her car, and she attacked me, immediately. It happened two or three times, and each time I'd get more relaxed. Eventually, we had a very nice relationship, but I wasn't deeply in love or thinking about marrying her and having children. She was way older anyway; I was only eighteen or nineteen years old, still a young boy.

Occasionally I'd have to fight my way home in Philadelphia. In South Philly there were a lot of gangsters who used to grab little guys, little colored guys, off the street and beat 'em up and throw 'em out in the woods half dead. One time, coming home from work, when I was living at Seventh and Pine, three white guys in this car pulled up to the side and told me to come over to the car. They kept cruising alongside me, but I kept walking. I was ignoring them. "Leave me alone, I'm not bothering you," I said. At that time, I used to carry a knife opened in my pocket. It was pretty sharp. They pulled up too close to me by the playground, and one of them reached his hand out to grab me and that's the last thing he remembered. I tried to saw his hand off. When I finished, this guy's hand was hanging there loose on the end of his arm: like if you've ever seen somebody cut a chicken leg where the joint goes together, and the meat is left there hanging. That's what he had. They started trying to catch me, and I ran. I ran down Lombard Street with this car trying to catch me. This guy was screaming from the back seat, "Take me to the hospital. Take me to the hospital!" They finally gave up trying to catch me. It was still dangerous to mess with me then.

Tiny Bradshaw came through town again and needed a trumpet section to go to Baltimore to play in the Astoria Ballroom down there. He was offering a nice little piece of money. We hadn't been making that kind of money, and since Charlie and Bama weren't at home anyway, they accepted the job and tried to get me to go along with them. "Man, come on, let's go, we've got a little clique going." I wouldn't go because I didn't want to leave home. I was still scared to leave Mama. Since I wouldn't go, they took Frank Galbraith, and I stayed around Philadelphia playing with Frankie Fairfax until 1937. For a while, I didn't see Charlie and Bama too much, but I used to go over and visit them when I was in New York because my brother J.P. had moved there. By then, they had left Tiny Bradshaw and were working with Lucky Millinder.

Charlie and Bama cruised me out of Philly to go with Lucky Millinder. They called me on the phone and I came over to New York to go with Lucky without him having heard me play. Lucky paid me for a while, even though I wasn't playing. He kept me on standby. Lucky Millinder's trumpet section was boss at that time; Charlie Shavers, Carl Warwick, and Harry (Sweets) Edison. I was supposed to take Harry Edison's place, but Lucky liked Harry, didn't want to fire him, and just kept paying Sweets and stopped paying me.

I was pretty ashamed. That was a big thing to go to New York to get with the big band, and then fail to get the job. That was the epitome of playing—going to New York to play. The offer to play with Lucky was my chance to go, so I cut out like a real musician, going to New York, not to Baltimore, Maryland. It wasn't so hard to leave Mama, because I had a room in New York with my brother where I could stay. My brother J.P. was over in New York at 142nd Street and Seventh Avenue, between Seventh and Eighth avenues, in the two-hundred block, and I figured I'd have a place to stay. I moved in with him, and later we moved to 216 West 139th Street. It wasn't hard to leave Philadelphia. The time had come for me to get out of there. Trying to survive in New York without any job was risky, but it was the only way to make the big time in jazz. Nothing seemed risky to me, since I was already known to be crazy.

Glory Road

For a little guy from down South up in the big town, trying to make the big time, I felt pretty sure of myself. How well could I play, though, when you stacked me up and measured me against all the other young musicians out there playing?

Charlie Shavers introduced me to a whole bunch of new cats, and we'd go to all these places, every night, making the jam sessions—Charlie and Bama, whenever they weren't working, little Bobby Moore and me. Sometimes, little Benny Harris and Kenny Clarke went with us; we'd just go and blow all over, everywhere. We'd go and get in a place and go fool. We were always looking for someplace to play.

Little Bobby Moore was the best of our crowd. He was better than any of us, really, and more advanced. He's down in Ward's Island at a mental institution now. I took him a trumpet out there once. Bobby had the advantage over me of being born and raised in New York City. That didn't give him any exclusivity on talent, but it did give him an edge in the kind of music he was hearing, against the music that I was hearing over in Philadelphia.

Bobby was more advanced than I was in Philly with the technical aspects of the trumpet, but as far as being musically sophisticated, I had the sophistication because I was a piano player. I don't think little Bobby played the piano at all, but he sure played that trumpet. He had really, really beautiful technique, and a whole lot of fire which you can hear on a Count Basie record called, "Out the Window." Lester Young is on it too. Bobby went with Count Basie, and that was his most famous solo. That may be his only solo (on record) because at the time he was there, Buck Clayton was in the band and got most of the solos. But little Bobby was baaad. He knew all of Roy's solos— all his licks—and could whup it. Bobby was the best in our crowd, he heard more.

We used to go to play jam sessions at a lot of places. We'd go in a place and find out if the union man had been there. If he hadn't been there, we'd cut that one aloose and go to someplace where he'd already been and play there. 'Cause if he'd catch us there, he'd want to fine you. Fifty or a hundred dollars, that was a whole lot of money—and fine the whole band too—but they'd run you out most of the time.

It cost much less to eat then. Eating cost twenty-five cents a day in 1937. You could eat breakfast, and get a big ham and egg sandwich for a dime, and drink some water. There was a big guy named Pike on the corner of 142nd Street and Seventh Avenue in a bar who had this concession for food and for twenty-five cents you could eat enough to fill a sow. So I wasn't worried. My money from Philly hadn't even run out, and I wasn't the type to worry, as long as I could get enough food to have enough energy to play my horn. I just went on and played with all these bands, made all the sessions, until my chance came. When I first came in town and Lucky Millinder disappointed me, I refused to go back to Philly. I just stayed in New York.

JAMES PENFIELD GILLESPIE:

"When he came to New York, he came here to me, and that was my baby brother. And we always got along all right, just like any other brothers. He came to me here and respected me as his older brother, almost a father.

"I paid the rent, $6.50 a week, and I'd leave thirty-five cents up on the table for him to eat with, 'cause you could go up on the corner and get a big meal for thirty-five cents. I had a job making $12.50 a week, $25.00 every two weeks, working as a tray boy down at Fifty-seventh Street and Sixth Avenue. This was at the height of the Depression, you know. I had to go to work at seven o'clock in the morning. Directly after he came here, then he was gigging right away at the Savoy, with different bands. He would be out and come in four or five o'clock in the morning. I would get up and give him the room and go sit in the park until time for me to get the subway to go to work. Most of the time he'd have some little chick with him. So I would get up and let him have the room."

Things were rough, but that made me feel real excited. Those were exciting times. I stuck around and was going up to the Savoy Ballroom on Lenox Avenue every night. I finally got an entrée into the Savoy without paying, just from coming up there all the time.

Charlie Buchanan was the manager of the Savoy Ballroom. There's a man I remember. Charlie Buchanan was in partnership—maybe a small partnership—but in enough partnership that now he's one of the richest men in Harlem. His wife, Bessie, went to the New York State Assembly, and he had enough money to back her, so he must'a been pretty cool. Now, he owns a whole lotta real estate in Harlem. Charlie Buchanan used to let us into the Savoy free. Since we all were musicians, it was in his interest.

CHARLIE BUCHANAN
(former owner/manager of the Savoy Ballroom):

"I was manager of the Savoy from its opening on March 12, 1926, until it closed in July 1958. Those who worked for us we would let them in. The Savoy was a funny place; everybody paid. But I mean there were certain musicians who worked with various bands who just came in. If you played in Tommy Dorsey's band, and we didn't know you, and you say you're a musician, we'd show you the box office. Fellows like Shavers and all those fellows would play one week with one band, the next week they might be with another band. They were regularly known musicians at the Savoy. The Savoy was owned by a corporation. I had a 35 per cent interest in that. Moe Gale and his father had the balance."

CARL "BAMA" WARWICK (trumpet):

"We used to go around to all the clubs and jam. There was a club called The Bit. Chu Berry was working there then. There were so many places where a guy could blow. That's how any musician develops. You have to apply yourself. That's the one thing wrong with the scene today. You have some great young musicians coming out of the colleges today, but you don't have that workshop type of thing, no jam sessions. I remember again around in the fifties the union stepped in and tried to stop us. 'We don't want to catch you guys jamming. If there's five guys working, we want to see five on the stand.' We went through a thing with the musician's union during a certain period when they tried to stop jamming in the late forties and early fifties. They tried for a period of six months or a year to frighten the guys, but this was the kind of practice that was giving cats experience."

So we were going to all of these different places, ten or twelve places a night. We'd go down to the Village to a lot of places, then finish off uptown: George's in the Village; the Yeah Man, and the Victoria, the Britwood, and Hollywood on 116th Street; Smalls, the Big Apple and another place over on 111th Street. We'd play at the 101 Ranch on 139th Street, and then Monroe's Uptown House and Dicky Wells'. Those were after-hours joints.

Since I could get into the Savoy free, I'd blow my horn with the Savoy Sultans, Willie Bryant, Fess Williams, Claude Hopkins, and anybody who'd come to the Savoy. Chick Webb took a liking to me and used to let me sit in with his band. That was strange. Chick Webb used to let me sit in, in Taft Jordan's place, and take solos. I think I was the only one he used to let sit in like that. I ain't lying. I'd never seen anybody sitting in, in that band. Everytime, he'd ask me, ". . . play some?" I'd say, "Yes, sir, I wanna play some!" I could read very well then. Chick Webb must have really liked the way I sounded because he never let nobody sit in, in his band, but me. That's how I met Mario Bauza, the Cuban trumpeter. He was playing first trumpet with Chick Webb. Mario liked me, and I got a good introduction to Latin rhythms from him. I always had a feeling for Latin American music. Teddy Hill heard me up there playing someplace, and he let me sit in with his band a couple of times too.

MARIO BAUZA (trumpet):

"I first met the 'Crazee' in 1937 when I was in the Savoy. I thought he was the greatest thing that I had ever heard.

"At that time, he was no different than he is now, not to me. I was a trumpet player, knowing that category.

"The difference was, he came with a new approach and confirmations and a different pattern than the old jazz. It was a new approach into the jazz. Later on, they started calling it bebop. In it, there was the evolution, the evolution of American music. In the last fifty years,

they have two moves. Louis Armstrong was the first move. Dizzy Gillespie set the example for the second move of trumpet players in my esti-
mation."

Teddy Hill was getting ready to go to Europe the day I ran into
him at the Savoy, hanging around there with Lucky Millinder.
Frankie Newton was playing with Teddy at that time. He replaced Roy
Eldridge on second trumpet in Teddy Hill's band when Roy went to
play with Fletcher Henderson. Frankie Newton used to play in a buzz
mute all the time, and he didn't want to go to Europe. Teddy said,
"I'm going to Europe, and I need a trumpet player. You know where I
can find one?"

"You're looking at one . . . yes sireee!" I said. "Ha! Ha! Ha! Ha!"
Europe . . . ? For $70 a week? Yeah! I was twenty years old, single
and insane!

Really, I was only nineteen, going on twenty, and I had to go back
to Philadelphia to get Mama to sign an affidavit so I could get my
passport. Mama said O.K., anything I wanted, since I was in New
York anyway, away from home. That's how I got the job with Teddy
Hill. Some people have told various writers, who have had the effron-
tery to set it down in print, that Teddy Hill hired me because I used
to baby-sit for him. That's not true. I deny it categorically. I used to
go over to his house and play with his little daughter. She was a baby.
And if I'd be around long enough, well . . . But that was afterwards,
after I'd come back from Europe, that I'd go over to visit them. I'd
never been in his house before I went to Europe with Teddy.

The real reason Teddy hired me, I believe, was because I sounded so
much like Roy. He wanted to keep a solo trumpet that sounded like
that in his band, someone who could play high, fast, and with fire. I
had been practicing playing Roy's solos for almost three years; they
were like second nature to me. All I had to do was read the parts that
I didn't already know and learn how to execute certain phrases better.
I played the hell out of them, and I could read 'round the corner, look
at it and just go.

A couple of guys didn't like my just coming in the band and getting
solo work. I had become a pretty competent professional musician by
this time. But being able to read and play well wasn't enough to keep
some of the older, gloomier guys in the band off of my ass. I couldn't
hardly sit down before they started on me.

TEDDY HILL (bandleader):

"First time I heard Dizzy was in Philadelphia. At that time I had Roy Eldridge and Chu Berry. Then Roy and Chu left to join Fletcher Henderson in Chicago. Dizzy had come to New York in the meantime, and along with a lot of other trumpets, he spoke to me about getting Roy's chair. I asked him to come to the next rehearsal.

"I called the brass section for rehearsal a couple of hours before the reeds. I'd been using Bill Dillard on first trumpet, Shad Collins on second, and Roy on third. I switched Shad to third and gave Dizzy the second book. He got on the bandstand with his overcoat on, gloves and everything.

"Some of the fellows resented Dizzy. When the possibility of a European tour came up, there was some talk of getting a man with more of a reputation. Some of the men even threatened to leave if Dizzy was kept in the band. I thought Diz had possibilities, so I called their bluff and told them to go ahead and leave. They stayed.

"Dizzy made my home his home. He'd come in almost every day. He was very fond of my little daughter, Gwendolyn, who was five or six years old; he'd wallow all over the floor, tell her candy wasn't good for her, then eat it all himself. Still a big kid . . ."*

Shad Collins, Dicky Wells, and some other guys had worked with other big bands, like Fletcher Henderson, and none of them believed in giving young guys a break. They had an *old* clique. In New York when the big bands of Chick Webb, Fletcher Henderson, and Teddy Hill were in their heyday, a young musician couldn't get in those bands. That was a drag because it kept a whole lot of guys out. If you were lucky enough to get into a band, some guys felt it was their duty to make it hard for you.

Shad Collins was very nasty. During my solos, he and Dicky Wells tried to act like I was playing absolutely nothing and looked around at me sneering. They even tried to start a little protest and threatened to quit if Teddy took me to Europe. That's what they *said*, but they didn't. Today, I'm a world-renowned trumpet player and Dicky Wells is a bank guard. I see him every now and then. Shad Col-

---

* Excerpted from an interview with Hill by Leonard Feather, published in *Metronome*, April 1947. Dizzy actually replaced Frankie Newton, not Roy Eldridge.

lins is a cabdriver. When I get to be his age, I'll still be where I am now; I have that feeling. I'm sixty years old, I'm no thirty-year-old, and I'm getting ready to go to Europe again. I'm at the top of my profession and playing better every day. All the musicians respect me and I respect them. I respect talent. The older musicians are the guardians of the music, but that's not an excuse to keep people down and try to destroy their talent. Those guys were just keeping our music motionless, trying to stop it from moving forward so somebody old could sit there and hold a horn. I did nothing against them. Nothing but play, and they didn't do anything to help me.

DICKY WELLS (trombone):

"It's a damn lie . . . damn lie . . . worst lie in the world. We were crazy 'bout Dizzy. Me 'specially. But Dizzy was playing, trying to copy. He was playing a little of Roy's stuff like I told you, but he was erratic on his horn, which proved out to be one of the best things in his life, you know. And cats'd say, 'cause they were doing this—'one-two-one-two—not 'bla-de-dah-de-de-dip.' They didn't want that then. But Dizzy was way ahead, and he was the prettiest person in the world, and he still is. But he accelerated—he did—he accelerated, which proved to be the best. Now he's more than Roy, but, then, he was copying Roy.

"People were dancing then. They don't dance now. Instead of sitting and looking then, you were dancing. You had rhythm in your bones, man. I used to watch those Lindy Hoppers throw those women all the way to the roof in the Savoy. Man, they would throw them all the way to the sky and grab 'em when they came down. And doing all the stepping, up they go again.

"Sheet! Dizzy tried to play like Roy then. And then he ventured off and went into Charlie Parker. Dizzy's pretty smart, you know, very smart. He went from Roy to Charlie Parker. I'm telling you where Diz came from. He came from Charlie Parker. A whole lotta Charlie Parker in Dizzy, you know that. If it weren't for Charlie, it wouldn't have been no Dizzy, I don't suppose, because he'd be right back stomping."

But he hadn't even heard of Charlie Parker.[†]

"Will you hold tight. Charlie had rhythm, boy; he was playing that horn, but he had this beat. So Dizzy brought a new little thing on, you know, which is very brilliant. He plays that horn. That cat knows that horn backwards. Shooo, Dizzy Gillespie? Now, if you go somewhere

[†] Questions and comments in italics throughout are those of coauthor, Al Fraser.

and listen and want a feeling, where you gonna get it from . . . if it's too erratic? If you got a broad, trying to make a broad and you're sitting next to her, 'one-two-three-four' . . . she's liable to say, 'Come on, daddy.' You know. You gotta have rhythm!

"These are facts. Dizzy brought a new style, and it's popular. You know, Roy Eldridge's jaws used to come out like this. I said, 'Roy, pull your muscles together, please,' and he did. Now, no air comes out. But Dizzy, 'puff, puff.' I can't talk to Dizzy. You can't tell him nothing."

On the other hand, Bill Dillard helped me tremendously. Bill was a trumpeter and singer, and he was beautiful. Bill played first trumpet and was one of the earliest guys to assist me. A beautiful trumpeter and singer, he'd show me how to hold notes out, how to sing on the trumpet, and how to use a vibrato. I was young and fly and could play. I could read like hell, but I didn't know a lot of the fine points of music. Bill helped me change the little things that I did that weren't professional.

BILL DILLARD (trumpet):

"I first met Dizzy at the Savoy Ballroom, prior to the time that we went to Europe in 1937. He used to come up to the Savoy, and he sat in with the band several times. Teddy let him sit in and play with us. And that's the first time I met him and the first time I heard him play. That was before we made arrangements for him to replace Frankie Newton in the band and go to Europe with us. It was several months before we left for Europe.

"It was a very complete change. As a matter of fact, we were all impressed with Dizzy, even before he joined the band. At least I was impressed with him because he had a whole different conception of solo trumpet playing. And I'm referring to the height, his register, how he employed the top register, very often above the C's and the D's up to the F's, and the ease with which he was able to play in the top register. And the next thing was the speed with which he played. He was able to play very fast, and that impressed me also. I did recognize the fact that he was inexperienced and that he was trying to say something that was a little foreign to me. His whole conception of playing trumpet and what he was trying to achieve was foreign to me, and I found it very interesting. But it was quite different from what Frankie had done, and of course Frankie was a tremendous musician, a great trumpet player. And Frankie had a tremendous style, he had great control and a wonderful conception of playing trumpet. But Diz was like something I had never heard before, even then.

"It was customary with the big bands of that era to have little cliques among certain musicians, older guys who had been in the band. When a new man came in the band, there was always a little feeling of jealousy and the older guys exerted their superiority or authority over the newcomer. And the newcomers were usually the butt of jokes. I think I do remember noticing that in the band at that time. He wasn't too popular with a few guys. Not that there was any serious difference, but there was always a little dissension going on. Some guys were the butt of the jokes and so forth. I think for a time Dizzy was that guy.

"In those days, the brass section was a separate unit. The rhythm section was a separate unit. We all rehearsed our parts separately, and later we'd put the different groups together.

"When we first started breaking Dizzy into the band, some of the phrasings and some of the sustained tones and style of playing that we were accustomed to, he didn't have any experience in. I was playing first trumpet, and it was my obligation to keep the section together. So I proceeded to show him and tell him how we played. I guess it gave him an idea. I had forgotten all about that, but it seems that he mentions occasionally that I helped him a lot. But I didn't do it deliberately. I was only doing it because I was the first trumpet and to keep the section tight. But he picked up on everything and he contributed tremendously.

"Roy Eldridge had great facility. He could play very fast passages, and it's possible that Dizzy in referring to Roy could have been relating to that flexibility and the speed that Roy used in solo playing. But other than that, I don't think that there is hardly anything that would make me feel that Dizzy and Roy had anything in common. Diz was always something aside from anybody else. I realize today that he was working on his conception of modern jazz, or the modern music, which was beyond most of us at that time. Later bebop and this progressive music employed flat notes and sharp notes and clichés of very fast notes which was foreign to the type trumpet playing that had preceded that. And I'm pretty sure it was an original idea, an invention of his own mind, something that he wanted to project.

"I never detected anything about his breathing. I only noticed, as all of us had, that his jaws were extended beyond the normal position. And that in itself possibly implied that he used a completely different kind of breathing technique to play. Now, why he started playing that way, which normally would be considered improper, to have the jaws bulging that way—you were always taught formally to keep the jaws in—I don't know. He always played that way. The first time I saw him, the jaws were bulging. And whether it was considered right or wrong, the results were the only thing that matter. Maybe with the correct or normal-type breathing, you couldn't produce what he's producing.

"And he always had a tremendous sense of humor. I don't know where he got the name Diz, but you got that impression from him. He was really 'dizzy' at times, and that meant he really enjoyed life. He was ready to laugh and giggle at almost the slightest little thing. And his playing reflected that too. Because I remember when I first heard him play, he would attempt to play something in the 'stratosphere,' and occasionally it didn't work out. He would take his horn down and laugh. Now me, not understanding what he was trying to achieve, thought it was weird. It was kinda dizzy, but that was the way he was. But I realized that he was working out his thing, and he had the reckless kind of abandon to develop that type of style, where most of us had always been taught that you should be very careful and precise, make sure you didn't make any bad notes. If it's something that you thought might be a little too fast, play it slower, but play it clean and precise, you know. But you could never achieve what he was achieving with that conception. I think you have to have a reckless kind of abandon, at least when you're trying to develop in the early stages, or you would never accomplish some of the things that these modern trumpet players have done."

HOWARD JOHNSON (alto saxophone):

"I don't know where Teddy heard about Dizzy or who told him about Dizzy, but Dizzy came. We wanted to try him out, so he sat in the section and started playing. He played a chorus, and in those days trumpet soloists didn't get a chance to play as many choruses as they wanted. In a big band, you only had a chance to play eight bars a lot of times, or one chorus, and a lot of the musicians had their chorus down, so everybody knew what chorus they were gonna play before they played it. Now, on the other hand, some of them had a helluva chorus down, but after that chorus they were no more good. They really couldn't improvise too much because they hadn't studied the stuff.

"Well, Dizzy sat in and he took a chorus, and a lotta the fellas, who shall be nameless, started pushing him. 'Take another one,' somebody else said. Trying to stick him, you know. They didn't know they were throwing Dizzy in the briar patch. The more he took, the better he'd get going. It kept building up and building up until they let him alone. This was just before he joined the band. They were testing him.

"Right away he sounded very good to me. I could tell that he knew his instrument. He could go down low, or up high. He was flexible. I could tell he had it right away. So next we had to find out whether he could read. That's another story. I really don't remember what happened. I don't think he had much trouble with it because I think he had good musical training before he joined the band.

"Dizzy's name was aptly applied. I remember after our first meeting, I spoke to him and said, 'You sound good, what's your name?'

"'My name's John Gillespie,' he said, 'but everybody calls me Dizzy.'

"Just as happy-go-lucky and free, and so, 'dizzy.' I always felt funny calling him 'Dizzy' at first, but I mean he told me it was Dizzy, and so . . . ? That's the way Dizzy acts, not crazy. 'Cause he was always smart. You could tell he was smart if you talked to him. He was just sorta flighty.

"I never wrote out Roy Eldridge's solos for him while he was in the band. I might have written an arrangement and left a spot open for Dizzy, but if Dizzy played Roy's solos, he played 'em on his own. Dizzy admired Roy greatly. Although his style is different, he admired Roy. Roy played fast, and Dizzy played fast, but it was a different kind of fast. Now how do I explain this? Roy would play fast in spots, in spurts, and go to a more or less Louis Armstrong style of punch in phrasing. Dizzy played fast almost all the time. He'd double up, what they called 'double up,' anyplace in the arrangement. Roy's style was more understandable to the people at the time because Dizzy was way ahead of his time, even then. But it was still patterned after Roy's style."

ROY ELDRIDGE (trumpet):

"I was with my own band at the Savoy. And Dizzy, Charlie Shavers, Bama, Joe Guy, and another little cat that was bad, named Bobby Moore, all used to come around. They could play all the things that I had made better than I could, you know. But Dizzy had his thing going. I talked to him once down at Minton's and he was asking me how I did certain things and I told him. And the one thing I appreciate about Diz, even though he used to play something like me, is that he went on and got his own thing together, which started a whole new kind of thing. And he's contributed a lot. Most all of the cats are trying to play like Diz now. He's still playing great and he deserves a lot of credit because the cat really stuck to his guns. I remember when they didn't like him and said, 'Awww, he's playing off key. . . .' But he stuck to what he was doing and he came out all right."

We had some all around good musicians in that band. Shad Collins, the other trumpet player; Dicky Wells and Wilbur De Paris, two trombones; Howard Johnson, alto; Russell Procope, alto baritone; Bob Carroll, tenor; Teddy played the alto saxophone; Dick Fullbright, bass; Bill Beason, drums; John Smith, guitar; and Sam Allen, piano. And you know Melba Moore: her mother, Melba Smith, was the singer with Teddy Hill's band. Later on she changed her name to Bonnie.

I made my first recordings with Teddy Hill's band, just before we went to Europe in May 1937. I played solos on two songs, "King Porter Stomp," and "Blue Rhythm Fantasy." They paid union scale, $33, something like that. The union had been fighting about that, to give us more than scale for recording dates. There was a ban on recordings shortly afterwards.

On those records I sounded funny. I was doing the best I could, trying to sound like Roy Eldridge. That was 1937. I was really into a Roy Eldridge bag, and added a little. I just put a little bit of me in it and a whole lot of Roy. Nobody noticed it. I guess nobody knew I made it.

I was just nervous and I couldn't keep my horn straight. I had never made a record before, they kept telling me to point toward the microphone. I didn't have the technique of recording, but I finally got it together. I was excited about it, but I had confidence; I can tell I had confidence by listening to the records, but experience? I played up to what I knew.

I try to play up to my level at all times. Whenever you hear me, that's the best I can do at that moment, considering all factors.

I was safe and didn't try anything challenging, but at that time I'd probably try anything, anything that came to my mind. It's only when you get older, and you get set, that you want everything you play to be a gem. That's why I try not to curtail young musicians when they play with me. If I want an older, experienced musician, I go and get him, and I know that he's got the taste. But when I want to see somebody developing, I get one of the young guys. But I don't handcuff him. I help him, yes, but I don't handcuff him.

Parlez-Vous . . . ?

We sailed to Europe, and I was the baby of the trip, the youngest person in the band, the youngest in the whole troupe with the exception of Warren Berry. And those older guys who had threatened to quit were right there on board. It was a whole show—The Cotton Club Show. We played all the music from the original show, but ours lacked the big stars who appeared in Bill Robinson's and Cab Calloway's Cotton Club Show. We used the name "The Cotton Club Show" because they had Clarence Robinson, the original producer and director, in our troupe. Bill Bailey danced Bill Robinson's act, and the Berry Brothers danced too, Ananias and James, and the new one, Warren. Warren, the young one, could do his own act and both of his brothers'. He was "meeeean," just a little bitty cat, about thirteen years old. His mother had to come along with him.

I had a lot of fun jamming on the ship with Smitty, the guitar player and the guys in the "Tramp Band." Buddy Johnson was with the Tramp Band then. Buddy and Rasputin, one of the guys who sang, were always ready to jam. It was quite an experience; they had a whole line of chorus girls, and everybody was having a ball. We spent seven days on the ship, and then we saw the land coming into le Havre. It was beautiful.

Paris, London, Dublin, Manchester. Six weeks in Paris, four weeks in London, two weeks in Dublin and Manchester. Whew, it was a dynamite show! We also had Jessie Scott (Bill Bailey's wife); Roland Smith, who used to sing "Ol' Man River"; and Alberta Hunter, an international singer who stayed in Europe for many years. She was very well known in Europe. I found that strange, how blacks who had talent and couldn't get any recognition in the United States would go over to Europe and immediately be appreciated and become big celebrities.

Our show was at the Moulin Rouge, the big nightclub on the boulevard de Clichy in Paris. It was shaped like a big windmill outside, and I'd never seen anything like that. The band would play for a big show with the dancers and singers on the stage, and then play a set of dance music for the audience. The French people didn't know what a big swing band was. It hadn't soaked in yet. They'd seen our shows before, like *Blackbirds, Shuffle Along, Green Pastures,* and *There's a Cabin in the Sky.* The original Cotton Club Show had also played there, but big band jazz was still a pretty new thing in Europe, and the ordinary Frenchman wasn't well acquainted with it. The only jazz musicians I knew who had been to Europe at that time were Benny Carter and Coleman Hawkins. Willie Lewis was a bandleader in Paris who had a big band and played at Les Ambassadeurs. France also had some jazz afficionados, collectors like Charles Delaunay and Hugues Panassié, who collected mostly New Orleans-type jazz.

The French loved Bill Coleman, a trumpet player who used to work with Teddy. He was living over there. He and Dickie Wells and the old clique were pals; same age and everything, from the same school, played alike, from the same era. Shad Collins, Sam Allen, and a lot of the older band members were doing record dates over there. They never recorded me on that trip to France. One of the things that the French have never forgiven themselves for is ignoring me in Paris when I came over there in 1937 with Teddy. Now, I'm one of the main people who has turned music all the way around, and they had a chance to catch me in my infancy and blew it. How? These guys in the band. The French probably asked them, "How about this new little trumpet player?" And they probably said, "Oh, man, he can't play nothing, don't get him." They probably said that, or refused to recommend me when somebody asked. I never got one record date while we were over in Europe. Not one single record.

DICKY WELLS:

"Oh, man, it was beautiful. That was the prettiest trip I ever had in my life. We went on the *Ile de France.* We had sixty-two people, twelve chorus girls, and twelve dancers, plus a tramp band.

"Now Dizzy got mad with me. He made a little crack, he said, 'Look, man, you cats made all these records. You went to Europe and you didn't feature me.' He got kinda hot at me. Well, Panassié formed the recording band; I didn't have nothing to do with it. He told me who to get. It was my band, but he directed, so he said, 'Get Roy Eldridge, bring the Roy.'

"I say, 'Roy didn't come.'

"He says, 'No, Bill Coleman then. Bill Coleman's here tonight, so let him play.' That's who they wanted, because we're from Cincinnati. He's from Cincinnati. He's been a citizen in France for about twenty years.

"I showed Dizzy what I'd written in my book about that tour. He said, 'Yeah, but you didn't say nothing about me playing in it.'

"I said, 'Dizzy, I didn't organize the band, you know. I ain't got nothing to do with that.'"

BUDDY JOHNSON (piano, bandleader):

"We 'tramps' dressed up in funny kinds of clothes, and we didn't have any musical instruments other than the piano. The piano was the only musical instrument used in the Tramp Band. The 'drummer' was a washboard and the horns were kazoos. You know, you blow, it sounds like blowing a paper through a comb. Those fellas knew how to do that pretty good. I hadn't played with the Tramp Band before leaving New York, but they were going to Europe. I said I'd play with them.

"We met on the boat. Diz was just one of the fellows in the band, and I was just one of the members of the Tramp Band. But I thought that was great to be going to Europe, because during those times if you ever went to Europe you were great after that, man. Dizzy stood out in his action even on the boat. The Cotton Club employed so many beautiful girls, and Diz was going like a bee, not stopping exactly anywhere, but always buzzing.

"When we got to Europe and started playing, Diz really stood out from the usual way the trumpet players play it. Teddy Hill was the leader of the band, and I'm not certain if he really recognized it at that time, maybe I shouldn't say that, maybe he did. But I know that Diz didn't have as many of the solos in the band that he could have had, you know.

"I became acquainted with Diz in so many ways, ways I can't even speak of now. I, too, was taking piano lessons, because I learned my music, not in Darlington, South Carolina, but after I got to New York, and learning those notes was something different.

"We worked at nighttime in the Moulin Rouge, and during the day everyone went out to see Paris. But I was a bit studious in order to get this music. So I'd go down as soon as the place opened in the morning and start on the piano. No one would be there but some cooks getting their work straight for the night. I was doing pretty good with my scales and everything. After a while, here comes a young man with his trumpet.

"Diz started playing his trumpet over on the other side of the room. I didn't know those notes at that time, and he would bother me, although I didn't say anything. But it impressed me because here is a musician playing in a great band, and he played so well; yet here he was rehearsing himself, practicing. After a while, he came over to the piano and told me, 'Yeah, now play this.' I think the song was 'After You've Gone.' And I played it with the chords that I knew. That's the way the man wrote it. But Diz said, 'No, don't do that, put this chord in,' you know, 'No, come on this way.' And the way he would play it was something new to me. I really didn't dig it, but it sounded pretty when he played it. But it never sounded pretty when I played it. So after a while, I began to understand that this young man was way out."

Sheeeeeeit! With no records I was going to be a big celebrity somewhere. I walked into the door of the whorehouse, and all the whores rushed to the door. I was a big tipper. I was young; I'd have 'em two at a time. Party! Party! Party! Smitty, the guitar player, and I hung out together. After we left the whorehouse, we'd go and take pictures. Smitty wasn't making too many records either. I took a lot of pictures, Notre Dame, the Eiffel Tower, le Louvre. I was taking everything in Paris, things I'd read about. That's all we did, take pictures, see the Eiffel Tower, lay up in the whorehouses, and go to work. In that order.

We used to hang out after the show in a little bar in Paris. I found out later that the owner was a collaborator with the Nazis. We used to have a whole lotta fun with him. He had this little bar near boulevard de Clichy, and he was just a nice little short guy, jolly all the time.

DICKY WELLS:

"Roy Eldridge didn't wanna go to Europe. We got Dizzy, and every time we'd look, Dizzy was coming out of a whorehouse in Paris. So that's Dizzy.

"But he was blowing. He was blowing his ass off. That's the first time we saw Josephine Baker. We were playing at the Moulin Rouge; Josephine was on, and I saw this cat in a corner patting his hands. I said, 'That cat looks like our bass player.' We were onstage, and this cat was standing in a corner patting his hands. He said, 'Man, you cats sound so good, and Miss Baker looks so good, I'm just gonna stand here and look. . . .'

"I said, 'Man, come on in here . . . !' Nigger had to bring the bass out on the stage. He was clapping his hands and having a ball."

JOHN WILLIAM SMITH (guitar, banjo):

"Me and Howard Johnson persuaded Teddy to take Dizzy. Before the trip to Europe, we made a record, on Bluebird, and Dizzy played a helluva solo on 'King Porter Stomp.' I liked the way he followed his chord progressions. Being a guitarist, I appreciated that.

"He was just like he is now, always jolly. Always kept something going. He used to wake me up with that record, Roy Eldridge's 'After You've Gone', every morning. He idolized Roy. In London, when we were playing at the Palladium, we roomed together up on Tottenham Court Road.

"He didn't spend no more time in the whorehouses than anybody else. Everybody spent time in the whorehouses, the whole band.

"One day we were walking down the street in Paris and this fine young French chick was passing by. Diz and I was standing in front of the Moulin Rouge, and with the little French we knew, we were jiving her and telling her how beautiful she was, and she was smiling, digging it. And this guy who was with her started cussing us out, *in English.* She was taking it up, smiling; she knew we were in the show. This guy said, 'You muthafuckas, you black sonofabitches!' Boy, we fell out."

Then, we went to London. I liked London very much, and we played at the Palladium. I used to jam in a place called the Nest Club. A lot of English people say they remember me from that. They say it, but I don't believe it because it was such a long time ago, 1937. Interesting how much the Europeans liked our music, even that far back. They took it seriously. They studied it and collected a lot of records. That's how most of the European jazz musicians and, afterwards, the rock musicians first learned how to play our music, by listening to records. They treated you nice over there too and gave you the respect due an artist. They still do. The Europeans are much more serious about jazz than most white Americans.

Our music had already begun to travel some places you wouldn't imagine. Teddy Weatherford, a piano player, had died in China prior to 1937. Once in Warsaw, Poland, I was talking to a Soviet composer who said Sidney Bechet had played in Russia before the Revolution, around 1914. That's before I was born, before 1917. Yes, sir! Our music can really get out there.

Lorraine

Cats still remember that green tweed coat from England that I wore after I'd come home from Europe. I went over to Philly with lots of clothes to show off. I'd already saved up a lot of money and for the first time in a long while I wasn't hurting. I'd been making $70 a week in Europe, in 1937, and that was a lotta money to be making. My pockets had the mumps. I came back here, clean as the board of health, gave Mama some money and partied over in Philly, then I came back to New York and found out that I couldn't work because of a three-month waiting period to join the union, Local 802, a protection against foreign musicians, purportedly.

The union wouldn't let me work; boy, was I in trouble.

All that time while I stayed in Europe I left my transfer in; I just let mine run. When I got back from Europe, I was almost ready to join the union. Heh, heh. But they found out that I was out of the country, they took my old transfer from Philly and tore that up, and I had to start all over again. I had to wait three months before I could get a steady job, and couldn't work with Teddy in the Savoy. For three months I couldn't work with Teddy Hill.

I could take single jobs, but no steady job without the union charging the whole band a 10 per cent tax. I could do little gigs, and then when three months went by I could join a band. They had a pretty tough rule against those "foreigners."

The best gig I could find during that time was with Cass Carr, a West Indian guy who played the musical saw and paid well. Cass had a band that played for all the ethnic things and the communists; they used to get some good gigs at the St. George Hotel in Brooklyn. Cass was probably from Trinidad. Most of the early West Indians were from Trinidad, so I guess he was from Trinidad. That's a coincidence: most of the money situation in Harlem at that time was in the hands of West Indians. I mean, under or next to the whites, the most money was controlled by the West Indians. When you looked at somebody who had a position of influence, a black man, most of the time it was a West Indian. Remember the guy who was later president of the borough, Hulan Jack? Well, with the exception of Adam Clayton Powell, Jr., most of the influential blacks were of West Indian descent. The parents, mostly, were second generation. I guess it was the influence of Garvey still there in Harlem. Maybe that's why the West Indians had so much money.

Cass Carr played the bass violin most of the time, but then he came out and did a specialty. He played "My Buddy" on the saw. I couldn't believe it. I went into hysterics the first time I heard it. All the time that I couldn't work, I played with Cass. We used to play for all the communist dances. Just weekend gigs, nothing regular. The communists held a lot of them, in Brooklyn, the Bronx, and Manhattan. At those communist dances they were always trying to convert you. As a matter of fact, I signed one of those cards; I never went to a meeting, but I was a card-carrying communist because it was directly associated with my work, the dances, Camp Unity and all that kinda stuff.

We played up at Camp Unity one weekend, and all kinds of stuff was happening. Most of the guys, most of the musicians, almost everybody up there was mixed. White-black relationships were very close among the communists. I think they were trying to prove how equalitarian they were by throwing together the white or the black counterparts of the opposite sex. A lot of white girls were there, oh yes. I thought it was pretty funny myself, being from the South. I found it strange that every couple, almost, was a mixed couple one way or the other. That was the age of unity.

Before I got back with Teddy Hill, I started playing gigs with Edgar Hayes, the "Stardust" man. Edgar didn't write "Stardust," but he played it better than anybody. Edgar Hayes is a hip musician, a pianist, who made a big hit on "Stardust." He's still working in a lounge out in California, at seventy-four years old. I could play with Edgar Hayes whenever he went out on the road, but I had to get permission from the union each time. After I'd put in my transfer card again, I wasn't supposed to leave this jurisdiction to play anywhere.

One time I sneaked and went to Washington with Edgar Hayes's band and didn't tell the union. They came looking for me when I got back, and I told them that I went over and spent a couple of days in Philadelphia with my family because my mother hadn't been feeling well. They went for it. They wouldn't take my card out again; they were ready to snatch my transfer. I went down there and made that gig because my money was beginning to run low.

I met Lorraine on that trip, in 1937. She was a dancer in the chorus that went from the Apollo to Philadelphia, Baltimore, and Washington, the TOBA* (Tough On Black Artists) circuit, and I noticed that she never went to the after-hour joints and places like that with the other girls. She would never hang around on the stage. She was down in the dressing room; she was never up grinning in somebody's face all the time. That created something, curiosity. Lorraine was brown and pretty, too, and had a nice little figure. So I said, "I wonder where she is all the time? I think I'll send her a note." I sent it through a girl named Alice Lyons (now Alice McLemere) who I figured could get us together.

The note said, "Would you like to have a Coca-Cola with me afterward?" Something like that. Lorraine sent it back. Lorraine thought I was kidding around with her, so I went down to Baltimore when she was dancing down there and she sent another one of my notes back to me. After that, I came back to New York and called her up at the theater, and she didn't even know who I was. Finally, I left a message at the Apollo for her to call me. When she did, I answered the phone, "Well, it's about time you called!"

"Say, man, you're lucky I called you at all," Lorraine said.

Everybody was telling her, "That Dizzy's just trying to play; he ain't never gonna be nothing." People tried to tell her not to bother with me, you know, like, "Get yourself somebody like Rex Stewart, a real boyfriend, that's working."

Lorraine was working at the Apollo, so I started hanging out back there, but still couldn't see her very much. Then after I had finally talked to her a couple of times, things really started getting bad. My brother J.P. moved out on me. We were living on 139th Street, and he moved down to 126th Street without telling me. I really had nothing, nothing even to eat. Nothing. All the money I had saved in Europe was gone. Sometimes I went a while without having something to eat. Those were pretty hard times, but I never even considered taking another kind of job. Hell no! That never even crossed my mind. I was going to make my living as a musician, even though I wasn't making any money. A lot of guys did that, wash dishes. Nnh, nnh. I wouldn't

* Actually the Theater Owners Booking Association.

ask my brother for anything either, shit, he moved out on me. All I did was hang around backstage at the Apollo. One time I got so low, I was begging somebody for fifteen cents to buy a bowl of soup.

LORRAINE GILLESPIE:

"When I met him at the Apollo, he said he was hungry. I said, 'Well, this is something different.' I thought all musicians were really rich. I didn't know they were as poor as this critter was. I couldn't believe it. I got mad with Dizzy's brother and with Dizzy's boss. Yeah, I got mad because Dizzy asked his boss for some money, and he said, 'Your girl is working, why don't you ask her?'

"I told Dizzy (I'll never forget this), 'Would you go and tell him that you don't have to ask him for fifteen cents. I don't make that much money, but I'll give you enough money to buy a bowl of soup with.' I mean I was raised that way. I didn't feel sorry for him. I did it the way I was brought up. If I had a roll, and you didn't have anything, I was supposed to give you half of it, whether I wanted to or not. That's the way my parents brought me up.

"I had many musicians that liked me before I met Dizzy. I never liked them because we lived in the same hotels and I knew what the chorus girls and all of them were doing. It wasn't exactly my stick. I was a little old-fashioned. I mean, they liked to ball and have a good time and weren't doing anything that was different from anyone else. But, I mean, I just liked to work. I was old-fashioned. I either went home and read the Bible or crocheted or knitted, that's what I was doing. By myself. I had roommates and never saw them except at work. They went out and stayed with their boyfriends. They even sent me money to pay their part of the rent. That was funny; I had the whole room to myself every week.

"When I first met Dizzy I didn't think nothing of him. I wasn't thinking about anybody. I saw a lot of guys, but I told the man, 'I am here to work, not to flirt.' I was working and didn't take time with nobody. You saw me on the stage and coming to work and going home; after that, later.

"We didn't have any courtship. He was working in the band when he was working, and I was working on stage. When I got finished rehearsing all day and working all night, we couldn't do much going out, because I was dancing. Dizzy could see me between shows for about half an hour.

"I really came to pay him some mind when this chorus girl who worked with me in Washington, Alice Lyons, started bringing me notes from Dizzy. 'I don't want 'em,' I'd say. 'I don't feel like being bothered.'

"So one day she came and said, 'Lorraine, he's a nice boy. I think that if you're gonna fool with anybody, he's more suited to you than to the rest of these chorus girls.' She said he was around my age. 'He's nice because he keeps giving me these notes, and giving me messages. Just see what he's got to say.'"

Despite what others may say, my wife, Lorraine, was the one who saved me because I don't know what I would have done. After we started going together, I found out Lorraine was giving her mother $10 a week out of the $22 a week she was making as a chorus girl for her part toward the household. When Lorraine's mother found out that she was going with me, she said, "Here, take the $10 and help yourself. You all need it worse than I do." I'll never forget that because most mothers-in-law just grab money.

Stompin' at the Savoy

There was a poolroom under the Savoy, where cats would shoot "one pocket" pool for money. Shooting one pocket means you have to make all your balls in one pocket; none of the other pockets is cool for you. You pick a pocket. If you make one in another pocket, you put that one on the spot and lose your shot. Those guys were playing, and one night the Savoy caved in from the dancers upstairs. This was in the late thirties. Those hustlers and pimps ran outta there like rats running out of a ship. It caved in up there with the dancers because the Savoy Sultans were playing at the Savoy.

CHARLIE BUCHANAN:

"How ridiculous, how stupid for anybody to make that statement. Don't you know that if the floor was to cave in, thousands of people would get killed, and they would close the Savoy for life. How would the floor cave in? Who said that? That's absolutely false, stupid, and malicious. That's not true. The Savoy's floor was built so that it would never fall. They had enough beams, and there were two dance floors, three floors, wood to give it a spring, which was good because had it been rigid it would have been dangerous. When an army is going across a bridge, they don't march, they break ranks because they don't want the regular beat to sway anything. That's a malicious type of thing to say that the floor fell out."

Whether true or false, the moral of that story is, Don't play the game so you have to put all your balls in one pocket because you can never tell when the roof might cave in. Ha! Ha!

The Savoy Sultans were the house band at the Savoy and anybody who'd come in there had to play against them. The Savoy Sultans had enough rhythm for a thousand-piece orchestra, that's what they really generated up there on the bandstand; and the dancers were always with them, up and down, up and down, with the Lindy Hopping. I grooved with the Sultans. The Sultans were from Newark and I knew that crowd when they first came over here. In Newark, they had a crowd that was much more advanced than the musicians' crowd in Philadelphia because it was closer to New York. Those cats could get right on the subway and come over to New York and get everything musical they wanted. The Savoy Sultans were some boss musicians. Al Cooper was the leader of that band; he's down in Florida and Nassau now, doing very well. But the main cog was Rudy Williams, the alto. Without being the bandleader, he was the leader in spirit. Boy, there was a big change in Rudy later, after he'd heard Charlie Parker. He tried to copy Charlie Parker and said, "Man, I want to play like that." He had a good sound, himself, on the saxophone. His style was based on Willie Smith, like that . . . that kind of fire. Maybe, if Rudy had pursued his particular track, we would have had another completely different sort of style coming out of jazz around the same time as bebop. Later on, he was drowned up in Massachusetts; that's how he died.

The Sultans had two trumpets, three saxophones and full rhythm. When they went into the Apollo to play a show, they had to add a trumpet. I was always their added trumpet player. There was Pat and Sam, trumpet players; Lonnie Simmons and Pazuza, on tenor; Cyril Haynns, on piano; Jack Chapman, guitar; and Razz Mitchell on drums. Brother Moncur, Al Cooper's brother, played bass. Brother Moncur is Grachan Moncur's father. That's one reason Grachan has such a good background in music. These guys used to jump.

Besides the Sultans, there was another band in Newark called Pancho Diggs, and another called Hal Mitchell. Hal Mitchell was a trumpet player, a marvelous trumpet player. We made the mistake of coming over from Philly to play a dance with Frankie Fairfax's Band, and Pancho Diggs was there. We made the mistake of showing up, and they washed us. Another guy from Newark who came up the same time that I did, and didn't get enough recognition, was Willie Nelson.

He used to play trumpet with Buddy Johnson, played a lot of solos. Was he baaad! I think I'm gonna start collecting little Willie's records.

The Savoy Sultans were a permanent band at the Savoy, other bands rotated; Erskine Hawkins was a house band, Teddy Hill, Chick Webb, and Willie Bryant, and, one time, Fess Williams. I played with that band too. Whenever the Sultans went out on the road, Chris Columbus came in and filled their shoes very well. Chris Columbus had a jumping little band too.

I also played with Alberto Socarras, a Latin band. Alberto Socarras was the premier musician out of Cuba of classical background. He played with the Havana Philharmonic Orchestra. When he came to the United States, he had a Latin band which was pretty good at the time of the conga and the rhumba. Then he organized a small band and went into the Savoy Ballroom to play. When the Sultans went on the road, Socarras was a house band, and he hired me around 1938, before I worked with Cab Calloway.

Socarras was more classical oriented, but he played some jazz and could play that flute. He has the most perfect vibrato of any flautist I've ever heard. Man, he sounds like a bird with his flute. I played maracas and trumpet with him, and that's how I first learned the "clave" beat. The clave is the same thing as our sock cymbal beat. You can start on "one," or you can start on "two," or you can turn it around, invert it. The experience in Afro-Cuban music I got playing with Socarras was very, very useful to me later on.

Things went from nothing at all to as much as I could handle, once I really started looking around hard for other jobs. After three months was up, I went back with Teddy Hill, gigged with the Sultans, and also worked as a regular with Edgar Hayes and Socarras. Whenever Teddy wasn't working, Edgar or Socarras might have a gig some place.

ALBERTO SOCARRAS (flute, bandleader):

"I met Dizzy a long time ago. I heard him playing and was very impressed. His style and his way of phrasing was, to me, perfect. So later on, I had the opportunity to use him in my band, and I was very much satisfied with his performance. We became very good friends. It was in the days of the Savoy Ballroom, around 1938.

"I like his style, and I like the cat very much. He was a marvelous musician. I want my band to play everything, Spanish music, Brazilian music, Argentine music, Cuban and American music. But I wanted my music to sound American. So when trumpet solos came, Dizzy took them. It sounded American because an American was playing it. It was easy for Diz to go from American music to Cuban music, see. Also, I wrote my own arrangements, and Dizzy's solos were very nice, very Cubanlike.

"I found him different from every trumpet player that I had heard before. Every time he took a chorus, it was something different. He did not stick to one particular thing, and the style changed entirely. That's what I liked about him. We played Cuban music first, like boleros and things like that, and he phrased his solos marvelously. Then we played rhumbas, fast numbers, and his style was very Cuban. To him it was easy as American music was to me. So we have a lot in common in that respect.

"Some nights at the Savoy Ballroom, we opened at nine o'clock, others at ten. Dizzy was always on time, but he made me nervous. I'll tell you the way it happened. At about quarter to nine, all the musicians were on the stand to hit at nine o'clock sharp, see. But at ten minutes to nine, Dizzy's not there. Seven minutes, Dizzy's not there. Five minutes, Dizzy's not there. Now I start getting nervous. Two minutes to nine, Dizzy comes running, sat on the stand, takes his trumpet, and, wow, I don't know how he tuned his instrument, but he was there. He made me nervous because I thought he wasn't gonna be there. But about two minutes to nine, right in the door, somebody comes running like nobody's business. That was Dizzy. After taking his trumpet out, he sat there and started playing. The next night we opened at ten, so he has one more hour, but the timing was perfect. Again, two minutes before the time, Dizzy was there. The only thing I didn't like was for him to get there two minutes before I hit. But he was always on time."

We started getting into the new style of playing when Kenny Clarke came into Teddy Hill's band. Kenny really drew a different kind of sound outta those drums. That's where he got his name, "Klook-Mop."

Teddy said, "Man, every time I turn around, he's going, 'klook-mop' 'klook-mop . . . !'"

"Teddy, man, that's the thing," I said, "that's the thing!"

Teddy said, "Yeah, but it breaks the rhythm."

"Yeah," I said, "but when he drops one of them bombs, he drops it on the fourth beat, and it leads over, the rhythm's still going. That's the new way!"

"I don't like it too much," Teddy said.

One time he wanted to fire Kenny, but I said, "No, man, don't do that, man, don't fire him."

World's Fair

By then, I was supposed to be the lead trumpet player, and I played solos too. Joe Guy was with the band and couldn't read well; I used to teach him his parts, Al Killian and Joe Guy. Al Killian was the high-note trumpet player. That was a nice band. After we came back from Europe, all those older guys left, most of them, and you had a new breed coming in. This was after I was able to get my card back, about six or seven months afterward. We had Sonny White on piano, Kenny Clarke, Ted Sturgis, the bass player, and had Earl Hardy (fat jaws Earl) on trombone. Teddy had to break up that band in 1939, just when everything was about set for us to go into the World's Fair.

That was some *weird* shit. They built a Savoy Ballroom, a pavilion, out in the World's Fair for a "Lindy Hopper Show." They used Teddy Hill's band; no dancing was allowed, just a show. It was out in Flushing Meadows. Then we got into a dispute with the union.

This is *some* shit. Moe Gale and Sam Suber were related in some way. Moe Gale was the owner of the Savoy Ballroom, and Sam Suber was an official of the union. They got in cahoots and made the pay scale at the World's Fair third-class scale, instead of first-class, which it should have been. We were doing about "eighty" shows a day; on-off, on-off, on-off, so the whole band, all of us, went down to the union to protest against this.

Suber came in, and Bob Carroll saw Suber come in. Bob was big and black and mean. Bob went at Suber and we had to restrain him.

Suber almost fainted. He had been sick, and I could see big beads coming off his face, sweat. He asked everybody, "Who's this guy? Who's this guy?"

I said, "Never seen him before in my life."

He was Bob Carroll from in the band, a tenor player on that first record date I made, "King Porter Stomp," and "Blue Rhythm Fantasy." I'd known him for almost two years.

So because Teddy Hill went to the union, they fired Teddy's whole band and put some other band out there at the World's Fair. I forget what band it was, they'd been working at the Savoy. And they told Teddy, "You won't work at the Savoy anymore." That broke up Teddy's band because the Savoy Ballroom was his pound cake.

After we got fired, Teddy didn't have too many gigs except at the Apollo every now and then. Teddy told us, "You know the guy ain't gonna give us no more gigs. So ya'll, if you get anything, go ahead." The cats just went out and looked for other jobs, that was the business. It was a damned shame that band had to break up because we were just beginning to get into something new.

Teddy got out of the business. He went to Mr. Minton, who owned the Rhythm Club. Minton knew that Teddy was a good businessman and put Teddy in charge of Minton's Playhouse. So that's how Teddy came to Minton's. Teddy hired Joe Guy, Kenny Clarke, "Scotty" (Kermit Scott), Monk, and Nick Fenton to work down there, and that's how they got that gig. This was in 1939.

◫

CHARLIE BUCHANAN:

"Teddy Hill's band was never banned from playing at the Savoy. In fact, I don't even know if I want to divulge anything that has no interest in Dizzy. That has no meaning. What am I gonna tell you about why we hired Fess Williams, why we didn't hire Teddy, why we didn't do it?

"Listen, a businessman fights with nobody that he can make a dollar out of. Remember that. That's basic. Teddy Hill was a well-liked band. You know, Teddy wasn't able to play for a time there. His fingers were a little stiff. I don't know . . . but that's not true. They'd come and go, come and go. It was hard enough to get good bands. He might have gotten the wrong understanding of it. Maybe it was something else, why Teddy had to. Teddy and I are still friends.

"Teddy had a substantially good solid band—nothing exceptional, good music—but nothing unique. Now Dizzy was unique later in his operation, in his own band. Teddy's was just a good, sound band."

In general, what did you think about the men in the bands who worked at the Savoy?

"Not too much. Remember, they were musicians, they were band-leaders. They got paid. They'd come and do their job . . . nice fellows . . . give me a good job, and that's all. I mean, I didn't go out in the nighttime in the bars and have drinks with them. I don't know if Dizzy ever drank. He might not know I never had a drop of liquor in my life. An acquaintanceship of good fellows, striving to do the right thing, friendly, but not a buddy. You have to be careful how you say the word, buddy. No social friends. We knew a lotta people alike."

The best proof of what happened at the Savoy is that we didn't work there anymore.

The Flatted Fifth

Hard times stayed away because, through Kenny Clarke, I had gotten this gig with Edgar Hayes. Kenny was working with him too. Edgar knew me from New York because Edgar used to be with the Mills Blue Rhythm Band, Lucky Millinder, so he knew me from being around. Edgar Hayes really respected my knowledge of music; he made an arrangement on "Body and Soul" just for me. He wrote it himself and asked me what changes I wanted to play. This was in 1938 before Teddy's band broke up.

Edgar Hayes respected Kenny and me, and he could see something happening with our music. Man, Kenny played vibraharp with Edgar, used to be a big star with him. Several very talented guys were in that band. Edgar had Joe Garland who wrote, "In the Mood." That was a big hit for Joe Garland. Bama was in Edgar Hayes's band then too. I remember one time we had a gig in Trenton, and another time Bama and I went to Detroit. The hotel owner's daughter took a liking to Bama, and that was Bama's pound cake while he was out there. She was one of the prettiest girls in Detroit.

Rudy Powell was a nucleus of Edgar's band. He was rough, too, until he started to study saxophone with the same teacher who used to teach all of the white saxophonists who played in the big bands. His whole style changed to a fast vibrato, very reedy sound, like singing, and he seemed to lose a lot of his original fire and feeling for invention. But before that happened, he taught me something.

Rudy wrote this arrangement for Edgar Hayes that had this weird change, an E-flat chord built on an A, the flatted fifth. When I ran across that in the music, it really hit—boom! The flatted fifth. Oooo, man! I played that thing over and over, and over again, and started using it in my solos. My solos started taking on a quality where there were long runs and points where the playing was sort of behind the beat. Sort of like the style of Dud Bascomb, another great trumpet player of that era, who didn't get the proper recognition during his lifetime.

Edgar Hayes had this arrangement, a ballad arrangement, and the chord was an E-flat. You see, I was always aware of where the chord was and also the time. I figured that was fundamental, but you don't stick to fundamentals. He had an E-flat chord in there, and I heard this A concert going up a scale, and I played it, and I played it again, played it again, played it again. I said, "Damn! Listen at this shit. Listen at this, man!" That's when I first became aware that there was a "flatted fifth." Before that time, until 1938, that was not a part of my musical conception.

It wasn't considered a "flatted fifth" then, it was considered a half step. We always looked on that simply as a half step, not as a "flatted fifth," which is a half step.

From doing this, I found out that there were a lot of pretty notes in a chord that were well to hold, instead of running over them. That's what Rudy taught me, and that has governed my playing ever since. And that's one of the things that's distinctive about Miles Davis, that he learned from me, I'm sure. Because I showed him on the piano the pretty notes in our music. There are a lot of pretty notes in a chord, and if you hold them for an extended time, it adds a hue. It adds a hue to your solos. He really went for that.

▉

EDGAR HAYES (piano, bandleader):

"We went to Detroit, and I needed a trumpet man in my brass section, and in doing so I tried to get one man and he would tell me about another one, and so it went on until we finally got a brass section together. Dizzy was one of them. I liked Dizzy very much. He was very apt and very fast on his horn. He knew another boy—there was two or three of them that kinda worked together—Carl Warwick and Benny Harris. So we finally got together and those three worked.

In the saxophones I had Earl Bostic and different ones, and we formed this group. But I liked the unique way Dizzy played. I liked it very much.

"I liked Dizzy's 'terminology,' the way he phrased his music, what we term in music sometimes, his 'curves,' musically. These other two boys worked along with him, and we formed a very nice brass section. I forget now who was on trombone, but he was very, very good. And then Joseph Garland, a saxophone player, liked Dizzy and started making arrangements. So did I, and I would make arrangements built around Dizzy because Dizzy took a lot of solo work. You know how those big bands used to play with those big tenor saxophone solos and trumpet solos. So Dizzy would take the trumpet solos.

"Sometimes I would give the solos to one of the other trumpets or the trombones. But be sure you're on your P's and Q's when you get your solo. Take it, and on time, because if you didn't, I wouldn't have to worry about it, because Dizzy would take that person's solo.

"You understand what I mean, being on time? Knowing where you're supposed to come in. If you happened to be just doing something, didn't pick up your horn, don't worry about it; Dizzy had the solo 'n gone. Sometimes I'd have to raise my hand and point at Diz to get outta there, you know, and let the man take his solo. The man would be getting ready to play his solo, to jump in there, and Dizzy'd have his solo 'n gone. Not meaning any malice or anything, he just didn't want the music to drop. So that's one thing I'd like to emphasize with Dizzy. He was very, very shrewd in the way that he came in on solos, and the way that he could get in and out of it without anybody being hurt.

"He loved his music. He'd sit up there with his horn all the time. He'd always have his horn ready to fill in on something—to the extent of filling in on what you call 'breaks.' My band was unique in having that break made up of the three trumpets of the brass section. Not just one man takes the break all the time, you know. Diz kinda led the section. Sometimes, if I were writing, I could almost hear Diz doing something, and I'd write it that way. I would interpret it as Diz playing it. Then when I'd bring it to rehearsal, Diz would take it and rehearse the brass section on it. We got along real well. Dizzy was the type of man that, when he looked at his music, when you broke open that arrangement, and he'd see those bars up there, broken up, and it read 'four'—that means he's out for four bars—somebody else was taking those four bars. Well, he's not out on those four bars. If you didn't take 'em, Dizzy was right in there on those four bars. But it was a feeling that somebody else was playing.

"Diz and the guys used to come when none of us had soles in our shoes, but we'd get on that bus and make that rehearsal, from 110th Street up to the Savoy Ballroom to rehearse. And it'd be snowing on the ground or raining, but we'd make that rehearsal. All of us would be there scuffling like the devil, practicing to bring the music. And we'd have it—my dear man—we would have it when we came outta there that night. We'd start rehearsing maybe round one o'clock, and we wouldn't get outta there until around six or seven o'clock at night. Sometimes Diz would have his horn coming outta the door, blowing a little something, just a little something. It didn't mean anything to maybe the other musicians, but it meant something to him. Sometimes I would catch it, or maybe Joe Garland, or one of the other arrangers in the band would catch it and put it in an arrangement. Those kinda things meant something. But nowadays, these guys don't mean nothing. They got their horns, all they wanna know is what the dough is gonna be on the job. How much it's gonna pay and all that kinda stuff. That's all they're looking for. Then they get on the job, and try to blow their brains out with one note. And you know how many notes Dizzy puts out. Those kinda things you remember. Sincerity, nobody had any more sincerity in the band than Diz.

"Now Kenny Clarke was another one. I think he picked a little of it up from Shadow Wilson, a great drummer in those days. But Kenny was a great one to jump in on open beats; he would jump in where the whole band was playing ensemble work. He would jump in on those. I have some of the records where Kenny used to play with me before Diz. But Kenny used to jump in there on those beats like some of the drummers today. Kenny started off that beat, drumming like that, Kenny and another drummer named Shadow Wilson. They were great drummers, jumped in there, just like Diz jumped in on other solos. Right between those beats, they would put a stomp beat in there and it would go over nice. You hear some of those big bands of yesterday, you'll hear those beats in there.

"We tried all things, all different patterns. Sometimes I lay here in my bed and think about the different things that we all did, and what they do now, and we had a fine group. We had one of the best bands in New York. And when those guys come out of that type of band, they try to inject into another band, and they can't do it. Because you don't have those kinda guys and leaders. I'm not patting myself on the back, but a leader like me tried to give the other guys a chance to play. When you go out into another band, maybe some guy'd wanna try to make himself the whole cheese, you know. And doing that, you can't have a band; you gotta let someone else in there. Just like the President of the United States, he's got the name, but he can't run the United States.

"When a lotta bands would be off from work, we had a little place up there, I think it was on 140th Street, a little gin mill or night spot. And I'd have Diz and Rudy Powell, I forget now who the drummer was, but there were four or five of us, it was contracted. I had a contract for every man to play on a job. That's when I wasn't using my big band, I played this nightclub. We'd come in there at ten o'clock and play until four. The place got so hot. We'd jam in there until two-thirty, three, and four o'clock. The people across the street was hanging out on the windows, you know, listening to us blow.

"I had to talk to Diz, I said, 'Diz, you'd better soften down a little bit.'

"'Okay, okay, we'll do that.'

"Diz looked like he'd blow louder, and the manager would come up and say, 'You'd better tone Diz down a little bit.'

"I said, 'I done told that guy . . . Diz, the people can't sleep, they gotta go to work across the street.'

"'Okay, Fess, I'll knock it off right now.'

"When I'd get finished, Diz maybe would put his mute in there for a minute or two then bring it out again. You see the music was just in the man's soul. It's still in there.

"This white guy was working downtown, somewhere else. He used to come up there right at ten o'clock on the subway. He'd say, 'Fess, I'm sorry I'm late.' He'd sit up there with his guitar and play with one bottle of beer all night long. Oh, he came out later, he and his wife with this fabulous guitar work. Both of them sang, Les Paul and Mary Ford. He'd come in the back door. Sit up there and play guitar with all these guys. Tommy Dorsey, Jimmy Dorsey, Benny Goodman, the only one that didn't *play* up there was Louis Armstrong, and Louis, he used to come in there. Now, when you come in there, I couldn't tell you who was gonna be in there, or who's gonna be there tomorrow night, I couldn't tell you. But it was gonna be somebody good, because I didn't allow nobody playing around there that couldn't. But they'd come in there, bring their horn, sit at the tables. Like you and your wife come in, you bring your horn, order a drink. We'd just jam all over the place.

"Roy Eldridge used to come in there. Roy used to come in there all the time. Dizzy did something like Roy, but not too much Roy. He was more dear to himself; it was a new thing. What he's doing today, he used to do that years ago, but he's just perfect today. He's more sure of it today. It's just like a preacher. A preacher starts out asquirming and scrambling for words, but that was twenty-five years ago. Now the preacher gets up there and just knocks off his words in a minute or two. His tone of voice and everything is perfected, you know. This is what I had, and this is what I'm proud of that I had.

"I arrived at the feeling afterwards, that the music was really gonna change, but at that time I didn't have any feeling. I knew we were going someplace, but I didn't know where we were going. I knew the music had to change to the extent that we wanted to arrive at a point where somebody would say, 'That's good.' "

Something really nice was bound to happen to me; I knew it, I felt it. Lorraine and I were getting closer and closer, so much that I was staring at walls and feeling a glow and having fantasies about getting married. But work was still too unsteady. I had to find something more stable that paid more money than the little gigs I was playing. Then I ran into Mario Bauza. He had just the thing. We had to make up a little scheme for it though.

Lorraine was very friendly with Rudolph, Cab Calloway's valet. She knew him very well, and she told Rudolph, "Please get that nigger a job, because I'm tired." Lorraine was still dancing at the Apollo, but that was getting harder and harder. I needed a job like that to stop her from working so hard in the Apollo, and she understood that, too, and told Rudolph, "Get Dizzy a job with Cab Calloway."

Mario was playing with Cab Calloway and he knew Cab wanted a solo trumpet. So one night, he sent me down to the Cotton Club in his place and told me to let Lamar Wright take all the first parts, and then when it came time for a solo, blow. Cab didn't know me; I didn't even report to him, just put on the uniform and sat down. I could play fly then, from being in Teddy's band, so when I took my solos, everything would be fine. In those days, the solo trumpet would accompany soft-shoe routines. I stood up when it was my turn. Bill Robinson and the chorus girls were looking back at me, "Who's that?"

Those dancers were moving the first night I played, so I knew I'd done a good job. But I still didn't know if the scheme had worked. Cab Calloway's band was the big leagues for a black musician. The money was good, and the traveling was easy.

Rudolph called me when I was at the Apollo working with Teddy Hill and said, "Come on down here."

I had never spoken to Cab, so I asked him, "Should I bring my horn?"

"Yeah, yeah. You start tonight."

I went downtown to the Cotton Club, put on a uniform and blew, didn't even ask what salary Cab was paying (I found out later it was $80 a week, $100 a week on the road). I tore up one number "Cuban Nightmare," a Latin-type thing that Cab had in his book. I was playing that one for Lorraine and, in a sense, for Mario. It made no difference that my hand was hurting, still sore as hell from where I'd cut it in a fight a couple of nights before.

With all the good luck, the circumstances of my leaving Edgar Hayes were pretty weird. The week before I went to try out for Cab's band, I'd played three days with Edgar Hayes's little group in the Victoria Cafe on Forty-second Street. That Friday, I went into the Apollo with Teddy's band, and after I'd tried out for the job in Cab's band and made a good impression, I went up to the Victoria to collect my few days' money from Edgar Hayes. He started jiving around with me about my money.

"Man, you got a good job," he said.

"Man, that's got nothing to do with it," I said. "I worked three days for you, and you're here balling it up at the bar. Spending my money on the bitches at the bar, spending my money that I worked for. Gimme my money!"

I went up there a couple of times more and didn't get my money. One night he was sitting up there at the piano with his glasses on. I walked up and grabbed his glasses off and said, "Okay. If you want your glasses, give me my money; you'll get your glasses back." Oh, it was only a question of about $19, for three days. The Victoria paid about $35 a week. He wouldn't give me my money, was spending my money, so I walked outside with his glasses, and he came outside behind me.

"Look, give me my glasses."

"Here, they're right here in my hand. You give me my money, you'll get your glasses. That'll be the end of that."

He swung at me, and I hit him with the hand with the glasses in it. He had rimless glasses. That's the kind of glasses he wore. Man, my hand was bloody, and Big George, the bouncer, had to pull me off him. I had him down, I'd knocked him on the ground, and was really ready to go to work, but George pulled me off. I got my satisfaction, though. I got some ass. I've had to say that so many times, "Look, my money or a piece of your ass. Take your choice!" That happened in 1939, just before I got the job with Cab. I could have really hurt myself and messed up my playing hand for life, but I just hate somebody taking advantage of me, so I donated that money to his coffin.

"Klook-Mop"

By far, the most important thing that happened to me musically during this period (1938–39) was my friendship and association with the great drummer, Kenny Clarke, who as you can see was hardly considered great by certain people in those days. Kenny was modifying the concept of rhythm in jazz, making it a much more fluid thing, and changing the entire role of the drummer, from just a man who kept time for dancers to a true accompanist who provided accents for soloists and constant inspiration to the jazz band as a whole. Kenny's style of drumming, with "bombs" and "klook-mops" in the bass drum and regular rhythm in the cymbals was ideal for me. It furnished just the right amount of support, push, or embellishment I needed. These were important changes. A lotta people didn't like them. Kenny had to suffer a lot to make those changes, but in the end, he turned out to be right.

Kenny initiated a new language into the mainstream of jazz drumming. You know, like you "infuse." He infused a new conception, a new language, into the dialogue of the drum, which is now *the* dialogue.

The trumpet and the drums are cousins. That's why you find a lotta trumpet players can play drums. You find quite a number, because it's a closeness there, with the brass.

When Teddy used to talk about firing Kenny, I told him, "Man, you ain't hip, man." Teddy used to say about Kenny, "Man, he breaks up the time."

I said, "Man, it's new shit. What the fuck are you talking about, man, come on."

He'd say, "Man, well he does all them old klook-mops 'n shit." So that's how he got his name, "Klook-Mop," because Teddy Hill said he was playing all them "klook-mop" beats.

There were always discussions, all the time. Kenny would run up to me—he played piano, too, all of them played piano—and say, "Look here . . . bam!" Right to the piano. I'd say, "Yeah, yeah," because guys were very generous in those days with their ideas, man. They didn't think and worry about anybody taking something and claiming it for their own.

The reason for the music sounding like it does now, the simple reason, is that whatever the present guys are doing, they are doing it like we did it. There's very little variation in presentation, presentation of notes, and how you phrase something. It's a little different. Trumpet players today play a little different from trumpet players my age, but most of the time, they play exactly as we played it. So it sounds like what we played.

KENNY CLARKE (percussion):

"I used to follow Diz around to all the jam sessions and hear him blow against other trumpet players. He was young and he was blowing. Everybody was asking me, "What is Diz playing?" I was just telling them to "Listen. . . ." We were with Teddy Hill's band together, Ella Fitzgerald, Claude Hopkins, so we've *been* barnstorming, early, you know.

"I noticed something unique about Dizzy's playing, that's why I was hanging out with him. His approach to modern harmonies, but rhythms, mostly. He could take care of all that harmony, but his rhythms interested me real profoundly, and I just had to find out about that gift he had hidden in him, the gift of rhythm. It wasn't only his trumpet playing, he was doing a lotta other things that some people didn't see, but I saw the rhythmic aspect of it. The way he played and the way he would hum time and things like that. I knew it was avant-garde, ahead of time, so I just fell in line with what was going on.

"It was the idea of the cymbals, which blended with the trumpet. It was a certain way to play the cymbals, that Dizzy liked very well, and

I just happened to be playing like that at the time. The cymbals and the trumpet have something in common, they're both brass. It's a perfect blend, and when the cymbals are played according to what the soloist is playing, something that corresponds, it's really beautiful. That's where the whole thing happens, right there.

"Yeah, those are the early days. We had a trombone player once, with Teddy Hill, and he didn't like the way I broke up the rhythm. He couldn't hear. The cymbal was keeping the rhythm, and my feet were playing something else, but I knew where the rhythm was. But evidently—I don't know whether he was listening to the cymbal or listening for the bass drum, I think it was the latter—he was listening for the Boom—Boom—Boom on the bass drum. And what the band was playing at the time didn't correspond to just four beats on the bass drum. Hardly anyone played four, they usually played two, and the music had progressed a little too far to adhere to old habits. So something had to be changed. And this trombone player couldn't accept it, and told Teddy, 'Man, we can't use "Klook" because he breaks up the time too much.'

"His name was Woody, and he was straw boss at the time. Teddy fired me through Woody.

"The most important characteristic of this new style of playing was camaraderie, that was first because everybody, each musician, just loved the other one, just loved them so much they just exchanged ideas and would do everything together. That's one characteristic about it I liked very much. Another word for that is unity. That's right, and I think that era of jazz had more enemies than any phase of jazz.

"It was sort of esoteric from the beginning. Only a few people understood what was going on. Everybody knew it was good, but they couldn't figure out what it was. And when somebody doesn't understand a thing, he has a tendency to dislike. But I mean the music has been so strong and was strong, and is strong now, until it's the best thing we have to offer today. And by our pioneering, the young boys come up.

"It was different from the 'swing' music that had preceded it, the technology of the whole thing. Musicians, by the forties, were going to universities and music schools. I think it was the most intelligent era of jazz, and they still haven't caught up with it. It's still modern. We play records we made thirty and thirty-five years ago, and it sounds like you made them yesterday. Just the technical side of it, the technicalities of recording. It wasn't on stereo, but if you just listen to the music. Whew! Oh, yeah, we used to discuss it on the bandstand sometimes and write out little things. I would say, 'Hey, Diz, whaddayou think of this?', you know. I think when we left Teddy Hill, we definitely knew that it was gonna happen. We were pretty sure of it, and everybody worked toward the same goal. That's what made it happen."

So when I left Teddy Hill's band, shoot—I had been playing with Teddy and Edgar; when I went down there and took that job for one night in Mario's place—man, I was ready. Ready and cocky about it. I was really cocky about it, because I knew where I was coming from. I knew those guys would say, "Damn, what is this shit?" I figured they'd be saying some shit. I figured all that. But I was ready.

"Hot Mallets"
(9–11–39)

Just after I went with Cab Calloway, I had a record date with Lionel Hampton; somebody wasn't in town. Lips Page was probably out on the road, Charlie Shavers was someplace else. Charlie and Buck Clayton had most of the record dates that Roy didn't get. I had just joined Cab Calloway's band.

Milt Hinton and Cozy Cole probably told Hamp there's a new trumpet player in Cab's band. If you need a trumpet player, why don't you get him? I had never met Hampton. They brought me down to this record date, and talk about giants, man, this was superroyalty. On alto saxophone was Benny Carter; tenors, Chu Berry, Ben Webster, and Coleman Hawkins; on guitar, Charlie Christian; Milton Hinton on bass; Clyde Hart on piano; Cozy Cole on drums; Lionel Hampton on vibes; and one trumpet, me. I was so nervous my hands were shaking. What a date. Man, I was so scared, I was nervous as a sheep shitting on shingles. All them kings were in there, and I was just a young dude.

"What's your name?" Gladys Hampton asked me.

"John Gillespie," I said. She thought I said Charles, and when my record check came out, it was C. Gillespie. She thought I was Charles Gillespie. I run into a lot of people, discographers, who ask me where did the "C" come from.

It turned out to be a great session, and on that date we made a record called "Hot Mallets." I played a thirty-two-bar solo, in my mute, and the style sounded very much like Roy Eldridge. As a matter of fact, Roy thought he'd made the record, he was making so many records at that time. It was funny when he found out he hadn't made the record. "Hot Mallets" established that I had something that was a little different. It sounded like Roy, but there were certain things in there that he didn't play, phrasing. We don't phrase alike. I used to phrase just like Roy; I used to try to breathe and do everything like him, but by that time, I'd discovered that there was something else. I wanted my own style.

When I joined Cab Calloway, I was in a style somewhere between Roy Eldridge and a style of my own. The most unique thing about me was I was always with the piano. Before I started really getting into myself, I was a great fan of Roy Eldridge. I am still a great fan of Roy Eldridge. But I figured that there was something deeper, there was more to me; and there was more to evolve from the instrument, the trumpet, than what Roy had created. Being a piano player, I was always a student of chord changes, or progressions. I would always recognize chord changes.

Roy Eldridge was a French-style trumpet player. Eldridge was in a direct line from Louis Armstrong, and he was the voice of that era, the thirties. I hardly ever listened to Louis, but was always aware of where Roy's inspiration came from. So I *was* looking at Louis Armstrong, you see, because they are one and the same. My inspiration came through Roy Eldridge, from Louis Armstrong and King Oliver and Buddy Bolden. That's the way it happened. The breakaway from the Roy Eldridge style is documented on recordings I made with Cab Calloway; it's right there on records. I have to read my discography to look up the names of the tunes that I played, but there was a definite break from the Roy Eldridge style, you could hear it on the records. My style kept going, getting away, but still maintaining those roots. You never lose the influence, no, never. Roy sounds like Louis now, and he's away from it, but you never really get completely away from them, the things that you did.

When I was with Teddy Hill, I sounded more or less like Roy, but with Edgar Hayes, and that arrangement in the book by Rudy Powell with the flatted fifth, I really got turned on. And from that one phrase —just one bar—I started developing that passage and listening to it, and before you knew it, I was trained like that. I was excited about the progression and used it everywhere. I sort of slowed down a little bit from hearing those pretty notes, and the young trumpet players loved it. They'd play a whole chorus of flatted fifths—a whole chorus— everything was flatted fifths. I used to hold on to those pretty notes. I'd be coming down, and I'd hold on to 'em. There are some nice notes in a chord, man, so now Miles knows how to hold one note for hours. That's how Miles got all those pretty things he plays. It resolves all the time. That one note. To find out where notes resolve, you don't have to play every chord. You can hold one note, and it'll take care of three chords, because it's in all of them. And pretty notes, too.

The younger trumpet players are still doing that now. They used to ask Clifford Brown, "How do you think of Dizzy?" He'd say, "Oh, man, he's the end, and I was inspired by him." But not really. When you look at it in terms of artistic development, Clifford was inspired by me, but through Fats Navarro.

After "Hot Mallets," I started making records with Cab Calloway, like "Papa's in Bed with His Britches On," "Bye Bye Blues," "Boo-Wah-Boo-Wah," and "Come On with the Come On." On all of those, I had eight bars and was pretty swift. I put in less notes and tried to make more content. All the young trumpet players who dig it say, "Ah!" because I had cut away from Roy by that time. My style was still developing, but by 1939–40, it had jelled, the development had jelled. Where my style is concerned, I'm almost playing the same way now that I played then.

On the "Hot Mallets" date, I didn't know too many of the guys. I just knew Chu and the ones in Cab's band, so I don't know how they felt about my performance, but I felt really great.

⬛

LIONEL HAMPTON (vibraharp, bandleader):

"I went down to the Apollo Theater, somebody was singing, and Dizzy was playing some background behind him. That's where I first heard him. I was sitting behind the stage, man, and heard this guy playing all this trumpet, you understand. I said, 'I wanna hear him at this recording session.' I had a contract at this time, and these were all-star guys.

"He came out with a new style, came out with a bebop style. He came out with a different style than we'd ever heard before. A lot of people don't know that was the creation of bebop, the beginning of bebop. After that, he left Cab and started hanging around Minton's, and him and Charlie Parker got to playing, and then they got into it more, you understand. But the first time I noticed, the distinct style, something new coming in outta trumpet was that time in the recording session with 'Hot Mallets.' You'll see it's a different style of playing. You know he left that Roy Eldridge style and left the Louis style, left all those guys' styles. It was a complete new style in trumpet playing.

"It was new, and it was fresh, and here's a guy who was creating a crazy sump'n entirely new, but it was so inventive. The harmonies, the chord structure, and the skill with which it was being played. He had a part where he jumped a couple of octaves, 'Baa-Bee!' Like that. And it was really outstanding playing.

"It just amazed me, and I knew that Dizzy was gonna keep right in the style. This was the style he cultivated, and I was glad to see it. I like execution, and here's a guy playing fast as a cat playing a saxophone. On a trumpet. I mean, a fast saxophone player. Here's a guy (on trumpet) playing faster than the fastest saxophone player. Of course that first day I heard him, when he played on 'Hot Mallets,' he amazed me, because that's about as fast as I've heard a trumpet played. I had never heard a trumpet played that fast before.

"The first time I heard bebop played on a trumpet—I mean that style later called bebop—was when Dizzy played 'Hot Mallets' with me."

MILTON HINTON (bass):

"Yeah, that was on Victor, down on Twenty-fourth Street. He had started the flatted fifths and the things which we hadn't been into, and it really sounded fantastic. We just couldn't quite understand it. And it sounded so good. It was so much over what we were doing, it filled out the chords so, and we just stood back in amazement at it. That's the only thing I can say about it.

"I remember the date; I remember 'Hot Mallets' very well, Ben and Chu being there. Lionel had gotten him (Dizzy) because we knew he was the new thing, and Lionel was always searching for something new. And that was the one thing that I got out of it. We say, 'Jeezus Chris', here this kid is . . . well listen at this!' It was quicker, and more notes and more harmony than we had been accustomed to having in the thing.

"I won't call that session the 'beginning of bebop.' It was one of the most progressive sessions. He had all of the giants there; I think Hamp really planned it that way. That's the one with all the saxophones on it, with Ben and Coleman, and Clyde Hart on piano. Charlie Christian was on guitar. It was one of the first sessions I'd ever been on with all the guys together, the real biggies. And I thought it was one of the most progressive as far as the 'giant steps' sessions were concerned. We weren't even using the word 'bebop' then, you know. And then when Dizzy walked in with this new innovation, it really tied in with everything that we had there because we had all of the soloists. We had Chu with the great line, you know, this great swinging line that he played with. And we had 'Bean' (Coleman Hawkins) with his big sound, and then Diz walked in there with all these chord changes to throw on us. Man, it was just unbelievable. I would call it a giant step or something like that. But Hamp deserves so much credit for having the forethought to surround himself with all of the great guys that he'd come up with, you know.

"I'll tell you one thing that nobody mentions: a guy like Cab Calloway, at that particular time, didn't want his musicians recording with other guys, and he raised particular hell about it. Not that particular session, but about Ben Webster and me doing sessions with Billie Holiday. And Ben threatened to quit. Cab said, 'I don't want you guys working in my band going out and making other people great.'

"He raised so much cane about that Ben told him, 'Man, you gotta be outta your cotton picking mind! We're trying to make a name for ourselves and get out here and be known.'

"And then Cab had a complete reversal, and the next thing you know, he was saying, 'I'm proud I got the type of men that everybody else wants to record with.' It turned into a complete reversal. The outcome of it was this kind of thing that Lionel and Teddy (Wilson) had been doing, pulling guys out. They were playing with Benny (Goodman), and when they got sessions, they would pull out all the guys from different bands that they thought were qualified and would improve their sessions."

Within the next few years, because I was such a nut about piano, I would exchange ideas with Thelonious Monk in jam sessions at Minton's, and learn about Monk's use of chromaticism. I learned rhythm patterns from Charlie Parker and Benny Carter, the drummer. I learned a lot about harmony from Benny Carter (the saxophonist), Art Tatum, and Clyde Hart. You see, you are the sum total of what you know. So I tried to analyze a lot and understand what they were doing.

The style of music that we created was a direct development of what had gone on before. All those ingredients we plucked from the musical atmosphere of the late 1930s went into it. Sort of like a musical gumbo. Gumbo is indicative of New Orleans. One night I was in New Orleans and I walked into a restaurant. On top of the menu the entrées said "gumbo." I said, "Bring me a bowl of that gumbo." They brought me a bowl, and it was so great that I ordered another bowl and then another and another. It was so good, I must have eaten five bowls of gumbo. They started to bring me another one, but I said, "Hold it." Musically speaking, "Hot Mallets" was just like that gumbo. It was such a good, even a great, and a marvelous beginning. But just like that gumbo, I wanted and needed some more to express myself completely.

Diz the Wiz

While I was with Cab Calloway, from 1939 to 1941, I used to sing, "I'm Diz the Wiz, a swinging hip cat. Swinging hip cat, Diz the Wiz." Then Cab would say something, and then I played.

Another guy, Lamar Wright, would say, "I'm Slop the Hop . . ." Those were the words of "A Bee Gezindt," one of Cab's tunes. Cab gave me a featured role in his band. I was the only trumpet soloist in the band.

Playing with Cab, I was always doing my damndest to be hip. I was a wig, and I was always doing crazy things. Always giving guys the hotfoot. If I found them asleep, I'd put a lighted cigarette in their mouths. Of course, they'd choke! Or I'd put some cellophane on a guy's chest—then light it. I don't do those kinds of things anymore, but then I was cocky, I could play hot and fly and I knew it. I even dressed the part.

Past 1939, we'd wear the bebop jackets with berets. Before Cab, and with him, I dressed conventionally; double-breasted suit and long coats coming down almost halfway to my knees; zoot suits at that time. Long-collar shirts with an ordinary hat.

It was the best job that you could possibly have, high class. Cab's band always traveled in the best way, by private railroad car or chartered bus, and I remember how we would go on the road then for eight, nine, or twenty weeks, in those private cars, and know where we were going to be for the next three years. Boy! Wouldn't I like that now. Yessir, no jim-crow coach for Cab. That experience taught me, and I learned so much from Cab Calloway. Working in his band taught me to do what I was supposed to do. You don't fuck up. You don't fuck up with Cab Calloway's job, especially with time. Be there a half-hour before time. I used to be there an hour before because I had to warm up, and I had to be sure to wear the proper uniform. Discipline! That's the word—and with no deviations from it. You were disciplined with that band.

We traveled all over the country. We played the Cotton Club, then we'd go out on a long theater tour with the "Cotton Club Show," and a new show would come into the Cotton Club. Cab would leave, and Bill "Bojangles" Robinson or somebody else would come in. The show that went out on the road usually featured Cab's band; Avis Andrews, singer; Moke 'n Poke, comedians; the Choclateers, three dancers; and the "Cotton Club Boys," dancers, six sharp, tall black guys. They looked like Navy captains and wore uniforms, with caps and brass buttons, white suit and white shoes. And all of them had to be absolutely spotless; there could be no marks on their clothes.

The whole thing was high class, very high class. Inside the Cotton Club, they had silken drapes, man, and so many showgirls in the chorus. They had a line of about sixteen girls, a big production like a Broadway musical. In fact that's what it was, a musical, because they rehearsed that show. The "new" Cotton Club was located on Forty-eighth Street, where the Latin Quarter is now. But the old Cotton Club was uptown in Harlem, at 142nd Street and Lenox Avenue. Blacks couldn't even go in the old Cotton Club, unless they worked there, and downtown the clientele was only the well to do. The 'ireenie'—the well to do—was all they would allow in there with exceptions made for a few black elected officials. Connie Immerman owned the place, he was very famous around New York during prohibition, and also owned Connie's Inn which was styled like the Cotton Club. Don Redman worked there.

Cab's band had five reeds, eight brass, and full rhythm. In the saxophone section at different times was Hilton Jefferson, Chauncey Haughton, Rudy Powell, and Andrew Brown. Those were the four alto saxophonists while I was there. The tenor players were Chu Berry and "Foots" Thomas, and Jerry Blake played clarinet and baritone saxophone. The trombone section when I first joined the band was Claude Jones, Keg Johnson, and DePriest Wheeler. Then we changed to Tyree Glenn, Quentin Jackson, and Keg Johnson. I think they always had three trombones when I was with them. The trumpet section was Mario Bauza, Lamar Wright, me, and then Jonah Jones came later. The rhythm section was Danny Barker, guitar; Cozy Cole, drums; Milt Hinton, bass, and Benny Payne, piano.

Cab wanted a good band behind him. He wasn't interested in developing any musicians. He always hired established musicians, who were already of high caliber. Cab could get anybody he wanted because he had the money to pay them. He really wasn't interested in developing any musicians; his band was the highest that you could get in New York. One alto saxophonist, Hilton Jefferson, was bad enough to play with Benny Carter, and Benny Carter would pass all the first alto parts to him and play third alto himself. That's how bad Hilton Jefferson was, but Cab didn't know it. Hilton put little different things in the arrangement, little notes, different trills and things. Rudy Powell joined the band, and Cab expected to hear that with Rudy. He didn't hear it. He thought something was wrong with the music. "Man, you're sure you're playing that right?" he said. Ha! Ha! Rudy was just playing what was written.

Cab is a showman. Cab is Mr. Showman and knew what to do with a stage. He'd conduct the band, waving, shaking his head and making the hair fall down on his face. It was the heyday of guys that danced out in front of a band during that time. They had a whole group of those guys, Lucky Millinder, Cab Calloway, Tiny Bradshaw, Baron Lee, and Bardu Ali who was in front of Chick Webb's band. They'd have someone out in front to wave a baton and jump around and dance and maybe sing a song. Some of them didn't even sing, some of them didn't do nothing. Jimmie Lunceford didn't play anything; at least Cab would sing and dance. Cab'll dance his ass off, right now.

A small group in Cab Calloway's band called the "Cab Jivers," comprised of Milt Hinton, Cozy Cole, Chu Berry, and Danny Barker, snubbed me and tried to overlook me when I joined. When I came in the band I should've been in that group, but I wasn't.

Now, under any other condition, when I came into the band, as far ahead as I was with that kinda shit, jump 'n jive, I would've gone right into the Cab Jivers, but Chu stopped it. There was a thing on his part against me, because I always respected Chu Berry's playing. But he thought I was too young to have that important a job. "There should be a major league and a minor league in music," he said.

When he made that statement, I said, "Tell me one thing. I know you're speaking of music, but what were you doing before you came here and got this good job? Thirty-three dollars a week in the Savoy with Teddy Hill, eleven dollars a night on the road with Fletcher Henderson? What did you get before you came here?" He was a big guy, and I was little then. I weighed about a hundred forty-five pounds; I'd speak up and didn't care because I was always ready. I had my shit all the time, you see, and if somebody wanted to take advantage of me, I'd have to protect myself. I should've been in the Cab Jivers; it was that thing with Chu that kept me out of it. I never did play with those guys, but I could've added so much to their group.

I would've been a good addition to the Cab Jivers, you see, because I used to practice all the time with Milt Hinton. I used to teach Milton Hinton solos with all those chords I was working on. They played a tune called, "Girl of My Dreams," and I showed Milt a whole chorus, two whole choruses. Do you know, Milton Hinton knows those two choruses today. Right now if you ask him, "Man, play those two choruses," he'd play 'em. I used to practice with him, we used to get it. Yeah, man. We used to go on the roof of the Cotton Club between shows and get it on. Nobody else was interested in anything like that. Most of the band was just sitting there making that money.

Cab had a good band: Andy Gibson and Buster Harding wrote some nice arrangements for him. And he had some cats who could get it. He had the best jobs, so, naturally, he had the best musicians. He always had some exciting musicians. He had Tyree (Glenn), Chu, Cozy, Hinton, Jerry Blake playing beautiful clarinet, and me. Man, these cats were cracking. But a band is never any greater, musically, than its leader. You have to be a superorganizer-administrator like Jimmie Lunceford, or you've got to be a top man on your instrument, to command respect from musicians and get them to play for you.

I never found myself becoming uncomfortable musically because I was always into something else outside. Playing with Cab was my job. Cab frowned on the idea of guys going out blowing, but I went anyway. In the different towns we'd visit, I'd go out and blow. People would say, "He's with Cab Calloway." Cab didn't like that. But I'd sneak out anyway. Shit, fuck Cab! I was thinking about my own development. When we were in New York, after the show, I'd go to Minton's and then to Monroe's Uptown House and jam until seven o'clock in the mornings.

I have no idea what "Hi de ho" meant, you'd have to ask Cab that. As far as I know it was just a scat for somebody to answer to him, "Say, hey, hey." And somebody'd say, "Hi de hi . . ." You'd have to ask the creator of the music what he meant by that. I can tell you what bebop accents are. I know why they happened. Those are accents, like drums.

CAB CALLOWAY (bandleader):

"Well, now, Hi de ho is really a nonmeaning expression. I mean it was just what came to my mind at the time that it happened, you know. I just can't explain what it was. It was just an expression. It's like Diz would say, 'Ooo-de-dah.' He would improvise something.

Well, that was my form of improvisation. It was just a scat expression.

"Dizzy was in Teddy Hill's band when I first heard him. I think he was recommended to me through, if I'm not mistaken, Jonah Jones. Of course, I went out after him and I landed him. A lotta people really don't understand Dizzy. Dizzy is a fine musician—a very, very fine musician—and a very intelligent, fine-thinking person. A person that really knows what's happening in life. And he digs life more than anything else. His whole outlook is entirely different from what the average person would think of him if they just look at him and watch his reactions and things that he says and does. They just don't dig that this man is real—he's really got something—he's really there. I've always respected him for it, of course, and we had a wonderful association. He really filled the bill, being a fine musician, and added as much, or more, to my band as anybody I know.

"When I first hired him, he was still a young musician but the premier thing about him was the fact that he was a good musician. He could read his parts. He could play his parts. That was the important thing. His interpretation of jazz was originally wild. It was really wild, and it was something that I really had to get used to. I used to call him on it. I'd say, 'Man, listen, will you please don't be playing all that Chinese music up there!' See, he'd get something in his mind; he'd get something that he wanted to do. His improvisation of jazz was just what he was thinking all that time, and he put it into his playing. And all of these intricate changes that he would make on his horn, man, which were way out; nobody had ever heard anything like this before. He played it in my band, and he, himself, didn't know what it was. He didn't know what to call it or what to say it was.

"His style developed. He developed this thing to be a trend that just adds so much to jazz that it's just unrealizable. You just can't realize the fact that this guy has done all of this.

"After he left my band, I don't know who he went with. Later, I can remember when we were playing at the Strand Theater, and Dizzy came down to the theater to see me, to see if I could get my band to actually play the first arrangement on bop that ever came about. Brought it down to the theater and asked me if I could get the guys to go up to the rehearsal hall and play this arrangement. He and Tadd Dameron, I think, I forget the other boy's name. He brought this arrangement down you see, and he says, 'Now, Fess, I want you to listen to this jazz here. It might blow your mind, man, but, you know, dig it, you just dig it.' And I sat up there and dug this stuff, man. Well, I went outta my mind.

"They blew my mind because some of the jazz they were playing in there, boy, the chord formations, I mean, the notes them cats were hitting, boy, were something else. They were really something else, in another world, see. And so afterward—we played it over quite a few times—he was pleased, I was pleased. 'This is it, man,' I said, 'this is something else.'

"My band never played it. But Diz's band played it. He had a band later on. He wrote a few tunes when he was with my band. He wrote a thing called, 'Pickin' The Cabbage,' and another one too. Ageemenetti, I can't think of it right now.

"Yeah, Diz the Wiz, a real rug cutter. Very good friend of Mrs. Butter. Butter schmutta a bee gezindt. Yeah, I think the tune was 'A Bee Gezindt.' 'I'm hap-a-mop a mocho. I'm a cat that's in the know. We the cats shall hep ya to dig this righteous riff.' Anyway, we had that line in there. 'Diz the Wiz, a real horn tooter.' And then he'd play about sixteen bars and blast out. Yeah, yeah, he was a rough man then, real rough.

"Musically, the most important facet of Dizzy's playing is not just his rhythm, harmony, chord changes, or his technical facility alone. It's the whole thing. Knowing that horn, he can do anything with it. You see, he knows the horn; anything he wants to make with it, he can make. Anything. And so that's sort've the key to the whole thing. That's the whole thing, the crux of it all. He knows the horn. He studies. He ain't no fly-by-night musician. This man is, I mean, Diz could sit down in a symphony and play in a symphony, just as easy as he blows what he's blowing now. You know what I mean, he can do that.

"I dunno why he never got in the Cab Jivers. Well, you see, it was only four of them. It was Chu, Cozy, Fump, and the piano player. Dave Rivera, I think, was the piano player at that time. It was only four. It was a quartet. It was only four, and I used them as a little jazz outfit to feature Chu. And of course after Chu died, why I never . . .

"No . . . ! I don't think it was because of anything Chu had against Dizzy.

"Man, Dizzy was major league all the way. He was major league all the way. I'm telling you, I'm sorry, but he was. And of course Chu was a very nice guy, but they all had their little things going. You know Chu and Tyree and Fump and Cozy, oh, Lord, and Keg Johnson, and all them guys. They had their little things going.

"Dizzy's playing gassed me all the time. He never sounded bad to me, never, never. I liked to listen to him play all the time. Beautiful. I wish I had been the musician that Dizzy was.

"But, I'm a musician; damn right, I'm a musician, all the way through. I can't arrange, I'm not an arranger. I mean there's ninety-nine thousand musicians who are not arrangers. But, my God, I've done everything that you could do, everything. I've written nine hundred songs. I'm an ASCAP member, I mean I gotta be a musician. I gotta know what's happening.

"I wasn't just fly by night, just skidding by. Oh, yes, I was a musician. I was a musician from the word go. I studied, yes, I played. I played saxophone with my band.

"But I still say I wish I was as fine a musician as Dizzy is. I wish I could've played. Of course, he told me many times, Calloway, put that horn down. You put it down. See, and I did. I put it down."

MILTON HINTON:

"When I first met Diz, he was the equalizer, the thing that really first impressed me as far as creative playing and modern playing. I met him when I was in Cab Calloway's band. It's been a lot of years—1937, 1938, or 1939. And he came into the band right after being with Teddy Hill. And he was the freshest and the most remarkable thing that ever happened to the band because we had been together, and we were strictly a show band. Very fine, musically, everybody, the musicianship of the band was tremendous. All the guys were technically perfect. They had been together. Most of them had been together from the Missourians. I had joined in 1936 as one of the newer things that had entered the band, other than the straight Missourian-type band which had been quite organized, a black band that was quite well off and worked consistently and made good money. And everybody was quite secure. The creativity had sort of, in my thinking, waned because it would always be such a set thing. There was always a place to work. They were accompanying Cab in these years. They were just really background for his hired host and for him singing, even though the musicianship of the men was tremendous as far as being musically, technically skilled on their instruments. And when I came in, I was out of Chicago, out of the rat race. I was fresh and trying to still be creative, and I came into this organization a kid, off the streets, you know, and not too many togs. And from a $35 a week job to $100 a week overnight, which was just absolutely shocking in 1936. And I thought I'd be rich, of course, in three months. And here I was in this band. And then I was amazed at the complacency. The guys didn't socialize with one another. They didn't go around to the jam sessions. At night, they got dressed. They got very sharp and dignified and split with their chicks; and they didn't go here and there. And if they were in a town, they didn't go by the big nightclub to find out who was blowing or what was happening in this locality because they had to come back to the theater and play their beautiful background standards for Cab Calloway or for the dancers.

"There were no drum solos. It was catching the singers, as they sang, or the dancers. So I was sort of lonesome. And here in 1938, here comes a fresh new entity which was everything that the word implies,

Dizzy! He was about as crazy as you can find, and always like Peck's Bad Boy, always trying something new. Whether he could do it or whether he couldn't, he was going to make this tremendous attempt at it, and take all kinds of abuses. If he was not successful in his attempt, everybody would talk about it. He shook me up tremendously. And it upset our whole band. It upset the whole dialogue of this Cab Calloway band. The older men looked on him as, 'What's this? What is this young upstart coming in here carrying on like this?' And the ones that must've felt a little differently about it said nothing. I was amazed because he knew more, even though I'm older than he is. But he had been more involved in this New York and Philadelphia rat race. And he had been playing with some very sharp cats; and he was very deep into his chord changes and his substitutions which hadn't even hit this band yet, not at all. Nothing like a C chord, to compare with it. Anybody making a substitution for a C chord? Nobody ever dreamed of that. If it was a C, you just played it, baby! And that was it.

"So here we had this new entity, and me, being flushed, I naturally took his side. I said, well here, I finally got some sort of relativity, somebody I can talk to and somebody I can learn from. And Dizzy felt the same way. Now, I was sort of a senior, because I'd been in the band a couple of years now, and I had a couple of dollars. I'd bought me a few new suits and a portable radio and other delicacies and joys of the day, and met a couple of nice chicks. So here I am, pretty well together and, now, I got Diz.

"'Man,' I said, 'that sounds nice, what you're playing. But I missed that change. What was it, Diz?'

"'Well, look,' he said, 'I'll tell you what after the show. If you'll come over, come upstairs, I'll show you what that was.'

"My bass was very portable. This was backstage in the Cotton Club. There was a stairway that led upstairs over the Cotton Club, a fire escape to the roof. And it was one of those spiral iron staircases and it took quite a bit of doing to take a big cumbersome bass fiddle around this thing to get up to the roof. But Dizzy would get in front of me and take the bass, and I'd get on the bottom. And then we'd get up there on the roof between shows, and Dizzy would show me these different changes. And it was just a revelation to me. And it was a joy. So now, when he played his solos, when he had a solo again, I could play the changes that Dizzy wanted to play, which made quite a difference, you know. And we got this thing going.

"There was a group in our band called the Cab Jivers. We were like the 'seniors' of the band. So during the radio show, Cab would always give us a little spot in the show. The Cab Jivers got a chance to play a little tune by ourselves. Like Benny Goodman had his quartet, with Teddy Wilson and Lionel Hampton, Cab had a little group called the Cab Jivers. Dizzy, of course, wasn't in it. But he was so hip,

I said, since I'm in it, since I'm one of the 'seniors,' I'll go to Dizzy and say, 'Hey, jazz, you better show me one of them chords, 'cause I gotta play a solo, and I want you to show me the changes and how I can play it.' One song was 'Girl of My Dreams I Love You.' And Dizzy showed me these new changes. Aw, man, you know! Well, instead of going right straight to the C, I'd make the D-flat chord: de, da, da, da, de, D-flat da, da, then go down to the C, and, man, it knocked me out. But it was a little foreign to my ear. Dizzy had me trying to attempt to bow it, because Slam (Stewart) was now quite a sensation on Fifty-second Street."

My roommate and best friend in Cab Calloway's band musically, besides Milt Hinton, was a Cuban, Mario Bauza, the former trumpeter with Chick Webb. Mario was like my father. He took off one day from his own job with Cab Calloway so Cab could hear me play. Mario helped me a lot, not just by giving me an opportunity to be heard and land a good job, but by broadening my scope in music. Mario was the first to impress me with the importance of Afro-Cuban music. Once I said to him, speaking about those large drums the Afro-Cubans played, "Man, I like them tom-tom things."

"You mean the conga drums?" Mario said.

"Yeah, if I ever get myself a band, I want one of them things, a tom-tom."

At the same time, Cab Calloway was dabbling just a little bit in Latin rhythms. I suspect because of Socarras' presence at the Cotton Club. Socarras, the Cuban maestro with his magic flute, with whom I'd played at the Savoy, sometimes played at the Cotton Club too. Socarras was such a marvelous flute player, and his Latin band was so good, Cab sorta liked it. I really liked it. Eventually, when I got my band together, that was the first thing I thought of. I had to have a conga drummer.

With Mario Bauza in the band, I really became interested in bringing Latin and especially Afro-Cuban influences into my music. Afro-Cuban influences, because there was no outside influence in our music, not in jazz. No one was playing that type of music where the bass player instead of saying, "boom, boom, boom, boom," broke up the rhythm, "boom-be, boom-be, boom-be, boom-be." No one was doing that. I became very fascinated with the possibilities for expanding and enriching jazz rhythmically and phonically through the use of Afro-Cuban rhythmic and melodic devices. But I was still unprepared to attempt anything that heavy, and so was anyone else in the field of jazz.

Cab had one or two of the usual Latin type numbers in his music book, but these were nonauthentic, watered-down adaptations of real Afro-Cuban music, which had been abandoned in its pure form and set to more simple rhythm so Americans could play it and dance to it. You know, like the rhumba and stuff. I much preferred the real thing, but over here, no one could play that except in a totally Afro-Cuban context. Living and playing with Mario, I found out that despite the language differences, Afro-Americans and Cubans were not destined to be total strangers, musically. In fact, they could sleep in the same bed, at least in the same room.

MARIO BAUZA:

"It was the funniest thing. I tell you that. He happened to be my roommate and he didn't let me sleep at night. Dizzy used to go asleep reading funny books, every night. And when he did get to sleep, he had nightmares. He'd start jumping and rolling and stuff like that.

"Cab had made one record using Afro-Cuban rhythms, and that was my idea. I forgot the name, but it was nothing complicated. It was something melodic with a little Cuban rhythm, but nothing complicated like what we're doing now. In those days, those American musicians didn't have the slightest idea about Latin music. The rhythms were too complicated for them."

We used to play at a theater in Kansas City where black people had to sit up in the balcony, called the "buzzard's roost." Colored people (at that time they were called that) weren't even allowed to come and hear us play unless they sat in some out-of-the-way place. It was the same way in St. Louis, at the theater there. I had another friend, a trumpet player in Kansas City named Buddy Anderson when I was with Cab. Buddy Anderson played trumpet at the Booker T. Washington Hotel in Kansas City and was going in the same direction as I. But eventually Buddy got sick and had to stop playing trumpet and started playing bass. A gifted musician like that lost out on the physical part. We used to play together whenever I visited there because we were on the same track and used to enjoy one another. We still do. Buddy Anderson used to come and hang out with me in the dressing room. We'd talk between sets and exchange ideas, and he told me once, "I got somebody I want you to hear, a saxophone player. You've got to hear this saxophone player I know, an alto."

"Oh, *man*," I said, "a saxophone player? I'm playing with Chu

Berry; and I know Benny Carter and played with Coleman Hawkins, and I know Lester Young." I was just on a record date with Chu, Coleman Hawkins, Benny Carter, and Ben Webster. "Saxophone? Wait a minute," I said, "I'm talking about saxophone players . . ." I'd played with Don Byas and Lester and Herschel (Evans) around New York. I'd known all these guys, great saxophonists, you know, and I said I wasn't too interested.

"Well, look," Buddy said, "I'm gonna bring him by the hotel anyway."

And I was astounded by what the guy could do. These other guys that I had been playing with weren't my colleagues, really. But the moment I heard Charlie Parker, I said, there is *my* colleague.

Buddy and I and Charlie Parker went up into this hotel room and locked up. We locked up in that room, and Charlie Parker played. I never heard anything like that before. The way that he assembled notes together. That was one of the greatest thrills because I had been a Roy Eldridge fan up until then, but I was definitely moving on into myself. Charlie Parker and I were moving in practically the same direction too, but neither of us knew it.

Later on, about 1942, Charlie came to New York with Jay McShann, and we became friends. We used to go to the Uptown House. Charlie had the job there at Monroe's Uptown House, an after-hours place, with Vic Coulson and George Treadwell. I used to go there and play. When Ben Webster first heard him, he almost fainted. Ben Webster was a big fan of Benny Carter's, you know. When young cats listen to Charlie Parker, now, they almost faint because he was that far in front.

BUDDY ANDERSON (trumpet):

"Yes, I introduced them.

"Diz came here with Cab Calloway, in 1940. We were the house band, and Cab played it as a one-nighter. And I went out with a group of the fellas in Jay McShann's band to dig Cab's band. Orville Minor, a trumpet player who was with McShann then, and I went out to dig Cab and dug Dizzy. He knocked us out. He was different from anything we'd seen. So at intermission we got to talking with him and told him about a jam session down on the streets, you know, Nineteenth and Vine. It was called the Kentucky Club.

"Sure 'nuff, Diz showed up and he was real different, every moment. So we talked with him a little bit after he got off the stand. I was telling him mainly about Charlie Parker, but Charlie didn't show that night for some reason. But that next day, everybody got up about twelve, as cats do, and we met again, right in front of that Kentucky Club; that is, Diz and I met. We were talking and Charlie showed up, just outta the clear, showed up with his horn. And we talked a little while, and Dizzy wanted to hear us play. So we went over to the Musician's Local, 627. We went upstairs to the piano and Dizzy sat down at the piano; he played. He wanted to hear me play trumpet and Charlie play saxophone. So we went through several numbers with him, but Diz was really feeling his oats then; he was coming through. He really didn't dig Bird, or me either, at that time. But it was a fine meeting.

"Then McShann's band, which Charlie was a part of, went to New York. We were in the Savoy, and Diz would come and sit in the band, which was unusual. But Jay dug him and let him make it and everything. Things just rocked on like that.

"It wasn't a hotel room, it was at the Musician's Local where there was a piano, and Dizzy sat at the piano and played piano for Charlie and myself to play. He didn't play trumpet, he just played piano. He wanted to hear us.

"I didn't dig Charlie myself when I first heard him. I dug that he was different, but I'd heard some cats that was different. I knew one in Oklahoma City was just as bad as Charlie, man, cat named Harold Tillman. He played alto, and he was very, very rough, man. He was a very fine alto-saxophone player. But Charlie was something you had to kinda keep listening to before you could really dig what's happening. He was altogether different from what was going down as a thing. Although, this other cat was doing practically the same thing Bird was doing, just different. There was a lotta different cats during that time.

"I would just say that Diz and Bird were on the same line, man. I happened to be in that same bag, at least that's what Jay McShann said in an interview in *Jazz Today* magazine that came out in the forties. It was a special issue on Charlie Parker, and they sounded different cats about Charlie Parker. In McShann's interview, instead of him talking about Charlie, he was talking about me. He said I was the same thing as Charlie Parker, only on trumpet.

"But Dizzy was far more advanced, musically, than I was. But 'Bird' was highly advanced theoretically too. But Dizzy was then and always has been out front, theoretically, of most of the cats, if not all of the cats. Diz is something else. I mean Diz is a terrible rhythm man. Max Roach made a point of saying that.

"Diz didn't play trumpet at all in that first little meeting. Bird had his horn up under his arm, and I had my horn. And we went directly over to the musician's union, went upstairs to the piano, and that is actually the way it was, really, honestly and truly. I know that like I know my own name.

"Diz didn't have too much to say; he just dug it, you know. It's hard to impress Diz, you know. Especially at that time. He's easier to impress now, much more now than he was then because he was younger and all 'dizzy.' He's wide open now; he digs everything. But he couldn't dig nothing but Dizzy at that time. I mentioned Charlie Christian to him. I was with Charlie down in Oklahoma City when John Hammond came down there and got him out of the band we had down there. And I mentioned Charlie Christian, and Dizzy mentioned that he knew him and everything, jammed with him, but it didn't mean much to him. Didn't nobody's name mean much to him but Dizzy's then. He was stuck on Dizzy.

"His personality was so scintillating. Cat would just keep something going. I could dig that, even in Cab's band. He was going!

"Diz and Bird seemed to me like two different things altogether. Diz, as one cat expressed it, made it up through hard work, and Bird's was more a 'natural' thing. He worked, he had to, but he didn't dig like Diz. I mean, Diz had to work hard for what he got. Bird's was more a natural thing. And he was highly collective, Bird was. Bird paid strict attention to what people did, and if he found anything that they did that struck him, he brought that into his thing. That's the reason he had so many 'outs' because he borrowed from everybody he could, and he'd embellish it and what not. But Diz is damn near all Diz, and it's a little bit studied, but nobody could do it but Diz. They couldn't copy Diz. They copied Charlie, but couldn't nobody copy Diz. I mean it took a long time. I just heard one of those Candoli boys. At first I thought it was Diz, but he was the first one I ever heard that sounded like Diz. They could copy Miles and cats like that, but they couldn't copy Dizzy. A lot of them started to try back then, but them cats couldn't make it because they didn't have the technique to do it with."

World War II was also on about that time and the general attitude among the musicians was, "Ahhh, they got me!" There were all kinds of stories coming out. I saw a lot of stories about how they wouldn't respect a black U.S. soldier down South. He had to go in the "colored" entrance and everything, and he's out there dying for his country. It was awful. It was a general thing. When he'd come up North to come home on furlough, he'd have to ride in a jim-crow car to come up, jim-crow buses too.

I already had in mind what I would do if they called me. I wasn't gonna make it if I could. My idea was not to go to the Army at all, and being on the road all the time, I figured they might not catch up with me. They did. They delivered my "greetings" when I was in

Pittsburgh with Cab in 1940, in the mail c/o The Cab Calloway Band.

To tell the truth, I was always somewhat of a pacifist. I didn't believe that it was necessary for people to be killing one another. After they gave me my greetings in Pittsburgh, I had to come back to New York. They said bring enough clothes for three days. Remember that song, "Bring Enough Clothes for Three Days"?

So I took my horn down, that was enough clothes for me. And when they told me to take off my clothes, I did, but I kept my horn. That's how I got into the psychiatrist, being there naked with my horn in a paper bag. That was pretty weird, to them, anyway.

They said, "Well, do you know if you're accepted into the Army, you'll have to be down here for three days?"

"I'm aware of that," I said. "My horn is enough."

So they asked me a lot of silly questions. They asked me about drugs. Every now and then, I'd smoke a joint or something like that. At that time, if you told them that you smoked a joint, they'd look at you a little bit funny, but most of the time they'd take you anyway. This was during the "second front," brother; this was when they were taking almost everything.

Then they asked me all kinds of questions about homosexuality and things like that.

"Don't be kidding, man," they said.

"I don't even know a jazz musician who's a homosexual," I said, "a real jazz musician."

Then they started asking me my views about fighting. "Well, look, at this time, in this stage of my life here in the United States whose foot has been in my ass? The white man's foot has been in my ass hole buried up to his knee in my ass hole!" I said. "Now, you're speaking of the enemy. You're telling me the German is the enemy. At this point, I can never even remember having met a German. So if you put me out there with a gun in my hand and tell me to shoot at the enemy, I'm liable to create a case of 'mistaken identity,' of who I might shoot." They looked around at one another.

After that they started trying to act friendly and asked me had I played with some band out West, some Western band.

"Man, you silly muthafucka," I said. "I'm a New York musician. We play in New York bands. It's a different caliber of musicianship in New York than it is out West there. I'll never play with no band out there."

They finally classified me 4F because I was crazy enough not to want to fight, in anybody's army. And especially not at that time. Shoot, I was just beginning to enjoy life.

Wholly Matrimony

As soon as I got the job with Cab, I immediately snatched Lorraine out of the Apollo. I stopped my wife from dancing, because the work was too hard for her, and took her out on the road with me. The place for a wife is with her husband, so I wanted Lorraine to go everywhere I went. The only strange thing about that was we hadn't yet been officially, legally, married.

One time, we were up in Boston with Cab and I started trying to talk her into it. "Let's get married?" I asked.

She said, "Yes," so we went to the clerk there and got our papers. We stayed up there for a couple of weeks, and that was enough time to get everything arranged; so we got married in Boston.

It was funny, the clerk didn't put the seal on our marriage certificate. We'd just gotten married, and we didn't know. We thought we were married, but we didn't have a seal on our certificate, and neither one of us knew that the guy hadn't sealed our marriage certificate. So nothing happened until later on; I made an application to join the Masonic order, and one of the Masons came to investigate me.

"Well, may we see your marriage license, please?" he asked.

"Yes, of course," I said. "Lorraine go and get the marriage license." She brought the marriage license, and he looked at it, and he looked at me, and then the guy cut out. Then we found out that they turned down my application. I asked the guy who had recommended me about it.

"Man, why didn't you tell him that you were just shacking?" he said. "We don't mind you shacking up, but admit it! Don't be jiving around talking about you're married, and you got a piece of paper with no seal on it."

"Whadda you mean? I'm married, nigger!"

"Uh, well, there's no seal on your marriage license."

So I looked on the certificate and sure enough, there wasn't. So we sent it back to Boston, and now we've got a seal; Seal of the State of Massachusetts, May 9, 1940. We finally got it straight, but that was funny that they didn't put a seal on our marriage certificate. We just made it legal; we were already married.

From the beginning, Lorraine was a woman with a very strong personality. As a matter of fact, Lorraine's own mother looked at her like Lorraine was the mother. Lorraine's grandmother was such a strong personality and she had a great effect on Lorraine's life because Lorraine was raised by her grandmother. Lorraine's mother didn't have the opportunity to pick up all that inner strength from her own mother because she moved up North to work. So Lorraine got all the grandmother wit. Right now, there are no problems that come up that she can't cope with. There's a right way and a wrong way for everything that you do; and no in betweens. Lorraine will take the right way, and there's no dillydallying with right—it's straight ahead. She's the most incorruptible person. My wife gives me the proper perspective. She gives me the anchor I need. She has real mother wit, and besides, she knows all there is to know about show business.

Another thing about Lorraine is she keeps my ego at a minimum. If my ego should happen to soar a bit, unprofessionally, or professionally, she will bring it right back down to normal. I'm quite popular in Harlem, and when I walk up the street, I have to make a million stops. I came home one day and told Lorraine, "Hey, I just came through Harlem, and, boy, those people up there really dig me. One thing about me, Lorraine, you have a husband who has that 'common' touch."

"You're right," Lorraine said. "You're one of the *commonest* muthafuckas I ever saw in my life." That really straightened it out for me, one sentence. She's got one sentence that'll straighten out everything.

LORRAINE GILLESPIE:

"He just asked me to get married. Dizzy didn't fool around with all that other stuff. He just asked me to get married, and I said, 'O.K.' I

Asleep on the road with the Earl
Hines band, 1943. COLLECTION OF
DUNCAN P. SCHIEDT.

Introducing "bebop" at the Onyx Club, 52nd Street, 1944, with (l to r)
Max Roach, drums; Budd Johnson, tenor saxophone; Oscar Pettiford,
bass; and George Wallington, piano. COLLECTION OF DUNCAN P. SCHIEDT.

"Bebop Incubator," Earl Hines Orchestra, 1945, at the Apollo Theater, (l to r) Diz; "Little" Benny Harris, trumpet; Howard Scott, trombone; Gail Brockman, trumpet; Shorty McConnell, trumpet; Gus Chappell, trombone; Earl Hines, piano and leader; Bennie Green, trombone; Shadow Wilson, drums;

Sarah Vaughan, piano and vocals; Andrew Crump, tenor sax; Jesse Simpkins, bass; Andrew "Goon" Gardner, alto sax; "Scoops" Carry, alto sax; Huey Long, guitar; John Williams, alto sax–baritone sax; Julie Gardner, accordion; Charlie Parker, tenor sax. FRANK DRIGGS COLLECTION.

Having a ball with Louis Jordan and guys from the band of 1946, (l to r) Milt Jackson, Louis Jordan, Joe Harris, Ray Brown, me, Dave Burns, John Lewis, Aaron Eisenhall (Jordan's trumpeter), Kenny Hagood, Joe Gayles, Elmon Wright, Marcelles, and Bill Frazier.

I just loved the sound of Ella Fitzgerald with my band in 1946. Ray Brown, bass, is in the background. COLLECTION OF DUNCAN P. SCHIEDT.

Blowing at the Savoy Ballroom; my band, 1946. Visible with me is Teddy Stewart, drums. FRANK DRIGGS COLLECTION.

Just partying with our wives, Chicago, 1946.

Bebop broke the attendance records at our Carnegie
Hall concert in 1946 with Ella Fitzgerald.

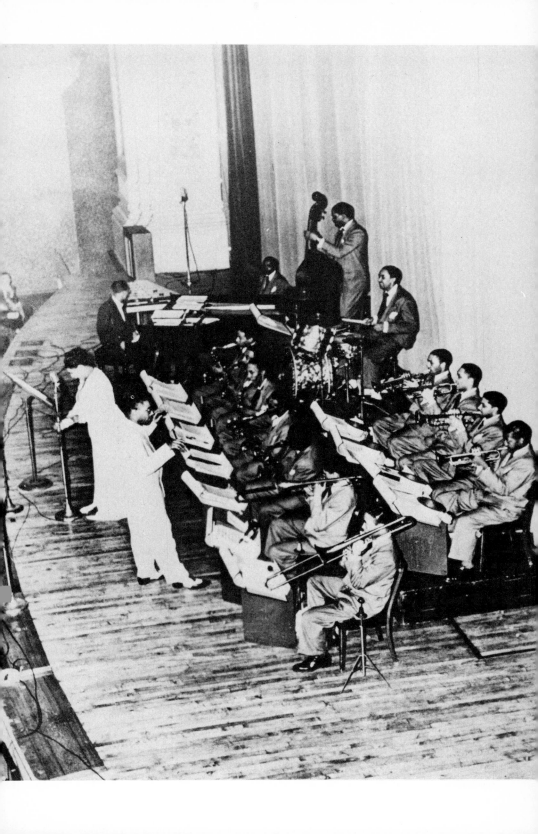

The band featured Chano
Pozo on conga drums.

And James Moody on
tenor saxophone.

went with him to Boston with Cab Calloway. In Boston, you can't be staying together in the first place, without being married. But there's plenty of them that's doing it. Dizzy just wanted to get married, anyhow. I think he thought that was a good excuse to get married. He thought I'd get afraid, you know.

"'Girl,' he said, 'you know you can't stay together in Boston and not be married. You gotta be married.' I guess he figured since I was already there, that was a good way to get me into it; I think that's what that was. We just went right on down to the courthouse and got married, and that was that. Somebody in the courthouse stood for us, we didn't even know who the man was. We didn't make any kind of to do out of it, because he was working and didn't have time for all of that. I wasn't working then. I'd stopped dancing temporarily.

"My mother's name is Lydia, and my father's name is Gus Lynch. My mother's other name in marriage is Willis. Willis is her last marriage name. I was born in Long Branch, New Jersey, but I was raised in New York. I don't know nothing about Jersey. My mother just went to that hospital; she was living in New York.

"I studied dancing with Grace Giles, her studio was at 132nd Street and Seventh Avenue. Like other kids in New York, you start when you're five or six years old and just go on up. Till you feel like stopping. I took everything; I took dancing; I took music. When I didn't feel like it, I just stopped the music. I went to dancing because I'd have more fun; I'd have a ball taking dance. Music, you had to go by yourself.

"Told my mother a lie. I told my mother that the man said I should learn how to sing as well as play, and he put some books on my chest. That man didn't do nothing. I'd heard that's the way you went through the singing scene.

"My mother said, 'Well, you most certainly are not gonna put nothing else on your chest.' She stopped sending me, and that's just what I wanted. I'd heard somebody saying that they have to train your diaphragm to breathe deeply. But they don't put books on your chest, I don't think.

"I spent my childhood down South with my grandmother in Darlington, South Carolina, but I don't know nothing about it. The only thing I knew was the block she lived on and that was all. Boy, every time somebody would invite me to something, my grandmother would go and investigate first. That's right! She'd wanna know who was gonna be there, why, where did they come from, and then wanna know their families. And then she'd start checking out the family. If she said, 'I don't know them,' that meant I was gonna miss the party. So I said if things are gonna be like this, I can really forget it.

"My first husband was from down there. He was from Hartsville. His sister still comes to see me. And his little nephews and nieces—

they call Dizzy, 'Uncle Dizzy,' and they mean it too. They call him Uncle Dizzy, right now.

"I was only married to my first husband a year—he died. He had a brain tumor. He died too fast. In the first place, we were so young, we had no business to even get married as young as that. But he did other type work. He was a chauffeur. When I was dancing, see, I wasn't even together with him that much, because I'd be traveling, dancing, and he was working. He was working for some rich family or something like that. He died with a tumor on the brain.

"When Dizzy and I first got married, we lived in hotels, because we were always out of town. There wasn't any sense in trying to call no place, home. The first place we stayed was 2040 Seventh Avenue in New York. Everybody was in there. 'Puerto Rico,' from the Apollo, lived right downstairs under us; Clyde Hart, the musician, lived upstairs. Elsie Blow, she was a chorus girl, lived there too. Oh, 'Cook and Brown,' a dancing act, they lived there. Cookie still lives there. Nearly everybody that lived there were show people—Erroll Garner, Billy Eckstine and his wife, June Eckstine.

"Things worked out all right when we first set up housekeeping, just as good as it is now, as far as I'm concerned. It's never been no different, because Dizzy is doing the same thing. Now, he's older and he's learned all that foolishness out there don't mean anything; but before, he didn't give a kitty.

"We had hard times in the beginning, and little money. When they took your social security and withholding out, you didn't have anything left. Remember, Dizzy was hardly making anything. He was a sideman. That's different from him being a bandleader. Dizzy was only making a hundred bucks a week. That hundred dollars did just as much as you can do now after they take out a lot of it for the government.

"The only thing amusing was trying to get to my grits, that was amusing enough. That's right! When you're working, maybe a whole lot goes on, but it probably went on with me on my job with the chorus girls, and him on his job. When you get home, man, you're tired, you're just like anybody else, 'Hello, good-by, and don't ask me nothing, I'm tired.' You gotta get up early to go to the theater the next day, and you gotta rehearse between shows, and all that. It's the same thing as with anybody else.

"What are the things I like about him the most? Well, everybody else sees all these things that he does and what not. Usually, I'm arguing about the things I don't like; it's hard for me to find what I like. Oh, my goodness, you made this pretty tough because I'm always on Dizzy about trying to do this and trying to do that right. He can do so many darn things wrong, till I don't know. I'll tell you what, one thing that I like about him. I never had any trouble with, like, if I wanted something, I don't have to ask him for it. Unh, unh. When I wanted something, I could go get it. I didn't have to say nothing to him. A lotta times if I wanted something and said, 'Oh, no, it costs too much money,' he'll get mad. 'You could get it, why don't you? You never get nothing for yourself,' he'd say.

"Now, I like that because I don't have to be like a child. Like a lotta women, when they want a pair of shoes or something, they got to ask their husband for the money. Unh, unh! None of that, because I don't think I could take that. When I met Dizzy, I was working for myself, and I didn't have to go through no questionnaires to get a pair of shoes. When my parents brought me up, like when I was five or six years old, I used to get twenty-five cents allowance. Oh, I thought I had a lotta money. Then, when I got to be about seven or eight, they used to give me fifty cents a week allowance. Then they went to a dollar. And then they went up as high as five dollars. Man, you couldn't tell me nothing when I got five dollars a week. I really learned how to take care of my money from that. I learned not to throw away my money, because I had that to take with me to school, or buy candy, or do the few little things I wanted. But one thing about my mother, if I ran through that money foolishly, shame on me; I wasn't gonna get another nickel for anything I wanted until the next Friday when I got my allowance. So I had to figure out how to budget it, you know. And you talk about a strict and tight budget! Man, I had some budgets going from way back. It taught me a lot.

"Yeah, I like his generosity; he doesn't like to limit me. I don't even say anything; I go get what I want. Of course, I don't want very much. I'm always talking about saving something. Dizzy'll spend more money on me than I do on myself.

"The funniest thing to me is when I have to tell Dizzy something. Like I'd say, 'Dizzy, don't do so-and-so.' Man, do you think he would stop? He's just like a kid, even a little worse. You have to say, 'Don't do so-and-so!' Then he'll say, 'Well, looks like she means it.' Then he'll stop. But he's beginning to get different, now that he's getting older.

"People on the outside say, 'Oh, the way she talks to him,' and 'Blah, blah' this and 'blah, blah' that. I was living with him, and I knew how you had to handle him. They just come to see him, you understand. It's quite a difference. That's right. I knew what I was doing. They handled him their way because they didn't have to live with him and go through the ups and downs, but I did.

"No, we just couldn't have any kids. But I don't regret not having any kids. See, that's why people don't understand me. I feel like if God wanted me to have children, I woulda had plenty of them. So he had a reason for me not to have them. And I can dig that reason, right now, fooling around with Dizzy.

"Well off? From a kid I never had to want for nothing, 'cause my family did have a little money, for colored people. When I was a kid, I had a nurse and I never had sense enough to know what she was. I just thought she was a playmate, but I knew she was older. But my people taught me that what they had was theirs, and they were gonna try to do what was right by me, but I wasn't supposed to get carried away in my mind with what belonged to them. I had to learn to work. So they taught me to enjoy what I could get, and I also had to learn that money didn't grow on trees; and I had to take care of what they got me. Not only that; they taught me when my warts got up a little high that I had to work and buy what I wanted. That's right. I had to take care of what they got me and work to buy what I thought I wanted.

"People think that I was well taken care of. All those chicks out there. 'Oh, she's well . . .' I had to work just as hard as Dizzy, or I would've been in a room today. Because he wouldn't have a quarter today. He would have spent it all. Before he could make it, he would've had it spent up, you know. Just like he can't understand it when I tell him, 'Don't use too much soap powder. Don't use too much this. Put out the lights.' All that's money going out there in the wind, and I save it.

"People don't see that, you know. I mean, when you owe a bill to any of these big concerns and you owe them a nickel, they'll write you a fifty-dollar letter to send the five cents that you owe them. So why can't you learn how to protect your nickel and dime, yourself. I mean, there's nobody to write to when you run through it. But if it's valuable to somebody else, it should be just the same to you. It ought to be just as good in your pocket as it is in somebody else's.

"The major problem with a man and wife getting together and adjusting to each other, most of the time, is that they just don't have respect for one another. That's the main thing. You don't have to have love for nobody. When you respect somebody, that's as much as you owe, and you don't give a kitty who they love. Look, if you love me and every time you see me, you're doing something to embarrass me or disrespect me, where is the love? Would you kindly tell me? Silent? No, I like you to show me what I'm getting. I don't want no pig in the sty. I wanna see what I'm getting. I mean—to respect somebody—you can't tell somebody to love you. Maybe they might love somebody else, but they got so much respect for you that they'll even forget about this. In the first place, what is love, anyway, if you don't have respect? I wish somebody'd just tell me what love is. The main thing people should look for and should ask for is respect. If you don't have that, man, you don't need no love."

See, what I told you about Lorraine? Mutual respect is so important because as soon as it disappears in relations between you and the next person, there's trouble. The tiniest thing can set it off, the tiniest thing.

Spitball . . .

My style of playing still hadn't really been established. To say that my style had reached a point that when you heard me play you would definitely know it was me would be untrue. But I knew where I was heading and kept on trying to achieve that, so my progress was rewarding, especially in the jam sessions at Minton's. I worked hard while I played with Cab, and practiced constantly. I could seldom get much encouragement from the guys in Cab's band. Mostly, they talked about real estate or something, never talked about music. That atmosphere kept me acting wiggy and getting into a lot of mischief, so I was a natural suspect when anything weird happened or went awry in the band.

We were playing at the State Theatre in Hartford, and no one knows what mood Cab was in that particular day. Cab loves the horses. He could've been playing the horses; there were times when he lost large sums on the horses. During those days, he was really a big horse lover. He still loves horses, but he uses the proper restraint now. But at that time, man, this money was coming in, and he'd call his bookie, "Hey, put me so-and-so . . ." on the horse races. So he might have already been in a bad mood.

The Cab Jivers were out onstage that night, about to finish playing, and the curtain started coming down. Jonah Jones, back in the trumpet section, started throwing spitballs out on the stage at the

drummer, Cozy Cole, while the Cab Jivers were out there. The spitball didn't hit Cab. Cab was nowhere around. But then he came out
there and saw the spitballs and accused me of throwing them.

I told him I hadn't thrown any spitballs, and one word led to another. Cab got so mad, he ran up in the band to get me and stumbled
all over the trombone players. He fucked up the trombones trying to
get to me. Of course, this happened after the curtain came down because Cab Calloway has too much class to do that kinda shit onstage.
You'll never hear of him losing a job on account of some shit like that.
Anyway, he tried to get me, and they pulled him off, and he went on
to his dressing room. On my way to the band room, I passed Cab's
dressing room. I heard him say that he'd wipe my ass all over the theater. "You ain't gonna do shit to me!" I said. In the meantime, I had
my hand in my pocket. He rushed out there and grabbed me in my
collar. I just let him grab me, but he turned me loose very quickly,
like I was red hot. I must have burned his ass when he grabbed me.
He put his hands up in my chest and pulled me up, getting ready to
hit me. He didn't know I was getting ready to kill him. Oh, yes, I
nicked him. He turned me loose, quick. When he saw that blood,
nobody had to tell him to turn me loose. Milt Hinton grabbed my
hand to keep me from really injuring him. I coulda killed him, I was
so mad. It was a serious fight, a very serious thing, and somebody
could've gotten really hurt because I'm a firm believer in nonviolence
when it comes to me.

And then Cab told them, "Get him outta here!" That's how I lost
the job. They paid me, and I cut out. I forgot all about it, grabbed
Lorraine, caught a bus and came on back to New York.

MILTON HINTON:

"I'm pretty good with my bow, but I didn't know anything about
the jazz. I had studied academically to play. Dizzy was showing me
these hip changes, which were even more hip than the thing 'Slam'
Stewart was playing. See, Slam's was more swing, but Dizzy was trying to show me some very hip changes, and they were a little foreign
to me, and nine times out of ten, I didn't get it. So every night, every
time the Cab Jivers would play it in the show, I would look back at
Dizzy when I got through playing, and say, 'Diz, did I make it?'

"And Dizzy would give me the O.K., if I was cool, by nodding or
he would stick his fingers in his nose and tell me that I stunk.

"And this is exactly what happened the night up in Hartford, Connecticut, when Cab Calloway accused Dizzy of throwing that spitball

which Dizzy did not throw. Dizzy put his finger in his nose to tell me I stunk, because I missed my solo a mile. When I looked back at Diz, Diz put his nose up and took his other hand and waved it at me to tell me, 'You stink!' And at the same time, somebody came along and 'thump!' a big blot of paper landed right in the center of the stage.

"It was Jonah. Jonah threw it. He just thumped it up in the air. It fell right in the spotlight. And Cab was in the wings. He saw it, and he saw Dizzy wave his hand at me, just at that moment. Man, Cab flipped! Of course, when the show was over Jonah and all the band walked off. Cab didn't say nothing to nobody but Diz. And the reason I happened to hear the argument is because the drummer and the bass player are the last ones off the bandstand. I gotta put the bass up, you know. As I came across the stage and saw it was getting uptight, I kinda laid back to see what would happen.

"There was *no* reason why he should have thought that Dizzy did it, since Dizzy was always doing something wrong. He would play a solo and he would get involved in it, 'ba-do-ba,' and he didn't have the chops he acquired later. He had the ideas, but his chops weren't always up to his ideas in those days. He was making an attempt at something, and he'd get about two thirds of the way through it and just run right out of chops completely, and it wouldn't be nothing but hot air coming out. The trumpet players, mostly, would be in awe because they would be admiring him for even attempting this. And even if he didn't make it all, they could envision what it would sound like if it had been finished. Of course, Cab, not being that kind of musician, all he heard was the last two measures were just hot air. And he'd say, 'Man, why can't you play the solos like all the other cats who just play what's on the paper? And play the thing nice instead of going all up there and missing all them notes.' And Diz would hang his head while Cab bawled him out.

"We would sit on the bandstand sometimes, and Cab would be singing a ballad. He'd be singing something like, 'I got you under my skin . . .' By now, we had J. C. Heard in the band, Dizzy's in the band, and Tyree Glenn is in the band. The trumpets sat on the left, and the trombones sat on the right, and Dizzy would be sitting back there. The lights would be low, and Cab would be singing his beautiful ballad, with his pretty white suit on: 'I got you, deep in the heart of meee . . .' And Dizzy would look out in the audience like he was playing football, and go like he was making a forward pass. And Tyree would be sitting on the other side of the bandstand in the trombone section, and he would act like he caught them. And just as he caught it, J.C. would hit a little bomb on the bass drum, 'bomm,' and the audience would crack up.

"Cab didn't understand. His back is to us, and the people would be laughing. And here he's singing this beautiful ballad, 'My darling, I love you . . . ,' and the people were laughing. He's wondering what in the heck is going on. And when he turned around and looked, of course everybody was acting just like absolutely nothing was happening. And this would drive him crazy. It was driving the poor man up the wall. Dizzy and Tyree were really the instigators of this thing, and the drummer is catching it, a 'bomm!' J.C. would just give a little accent, not a big boom to upset the tempo of the piece Cab's singing, but just an accent to let you know that the pass had been caught. And all of us would be dying.

"So it was just Dizzy's nature. He was Peck's Bad Boy, and he would look out in the audience like he saw somebody he knew. Cab was singing this beautiful ballad, and he'd put his hand up and dip his head like he'd seen somebody. And the people would start snickering and Cab would wonder, 'What in the world am I? What in the world is going on here? All this carrying on? The people are laughing, and I'm trying to take this thing serious.' And of course, when he turned around to see if the man was doing anything, we would all be very quiet. And, of course, when he came off, he would bawl the daylights out of us. 'Well, fellas, something is happening back there, and I don't like it at all!' And nine times out of ten, he would finally find out it was Dizzy. And he would bawl Dizzy out, and Dizzy would take it.

"Consequently, that one time in Hartford, when Dizzy was not wrong—he'd not done what Cab accused him of, throwing that spitball —Dizzy was terribly upset about it. And Cab was terribly upset, because Dizzy had said he didn't do it. That Dizzy would deny *doing* this thing. And of course Cab had a coupla nice fine chicks sitting back there waiting for him too. And he's got on his pretty white suit, and he's the bandleader. So when he says to this dumb trumpet player, 'Man, what the heck are you doing, throwing them spitballs out there in the middle of the stage, when these fellows are out there trying to entertain the public? What kind of fool are you?'

"And Dizzy says, 'Well, Fess, Fess, I didn't do it.'

"Cab said, 'You're a damn liar, you did do it.'

"'I didn't do it,' Dizzy said.

"And Cab couldn't have that kind of talk coming from this little upstart trumpet player, with these pretty ladies sitting up there waiting for him to come out, and his pretty white suit, and he's the boss. He just ain't gonna have that kind of break from discipline. And he's a pretty big guy too. And so Cab says, 'Well, look, now, I say you did it. You did it! Now, go ahead on, or else I'll slap you down.'

"And Dizzy was a pretty strong kid too, and for once, he's right. 'You ain't gonna do nothing,' he said.

"And Cab turned around and laid a hand on his face. And Dizzy turned around and laid his knife right back at Cab. And I sort've deflected the knife, because Dizzy was gonna tear him up, man. He really meant to get him, but I stood there. I wasn't as big as either Cab or Dizzy; I only weighed about a hundred twenty pounds, soaking wet. But I deflected the knife to keep it from going in his side. By that time, Cab's hand grabbed it, and it hit him in the leg. But the scuffle was going on so fast, Cab didn't feel it. And by that time, the big heavyweight guys like Chu Berry and Benny Payne heard the scuffle, and they got there and pulled them apart.

"We pushed Cab into his dressing room, and Dizzy went on in his dressing room. Well, by the time Cab got in his dressing room, his pretty white suit was stained completely red. The knife had gone into his thigh. And then he looked, and where he had been scuffling, Dizzy had kinda scratched his waist a little bit with the blade. Not too much, but just a little bit. But the blade had done in his thigh, and that pretty white suit was ruined, you know.

"So he walked on back to the band room and said, 'Hey, I guess you cats know this cat cut me.' He pointed at Diz and said, 'Now you just get your things and get on outta here.' And Dizzy put the cover on his horn, and he and Lorraine walked on out. They took the bus. This was in Hartford, Connecticut; we were coming home to New York that night when the show was over. A bus always met us at the Theresa Hotel to take us everyplace, and it always brought everybody back to the Theresa Hotel. That night, when we got back to the Theresa, who was there to meet the bus, but Diz. He said he had no hard feelings about it. When the bus opened, and Cab stepped out, there was Diz. Cab just hit him on the hand, and I'm just so happy to say that they are friends today. Because it wasn't until recently that it became known who really threw the spitball, but we know now that it wasn't Diz."

CAB CALLOWAY:

"Dizzy was a devil, a playful devil, you know. You wouldn't expect nobody else but Dizzy. You could put twenty guys up on the stand, and if something like that happened, you couldn't look at nobody but Dizzy. You'd expect it, and I did, and I was so wrong.

"Man, I went for fifteen years, and I never knew he didn't do it. I never knew it. But I'll never forget it. I'll never forget it, man. I'll carry it right on to my grave.

"He hit me in the rear.

"I admire the way he has lived his life, the way he has believed in God and the way he accepted religion and continued to be the man that he always was. That is the outstanding thing to me, and he'll never change. It's there, and God loves him for it. And that marvelous wife of his, Lorraine, is a wonderful, wonderful girl. You got to go along, man, you got to go with it. That's it. That's it all the way. You sit down and talk with Diz, man, you have no idea the things that'll come out. You'll think he's gonna sit there and start talking a whole lotta jazz and la-de-dah. No way, man. No way. Not that way, no indeed. And I love him for that."

I didn't look back. People were a little reticent in dealing with me, however, after word of that fight got around. Especially out of town bands: the Jimmie Lunceford band, for example, never hired any New York musicians because you'd have to pay them. They demanded money. And Jimmie Lunceford was notoriously known as what we call a skinflint. As a matter of fact, I remember once, in Boston, Jimmie Lunceford's band struck, and they got $2.00 a night more. He was probably paying about $14 a night. They had a lot of élan but no money. So did I for a little while after that fight.

Right after I left Cab, I played with Ella Fitzgerald's band. Chick Webb had died, and Ella took over the band. I played a couple of weeks with them in a place called Lavarge's in Boston, and then came back to New York. That stint with Ella Fitzgerald was pretty funny too, because at first Teddy McCrae was the leader who took charge of everything; Ella just sang. It was Ella's band, and the money went to the Gale Agency, which paid Ella, but the musical directorship of the band was in the hands of Teddy McCrae and he hired me for those two weeks. After that, they fired him, and Taft Jordan, a trumpet player, took over the band. And so I was no longer with Ella's band after that. But I wanted to stay in New York anyway.

Minton's Playhouse

In those days we had several means of access to experience: big bands were one, jam sessions were another. I tried to get plenty of both. Musical happenings at that time were an excellent reason to want to stay around New York. Amongst musicians when I came up, we had a very close feeling of camaraderie. We were all trumpet players together—Charlie Shavers, Benny Harris, Bobby Moore, and I—and we were unified socially; not just trumpet players, other musicians too. We traded off ideas not only on the bandstand but in the jam sessions. We had to be as sensitive to each other as brothers in order to express ourselves completely, maintain our individuality, yet play as one. Jam sessions, such as those wonderfully exciting ones held at Minton's Playhouse were seedbeds for our new, modern style of music.

Monk'd be asleep on the piano. To wake him up, I'd mash the quick of his finger and wake him up right quick. He'd say, "What the fuck're you doing, muthafucka!" He'd wake up and go into his thing.

I first met Monk during the early days, 1937 and 1938. Monk used to be with Cootie Williams up at the Savoy, and then, in 1939, he got the gig down at Minton's. I learned a lot from Monk. It's strange with Monk. Our influence on one another's music is so closely related that Monk doesn't actually know what I showed him. But I do know some of the things that he showed me. Like, the minor-sixth chord with a sixth in the bass. I first heard Monk play that. It's demonstrated in some of my music like the melody of "Woody 'n You," the introduction to "Round Midnight," and a part of the bridge to "Manteca."

There were lots of places where I used that progression that Monk showed me. You see, I give people credit; I don't try to take nothing from nobody. If I get something from someone, and I expand on it, I give them credit for it.

Now in my ending of "I Can't Get Started," there's an expansion of a minor-sixth chord going to the first chord of the ending of that song and also to the introduction of "Round Midnight." It's the same progression. Those are two of my most well-known solos on ballads, and the first time I heard that, Monk showed it to me, and he called it a minor-sixth chord with a sixth in the bass. Nowadays, they don't call it that. They call the sixth in the bass, the tonic, and the chord a C-minor seventh, flat five. What Monk called an E-flat-minor sixth chord with a sixth in the bass, the guys nowadays call a C-minor seventh flat five. C is the sixth note of an E-flat chord—the sixth in the bass—the bass plays that note. They call that a C-minor seventh flat five, because an E-flat-minor chord is E-flat, G-flat, and B-flat. So they're exactly the same thing. An E-flat-minor chord with a sixth in the bass is C, E-flat, G-flat, and B-flat. C-minor seventh flat five is the same thing, C, E-flat, G-flat, and B-flat. Some people call it a half diminished, sometimes.

So now, I extended that into a whole series of chords. B minor, E seventh, B-flat-minor seventh, E-flat seventh, A-minor seventh, D seventh, A-flat-minor seventh, D-flat seventh, and into C. We'd do that kind of thing in 1942 around Minton's a lot. We'd been doing that kind of thing, Monk and I, but it was never documented because no records were being made at the time. There was a recording ban.

The union wanted a trust fund for the musicians and wanted the record companies to pay for it, but they refused to pay. So the union stopped us from making recordings. I don't think it was a question of stopping the new style of music from coming out. They just wanted some benefits for the musicians. It was a good move for the musicians trying to get some of the money that was being made by these people who were making records. The recording ban lasted three or four years, I think 1942, 1943, and 1944. I was recording again by 1945.

The only reason some of the new things we were doing musically were never documented is because there were no records made at the time to show what we were doing. So later, when I recorded "I Can't Get Started" (Manor 1047), I didn't play the regular progressions. I went E seventh to E-flat seventh, D seventh to D-flat seventh, to C. And then we'd do the flatted fifths inside of that. Tadd Dameron used to do those kinds of things too.

I asked Monk one time, "Hey, man, show me something that you learned from me that you used countless times in other works."

Monk said, "A Night In Tunisia."

"Not a tune." I said, "I'm talking about progressions." Then I showed him what I'd learned from him the first time, that one particular thing that opened up a whole new trail for me. But he couldn't remember one particular thing that he'd heard me do. I was always a piano player, so I was always finding things on the piano and showing them to the guys. I'd show Monk. And I know that there are hundreds of things, because we used to get together. I'd say, "Look, here . . ." and show him something. But Monk is the most unique musician of our crowd. He was the one least affected by any other musician, unless he's affected by piano players like James P. Johnson and Fats Waller or Duke Ellington. I never heard him play like Teddy Wilson. I never heard him play like that. When I heard him play, he was playing like Monk, like nobody else.

Also, by that time, I was getting my chops together. And Roy used to come by Minton's. Roy is the most competitive musician. Roy used to just shower trumpet players with chops and speed. I'll never forget the time, the first time, Roy heard me make an altissimo B-flat. Boy, his eyes went up. I always had my speed, but didn't have too much chops. But I was getting them together at that time. One time, we were playing "Sweet Georgia Brown," in A-flat. I played about two choruses and hit a high B-flat. Roy looked!

"Look, you're supposed to be the greatest trumpet player in the world," Monk used to tell him, "but that's the best." And he'd point at me. Monk will tell you that. Ha! Ha! "You're supposed to be the greatest trumpet player in the world," Monk said, "but that guy is. He'll eat you up." Monk'll tell anybody. He'd tell Coleman Hawkins. Anybody. Monk would tell anybody how he feels about his playing. Monk'll tell you the truth, whatever he thinks about it. He's not diplomatic at all.

THELONIOUS SPHERE MONK (piano):

"I first met him at the Rhythm Club."

How did he sound when you first heard him?

"He sounded good."

Was it different from what you'd been used to hearing?

"Yes, I mean it sounded original."

Did you hear anything of his that you especially liked?

"I heard a lotta things."

Which things?

"Well, I don't know all his tunes, so I can't say which one I like the best."

If there's any great contribution that you think Dizzy's made to our music, what do you think that contribution would be?

"I mean that is hard to answer. That's hard to say, you know."

Are there any incidents you can recall, let's say from the days at Minton's or the Savoy when something Dizzy did or said to you struck you as particularly unique, that really knocked you out?

"I don't know what you mean when you say 'knocked you out.' Well, he was amusing to the people on the stage."

What do you like most about him as a person?

"His musicianship. That's what."

Monk's contribution to the new style of music was mostly harmonic and also spiritual, but Kenny Clarke set the stage for the rhythmic content of our music. He was the first one to make accents on the bass drum at specific points in the music. He'd play 4/4 very softly but the breaks, and the accents on the bass drum, you could hear. Like, we called them, dropping bombs.

The most distinctive bass player among us was Oscar Pettiford. Ray Brown came on the scene afterwards, but Oscar Pettiford was the bass player for our music. I can't talk about what happened on bass before Oscar because I never did play with Jimmy Blanton too much. But Oscar was a great devotee of the guitarist Charlie Christian. He played a lot like Charlie Christian; his style was based on Charlie Christian's. A lotta bass players, when they play a solo, are always thinking in terms of tonics. Jimmy Blanton was the first one that I heard playing differently, but they tell me Oscar was playing the new way in Minneapolis before he came to New York. He'd picked up on Charlie Christian and was playing melody on the bass, like a soloist, like a trumpet, or any other melody instrument. A lotta bass players, right now, when they play a solo, you can hear them always, boom, the tonic. Then they go and play a little something, and then they jump back when the chord changes. They change on the melody because they feel a need to play a supportive role. You don't need the tonic when you're playing solos. You don't need the tonic. A lotta bass players, except the new bass players, don't understand that.

Charlie Christian was baaad! He knew the blues, and he knew how to do the swing. He had a great sense of harmony, and he lifted the guitar up to a solo voice in jazz. But he never showed me a total knowledge of the harmonic possibilities of the instrument. His har-

monic sense wasn't on a level with a guy like John Collins. John
Collins practiced hours and hours, man, different variations of chords.
John Collins is about the most, the deepest of the guitarists because he
knew a thousand ways to play one thing. And you have to practice
like that; you just can't get that on the guitar because of the positions
on the instrument. You've gotta find out where the positions are,
where the best positions are, and once you've learned that, you can go
on and get a new one, and another one, and another one. That's how
John Collins played.

Other musicians came to Minton's in the early days (1939–42)
such as Kermit Scott, a saxophone player, and Nick Fenton, a bass
player. Kermit Scott had his own little style going. He lives in California now and came out on the stage with me in Monterey, in 1974, and
played "Manteca." He went right on out there and took care of business. I introduce him every time I go out to California as one of the
founders of our music. He gets a little play behind that. He used to
play with Coleman Hawkins too.

A whole group of tenor players came to Minton's—Don Byas, Lucky
Thompson, Horace Hoss Collar, and Rudy Williams. A lotta trumpet
players came too, and pianists; but these were the ones who impressed
me most in the very early days at Minton's. Some great musicians
would come afterward, and certain ones who were there at the beginning didn't make the transition with us. Clyde Hart played a lot of
gigs and record dates with us, but Clyde Hart had developed as a
piano player along the same style as Teddy Wilson. So he didn't play
like us, but he knew what we were doing, and he was right along with
us all the time, you know. He adapted himself, but he never broke
away from the older style of playing the piano. Bud Powell never
played at Minton's. Bud was inspired first by Billy Kyle and then
Charlie Parker. You see, Bud Powell didn't play the piano like a piano
player, he played like a saxophonist, like Charlie Parker, a-diddle-de-
diddle-de-diddle-a-diddle.

My own contributions to the new style of music at this point were
rhythm—Afro-American and Latin—together with harmony. I built
most of the harmonic structure and showed the piano players how to
play comp with the soloists and generally whatever was needed with
our music for accompaniment. As far as my own style of playing was
concerned, I always went for effect. Whatever the effect was for me
at the moment was what I played. Now, a lot of things are played
when music is written, and if you play every note that is down there,
it will become involved and stiff. So rather than bother myself with
that stiffness, I eliminate those notes and make it so that the note will
be heard without being played. I see some guys try to transcribe my
music on paper but if you play it like that, sometimes you'll sound real

corny. That's because they hear notes that I didn't even play. It's there, without being there. It's implied. And although people can't really hear it, they feel it. It's an auditory illusion.

What happened down at Minton's anyway? On Monday nights, we used to have a ball. Everybody from the Apollo, on Monday nights, was a guest at Minton's, the whole band. We had a big jam session. Monday night was the big night, the musician's night off. There was always some food there for you. Oh, that part was beautiful. Teddy Hill treated the guys well. He didn't pay them much money—I never did get paid—but he treated the guys nicely. There was always some food there for you. He had a kitchen, you know, and you could eat there.

We had a lot of fun. Hoss Collar (who was really an alto player) and I used to have this routine. Let's see, you'd hold out your hand and say, "I'm hitting. You're an ass." No, that wasn't it. Now I've got it. When you held out your hand, he'd say: "I'm hitting. You're an ass." You'd reply, "That's what *you* is." And he'd say: "That's what you *want* me to be." Right now, I walk up to some of the cats and say: "That's what you want me to be," and they go to pieces. Me, too.

Then there was a guy they used to call the Demon. He came to play, but he never did. Couldn't play to save his life. But he played with everybody—Lester, Charlie Parker. He was the first freedom player—freedom from harmony, freedom from rhythm, freedom from everything. The Demon was from Newark, and he never stopped playing.

Johnny Carisi was the only white boy up in Harlem playing at Minton's. He'd learn all the tunes. Played all of Thelonious Monk's tunes, all of mine. I'd play a chorus. He'd be right behind me. Roy? Right behind Roy. Right behind everybody. He was welcome so long as he could blow the way he did.

Jerry Newman, among many others, recorded us in Minton's with Charlie Christian. He had a wire recorder. He just brought it down there and went home and put out a record.* He never gave any of us a dime, not me, Joe Guy, Don Byas, Chu Berry, Charlie Christian, Nick Fenton, Ken Kersey, nor Kenny Clarke.

There were big fines for playing jam sessions, and the union had "walking" delegates who would check on all the places that were frequented by jazz musicians. So we were taking a big risk. One guy in California would follow you around to see if you were going to a session. He belonged to the "colored" local out there at first, and then they merged and put him in charge as "walking" delegate for places where the "colored" musicians would be playing. He'd follow you around just waiting to see you pick up your horn without a contract,

---

* "The Men from Minton's," May 1941 (Esoteric ESJ4; ES548).

and fine you a hundred to five hundred dollars. We were somewhat immune from this at Minton's because Henry Minton, who owned the place, was the first "colored" union delegate in New York. Unfortunately, to the young jazz musician, the union has always been just a dues collector. On our level we never saw it as being of any real benefit, and sometimes it kept us from gaining experience. The union benefited the classical musicians and created things for them, but the jazz guys got nothing. There wasn't much help you could expect from the union. Guys were saying, even back then, "You don't do anything for jazz musicians. You do everything for classical musicians." That was under the "unity" program which still exists now, every election. We've always had movements within the union to kick out the officials, but they've never made any headway. In the first place, they controlled the composition of the membership through regulations like the three-month waiting period to keep "foreign" musicians out. That meant anybody, even from next door in New Jersey. A lot of situations like the one I mentioned at the World's Fair in 1939 arose with the musicians, and from my angle, it looked like the union was siding with the employer instead of employee. The president of our local now, Max Aarons, has been a very close friend of mine and has done a lot of things for me, personally. I'm not saying that the union hasn't done anything for anybody. But I can't remember one thing the union has done to benefit jazz musicians generally. As far as jazz musicians are concerned, the union is still only collecting dues.

Though the tale is told that somehow we all wound up in Minton's, gigging, that isn't really true. I never worked at Minton's. I went there to jam. Charlie Parker never worked at Minton's either; only Monk and Kenny Clarke, who had the house band, actually *worked* at Minton's. The sessions were nightly, and I couldn't go to Minton's when I was playing with Benny Carter on Fifty-second Street because we worked at the same time. I wasn't working with anybody when I was going to Minton's to blow, unless I was working with Cab at the Cotton Club or someplace else where we got off early.

After hours, I'd go to the Uptown House to jam. There was as much creativity going on at Monroe's Uptown House as they had at Minton's. That's where we all used to go after hours, until daylight, to play. Clark Monroe had a warm feeling for musicians, and he also used to feed us. He didn't pay you any money, but you could eat and he had a band there, a non-union band, a "scab" band, they called it. Charlie Parker played in that band after he came to New York.

What we were doing at Minton's was playing, seriously, creating a new dialogue among ourselves, blending our ideas into a new style of music. You only have so many notes, and what makes a style is how you get from one note to the other. We had some fundamental background training in European harmony and music theory superimposed on our own knowledge from Afro-American musical tradition. We invented our own way of getting from one place to the next. I taught myself chords on the piano beginning at Laurinburg because I could hear chords in European music without anybody telling me what they were. Our phrases were different. We phrased differently from the older guys. Perhaps the only real difference in our music was that we phrased differently. Musically, we were changing the way that we spoke, to reflect the way that we felt. New phrasing came in with the new accent. Our music had a new accent.

KENNY CLARKE:

"The leaders of it were Diz and Bird."
You wouldn't include yourself?
KC: "I'm thinking from a modest . . ."
Please don't be overly modest.
KC: "Well, the overall thing . . ."
DG: "Everybody had a part to play, and he had a big role. His part was just as important a contribution as mine or Charlie Parker's or Monk's. His contribution is on the same level. No one is more than the other. I'd think of something and bring it, and say, 'Hey, look, Klook, look at this, here, man,' and show him on the piano.

"He'd say, 'Yeah, lemme try that.' And in trying it, he'd do something else, something to aid this; and by him doing that, I'll think of ten other things to do."
This new style was something free, definitely, something that was flowing naturally from you, but at the same time, it required a great deal of technical study. Some of the older guys I talked to said, "Well, after Diz and them, just anybody couldn't play, you had to be a technician." Why?
KC: "Well, it's like I said in the first place. It was the most intelligent phase of our music. It was the most intelligent, before or after, and up until now. If we had remained on that same plane, it's no telling what we'd be playing today, instead of deviating into something else.

"Yeah, they were coming along, everyone. It became almost a cult after a while, and the ones who felt themselves musically strong enough would enter it. I mean, later, Miles came here to New York to attend Juilliard. I mean everyone was studying. Max was studying over at the New York School of Music. These young guys that were coming up under us, we were teaching them that whatever you do, get an education. Then you can do whatever you wanna do."
Speaking about the social aspects of this era, Kenny, you were also

*known to be one of the more militant of the men who were creating
this new musical style.*

DG: "The word is vociferous. . . ."

*What kind of statement, if any, were you making about the social
scene around you?*

KC: "It was an economic thing because we were already together
socially."

But were you making any statement about the world around you?

KC: "Yeah, in a way. The idea was to wake up, look around you,
there's something to do. And this was just a part of it, an integral part
of our cultural aspect. It was just more musician, to respect somebody
that's doing something. And somebody'd say, 'Yeah, that Dizzy, man,
sure gave us the word.' Things like that."

What was the word?

KC: "Wake up."

*"Bebop" was later publicized as a "fighting" word. Was this a
"fighting" music?*

KC: "No, no, by all means no!"

DG: "It was a love music."

KC: "'Bebop' was a label that certain journalists later gave it, but
we never labeled the music. It was just modern music, we would call
it. We wouldn't call it anything, really, just music."

Did this music have anything special to say to black people?

DG: "Yeah, get the fuck outta the way. . . ."

KC: "Yeah, like I said it was teaching them. I mean people who
you idolize. It was nice when you'd see a brother, ballplayer on the
field, and you knew that he'd just finished college. You'd have a certain amount of respect for him, more than you'd have for some dumb
cat outta the cornfield, and because he can play baseball, they put him
on the team. There was a message in our music. Whatever you go
into, go into it *intelligently*. As simple as that."

*Can you think of anything amusing that happened between you two
during those early years jamming at Minton's?*

KC: "Well, I think that we've known each other for forty years, and
I don't remember us passing one harsh word. And I think about that
often. I say, 'Here's a man I never disputed with, never had any con-
trary thoughts about.' Seems like what he was thinking, I was thinking
too. Never one harsh word. The thing he didn't like—I knew he didn't
like—was when he was playing, and I'd drop a stick. That was hell to
pay then."

DG: "Muthafucka, do you want your sticks glued to your hands?
Get some Elmer's Glue and . . . Ha! Ha!"

KC: "Anything else but that. That was unpardonable."

MILTON HINTON:

"I made many sessions up at Minton's. I thank Diz for that. What really happened there for me was the outcome of this thing on the roof, where Dizzy showed me these new changes. Everybody used to come to Minton's to blow at night. I lived right across the street from Minton's, so I was kind of like the house bass player. I was the handiest one, just because I lived there and eventually wound up living in the Cecil Hotel. But so many kids from downtown, kids that couldn't blow, would come in and they would interrupt. Monk would be there, and Diz would be there, and I'd be there, and kids would come in there that couldn't blow, just bought a horn. And we're getting ready to blow, 'How High the Moon,' and these kids would jump in and they would just, you know, foul up the session.

"So Diz told me on the roof one night at the Cotton Club, 'Now look, when we go down to the jam session, we're gonna say we're gonna play, "I Got Rhythm," but we're gonna use these changes. Instead of using the B-flat and D-flat, we're gonna use B-flat, D-flat, G-flat, or F and we change.' We would do these things up on the roof and then we'd go down to Minton's, and all these kids would be up there. 'What're y'all gonna play?' We'd say, 'I Got Rhythm,' and we'd start out with this new set of changes, and they would be left right at the post. They would be standing there, and they couldn't get in because they didn't know what changes we were using, and eventually they would put their horns away, and we could go on and blow in peace and get our little exercise."

JOHNNY CARISI (trumpet):

"About me being the only white guy at Minton's, I think I lucked up on getting in there at the beginning of it, because later on a lotta cats came, mostly because I told them, Kai Winding and a coupla guys.

"The only 'thing' I ran into was really a backhanded kind of compliment, in a way. There was a lotta getting loaded there. I remember one time we took a walk outside, and Joe Guy was pretty stoned. I guess the previous set I'd managed to keep up with them, whatever they were doing, and Joe Guy, half-hostile, and half-familiar, family kinda style, grabbed me and says, 'You ofays come up here, and you pick up on our stuff.' And the other cats were saying, 'What're you doing, Joe?' They cooled him out. He was loaded and everything. But it was kind of a compliment, because he was really saying, 'Man, you're doing what we're doing.' I wasn't anywhere near the player I could be as far as the ax was concerned, but I guess I had good instincts as far as, like, what to play. Never mind how I played it.

"At Minton's there was a lotta getting loaded. As a matter of fact, Monk taught me how to drink. At the end of a set, he'd say, 'Come on, come to the bar.' I'd say, 'Monk, I don't drink much.' He insisted. He'd say, 'What? Call yourself a jazz player . . .' And the next thing you know he had me drinking double gins. It was very funny."

ILLINOIS JACQUET (tenor saxophone):

"The first time I met John Birks Gillespie was in Chicago, I think, in 1940 when I was appearing at the Grand Terrace with Lionel Hampton's band, and he was, I think, at the Sherman Hotel with Cab Calloway. They would get off a little earlier than the place we were working on the South Side of Chicago. We went until four o'clock, and I think the Sherman Hotel got off at like one. So he got a chance to come out and hear the Hampton band, and afterwards, he and I went out. He came up to my room at the Ritz Hotel and started playing his trumpet, right in the mute. And I thought that was just phenomenal, you know, that a musician could just pick up his horn and want to play, any time of night or any time of day. That's how I first met him.

"Most people will hear about a musician like Gillespie before they probably even meet him. His playing, the way that he'd convert chords, and his progressions were different from the trumpet players at that time. His style was completely different than anyone I'd ever heard. And then you could hear one change in his playing in 1940, when I first heard him. I could hear the whole concept of the changing of the trumpet, the style was changing. I could tell that there was gonna be some difference.

"I could tell that he knew what he was doing. It was just that it was so different, his technique. You could tell that it was a well-developed brain, jazz music wise. You know when you study music, and you play this type of music, you can almost tell if a person has studied his instrument or if he's just, like, gifted and he can go along with certain things. And I could tell that he was well developed with progressions of chords and the fundamentals of taking a solo. You tell a story, and I could tell that his story was already written before it was told, you know.

"Working in the bands, that was your college. If you played music, the big bands were your college. Cab Calloway's band, Duke Ellington, Count Basie, the late Jimmie Lunceford, and all those big bands. And most of those people in the bands, the musicians, were college graduates or started out to be doctors and started playing music. But they were all educated musicians, mostly, in their fields. You got in a band, the discipline was there. The band itself was a school. Maybe a lot of them didn't finish college, but most of those guys had been to colleges. So when a youngster like me would join a band like Lionel Hampton or Basie, everybody was like professors.

"Nobody else would be acting a fool, and drinking. Everybody was so busy reading their music, some of that would rub off on you. And after a year or two of that, you would begin to act that way, live that way, play that way, and get more ambition about your music, your job, you know. And it made a better musician out of the individual. See, you need a lot of discipline out here too; all that is required in being a better musician. And I think this is what is missing today. A lot of the younger musicians today don't have the outlet of being able to join some of the big traveling bands. Most of the big bands, today, a lot of the big names are gone. They're no longer with us, some of them; and the economy is different. There are different changes; times have changed, prices are higher. To have a big band today costs a fortune in hotels and what not. So they are missing something by not being able to get the experience out of the big bands. Before, when you were able to leave the big bands, you could go out on your own, because you had been with the band, you had the experience. That's why Dizzy is still going strong today, because he's been with a lotta big bands. That was a school for him. He couldn't have gotten that in school. He couldn't have gotten it nowhere. That's the only school he could've gotten it from—the school he went to.

"During the time in the forties when Minton's was operating, we used to go up there and jam. I was with the bands at the time, and I would come in and out of town. When I was in the city, we were appearing at the Apollo or downtown at the Paramount or the Strand. After the last show we'd go to Minton's and sit in or listen to some of the guys play.

"It was sorta like a free-for-all. People that could play would wanna sit in. They could get up and play. Take a chorus or join the session. Sometimes these would be guys that couldn't play as well as some of the other guys. Still, they had the opportunity to get up there and play. But sometimes they would be a little off key. They would think that Monk would be in the key of B-flat, and he would be in the key of F-sharp or D natural. And then these guys wouldn't stay on the stand too long because they could never find the keys that Monk was playing in. So right there he knew that they would probably not be qualified to take up all that time with those long undesirable solos. And like Monk and the others would get into some weird keys sometimes, and while they'd be changing keys, things would be getting modern all the time, because the keys were sorta hanging *them* up a little bit too sometimes. But a lotta guys just wanted to get up there and pose, and the music was not coming out; quite naturally they

tried to get into another key when they saw them coming. You'd mod-
ulate into another key, and they wouldn't stay up there *too* long. Then
when they disappeared, the regular guys would come up that could
really play, and they'd go on and finish what they were trying to do.
So, like, you would get a chance to play things that you would ordinarily play in B-flat, in D natural, see. But you were schooled
enough to play in those keys because you knew when you were in a
different key.

"There were many, many giants that would come in there to play.
People like Dizzy, Charlie Parker, Denzil Best, Harold West, Shadow
Wilson. Sometimes the late Sid Catlett would come in. Monk, Sir
Charles Thompson, Bud Powell, Freddie Webster, Don Byas. It was
just like a jam, somewhere to go and play. There was not any strain on
being a cutting session or anything like that. Nothing like that. People
just came to play. The musicians came to play, late at night, because it
seemed like the music would sound better that time of morning. They
didn't have nothing to do but go to bed. They didn't have to make no
shows or be between shows. The job was over.

"So the music would be sounding good. If you could play and the
guys knew it, they would ask you to play. You know, 'Come on, man,
take your horn out and play something.' But, I mean, there would be a
lotta other musicians that would be there who weren't qualified to get
up there, but still, they would have their horns. They were trying. So
to not be no drag, we would let them up there, but it would be kinda
tough when they'd get up on there, and they thought they were in B-
flat. Sometimes they would think and they would go home and woodshed and come back, and they would know how to play in all the
different keys. That would make a change, right there, because they
thought that if you could play in B-flat, you had it made. You'd see
guys up there trying to tune up because they'd be in B natural. It
would make them think twice if they were in the wrong key, and
they'd go home and woodshed. And if they ever came back, they'd be
ready to play in all the keys. And that made them better musicians.
That changed a lotta musicians into better musicians. That is one way
there was a change in music, in jazz music, during that period.

"The major difference in the new music was the chord changes. You
see, in Louisiana, where I think that jazz was born—I was born in the
state of Louisiana, so quite naturally ever since I can remember, we've
been listening to jazz music—from the times when they played right
from the ear, because there was no time for people to study music, I
imagine, they just played. Pick up any instrument, and if you had
some kind of a soul for music, you'd just learn it sideways, any kinda
way. Learn that song, learn it fast, learn it slow, play it in waltz time.
It was the same song, you know. There was nobody to teach you. And
so quite naturally when you heard those bands back there, they were

just all playing together. You hear a Dixieland band playing today, everybody's playing together. They're going for themselves, you know. And I think what happened was that people started playing on the chord line, and started getting more progressive, then they started to realize that all those people didn't have to play together, like solos. If one was good enough, then he could play without all that interruption, like Louis Armstrong. That means when you hit Coleman Hawkins, you'd hear just the saxophone and the piano and the rhythm section. Because now they were getting together, and they were playing on chord lines. So it was sorta like you knew where you were going, and you knew who you were playing with, and you knew what they knew. Say, for an instance, your piano player. You're listening to him, and you know he knows what he's doing because he's running what you're playing. He's listening to you. If you two don't co-ordinate together, somebody's worried, and your piano player says, 'Man, what was that you were playing? Because I wanna play that with you.'

"So people started playing together and chord changes became more understandable to soloists. And then they start to hearing people like Roy, before Diz, and then Diz. Dizzy started changing the progressions, and started playing the whole chord instead of the melody. Play the melody too, but you can play the chords, and you don't even hear the melody. And you could take the chord changes and make other songs out of the same melody. You wouldn't even know your own song after they got through with the chords, and wouldn't play your melody. We started doing that later in the forties, Charlie Parker, Dizzy, and myself—all of us were doing it that way. And that changed the pattern from Dixieland to swing, and from swing to the progressive era. The music was progressing into chord changes, and if you didn't know your chords, well then, you couldn't play certain songs with these guys. They weren't playing the melody to the songs. So, like, it went from playing just with the ear to where a person would tell you just what he's gonna play. And if you're playing with him, that's what he wants to hear on the guitar, on the piano, the bass line. Most drummers at the time were hip enough to know what was happening anyway, because they could hear. The change was away from the old pattern of solos in Dixieland style into more of a studious musician's sureness, someone who had studied a little deeper into what had already been done. And then they took it and started to play the chord changes, the correct changes, and that helped change the style of music. Diz and the others were well schooled in that change. They were well schooled, knew where they were going with it. Because today, I mean, you have to be accomplished on your instrument to play with Dizzy now, today. He would know right away if you were not capable of playing the piano with him, or the guitar, because you're involved in chord changes. Just any gifted musician could not sit there, unless he was able to hear everything. And it's hard to be that gifted. You have to put it together a little bit. Sometimes you have to go into the woodshed. You have to get into the books. It's good to have talent, but you must put something with it. And I think that's what Dizzy has done. He has the talent, and he always had it, but he put something with it. He put some knowledge with it.

"And then they called it bebop. Well, people give things all kinda names, you know. But it is music, and it's progressive music, music that has moved from where it began to where it is today. Now, there is not much change in progressions, because that's always gonna be there, the foundation. But it's how you play it. How you're gonna write for it. How are you gonna play? Are you gonna play like Coleman Hawkins? Are you gonna play like Louis Armstrong? Or are you gonna get your own creation, your own painting, or your own style? And this is what Dizzy has contributed to the world of music—his own style. And that is one of the hardest things to do in music, to be an individual stylist. We have to give him that edge, because he really worked for it, and I saw the development. I saw him develop it. I saw him developing a style from the early forties up until now. And he has not changed, spiritually, from the time I met him up until now. And this is one great thing that I admire in him. That he has maintained dignity and discipline as a jazz musician, as a trumpet player, and as a man."

MARY LOU WILLIAMS (piano):

"After I had left the Andy Kirk band, I think it was around 1940 or 1941, we were working in Kelly's Stables, and I decided to stay here in New York. During that period, I was living at the Dewey Square Hotel, and that was the beginning of what they later called 'bop.' I used to go around the corner to Minton's and I met Dizzy there.

"Well, you know he had that name—Dizzy—and so when people hear such a name, they actually think the person corresponds to the name. But I thought he was wonderful; he's always been great to me and he was very charitable, even then, you know. He knew that I was in New York and wasn't working, and he began to give me some of his gigs. And most of them were non-union gigs. He sent me on a gig up here, on 149th Street, to play a ballroom for him. He left and went with another group to play, and he put me in charge of his group. Illinois Jacquet was there, and Oscar Pettiford, and Klook, Kenny Clarke, was on drums. Just one horn, Illinois Jacquet, the rhythm section, and myself.

"And so they featured me at this ballroom, and they had a big plac- ard out front, 'Mary Lou Williams, blah, blah, blah.' About how I'd just left Andy Kirk's band. We were very popular. Andy Kirk's band had quite a few followers in New York. So I went to this gig, and the place was jammed and packed. And these little gigs that Dizzy was getting weren't paying too much money, only five or six dollars per man. I saw this big crowd there, and I told the guys, 'We're not gonna play any more. Let's take intermission,' I said. And I told the manager, 'We can't play for this kinda money; you'll have to give us more money.' I think he gave me $20 as the leader but the big surprise was that the delegates from the union happened to be there that night. I guess that was about the biggest crowd they'd ever had. This was the first time union delegates had ever been there; it was such a big crowd. And we didn't know what was happening until about a week later; the Board called me downtown to the union for playing a non-union gig. They talked about it, and they were saying that I really was an asset to the union. 'You know what she did?' the musicians said. 'She stopped the boys from playing, and she wouldn't play any longer until they gave them more money.'

"And that's actually how I got into the union. Otherwise, I would have had to wait three months or six months, you know, whatever the time. That was one of the good things that he did for me. He always looked out for me, and I never realized how wonderful he was until years later. Anytime he thought I wasn't working, or something wasn't happening right, he'd always come to my rescue.

I went to Minton's every night. When the thing started, Thelonious Monk and the others had a little band going. They were afraid to come out because they were afraid that the commercial world would steal what they had created. So they stayed in Harlem, at Minton's, and the downtowners began to come up, writing their notes on their little pieces of paper and everything, you know. I detected that in the club. It finally got downtown about this new music that was going on in Minton's. And these sessions were really terrific. The cats would come in around nine-thirty or ten o'clock at night, and even later, and they'd jam there all night. The house only paid for maybe a small trio, and the place was jammed. And in no time, the commercial world from downtown was coming in on it, and they tried to learn it. I heard some of the guys speak about not wanting to play downtown or play in the open so everybody could take it from them. Because you know the black creators of the music have never gotten recognition for cre- ating anything. The music is so heavy. I don't think anybody is look- ing for any big applause or anything about what they've created. But after a while, you get kinda really disgusted and dried out because ev- erything you create is taken from you, and somebody else is given recognition for it. But the music is so great, I think half of them could care less, except they have to eat and sleep, you know. But Minton's was really a good scene, and it all started there until they began to play on Fifty-second Street.

"Dizzy did not receive a warm, open reception when he was coming up. He came up the hard way. And I know of at least ten musicians that have become bitter, and they're just not doing anything, you know; they're working off an ego and all that. Well, he doesn't. He's just a nice guy. He's so nice to everyone else until it added to his power as far as being the greatest in the world. He is, in fact, and you can't deny it. And I've seen him go all the way out for someone in order to make them a success, and continually do it. I've gone out when he has asked me to come and help him to do things, and he'll sit there patiently—he has a lotta patience—and he'll teach musicians how to play. Someone made a remark once that every musician that was playing with him during this period should be paying him two or three hundred dollars a week because he teaches all of them. He'll sit there patiently with them until they learn what he wants them to learn. And he'll keep people; seems like he just hates to fire them if they're not good. I've never seen such a great giant like him before in my life.

"Oh, I forgot to mention the number of jobs Dizzy has gotten for people, people who are now big movie stars, writing for the movies and everything else. Yet, he goes along just being nice, playing his instrument. The rest, they'll just go on their way and think about what *they* wanna do in life, you know.

"I played through all the eras. I changed. In the 'modern' era, there were more notes, you know, like, the 1930s era was the feeling. You see, the blues stayed in it from the beginning of the spirituals. The blues feeling has always been there, even with Coltrane. I could hear that in his music, although he went way out, but I could still hear that feeling in his music. Well, it was still in bop except it was just millions of notes. You know, when we first heard it during the forties, it sounded like a musician, like *Dizzy was playing a million notes in one bar*. See, and that was the change, and they still had their own beat going; you could still move your head or your body with it. That was the only change; and the phrasing every other note. That was the big change for that era, but the other era was practically all swing. During the swing era, as far as a pianist goes, you had to have a great left hand. You could play all the notes you wanted to play, but if you didn't have a great left hand, or two hands, you weren't considered a great pianist. And it was practically all swing, you know, like a Basie kind of a thing. But bop came along with a more modern thing, and the blues and the swing part, but it was just more colorful.

"Oh, yeah, and the harmony structure of the blues changed from the plain old C seventh, and what not, to major seventh and many other beautiful modern harmonies. But they were beautiful, like riding around and taking in the scenery, rather than just having a steady beat going."

Charlie Parker deserves special mention because he was not actually here at the beginning. When Charlie Parker came to New York, in 1942, the new style of music had already begun, but he made a gigantic contribution, which really added a new dimension to the music. It's hard to describe it exactly, he contributed so many different elements. A lotta guys played fast. Rapid! I mean *in one,* these cats. But they didn't play the notes that Charlie Parker played. His modus operandi was different, how he attacked and how he swung. I was always a piano nut, from a little boy; I'd show "Yardbird," too, things on the piano and how our music was structured. But Charlie Parker played very syncopated and sanctified. There was nobody playing like that in our style. I always thought like that too, though most guys went more straight and evenly from one note to another because I, also, aside from my piano playing, was always the teacher of the drum. So I'd hear that in the drums, and I played like that, with accents. But Charlie Parker, when he came on the scene, had it down to a T personified.* Charlie Parker's contribution to our music was mostly melody, accents, and bluesy interpretation. And the notes! "Bird" has some notes in his melodies, the lines that he wrote, that are deep, deep notes, as deep as anything Beethoven ever wrote. And he had little things that he used to play inside. He'd play other tunes inside the chords of the original melody, and they were always right. The little inside tunes that he played were always on the right chords of the original melody. The press, when we later started getting some notice, always tried to pretend we were angry with each other, envious, jealous, and things like that, but that's absolutely false.

My wife used to tell me all the time, "I like the way that Charlie Parker puts them other little numbers in there. Why don't you do something like that? Play 'O Solo Mio' in the middle of 'Dizzy Atmosphere' or something like that."

Yes, Charlie Parker was something else, and he jammed with us at Minton's too.

---

* Charlie Parker's bluesy, syncopated style is often attributed to the influence of "Old Yardbird," Buster Smith, a saxophonist out in Kansas City. I never heard "Old Yardbird" play, but I've heard about him.

Little John Special

       Despite losing the "good job" with Cab, I was quite self-assured, knowing that many musicians considered my style of playing to be very new, original, and distinctive. I felt I had something new, a real chance of creating some beautiful music and gaining the proper payment, respect, and recognition for it. Realizing that I had something very imaginative and unique going for me, I stopped accepting jobs where the salary was too low and unreflective of my talents and contributions as a soloist. Jazz musicians were paid some pitifully low wages at that time, as sidemen, and since I had no group of my own established, people considered me a sideman. That status—and the little money that went along with it—I refused to accept. I ended up working at a furious pace for about a year with over *ten different bands,* trying to make each one give me what I wanted. I refused to stay in any one place for too long, demanded special treatment, and if I didn't get it, I'd leave and go someplace else.

    In New York, in late 1941, I went to work at Kelly's Stables on Fifty-second Street with Coleman Hawkins for a week. That was funny. I told Coleman, "Look, Coleman, I'm not gonna work for $66. I want $75 a week."

    "Yeah, yeah," Hawk said, "you deserve it." But Hawk wasn't the one who was paying the money, and things just kept going back and forth between him and the owner. So at the end of the week, they gave me $66.

"Look, you're gonna miss a trumpet player around here," I said, "because I want $75." A little over scale, I figured, because I was a good musician, a soloist. I didn't show up anymore, and that was the end of my engagement with Coleman Hawkins.

They paid Coleman the money he asked for. He'd just come back from Europe, and he was getting his money by saying, "I want so-and-so for myself. Those other musicians work for scale." I couldn't accept that, so I left. Of course this is in no way intended to be a negative comment on Coleman. He wasn't the one who contracted the job. I feel sure Coleman Hawkins would've paid me my money if it had been left up to him.

Benny Carter picked me up and took me into Kelly's Stables with him and a marvelous little septet: John Collins, guitar; Charlie Drayton, bass; Sonny White, piano; Kenny Clarke, drums; Al Gibson, clarinet; Benny Carter, and me. We were getting it, playing all kinds of music. We played a lot of Benny Carter's music, but my music too, Al Gibson's music, John Collins' music. Everybody was making up tunes. It was Benny Carter's band, but we played a lot of things in the modern style, especially with Kenny Clarke and Sonny White in there. Sonny White was a devotee of Teddy Wilson, and he never did get all the way into the modern sound like Bud Powell. He never got into it, but he was beautiful, like in the classic mode of jazz pianists. Kenny Clarke and I had already established our own style, and as leaders in the modern trend, Benny gave us a great deal of freedom to play the way we wanted. Benny Carter is a master musician and he understood. He knew what we were doing was valid. We never had any hangups with Benny Carter. It was just a long honeymoon.

Apparently, I made a deep impression on Benny Carter. Benny Carter didn't play in our style, but he played. Benny Carter is a multi-talented musician. He played all of the reeds and played trumpet too. Benny is a magnificent trumpet player. He'd pick up the trumpet, take it, and go to town! Beautiful sound too. He used to blow out his trumpet players. He used to pick up his horn and play solos and wash out the trumpet players, man. He was always the best trumpet player in his band.

I noticed when Benny brought me in, he got on a new kick. He went to the tenor saxophone. He brought the tenor down, and he played that a lot. He sounded like Ben Webster. Ben Webster was greatly influenced by Benny Carter who is the bellwether of the saxophone. Many people don't know that Benny Carter was playing tenor before Ben Webster. Everyone knew Benny Carter played alto, but the sound he made on tenor sounded like Ben Webster.

Anyway, I noticed while I was there that Benny wouldn't play trumpet with me. He never did play with me. One night, I went back into the band room, and his trumpet was laying there. I picked it up, and he hadn't played it for so long that I couldn't push the valves down. He hadn't touched it. That's a form of respect, from one musician to another. That was beautiful, you know. I cleaned out the valves and oiled them for him, and brought his trumpet out on the bandstand and handed it to him.

"Man, what am I gonna do with this?" he said.

"No, come on," I said. "Let's play some. I wanna hear you play, man." And then we played fours and eights.* That one night, we had a ball there, boy. We had a good time with two trumpets. That was a beautiful night, the night Benny Carter played with me on trumpet.

JOHN COLLINS (guitar):

"I pulled Benny Carter's coat to him. I say, '*Hire* this cat.' So he hired Diz. We had a little band, a small band; and he needed a trumpet player. And so I had to tell him, 'Man, you gotta hire Dizzy.' It was around 1941 or 1942 because after that Benny took a big band into the Apollo.

"'Who is Dizzy?' he said.

"I don't remember much about the Fifty-second Street gig because I left shortly after that for the Army. Benny went to the draft board with me to try to keep me out of the Army, and they almost got him, you know. They asked him, 'Well, how much are you making? Are you paying any income tax? So-and-so and so . . .' So he had to back off.

"Musically, the major changes Diz was making was the chordal forms. He was the first one to really play a chordal form of trumpet. Everybody was following Louis, and then Roy came through, and he was a little more modern. He took Louis' sound, and he was a little more modern. But Dizzy came along with his own things. He was playing chordal forms. He pulled everybody's coat. He used to come up to my room, and we would play, Dizzy, Ben Webster, and I. Just the three of us would just play. And he was way out as far as structure was concerned."

---

* Fours—playing four bars of improvisation in tandem with another instrumentalist. Eights, eight bars.

BENNY CARTER (saxophone, composer, bandleader):

"I first met Dizzy in the early forties, after I had returned from Europe. Gee, I think at the time I met him, he was probably playing with Cab Calloway. And I heard him with the band, heard him around at different sessions and things, and I got kind of excited about him. And then when I was able to offer him a seat in my band, and he was available, and he accepted the offer, I was very, very pleased and excited. Because I knew he had something that was new, fresh, creative, imaginative; and doing great things with the instrument, things that had been considered impossible before, you know.

"I think we played at Kelly's Stables, and we followed that with a stint at the Famous Door. And that's where Irving Alexander, one of the owners at that time was always asking, 'What is that trumpet player playing? Where did you get him?' He didn't quite dig what Dizzy was doing. A lotta people didn't, but of course everybody digs now.

"I told Irving Alexander, 'Oh, that's music, music, the new music, you know.' So, finally Dizzy gained great acceptance, and he is certainly a great influence on every trumpet player that followed him. I mean, like, in that day, you'd hear a little of Louis from all the trumpet players and from others too. Just like now you hear Dizzy in other instrumentalists as well, you know, trombones and piano and drummers. Sure. So when Dizzy and Bird got together, which was just a natural association, they kind of turned the whole picture around."

Dizzy was playing this new style when you hired him, but he was playing in your band. How did you like it, musically?

"Ah, yes, he certainly was. This was quite new to me . . . particularly what he was doing with the instrument. The man who devised or designed or invented the trumpet knew there were certain things on the instrument that were supposed to be impossible to do, but they never thought to inform Dizzy of that. So he just went ahead and did them, you know.

"Well, I thought it was interesting. I could not tell where it was going to go. I certainly couldn't forecast that the public was going to reject it or accept it. I had no way of knowing. And strangely enough, would you believe that I never attended a session at Minton's? I was never in Minton's. Why I never got to Minton's, I can't even think at this moment. I think I was pretty busy writing, and I used to go in nights. I didn't go much to sessions after my gig was over, you know. And if anybody that reads this can remember seeing me at Minton's, I would say let me know.

"We will certainly acknowledge that Dizzy's been a major contributor, and he certainly revolutionized the playing of the instrument. He plays the instrument differently, probably devised a new system of fingering. Being a sometime trumpet player, I just have to feel that he must have. I don't know *what* he does, but what he does . . . well, I don't call it false, I'll call it 'alternate.' I'll call it alternate fingering. They usually call things like that false fingering, but we'll say alternate fingering. Yes, I think he's really explored a lot in that area.

"Dizzy's not correct saying I used to wash out my trumpet players. I had some pretty good trumpet players, really. But of course I did love the instrument. I still do and I used to pick it up and play. Of course when Dizzy was in the band, I thought it was time to put the trumpet down and leave it down. But what he said about coming in, taking the trumpet, and making me play some duets with him was quite right. Of course I came off second best as I expected to, but it was fun playing with Dizzy. And one of these times, now, I'd like to catch him and play a duet with him, if I ever get any chops. But I mean just for the fun of it; I'd love to do that with him sometime. I'm playing trumpet now, on my gig, but just a little because I don't have enough time to devote to the instrument. I'd better concentrate on that saxophone, which I haven't been involved with in years. But playing with Dizzy under any circumstances is a ball."

During this time with Benny Carter, I had a reunion with Cab Calloway. After I'd left Cab Calloway, he wouldn't speak to me for about two or three years. I'd go by him and say, "Hello . . ." and he'd turn his head. Jive! We didn't get back together for a very long time, but it finally happened. I was living in 2040 Seventh Avenue, and Cab had a gig up at the Westchester Community Center. His band left from the Theresa Hotel, and I was just passing by that day and saw all the guys. All those guys were glad to see me because I was doing pretty well by then. My name was getting around on Fifty-second Street. I went in the bus to talk to them because Cab wasn't there, and Tyree Glenn, who's a signifying monkey, and Milton Hinton, another signifying monkey, touted me up.

Tyree asked, "Hey, what're you doing?"

"I'm not working tonight," I said.

"Come on, go up to Westchester," Milt Hinton said.

"Oh, man, you know how Cab is. You know, I don't wanna . . ."

"Whatsamatter, nigger, you scared?"

"No, I ain't scared of Cab; fuck Cab Calloway!"

Finally the bus driver just pulled off with me in the bus, and when we got up there, and I got outta the bus, Cab's limousine was sitting there. He got out of his limousine at the same time the bus pulled up.

When I stepped out, he saw me, and his eyes went up; his eyes bucked and he walked over to me. The guys in the band didn't know that he had that funky attitude towards me. They didn't know it because I used to come by the Apollo where Lorraine was working for him. I had seen him, and they didn't know that Cab had this funny attitude. But now he was in front of all the guys, so he walked up to me and put a hand on me and said, "Hey, kid, how're you doing?"

"I'm doing all right."

"Yeah, I've been hearin' a lotta things about you. I'm glad to see that you're doing all right."

I started to say, "The best thing in the world, my most significant move, was when I left your band." I didn't say it and from that time on we were tight.

I had a chance to make some money by going out on the road to Canada and the Midwest with a white band, the Charlie Barnet Orchestra. At that time, there was less discrimination in the field of jazz than in any other part of American life. But it still existed, because they had only one major white band that hired black musicians on a permanent basis to play with them, and that band was Benny Goodman's. Of course, the white bands got most of the jobs that paid best, and the black musicians, the major creators, as a rule were frozen out. They used all kinds of excuses to justify this evil, such as the trouble mixed bands might provoke among racist customers and employers, the problems of finding restaurants, hotels, water fountains, toilets, and other public accommodations for the black members of the troupe. But the main reason those forms of discrimination persisted was because the bands themselves accepted it, and profited from the injustice, because they were insulated from competition with black bands and musicians. So this job provided a way for me to help break down some of that racial discrimination too.

Charlie Barnet had a reputation for being a liberal. Earlier, he had used Lena Horne as a female vocalist, and then he had Oscar Pettiford at one time and Trummy Young at another. When I joined the band, I was the only black person in the show and we played at a place in an Indianapolis hotel. Indianapolis used to be a cracker town. At the Circle Theater there, colored people weren't even allowed to come in. One day, as I was going up to the band room at the hotel, the security officer stopped me and asked me where I was going.

"To the band room."

"What are you going in there for?" he asked.

"I'm a member . . ."

"Come on . . . !" he said. They had to go and get somebody to tell

him to let me come up to rehearsal. After that incident, I talked to
Charlie Barnet and made him give Joe Guy a job. I told him I was
lonesome, and really I figured with at least one more "member" in the
band, security guards and people like that might get used to seeing
"members" around. Joe Guy and I went out on tour together with
Charlie Barnet and with two "members" in the band. I had a good time.

Another incident occurred in Detroit. There was a white trumpet
player in the pit, and I used to have a habit of holding my horn down
reading music.

"Your horn is supposed to be way up over the stand for the tone to
come out," he said. "You should hold your horn up."

"O.K., I'm gonna try to remember that," I said.

He'd sit there in the pit, and I'd look down, and he'd be raising his
palms up, saying "up, up." My horn was down, and he'd sit there and
remind me. By the time those two weeks were finished, I was in the
habit of holding my horn up. So white boy *is* good for something.

Touring with Charlie Barnet, I discovered some of the differences
between working with "white" and "colored" bands. In the different
black bands, you had to play differently, because every "colored"
band played, or phrased, in its own unique way. So you had to adapt
yourself to many peculiar styles of playing. In the white bands I
worked with, Charlie Barnet and Boyd Raeburn, everything was more
standardized, and a musician didn't have to change too much as he
moved from one band to the other. The black bands, on a whole, were
much more unique stylistically and in the way they sounded. That experience playing in black bands I wouldn't trade for anything.

Another thing I found out about the difference between our bands
and white bands at that time was that in white bands the musicians
were on salary. If there were any extras, they also got the extras, but
every week, Tommy Dorsey and Benny Goodman would pay their
musicians a salary. In the black bands, if you were playing someplace
for a week, you got paid by the week. If you were playing one-
nighters, you got paid by the night. If the band was out of work five
nights, you received no money for those five nights. You could borrow
some though; you could make a draw. Les Hite had the first band, the
first black band I knew of that paid you whether the band worked or
not. That was something beautiful.

Les Hite came from California and had a rich white woman, an industrialist, as his sponsor. She put money into the band, which ena-
bled Les Hite to pay salaries whether the band worked or not. You
got a salary every week—which was pretty nice, and the first time it
had ever happened to me—not much money, but still it was money
every week. Les had the house band at the Cotton Club and played
all the shows in Culver City, California. He had the premier band in

California; Lionel Hampton had played with him. I got the job through a good friend of mine who later became even more important to my development. But at that time, April 1942, he was running Les Hite's band and his name was Walter Gilbert Fuller.

Les Hite appreciated our music and liked my playing, but he was afraid of me because of the incident with Cab. He had heard about that scuffle, and Les Hite thought I had to be some kind of nut, so we didn't have too much to talk about. He paid me and everything was fine, but he was reticent.

Oscar Bradley, Les Hite's drummer, used to play paradiddles and flams and double flams behind my solos. He was one of those "school" drummers, sorta on the order of Cozy Cole, that studied, right on cues and paradiddles, "a-ra-ta-ta-drrr." I was used to Klook with "chink-a-ching" and the bass drum accents. I liked to hear the bass drum doing things, and Oscar Bradley was playing these paradiddles. I said, "Man, don't do those paradiddles in my solo. Just gimme some chink-a-ching."

So Oscar said, "O.K."

One time, we were playing the Apollo. I stood up to play a solo, he went into one 'a them ratamacues. I sat right back down. He wouldn't back off, so I sat down in the middle of a solo. I just sat down. Les Hite *looked* at me, but he was scared to say anything because of my reputation, so he fired the whole band. Les fired the whole band, and then hired back the men he wanted. Bandleaders used to do it like that, and it's a good idea. You say, "I'm breaking up my band, everybody's fired," and then say, "I want you, you, and you in my new band." That's better than pointing at one person and saying, "It's you I wanna get rid of." Can you believe Les Hite fired a whole band to get rid of me?

WALTER GILBERT FULLER (arranger):

"When he left Cab's band, Dizzy was running around New York playing with everybody, and we'd meet occasionally, and then Les Hite's band came here. I came back to New York with Les Hite's band, and we hired Dizzy to work with us. I was writing and running Les Hite's band.

"We had a pretty good band. I was the arranger and I ran the band. I hired and fired the men in the band, wrote the music for the band, and was the arranger. Everybody got paid by the week. We had a stipend, it wasn't that much, but in those days . . . We'd pay everybody $35 a week. If there was a period when the band wasn't working, you'd still get $35 a week. We paid the cats like that on the road, you know, and if we didn't have work for a week, two weeks, three weeks, they got paid, no matter.

"Les wanted to know, what the hell did you send for him (Dizzy) for? He was really afraid and uptight about him. I told him, 'Man, the cat can read the music, and play the stuff. Ain't no sense in talking like that, we need somebody who can do that. And we need somebody that can play solos.'

"We were in New York, and we were coming to New Jersey to play the Flagship. We had just come down from Boston, and came back to New York. I came over here to Newark to lay dead, and got Dizzy and put him in the band. He came in, read all the music, and ran it down and everything. Les was still unconvinced until Dizzy sat in and read the music. When he read the music, you couldn't say nothing, because he could read fly shit! Whatever it was. He could read anything that you put in front of him. A lotta guys didn't know that he had that kind of facility, except for the people that were in the band with him, in Cab's band. And Dizzy always had facility on his horn. He didn't have the best tone, but you couldn't find a better technician. Because that's what he was. When it came time to playing what he later called bebop, he was able to do it because he had that technique already. He had come with that. The things that he recorded with us, with Les Hite's band, back in 1941 and 1942 show that.

"When Dizzy decided to sit down in the middle of that solo, Les just looked and got mad. He got hot about it. He gave everybody notice. He fired the whole band except me, and then told me to go back and rehire them.

"He got hot, really got hot. Fluffy got hot. She got mad with the band. She was the one that was putting up the money for the band, and she got hot with us.

"Around 1941 and 1942, we used to hang out together. We used to go all over. I can remember now, going around. Dizzy had a leather jacket and a tallyho-type hunting hat. One of the English-style hats that the cats riding on horses talking about 'tallyho!' wear. I call it a tallyho hat. Dizzy always had him some strange type of hat. And that was back in 1941 and 1942 that he had this leather jacket. I'll never forget the leather jacket. And the other thing that I remember that he had was this knife which came out from a rabbit's foot. He never thought I remembered, but he had this little rabbit's-foot knife that he always kept in his pocket. The handle had fur on it. It wasn't a switchblade. He could take it out of his pocket and flick it open somehow. It opened like a switchblade. You'd think it was a switchblade. Pull it out of his pocket, completely closed, and before you knew it, he'd snapped it open.

"I can remember it was cold in New York, and we'd be going around backstage at the Apollo. He'd go around there and see Lorraine or something like that. And we'd go in and out of different guys' places in 2040 Seventh Avenue. Hanging between there and the Theresa, or down to Minton's, downtown and places like that. We hung out, you know, the guys, during those days. I went in the service around 1943, and so we hung out during 1941, 1942, and 1943, and then I went in the service and I didn't see him until I got out. When I got out of the service, I came back to New York. Where else? There was no place else in the world to go."

While I was in that band, Joe Wilder, another trumpet player who I knew from Philadelphia told me, "You watch Les very closely. He has three different sets of false teeth."

I said, "Whaddayou mean?"

He said, "Well, one of them is called 'grin wells'; another one is called 'sneer afters'; and another one is called, for quizzical expression, 'I don't believe its.' These teeth are set in his mouth, and all he has to do is open his mouth to get different expressions." Ha! Ha! I found Les Hite too bizarre.

After that, I moved around pretty fast among the bands; Claude Hopkins, Fess Williams, Calvin Jackson, Boyd Raeburn, and Fletcher Henderson. I made Fletcher Henderson stop playing "oom-pa, oom-pa, oom-pa," on the piano during my solos. I stood up to play at the Apollo, and said, "Stroll!" Stroll, is without the piano, just the drums and bass and, if there's one, the guitar. Prez used to stroll a lot; Roy Eldridge used to stroll a lot—piano out. That's where I learned it, because Roy would say "Strolluh!" in a minute. The piano would be getting in his way. I worked a weekend with Fletcher Henderson in the Apollo and then some one-nighters, but I had to tell him to lay out because the style of piano he played was getting in my way. Being determined to play my own style, I wouldn't let anything stand in the way of that. Nothing.

Progressions actually were one of my major contributions to our music. I showed Bird, Al Haig, George Wallington and scores of piano players who voiced the chords like I did how to play comp. The new pianists that have come out since, like Herbie Hancock and Chick Corea, have got some other things going too, but actually when they get down to basics, they jump right back down on it. They do a lot of things upstairs, but they must recognize the foundation that was laid down during the forties in our music, bebop. I figured out that saxophones could be voiced that way too.

Probably the best thing that happened to me with Les Hite's band was a solo I played when Les Hite recorded "Jersey Bounce." (Hit 7001) in June 1942.

That summer, 1942, I got another job with Lucky Millinder. This time, I had no problems, because Lucky had heard me play with all the bands in the Savoy. I'd already made a name as a modern stylist and had just recently left Cab Calloway.

Lucky Millinder acted weird, but he was the greatest conductor I'd ever seen. He had the biggest ears of anybody. He didn't know anything about music, and all he could do was rely on his memory—but his memory was astounding. He knew arrangements. He knew what everybody was playing all the time—the whole band—and if you missed something, he'd look at you. Yeah, he'd look at you. He couldn't read music, but he knew where everything was, and he'd bring you in. You didn't have to count. Like, suppose you had five bars out, or seven bars out. When you stopped playing, you could just cool it. Two bars before you're coming in, Lucky's waving his hand, getting you ready. And then you'd put your horn up there, and he'd bring you in, understand—on that beat—wherever that beat was. Sometimes that beat would be on the second note of a triplet, and he'd bring you in. Yeah, Lucky'd bring you in, and all you'd have to do was read from there on. He was great! Just read from that point on, just keep on reading. Lucky was great. Lucky was great!

I recorded a tune called "Little John Special," with Lucky Millinder (Brunswick 03406) and the arrangement incorporated one of my licks. This riff in "Little John Special" was something I'd been playing for a while to set a rhythm behind the saxophone soloist. The saxophones would set the same riff behind the bass player to form a pattern. That riff later became very important as the basis for one of my most well-known compositions, "Salt Peanuts."

Lucky Millinder was also nuts. He had this weird idea of how to run a band. He had a fire complex. I guess Lucky fired everybody that he'd ever had at one time or another. He'd fire anybody, look in the mirror and fire himself. Lucky fired me. He said I'd lost my chops. He actually moved the word around that I'd "lost" my chops, and while we were working in the Earle Theater in Philadelphia, he gave me two weeks' notice.

The way you find out you're getting ready to leave Lucky's band: You look up, one night, you're sitting in the Savoy, and there's a chair next to yours, and another trumpet player's sitting there playing your parts. That means you should know that you're on your way out. Then they'd check out the guy's solos. When you're getting ready to stand up and play your solo, Lucky would point to the other guy to play your solo, checking him out. Lucky fired me; he gave me two weeks' notice. He just fired me, and I don't know what his actual reasons were. He didn't have to have a reason. Lucky didn't need a logical reason to fire you. He just had this firing syndrome.

During my last week at the theater, the situation came to a head and, man, I played my heart out. That whole week I got up and played whether Lucky pointed at me or not when the time came for solos. I just played and played and played.

Lucky called me into his dressing room and said, "About that, um, notice, I'd like for you to stay on."

"But, Lucky," I told him, "uh, I can't stay on because I've got another job."

"O.K., I'll tell you what. I'll give you five dollars a night more." That was unheard of, man! I already had a salary of eighteen dollars a night for one-nighters. They had a certain salary in theaters, a certain salary on the road. Lucky offered me some more money. He'd do that. He'd fire a guy, then have to pay him more of a salary to get him to stay. Lucky was freakish that way. But I wouldn't accept it; I told him that I had this job, so I couldn't stay. And he said, "Man, you mutha—"

I said, "Nooo, Lucky, *you* gave me notice. I didn't put my notice in. You gave *me* notice. So I'm awful sorry, but I gotta leave."

Lucky didn't know me that well. Having been a resident of Philly, I already had a gig lined up at the Downbeat. Nat Segal owned this place, and he had a bar downstairs with a club upstairs. They'd heard about me over in Philly. I was a star. When I discovered Lucky had put me on notice, I contracted the job at the Downbeat. Nat Segal promised me what I wanted, a hundred fifty a week, for seven weeks, and I could use a local rhythm section which he'd also pay. A lotta white musicians were very interested in me and the modern style then, and there were some good musicians around Philly, like Charlie Ventura, Buddy De Franco, and a guy named Ellis Tollin who's got a large music store in Philly now. He used to be a drummer. So I went to work in the Downbeat for seven weeks with a local trio. I remember Jimmy Golden played piano. Another musician, Red Rodney, the little trumpeter who later played with Charlie Parker, would come to the Downbeat, but Red was still a kid, not even old enough to get in the club. He used to stand on the stairs to listen, and they would run him outta there. That's how I met Stan Levey, during that engagement over in Philly. Stan was a left-handed drummer, a white boy, who in a few years picked up on Max Roach's style, and he sat in with the group sometimes. Stan came over to New York and later worked with me. He had the most feeling of any of those white drummers who picked up on modern jazz early, guys like Shelly Manne, Irv Kluger, and Dave Tough. It's a shame that Dave Tough wasn't born the son of a sanctified preacher; there's a kind of soulfulness within him. He played with Tommy Dorsey and was the star of Tommy Dorsey's band. Dave Tough married a black woman and took her everywhere he went. This happened long before the era of Martin Luther King and the sit-ins in North Carolina at the lunch counter. I think that period was the beginning of this current age of civil rights. Paul Robeson ushered in that age and was a forerunner of Martin Luther King. But ironically, blacks at that time seemed to be awfully slow to pick up on anything new that came from one of their own, and that included our music.

On the other hand, Norman Dibbles, the drummer in Frankie Fairfax's band, while I was there, came over here to New York and passed for white. Norman Dibbles and Bama looked alike, but they didn't favor one another because Dibbles was blond, and Bama had black hair. But the skin color was the same. Bama played in a lotta white bands, and they didn't know he was colored.

Bama would see me talking to somebody and say, "Man, what you talking with that greasy muthafucka for?"

"Well, I thought he was all right."

"Man, that muthafucka hates niggers."

They'd say things in front of Bama and they didn't even know he was colored. Bama's heard a lotta things from people that didn't know he was colored. Dibbles, when he came to New York, immediately, became white. He never worked anyplace in Harlem, and he lived out in Forest Hills with his wife, Isabel, and called her "Doll." She's just as white as he is, or whiter. Dibbles' wife and his mother, both are as white as he is. Dibbles builds model trains very well. In his house, he has them going all kinds of ways, up, under, inside of tunnels, and over waterfalls. Dibbles didn't want any problems from white racism, so he even changed his name to Dibb Norman. That's the way he's listed in the union directory, Dibb Norman, but his name is Norman Dibbles. He went the route, he really went the route.

So after Lucky said, "His chops ain't no more good," I proved him wrong because I went to work by myself after his job.

Pickin' The Cabbage

Really, the way that I began writing arrangements came from the piano. Often, when I'd find myself strapped for vittles, I'd write an arrangement and fend off starvation.

Sometimes I see guys who write music, just sit down cold and write. When I make an arrangement, man, I sit down, at the piano, and test out all the chords and combinations. There's a limited amount that I write "biing!" just outta my head. I test it, and so it takes me a little time. That's why I used to charge a lot of money for my arrangements.

Jimmy Dorsey's manager wanted to buy some of my arrangements once, and I told him, "A hundred dollars an arrangement."

"A hundred dollars . . . !" he said.

"Well, pass me my music. Pass me the music. Ain't no argument about it." And I started gathering up my music.

"No, wait a minute, now, let's talk."

"No, no, there's no talking about it." I knew that he wanted the latest things. He paid me the money.

The first arrangement I wrote for a big band was "Good Night, My Love." I had Ella Fitzgerald sing that with Chick Webb, and I love that number. "Good Night, My Love" is one of the most perfect tunes ever written because of the way the progressions move. I made that arrangement for Frankie Fairfax in Philly. Charlie Shavers and Bama were there when I wrote that arrangement.

When I moved to New York, I'd compose little things for Teddy Hill, "headers," mostly. I created the head arrangement on a tune they called the "Dizzy Crawl," and later on when Shad Collins left Teddy's band, he took it over to Count Basie. They recorded it and named it "Rock-a-Bye Basie," but that was my composition. I heard it on a Count Basie record; the moment I heard it, I knew it was mine. It was just a riff, but a riff is a tune. All you need is a riff, and you've got a tune. I didn't copyright it; it was a head arrangement. I just set a riff and told them what to play. Anytime you write something, copyright it or look out. At first, they took it, just stole it from me, and I didn't get any royalties from it until way, way, way, way later. Later on they acknowledged it and gave me some money. Shad probably told them—way later on—and then I started getting some royalties, a little chump change.

Basie said, "Well, Shad brought that here and said it was his."

Muthafucka. They put me down later on, as cocomposer, and I got a couple of royalty checks, but I haven't received any royalties on it in the last fifteen years.

A lotta tunes got stolen by the bandleaders, too, that way. I probably did it myself a couple of times, but not completely. If you have a lotta guys on a record date and play a head arrangement, and you set the melody and someone else adds something and someone else, something else, well, you set the melody, so it's your tune, but the arrangement is another matter because the other guys contributed to the arrangement. The head arrangements go right into the band's book, and if nobody bothers to write them down, they always turn out to be the boss numbers. Head arrangements are just feeling. You don't have to read. You run into trouble though when you replace someone because he takes his notes with him. We used to do head arrangements a lot at Minton's and Monroe's. Basie's band was built on head arrangements. When he first came out with "Jumpin' at the Woodside" and most of his things that became big hits, like "One O'clock Jump," they were head arrangements. You know a dance is from nine to one. One o'clock means getting outta there. So when one o'clock jumped, you played that.

COUNT BASIE (piano, bandleader):

Diz says that Shad Collins brought into your band one of Dizzy's riffs called the "Dizzy Crawl" and that you recorded it as "Rock-a-Bye Basie." How did that happen?

"I don't know, really, how it happened. It's been so many years ago, I don't know how it happened. Who claims it?"

Dizzy Gillespie. He says that later on you put his name on the tune.

"Well, that's it then. That's the way it goes. If it's Dizzy's tune, and I put his name on it, that's it. Diz don't go around just claiming tunes, just dry.

"Diz? I think he contributed 75 per cent of modern music, as far as I'm concerned. That's right. I think he's one of the greatest."

A couple of my early compositions and arrangements, "Pickin' The Cabbage" and "Paradiddle," were written for Cab Calloway and Cozy Cole and were recorded in Chicago, March 1940. (Vocalion 5467). I felt they had some effect on Cab's band, and if you listen closely to my arrangement and solo on "Pickin' The Cabbage," you'll hear the seeds of some of my later and more well-known compositions like "Night In Tunisia" and "Manteca." If you really have good ears, you'll hear more than that. A careful listening to "Pickin' The Cabbage" will show you the musical direction I'd follow for the rest of my career. It's a real beginning of Latin jazz and possibly the first use of polyrhythms in our music since the very beginning of jazz. All of the elements for fusing and synthesizing Afro-American "swing" with the various Latin and Caribbean beats are right there in that one composition, "Pickin' The Cabbage."

MILTON HINTON:

"But he revolutionized Cozy's band when he came in. He was the one that first started Cab—he and Chu Berry—thinking along the lines of playing some music other than 'hi de ho.' Something other than a vocal to exploit the band—to let the band do a couple of things. In fact, Chu Berry once said to Cab, 'Look, man, if you get a good band and let these cats play, you know, if your hair falls out you can still be a big star. The people will still come to hear your band.' Chu had that kind of thinking, and Dizzy was doing his little experimenting with writing. We'd get three or four other guys and we'd rehearse back-stage, and Cab began to hear a few of these things and it sounded good. And then he'd say, 'Throw that in.' And finally, I can remember, in Chicago, the first time Cab ever had a record session where he used instrumentalists, you know, something other than vocals for himself. And he let Dizzy do a thing called 'Pickin' The Cabbage,' which Dizzy wrote. Tyree later did something called 'Bye Bye Blues,' and Cozy Cole was given a drum solo called 'Crescendo and Drums' and 'Paradiddle.' They got me playing a bass solo, especially on one side featuring the bass, called, 'Ebony Silhouette.' And these were all because of Dizzy and his creative nature that had shown Cab that, 'Hey, this band you got is a good band, here, and they can do something too, baby. So you can rest your vocal chops for just a minute, cat, and let these cats work, and then come on back and it sounds better.' Of course, that's the way the program stayed. The format stayed like that even after Dizzy left. But he was the innovator who started it."

Yeah, the music started becoming a fad. Everybody was calling me, and I was busy trying to blow. They all wanted some bebop in the book. Tadd Dameron became the leading bebop arranger, but he didn't play much; he just wrote most of the time. I played as much as I could, so I didn't have too much time to write. Just when I needed some money. BOOM! I'd make an arrangement. I preferred playing at different places on the Street like the Yeah Man. The Yeah Man was fabulous. A guy named Fletcher Smith used to play piano there, and oooh, could he play some piano. He played with Cootie Williams for years.

Composing new songs flowed naturally from writing arrangements. In 1942, Woody Herman commissioned a tune from me that he called "Swing Shift." They named it, because I didn't put any names on them, and then it went into Charling Music Publishers. When you'd write something for Woody Herman, it automatically went to his music publisher, and they'd copyright it and give you the royalties. I don't even remember how that tune went. I wrote another tune for Woody that he called "Down Under," as a tribute to Australia. Woody had one of my compositions in a movie of his, but I forgot the name of that one too. Then I wrote one for Jimmy Dorsey. They named it "Grand Central Getaway." The peculiarity about these things I wrote for bands like Woody Herman, Ina Ray Hutton, and Jimmy Dorsey is that it was just like the current craze, the rock craze. They had to have some bebop in the book. But when I'd bring these arrangements and songs, sometimes they'd have a hard time playing them.

I remember Jimmy Dorsey's band being very conservative in their approach to playing. In Woody Herman's band they had no trouble, because the guys were getting into the music and they wanted to really play bebop. We articulated differently from the older guys—that's what made it different—and you'd have to tell them how to phrase it. You couldn't write those phrasings down, so you'd just tell them how to phrase it. Woody didn't have too much trouble with his trumpet section because he had a bunch of younger guys like Markowitz. But Jimmy Dorsey's band—when I brought the music over, and they went over it—I had to say, "Nooo, trumpets, that ain't how it goes!" I tried to hum it for them, and they still couldn't get it.

Jimmy Dorsey finally said, "Let's hold this one until tomorrow night. You bring your horn over. The guys said it was too hard."

"It's not hard," I said. "It's just the way that you articulate." So the next night I went over and showed them how it went. They made a record of it. They finally learned to play it because they were professional musicians. They didn't play it like a band that I'd have would play it, but they played it very well.

With Woody Herman's band it came more naturally. All the trumpet players in the band wanted to play like me; all the drummers wanted to play like Kenny Clarke or Max Roach and so on. Woody had a band trying to sound like us anyway and he probably said, "Well, shit, I'd better get some music like that for these muthafuckas to play. They're gonna play like that anyway. They don't wanna play no 'Evil Blues.'" So he tried to get me to become his arranger.

WOODY HERMAN (clarinet, bandleader):

"I don't think there was any competitive spirit. As a matter of fact, we were all very groovy friends. We all, to a great degree, tried to find the same things, musically. So I don't think it was anything more than a warm kind of thing.

"Of course, I've given some very strong advice to Diz on a couple of occasions. When he was writing some charts for me, back in the early forties, Diz wrote this thing called "Down Under." It was supposed to be like a tribute to Australia or something. But anyway, it was typical of what he was into when he was writing in those days. And Diz, every once in a while used to help us out, like if we were uptown in the theater, in the Apollo or someplace, and we needed somebody, Diz would leap in. He jumped in and had fun with us, you know. But I always insisted, like when we sat around just talking and saying things, that he was such a great writer. 'Man, why do you waste time playing a horn when you're such a good writer?' I said. So you can see how wrong I was. Right? That's the way it was.

"Diz to me was the beginning of an era. And Pops (Louis Armstrong) was the beginning of an era. And during that span from

Pops, from when he was a young man, everyone else in-between is not
that terribly important. In other words, these were two terribly important giants. And of course Diz associated with Parker and Monk and
other guys, you know. And the point is that they were the beginning
of that particular era which is still in existence. Because the average
youngster in America, or anyplace else in the world, is not aware of
that. They're hearing something that was originally invented by a particular hard core of guys. Yet today they think of it as music in a commercial, on television, on radio, anything. Right? I think that one tremendous giant was Pops (Louis Armstrong) and then the next
tremendous giant was Diz. And I mean that sincerely.

"My band was one of the first to use his arrangements. And I thought
that his possibilities were endless. At that point there were a lot of
guys blowing, right? And some blew more than other cats, and I
thought he had a particular genius for arranging; and I think he
proved it many times with his own big band, when he got to that
stage in his life, and many other times. But yet, once about two years
ago (1974) I called him about doing new versions of some things he
wrote years ago. 'Are you kidding?' he said. 'I don't wanna mess with
that.' You know, he just doesn't feel it's important to him now. I certainly understand it because everybody goes through different kinds
of changes, different ways of maturing. But I have the utmost respect
and love for him. And I can't make enough of the import I feel he had
on American jazz."

In music, I don't see too much difference between head arrangements and written arrangements. The jazz musician, though he
practically never receives credit for it, is constantly composing
during his improvisations, and most of the melodies he creates are
never set down on paper, nor on record. There's such a tremendous
volume of original music created during every good jazz performance, it's utterly fantastic; and there should be some way to save
it and use it. All jazz performers should carry pocket tape recorders to
provide them with feedback and material for future compositions. If
they had those midget tape recorders on the market back in 1942, I
could've written a song a week without taking off any time from what
I believe is the essence of jazz composition, playing and improvisations.

Some of my best compositions, especially during this early period,
came out of my improvisations. "Salt Peanuts," for example, was a riff.
I set that riff way before, in some band. A riff goes back because you've
gotta have something that you know, when somebody says, "Set a riff."

You've gotta have something you know because there's no time to do it then. You have to reach back and try to figure out what you know. I co-composed that tune with Kenny Clarke. But before the written composition, I set that riff on a record date with Lucky Millinder in 1942, in an arrangement called "Little John Special." "Salt Peanuts" wasn't officially credited as a composition until 1943. I first recorded it with my own group in 1945. (Manor 5000.)

I don't recall how the tune got that name, "Salt Peanuts," but as a tune on its own, it became more elaborate than just a riff. Regarding the co-composition with Kenny, we'd get together and somebody'd think of something to play, and you'd say, "No man, let's try this." And if that didn't work we'd try something else and something else until we'd finally say, "Yeah, man, that's it!" That's how you do it, by common agreement. Kenny and I came to a helluva agreement on "Salt Peanuts."

Very early, the tunes I wrote, like "Pickin' The Cabbage," sounded Latin oriented or expressed a Latin feeling, like putting West Indian hot sauce in some black-eye peas or hot Cuban peppers in a dish of macaroni. This in part shows the influence of Mario Bauza and Alberto Socarras, but instinctively, I've always had that Latin feeling. You'd probably have to put me in psychoanalysis to find out where it came from, but I've always felt polyrhythmic from a long way back. Maybe I'm one of those "African survivals" that hung on after slavery among Negroes in South Carolina.

In 1941–42, during my engagement at Kelly's Stables with Benny Carter, Benny had a date to make a "soundee" movie. They used to have movies then, I believe they called them nickelodeons, where you could put a penny in the slot and watch. Maxine Sullivan and Benny were making the movie, and I played in it, as a member of Benny Carter's band. During the break I sat down at the piano to improvise some chord changes. Actually, they were thirteenth chords—A-thirteenth resolving to D minor. I looked at the notes of the chords as I played the progression and noticed that they formed a melody. All I had to do was write a bridge, put some rhythm to it, and I was over. We didn't play it in the movie, but I remembered it, after I got away from there, and jotted it down. The melody had a very Latin, even oriental feeling, the rhythm came out of the bebop style—the way we played with rhythmic accents—and that mixture introduced a special kind of syncopation in the bass line. In fact, for the first time in a jazz piece I'd heard, the bass line didn't go one-two-three-four-, "boom, boom, boom, boom." Afterward we played the tune on Fifty-second Street and called it "A Night In Tunisia."

The heavily syncopated rhythm in the bass line probably gave a whole lotta cats ideas. From that point in jazz, the bass didn't have to go "boom, boom, boom, boom." Instead it went boom-be, boom-be, boom-be.

This tune sounded so exotic that it didn't seem right to call it "Interlude." I never cared what people called it as long as they played it. Some genius decided to call it "Night In Tunisia," which sounded quite appropriate, and people have been calling it "Night In Tunisia" ever since. Later on, Frank Paparelli transcribed my solos for publication, and my putting his name on "A Night In Tunisia," as co-composer, was the payoff. But he didn't actually have anything to do with the writing of the song. It was my way of repaying his favors to me.

Earl Hines claims he named the tune, but that's a lie because I played "A Night In Tunisia" with Boyd Raeburn on a record before I went with Earl Hines and had played it in 1942 on Fifty-second Street in Benny Carter's band.

Incubator

By the time I joined Earl Hines in late 1942, our new music, a premature baby, had grown to quite some size. The music had developed well-defined characteristics; its major organs, the players, were creating and producing consistently, and a group of followers, small, but growing and fervently dedicated, had emerged. But could the new style survive alone, commercially? After leaving Lucky Millinder, I tried to answer that question by going out as a single attraction when I accepted the engagement at the Downbeat in Philly, a little stint which commercially and personally was quite rewarding to me. The public dug it enough for me to be invited there as a star in the first place, and we attracted good and enthusiastic crowds. But could we all survive as modernists, without any further ties to the mother dance bands? Would the public reward us with that much commercial acceptance?

At home for a while with Mama, making a nice salary as the star attraction, and playing my own style of music, I hadn't given too much thought to joining another band until Earl Hines came through. Years before, Trummy Young tried to get me a job with Earl. Trummy was with Earl while I was in Philly playing with Frankie Fairfax. I've known Trummy Young since 1936. But I wouldn't leave Philly then and wasn't particular about leaving this time just to go with another

band. But Earl Hines's band had something a little different. He had a
lotta young guys who all wanted to play in the modern style. Two of
those guys were Billy Eckstine and Shadow Wilson. Shadow and Billy
were tight buddies, and both were friends of mine. I'd known Shadow
from Frankie Fairfax's band. Shadow was the drummer in the band
that mutinied on Frankie when everyone quit just before I joined.
And I'd met Billy in New York. These greasy muthafuckas cruised me
out of Philly to go with Earl Hines.

They told Yardbird, "Well, Diz is coming over here." Then to me
they said, "Well, you know we're getting Yard." And then Billy Eckstine and Shadow got Earl Hines to offer me $20 a night on the road.
So I took it. They got Charlie Parker the same time—cruised him in
there. Billy Eckstine talked Charlie into joining the band. Earl needed
a tenor player, and Charlie Parker played alto, but they got Charlie to
pick up on tenor. Earl bought Yard a horn and he played tenor with
Earl Hines. I came in a couple of weeks before Bird.

BILLY ECKSTINE (trumpet, vocalist):

"Diz and I became friends somewhere around 1939 or 1940. Even
then, you could see that Diz had his head on straight, man, he was completely into studying. Completely into knowing that music is something
that's got to be studied. Dizzy was never one who went on just what
God gave him. He always embellished it with studying and understanding. And then we lived together in the same apartment building
there at 2040 Seventh Avenue. I had one apartment and Dizzy was
up over me, and Dizzy had an old piano. Diz was constantly working
out things at the piano.

"See, that's the problem with a lot of kids, now, who try to copy
Diz. They hear some of the clichés and things that Diz plays and they
try to play that and they do all right. But once they leave that, they
have to go into the improvisations that he does himself. He has pure
knowledge of what he's doing! They don't have any knowledge or
maybe are not that deep into their knowledge as Dizzy, so they get
lost out there. But Diz, you're not gonna lose him, you're not gonna
lose him. The man's master of his instrument.

"Dizzy worked on chord progressions, things like that, finding
different ways of doing things. Finding different progressions, alternate ways of using the musical chords, not just the given things that
are in the songs. He would work out the alternates and the prettier
themes, different progressions to them, and countermelodies, which he

still does. Man, there are some beautiful passages that Dizzy has created."

EARL "FATHA" HINES (piano, bandleader):

"I met Dizzy when he was with Cab Calloway, when I was at the Grand Terrace. And then after his separation from Cab, he joined me. He wanted to join the organization because we had some boys in there that he knew—little Benny Harris and Budd Johnson—and so he was very much interested in joining the band.

"You see, I'm a funny fella. I don't hire a person just to hire him. They have to have something. At that particular time I happened to have a band where everybody had a spot. Dizzy was one of the fastest guys as far as execution on his horn. I had other men in there for tonation. I had men for first position; I had men for second trumpet. Dizzy was always the man that played all of the fast numbers and numbers that had a punch to it. And when it comes to that type of musician, you can't beat him. Dizzy was always a man that realized he wasn't much of a soloist as far as tonation was concerned, as far as trying to sing a song, but he can put a mute in there and make you like it. But that's the kind of guy he is. He's a great artist and knows how to get around those things, so I have to give him credit for it because he's a helluva musician."

We had a beautiful, beautiful band with Earl Hines. He's a master, and you learn a lot from him, self-discipline and organization. One time we had a Christmas show. Earl Hines organized it, everything we would do on the stage. Earl Hines put on a show. He had Don Redman, another giant, to make an arrangement on "Jingle Bells" with everybody in the band singing. I'll never forget those lyrics:

> Jingle bells, jingle bells, away, away, away,
> Don't cha know that Santa Claus is hip
> He made this trip
> Just to drive your blues away
>
> Say, daddy, you're gonna have a ball
> And you're gonna get tall
> As a Merry Christmas candle on a Santa Claus
> Fall right in, laugh and grin
> And be happy

A Merry Christmas to you, you, and you
And you, and you, and youuuu too.
Ah, we all wish the best to you
And you, and you, and you
A Merry Christmas to you.

We'd be pointing at the audience all the time. You'd get a lotta work that way, if you pointed at the same broad all the time. In the trumpet section, we had Gail Brockman, Shorty McConnell, Benny Harris, and me; at one time, too, Jesse Miller. Trombones, Bennie Green, Junior Chappell, and Howard Scott. On saxophones, "Scoops" Carry and "Goon" Gardner, altos; and Charlie Parker and Thomas Crump, tenors. John Williams, Mary Lou Williams' ex-husband played baritone sax; Connie Wainwright, guitar; Earl Hines, piano; Shadow Wilson, drums; and Jesse Simpkins, bass. Billy Eckstine, male vocalist, and Sarah Vaughan, female vocalist.

Earl Hines was the pianist in his band, and I mean he played some piano. We used to make him play longer solos. We'd say, "Play another one, Gates." And he'd go again. They'd say, "Lay out, lay out, lay out . . ." and we wouldn't come in. Earl had to play again. He'd look up and keep playing and grinning. You couldn't flush him, you couldn't flush him, no matter what you did. We wouldn't come in when we were supposed to and make him play another chorus. He'd be sweating, man, and he's so cool. He is the epitome of perfection.

Earl Hines is the master of composure. He is class personified. I don't know a classier musician, or a classier person in any field, than Earl Hines.

Charlie Parker picked up the tenor to play with Earl Hines, and since I was in that band, we became close. Out on the road with Earl, things started happening between Charlie Parker and me. Yeah, man, we hung out together. We were together all the time, playing in hotel rooms and jamming. We were together as much as we could be under the conditions that the two of us were in. His crowd, the people he hung out with, were not the people that I hung out with. And the guys who pushed dope would be around, but when he wasn't with them, he was with me. Yard was very funny about that. He never did use in front of me. He might smoke a joint or something, but he would never take off in front of me. So I couldn't swear that he was even using or addicted to dope. I couldn't swear on it because I never saw it, and I became as close to him as anybody.

One time, we were with Earl Hines in Pine Bluff, Arkansas. I used to sit up on the bandstand during intermission. We were playing white dances, and during intermissions you couldn't go out in the audience, so you stayed backstage. I was sitting at the piano, fooling around with something.

Some white guy said, "Hey . . ." to me and thumped a nickel on the stand. And then he said, "When you come back on, play so-and-so." I don't remember what tune he wanted us to play.

I looked down at the nickel, and looked at this dude, and picked up the nickel and threw it someplace, and just kept playing. Later on that night, after the dance was over, I thought everyone had left and we could go to the "white" men's room. While they were dancing, all the men's rooms were "white" and the ladies' rooms too. Anyway, I went in and came out of the men's room, and as I was coming out, I saw this shadow behind my head, coming down. This bottle was coming at my head. So I just happened to turn, just in time, just a little bit, and the guy caught me in back of the head with this bottle. And, boy, I really saw stars! But he didn't knock me out. I reached on the table and picked up one of those big, big bottles, a magnum bottle. I turned around and was just getting ready to hit this guy when about five guys grabbed me. And about this time, the blood, oh, the blood was coming from my head, all over everything, and I was trying to get away from these guys. And then Charlie Parker came along. Charlie Parker walked over to the guy who hit me and said, "You took advantage of my friend, you cur!" He called the guy a "cur." The guy probably didn't even know what a cur was, man. That was funny, because I know that peckawood didn't know what a cur was. So then I went to the hospital and had about nine stitches put in the back of my head.

I guess Charlie Parker and I had a meeting of the minds, because both of us inspired each other. There were so many things that Charlie Parker did well, it's hard to say exactly how he influenced me. I know he had nothing to do with my playing the trumpet, and I think I was a little more advanced, harmonically, than he was. But rhythmically, he was quite advanced, with setting up the phrase and how you got from one note to another. How you get from one note to another really makes the difference. Charlie Parker heard rhythms and rhythmic patterns differently, and after we started playing together, I began to play, rhythmically, more like him. In that sense he influenced me, and all of us, because what makes the style is not what you play but how you play it.

EARL HINES:

"They used to play out of each other's books. He used to play out of Charlie Parker's exercise book, and Charlie Parker played out of his exercise book, when we were in theaters, between shows. This is where they got all these ideas. And a lot of younger guys thought that the more mistakes you made, the more modern the musician you were. They didn't realize that these were actual *facts* that those boys were playing; this was written. Later on they found out that you had to study to do what they were doing.

"Dizzy created a new style. It was peculiar to all of us at that particular time. But it wasn't that exactly. I knew what he was doing because he took it out of the exercise book.* But to insert it in tunes was where the difficulty came, and you know that he was crazy enough to know where to put it, and had a photographic mind, and could remember all those things, you know. He could remember to put it in those changes that they had in the tunes.

"There have been several different people who've been trying to come up with new ideas, but, you see, what Dizzy did, and Charlie Parker, they both were together—having a photographic mind—on these jam sessions; they remembered the chord structures and would insert these passages that they found, that they rehearsed. That's what made it sound so different. A lot of people, especially young musicians, thought the more mistakes you made, the better modern musician, or bebop player you were. They didn't realize that this man was actually playing music.

"If you're a leader, if you've had any experience at all, this is what you're in this world for. If you find people that are capable of doing things, the idea is to give them that opportunity. Somebody gave me an opportunity, or else you would have never heard me. And so you pass it on. This is where the mistake has been made. So many people get in their shell, and they say, 'Hurray for me, and the heck with everybody else!' That's not right.

"When you see my little group now, you'll notice that everybody has a spot; I feature everybody. So that when I'm not around, they still can use the idea that I had and create something of their own. That's what happens."

SARAH VAUGHAN (vocalist):

"Dizzy was in the band when I joined Earl Hines in 1942. That was my first job after I had won the contest at the Apollo Amateur Hour. Yes, Billy Eckstine brought me in the band and there was Dizzy and there was Charlie Parker. I don't know if Bennie Green was there then, but during my stay there, there was Fats Navarro, Gene

* Earl Hines's remark about our improvisations coming from the exercise books is untrue.—DG

Ammons, Dexter Gordon, and little J.J. (John Jackson) from Kansas City. Oh, so many musicians. How fortunate I was.

"Well, that was the beginning of bebop. Yes it was. Yeah, that was the beginning. People would stand around and stare at us a lot because this music was so new and everything, but they finally got the message.

"I loved it. Oh, listen, I was going to school. I really didn't have to go to Juilliard, I was right there in it. But I took piano lessons when I was about seven until about fifteen, then I took organ for a while. I used to play in church. Anyway about Dizzy, I loved it, the harmonies. And I loved the way Charlie Parker just flew all over that horn. There ain't but a few notes, but look like he added a few more to me. Played so fast and so swift. And the same thing for Dizzy. It was just something I never heard before, and since the first time I heard it, I haven't stopped listening to it since.

"I don't think it affected my style any; I just learned a lot. Lots and lots, a whole lots. I used to stare at them in amazement. But I used to feel it; you know, both of us used to sit on the stand and we'd get to swinging so much, Dizzy would come down and grab me and start jitterbugging all over the place. It was swinging.

"Dizzy is truly simple as he wants to be, but he's sly as a fox and smart as a whip. Now that's why we call him Dizzy."

BILLY ECKSTINE:

"Well, I will say that we had our fun. We were wild, but wild in a good way. I mean it wasn't wild to the point of anything detrimental. I think the guys were full of enthusiasm, everybody, and it came off. New things, learning, everything was new in this concept. And it was a beautiful study. I mean, I've seen the times, heck, when we were in the Booker T. Washington Hotel in St. Louis, and hell, we'd rehearse at three o'clock in the morning, right in the room. Heck, Bird would take the reed section, and, man, nobody knocked on the wall, things like that. We'd rehearse any time, all night long. Just play! It was definitely a schooling period for everybody concerned.

"Earl Hines was a brilliant man in this respect: Earl has always believed in something new. He's never a person that stands back and lives off his past laurels. Like in my particular case as the singer with the band. During those days, the vocalist in the band was something to separate the instrumentals. In Earl's case, it was entirely different. He used his vocalists as a part of the orchestra. Earl didn't throw any clogs in our wheels at all.

"Bird was so full of spontaneity. It just . . . boom! . . . came out.

Bird was just a genius, that's all you can say. And Diz was a person who would work, who was also just as apt, but Diz knew methodically what it was. He was more of a technician, as far as the knowledge end of it was concerned. He pursued it. I don't think it came as easy with John as it did with Bird. For about seven years when we were together through Earl Hines's band and my band, I'd hear Bird every night play his solos and never play the same thing, at no time, at all! If he played a hundred choruses, he'd play a hundred different ones, you know. Well, those kinds of people are just . . . When you read up on the masters and the geniuses, they all had these little ways about them. These little idiosyncrasies that maybe were strange to some people. Well, Bird fit right into that same category. Totally gifted! Totally!

"We were in Chicago once, and Bird had pawned his horn, and Bobby Redcross, a friend of ours, had one of those little sweet potatoes, ocarinas. Looks like a sweet potato. Bird was sitting up there in the room with him that night. Next thing, we went over to the Club 65, right across the street, and Bird was up there in the mike playing this ocarina and swinging the hell out of it! And he'd just picked it up in Bob's room. So those people are just put here, I believe, for a certain time, to do what they're supposed to do, and then they leave. I've always noticed it; and they don't stay long.

"But John is still creating, and with the writing that Diz can do— See, if Diz would have the time and want to, he could put that horn down and write. He would still be just as great."

BOB REDCROSS (recording engineer, road manager):

"I first met John in 1942–43, when he was with Earl Hines. Earl had been out on tour, out East, here in New York. Billy Eckstine and I always stayed pretty close and the band was being reorganized; and in the reorganization, Billy and a few other people in the band, Budd Johnson, and a couple of other guys, had a little clique in the band. I guess they made some moves and influenced Earl to put Diz in the band. And so when they came back to Chicago, that's when I first met Diz, though I had seen him a few years before then. I'd seen him when I was in New York.

"Chicago was a little funny during that time. Roy Eldridge had gone out on his own and had set up a band that worked at the Three Deuces right after he'd left Fletcher Henderson. And I mean it was pretty rough for anybody playing a trumpet to gain any recognition around Chicago. Roy was completely into it. At the time it was a completely different thing altogether. In fact, Diz had even been influenced to a great degree *earlier* by Roy. It was beginning, I guess, the nucleus of the formation of bebop. And there was just a few of the guys who were able to play that progressive style, you know. And John fit right in with Bird and just a very few other people. But John's virtuosity as far as I was concerned, man, was his ability to get over his horn. I mean and play extremely fast and very high, which was à la Roy, to a degree. But by this time, his whole thing went completely out of the realm of Roy because you begin to go into the thing which bop evolved from.

"I had a joint there I was running, where a lotta musicians and entertainers used to hang out. Plus, I had one of the only recording machines around. A private machine—like a home machine. And guys would get through work and come by and sit in my hotel room and jam. And plus, I'd take off the air, just as long as people were playing in places that were on the air, like The College Inn or some of the bigger hotels, like when John Kirby would come in, Duke Ellington would come in, different bands would come in and they had air time coming out of those places. I would take them off the air every night. I'd take air takes of different people who were in town. Back in late 1939 and early 1940, 1941, I used to know all the little joints where I could take guys, and they could sit and jam. Because it was against the union rules for a guy to play anywhere (without a contract) to jam. They was very, very strict on that. So we had a few hideouts and what not. I knew the guys, and I'd always take them where they could sit down and have sessions. I was running a joint, a little cocktail bar, called Tootie's. But I did all my recording in my hotel room. All my sessions were in the hotel.

"The Savoy Hotel, that's where Bird made that thing called 'Redcross' that he did. He made it in there. Yeah, I got the original record. I saw Teddy Reig recently and Teddy said that he's reissued all those things on Savoy. He had the dates on Bird, you know. He reissued them on Savoy, and 'Redcross'† is one of them. But I know I got a copy somewhere. See, I got a bunch of 78s I refuse to get rid of. I just keep carrying them from one place to another, year to year. I was telling Diz I had some of those things that was made in the hotel room; I don't know if they will even play anymore. Last time I saw some of them, the wax was beginning to come off. These were made during the war, you know, back at the first part of the war, when all metal had been conscripted for the defense effort. Some of them are glass based, made with wax on top of the glass; and some were remnants or combinations of metal with wax. These were home recordings. These were regular 10-inch discs, and some of them weigh about as much as six or seven 10-inch regular wax recordings of the day. They were very heavy base. Some of them were aluminum; and they were made of whatever

† Later misspelled "Red Cross" on records.

metal they could get. Then after a while, they couldn't even get metal. They got to putting them on glass. I think the name of the machine was a Silvertone. It was made by Sears, and it was a disc recorder. It cut wax. Your discs were made from a base with wax poured over it. Then it had a recording cutting arm that you set down onto the record, and it began to cut these grooves. And whatever they were playing, it would be transcribed right into the disc. They were just a lightweight edition of the present way of recording. The only thing is, naturally, there's been a lotta years of refinement added to it.

"The one Bird made, Bird called it 'Redcross,' but it was originally called, 'The Devil in 305.' That was my room number. That was a riff, and they got up on a riff, and they start playing it. Diz was on that. This was during the time they were with Earl's band. But when Billy left Earl, he took all them same people with him and got his own band."

BILLY ECKSTINE:

"When I left to go down on Fifty-second Street, and then later to start my own band, the guys that I got in the band, all came with me, including Sarah. We just happened to be guys that hung out in the daytime together.

"I happened to have had a little luck with some recordings and things like 'Jelly, Jelly, Jelly' with Earl Hines, and I had a little bit of drawing power in the black circle. So I got my band together on that pretense. And when I left and started my band, all the guys left with me, Diz and Shadow and Bird all left. Diz was my first musical director with my band. We were working Fifty-second Street, and the offices wanted me to get a band, which at that particular time was about the only way a black person could excel in music, having an orchestra. So Diz was my first musical director, and some of the earlier things that later he became very famous with were written in my band, 'Bebop,' 'Groovin' High,' things like that.

"I chose Dizzy as musical director because I didn't see anybody more apt at that particular time. And that was the style of music we wanted to play."

Earl Hines gave us all kinds of leeway, and he became quite instrumental in seeing that we had a chance to develop. Earl Hines, as a musician himself, an innovator, could understand another innovator when he saw him. He'd see him and know him, right away. Working with Earl Hines ended as a delightful and beautiful experience. The only reason I left his band was because I felt very close to Billy who offered me a job as music director of his band at $25 a night, which I think was what he was getting paid with Earl Hines. Billy was making $25 a night, as the star of, 'Jelly, Jelly, Jelly,' 'Stormy Monday Blues,' and 'I'm Falling for You!' I think I'll start singing ballads. Yeah, the more I think about it, because while the booking agents and managers were deciding whether to name Billy, 'X-tine' or 'Eckstine' (for fear someone might think he was Jewish?), I was out on the street.

No Dancing

Maybe Wallace Jones recommended me to Duke Ellington. Wallace Jones, the lead trumpet player with Duke, formerly played with Willie Bryant, when I used to play at the Savoy with Willie Bryant, and it was probably Wallace's recommendation that steered me to Duke's band to sub for four weeks. Those four weeks were very strange. The most enchanting thing about it turned out to be Lena Horne. She starred those four weeks with Duke Ellington, in the Capitol Theater on Broadway, and came across beautifully.

Playing Duke's music, the music of a master like Duke Ellington, is another kind of experience. To play with Duke you have to forget everything you know. You can't use your own experiences because Duke has some new shit for you when you go in there. You don't rely on what you know from someplace else. This is a new experience! You have to conform to his approach and be receptive; just be receptive enough to take it.

The guys in Duke's band weren't too nice, either. They didn't help anyone. In rehearsal, they wouldn't tell me that you had to jump from "A." I'm supposed to remember all that, that you jump from "A," to the first three bars of "Z," and then jump back to "Q," and play eight bars of that, and then jump over to the next part, and then play the solo. Nobody would tell you anything. Cootie Williams, Rex Stewart, and Wallace Jones were sitting up there, as silent as high priests in a temple. I had to guess what it was.

Duke had his band set up and used it as an instrument to get certain musical effects, especially tonal colors—but not just that. Duke accomplished so much, you just have to grab one phrase of his artistry and try to deal with that. What he did for the instruments in the band —the sounds that came out of his band—were unprecedented in the history of jazz, and you will never hear sounds like that again. Never in life will you hear such sounds again, live. It's the same with the others, like Lester Young and Charlie Parker. All of them were kings, and you can't get any higher. When the king is dead, long live the king, he'll be there. You don't have to worry about him, he'll be there.

Before he passed on, no one had ever seen any of Duke Ellington's scores except Billy Strayhorn, and Strayhorn, I think, probably never showed any of their scores to anyone. Because of unity, what they did, nobody knows, even the guys in the band. The Baha'is believe in unity, but unity with diversity, to make it prettier. You always think about what you can do to make it prettier. Duke had that band unified, and he could drop anywhere in the band and get a masterful performance. He used his band like an instrument; he revolutionized it, but nobody can follow that, because nobody knows what he did. You see these Ellington experts going round here getting and trying to get. They don't know what they're doing because nobody knows. It's the guys who played it that portrayed Duke's music. They have to go back in the grave and dig up Bubber Miley and Johnny Hodges, Harry Carney. You've got to have those three in order to get it together. Oooooo! That's the history of our music. When the king is dead, long live the king, he'll be there.

Very funny. I didn't play any solos in Duke's band until one guy, I don't remember who, missed the show, and somebody had to play his solo. And then Duke pointed to me; and he pointed to me again, again, again, and again. I kept playing. I don't know how many choruses. He just kept pointing at me, saying, "Another one . . ." Until I just sat down.

Around that same time, I wrote "Woody 'n You." The tune just popped out on a record date I had with Coleman Hawkins. Coleman Hawkins picked up some guys, most of whom worked at Monroe's or somewhere around New York, for this record date: Max Roach, Victor Coulson, Don Byas, Budd Johnson, Leo Parker, Oscar Pettiford, Ray Abrams, Clyde Hart, Leonard Lowry, Ed Vandever, Coleman, and I. On this Coke break, I started fooling around with the piano. I had been playing the progressions a long time, and I said, "I'll make a tune outta this, right now." Bam! The melody turned out great, and after hearing the melody, I found it easy to write down a counter-melody.

The song came right from the chords, and I named it "Woody 'n You" after Woody Herman because he liked my writing so much.

"Woody 'n You" came from a minor-sixth chord to the dominant seventh. That's one influence of Monk. B-flat-minor sixth with a sixth as the bass to C. A-flat-minor sixth with the sixth the bass to B-flat. It's a natural progression in fourths. From G to C is one fourth. You jump down to F which is a fifth from C to another fourth and then jump down a fifth to another fourth, and then the tonic, which is D-flat. And that's the key you're in.

Looking at the notes in my right hand, I discovered a counter-melody. There were two melodies in it—a melody, and a counter-melody. That's how I wrote "Woody 'n You." I didn't try to express anything particular, just music, just what the chords inspired; and it turned out so well, we recorded it that same day, February 16, 1944. (Apollo 751.)

The front-office fellows still hadn't made up their minds about what to do about launching Mr. X-tine's new career. But I recorded again, April 13, 1944. With Billy Eckstine and some of the guys who would soon become members of his band. We only recorded three sides, among them an arrangement of "Good Jelly Blues" that I'd written for Billy.

That arrangement on "Good Jelly Blues" (Deluxe 2000, 3000) is one of my best and was the first "double up" arrangement. In our style with all the riffs, we played very few riffs slowly. Very few phrases weren't "doubled up," double the time of the music, except for whole-note phrases. So on "Good Jelly Blues," when we were playing behind a vocalist, Billy Eckstine, the saxophones would hold the harmony behind him. It was nice, and we had some good players on that session: Al Killian, Shorty McConnell, Freddie Webster, and me, trumpets; Budd Johnson and Jimmy Powell, altos; Wardell Gray and Thomas Crump, tenors; Rudy Rutherford, baritone; Clyde Hart, piano; Connie · Wainwright, guitar; Oscar Pettiford, bass; and Shadow Wilson, drums; and Billy Eckstine.

That spring, at the Aquarium on Fifty-second Street, I worked with John Kirby in a sextet. John, a bass player, had George Johnson on alto, Ben Webster on tenor, Billy Kyle on piano, Bill Beason on drums, and I played trumpet. Someone recorded us live over the radio on May 23, 1944, when we played some numbers in the new style, but the gig with John involved playing mostly traditional jazz standards. I still hadn't found what I was looking for, a place downtown, on "the Street" where I could play strictly modern. Jamming at Minton's and

Monroe's we had our fun, but with the level of music which we'd developed by 1944, it wasn't very profitable, artistically or commercially. We needed to play to a wider audience and Fifty-second Street seemed ready to pay to hear someone playing something new.

PETE MIGDOL (critic):

"Around 1939 or 1940, we were both the same age and he was in uptown clubs, the Savoy and most others, with Teddy Hill. And at that time, I was with *Metronome*. And I covered Harlem for *Metronome*. And being seen up there a number of times, Dizzy and I somehow met and we clicked together and we became very friendly.

"The sounds that were being brought out in those years were all fresh new sounds. I knew the people that were involved with the publishing of *Metronome*, and I asked if they'd like to have Harlem covered. *Metronome*, which was a national magazine, had every area of music supposedly covered except where there was probably ten times as much music as any other area, any place. They grabbed at the idea, and I started to cover Harlem for *Metronome*. And that's how I met with Diz.

"Diz turned to bop, if my memory serves me right, around 1940 or 1941. Yeah, it's early, early. He worked with the Benny Carter group at Kelly's Stables. After that, he made such an explosion on the Street. Later, he was able to get his own combination working on the Street, and that was his start.

"The music with which Diz evolved, a lot of people think was an overnight affair. It wasn't. It took about three years before the Street itself, which was the hippest block with regard to its short distance and that amount of music, dug what was happening. . . . The Street was a very, very exciting thing. There's nothing around today that you can even . . . you can't put nothing back together like it was. It was a Street of stars. It'll blow your mind walking in from one club, into another club, and each one had a star of greater magnitude than the one prior. This was the top talent street, and it was, of course, discoverer of a lot of the new people for that era.

"I would be lying if I said I came right on with the new style, because they were playing sounds that lots of ears weren't prepared for. I was honestly listening to it very, very often. I heard it in Minton's on a half a dozen occasions. I think it broke out on the Street. That's when it had to be proved. Minton's was basically, you could say for all intents and purposes, let's-see-what-comes-out. It had to be proved on

Fifty-second Street. And I waited until it got to that. It did take me six to eight months to really fall in with the sounds that were coming out, because they were that new.

"Dizzy's the one that about turned the music industry around. Some of his Latin beats. His writing, I love his writing. At one time it would've been a toss up, except that his ability shone through so strong on the trumpet. There was a toss up that he wouldn't stay as a writer. . . ."

Finally, Billy Shaw, the booking agent, decided that Billy Eckstine should definitely have a band. First he put him on Fifty-second Street as a single, and then he put out feelers for deposits from agents in other cities, and with the money from the deposits, he built a band. At that time, you didn't have to pay musicians for rehearsals. Bands, now, are full of shit, you have to pay to rehearse; but, then, they used to rehearse because practice made perfect. After rehearsals, we had some new music. Our breathing and phrasing were different from all the other bands, and, naturally, we sounded very different. There was no band that sounded like Billy Eckstine's. Our attack was strong, and we were playing bebop, the modern style. No other band like this one existed in the world. That was the strangest band.

I was playing with Billy Eckstine, and a cat took me in the basement one time in St. Louis, at the Plantation Club, and says, "I want you to turn on the light, now. When I give you the sign, turn on the light." He say, "O.K., turn it on!" He took out his gun, and a big rat ran across the basement. "Pow!" He shot that rat dead.

The Plantation Club in St. Louis was a white club. They fired Billy Eckstine's band because we came in through the front door, and they wanted us to come through the back. We just walked right in with our horns, in front. And the gangsters—St. Louis was a stronghold of gangsterism—said, "Them guys got to go." So we changed jobs with George Hudson. He came over and played for them. Clark Terry was with that band. We went over to work at another place.

Then during wartime, we were on the train going to play a gig, and we were riding in the "colored" part of the train. This Uncle Tom porter was reporting what we were doing back to the white conductor.

"We got some smart 'uns dis time, suh! Got some smart 'uns on heah. . . ."

We were gonna throw him off the train. We saw him back there with his mop, listening; and somebody in the bathroom saw him talking to the man and pointing back at us. We were waiting for him to come back to our compartments so we could throw him off. That train was going ninety miles an hour. The guys in that band didn't dig no rats.

My main problem in that band was getting those guys to make time, especially Yard, and he wielded such a great influence over the others. Yard had a problem, a timeliness problem. Once, with Earl Hines, he decided to sleep under the stage so he could be there the next day. He slept right through the first show. Up under the stage. Everybody was looking for him, and he was asleep up under there. Another time, the whole saxophone section didn't make a job in Louisiana. Just the brass and the rhythm section showed up. Leo Parker, Charlie Parker, Junior Williams, Gene Ammons, Dexter Gordon, none of them showed up.

Sarah Vaughan acted just like one of the boys. She put herself in that position, one of the boys, just another musician, and she was as good a musician as anybody in the band. She could play the piano, knew all the chords, and played terrific chords behind us. I remember Ella never acted like one of the boys; she always played the role of a lady. But you could say anything you wanted to in front of "Sailor," uh, I mean, Sarah. She'd use the same language I used with the guys.

A lotta shit happened to us in St. Louis. One time there, in the Club Riviera, Billy punched a guy down the stairs, and this guy had a pistol and everything. All of us had pistols, too, so it didn't make any difference. Everybody in that band had a pistol. If you went down South, you'd better have one and a lot of ammunition. We were musicians first, though, and fun-loving peaceable men. But don't start no shit. Gangsters—did I ever run into some gangsters in my career!

BILLY ECKSTINE:

"Dizzy was with me for about seven months. He was the first musical director I had with my band. He's the one who gave me the idea of getting a band in the first place.

"It was a new sound. Well, not a new sound, I shouldn't say that. But it was a new feeling, better than that, and then new usages of chords that Diz worked out. Then with Bird in there, they had some things that were going together. You could sing countermelodics. You see, everybody in my band, including the vocalists, was working on that same kick. Sarah Vaughan was my girl vocalist, and we worked on the same type of things. Of course, we got rapped a lot about it, in those days. They said that we were singing . . . some dummies would say we didn't even know where the melody was. But we were singing improvisations around the melody, which they couldn't hear at that time. That was the reason why my band wasn't successful, because it was a little too advanced for the people at that time.

"During those days, there were battles of jazz, and we played the Brooklyn Armory in a 'battle of music' against Jimmie Lunceford. At that time, nobody gave us any notice. We were the redheaded stepchild of the orchestra world. But, man, we lit into them. It was all over, once people who had any knowledge of music would listen to that band. I can truthfully say it now without any type of conceit; there was no band that ever swung like that band I had. We used to get on one-nighters sometimes, boy, and it was unreal how that band sounded. But we never got anywhere because they couldn't hear it, and they wouldn't let me through with it. But, hell, I knew what we had! And everybody else in the band knew what we had.

"We didn't have it easy; our type of music was more or less a concert style of jazz. People would start to dance, and then they'd turn around and listen. Sometimes our tempos were almost not danceable either. Diz made an arrangement of 'Max Is Makin' Wax,' which was way up there, featuring him and Bird. You couldn't dance to that at all, but people would stand there and watch. But I think that one of the main things is that it was at the end of the war, and during the war, and people weren't ready at that particular time for a concert style of jazz.

"We never had any problem with the young musicians; they loved it; they loved the band. Everywhere we'd go there was a following of young musicians. But the populace, in general, and the powers that be, that booked the bands, and the clubs were used to listening to a certain type of music. They were not thrilled by us coming in; young, wild, crazy young cats playing this style. I remember one place we worked the man wanted to give me some money to go downtown and buy some stock arrangements.

"'Man, I've got money to go downtown and buy some stocks, if I wanna buy some stock arrangements,' I said. 'I don't want no stock!' All those kinds of things happened. We ran across all that, but the youngsters always dug the band.

"No, I don't think Diz influenced me as a singer. But Diz did influence me. I guess he and a lotta the other guys did, Bird and everybody else. It was a trading-off point, musically, which helped my singing. Not as far as the style was concerned, but it helped it musically. I think to everybody concerned, it was a school we were in. You could hear things, and when you'd hear certain chord progressions, you automatically heard another countermelody to sing along against it with the same type of feeling, as of togetherness.

"Man, I'd be out on the stage singing, and I used to notice people laughing, or something like that. And then I'd turn around and look back at Diz, and he's just looking straight ahead. Well, all the time that I'm singing, he's doing pantomime to the audience—pointing at me saying that my teeth are false. And he's pointing, saying that I'm a faggot, and that I go with him and all. And when I turn around and look, he's just looking straight up in the air. He used to do all of this stuff with me, and we had a million laughs. Diz is my baby, I love him.

"Dizzy's contribution to modern music is so vast. There is really no description of what Diz has contributed. Diz is a master at what he does, and I mean a *master*. You can stop him at any time while he's playing, and say, 'What was that?' And he'll tell you all about it. It's not that he's out here winging. He knows what he's doing, he's done his homework. You could go on for days about what Diz has contributed to his music; his style of playing; his style of improvisation; his usages of chords; his style of arranging. He's contributed so much.

"Oh, man, he changed the trumpet all the way around, completely around. He made it an instrument that's unlike playing just the things that the books tell you about in order to be very fluid. Diz has done things with the horn that nobody's done before. The speed of his instrument, the clarity of the instrument. He has been the backbone of practically every young musician that comes along now, playing his instrument. You go through Miles. I remember when Miles used to follow us around in St. Louis. And Miles, you couldn't even hear him past the reed section. That's before he even left home. Well, Diz was such an influence on him; on Freddie Hubbard. Everybody you name today, practically, Diz was the influence on him as a trumpet player. Regardless of how, maybe, they wanna stick their chests out at some little bit of affluence they've had; if they go back to their roots, Diz is there with them. Diz is the one who put them there, and sooner or later, they play something of Dizzy's and don't know they're playing it.

"Diz and Bird were the biggest and most important contributors to modern jazz. And in the vocal field would be Sarah Vaughan. And on bass, the style of bass that's being played today, its egg was Jimmy Blanton or Oscar Pettiford. And my baby was Art Tatum. You can see a lot of Art in Oscar Peterson, which is only right. Somebody's always being inspired. But you take it and you go from there. You don't constantly live off of somebody else. Monk is another great mind. He brought in a style and the way he comped, his rhythming things. And Bud Powell, of course, brought the sound of the new music through his right hand. Bud was a great innovator of his end of it, on the piano end of it. But see, when you look at those things, regardless of what instrument it was, the style and the improvisations came from either Bird or Diz.

"I don't think that either Bird or Diz was more important than the other. I think it was both of them together. I think it was a thing that came together for a happy meeting of minds, and I really believe they learned from each other."

WALTER GILBERT FULLER:

"Jimmie Lunceford was on one side of the stand, the bandstand was in the middle of the Brooklyn Armory, and Billy Eckstine was on the other. And that was the night I knew that the whole thing had turned around. Because Lunceford was the boss, say, from 1936 to roughly 1944. Every time Lunceford would play, that sucker would sound bad. And after a while the people would be around Eckstine's side of the stand when Lunceford was playing. When Billy Eckstine's band was playing, everybody ran around to that side. And you could see the whole crowd moving, shifting around. After a while the shift stopped. The people stopped going back around to Lunceford's side and stayed on this side with Billy Eckstine. Diz was *the* musical director, right then and there. So that's the first time that I got the inkling that the real change had taken place. . . . That was the first night that we knew. Jimmie Lunceford wasn't doing anything."

SARAH VAUGHAN:

"I don't think the band was any experiment; it wasn't no experiment; they were just playing music that they knew. They weren't experimenting on anything. If it didn't work, it just didn't work. But it worked. They were getting out there and playing what they knew to play.

"We tried to educate the people. We used to play dances, and there were just a very few who understood who would be in a corner, jitterbugging forever, while the rest just stood staring at us. But we didn't care, we didn't care. Maybe, we just knocked each other out. Yeah, we had lots of fun.

"It was a very rough band. They kept me in order. I'm telling you they used to beat me to death if I got out of line. I mean, literally, kicked my what's-its-name. Oh, my Lord, my arm used to be so sore. But I would never do that again, whatever that was.

"We were just trying to play some music for the people, that we knew was together. We were trying to educate them. And it took a while! Jazz might not do as good as it's supposed to do, but it's still here. And it's going to be here, you know. We didn't care whether anybody really, actually, enjoyed it or not. We *were*, you know.

"Dizzy's main contribution to music? Good harmony. But nobody can play as fast as him, and it means something. I've heard a lot of people run up and down all over their horns, but they say nothing. But Dizzy and Charlie, all those guys used to do that, and they were really saying something. Chord changes and harmonies, stuff like that. It looks like they invented harmony, to me. But you know it was going on long before, but not as much.

"You had to sing within whatever the chords were they were playing. You had to know a little about music or have a hell of a good ear to stand before that band. I loved it, loved it! I could do it over again.

"The things that we used to do on the road! One time we were on a train, we were coming from down South. You know that train was split, colored and white, segregated. One white fella was sitting by the train door eating chicken, and he threw the chicken bones back in our part. So we had some friends of Billy's who came from Washington that used to just travel around with us, just for the hell of it. Very tough hustlers from Washington. They didn't say nothing, didn't bother him until we got in. We pulled into Washington, and that's when it all started. I really don't think that man will ever throw no chicken bones back in anybody's . . . That's just one of the little things. And another time, we were in Wilmington, and after the dance, we went to the station to wait for the train. There was a young white guy back there shining shoes, so 'B' went to get a shoe shine. He said he didn't shine no nigger's shoes.

"So 'B' walked back there and said, 'Hey, guys, young kid back there said he don't shine no nigger's shoes.'

"So everybody said, 'Oh, damn, that sure is a shame,' started stretching, and walked off to get their shoes shined. We left town by foot. Everybody spread out and said, 'I'll see you at the next gig.' Well, he shouldn't have said that.

"Dizzy's funny when he sings. He makes me laugh, but I love it. I love when he sings, and Dizzy's a good arranger, he's a great arranger. Dizzy's what a good musician's supposed to be. There's nothing Dizzy does that I don't like—music, singing, playing, or humming. Because when he sings and he hums, it's funny. And he plays serious. And he can be funny playing sometimes if he wants to be. He's just excellent. I wish I could sing like he plays, but that's impossible. If I could do that . . ."

ART BLAKEY (drums):

"I met Dizzy through his music. I had listened to him on records
with Cab Calloway and different bands he played with during those
days. I heard him then, and that's how I got acquainted with him.
And then I met him in person, in 1944, and we worked together with
Billy Eckstine.

"I didn't know what to think of the new style of music when I first
heard it. Things were moving so fast, I didn't have a chance to think.
All we could do was play. All we thought we were doing was playing.

"When I first joined the band, he was the musical director. He
wasn't the straw boss, he was the boss. It was Billy's band, but he'd
stand up in front and sing. Dizzy was the master of all the music. I
came in the band, and I was doing some funny stuff on the drums, trying to play shuffle rhythms, I thought. And he stopped me right in the
middle of it. The band was still playing and people were still on the
floor dancing.

"'Blakey, what are you doing?' he said.

"'I don't know,' I said.

"'Then why do you do it? If we had wanted a shuffle here, we'd
hire Cozy Cole. We want you to play your drums the way *you* play
them.' That's the kinda man he is. A beautiful man. It was very funny
to me.

"Dizzy, Monk and Bird, Bud, that's it. Coleman Hawkins, Don
Byas, that's it. Those are the guys who brought it out. Lester Young,
all them cats contributed. But Dizzy was there, he was one of the
leaders. And it was a beautiful thing. Nobody cared who was leading
what. They just got together and played. And they passed around
their knowledge, what they had, to the rest of us. And they were
beautiful people, and Dizzy's still doing it. And he's one of the world's
greatest—not just trumpet players—he's one of the world's greatest musicians. Plus one of the world's greatest personalities. Plus, he's a guy I
love. I really love him because he's responsible for me in a large way.
In any sense, especially musically.

"Dizzy and Bird? All people are different, like fingerprints. They all
came in, and they put it together, and they played very well together.
And it turned out to be like a school. And they were both very young
men, and they became legends within their own time. And they
turned the tide of music around. And these guys were the leaders.
Now, they didn't do it by themselves. Others were with them. But
they were in the forefront of it. They were in the forefront of all this
stuff that was going on, and they did it. I think they were wonderful,
Monk and Bird and Dizzy and all of them. And there was another

I started singing with the Ravens.

Riffs with Dinah Washington.

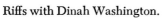

My band in 1947, (l to r) Milt Jackson, piano; Howard Johnson and John Brown, altos; Chano Pozo, conga; James Moody, tenor; and Cecil Payne, baritone. The others . . . ?

With Nelson Boyd, bass; and Joe Gayles, tenor; from the band of 1947.

he great Chano Pozo with the band of
948, at the El Cino Club, Detroit.

Beboppin' with scat singer Joe
Carroll. FRANK DRIGGS COLLECTION.

Aboard the S.S. *Drottningholm*, en route to Europe in
1948, (l to r) John Brown, alto; Milt Shaw, manager;
Lorraine, and Pancho Hagood, vocalist.

My band of 1949, (l to r) Jimmy Forman, piano; Joe Gayles, tenor; Ernie Henry, alto; Al McKibbon, bass; John Brown, alto; Cecil Payne, baritone; Teddy Stewart, drums; Johnny Hartman, vocalist; Sabu, conga. I'm directing. The trumpets are Dave Burns, Willie Cook, and Elmon Wright. Trombones, Jesse Tarrant, Sam Hurt, and Andy Duryea.

A whole show . . . at the Strand Theater, featuring my band and (l to r, in foreground) the Berry Brothers, dancers; John Mason, the "fall guy" in blackface; Maxine Sullivan, with Joe Carroll and me at center stage, and the Deep River Boys, quartet.

Bebop really hit Broadway in 1948!

Grabbed by "Rubberlegs" Williams behind the Apollo Theater while Wesley looks on grinning.

The band I had by the end of the 1940s was the greatest, musically. But I had to break it up. . . .

great, great musician who has passed, Oscar Pettiford. Bud Powell, all these guys had a hand in it, but the forerunners were Dizzy Gillespie and Charlie Parker."

BOB REDCROSS:

"Diz always impressed me . . . Diz always impressed me as *not* being 'dizzy,' if that means anything. Because as soon as you say dizzy, you get the impression somebody's being kinda flighty and not altogether, mentally. But man, it was as far from that as—anything in the world. I mean much deeper. And when you began to see where he was coming from, he's much deeper than anybody, even his contemporaries. Because there was a lotta guys at the time, young fellas, and all of them were on a giddy type of kick. Light, like a whole lotta horseplay, or a lotta playing around, just in general. Most of the guys were in their twenties, some of them were even younger than that. And nobody seemed to be very serious, because if a person would be serious, they would stand out like a sore thumb. Diz has a way of popping his eyes, looking at you, double-taking, you know. Like he's in a trance and coming out of it. And a lotta people look at him like this is some kinda strange cat, but the man would be preoccupied in thought, I found out. And another thing I found out about is his power of concentration on something. I mean, if something struck him as being intriguing or fascinated him, it would stay right in his mind.

"I remember one time we were playing a show, I don't remember where it was now, but there was some girl singer. I think it might've been in St. Louis. This girl had some pretty songs, I mean, that were standards. She had some pretty passages and what not. And there was one song that she sang and she would come to an interlude. Between that and the next passage, there was an interlude, and the interlude, it seemed to Diz, always needed to be filled. We didn't play too many shows with that band; but it had to be somewhere we were playing a show with a singer who was already on the bill, because what the hell would Billy need with a girl singer and he's already got one. Anyway, in this interlude, Dizzy just felt like he had to play something, and it was pretty. But what it did, it distracted this broad.

"After the first show, the girl said, 'Listen, would you tell your trumpet player to stay outta that thing right there.'

"So, 'B' pulled Diz aside and said, 'Lay out, Diz.' Man, the whole damn week, Diz was in that thing, and he couldn't get out of it. And I was watching. He'd take and put his horn down; he'd take his horn and put it sideways, and turn it down, put it down below everything, and he'd still be playing that passage, whatever it was. He heard something; you could say that would be Dizzy.

"You couldn't hear him. I could hear him because I would listen for him, and some of the guys in the band would hear him too. It was pretty and something he wanted to play.

"And the other thing I remember emphatically about him. I personally believe he was responsible for some of the development of Art Blakey. Because I've watched Diz. See, I was always a trumpet player's man, trumpet players and singers. Roy was my buddy since when he first came to Chicago with Fletcher Henderson's band. I always liked trumpets. I remember watching Diz, and I saw the same thing with Diz I used to see with Roy. Roy used to fool with Harold West, God bless him. He used to emphasize certain beats with West, like make him try to get in on certain beats. And I used to watch Diz. Diz would get up outta his chair and go put his head right in Blakey's bass drum and stand right down in front of him and be going, 'Ooo-bop-she-dow-ooo-bop-bop,' hollering out licks for him and accents for him to play.

"Diz did a lot of writing for the band and was musical director, and then you had Gail Brockman, a boy from my hometown. Gail used to do a lotta writing, and so, naturally, he'd conduct some of the things. And you had Jerry Valentine, the piano player, who was also a trombone player. He also did some directing. Then you had Budd Johnson, who was quite a straw boss in the band. I mean it vacillated between them; it was pretty loose; it was flexible. I mean everybody got along. You had some guys in there who couldn't play nothing for listening to what was happening around them. I mean, they were scared to death. Man, I've seen that reed section completely stop, and there was nobody playing but Bird. They'd be playing passages and Bird would run into something that'd scare everybody to death. And the same thing would happen with Diz. Diz would be playing, man, and the brass section would damn near quit. What was that shit?

"Diz and Bird were almost like feed to each other. They would feed each other. They would feed each other ideas. I'd hear Diz run across an idea, maybe they were playing solos, running across a passage, and you'd hear Bird maybe later on come up with another treatment of that same passage, taking it somewhere else where it would fit. They really were a complement to each other. They fed each other ideas. They both respected each other.

"Diz had a personality that was natural. He wasn't as wild as most of the musicians of that era were. He wasn't that wild, I mean, in his private life. I mean, see, everybody knows Bird was very far out, you know. Very far out in his personal habits and things. And this, Diz has never engaged in. He never indulged in none of those type of things. I used to watch some of the young ofay guys who were very much influenced by both of them, particularly those guys who were in

Woody's band, you know. And they were running around all gog-eyed with bulging eyes just looking at them like they were God and everything. And they thought that they had to do things that they did. And a lot of them were doing things that they thought Diz was doing, and Diz wasn't doing none of it. I mean, like Red Rodney, the little ofay trumpet player who was with Woody Herman before he went with Bird. That whole group, they always thought these guys were real far out. Well, Bird was far out. And Bird used to put them on. Bird would put them guys on. He would lead them into doing a lotta bs'ing and what not and laugh at them. But Diz didn't go in for a lotta the things that were considered the 'in' thing to do.

"He was always deep. Diz was always deep. I remember when he was one of the first ones to delve into Masonry. He read a lot. Well, that's where they were similar. Bird was a deep person as far as mind was concerned too. Man, he could converse on any level about anything, and I mean with in-depth study. And you say, 'I wonder where the hell he got time to read, or to know about this?' Because you couldn't figure where he would get the chance to know. When would he have the time? They were dissimilar as far as I can see. Musically, they were similar, because musically, they were very innovative. Personally, I'll put it like this. When the gig was over, and there was nowhere else to go to play anything, Diz would retire to go home. And Bird would be looking for somewhere to indulge himself in a mind battle or something, some kinda mind-entanglement things. Where he could do something to his head. That wasn't Dizzy's stick.

"I'd say there was more than respect between them. There was a great deal of love there too.

"Another thing about Diz, and it all fits right in. Diz was never envious. Like, he could see someone who had limitations, somebody else would say, 'Man, that cat can't play!' 'No, man, don't say that because he's got some beautiful ideas,' Diz would say. Somebody'd make a blanket statement, say a cat couldn't blast, or couldn't play out with a lot of fortissimo. But it's obvious. Diz could appreciate that. He would show you where, in that, you were wrong too. I remember a little guy that used to be in the band that loved Diz, and Diz loved him too. Remember little Benny Harris? Benny's little chops was nowhere near, he didn't have nearly the flow nor the power that John had. But, man, Benny could say a lot in his register. Diz would stand and look, with awe on his face, and smile, encourage him. This is the way he is now. He can see something in things that a lotta people would go right over the surface of and not even look in depth to see the real values. That's another thing that they had in common, Bird was the same way. If you were sincere in doing what you did and did it to the best of your ability and said something, he would recognize it and encourage it. Ain't no put down. Wouldn't be no put down at all.

"Up in Boston, I think, Diz draped his horn around somebody's neck. That band used to have fights all the time. Man, we'd fight the people and the bosses and everything because when they started playing, man, that was the first band that ever played that people couldn't dance to. We opened at a place in St. Louis, and the man, after the first set, came and said, 'Look, you all play "Stardust?"'

"B says, 'Yeah. . . .' So B played it, but they played it in the way that *they* played it.

"The man came back and said, 'That ain't what I'm talking about. Play some pieces with that beat.'

"B says, 'Look, this is the way we play.'

"The cat say, 'Well, I don't like your music.'

"B says, 'We don't like your joint.' So they packed up and left. And it was the same way in a lotta different places because people hadn't been used to that. See, people were used to patting their feet and dancing. This was new, and it was like they were going around educating people. In some of the places, the younger people were so amazed at the virtuosity of the instrumentalists. And they were showcased with these new types of arrangements. A lotta younger people were more flexible. Man, they were awed. They would stand there and just go crazy. But nobody was dancing.

"Once I had to leave them down in St. Louis. They fought for two hours down there. The East St. Louis cabdrivers gave their annual ball, and the St. Louis cabdrivers came to break it up. We didn't know that, but that was the way they used to have it. They had an annual ball and an annual fight at the same time. They shot into the drums, and all. This was like mayhem. This was their custom. Then you had the places where you couldn't play the blues after twelve o'clock at night because that was the signal to start fighting and a free-for-all. All of the things I can think about are things that happened with the guys together. I mean, like on the bus or in a hotel or something. And some of the things you can't talk about.

"Diz was definitely the nucleus of the powerhouse in the band. But you also had a first-trumpet player, and a second-trumpet player in that powerhouse. And you had a little guy in there by the name of Shorty McConnell, who, I understood, couldn't read his name if it was written, as far as notes went, but he was a powerhouse. It was a powerhouse brass section.

"John had the real professionalism, that would put the cohesiveness to that thing. They were lucky enough after John left to replace him with 'Fat Girl' (Fats Navarro). It took somebody like that to keep it from being a hole that would be too damn big. Gail Brockman was a good trumpet player, but John, man, was just the powerhouse, and he gave it the touch of perfection that was class.

"Dizzy would teach guys. He would take a guy, like, say, Benny Harris. You know Benny was his boy. But now he had another little guy that came in the band in-between. Diz would take him aside too. Not only would he take him, but, you see, you had a lotta boys in that band who had just come outta high school. Gene Ammons had just come outta high school. Now, John would take them and say, 'Hey, man, that note goes like this,' and would play it for him. He was a teacher. Because whenever he got his, he got it, and I imagine it came from the company he was in earlier when he first started in the bands, here in New York.

"One of the most memorable things I ever heard in my life was the night that they played in Gary, Indiana. God Almighty! Man, I ain't never heard nothing like that. Everybody was on. Blakey was on; John was on; Bird was on; Budd was on; everybody. Man, they upset this place. They had people screaming and hollering. There wasn't no thing about nobody was gonna try to dance. These people were hollering and screaming like maniacs. And the band was up.

"And, incidentally, that band was never recorded. It was never recorded like it was. There were never any good recordings on that band, never. I mean, commercially; the band was never recorded well. And I never got a chance to record the band, myself, just the cats that came by—a bass player, drummer, and guitar player and four or five horns. That band never recorded well, and it never got a chance to record because of the damn studios and the technicians at National. They were from hunger.

"There was a recording ban on, and we slipped two or three different times. I know we went into a building on Fifty-seventh Street and Broadway, and there was an elevator strike. And they had to walk up eighteen flights and down eighteen flights, carrying their instruments and all, just to make this damn date. I don't know what the hell it was, technicians, or what. The band just never did come off well on records. Like all the things that Tadd Dameron wrote, and things that Dizzy wrote, they didn't record well. They didn't sound like that band. That band was tremendous, man.

"That night in Gary, they played everything that they had in the book. When B first got his band together, I think Basie gave him some arrangements. One of the arrangements I think Basie gave him was 'Air Mail Special,' and that was the same thing that the two tenors, Dexter Gordon and Gene Ammons, hooked up on. And you had several things that Tadd had written. Then you had some things that John had brought into the band. Budd Johnson had written a lotta stuff. Then they were heading some things too. But the guys, I mean, they knew what they had in that band, but the people didn't know. The public didn't know what they had. This band was way ahead of its time.

"We opened at the Downtown Theater in Chicago, and one guy at that time was a mainliner. See, all them cats that were trying to do that, they couldn't do it, like Bird. Bird would do what he was doing and stand right up, play his solos, sit down and go to sleep. And you touch him, and he's playing, come right in where he was supposed to be. Other guys? Man, they were playing 'Air Mail Special,' the intro. It was the opening tune. So after they got through the intro, the first horn to come out is supposed to be this mainliner cat. He gets up and walks right to the footlights, and takes his horn and puts it to his mouth, and upped his head back to blow, and instead of blowing, put his horn right down and puked right into the front row. It was all we could do to keep B from "shooting" him. B was angry and was gonna punch him out when he came off. B got off the stand and was waiting for him to come off. He went right up to the footlights and puked. That was his way of saying hello to the people."

BUDD JOHNSON (tenor saxophone, arranger):

"Billy Eckstine and I are very, very good friends. I was responsible for getting Billy Eckstine in Earl Hines's band, and I used to write all his music for him. After I left Earl, Billy stayed on for a while, then he decided to go for himself. And he always told me, 'Well, Budd we are gonna be partners whenever I get a band. You can write all of the music and everything, and you'll have 20 per cent of the band.'

"I say, 'O.K., that's good, that sounds great to me, whichever is greater, the money or the 20 per cent. No less than 20 per cent of the take.'

"We went up to Billy Shaw with that idea, at the William Morris office, and they cut me right out. No way was I gonna get 20 per cent. In the meantime, Billy hired Dizzy as musical director. I dunno what kinda deal, flat salary, or what. So Dizzy went out with the band. Well, this band went on; they're becoming good. I was still doing some writing for the band. When they would come into New York to record, I would make some arrangements. And the reed section, most of the reed section were junkies, and they were messing up, missing trains and what not. Finally, Billy Shaw called me up to the William Morris office.

"He said, 'Budd, I want you to go out and take over the band, because Dizzy is leaving and maybe you can whip these cats into shape and keep them from missing planes. People wanna dock us and sue us and everything because the full band is not there.'

"'I'll have to have at least $300 a week,' I said, 'whether I work or not.' O.K., the salary was agreed upon. Bam! I probably could have gotten more. Anyway, that was pretty good money at that time; this was 1944. So I got the job and I went out as musical director. And this is when Dizzy left the band to go on and do his own thing. I stayed with the band close to a year."

Recently, after becoming an adult musician, after forty years, you realize that your music reflects the times in which you live. My music emerged from the war years, the Second World War, and it reflected those times in the music. Fast and furious, with the chord changes going this way and that way, it might've looked and sounded like bedlam, but it really wasn't. Because we always kept in mind the fundamentals of the music, like, in the cycle of fifths, C, F, B-flat, E-flat, A-flat, D-flat, et cetera, we went through a cycle, and all of my music is built on those. Sometimes, when you know the laws, then you can break them. But you've got to know it first. And it's the same way with all the laws of living, break them flagrantly, and you might hurt yourself, or someone else, or even blow your own mind.

The Onyx

        Leaving Billy Eckstine in 1944, I recommended Fats Navarro for the job, and he proved to be an ample replacement for me in the trumpet section. I took a job with Oscar Pettiford. We became co-leaders of a group at the Onyx Club on Fifty-second Street. Of course the ideal group was always Charlie Parker and me, but the first group with Oscar Pettiford was magnificent, and that was the thing that put us on the map. The opening at the Onyx Club represented the birth of the bebop era. In our long sojourn on Fifty-second Street we spread our message to a much wider audience.

    Oscar and I decided to get Charlie Parker. We sent him a telegram in Kansas City, because he'd gone back home for a while. Didn't hear nothing for months, so the initial group consisted of Max Roach (drums), Oscar Pettiford (bass), George Wallington (piano), and me. We really wanted Charlie Parker, and we sent him a telegram, but he didn't get it. Yard said later that he hadn't received the telegram, because I know he would've come with Max Roach and George Wallington in the group. For a short while, we had just a quartet, but in the meantime they hired Don Byas as a tenor-saxophone soloist in the Onyx. We were cooking so much that Don Byas, who was supposed to play with the Al Casey trio opposite us, said, "Unh, unh," and he came to our rehearsals and joined our group.

    I had an argument with Don, once. He'd occasionally get drunk. He

couldn't play shit when he got drunk, but, man, when he was sober!
So I'm sitting and looking at him. He was playing a solo and slobbering all over his horn. I kept looking and going tsk-tsk-tsk. He says,
"What the fuck you lookin' at?" Same words! I said, "I'm just looking
at you." He says, "Wha's wrong?" And I said, "You ain't playin' shit."
He says, "Well, you're not doin' so hot yourself." I said, "Well I'm
doin' the *best* I can; I'm sober." He says, "Fuck you!" I said, "Fuck
you." He says, "Mother-fuck you." And I told him, "Don, if you think
for a minute that I won't take advantage of you while you're drunk,
you've got another think comin'. You're drunk and if you get up and
act like you wanna do somethin', I'm gonna smash you! I'm gonna
take advantage of you—you're drunk, you can't do anything. You can't
fight!" So he started to cool down. That was really a beautiful group.

Sy Barron, the owner of the Onyx, asked us to get a group together
because Oscar had won the Gold Award, and I had won the New Star
Award in the *Esquire* Magazine Jazz Poll—1944. Everybody down
there at the Onyx was an award winner that year. Billie Holiday had
won the Gold Award, and the Al Casey Trio had won an award, so
the Onyx had three, really four, award winners. They didn't even include my name on the bill, because as "new star" mine was the least
award. It was my band, together with Oscar, and we were playing in
the modern style which I had heavily contributed to since the
founding.

Maybe I should've been satisfied. We had finally come through to
an age of concerts. Our music had developed more into a type of
music for listeners. Whenever we played in a club, they had a stage
set aside with all the tables there. People sat at the tables, with no
dance floor. They had another area where you didn't have to buy
drinks. You could sit there and listen to the music. So it became a listener's groove, instead of just grooving with the dancing. I always
liked dancing, but you can have a good time without dancing. Dancing won't make you cry, and crying is a strong emotion. Somebody
plays or something, and you say, "Man, I cried. I sat there and cried."
Sometimes you can listen to a groove so strong that it'll throw your
back outta whack.

Billie Holiday worked opposite us, and Al Casey used to play for
her. Billie Holiday had a great following amongst the film industry. I
guess that's because of the type of woman she was, very warm. Billie
Holiday was one of the warmest people I've ever seen. There was an
incident every hour. Every hour, there was some kind of an incident.
Somebody'd get drunk; women and men drooling over Billie Holiday
—all kinds of shit—with the movie stars and things. I played behind
Billie Holiday several times, sitting in, but we never recorded together.

I remember Leonard Feather always came by the Onyx. "Hey, why don't you write something about Dizzy sometimes, man?" Oscar told Leonard.

"Huh . . . ?" he said.

"Yeah," Oscar said. "Write something about him; that guy's something else, you know." Oscar Pettiford used to make him feel embarrassed. Leonard Feather wrote mostly about the older guys, Coleman Hawkins, Teddy Wilson, and Benny Goodman. He wasn't really hip to us and what we were doing musically.

LEONARD FEATHER (jazz critic, promoter):

"I was producing a record date with Helen Humes, and it was a blues date. Pete Brown was the featured instrumentalist, an alto saxophonist, and I took Jimmy Hamilton, the clarinetist with Benny Carter's band, and Dizzy, who was playing trumpet with Benny Carter. I used them both on this record date because they happened to be in town, and I was hanging around that band in 1942. To my eternal regret because it was a blues-oriented record session, I decided that it would not be appropriate to have Dizzy take any solos. As much as I'd begun to admire his work, I didn't think he fitted into that contest. So that is one thing that history has lost, a very early example of Dizzy in a small combo context, when he could've been featured and wasn't, and it was my fault. He had never made any combo records at that time.

"Then I really got to know him much better during the Earl Hines and Billy Eckstine eras. One day I ran into him on Broadway near Fifty-second Street, and he was carrying a record with him. It was a demo record. He said, 'Have you heard this girl with Billy Eckstine's Band—Sarah Vaughan?' And I had heard Sarah and had been very much impressed with her, and Dizzy was trying to do something with getting her a record. He took me up to the studio, it was Nola's Studios, that night, and he played this demonstration record for me—I think it was 'Night In Tunisia.' Anyway I was tremendously impressed. I started going around to very small companies trying to get a record date together, and it was not easy. Nobody cared that much about an obscure big band singer with Earl Hines or Billy Eckstine. But eventually I did get her a date with a company called Continental Records, and we recorded that on New Year's Eve of 1944. We made four tunes, and Dizzy was on the date, and Georgie Auld played tenor. It was sort of an all-star band. I had a very small budget for the session, and there wasn't enough left over for a piano player, so I had to fill in.

And one of the tunes that we did was 'Night In Tunisia.' My ears were not quite up to that, and my reading wasn't that good, and I couldn't cut the parts to 'Night In Tunisia.' Diz had to come over and take over the piano for me and play on it. He played trumpet and piano on that track.

"Five months later I produced a second date with Sarah, on which both Bird and Diz played. I was frustrated at having to record Dizzy for these small companies, but finally toward the end of that year I talked Steve Sholes at RCA into letting me produce an all-star session headed by Dizzy.

"By that time my respect for Dizzy's artistry was coupled with an admiration for his social and racial views. He was one of the first black musicians to hire sidemen without regard to race and to speak out fearlessly against the bigotry that was then rampant even in the music business."

Oscar Pettiford was an Indian—mostly black—but at least part Indian. He came from a family of musicians that had a band called Doc Pettiford that used to travel around down South. They came through my home in Cheraw a lot, but I didn't even know Oscar then. Musically, his whole family was very gifted. His sisters, mother, father, brother—all of them—played in the same band. Oscar became the definitive bass player of our music.

I first met Max Roach at the Uptown House where he played. He was just a young kid from Brooklyn, playing with Ebenezer Paul, Allan Tinney, Ray Abrams, Victor Coulson, and George Treadwell. Those cats were getting it. Boy! And then Charlie Parker joined their group. It was a non-union gig, a "scab" place they called it. We used to play there after hours. Damn the union! After hours, the union didn't have no business in there.

When I first heard Max, I said, "I'm gonna get him. . . ." If I couldn't get Kenny Clarke, I had Max. Kenny, I think had left for the Army. I sent for Max one time though, and he'd gone on the road with Benny Carter. Max knows how I feel about his playing because even at that time, when he was young, I said, "Look, now, you're in my band. Never mind if Gabriel comes to ask you to play them drums. Don't you get off of them damn drums! You sit right there." At the Onyx all the drummers wanted to sit in, and I wouldn't let them. All the big guys—Big Sid Catlett—I wouldn't let nobody sit in. They could play, but Max knew all of our arrangements. I said, "No." Because it was a major debut for modern jazz, and I wanted it to sound just perfect, so only Max could play with us.

MAX ROACH (percussion):

"I first met Dizzy, musically, actually, by hearing some work of his that another trumpeter would play. He'd play certain things, and he'd say, 'These are some of the things that Dizzy Gillespie played.' And so it was always something for me to go to Minton's or go to the Apollo Theater when he was working with Cab Calloway. And we, our group, would wait for Dizzy to play a solo. We'd go to Minton's and listen to Dizzy and Thelonious Monk and Scotty and people like that who were jamming. And then later I met him. Dizzy, of course, paid me a great compliment at that particular time, when he was with Cab. There was a group of us around New York at that particular time, Bud Powell, Allan Tinney, and people like that. And I think Dizzy had heard me play, either at Minton's or Monroe's Uptown House, and he said when he left Cab Calloway, he was gonna start a band and he'd like for me to play with him. That was to me a great compliment. Because even at that time, Dizzy was a legend, musically. He was already a legend at that time. When he did start the band, he called me, and we began to work together. His idea of a band at that particular time was to have Charlie Parker and Oscar Pettiford, Bud Powell and myself in that first quintet, that birth on Fifty-second Street. And as you know, the rest of it is history. That particular quintet, all of us, didn't play all together at one particular time, for one reason or another. But the first quintet did include Don Byas, Oscar Pettiford, Dizzy, George Wallington on piano, and me; and we played the Onyx Club."

George Wallington, a young white guy, following our style, was a quiet student of our music. He wanted to learn how to play modern jazz piano, and he'd heard about me and sought me out. Music school was always open on the job, so I brought him into the group as pianist. But every now and then, George would miss a chord, and Oscar would jump all over him, "White muthafucka, can't play—shit!" I had to spend a lot of time protecting him from Oscar.

George Wallington tried to play like Bud Powell. Bud's style, in turn, comes from Billy Kyle's, pianistically and technically. But Bud's main inspiration was Charlie Parker and me. We didn't need a strong piano player in there. We had Max and Oscar Pettiford. We really didn't need Bud. We didn't need a piano player to show us the way to go. Piano players up to that point played leading chords. We didn't do that because we were always evolving our own solo directions. We needed a piano player to stay outta the way. The one that stayed outta the way best was the one best for us. That's why George Wallington fitted in so well, because he stayed outta the way, and when he played a solo, he'd fill it up; sounded just like Bud.

Bud's importance was as a great soloist, not necessarily an accompanist. He was too much of a rebel for that. Bebop pianists didn't lay down the changes; some, like Monk, just embellished them. If you're playing with Monk and you don't know the changes, shame on you. You'll never hear them from him.

We were getting it, and we used to practice all the time. We'd take the chord structures of various standard and pop tunes and create new chords, melodies, and songs from them. We found out what the composers were doing by analyzing these tunes, and then added substitute chords to songs like "Night and Day," "How High the Moon," "Lover," "What Is This Thing Called Love?" and "Whispering." When we borrowed from a standard, we added and substituted so many chords that most people didn't know what song we really were playing. "How High the Moon" became "Ornithology" and "What Is This Thing Called Love?" was "Hothouse."

I was the first one of the boppers to play "How High the Moon." I learned it from Nat Cole at Kelly's Stables while playing with Benny Carter in 1942. At that time Art Tatum was playing there, opposite Nat and the King Cole Trio. I doubt if all three of them cost $3,000. Nat Cole played that number, and I liked the changes. I said, "Man, what's the name of that?"

"'How High the Moon,'" he said.

"Show it to me." He showed it to me on the piano, and I rushed uptown and showed it to Monk. I said, "Look here, man, look at this tune." And then we started playing "How High the Moon." In the interim, little Benny Harris wrote a countermelody to it that became quite a thing with bebop musicians.

We started developing more chords out of a single chord on a tune called "Whispering." Instead of E-flat to D seventh, we made four chords; E-flat, A minor, E augmented, and A minor seventh to D seventh. We needed a melody to fit that, so I wrote "Groovin' High." Of course there are about ten million tunes written on the changes of "I Got Rhythm," and Tadd Dameron came up with "Hothouse" from "What Is This Thing Called Love?" That was our thing in bebop, putting in substitutions.

This wasn't pilfering. In cases where we needed substitute chords for these tunes, we had to create new melodies to fit them. If you're gonna think up a melody, you'd just as well copyright it as a new tune, and that's what we did. We never did get any suits from publishers.

The pop guys were writing mostly fundamentals at that time. They didn't write any hip flatted fifths, and we considered our changes improvements on the sound of popular music. It added new sounds to pop music, and the arrangers now use it. I can hear a lotta the music that we created during those years now, in motion pictures and on television.

The most important thing about our music was, of course, the style, how you got from one note to another, how it was played. It's most important because you can play the same thing and not play it the same way, and you won't be playing bebop. We had a special way of phrasing. Not only did we change harmonic structure, but we also changed rhythmic structure.

In the Onyx Club, we played a lot of original tunes that didn't have titles. We just wrote an introduction and a first chorus. I'd say, "Dee-da-pa-da-n-de-bop . . ." and we'd go on into it. People, when they'd wanna ask for one of those numbers and didn't know the name, would ask for bebop. And the press picked it up and started calling it bebop. The first time the term bebop appeared in print was while we played at the Onyx Club.

The tune "Bebop" was written around the same time. We thought we needed a tune to go with the name. I'd composed a fast thing, and just named it "Bebop" later on the record date. (Manor 5000). It didn't have a name before the record date. I've written two more tunes, stolen from myself, "Things to Come" and "Things Are Here," which both came from the chord changes of "Bebop," the same changes. In a similar vein, "This Is the Way" was a ballad I wrote to show my sense of chord progressions and that I was sticking to fundamentals.

MAX ROACH:

"The only reason that the music of the Gershwins and all these people lived during that period was because all the black people, the Billie Holidays, Ella Fitzgeralds, Dizzy Gillespies, Charlie Parkers, the Monks, the Coleman Hawkinses projected this music, used this music and kept it alive. It's very patronizing and condescending to call the music of that period bebop, but that's something we seem to have accepted. Aside from the harmonies and the melodies being revolutionary, let's look at some of the titles—song titles such as 'Things to Come,' 'Woody 'n You,' 'A Night In Tunisia,' which is suggestive of Africa, 'Con Alma' (with soul). Look at Charlie Parker's, 'Now Is the Time.' You can read a lot of things into just the titles.

"When you get down to the music, there was a period when the music moved from uptown to downtown, and they had no name for it uptown when the music came out of Minton's. Nobody considered the music as 'bop' until it moved downtown. So to derogate the music and make it look like it was one of them things, they started hanging labels on the music. For example, don't give me all that 'jazz,' or that's 'bop' talk, this thing or the other. We argue these points because words mean quite a bit to all of us. What we name our things and what we call our contributions should be up to us so that we can control our own destiny.

"Economically, now, is another level. When the music moved from uptown to downtown, downtown meaning whites were now the clientele, a few more pennies were being made than when we were uptown, and the scene is changed radically because of the war and war taxes. The people who came into the clubs wanted to hear tunes that came out of their environment, things that they were familiar with. Prior to that point, everything uptown was completely original—blues, Basie, Jimmie Lunceford. All of that music, all of these tunes have a message—'Ain't What You Do, It's the Way How You Do It,' 'Straighten Up and Fly Right.' Well all of that is still continuing. But when we got downtown, people wanted to hear something they were familiar with, like 'How High the Moon,' 'What Is This Thing Called Love?' Can you play that? So in playing these things, the black musicians recognized that the royalties were going back to these people, like ASCAP, the Jerome Kerns, the Gershwins. So one revolutionary thing that happened, they began to write parodies on the harmonic structures. Which was really revolutionary. If I have to play it, I will put my own particular melody on that progression, and people would ask, 'Say, what is that?'

"And we would say, 'Well, you asked for "What Is This Thing Called Love?" and that's what it is.' So you see there were a lot of things that were going on revolutionary during that time. If you made a record, you could say, 'This is an original.'"

Some of the big names in music, like Jimmy Dorsey, started coming out to the Onyx to hear us and left completely flabbergasted. The music industry couldn't ignore the modern trend any longer, and Jimmy Dorsey wanted to find out more about our music since he couldn't hope to make the transition with just the one or two arrangements that he'd bought from me, not when the entire popular music field seemed about to turn modern. When he came down to hear us at the Onyx Club, Jimmy Dorsey got drunk because he couldn't believe

what he heard from this small group. And this was without Charlie
Parker. The first night he got drunk. The second night he stayed sober
and invited me down to his suite at the Astor Hotel which was at
Forty-fourth Street and Broadway across the street from the Paramount Theater.

"Boy," he said, "I'd love to have you in my band—if you weren't so
dark."

"You know any trumpet players, white ones, who play like this?" I
asked. "Well, make up your mind."

He just laughed.

Generally, there were few problems of racial discrimination in the
clubs on Fifty-second Street because most of the bands there were
black. Even among the clientele on Fifty-second Street there was very
little racist feeling. That was the one spot in New York where there
was not too much discrimination. But once you left Fifty-second
Street, look out.

I used to take the subway, because all of us were living in Harlem.
We'd walk to get the subway at Sixth Avenue and Fiftieth Street, just
around the corner. At that time, Mme. Bricktop had come back
from Europe, and one night we were standing in front of the RKO Theater talking to her. Oscar Pettiford, Bricktop, and I were standing
there. Bricktop's got red hair and a light complexion. Oscar, naturally,
was juiced, and three cracker sailors walked up. One said, "What you
niggers doing with this white woman!" Oscar hit at him and fell. The
Street was the jumping off point for all the crackers from down South
going overseas to different places. They'd come down to Fifty-second
Street to start some shit. And they used to get it too because everybody down there was ready at that time. I was standing there with my
horn but I used to carry a carpet knife, one that you cut carpet with,
with the crook in it. Yessir, I was ready for Fifty-second Street.

When Oscar hit at this guy and fell, I wanted to let Oscar and this
guy fight it out. If Oscar's drunk, that's his business. Let him fight it
out with the guy. But these other sailors started crowding around.
And when they did that, I stood over Oscar and pulled out my knife.
They started toward me, and one of them spied this knife shining.

"Look out, he's got a knife!"

"Get up, Oscar!" I said. "Get up! Get up, get up!"

"Anh, annh . . ." Oscar grunted. But he finally got up and ran out
in the middle of the street and tried to get a cab. He hailed a cab, and
I was holding these guys off. We got in the cab, and the cabdriver
wouldn't go to Harlem. More sailors were coming all the time now.
We tried to get the cabdriver to take us out of the vicinity, and he
wouldn't do it. He just stood there. And so we jumped out of the back
door and ran down into the subway on the other side of the street, on

the west side of the street. "Go ahead, Oscar, run, go ahead," I said. "I got them." And I let him run. He ran down and went on through. He jumped over the turnstile or something—he left me. I told him to go. I had a knife, so I say, "Well, I'll hold off these guys."

These sailors were taking off their coats, throwing them at me, trying to make me drop the knife. One of those coats hit my knife hand and knocked it down, and my knife fell down at the bottom of the steps. I was looking for it, and I couldn't find it. I turned around down there looking and when I looked up, one of those sailors, was making a flying tackle at me. Just in time, I raised up, tensed myself, and he hit my back and fell down at the bottom of the stairs. I carried my horn in a bag, in a trumpet bag. I grabbed him in his collar, and took my trumpet and knocked. I tried to move his nose where his ear was with the bottom of the valves. Blood was everywhere. And when I hit him with the trumpet, all these other sailors were pummeling on my back. Boy, they were pummeling me. And I was trying to protect my mouth, running with my hand over it, and they were beating me, all in the back and stuff, and I kept running. Finally, I broke through them, and they were right behind me. I jumped over that little fence at the end of the platform. I ran along that little catwalk there on the side where the workmen walk. I ran up in there and hid, and it was very dark in there. There was only a little space, only about two feet wide. Well, if anybody had come behind me, they had to come one at a time because the rest of it was the third rail. I was standing there, waiting with my horn. One at a time. I was gonna knock one out and throw him on the tracks, knock another one out and go ahead. But the SPs came and got them before they could find out where we were.

A little while later, Oscar and I split up. You see, Oscar would get drunk a lot. One time he was juiced and was playing. I said, "You know what's wrong with you? You're a prima donna." And boy, he blew up.

"My daddy called me a prima donna one time," he said. "And I quit."

"Let the doorknob hit you in the back," I said. "I was here when you got here, and I'll be here when you leave here."

Not long after that we decided to dissolve the relationship, and I moved across the Street. Budd Johnson and I started a band across the Street in the Downbeat, and Oscar hired Joe Guy to play trumpet in the Onyx. Whiskey made Oscar do all kinds of things, which had nothing at all to do with music.

The Downbeat

The Downbeat was right across the Street from the Onyx Club, and our group sounded just like the other one. We even played all the same numbers, but instead of Don Byas playing the saxophone solos, it was Budd Johnson. I knew Budd Johnson from Earl Hines's band; he and Trummy Young had tried to get me to go with Earl Hines before I left Philadelphia. Budd Johnson was around New York doing the same things I did, playing and writing arrangements. Budd was a first-rate musician long before any of us came up. Stylistically, Budd emerged from the same era as Lester Young and they played very similarly. Budd Johnson was probably one of the first guys to discover the cool, flowing style of Lester Young and was a number-one musician since I'd been knowing him. He was a first-rate musician and had been for a long time.

Budd Johnson didn't come up in our era, but he was one of us because the style he played blended easily with ours. In a musician, it's a choice of figures. It's not what chords you play; it's what you do with them. Of the utmost importance is timing and where you put it. Like with Ben Webster; I've heard Ben play in so many settings but to sit down and listen to him play a ballad—nobody who ever played a ballad does a better job than Ben Webster does on it. I don't care from what age they come in music.

Clyde Hart told Ben one time, "Frog, why don't you just come on

out and be a faggot!" As tender as he plays, man. But Ben is rough
and tender at the same time, and when he says "Oooo Wooh!" just in
the right spot, it hits you right in the solar plexus.

Clyde Hart, our pianist, was also well versed, though he didn't play
in our style, like Bud Powell. Clyde knew everything—all the changes
we played, but he played the piano like Teddy Wilson. Basically he'd
copped Teddy Wilson's style, though he'd put in his own licks. Leonard Gaskin, on bass, didn't have nearly the strength of Oscar Pettiford,
but for that gig, he was ample. Max, of course, was perfect on drums.

At the Downbeat I was very busy trying to create music and didn't
think much about things like publicity. Budd Johnson, on the other
hand, besides being a top player and arranger, had a very good mind
for business, and so we became coleaders of the group. Budd had
been playing with us in the Onyx, and earlier, February 14, 1944, we
recorded together on a classic album with Coleman Hawkins (Apollo
752).

During the time we played together, a lot of things were happening
musically. Besides the gig, there were Sunday afternoon sessions at
Kelly's Stables and down in the Village. Monte Kay, a producer, who
used to be the manager of the Modern Jazz Quartet and now manages
Flip Wilson, used to give these sessions, and I would play for them
even while I was working over in Philly. I'd get about $8.00 and I had
to pay my own fare on the train coming from Philly to play these sessions at Kelly's Stables for Monte Kay. Monte Kay, Pete Cameron,
and Jerry Hurwitz were some of the first guys around giving modern
jam sessions, and there was another guy named Ed Harris who presented the first modern jazz concert in New York around that same
time. There were sessions going on all night in the Village and at
Kelly's Stables and you could always pick up a little change from
them.

I stayed preoccupied, mostly teaching the younger guys how to play
the fundamentals of the modern style. The younger guys were willing,
but they'd get out there and forget fundamentals, like C, E, and G is a
major chord. And using flatted fifths—if you want to make a flatted
fifth, O.K. But to play flatted fifths all night! I'd show them what to do
and explain to them why.

Ray Brown is a good example. Years later, we were playing a tune
with Jazz at the Philharmonic, "I'm Through With Love," and on
one chord Ray heard me play certain notes and he thought it was another chord. He heard these three notes and thought it was something
else and said, "You're making an A-flat-minor seventh."

I say, "No . . ."

"Yes, you are," he said. "I heard it."

"Hmmph!"

"Oh . . ." he said. That's all he said because if you say something and you can't prove it, you don't have any business saying it.

Miles was the same way. He used to ask me, "Man, where do you get them notes?"

"Off the piano," I'd say. "That's your ass if you don't play piano, you can't find them. You might luck up on them sometimes, but if you know the piano, you'll know where they are all the time. You might get lucky and find one every now and then just from playing your own instrument, but if you know the piano, you'll know where they are all the time. You can see them."

My house used to be full all the time. Miles used to stay there. He didn't have a bed there because there was no room to have a bed for him. But as soon as he'd get up—boom, he was over there. Kinney Dorham, Max, everybody. Any one of those guys of that era, Monk, all of them came by my place which was a clearinghouse for our music. Teddy Hill used to let us rehearse at Minton's. We never rehearsed at my house because my apartment was so small, a little bitty apartment. We'd go somewhere else and rehearse. But we'd get into modern jazz theory because I always had a piano. Chu Berry's wife gave me the piano when Chu died. They lived downstairs, and we moved it upstairs. "If you want the piano, move it upstairs, it's yours," she said. Chu had died, but he didn't play the piano, anyway. I'd show guys; but when I was coming up, older guys wouldn't show you nothing—show you something wrong!

🎹

BUDD JOHNSON:

"Coleman Hawkins came in from Europe. He'd heard about this new music, so Hawk wanted to surround himself with the cats that were playing the new music, play with them and record with them so he could find out what was going on. The new music was so influential, until it almost—it even changed his style of playing. Anyway, Hawk hired me, and I wrote an arrangement. He hired Dizzy, and that's when Dizzy wrote 'Woody 'n You' for him. We had been playing it, but Dizzy wrote an arrangement for Hawk. He lined himself up with all of the guys that were from Fifty-second Street and made the recording. It wasn't a studio band, it was jazz musicians who were playing on the Street because he wanted his coat to be pulled with this kind of music, and he wanted to be in first. Hawk wrote some of the arrangements. At that time, I was living just around the corner from Coleman Hawkins. I used to live on 152nd Street between Convent and Amsterdam, and Hawk lived at the King Haven which was on

153rd. I used to go around to Hawk's house, I had always admired him, and he told me at that time, 'Well, man, I'm gonna do this— "Body and Soul" was such a big hit and it's my solo, so I'm gonna do that over and call it "Moon Mist" or something like that.'* So he made it all over again, and that was on this date too. Hawk, Dizzy, and I did the writing for that date. The thing that I wrote, Clyde Hart and me, was a tune called 'Buh De Daht.' Well, this was a beginning for this stuff being put down on paper because the cats used to just play it and teach each other. You make the riff and I find it. But, see, we started to writing it, and when you start to write it, you got to get the right voicing, and you gotta really know a little something about the harmonic devices. So I mean I learned a lot from Dizzy.

"Now the way that word bebop came about to my way of thinking is when Dizzy would be trying to explain something or show you how to play it, he would hum it to you. And he would say, 'No, no, it goes like this—ump-de-be-de-bop-be-bop-be-doo-dop-de-de-bop.' So they would come up to Dizzy and say, 'Hey, play some more of that bebop music,' because he would be scatting like that. See, and they just picked up that word and they'd say, 'Play some more of that bebop music.' This was the description, you know, this was the way—the only way they could identify it and tell him what they wanted to hear him play. And of course Dizzy, being as intelligent as he is, he just kept it going. So this thing went on and made him a fortune.

"Now, a lotta people say, 'No, it was Charlie Parker.' Well, I don't agree with that because Charlie Parker used to come to my house, Monk, all of them, you know. Of course, Charlie was able to put his own things down. But during that time, you know, Charlie Parker made me remember who he was and where he came from. Like, I used to live in Kansas City, and I played with a band called George E. Lee. Well, Charlie Parker said to me one day, 'You don't remember me, but when you guys used to rehearse . . .' We used to rehearse at George E. Lee's mother's house. He says, 'Well, we were the little cats that was playing stickball out in front of the house. And when you cats would start to rehearse, we would come up to the window and look in and listen to you guys.' And he was talking about 'we,' it was the Businessmen of Rhythm, L. D., and all those guys that turned out to have a very beautiful little dance act, and Charlie Parker. That was on Euclid Avenue in Kansas City.

"Well, when Charlie started to play the saxophone in Kansas City, when the cats would see him come around, they'd say, 'Oh, no, not this cat again, man! I mean look . . .' And they did the same thing with Miles Davis on Fifty-second Street. 'If this cat's gonna get on the stand,

* It was actually "Rainbow Mist."

I'm not gonna play, man.' That's how bad he sounded. This hurt his feelings, you know, and Charlie woodshedded.

"There was a man by the name of Buster Smith, an alto-saxophone player, whom I had known since I was a kid from Dallas, Texas. And he would play. This was before I even thought about going to Kansas City, or anyplace. I was just a young teen-ager, thirteen. We used to work in all the little joints in Dallas. And this cat Buster Smith was playing alto and clarinet and he could play some piano. And he would play that alto like 'be-oop-un-doop-be-oop-em-bop-be-oop-em-bop-deedle-e-oop-em-do-be-oogie-be-be-oo-gee-doo.' That was his style. So he went to Kansas City and he joined Benny Moten's band, and he was with the Blue Devils, which was Walter Page's band, which turned out to be Basie. Charlie Parker emulated this man, see, which is not exactly a Dizzy Gillespie style. But in the early years in New York, Charlie and Dizzy used to come and work together. I would say that Charlie learned quite a bit from Dizzy, and Dizzy got quite a bit from Charlie. But they had two different styles, and when they started working together on Fifty-second Street, playing all this fantastic music, naturally, they started to jell.

"I'm saying all this to say, Dizzy is playing Dizzy! And I remember when he used to say, 'Man, if I could just get a piano player to play these chords behind me when I'm playing,' he said, 'then I could really stretch out, because this is the way I think the music oughta go.' So this is why he would be teaching guys like Tadd Dameron and George Wallington and all of the different piano players. I remember Diz would come in where you were working and sit in the band. And, like, we'd be jamming. He'd let everybody else play first, and while they were playing he would be telling the piano player, he'd say, 'See, when you get to that chord you make a so-and-so, you make a so-and-so.' And so when it got to be Dizzy's time to play, now, the piano player has learned the new changes, and this cat would get up there and blow the roof off the joint. Just wash everybody away. And everybody would start to say, 'Man, play that behind me.' Oh, he was phenomenal, man. Dizzy is a giant!

"So Oscar Pettiford said, 'I'm taking the band in here.' [The Onyx.]

"We said, 'Well, O.K.'

"Dizzy said, 'Me and Budd'll get together.' So Dizzy and I formed a little group and we went across the street on Fifty-second Street to a place called the Yacht Club. Dizzy was the musical director, and I was the business manager. We hired some cats and we worked. We hired this cat Monte Kay and another guy named Mal Braveman. They were supposed to be doing the publicity on us. You know they were charging us $35 a week. Finally, they got us in Archer and Winchell's columns, but they didn't really do nothing, so I cut them out. And we went on together.

"Then, finally, Dizzy said, 'I got a chance to go with William Morris Agency. I'm gonna sign a contract with William Morris.'

"I say, 'Great!' You know we didn't have anything written on paper. We were friends, so that didn't matter. I wanted to see him go ahead. In the meantime, all of the guys who were interested in trying to improve theirselves and learn more about this kind of music would go by Dizzy's house. Man, you'd go by Dizzy's apartment and sometimes he'd have as much as fifteen or twenty cats up there sitting around. And Diz would be walking around all open and talking. Tadd Dameron at that time was one of Dizzy's students. Tadd would say, 'Well, Dizzy, I'm making an arrangement for so-and-so and look . . . and I'm doing this.'

"Dizzy would say, 'Look, don't use these chords. Lemme show you what to do.' And Tadd would get up from the piano. And Dizzy would sit at the piano and show him the changes. Actually, Tadd would have never been able to write the way he did if it hadn't been for Dizzy Gillespie. Because this was a system that you had to follow. He's got a headful of music. He's very smart, a very good arranger. I remember the time when we used to write for Boyd Raeburn's band together. And Dizzy would sit in the bands and show the trumpet players how to play the parts. I used to get a little peeved with him about that. I'd say, 'Man, what are you doing, showing these cats?' But he got a kick out of it.

"Diz would sit up there and play and say 'That's the way it was supposed to go.' And he would teach these guys how to play the part. Of course, he had made the arrangement, so he wanted his arrangement to sound good. And he showed them. They would get hung up on the fingering, when they'd get up above high C. Diz would show them how to do that. He's got the greatest fingering in the world. I don't know nobody that can finger a trumpet like Diz. He knows all of the short cuts for the pure notes, and everything, which is quite a study in itself. Dizzy also plays the bass very well, he plays drums very well, he plays the piano. This guy can just about play any instrument that he wants to play. That's how he was able to instruct all those young guys, like Fats Navarro. Fats Navarro first heard Dizzy, and he almost died. He said, 'Man, listen to this cat, man . . . !' I remember when we were in Billy Eckstine's band, even before Fats joined. Navarro, man, he was gonna do this or die. And finally he became a very great trumpet player, patterning after Dizzy. When I first met Dizzy it was like going to college. I mean he taught. Whether the guys wanna admit it or not, he taught. He really taught them all about what was happening. See, the reason I say Dizzy is as great [as], if he didn't have a little edge on, Armstrong—Armstrong could play and he had his great delivery and everything. But if you wanted to play, you had to have the ability to write down or copy what Louis had done. He wouldn't—he couldn't explain to you the theory of what he was doing. And it was only as a soloist. But Dizzy is a soloist in his own style, plus the fact that he knows all about music; he could explain what he's doing. He could lay down the form to carry it on for posterity. I mean, you know, this is very important, I think, to pass on your knowledge to someone. See, although they may have all been inspired by Louis, you know, it takes a little bit more than that to pass down through the ages. And I think what Dizzy has done is just that because of his great knowledge of music and being able to explain it, and get it over. He'd make a great teacher.

"Now, Monk was in there too. I gotta give Monk a lotta credit because, actually, at that time, Monk, being just a little bit different from Diz, had something going. And of course there is a familiarity between the two of them—that is, as far as modern harmony and the new things. But Monk actually had tunes down on paper. And I never will forget, in Minton's they had a guy named Scotty on tenor, from Texas. They had Joe Guy on trumpet, Kenny Clarke on drums, Monk, and Nick Fenton was the bass player. Anyway, these cats were playing these off-the-wall tunes, new music. Monk is an originator also. You take guys like Lester Young and Ben Webster. They heard about Minton's. So when they came in town, they tear up to Minton's. I remember Prez getting up there because Prez is supposed to be, you know, the President. And they lowered the boom on him with this new music. And Prez had never heard no music like this before. He couldn't get outta the first four bars, man, you know. You gotta have some music in front of you to read or something; your ear will not carry you to where these guys were going. And it was sort of funny and pitiful at the same time, but it was a good lesson.

"And then I remember when Ben Webster and Prez were there together, and they're gonna go up there and cut this guy Scotty, you know. Scotty knew that music backwards. He used to sound like Hawk too. But all the guys used to go up there and sit and play. And I mean they would get a good lesson when they sat in. Dizzy could play the music because Dizzy knew what was happening. He was into that, his bag at the same time, see, because they all come up together. They used to play not only at Minton's but Clark Monroe's Uptown House, and they had a little cat named Vic, Victor Coulson. Yeah, this cat was bad. He was mean! He was playing that style then, only he didn't have the range and the knowledge that Dizzy had. But he was in on this at the beginning also. I mean, the musicians used to go there and battle like dogs, every night, you know, and just playing for nothing and having a good time. I think those are the most memorable days of my first coming to New York. And seeing this and listening to this, I had sense enough to sit back and try to absorb, before I would yank out my horn and get washed.

"I mean they wasn't calling it bebop then. Even Monk couldn't explain it, but Dizzy could, and he could develop. But now, I do remember this about Monk. Monk's feelings got hurt because Dizzy and Charlie was getting all of the credit for this music, this style—I used to go over to Monk's house with him, drink some wine with him. 'Come on, I want you to hear what I'm doing,' he said. 'I'm gonna let them take that style and go ahead, and I'm gonna get a new style.' I used to go over to Monk's and sit down and drink. His mother would fix some food for us, and he would just play for me. All this funny-type music that he was playing. And he had gone altogether different from what he had been doing. I said, 'Hey, man . . . that's outtasight! What're you doing; whaddayou call that?'

"'I don't know, man, it's just—you know.' He couldn't explain it to me. And I never thought of Monk as a great piano player. But he would fumble on that piano and get these things out and made all the dissonant chords, and major seconds, and minor seconds.

"And I said, 'Hey, man, that's outtasight.'

"'Well, I'm going on now with my new music,' he said. And he did. He did go right on along with his new music. But at the same time, if you listen closely, Dizzy's style is different. I mean it was also different from the beginning when I first heard Monk. Dizzy's music was a little different from that. And I think along with what they knew, they picked up a lotta things from Diz too. When you have a lot of knowledge of music, and understand the theory and the new harmonic devices and everything, it's not very difficult to come out with a sound. But with a style of music, it's very difficult, man, because it's hard to play something that somebody has never played before. But, I mean, see this is what Diz had on all of these musicians. And he could sit down and play the piano so well. Even today, Dizzy says, 'Dig this, this little thing I wrote.' And the beautiful simplicity to it and with the way he is going harmonically, you say, 'Oh, wow, man isn't that pretty!' It's something that you haven't heard before. And of course, now, with his wide, wide world of traveling and picking up different sounds from different countries and really understanding their music, he can incorporate that into what he already knows and always have something new to present. You know Dizzy's been all over the world. He understands all of the different rhythms and things, of the black music, the drums, and the Africans, Cubans, Brazilians, you know, South American music. All of it, he understands. He knows where the beat is. And some of that music is so difficult, it's hard for the average

cat to find where 'one' is; because listening to it can throw you off. But
Dizzy knows all of this. He's a phenomenal man."

MAX ROACH:

"As a musician I think Dizzy has no peer. He's inspired perhaps
more musicians who are out here today than you can shake a stick at.
And I mean not just trumpet players or saxophone players but percussion people as well. Dizzy was always a complete musician, both as a
composer, orchestrator and, of course, one of the most innovative of
soloists on trumpet. So as a musician, I don't think Dizzy Gillespie has
a peer. He's in the same category I would say in the history of the
music, of our music, as certain people who add layers upon layers.
Like you might have a Buddy Bolden, and then you'd have, say King
Oliver and Louis Armstrong, Roy Eldridge and Dizzy Gillespie, all the
other people in between who became virtuosos and great musicians in
their own right, Dizzy is one of those. He's a cornerstone in the development and evolution of our music.

"It was always an inspiring and most challenging experience to
have been involved with Dizzy during that time, and even today. You
know most recently we've done some things with him. He's always
stimulating and his ideas about music are always challenging. Go back
to some of that earlier music, you know, his 'Night In Tunisia' and
many other things, 'Con Alma,' go back to the first big band that he
had. You know the music was always a challenge, it was always fresh,
and his personality, of course, exemplifies all of these things, and that
kind of creative genius is always stimulating and challenging. Another
thing Dizzy has always been—and this is the way it is with truly great
people, their security allows them to be—generous, you know. So
when I say this, and the way Dizzy would teach, oh, Miles Davis and
Clifford and Fats Navarro, all these people—all these folks and myself,
and all the others, the pianists and the bassists, the way he would take
his time to give you whatever information that he had, to use the way
you wanted to use it. My first record date with Coleman Hawkins was
a result of Dizzy introducing me to Hawkins. Since he was doing some
of the writing for that particular date, he asked Hawk to use me, I
imagine, because I got called on that first date. And that was the beginning of a whole new world for me, musically and also creatively.
Dizzy was in large part responsible for spawning people like Bud Powell—Dizzy and Bird and Monk and Klook were in large part responsible for spawning people like Bud Powell and J. J. Johnson and myself and Ray Brown, people like that who came later.

"There's no such thing. Who invented bebop? What kind of statement is that? How can you look at something and say who invented

it? That's coming from another kind of mentality. Who invented something else? Who discovered America, Columbus? No, I think that Dizzy is one of the African-American's greatest contributions to musical culture. We can talk about the music of the forties, fifties, sixties, and on into the seventies, Dizzy still prevails and his music is still as fresh. When I hear somebody say, 'Who invented bebop?' first of all I have to say I don't know what bebop is. But I know that during the forties that something happened to the music, and the people responsible for that happening were people like Dizzy Gillespie, Charlie Parker and Thelonious Monk, and Kenny Clarke and Clyde Hart. I'm talking about the forerunners; that crowd, man, they were something."

Hepsations '45

Bebop really jumped up commercially in 1945 and I organized my first big band. The same guy who got Billy Eckstine his band, Billy Shaw and his son, Milt Shaw, paid for this band. Milt Shaw became my manager. We were supposed to play behind some big stars in a road show which was called Hepsations 1945. The Nicholas Brothers, Harold and Fayard, after dancing through their own hit movie, *Stormy Weather,* had become big stars and were the featured headliners. The show also featured Patterson and Jackson, comedians; June Eckstine, the female vocalist who was then Mrs. Billy Eckstine; Lovey Lane, a shake dancer; and some chorus girls. I made a major effort to gather the best modern jazz talent available and to organize the band well so everybody could hear exactly how hip the cream of the crop sounded. Most of the guys in the band came over from Billy Eckstine, and it wasn't really too much of a problem. Billy had started getting ready to break up his band and he later gave me everything, all his music, all his stands and microphones, everything.

"You want some uniforms?" he said.

Billy got sick and tired of trying to run a modern jazz orchestra, having to beg the dancing public to listen, but I still wanted to give it a try. I'm not big band crazy, man, but it's beautiful to feel all the warmth of the guys playing in a large group rather than a small one. The Fifty-second Street public seemed ready to dig bebop on a small scale, so we wished to succeed where Eckstine had failed and quietly hoped that a big modern jazz band would finally catch on. We formed the first Dizzy Gillespie Orchestra, mainly for a tour down South. With a big band, a lot of musicians, instead of just a few, could play our music and make some money. To attract a mass audience to bebop, we had to first establish a feeling for the music among the large black population of the South by touring the southern states. Things didn't work out the way I'd hoped, and that first big band exists as a blur in my mind. I'd prefer to forget it.

This orchestra and our style of playing, generally, was geared for people just sitting and listening to music; nearly all of our arrangements were modern, so imagine my chagrin and surprise when I found out that all we were playing was dances. In New York, they told us that we were going out on a concert tour, but all they had was rock 'n roll audiences. That was something. They couldn't dance to the music, they said. But I could dance to it. I could dance my ass off to it. They could've too, if they had tried. Jazz should be danceable. That's the original idea, and even when it's too fast to dance to, it should always be rhythmic enough to make you wanna move. When you get away from that movement, you get away from the whole idea. So my music is always danceable. But the unreconstructed blues lovers down South who couldn't hear nothing else but the blues didn't think so. They wouldn't even listen to us. After all these years, I still get mad just talking about it.

WALTER GILBERT FULLER:

"When we got started, I came to Minton's. 'Lemme go see what my buddy's doing.' Man, he had eight cats sitting up there rehearsing arrangements.

"'I'm getting a band together, you know. I'm going out on the road with the Nicholas Brothers.'

"'Well, where is the band? Where is the music?'

"'That's what you see up there. That's it there.'

"'Man, you ain't got no band here.' I asked Milt Shaw, 'Can you get some money?'

"'How much money do you need?' he asked.

"'Well,' I told him, 'you need carfare for these cats every day. And you should give them something to buy a sandwich for some lunch. You don't have to pay them. Five or six hundred dollars and we can do that.'

"'I don't know,' Milt said. 'I'll go talk to my old man.' He went downtown and told him, 'Listen, Pops, we ain't getting this thing fast enough, and Dizzy's friend says that we can get the thing together if we get him $500 so that he can pay the cats for rehearsing and give them a little carfare.'

"Because the guys didn't have the money. Them cats were broke, nobody had any money. So we changed the rehearsal place to downtown, to Nola's Studios. Then I put out the word that we were organizing a band, and, man, we had fifty to a hundred cats coming there. Everybody wanted to play in Dizzy's band.

"The thing was to establish Dizzy with a style. So what I did was took all the records that he had made, like 'Blue 'n Boogie,' 'Salt Peanuts,' 'Shaw 'Nuff' and 'Night In Tunisia,' and we made arrangements on those things.

"It wasn't a matter of writing arrangements to suit me at all. It was a matter of writing arrangements for his band. And you couldn't write music for a black band that sounded like somebody else, because they wouldn't take it. So you had to try to set something with a style. Oh, you could write anything for a white band, and they'd take it, but you couldn't do that for no nigger band. You had to write in their style.

"And then Billy Shaw had misled us, talking about we were gonna do concerts. So we went out on the road with this thing and had to play for dances. Every damn thing they booked was dances. The people were out there looking to dance. One of them hollered down there, I think it was Bluefield, West Virginia, 'Can't you nigguhs play no blues!' The next thing we worried about was them throwing bottles and shooting and starting a riot. And one of those promoters called up Billy Shaw and told him, 'Don't you never send Dizzy Gillespie back out here again to us! We don't want it!'"*

"Let's set the record straight about what Tadd (Dameron) did for that band—Tadd didn't write no arrangements for that band, none whatsoever. Not the first band. The first band, we took all of Dizzy's records, and he and I sat down and wrote them out. My argument was, why give them the royalties off of 'Bebop' when we don't control the publishing, and give them everything, and they don't pay you anyhow. So, let's write something new, another melody on top of it.

"Dizzy and I sat down, and Dizzy, basically, did most of it. The

* DG: The guy in Virginia—Weinberg. He consolidated all the one-nighters for the bands. In the past, there was, like, a promoter in Raleigh, in Norfolk, in Richmond, in Charlotte, in Columbia, different promoters in all these towns. This guy, Weinberg, told Gale, "Look, I can give you a tour. I can give you sixty one-nighters if you give me the acts." So they sold all the acts to Weinberg, and then he had the colored guys in the different towns working for him after that. He could get a cheaper price on the bands than the colored guys. And that was the beginning of the end of the big bands. They put the local promoters out of business. Except they didn't fuck up Don Robie, a black promoter in Texas. It was very lucrative for the bandleaders, for a while.

lines on 'Bebop' were his. We changed the line, reversed the line on, 'This Is the Way,' and I made the arrangement for the band. We did that on the basis of Woody Herman playing 'Caldonia.' Because they had the hottest band out there, and everything that Woody Herman was playing was in Dizzy's style. They were taking Dizzy's licks and used Dizzy's licks to do it. People thought Dizzy had made the arrangement. Lots of times you'd write an arrangement for a band, the arrangers in the band, the cats in the band who were writing, would take your scores. And they'd analyze them, and then come back and write something else on top of what you did, using your exact figures, all the things, and then come out with an arrangement. They said it was their thing, but they had lifted what you had done the previous week. I went through that experience a lot myself.

"Now, we were trying to outdo Woody Herman's band, so that's why we later wrote 'Things to Come' which was much faster than anything that they ever played. And Dizzy—when he finally got the guys—when they learned to play it, then he kept bringing the tempo up, kept bringing the tempo up, until it went so fast, you couldn't even pat your foot that fast. In two, you were patting damn near as fast as you could pat. And people could never realize how in hell did they ever play that music? Couldn't figure out how in the hell the trumpets ever played that music so fast, but they had it.

"That first band, like I said, Tadd was nowhere around it. That was 1945 . . . Hepsations of 1945! Anyway, we went all over the South with that thing."

CHARLIE ROUSE (tenor saxophone):

"During that time, that whole interval was like a school for young cats. I had just graduated from high school, from Armstrong, in Washington, when I joined Billy Eckstine's band. John Malachi and Tommy Potter were in the band, but Dizzy was musical director. He was writing and doing all that, him and Tadd Dameron. I met him in the band during that time. So after he left, he told me he was gonna form a big band, and he asked me to go with him.

". . . I went home and came back to New York and Dizzy was forming a big band, his first big band. Max Roach was in the band. Bird was in the band for a little while. Leo Parker was playing baritone in the band. Leo Williams was an alto player. Both of them were from Washington. Freddie Webster was in the trumpet section, and Benny Harris. It was a helluva band.

"It was something that you weren't used to. They were playing harmonics that no one was playing before, like back in the days with Louis

Armstrong and Ben Webster and all. Bird and Dizzy and Thelonious had created a new set of harmonics. And it was scary, man, at first. But everybody was showing each other different things. It was like a school. It was really a school within the band.

"Oh, man, I learned how to count better. I learned how to project myself, playing the right chords and everything clearly. During that time, they were playing real fast, like, 'Bebop' and 'Salt Peanuts' and all. He taught me how to—so I won't get lost—how to count, so, I would always know where I'm at."

MAX ROACH:

"When he had that first big band, I got tied up into 'shit,' I mean heavily. Well, Dizzy took me off the streets then. We went down South; he took me down South with him and nursed me like a baby till I got over that shit. I was working every night; he'd see that I got some swimming in, that I ate well, and really took care of me, man. Sometimes I couldn't make it, man, he was right there. I shook the habit and everything. Really, with all the other responsibilities of leading that big band, rehearsing, playing for the acts—we had June Eckstine, the Nicholas Brothers, Patterson and Jackson. . . . I remember Lorraine saying, 'You oughta go to bed with him!' I'll never forget that. That was his way of making me feel like I meant something too. I forgot all about that shit. I said, 'This cat thinks that much of me, to spend that much time, with this bullshit I'm putting him through? Shit, I gotta be somebody!'

"And it's something that prevails in people who are of big stature, you know. They don't have any problems with saying: 'When I get my band, I want Clifford Brown and Miles Davis and Kinney Dorham and Fats Navarro in the band.' When Dizzy had his first big band, that's the kind of brass section we had. He had Freddie Webster, Kinney Dorham, Miles Davis, Fats Navarro. That's the trumpet section, right?"

MILES DAVIS (trumpet):

"He could teach anybody, but me. No, man . . . the shit was going too fast. I mean that was a fast pace, man. You know, before I joined the band, Freddie Webster and I used to go down every night to hear Diz. If we missed a night, we missed something. We'd go down to Fifty-second Street to hear Diz and get our ears stretched. Stand up at the bar, throw up a quarter, and name the note it came down on. That shit be going so fast; and we'd be testing ourselves.

"My style wasn't any different, I just played in a low register. I was asking him, 'Why can't I play like you?'

"'You can,' he said, 'you do. You just play in a low register, the same thing I play in a high register.'

"Also he told me, 'You learn how to play piano.' Because I asked Dizzy one time, 'How do you play that chord?' 'Muthafucka,' he said, 'learn how to play the piano.' That was it.

DG: "Now, Freddie Webster . . . Freddie Webster probably had the best sound of a trumpet since the trumpet was invented."

MD: ". . . that you ever heard in your *life*."

DG: "That was alive you know, just alive and full of life.

"Well, this was the regular hang out."

MD: "We used to all hang out together, man, every night. So the shit, you know, rubbed off."

DG: "Everybody shared everything. Miles would come and say, 'Look what I found at the piano, look what I found . . .'"

MD: "You remember that Egyptian minor scale I showed you all? I was going through some books. I said, 'I'll give this to Dizzy.'"

DG: "Egyptian minor, that's right. He was going to Juilliard then. You see, music is so vast, like rhythms and harmonics in our music. Imagine, if you just study that and study what it has done. And it's infinite."

MD: "See, so I stopped going to school. My father looked up one day and I was back in St. Louis. 'What the fuck're you doing here?' he said.

"I said, 'I'll explain. . . . A guy named Dizzy Gillespie and Charlie Parker, Yardbird—'

"'Yardbird Parker, and Dizzy Gillespie . . . ?' he said. 'What're they doing?'

"'Well, they're playing a new kinda music, and I can't get that—I can't learn that at Juilliard.' Because everything at Juilliard, I knew."

FAYARD NICHOLAS (dancer):

"Well, I first heard Dizzy's records in the forties. I think that was in 1945, and right away, as we say, I dug his music, which was bebop. They call it that now. I loved his style. It was different. It had something that was all his own, just like Duke Ellington. When you hear Duke Ellington's music, you can close your eyes, just listen to the music, and you know that's Duke Ellington. That's the same with Dizzy. You close your eyes and you hear that trumpet, and you know that's Dizzy. It's nobody else. You don't have to see him. Just listen. And this is what I love about Dizzy and all musicians who are original and have their own style, like I told you about Duke Ellington. That's what I liked about him . . . just how sensational he was.

"My agency at that time, William Morris Agency, told us that they wanted us to go on a tour, because at that time we were very big because of our movies. So they said, 'Fellas you're very popular in the South. We'd like for you to make a tour in all the southern states.' And he said, 'I think it'll be a good idea if you take Dizzy with you, with his orchestra. He has a new orchestra now, and I think he's gonna be big.'

"So we said, 'Sure, why not, yeah, we love Dizzy's music. That would be beautiful.' This was, you see, Dizzy's first break, being in our show. We got it together with Diz, and we toured, I think all of the southern states, like Alabama, Mississippi, Tennessee, you name it, Texas. And it was very successful, very successful.

"I would listen to this bebop music, and I tried it, maybe I would create different steps to it to fit the music. Then I would try and do something that I'd been doing before and see whether I could fit that to it. And it worked out. Sure you can do it, if you just put your mind to it and get with it.

"Dizzy; every night that he played in our show, instead of going to our dressing rooms and just relaxing while he was doing his thing, we'd come out there and just watch him and listen to him. Because there was something different every night. He never played the same way twice, and each time it seemed greater, which was remarkable. And Charlie Parker was with us too. Charlie was on alto sax, and the same way that Dizzy played on his trumpet, he could play on his sax. And it was beautiful.

"At that particular time, down South, the music was strange to them. I remember all the different places that we played, the auditoriums that we played, the theaters; they didn't understand it at the time because it was way ahead of its time. But we understood it; the musicians understood it, and so we were having a ball. And Dizzy played his heart out, you know, he was beautiful.

"I remember when we first opened. I don't remember if it was in Savannah, Georgia, or what. It was in one of those southern states. We played in these different places where the audiences could dance as well. They could see the show, and after the show they could dance, or they could dance before the show. Now, this opening night, they had the dance before the show, and everybody was there, all the people. The place was packed, and the band was onstage and the curtains were closed. So they opened the curtains, and then they saw the band. They were running up to the bandstand, saying 'Yeah . . . !'

"There was a voice from backstage saying, 'Now, ladies and gentle-

men, Dizzy Gillespie and his Orchestra.' So Dizzy strikes up with
'Bebop.' They were playing like mad. Everybody was listening. They
were dumbfounded at first, and then they said, 'Oh, man, you a drag!'
and walked away. Ha! Ha!

"They were ready for him, but they couldn't understand this bebop
music. 'How can we dance to that? What's going on . . . a-bla-blee-
bu-bu-a-blee-bla . . . !' And that happened everywhere we went.
They just didn't understand it. Down South, they wanna hear the
blues, get with it. And when you bring them something that's outta
their class, 'Well . . . what is this?' It was way over their heads. Now
when the show came on, they loved that.

"My brother and I were the masters of ceremonies, but, see, first,
we told Dizzy, 'You go on and be the MC.' The manager of the place,
after Dizzy did it the first time, said, 'No, you'd better do it fellows,'
because Dizzy didn't have this gift of gab at that time for emceeing a
show. He could talk, but when he got onstage, he'd clam up. He
wants to play, not talk.

"So, we'd bring them on, 'Now, ladies and gentlemen, Miss June
Eckstine.' And she looked good. Aww, that girl looked good! And before she started singing, all the boys were ready to say, 'Yeah . . . !'
When she started singing, the guys said, 'Aw, that ain't it . . . !' She
sang modern, and they couldn't understand her either. Brought on our
little dancing girl, Lovey Lane, shake dancer, see—oh, they liked that
—right on down with it, and they liked our two comedians, Patterson
and Jackson. Both of them weighed about three hundred pounds, and
they'd sing and dance. Oh, they were beautiful, yes. And then we
closed the show. Then we'd do a little finale with everybody on, and
we'd do 'Salt Peanuts' or something like that. We all did that with
Dizzy. That was our little finale.

"So after that, my brother and I, we'd go to the mike and thank the
ladies and gentlemen for coming, hope they enjoyed the show, hope
we'll be back with them again, real soon. They loved that, but they
just couldn't dance to Diz's music. They couldn't dance.

"So I told him, I said, 'Diz, why not play something that they're familiar with?' He said, 'Aww, no, no . . . this is my music!'

"I say, 'I know it's your music, but slip a little bit of that in too.
Make them happy. Then go back to your thing. Kinda compromise
with them.' So he tried, he tried it. Sure he wants to stick to his own,
that's his style. That's what he knows best. But I said, 'Play a little
"Stormy Weather," or something that they're familiar with. And then
maybe give them a little bit of jazz that they know. Then come on out
with your bebop, your modern jazz, maybe they'll appreciate it better,
a little bit more. But you don't give it all to them, something that they

don't know. They'll walk out on you every time.' But I'm so happy that Diz didn't get discouraged."

No, I couldn't get discouraged, and I wouldn't let it affect me because we never had a big crowd, anyway. Jazz never attracted a real big audience, like rock 'n roll or the singers that came along. We never carried big crowds because jazz is strictly an art form, and so there was always a division between jazz and what other people were doing who were not really participating in a creative art form. Those other things people were doing were not creative; they were like pretty, manufactured meaningless tinsel rolling off an assembly line.

When we got back to New York, I broke up that big band, almost immediately. People weren't ready for bebop in a big context, like they were if you played it in a small group. That's when I got the band together with Charlie Parker, Max Roach, Bud Powell, Ray Brown, and later Milt Jackson, at the Three Deuces. They say you always have to bend; if you wanna make money, you have to bend. As a very young man, I busied myself trying to create and I didn't have no time for bending at all.

Three Deuces

The height of the perfection of our music occurred in the Three Deuces with Charlie Parker. He'd gotten in touch with me, played in the big band, and finally we'd assembled in a setting ideal for our music, the quintet. With Yard and Max, Bud Powell and Curley Russell, aw, man, it was on fire all the time. And, then we changed. Max went with Benny Carter, and Stan Levey took his place. Stan was a disciple of Max.

Bud Powell was the definitive pianist of the bebop era. He fitted in with us more than anybody else because of the fluidity of his phrasing. He played just like we did, more than anybody else. Curley Russell started off with us and then Ray Brown took his place. Curley couldn't read well but he could swing. All of us used him—Yard, Coleman Hawkins—Curley got around, but his solos weren't in the vein of Jimmy Blanton, Oscar Pettiford, and Ray Brown.

Yard and I were like two peas. We played all our regular shit.* Charlie Parker and I were closer musically than Monk and I. Our music was like putting whipped cream on jello. His contribution and mine just happened to go together, like putting salt in rice. Before I met Charlie Parker my style had already developed, but he was a

---

* I made "All the Things You Are" with Charlie Parker and used a classic introduction that almost everybody plays (Musicraft 488). Later I got tired of this and built upon what I had done before, using other progressions.

great influence on my whole musical life. The same thing goes for him too because there was never anybody who played any closer than we did on those early sides like "Groovin' High," "Shaw 'Nuff," and "Hothouse." Sometimes I couldn't tell whether I was playing or not because the notes were so close together. He was always going in the same direction as me when he was way out there in Kansas City and had never heard of me.

The enunciation of the notes, I think, belonged to Charlie Parker because the way he'd get from one note to another, I could never . . . That was just perfect for me. I came from an age of Roy Eldridge, and Roy Eldridge got from one note to another much differently from Charlie Parker. What I did was very much an extension of what Roy Eldridge had done— Charlie Parker definitely set the standard for phrasing our music, the enunciation of notes.

MAX ROACH:

"When Dizzy wrote a piece, there were certain things that he wanted expressed. When Charlie Parker wrote something, there were certain things that he wanted expressed, and your technique developed along the line of music that you were engaged with at the time. When dancing, comedians and all these things became too costly because of the war tax, the spotlight came on instrumental playing. Instrumental playing was the source of entertainment during the whole forties period, and so the virtuoso instrumentalist was the one who worked. Everybody worked hard at developing themselves instrumentally, constantly; this was a constant thing because no beginners could be on the bill. The spotlight was on instrumentalists because of the prohibitive entertainment taxes. They had a war tax at 20 per cent; they had a city tax; they had a state tax. You couldn't have a big band because the big band played for dancing. Count Basie traveled with a small band. The only big band I think that survived during that whole period was Duke Ellington, that traveled during that whole period. The war broke everything down. A lot of things were lost, but instrumentally, things were gained because during that period the height of the kind of virtuosity that was exemplified by Art Tatum, Coleman Hawkins, Dizzy Gillespie, and Charlie Parker occurred. You had to really know your instrument. Those guys survived because people came to hear music. People began to sit down; they were sitting down listening to music because you couldn't dance in a club. If somebody got up to dance, there would be 20 per cent more tax on the dollar. If someone got up there and sang a song, it would be 20 per cent more. If someone danced on the stage it was 20 per cent more. In order to have any entertainment at all during that period, the people just had instrumentalists playing, and it was a wonderful period for the development of the instrumentalist. And you were constantly experimenting to develop new ideas and meet the demands that the new music required on your instrument.

"Because the groups were small, quintets, quartets and trios, in order to have a fuller sound, more was required. More open spaces for solo playing. All this meant that you had to work hard. When you came to work at night or on a record date, you were prepared to meet these demands in craftsmanship. When you look at the period before that, the men like Jo Jones and Sidney Catlett and Chick Webb had tremendous virtuosity. What we were doing was just an extension of that all the time. The people who decided to say this was a big change were the critics of the time. But we were just continuing in a tradition to meet the high standards that were set up before we came on the scene.

"It was an exciting change. You know Afro-Cuban musicians were playing with the small groups we had on Fifty-second Street even before the big bands came back, and it was exciting to listen to the rhythm section. Of course, Dizzy brought Chano in to play, this was just after the Fifty-second Street period. This was when they moved up to Broadway. But they were playing with us prior to that. I can recall playing a concert with just Dizzy and Charlie Parker at the Hotel Diplomat, right across the street from Town Hall in New York City. We played with a group of African drummers that was visiting the United States. It was just Dizzy, Charlie Parker, and myself and about six or seven drummers. No piano, no bass or anything. We just played the things we were playing on Fifty-second Street, 'Woody 'n You,' 'Tunisia,' things like that."

MILES DAVIS:

"But they played the same chords, the same chords. Dizzy and Bird played the same thing. They used to play lines together just like each other. You couldn't tell the difference. But naturally being a saxophonist, Bird was fast. Bird was a *fast* muthafucka. He used to do some shit, boy, you couldn't believe."

DG: "Remember when he used to 'cram?' He'd be at a tempo way up there and he'd 'cram' something. And that means triple the tempo that he was already playing. Muthafucka'd be way up at a high tempo, and then he'd cram, right in the middle of that, '. . . a waddl-le-laddlela.' Boy! Oooo, shit."

MD: "He'd be eatin' up those triplets. Yeah, well guys got faster, you know. There were a lotta trumpet players that were lazy, and after they heard Diz, man, they got up and tried to do something like it. Don't you think so?"

DG: "Well that whole movement was conducive to acceleration of everything. Chord changes going. Like a guy had one chord, he'd make two chords outta that, like the B minor seventh to E, to E-flat, instead of just a plain B-flat seventh to E-flat."

MD: "And it made you play a little bit faster, you know. I think he changed the whole thing. He changed the whole music around. You have clichés now on television that he used to play years ago. He changed the arrangements around, big band arrangements. And just the way he played them, man, just fucked everybody up. Except me. He fucked up a lotta musicians, a *lotta* musicians, man, trying to play like Dizzy Gillespie."

DG: "You did your share of fucking up musicians too."

MD: "Aw, shit. . . ."

DG: "Heh, heh, heh. Everybody who'd come along would fuck up a whole generation of musicians, everybody. Louis Armstrong fucked up a whole generation of musicians trying to play one hundred high Cs. Bam! Bam! Bam! Bam! Bam! Louis Armstrong was known to hit one hundred high Cs, right behind one another. 'Banh! Banh! Banh! Banh! Banh! Banh!' Like that. They used to count them, 'One! Two! Three! Four!' Muthafucka hit a hundred and then make a high F on the end."

The so-called "mystery" recording session with Diz, Bird, and Miles; they've got a couple of versions out about who played trumpet on "Ko Ko." Who played it?

MD: "You—Dizzy."

DG: "Yeah, it was me because Miles had never played 'Ko Ko.' Yard and I had been playing together, and Miles had never played that introduction. I knew the introduction." (Savoy MG 12079.)

MD: "That's the damndest introduction I ever heard in my life."

DG: "Boy, when this music is solidified with the contributions of all those guys, and they show those notes that Charlie Parker wrote, the notes that guys who play don't even hear. Boy, you talk about perfect! Perfect melody with chords. It's just perfect, man, the lines that he wrote."

Yard and I never had any kinda words, or anything. There was never any underhanded shit with us like the newspapers made out. Only one time. I think Yard asked me to lend him some money. He had my pipe and he threw it down and broke it. Babs Gonzales was trying to get me to fight him. I said, "Aww, shit, no. . . ." I knew nothing would come out of it. The pipe was just broken, so fuck it. I was mad though. I'd just get mad when Yard would come in late.

We were pretty close philosophically, but my closeness to him was mostly musical. I didn't hang out with the same people he hung out with. I didn't do the same things he did, so I wasn't actually one of the crowd, one of the "deep in the hat" boys. Countless thousands of guys that were using shit were probably closer to his other life. Yard always denied the fact that he was using shit to me. I used to say, "Muthafucka, you're high." He'd be nodding. "Man, when you gonna come down off that shit?"

"Oh, Diz," he'd say, "you know I ain't using nothing." Nodding all at the same time and talking about, "Man, I don't use no shit." And I never *saw* him use anything. All I saw was the symptoms.

MAX ROACH:

"Bird wouldn't be on time, and it would always harass Diz, although there were no fights about it because Diz's criticism of any of us, or even himself, doing something off was always a drag. Anyway, this particular night, I guess we had had it. Bird came in late and instead of coming right in and going to the bandstand—we were on the bandstand playing—Bird came in, went right to the bathroom. So we played one tune and went into another selection, and Dizzy played. Then while the rhythm section was working, Diz went to the bathroom which had swinging doors and was right next to the bandstand. The microphones were out there. Diz went to the bathroom and peeped over into the stall where you sit down, and Bird was obviously in there shooting some shit. Diz came out the door talking to us but really drugged about it. "Do you know what that muthafucka is doing?" he said. "He's in there shooting shit." It hit the microphones, and it went through the whole house to the speakers, and Bird heard it in the bathroom. Man you heard spoons dropping and needles, and Bird comes rushing out the bathroom.

"He said, 'Diz, man, why would you do something like that to me?'

"Now, this was something! But Bird understood the criticism because we were on him at that particular time about himself. We were all back there in the dressing room at the Three Deuces, and we were telling him how much he meant to us, how much he meant to black people, how much he meant to black music. And for him to just throw away his fucking life like that was ridiculous. And the way he countered us was with the story about, 'Well, listen! It could be that I'm attaining this kind of notoriety so that I can get the spotlight on me, just to show our people—young people and everybody else—that you're not supposed to use dope and throw your life away like this.'

"Diz's concern for Charlie Parker was of that nature, where he would jack him up just like that, even though it did seep out and everybody said, 'Wow . . . !' Because the 'man' could have come right in there. Everybody was scared to death. But that was Dizzy's way, because he had come down every way he could to say that you gotta take care of yourself; you gotta do this, you mean everything in the world. That's what a family really is, and that's the relationship that Diz and Charlie Parker had."

RAY BROWN (bass):

"I had just come to New York that same day. I was with Snookum Russell's Orchestra from down in Florida and had left the band to go to New York. I had an offer to go with the Andy Kirk Orchestra. When I got into New York, I went to stay with an aunt of mine who had a son who's about my age, and she said I could stay there with them until I got myself going, you know.

"So I asked him where Fifty-second Street was and he said, 'I'll take you down there.' We got some food and went down to Fifty-second Street, and I was looking in all the clubs. There was a place called the Spotlite, and Coleman Hawkins was in there with a rhythm section. Billy Daniels was singing, out in the middle of the floor, and Hank Jones was playing piano. I knew Hank because we both had stayed at the YMCA in Buffalo; and so I went over and reintroduced myself. He remembered me, and we sat down and talked for a couple of minutes. While we were talking, he said, 'Hey, there's Dizzy Gillespie coming in here.'

"I had heard about Dizzy and everything on records, but I had never seen or met him. And I said, 'I would like to meet him,' and so Hank called Dizzy and Dizzy walked over.

"Hank said, 'I want you to meet a friend of mine. This guy is a helluva bass player too.'

"So Dizzy said, 'Can you really play?'

"I said, 'Yeah!' What the hell can you say?

"So he said, 'You want a gig?'

"I said, 'Yeah . . . ,' you know.

"So he gave me a card that says, 'Come to my house tomorrow night at 1 o'clock for rehearsal,' you know, just like that. And I got there the next night, and it was Bud Powell, Max Roach, Dizzy and Bird, wow! Outta sight, just like that. The only thing is being in the right place. Yeah, and we went to work right away.

"It was mind blowing. These guys were playing something entirely different from what I'd ever played, you know. But the one thing, I guess, I had going besides enthusiasm was a lot of stamina. You see, they liked to play fast and it didn't bother me to play fast. I can play fast all night, that wasn't any problem. It was just a matter of learning the way they played changes. Because Dizzy played—he voiced his chords differently, and he wanted a different bassist. That's what I had to learn, you know, what notes to play, things like that. It was like going to school. That's one good thing about Dizzy, if you don't understand something, he'll take you to the piano and show it to you. That's how all of us learned a lot, you know.

"Everybody was in the group, and about two weeks later, Dizzy picked up another guy who said he was a 'bitch,' and when he got there, he was. That was Milt Jackson. So Dizzy, first of all, obviously had an eye and an ear out for 'dizzy' guys, you know. When you read about somebody's band you usually have some doubts. That particular group, you know what happened to everybody in that band. Everybody in that band did a lot in the music business, there was no question about it. Bud and Max and Milt and I were the youngest guys. Dizzy and Bird were a little older than us. But it's an experience that you retain for the rest of your life.

"What I love about Dizzy's playing is the melodic content of his ear. Dizzy relies on a rhythm section to play him the right voicings and right notes. And if you do play the right notes—see, this is a leader in a different way, which is good, because if you have any imagination, you give him different ideas, ideas he might not think of, you know. Of course, he had to train us to get to that point, but his melodic conception of how to approach a solo is fantastic. The ideas that he comes up with.

"Oh, I couldn't put [the best] on any one performance. Milt Jackson and I used to run together. We used to go to work and we'd be waiting outside to get in to start to play. And you know, when we first started playing with Dizzy, of course, all eyes were watching me from that front line, you know. And then in later years, the fact that I found out more of what to do back in the background, the lighting and leading, throwing some good notes at him, watching him grab a hold of it, seeing what he would do with it was a gas."

The most memorable thing about those dates on Fifty-second Street was the influx of bands, small groups, and the different sets. The sets weren't the same. You could go across the street and hear Coleman Hawkins, Art Tatum, Billie Holiday, Al Casey, Benny Carter—all of these great musicians playing at the clubs. Somebody asked Roy once, "Did you hear that group with Diz across the street?"

Roy had that feeling. He was from the old school and he didn't know the continuity of the music, how it happened, why a guy comes up like me, like himself. He probably figured he just got it out of the air, but he didn't. He was inspired by Louis Armstrong, Rex Stewart, Red Allen, and all these guys. He didn't know the chronology of the music, how these guys come, so he didn't treat me too well. Sometimes, I'd meet him out in front of the Three Deuces and say, "Hey, Roy." He'd make like he didn't hear me. Like he didn't hear me, and all the trumpet players were trying to play like me, instead of trying to play like him. Roy Eldridge is the most competitive musician I've ever seen. Every time he picks up his horn and another trumpet player's there, he wants to blow him out. I never was one of those. I always played what I had. Guys in a session, everybody's sweating, I'd do what I had to, but not with the idea of cutting somebody.

But Roy used to come into places, and we're on the bandstand, the younger trumpet players, playing gentlemanly. He'd take out his horn at the door and start on a high B-flat, the next chorus, and come walking in, and everybody'd look around. That's Roy, coming up on the bandstand walking with it. The cutting sessions were like that. When I first came to New York, Charlie Shavers, Little Bobby, Benny Harris, Bama, and I used to go out in threes and fours. We'd play eight bars apiece, the other one'd come in after that. We could play almost all night like that. Other guys would get tired trying to play chorus after chorus. We'd get some good things going on Roy, Lips Page, Red Allen, Rex Stewart, all of the famous trumpet players. That was great experience. Roy used to always get the best of us by playing real high; he'd challenge me. But now trumpet players who play high have to do something else within that. You just can't get up and scream any more, though it has an effect on a big audience like Jazz at the Philharmonic where people are out to make a whole lotta noise.

DUKE GARRETT (trumpet):

"I play trumpet. I was with Lionel Hampton for ten years. When I got with Lionel I was able to get Dizzy to play with the band. One time, Joe Morris played sick; he thought the band was gonna fall apart. He was a great trumpet player; he's dead now, but he and Cat Anderson were with the band, and he thought the band would fall out if they left. So I saw Dizzy up on 125th Street and Eighth Avenue; he was just coming from a recording session. I had him to go down to the radio station and he played the first trumpet book for Hamp. And the boy, Joe Morris, heard it on the radio and wanted to know who that trumpet player was. Like to had a heart attack. He thought he'd lost his gig. Dizzy just played that one day. When I got back up to the Braddock Hotel, Joe was up there with Billie Holiday and them, and they say, 'Duke, who was that playing?'

"I said, 'Man, you better go to see Hamp and get your job.' I knew if Joe kept his job playing trumpet, I would keep mine. 'You better go down there and see Hamp right away,' I said.

"Everybody in music, and everybody outside of music, knows that Dizzy was the brainchild of the turnaround of modern music. We were back there playing like Roy Eldridge, and Roy was playing off of Louis Armstrong. And then Dizzy came along playing off of all of them, plus what he had to offer. And it innovated the trumpet so, most trumpet players—they didn't commit suicide but they died off. They didn't go kill theirselves. I won't call their names but I've seen them stand up and cry at the bar and stand up outside the club and not go in. Ain't but one boy I know that would go in when Miles and them used to sit down there with their horns in their laps and look up at Dizzy like he was God or something. Fats would too when they first come to New York in 1944. I saw it with my eyes; I was right there. I got pictures in my house to prove it—me, Dizzy, and Charlie Parker. I got me and him at the Three Deuces, me and him running outta everywhere.

"Dizzy's playing—it was different and it was accuracy of chord structure. Before, we trumpets had just been screaming and trying to see who could play the loudest and who could get the highest. Then he came out with an intelligent way of constructing solos on the chord structure of a tune and then delivering it in a way that was not an easy way—it was a way that you had to study. And some of us right today never have gotten down to his technique.

"Dizzy and Charlie, I knew them both just like brothers, closer than a brother. Charlie Parker understood what Dizzy would be explaining because Dizzy is a technician and a musician. It's a difference in a player and a musician. Some people can play but they are not musicians; just like some people can drive a car but they are not mechanics. Now, Dizzy is a complete player and a complete musician. That means if I was comparing it to a mechanic, in layman's terms, he can drive the car, plus get out and fix it up. Now, Charlie Parker could drive the car and drive it well, better than anybody who ever played the saxophone. Right? But he was not—anybody would say—he was not the mechanic that knew what to do with the car. After he found out what to do with it, he could do it, understand. The same way as if you tell me to cross the wires, and you're a head mechanic, and still you can cross them too, you're a foot ahead. But Dizzy was always the brain trust, I would say, of modern music. Charlie Parker delivered it; Monk delivered it, and Dizzy might have traded ideas with Monk. But Dizzy is the one that put the foot in the door. And then Louis Armstrong, and even my boss Lionel Hampton converted. Dizzy converted Lionel Hampton. We never played 'How High the Moon' until I told Lionel about Dizzy. Yeah, I brought him over there, and he didn't believe it. Lionel's got it in a book now that I'm the one hipped him to the modern.

"After we got the sound, we hired Kinney Dorham, Benny Bailey, Fats Navarro in our brass section. You know, keeping it modern. Then we hired Charlie Mingus, brought him in from California.

"The best performance I've ever seen Diz give was some years later, when my friend Charles Mingus wrote a book and put on the back of it that Thad Jones was the greatest trumpet player in the world. Well, Dizzy got the word. Somebody gave him the word or he read the book; whichever way, he got it. Basie was at Pep's, in Philly, and they had just made this tune, 'April in Paris,' and Thad had played a remarkable solo on that. So Dizzy walks in, and all these trumpet players sitting up there, Reunald Jones, Wendell Culley, Joe Newman, and Thad Jones. Thad wouldn't take down. Joe Newman jumped off the stand and told Dizzy to play his book, and Diz just walked in.

"And we were all sitting there; we wanna see this out, you know. So Basie played a tune and give all the trumpets some. And Dizzy just start to eating everybody up. He started to doubling up faster than the music; I didn't know where he was myself. People from New York were screaming for their life, man. Charlie Mingus was there with his mouth poked out. They tried to play high on him. Everytime they go high, he'd bring them right on back down. Soon as they started to playing in the middle, he'd cut them up there. So Basie, Count Basie, just said, 'Well, Dizzy, you just go on and play.' And then he played, about fourteen choruses. Count Basie said, 'All right, band, come on in!' That big band flew in, Dizzy's still playing. And they walked off there, and somebody said to Charles Mingus, 'You think you won tonight?' Charlie Mingus was ready to fight because everybody was teasing him about how Diz had walked off with the trumpet section.

"Nowadays, they don't always go for battling, but when I came up, it used to be a battle. If Dizzy walked in, like, where Roy was, well, Roy would be waiting for Dizzy. And if he didn't beat him, Roy would get off the stand and get drunk, just stay at the bar and start to cussing and calling everybody different names, 'Muthafucka can't play a goddamn thing—hip-ass muthafucka—' like that.

"What Charlie Parker and Dizzy would do, they would put their horns under their coats and run in on Coleman Hawkins, and run in

on Illinois Jacquet and all of them, and start to playing, down on
Fifty-second Street. And they would just wipe out the session. But if
the cats saw them coming with their horns, they'd get off the stand before it started. And in the middle of a tune, they'd slip up on the stand
and eat them up.† Boy, those were the days; Fifty-second Street was
jumping."

In 1946, I first discovered that I could make a high B-flat. Roy was
there with Georgie Schwartz. Roy was with Artie Shaw at that time. It
was a session, we were playing "Sweet Georgia Brown," and I had the
shit going all up and down in the register. But Roy had never heard
me go any higher than an F, sometimes a G. I made an altissimo B-flat.
Roy's eyes went up. He turned around and said, "What is wrong with
this muthafucka?" Ha! Ha! Ha! Haaa! I remember that, man; I remember the first time Roy heard me make a B-flat. But I have this
deep feeling for Roy. Roy was my idol. I just wanted him to know that
his influence had paid off. After a while when my style started getting
together, you could tell the difference between the two trumpet players. When two guys are playing just alike, you can't.

"Fat Girl," Fats Navarro, was a guy like that, competitive. He used
to say to Benny Harris about me, "I'm gonna get him. I'm gonna get
him, now."

"Don't fuck with him," Benny would say.

"No, no, Benny, I'm gonna get that muthafucka tonight!" And I'd
come up with some new shit. Ahaa, ha, ha, I could go back further
than Fats, shit that he never heard, you see. He knew all my licks; if
you hear him playing now, you'd hear all those. When you corner a
guy, guys like Don Byas, Ben Webster, and Coleman Hawkins, Lester
Young, as long as you're a nice guy with them and don't try to get
smart, you're all right. But don't do nothing to make them think you're
trying to out shine anybody. You'll run into a cage of apes. You'll learn
not to try to back anybody into a corner, especially a guy that's a
master. They thrive on competition; they thrive on it. It bounces off
them like that.

† This was known as an "ambush."

California

We took modern jazz out to the land of enchantment, California. When I was playing with Charlie Parker for those eight weeks out in California, every moment was like magic, almost. Hollywood, we gave some golden, magic, never fully appreciated moments. I've often wondered where that element comes from that makes a phrase or a note coherent, spiritual, and meaningful to someone else besides yourself. How does it trip that valve in the listener? It could come from the audience, or from the musicians you're playing with, but sometimes it just hits and everything is just right. If you're lucky, that happens once in your lifetime, maybe.

Every bit, if not *all* of the magic during that engagement came from the guys on the bandstand. That little band we had was very skillfully assembled. Charlie Parker I hired, because he was undeniably a genius, musically, the other side of my heartbeat. Milt Jackson, on vibes, was someone new and coming up fast in our music, very rhythmic, soulfully deep, and definitely my most prized pupil. Ray Brown, on bass, played the strongest, most fluid and imaginative bass lines in modern jazz at the time, with the exception of Oscar Pettiford. People noticed I had two white guys in the group—Al Haig, piano, and Stan Levey on drums. I guess because it seemed strange during the time of segregation. Almost everyone disregarded the fact that both cats were excellent musicians and devotees of the modern style. I didn't hire them because of their color but because they could play our music. All those guys, white boys, like Shelly Manne, Irv Kluger, Jackie Mills, Stan Levey were drummers in the drawer behind Max Roach, and they knew all the licks Max played. There wasn't that much money in the gig either, so Kenny Clarke had gone with Red Allen and Max went with Benny Carter. Both of them had better jobs than playing for peanuts with me.

Lay to rest any rumors that Charlie Parker resented working for me. Hell no! Yard was glad not to have that responsibility because he might not be there. I actually took six guys to California instead of five I had contracted for because I knew—them matinées, sometimes he wouldn't be there and I didn't want the management on my back. Yeah, Charlie Parker was such a great musician that sometimes he'd get lost and wouldn't show up until very, very late. Then the guy would look up on the stand and tell me, "You got a contract for five guys, and only four guys on the stand, deduct some money." So I hired Milt Jackson as an extra musician when I went to Billy Berg's to be sure that we had five musicians on the line, according to the contract. Sometimes, when Charlie Parker wouldn't make a matinée, Billy Berg would come up to me and say, "Where is Charlie Parker?"

I'd say, "Look, you don't have Charlie Parker's name on the contract, and you want five guys. You've got five guys on the stage." So he'd get outta my face, you know what I mean, and then Charlie Parker would come up later. But it was my group, the Dizzy Gillespie Quintet, and Charlie Parker was just a prominent member of that. I paid all the bills and made the major decisions.

We hit some grooves on the bandstand at Billy Berg's that I'll always remember, but the audience wasn't too hip. They didn't know what we were playing, and in some ways, they were more dumbfounded than the people were down South. Just dumbfounded. There were a lotta dumbfounded people because a lot of them came to see us. We were on the bill with Slim Gaillard and Harry "the Hipster" Gibson, big stars on the West Coast.

I had a big fight with Slim Gaillard. Somebody asked me in the club one night, "How do you like California?"

"I'll be glad when this eight weeks is over with," I said. "I don't like this place."

"What about it—?"

"Man, it's a whole lotta 'Toms' and musicial nothings and all that."

Slim Gaillard's wife heard me say that. She heard me use the word "Tom," and she went and told her husband that I called him a "Tom," and he accosted me in the men's room.

"Man, I ain't even mentioned your name since I been out here. What are you talking about?"

"Don't tell me you didn't!" he said. And he wanted to get bad about it.

I was just oozing over to the place in the bathroom where they sell all the bottles of cologne, and he was just oozing up on me. Finally, he hit at me, and I ducked, and he missed. I hit him and he went down, and I was getting ready to walk through him. The fight spilled outside, and his wife must have seen the scuffle; she went in the kitchen and got a butcher knife and was getting ready to stab me in the back with it.

"Look out—!" somebody said. So I grabbed a chair, an iron chair. I was getting ready to crown her with that iron chair because she had this knife in her hand, but before I could hit her somebody grabbed both of us and that was the end of it.

I cold-cocked Slim Gaillard, just one lick, a big lick, but since that time we were great friends. I made some records with Slim Gaillard after that, Charlie Parker and I. We had all the Hollywood crowd there trying to get "in." Naturally, anything new that comes out, people wanna be "in" on it, but they didn't begin to understand our music much until a little later on. They were much more interested in singers out in California.

🎼

AL HAIG (piano):

"I was in Boston and I picked up a late radio show one night from New York, and I was interested in jazz before that, but this seemed to really be just exactly—it was just so new it appealed to me. I was very young, in my twenties. I'd listen to this strange music from New York, and I thought, Jesus, I've got to really follow that down. So I came to New York, eventually, and I started looking for Dizzy on Fifty-second Street. At that time, I don't think he was working, but he used to sit in a lot, so I'd run around to the various clubs looking for him. When I'd get through with my job, I'd immediately run up to Fifty-second Street, looking in every club for Dizzy, to see if I could find him sitting in somewhere. And then, eventually, on Sunday, I just met him, probably at Kelly's Stables. I introduced myself and told him I admired his playing. He indicated that he was working somewhere, and we should get together, or something. Then I started working on Fifty-second Street. I was working with Tiny Grimes, and he and Charlie Parker came in. They sat in with Tiny's group, and from there, I think that Dizzy said that they were starting a group and would I be available. I said I was.

"I was with Charlie Barnet's band, and I got a telegram from Diz saying, 'Would you want to join the band . . .' When I got to California, to Hollywood, I got a call from Dizzy, from the hotel, and I remember that I said, 'How is Bird?'

"Diz said, 'Oh, he's right here. He wants to say something to you.' And Bird goes off in a corner and played something. He played a little thing for me over the phone. It was very funny. So on the basis of something like that, I would say all was well. I imagine they just got together from New York and just went there. I think they were getting along well then.

"One of the problems, I think, was Billy Berg, himself; I think that somebody sold him a revolutionary-style group as it were. If you wanna call it that. And I think that Billy Berg was not interested in any kind of music except music that was commercial, that sold for him. I do remember that the club was off limits for musicians. There was no freedom; it was just a job. I think there was an odd bit of fraternization at the bar among musicians, the bar was up alongside the bandstand. But other than that, I don't ever remember sitting at a table with anybody there. I was never invited to a table. I don't even know whether I would have been permitted to sit without getting a squawk from Billy Berg. But after all, Billy Berg did buy it; he did buy the group. I never did discuss it with Dizzy, because of the new music that he was playing at that time, we were accustomed to reactions from people.

"It was harmonically very innovative and also rhythmically different, with Bird and Diz on the bandstand, you know. And we did very little traveling, which meant that I don't really have a deep insight into, particularly, Charlie Parker. I don't think anybody has an insight except Dizzy, maybe. I don't think that many people have any idea of what, you know, really motivated Bird or the inner workings of his thinking. Dizzy was more outgoing. There was a certain amount of intrigue with Charlie Parker too. You felt that if you were going to hang around with him, you were under a spell or something. I mean I've heard this from different people. If you wanna hang around with me, you gotta do what I do, man. It wasn't like that with Dizzy. Dizzy was just a friendly type of guy. But most of my relationship with them was musical; it was on the bandstand.

"It was very good, very understanding. Of course I was new to the type of music he was playing, and so I was more or less in the role of a pupil. They had to show me exactly how the charts went and so on and so forth. And that was my role for some time. Now, that I think of it though, that wasn't a great period of time because I actually did more playing with Charlie Parker, after Dizzy formed the big band. It seems strange, retrospectively, to think of it as just a few months. It was just about that time. We later did concerts, Dizzy and Charlie and myself, and Max and whoever was playing, but my role was always strictly that of a learning subordinate.

"Dizzy taught me a lot about the treatment of tunes, of songs, in the jazz context, in every aspect, harmonically, rhythmically, aesthetically, whatever the word is—intuitive learning, or something. He's a wonderful great guy, a very sympatico type of person, a sharp guy. He's a composite of a great deal of very great things, and he's also been very good at maintaining himself in the idiom of music, where a lot of people fell by the way. He's just maintained himself well. He doesn't drink. He does what he's supposed to do, and he's been a good influence on musicians.

"The only thing I can think of is that there was some mixup out there, and Bird just suddenly disappeared. I had the feeling that Lucky Thompson was brought in to supplement the group. My basic idea about that was that Bird resented another saxophone player. This would be a just-off-the-top-of-my-head guess. He was probably sick, you know, and I must say that in all naïveté, I don't really know, because I didn't even know what heroin was, or any of that; that came later. I didn't know what Charlie Parker was involved in, anything like that, believe it or not. I was only twenty-two or twenty-three, and I certainly wasn't interested in those kinds of things anyway; I was interested in music.

"I don't know what the problem was; I'm only speculating. Originally, it was like Dizzy and Bird playing those lines together. And it was very tight, the group was much more solidly integrated then—that is, the original group, the quintet, than the sextet or septet, or whatever it turned out to be at Billy Berg's. And as I said, this is speculative; there is a possibility that Bird may have resented that. But this is just conjecture and speculative . . . I don't know. I have no idea, and I never talked to Charlie about it. I never asked him because the next time I saw him, a year or so had passed. Billy Berg was forgotten, and when I saw him the next time was a completely different thing. The music had caught on then."

STAN LEVEY (drums):

"I must have been sixteen, and he was working at the Downbeat Club in Philadelphia, around the corner from the Earle Theater. Dizzy was young then too; he must have been about twenty-four; he's eight years older than me. Anyway he had the little band up there, just a quartet.

"And one thing about Dizzy, which is marvelous, and he still does it today: he encourages young musicians. Man, I never saw anybody that open and willing to give his knowledge to people. The guy is just marvelous in that area.

"I went up and said, 'I'm a drummer.'

"He said, 'Yeah, come on up and play something.' I did, and he liked what he heard. Right away, immediately, he starts, 'Did you ever hear of Shadow Wilson?' Of course, I hadn't; I'd never heard of anybody. Dizzy says, 'Well, Shadow does this,' and he'd sit down at the drums, you know, and play it for me. That was marvelous. I guess I had a spark of talent, and he was that open that he would give. He was giving, man, he was nurturing young musicians. I never met anybody like that. Tremendous. And I used to come around to the club and sit, and he'd say, 'Well, you wanna come to work?'

"And I said, 'Yeah!' I think the gig paid eighteen dollars a week or something, downstairs.

"I caught up with Dizzy again, in 1945. I went to New York, waited six months and put my card in, then ran into Dizzy again. We never lost contact; I'd call him or I'd see him everytime he came in town.

"As a drummer, the thing I learned from him, which was so important, is that the drums are also a 'musical' instrument. Up to that point, everybody was listening to Gene Krupa and the bangers. They were all good, but it was an unmusical situation. With Dizzy, it became very musical, the drums. Dizzy wanted the drums to punctuate, as in a paragraph, to punctuate what he was doing musically. So you become more of an integral part of his particular music, which at that particular time was called bebop, or whatever the hell you wanna call it. He was the only guy that took the drums outta the straight 'clunk . . . clunk . . . clunk . . . ,' or whatever the hell we were doing in those days, into a more musical situation where you really had something to say in relation to him and Charlie Parker, or whoever was on the front line playing the actual music. That was a giant step for drummers, because drummers, say, like Jo Jones and that type, never broke the stride. That was the thing in those days, to keep time. But Dizzy didn't want that. He wanted more statements from the drummer, which was great, man. It opened all the doors, and whatever ability you had. He said, 'Beautiful, do that, that's great!' Anything to contribute musically to the band, he was wide open to accept it. Very few people in those days would do that. It was unheard of.

"Of course everything was fast. He played very, very fast tempos. You had to have that ability to play with Dizzy, and somehow I was able to play as fast as anybody wanted. I was as fast as Max, and there was just a few guys who could do that. Very, very speedy tempos. But Dizzy had patterns, man. He was always rhythmically oriented. Like he was into conga drumming, in every way, twenty years, thirty years before anybody. He fathered these things. So thinking in rhythms, he would have things in mind for the drummer, and he'd just sing them to you. And if you couldn't play it, he'd sit down and play it. Incredible!

"On 'Salt Peanuts' he had that all set up. The drum part worked like part of a jigsaw puzzle 'Bop-be-da' the little figures. He had little parts in there that had to work together, and this was all going a mile a minute, man. He worked this all out in his head. And, hell, you can't do it? He'd say, 'This is the way it goes,' sit down and play it, just the way he'd sit down at the piano and play what he wanted. Incredible!

"We were the first mixed band, ever, to play in California in a nightclub. People were looking at us, 'What the hell? What's going— what is this?' They had Al Haig, who was white, and myself, who was white, and five black musicians. Well, right away, that was weird because at that time these things weren't happening, especially in California, which was in those days ten or fifteen years behind the times. So there were some weird vibes coming out of California on that scene. But the band was really good; the band was really excellent.

"Nobody got bruised or anything, but the reception was cool to the music. What they were used to in California was 'Slim and Slam,' Eddie Heywood entertainment as opposed to pure music. Everybody was asking, 'Well, where is the vocalist?' That was the thing, 'Who's going to do the singing, here? Who's gonna tell the jokes?' That wasn't it. The pure jazz enthusiasts were all there, but the numbers were small. But Diz had a lot of movie people come in and listen, as this was the place to go.

"We used to do a broadcast every night from Billy Berg's, and somebody has a recording of that, every broadcast. Someone out here has that.

"Oh, just get to the gig. The only thing that would get Dizzy is if you were late. That kind of thing got him because he was and he is a 'pro,' man. That got to him; don't be late. Be there! As far as your ability, you wouldn't be in the band if he didn't dig you. See, that was up front. It was never, 'Well, I'm gonna see how you do.' If there were any reservation, you wouldn't be there, so all that was straight. Just be there on time. And that was the thing with Parker that was so rough. In fact, when we came out here, for about four days they added Lucky Thompson because Charlie would get there at eleven-fifteen, and we'd be late all the time. He had many problems out there.

"Of course you know Charlie was really ill, man; he was strung out from the time all of us met. And Dizzy had his act together, even in those days. Financially, not that he was well off or anything, but his money went here and he took care of his business. He was a musician and a businessman, right? With Charlie, Charlie was the ragamuffin. You had to put a net on him to get him where you wanted him, but his ability, his gift, took precedence over anything. I mean, that ability, his talent, just made up for anything. So the attitude Dizzy had toward Charlie was, well, we have a child here who has a great talent. And whadda you do with a child? You have to look after him—not a father-son—but a kind of 'keeper' in a way. You can't give him all of his money. You gotta watch; you can't give him everything at once, he'll get rid of it and you won't see him.

"But of course Charlie had his—he was very strong too, mind you. His personality was extremely strong. He wanted what he wanted. So their relationship was rough because Diz was all business, and he says, 'We hit at nine-thirty, and goddamit, this is it, man! We gotta hit!' And Charlie wasn't hitting at nine-thirty. If he got there at eleven, that was good. So that ground their relationship kind of to a halt. Because it was just unbearable to Dizzy. Dizzy was voracious in his drive to succeed, to get to wherever he wanted to get with the bucks and the numbers, or whatever, and Charlie was oriented to drugs, to get his drugs. So there was a problem.

"When we finished out in California, at that point, Parker was a basket case, I mean really. He couldn't get the drugs that he was using, and he was using some Mexican drugs. I mean, he was a mess, practically ruined. You know he wound up in Camarillo. Now, we were closing on a Friday, and it was Wednesday, and we hadn't even seen him. Nobody at the hotel had seen him. He was out in the jungle somewhere, just lost, man. So Dizzy went ahead and bought five plane tickets, O.K.? And Friday came, nobody'd seen him. Dizzy gave me some money the last day and says, 'Get in a cab, here's twenty bucks and here's his ticket. Try to find him—try to—really see what you can do. All right?'

"Course I went all over the place, every place I could think to go, and of course we didn't find him. And the last thing Dizzy did was, he left Charlie's ticket at the desk in the hotel. I know a lotta bandleaders . . . Dizzy wasn't making big money out here . . . a lotta guys would say, 'Oh, screw him. The guy didn't show up, forget it, that's his problem.' But Dizzy would make an effort, even though Bird had jerked him around pretty good by not showing up and being late, causing many problems. And so he was trying to finish it off in a good way and do what he was supposed to do. That, I feel, was pretty good. By all standards, he was a man."

RAY BROWN:

"The music wasn't well received at all. They didn't know what we were playing; they didn't understand it, and a guy asked us to sing. We were supposed to be here more than a month, and after the end of

the first week, they said, 'You guys gonna have to do something. . . .'
A guy named Billy Berg, he said, 'You're gonna have to sing or something.'

"And I'll never forget, Bird wrote a couple of charts where the
whole band was singing, you know. I don't know how Dizzy felt inside, because I don't think he really cared for that. I'm sure he didn't,
but I'm sure he didn't transmit it to the guys in the band. The guy
said that we had to sing. Slim Gaillard and Harry 'the Hipster' Gibson
was the other two acts, and they were big favorites out here. And the
musicians . . . I know, I looked up and Art Tatum was in there four or
five nights a week. Benny Carter and other, very well-versed musicians
were out there, and I think they had an idea of what was going on. But
the average public couldn't fathom what we were doing at that time.
But you know Dizzy went back there a few years later and tore it up,
same chords, same crowd. So the music was valid; it was just a matter
of them catching on, you know, the times.

"We all know what Bird's habits were because he'd had them since
he was fourteen years old. That preoccupied a lot of his time off the
bandstand; it took up most of his social life; it dictated the type of
friends that he was to have. Unfortunately, he was relegated to just
dealing and running in certain areas to get what he wanted to get, to
keep up with his needs. Where Diz and Bird were compatible was on
the bandstand, musically. I mean it was like one guy with two heads
was playing together. It's hard to go back and find any two horns that
played together any better at any time. And such fantastic soloists.
And they were playing a different thing."

Tempted as I felt to go upside Billy Berg's head for demanding that
we sing as well as play, I stayed cool, and except for "Salt Peanuts,"
we didn't sing neither. Sea to sea, America in 1945 was as backward a
country musically as it was racially. Those of us who tried to push it
forward had to suffer, but some good people managed to survive by
playing loudly through it, and I don't feel that I disappointed anyone.
My own spiritual condition stayed pretty good—though I didn't have
an affiliation with any religious group—I felt pretty cool.

Charlie Parker never believed I let him down, and he remained my
closest friend and colleague until his death. When we got ready to
come back to New York, he wanted to stay out on the Coast, and I
gave him his transportation, the money. What he did with it, God
knows. I gave him all his money and his ticket, because my wife was
right there and she saw me. He suffered a nervous breakdown and
went into Camarillo State Hospital. When I got back to New York, I
hired Sonny Stitt, another marvelous musician.

The Spotlite
(THE BIG BAND, 1946)

Bebop took a great leap in popularity. My name hit the billboards as a great trumpeter before I knew it—and they had me getting ready to organize another big band. Two clubs on Fifty-second Street, the Spotlite and the Three Deuces, were begging me to accept extended engagements when I returned to New York from California in 1946, and we went into the Spotlite, a bigger club, instead of the Three Deuces.

Clark Monroe, a black guy who also owned the Uptown House, owned the Spotlite, and he told me, "Look, you come in here for eight weeks with a small group; you could get Sonny Stitt and then open up for eight more weeks with a big band. Build it in here." We did that. In the small group I had Milt Jackson, Ray Brown, Sonny Stitt, in place of Charlie Parker, Stan Levey, and Al Haig.

A major turning point in my playing, I think, happened one night at the Spotlite when Randy Brooks came in. Randy Brooks was a trumpet player/bandleader with a tremendous range, and then he had a cyst on his lip. He went to a doctor, Dr. Irving Goldman, who was the premier plastic surgeon and nose and throat specialist in New York. My lip was cut, and after playing at night, when I'd wake up in the morning, I'd squeeze it and pus would come out. Between sets, I'd go back in the kitchen and get some baking soda and boiling water and mop it up, go back out and feel good. But when I'd go home and come back out the next day, I'd still have that soreness. "Man, you need to go to a doctor,"

Randy told me. "Dr. Goldman is the best for what's wrong with you. I'll make an appointment for you," and he made the appointment.

Dr. Goldman's office was down in that neighborhood, 121 East Sixtieth Street, no niggers. As a matter of fact when I went there, the nurse put me in a little private waiting room. I noticed that, but I didn't say anything. A lotta magazines were back there. Dr. Goldman looked at my lip and said, "Umm, hmm," and went and got a small reamer. He got ahold of my lip and took some white stuff and cleaned it out. He stuck this reamer down in my top lip, and then he put this white stuff in there which burned a little bit. I went on playing, and very soon, my lip was all healed up from the inside. Dr. Goldman straightened it out; but every time I'd go to his office, he'd put me back in that little room, in the back. This is 1946, and since that time—knock on wood—I haven't had any serious trouble with my lips. My chops got together during the Spotlite engagement. My chops really got tight then with range. I could hit Gs and As, sometimes B-flat. Get on up there and ride. My playing was accelerating more and more and all the trumpet players were trying to play my style.

When I formed the new big band, I hired Bud Powell on piano and Max on drums. The money was a little erratic, and Bud was super-erratic, and I had to do something about that, so I got Monk. I had no trouble outta Monk, not too much, but Monk wasn't showing up on time either. It was against the law to show up on time.

Billy Shaw arranged all the business. We rehearsed the band in the Spotlite, and I took that big band out on the road in 1946, 1947, 1948, and 1949. We built this band to last permanently. Pulling it together was quite hectic; Walter Fuller, thank God, came in to organize and arrange things. No one can beat Walter at organizing and arranging.

A composer gets an arranger because he's lazy; he doesn't wanna sit down and write it all out himself. With Walter Fuller, I didn't have to do it all. I just had to write the melody, and sometimes a specific harmonic structure, and then say, "I'd like to see it moving like this." A lotta stuff you just leave to him, and he works with it, puts it up, and it'll be just like what you want done. Because he understands. But not fully, really—nobody understands you fully. You can tell the arrangements I made by myself and the ones someone else made; they're different. A composer should have someone that understands him real well. Like with Duke and Billy Strayhorn, it was just like Duke writing the arrangement because Billy Strayhorn was so into Duke. He was so in tune with Duke Ellington. Duke was fortunate to have Billy Strayhorn, and I was lucky to have Walter Fuller to write arrangements and organize that big band in 1946. I still arranged for different bands, Ina Ray Hutton, Jimmy Dorsey, and Boyd Raeburn, but mainly because I had to do it. I wasn't making enough money. We wanted to sound in the same idiom as the small bebop unit with Charlie Parker, like what we had played in the small group. We wanted the big band to sound like that.

WALTER GILBERT FULLER:

"Instead of having eight weeks to put the band together in the Spotlite, we had five days, because they went in there with the small band, and they wanted a big band in there, and they gave us a week or a week and a half to get it together. Billy Shaw said, 'Get the big band together.' Dizzy can't remember what happened. He didn't even know what the music was gonna sound like and never showed up for rehearsals until Friday, the opening day.

"Oh, yeah. They found some young girl, some young white girl on the Street that had been injured in the club, underage. And they say, 'Where you been?' She'd come from a good family someplace.

"And she says, 'I go to the club to hear the music, and I met all the musicians.'

"They said, 'Well, who do you know?'

"'Well, I know Dizzy Gillespie. . . .' That's all they wanted to know. They went to Dizzy's house and arrested him for contributing to the delinquency of a minor. Billy Shaw came and got him out right away. It could have been a setup, I don't know.

"Billy Shaw told us that we needed a band, so we got the money again. This time, I wasn't gonna have fifty cats down there auditioning. We picked the cats. Dizzy and I never had any arguments about that. We only had one argument with reference to who was going in the band and who was going out, Monk and John Lewis. I'll tell you about that.

"Anyhow we had some music already. And now, Billy Eckstine no longer had a band. So I went over to Billy and said, 'Hey, man, Dizzy's gotta be ready for the Spotlite next week. Why don't you give us some music out of your book? You know he helped you get your thing together, now why not help him get his thing together?'

"So he says, 'Well, Fuller, I'll give you whatever you want. Tell you what. Here's the key, and you go up there and take whatever you want. How many things you want?'

"'I want ten.'

"'You take ten things you want out of the band, copy them, and bring my music back.'

"After that he gave us all his stands and everything. Microphones, everything. Asked me if I wanted some uniforms.

"So I went to see what arrangements they had in the book. And I got 'Stay On It,' 'Our Delight,' 'Cool Breeze,' and 'Good Bait.' Those were some blockbusters, boy! See, I tried to pick what I thought were the best things that he had. He had some other things in there by other guys like Linton Garner's 'Minor Walk.' But I got the good things, and among them were those things that I named of Tadd's. Now, Tadd (Dameron) never sat down and wrote an arrangement for Dizzy because Tadd wanted to get paid, and we had no money. They weren't giving him money to get a book. That was the first mistake they made. Tell Dizzy to get a band then not give him money for a book. He had no money to put into a book; so we had to get it the best way we could.

"Now, our band didn't sound like Eckstine's band. Eckstine's band sounded like something else compared to ours.

"Billy Eckstine came with the beginning of this change in the music. Guys really hadn't heard Bird to the extent where he had influenced what it was. The biggest Bird influences came when Dizzy and Bird put their thing together and started recording together.

"We started writing ourselves, and in that first week, between Dizzy and I, we sat down and wrote 'Things to Come.' He and Lorraine came down to my office on Broadway, in the back around a long hall. Lorraine sat over on a chair waiting for him and fidgeting, while we sat there arguing back and forth over what we were gonna do. Finally, I got enough of what I needed, and said, 'O.K., you can go ahead; take Lorraine and go.' We did 'Things to Come'; we got 'One Bass Hit' together. We did 'Ray's Idea' and 'Oop-Bop-Sha-Bam.' Now, that was like Dizzy's first bebop hit. We did that with a small band, with Sonny Stitt. That was Sonny Stitt's first record date. 'That's Earl, Brother,' too. I know those two we did on that first date with the small band, with Sonny Stitt playing alto like Charlie Parker. And Sonny could play his can off during those days too.

"Anyway, for the first four days of the week, I rehearsed the band from one o'clock in the afternoon til about six, then went home and started scratching and writing, trying to get more music. Then we sat down and we got a theme song together. Dizzy and I sat down and made an opening.

"The opening had 'Shaw 'Nuff' in it. Max was back there rolling and carrying on, on those cymbals. And then Dizzy came on, outta nowhere. Max would overpower the band with a big old cymbal he had, and then Dizzy would come in from on the side of the stage hitting a F, and the band came in underneath him, real pretty and quiet. We opened that thing up.

"We had the theme song all ready, when this cat came in there. And from the theme song, we went into a lope, this pretty slow thing. Man, the people heard that band that night. But getting up to that.

"Five days, Dizzy always comes in and plays with the guys. I said, 'Get the fuck outta here. Don't bother me; I don't wanna see you. Lorraine, keep him away from me until Friday.' Knowing him, I knew he could play the music. I wasn't worried about him playing his shit. I knew Dizzy would play anything he saw. That Friday, I told him, 'You gotta direct it, they gotta get used to you, not me. Get on up there and do your shit.' Told him how it went and what it was. Dizzy looked at that music and he took off with it. I saw him grinning, so I said, 'Well, we got past that.'

"And then Dizzy played his parts. The cats had never figured out what the music was because they never had his stuff in there. It was always playing background and they got used to playing it, so they knew what it was. And, man, we had the most precision stuff you'd wanna hear. We stayed in there the whole afternoon. We'd been rehearsing all week, and this cat came in there in one afternoon and got it all, knew exactly what he was doing and ain't never faltered.

"That night, about ten o'clock, all these people were coming in, and Monroe had ballyhooed up the opening, 'DIZZY GILLESPIE'S BIG BAND,' and put a big sign in front of the club. You had the Three Deuces open, and the one next to the Three Deuces, the Yacht Club. So people had seen this sign, 'DIZZY GILLESPIE'S BIG BAND.' By this time he had people who liked him, they'd been seeing him on the Street and everything, so they all came there to see what the hell he was gonna do. And, man, he hit into that opening. Well, they weren't expecting that noise, the whole band, a little club, and this first thing started with the whole band hitting one note. And Dizzy brought his hand up, and everybody jumped. And by the time they landed on their feet, thinking it was over—no, he hit another one—another one—another one! And old Max was going, took off with the shit. Then Dizzy played his theme. Whatever the first tune was, it was like a loper. They played that and then they played 'Things to Come,' to wind it up. He had a whole series of things that he played. Some of the things we never recorded. He had a lotta pretty tunes.

"When we started hiring guys in that band at the Spotlite, we had Monk in the band, playing piano. Max was the drummer, Ray Abrams, Warren Luckey. Cecil Payne was the baritone at that time. Then we got Ernie Henry in the band, and we had Howard Johnson, the alto player. And Howard had a nice tone, knew how to lead a section, had all kinds of experience. The cats were something, man.

"Kenny Clarke brought John Lewis in the band. Kenny said, 'Hey, Walter, this cat was in the Army with me, give him a break.'

"I told him, 'Well, O.K., tell him to bring some of his stuff around. We ain't got no money. Tell him we can't give him but fifty dollars for his arrangement. If we buy it.' Fifty dollars was a lotta money then.

"He brought the arrangement, some of the original things he wrote. And he had a very strange way of voicing which was different. Like, his ideas were different from what we were doing, but it still wasn't what the old cats were doing. So you figure, 'Hey, man, maybe we got something here?' So I told Dizzy, we played the stuff, and it wasn't too bad. So, I said, 'O.K., we'll take him in.'

"Monk never would show up on time, but I didn't want Monk in the band for the sake of showing up, as much as I wanted to get Monk's things. Because Monk was a freak for tunes. He had all kinds of strange shit going on. And we got all the things from him, like 'Playhouse,' but I never did have a chance to write the arrangements on the things because everything was happening. I was writing for six or seven other bands at the same time, and I would never write the same shit for them that I would write for this band. They would try to get me to write Dizzy's shit. You know, 'Write them like Dizzy's.' I wouldn't write them. I wouldn't write the arrangement. Tell them, 'No, man, I couldn't do that.'

"Anyway, we had Monk for that, 'Ruby My Dear,' and all that stuff. We had all of the songs—all of Monk's tunes. We got all of Bud Powell's stuff. We were getting everybody's stuff. You remember 'Tempus Fugit?' Bud played with the small group after Dizzy came back from California.

"Anyway, Monk wouldn't show up. Dizzy's mad because Monk don't never show up on time. Anytime we got ready to hit, we'd hit without a piano player. 'Where's Monk . . . ?' He just wouldn't show up on time; he just didn't make time. So Dizzy's mad.

"So then John Lewis says, 'Dizzy, I can play better than Monk.' And the next thing I know, John goes up to Lorraine and tells her he can play better than Monk, and he's so nice and everything.

"Lorraine says, 'Aww, Dizzy, I don't see why you're going through all that hell. Why not just go ahead and hire him?'

"So then John Lewis got in the band. Boy, when John Lewis got in the band, that was the end of Monk. I never forgave Dizzy for that. I didn't think Monk was a piano player like Oscar Peterson, that type of thing, but he had material that we needed. And the idea was to collect as much music as possible.

"We had Charlie Parker in the band. He came back to New York. We played up in some theater in the Bronx. Had Freddie Webster, and

Miles and Kinney Dorham in the trumpet section. Up there in the McKinley Theater in the Bronx. That was the end of Charlie Parker in the band. Charlie Parker came in the place and had his shit in him and sat up there all through the whole thing till his solo comes, and when his solo comes, Bird put his horn in his mouth and . . . 'doodle-loo-deloodle-loo.'

"And Dizzy, on stage with people in the audience, said, 'Get that muthafucka off my stage!' Because he didn't want the whole band to be tagged as a bunch of junkies, you know. He wouldn't let me put him in there anymore; he just wasn't gonna have that. Because Bird would always get high, man, and then start to nodding right up on the bandstand. And you're playing the whole thing with no first-saxophone player. But, man, he couldn't keep his head up. So that was the whole thing in a nutshell.

"Dizzy didn't fire him. He actually didn't have to let him go. He came to me, telling me to fire him. He told me to get him off his bandstand. That's what he said.

"Well, he was a bad influence. In the first place, he'd nod on the bandstand. The younger musicians in there were looking up to him. A lot of times musicians would come to Diz and think that he was doing the same thing because he and Bird were like one person. So we had to cut that loose, but it really didn't make that much difference.

"That was a helluva band, but again we wanted Charlie Parker for writing the tunes. And I told Dizzy, 'Shit, man, it'd be worthwhile just to give him a hundred dollars a week and let him write tunes for us than to be worried with him.' But we didn't have the money at that time. There was nobody putting the money up. You couldn't do it. And nobody knew the band until we got the first hits, and then we were able to go out on the road together and do a tour and all that. And everybody was afraid that we were doing the same things that we had done before. But when we got the hits, that kinda erased it. We started going all over the place.

"We wanted it to sound like what Dizzy and Bird were doing, but the sound had to be translated into a big band sound. The real thing was to get Dizzy's sound into the band, nobody else's. In order to get that sound, and to keep the band from sounding like other bands, nobody in the reed section other than the first man could use vibrato. That was the first rule. We never let anybody in there use vibrato except the first man, so that when the saxophones played, they had a distinctive sound. When it came to the trumpet things, Dizzy would show them; so he had four cats doing exactly what he wanted them to do. The note is there, but it's not there. He had to teach each one of the guys how to do that, so it went right. That was our arrangement.

"And my thing was to develop a new and distinctive sound. The way Dizzy maintained and kept that sound was because I refused to write for any other bands. I wouldn't write for no white bands; I wouldn't write for anybody from 1945 to 1948, until I left that band. He had his sound. And whenever I wrote an arrangement for anybody else, I wouldn't voice the same way that I voiced for that band, because I didn't want anybody else to sound like that. That sound was ours, and I wasn't gonna write it down for anybody else, because if you did that, then they could take it and copy it for themselves. Once they all began to sound like Dizzy, I knew that meant out of business for me.

"I knew all of this from Fletcher Henderson who gave his sound to Benny Goodman; Sy Oliver who gave the Lunceford sound to Tommy Dorsey. I saw Eddie Durham who gave his sound to Glenn Miller by using the lead clarinet. He used to take the lead clarinet player, Willie Smith, outta Lunceford's band and put him on clarinet, on top of the band. He played so loud that he could dominate the reed section. When you wrote arrangements for Lunceford, you had to put Willie Smith on the lead, because if you put him on harmony, it wouldn't sound like nothing, because the cat was so strong, he'd overblow the whole damn band. His tone was so cutting and so piercing.

"In Dizzy's band, I used all open harmony for the saxophones all the way through, then close harmony for the trumpets, and spread out the three trombones. That's what gave the brass that big fat sound, with the close harmony in the trumpets. Like I said, nobody, not even Dizzy, knew what the hell I was doing. Even with Hepsations 1945, I took 'Blue 'n Boogie,' all the things, and wrote them for a big band. So when you hear things like, 'Well, the basic ideas came from Dizzy,' the idea was that it's supposed to be Dizzy's band, not my band. So I had to try to do something that would identify the band with what he was doing. That was to make the band be his; of course I never even said this to Dizzy either. Don't tell him that.

"The biggest criticism of Dizzy that I had was that he didn't have my background in terms of putting an organization together, running the business aspect of that operation the way I would have run it. In the beginnings when we started the music, I didn't have any problems in convincing him to do anything that I wanted to do. Most of the time when we went to the dates and things, I selected the music. I picked the music; he didn't give me no arguments about that because everything that I picked was what he liked. In other words we were in accord with everything. But nobody else would ever believe what I would say.

"Like I'd tell a guy, 'Hey, you didn't come in here on time!' Now, I did that to Freddie Webster and Max Roach and told them, 'You can forget it from here on. You won't be here.' Looked right at them, 'You're late, you didn't show up.' Make them pay. They had to buy everybody in the band wine, whiskey, beer, and cigarettes. Whatever the band wanted, you were the sucker; take it out of your pay for being late and wasting everybody else's time. So we did have good discipline in the band. Like this thing with Max Roach and Freddie Webster; we were in Chicago, we had to hit; one o'clock was the show, and they show up at ten minutes to one and hadn't rehearsed anybody else's music. Max is the drummer and Freddie is, like, the first trumpet player, so we couldn't get anything done. You just couldn't let the guys keep on doing that or you wouldn't have had anything. After a while in changing the fellows, we got all kinds of good little guys: Dave Burns, Elmon Wright, Matthew McKay. We had a lotta nice guys in the band who would make the time and things like that. We didn't have any real problems in the band in terms of things like that, later.

"I also didn't like Dizzy's choice of singers. He picked a girl named Alice Roberts. I didn't think she was a real blues singer because her voice was too light, but we still recorded her. And as it turned out, she didn't do like a Dinah Washington did. So the girl made records with us, but I don't know that she ever made any more after that. Things like that.

"As a musician, Dizzy didn't have the tone that everybody else had. He concentrated more on technique than he concentrated on tone and the kind of sound he got. His sound and tone wasn't as big as, say, Freddie Webster's. Or you could say that his tone wasn't like Miles's, because Miles tried to sound like Freddie Webster when he started out. And Miles had a softer tone. When you look at Miles as a whole, Miles didn't have the technical facility for getting over the horn like Dizzy had. So, I mean, like you either develop in one area and you don't develop in the other. It's like specializing in something. Dizzy specialized in technique. Other fellas specialized in tones.

"He had fully developed harmonically. He had totally developed technically, and the only thing—if you were gonna say anything about him—you could say that his tone wasn't, like, as developed as the other parts of his musical getup.

"I told him, 'You got a lousy goddamn tone.' But he didn't develop that, like he developed his technique, like he developed his harmonic knowledge and vocabulary, which is vast and extensive. But when it came to the tone, he didn't place that much importance on it at the time. Well, he never held a note that long.

"Also, he used to play all the time, because he wasn't at all concerned with whether you made the band this way. He'd be quiet for a minute, and with his nature of being a nervous type guy, with a lot of nervous energy, he'd sit down and play, or you'd get some guy in the band that couldn't play the thing and he'd go up and play it for him. What was bugging me with things like that was, If Dizzy's gonna play the damn thing, then let Dizzy stay up there and play it! What's the guy gonna do? I don't need him.

"Guys like Dizzy spoiled me. Because you could write an arrangement and give it to him, and he could read it down the first time flawlessly. He was always kind to the fellows, and he would always try to show them. But while he was telling them, he was killing the time. We only had three hours to rehearse, and I couldn't spend an hour or two hours with them.

"What I liked about Dizzy was his fingers. Dizzy had a lotta tricks in terms of fingering. False fingering, which a lotta guys don't even know. Where some guy would be playing like an A-flat with his second and third valve, Dizzy would be playing with one finger. Other cats sitting up there hitting two, this nigger was playing with one. Because he knew where it was. It ain't supposed to be there, but it is.

"And then Dizzy was playing around with the harmonies. You talk about Roy Eldridge; Roy Eldridge was playing the harmonies that Jimmie Lunceford and them was playing, seventh chords or ninth chords, stuff like that. And that's about the extent of where they went. And see, that's where the music started changing. This is why his thing started changing, because Dizzy was playing augmented elevenths, flatted fives, and all this stuff that people weren't playing. People weren't playing augmented eleventh chords, thirteenth chords, minor ninths—they hadn't heard such stuff. They called him the 'wrong note' trumpet player.

"Now this cat would stay up on the piano. He'd get in a place on the piano and work out. Say, 'Listen to the way I'm gonna change this.' So he'd sit down and change the changes on standard songs to something else. Now the melody is the same, but the harmony was entirely different. And if you heard us play a song, he had worked out the harmonies by himself or we had worked them out together. I'd tell him, 'O.K., what kinda chords you wanna use; what do you think?' And we'd sit down and come up with all this shit. This changed the sound of what the music was, changed the whole complete sound of what it was from them lousy major chords, with a sixth, and the ninth chord and the major seventh. It started changing the thing. When we did, like, say, 'One Bass Hit,' you had a thing in there where he went into the bridge, and the saxophones came in and hit a flatted fifth, or raised eleventh. Everybody was looking saying, 'What the hell is that?' But you couldn't say it sounded bad, and you couldn't say it was wrong."

HOWARD JOHNSON:

"When Dizzy first came to New York, I didn't call myself being kind to him, but I treated him nice. I was never antagonistic toward him. And years later he may have considered it returning a favor by having me in his band. That shows that he had a good memory and appreciates things. In 1946, I think that's one of the reasons he hired me, out of friendship. Of course, I'm not downgrading myself, I can play, but I think he did it a lot on a friendship basis.

"I came back to New York, and Billy Eckstine was playing at the Cotton Club, in 1946. I had just come out of the Navy, and I was there with a friend of mine. Dizzy happened to be there that night, and he came over to the table and sat down.

"'What are you doing now?' he said.

"'Well, just gigging,' I said. I was working at Smalls then, on weekends, with Harry Dial.

"'I'm getting another big band,' he said. 'We need a good leadman.'

"'O.K.,' I said.

"'As a matter of fact we're having rehearsal tomorrow.'

"I said, 'O.K., I can make it,' then forgot about it. At that time I was living on 124th Street near Broadway, and Walter Fuller was living right around the corner on LaSalle Street. By the time I got home after a night of carousing, I had forgotten all about the rehearsal. So Walter Fuller came around. Dizzy had called him and told him to come get me. So he woke me, and I went around to the rehearsal. That was the beginning of that.

"I first heard bebop when I came back from overseas. I was in San Francisco and heard those first records with Charlie and Dizzy. I said, 'Gee, the music sure has advanced. I'd like to play it, but I think the music has gone out of my realm now.'

"The one thing that bebop lacked was the beat at that time. They didn't have a good beat, and the general public could not follow it. I remember oftentimes we used to go to a dance, and the band would be great, and the people would stand around and watch instead of trying to dance. And a much lesser band—a lesser band—would come up and play, and they would dance because they could feel a pulse. Bop more or less showed people that jazz was something to just listen to, and feel, rather than dance to, because people couldn't move to it. As a matter of fact, the beat was lost for a few years until Fats Domino brought it back. Four or five years, actually, the beat went out of jazz music. That's a part of jazz, you know, and bop is jazz also.

"To me it was a new concept because I hadn't played that progressive music at all. But I mean, the notes, I could read the notes, and some of those fellows were not too good as readers in that band, but they had the progressive feeling. Dizzy had an idea where he was gonna have the stuff all written out. That's when he got songs like, 'Things to Come.' That's the reason why Dizzy was interested in accomplished musicians. I got in the band that way. It wasn't too difficult. After it got started, it moved along quite well. I made a couple of arrangements myself for the band with the new concept, because I liked what they were doing. It was wild. And then we opened up down at Monroe's on Fifty-second Street. I remember the night we opened, Duke Ellington came in, and so after we'd played 'Things to Come' and some wild stuff like that, we called on Duke to speak.

"Duke said, 'I love all music; it's saying something.' Which amounted to 'I don't dig it, but I appreciate everything.' You know he was very gracious. 'They've got something. It follows after the title of their theme song, 'Things to Come.'"

TED KELLY (bass trombone):

"Now, you know when you first start playing you're not too great a musician. Then you have more nerve than talent, you dig. I was living downtown, the next house to Thelonious, and I used to go uptown and play now and then. So one night I went up to Minton's, and sat in with the band. The nerve that you have when you don't have much talent. When we got through, Thelonious says, 'Man, come by the house tomorrow because you don't know what the hell you're doing. You don't know what you're doing.'

"So I started going by Thelonious' house on Sixty-third Street. I was living 247 and Thelonious was living 243. I used to go by his house and play every day. And I got to be pretty competent at the kind of things they were playing at the time. Finally, one day he says, 'Hey, man, you wanna work with Diz?'

"I said, 'Yeah!'

"So he says, 'Well, he's putting together a band.' And they were rehearsing up at Minton's. He took me uptown, and he says, 'Diz, give my man a job.' And that was the beginning of that. That was my association with Diz. So we rehearsed, this had to be about 1946, because I was supposed to be graduating from City College at that time. I was a chemistry major, but I had been pursuing music courses in high school and had been playing music from the time I was seven, violin and so forth. Diz decided he was going to go out and do sixty one-nighters through the South. So I was never even here for the graduation ceremony. I went out with Diz. I went down South, and we did these sixty one-nighters.

"We came back, and we played at the McKinley Theater in the Bronx. We worked up there for a week or so. And Sarah Vaughan worked with the band at that time. She was still relatively unknown. She had on her little blouse and skirt. We did a week or so up there. By then he had Freddie Webster, Bird, and Benny Harris in the band, good musicians. It was cooking by then."

ELMON WRIGHT (trumpet):

"I first met Diz when he worked in Cab Calloway's band. My father, Lamar Wright, Sr., worked in Cab Calloway's band. When I was a kid, my father used to take me to hear rehearsals and sometimes their gigs. So I met Diz when I was a youngster, even before I started playing. Then when I got interested in music I took up the trumpet. When I came out of school—I'd studied pretty hard—I worked with different bands, Don Redman, and then got a shot at Dizzy's band. They were making a tour, this was 1945, with the Nicholas Brothers; and Diz had the band. They were having tryouts, and they wanted a first-trumpet player. I passed the test, so I got the seat in Dizzy's band. Diz had known me when I was a kid. So that gave me a little booster right there too, you know. I was seventeen.

"The music was outta sight, man. Those first things, 'Disorder at the Border' with Diz and the 'Bean,' Coleman Hawkins. Oh, man, when I heard that, I like to went crazy, you know.

"People wasn't too hip to it, man. It was a little bit ahead of them except for a few people. This was 1945. We did a lotta tours down South. I remember, 'Why don't y'all get outta that old be-beop-a-de-bop . . . !' Things like that.

"Then after the tour was over, I left Diz and went with Roy Eldridge for about six or seven months and left Roy Eldridge and came right back to Dizzy's band. I happened to be standing in front of the Braddock Bar on Eighth Avenue and Diz needed a trumpet player.

"He said, 'What you doing?'

"I say, 'I ain't doing nothin'; I just left Roy Eldridge's band.'

" 'Come on,' he says, 'the bus is leaving in forty minutes.'

"I ran home and packed a bag. The bus was in front of 2040 Seventh Avenue and that was it. That was in 1946, and I was with the band up until the band broke up in 1950. You could say I was with him from 1945, but, like, I left for a period of about six or seven months, and I came back in 1946.

"In those days, Dizzy's prime, he was outta sight. Oh, he's still outta sight. I remember there was one occasion when he played Chicago, a hotel off of Sixty-fourth and Cottage Grove. Anyway, we had a featured guest, Charlie Parker. I'm trying to think what year it was, but anyway, during those times they didn't have tapes, they had wire recordings. And, man, that night was outta sight. Diz and Bird got together. Well, you know Bird, he's the master. Well, Diz says, 'I ain't going to let you do that to me,' and the both of them took off with the big band arrangements behind them. A fella took these things off on wire and played them back to us. When he played it back, it sent chills up my spine to hear this. That was one occasion. And then I think Miles played with us a couple of times. That was a gas. There were quite a few, quite a few.

"Diz contributed a style. Style, because before Diz started playing like he was playing—don't misunderstand me, I'm not putting them down—but everybody was playing more or less like Roy. And don't misunderstand me because Roy's my man too; I worked with him too. He's something else too. But when they heard Diz, man, the whole thing, overnight, the style changed. The phrasing, the way you go from one passage to another. The phrasing and then the syncopation. Like Diz was to trumpet players what Charlie Parker was to saxophonists. Overnight it changed. When you heard Diz—'Boom!' It just changed overnight.

"Just about every modern trumpet player, Diz played a part in your life as far as trumpet playing goes. In his upper register, he can do things that I haven't heard any other trumpet players do. You hear him do these things, and you say, 'That's impossible, man . . . ! How the heck can a guy do that? He ain't got but three valves.'

"Diz used to get mad at saxophone players. He'd say, 'Man, you guys got a key for every note, man. Say, we ain't got but three valves.' He was just joking with them, you know. He used to rib them. 'Man, you got a finger hole for every note, and we ain't got but three valves to make all of these notes.' I guess that's what keeps him on top. Seems like it's impossible, but he'll give it a try."

DAVE BURNS (trumpet):

"I met Dizzy in Minton's Playhouse, and I think I was about sixteen or seventeen years old; I was still a teen-ager. And we went over to hear this guy that was playing so different from anybody else, you see. We came over from Jersey, we had a teen-age band in Jersey. The leader of the band was an older guy, and he took us over there.

"He said, 'I want you to hear this guy, because you never heard a trumpet player play like this in all your life.'

"Of course, in those days, I was a Louis Armstrong fan, and my fa-

vorite guy was Roy Eldridge. I guess Dizzy's was too before he got
into the thing he was playing. Anyway, we went over to hear Dizzy at
Minton's Playhouse, up on 118th Street. And he was making it with
Monk, Kenny Clarke, and a guy named Kermit Scott. I think he was
from San Francisco. This was before Bird came to New York. This
was going back into the thirties, around 1938. Before Bird. That's the
first time I heard of Dizzy.

"Oh, my God! That's why we went over to hear him because he was
the most phenomenal trumpet player I ever heard in my life. He
turned my whole musical direction around so much, because nobody
was playing the changes and the chords he was playing. Now, when
you hear it, everybody plays like Dizzy. They don't play the same
style, but it's still patterned after Dizzy's, the way Dizzy plays the
trumpet, you see. And there's no trumpet player alive now that hasn't
been influenced by Dizzy. If there wasn't a Dizzy Gillespie, there
wouldn't have been a Miles Davis. He wouldn't have played that way
because he wouldn't have heard Dizzy.

"Dizzy was the greatest influence on jazz music, as far as the brass
instruments. And not only that. He was the greatest influence on
music, period. Period! He and Charlie Parker are the two greatest
influences on music, and I think that stands. Anybody that's doing
anything, playing anything as far as jazz is concerned, is playing like
Dizzy and Bird, or they have played off of what Dizzy and Bird had
created. This is what makes them the giants of today.

"I joined Dizzy's band in 1946, after I came out of the service. I was
with him from 1946 until around the latter part of 1949. Then I went
with Duke Ellington in 1950.

"I stayed with Diz a good three years; it seems like months because
we had so much fun together. It was a big band then, and the music
was adapted by Gil Fuller. He's great, great, great, very imaginative, a
genius of a man.

"And then after that, John Lewis came along playing piano. John
Lewis, from the Modern Jazz Quartet. I remember when John first
came in the band. After Monk left, then John joined the band. There
was quite a bit of a change, but John was so down in the things that
he wrote, you know, which were different from Monk's. John started
writing some charts for us, arrangements. Like he did 'Two Bass Hit.'
I remember John doing some real nice things for us. But I remember
John doing some things that didn't sound good too, when he was trying to learn. I think at this time he was really learning how to write. I
mean he knew how to write, but he didn't know how to voice. I
remember some things that John brought that we just turned our
noses up at. We said, 'Oh, my God, I don't think I could take another
one of these.' If I saw John now I'd say the same thing, and he would

laugh about it. I remember some things he used to bring, and I'd say 'Oh, my God, please, John, don't bring another one—no bullshit like this, no more.' You know I used to say that to John."

JOHN LEWIS (piano):

"I met Dizzy in 1946 through Kenny Clarke. Kenny Clarke and I were in the Army in France together, and after getting out of the Army in 1945, I came to New York around Christmas time. But before coming to New York, I heard a broadcast from Billy Berg's out in California, and it was quite a terrific thing. I guess they never did hear that group like that in the East, the group that Dizzy had with Milt Jackson, Charlie Parker, Ray Brown, Al Haig, and Stan Levey. That was really almost unbelievable. I was at home in Albuquerque, New Mexico. These were broadcasts we were able to receive from California. Well, that was one of the most marvelous experiences that I ever had. It was just unbelievable.

"I guess during the war there had been a constant search to achieve virtuosity; you know, with all the other great players, Lester Young, Ben Webster, and of course the greatest virtuoso was Art Tatum, already, before the war. And it was like this with that group that Dizzy had; everybody was a virtuoso.

"But then sometimes you'll have virtuosos, but you won't have virtuoso music to play. Only, that music that they had to play was virtuoso; it wasn't for just the ordinary run-of-the-mill musicians that had existed up until that time. They didn't have music like that. And that really is the big change as far as I'm concerned. It changed the music to a complete virtuoso music. Before, it was a functional music, for dancing, principally for dancing and also for shows, some stage appearances, and a few concerts, very few. Duke Ellington was the principal concert artist that we had. He was the best one as far as I'm concerned. But then that changed with what Dizzy was doing. That was something really completely different.

"So I came to New York to go to music school and met Diz in 1946. Kenny came home a little later; he came home in January, I think, of 1946. Kenny took some arrangements of mine that we played in the Army together down to Dizzy, and he liked them, so I started writing.

"Well, you know Dizzy is sensibly self-taught. So having the advantage of what he knew shown to me by Dizzy—anything I wanted to know, Dizzy would show me on the piano, or write it out for me —then the advantage of going to school to find out things you can't find out in the streets, because you can't find them all out there. And there are so many that you can't find out, of course, in school. I got both advantages. Dizzy brought a lot of exciting, wonderful new

"Klook-Mop" . . . his other name is
Kenny Clarke. WIDE WORLD PHOTOS.

With Milt Jackson in Detroit, before he came to New York.

Cutting the fool with Yardbird at the Royal Roost or Birdland, 1950. PHOTO BY
DUNCAN P. SCHIEDT.

Jazz at Massey Hall, 1953. Bud Powell, piano; Charlie Mingus, bass; Max
Roach, drums; me up front; Charlie Parker on alto saxophone. FRANK DRIGGS
COLLECTION.

With sculptor Dexter Jones and my head in bronze.

Celebrating with Sarah Vaughan and two Argentine visitors at Birdland during the 1950s; receiving an award for having the most popular record in Argentina, "Things to Come."

Relaxing with Carmen McCrae during the 1950s.

Concentrating on the
piano with John Lewis.

Sharing a smile
with Monk.

With Nat King Cole and friends. PHOTO BY HERMAN LEONARD FROM THE COLLECTION OF CHARLES STEWART.

"Professor Bogus," Charlie Roisman.

About my Nigerian ancestry . . . CHARLES STEWART.

W. C. Handy refused to O.K. our modern version of the "St. Louis Blues," but he gave me an autographed picture several years later, in 1953. COLLECTION OF DUNCAN P. SCHIEDT.

With members of a small band, 1953, Bill Graham, Lou Hackney, Wade Legge, and Joe Carroll, vocalist, Dusseldorf, Germany.

ideas, especially new melodic ideas, in the sense of creating very fluid lines, instead of the old lines, which were slower and based on popular tunes. He changed that; he and Charlie Parker both, of course. Then he had a unique way of voicing and he had a unique touch at the piano too. Actually, I thought he should've really done the bulk of the writing for the big band he had and found somebody else to do some of the other stuff. Then I would guarantee that that would probably be, still be, one of the most successful big bands. It would be the most unique one. But he didn't have enough time to do it all, with all that other business stuff you have to do.

"Gee, I guess I learned so much that I've forgotten. It's a collection of all the things, and it turns you into a creative musician. You just use the things naturally. It's been so long ago, I can't even remember all the things that I learned from the experience of being with Dizzy. There were an enormous number.

"I was really just mainly affected by the musical performances that I made with him and heard him play. I remember one night in Detroit, he played 'I Can't Get Started' and something else with the big band in back. Played so much, he did, after that set, I said, 'That's it. . . .' Thought it was time to go home, and put on my coat getting ready to leave.

"He said, 'No, no, we got another set to play.'"

JAMES MOODY (tenor saxophone):

"Well, the first time I met Diz was in Greensboro, North Carolina, when I was in the service. I was in the Air Force, and Dizzy came down there with his big band and played on our base. Diz played at the Big Top down in Greensboro. At that time the Air Force was segregated too. I was in the little band that they had there, and Dave Burns was too. Dave Burns and Linton Garner, Erroll Garner's brother. We met Dizzy there, and I think Dizzy was saying that when he got back to New York, he was gonna form another band, this was about 1946. We told him we would be getting out in a few months.

"He said, 'Come by and try out for the band.'

"We had records of Diz and Charlie Parker. We had things like 'Hothouse' and all that, and we'd be sitting in the barracks trying to play that stuff, you know. We went and tried out for the band, but I didn't make it. Walter Fuller was in charge of the auditions, you know.* But Dave Burns made it. Then I went back to Newark. And two

* WALTER FULLER: "Yeah, I remember when he didn't make the band. . . . Dave brought him down and said, 'Why don't you give Moody a break?'
"So I told him, 'Well, man, I'll be glad to give him a break. If he can play,

months later—not two months, not too long—I got a telegram one
night. My mother was ironing clothes, and she was smiling when I
came in.

"I said, 'What are you smiling about, Mother?'

"'I'm just smiling. . . .' She said, 'Look under that sheet.'

"And I looked under the sheet and there was a telegram that said,
'You start with us tonight.' And I think they were working at the
Spotlite. So I joined the band that night. And when I went with them,
they had Milt Jackson, Monk, Ray Brown, Howard Johnson, the saxo-
phone player, Talib Dawud. Oh, and I was in awe. I was awestruck.
Like, Jesus Christ, man!

"Well, see what I had listened to was Charlie Barnet, Jimmie Lunceford, Chick Webb, people like that. The first cats that I heard were,
like, Jimmy Dorsey on alto, and I like that. But when I heard Count
Basie and Lester Young together, I said, 'Oh, oh, hot dog!'

"And when I started hearing this other stuff, I said, 'What's happening out there?' I remember one of those first solos that Diz took. I
think it was with Cab Calloway. The bit he took sounded good, man,
and new. I liked it. Maaan, I wanted to play like that.

"Oh, I learned an awful lot, a lot musically, a lot intellectually. I
learned a lotta things from him. Musically, he told me about chords
and things, and then I noticed the way he spaced when he played.
See, you don't have to play in all the spaces. Play this chord and then
skip one. And then when you come back, skip the one you played and
play the one you didn't play the next time, the stuff like that. . . .
And then Diz says, 'You spend a lifetime playing music to learn what
not to play. You can't play every single one, so don't try to. Just take
your time.' And also I learned to play the piano. You play the
piano because everything is there, you can see it. Playing a horn is one
thing, but if you play the piano you can sit down and see all the notes.
You see what's there, and then you just apply it to your horn.

"Man, they thought he was nuts. They say, 'Here he come, playing
those wrong notes again.' Yeah, man, a guy told me one time, he says,
'See, people be listening to Dizzy and what Dizzy is playing; and what

he's got the job. It makes no difference to me.' So we told Moody to sit down
and tune up.

"Moody said, 'Peeeeeep . . .' you know, like a bird.

"'I'm playing as loud as I can,' he says. 'I'll do it again, man, Peeeep . . .'
And you could hardly hear him.

"I told him, 'Man, you got to play more than that. You got to put more balls
in your thing than that. We can't use that because nobody would even know
you're sitting there.' So he's looking all scared and everything, and we started
to playing, and sure enough, as we played, you couldn't hear him. So I told Moody,
'O.K., I'll tell you what, man. Whenever you get it together, come back again
and you'll get the job. You come back, but you gotta develop yourself some lungs
and a stronger tone, and then you can play.' "

Dizzy is doing is capitalizing off of his mistakes.' That's what the guy
says. 'See, Dizzy makes a mistake, and then he jumps off that and goes
on something else. So that's it, see, that's what he's doing.' That's how a
guy explained it to me.

"When somebody's talking like that to you, you don't say anything.
You just listen and say, 'Unh, hunh . . .' and say to yourself, 'What a
jerk!' And this guy was a musician. I don't wanna mention his name,
but he told me that. 'Dizzy capitalizes off of his mistakes, that's all.
He's a good musician, but he capitalizes off of his mistakes.'

"I said, 'O.K. . . .'

"I remember we went on tour with Ella Fitzgerald. It was Dizzy
and Ella, you know, and we toured all down South. It was funny to
see the reaction of the people to the band. Down there it was a little
different because the people weren't quite aware of bebop, and they
didn't know how to dance to the music at that time. So they would
stand and look up at the band as if we were nuts, you know. One
time, down South, this guy was looking up and he said, 'Where's Ella
Fitzgerald?' He was mad because he didn't see Ella Fitzgerald yet,
you know. 'Where's Ella Fitzgerald?' And we were playing. I think
that night we kinda had to band together, to get out and leave there.
It was down in one of those little towns down South somewhere. They
didn't know what was happening. But, man, when we were like out on
the Coast, in Chicago, and Detroit. Oh, man; people, boy, they'd be
wild. Lines would be all everywhere. We were playing the Paradise
Theater in Detroit. Man, the people! Just lines, crowded, coming in to
see Dizzy. It was outta sight too, beautiful.

"We used to play places and people used to look at us. But then I
was naïve myself; I didn't know what the heck was happening. I
stayed with the band just about three years from about 1946 to 1949.

"Oh, I became an alcoholic. That was the first time it began, because I was an alcoholic for a few times. But he was always nice to
me.

"I remember my mother said, 'Would you kindly take care of my
son, please, on the road?'

"Diz said, 'Sure, sure, I'll take care of him. . . .'

"One night on the road, some faggot was trying to rape me, man.
Really!

"I said, 'Look, man, why don't you cool it.' This faggot was a big
nigger too. I wound up sleeping with Dizzy that night.

"Dizzy said, 'Come on, Moody, let's go . . .' because this faggot was
not taking no for an answer. He wanted this young boy.

"Another time, we went on a tour with Ella Fitzgerald and my
whiskey told me to dance. And I was dancing with a white girl down
in Texas, somewhere, in 1947. Dizzy and Lorraine, both of them had

to go out there and pull my butt outta there. 'Nigguh, you better get on this bus. Come on, we have to leave town, quick!' Dum-de-dumb-dumb! I went back with the band later, and then after that I went with Dizzy, with the small group. I stayed with him almost eight years."

JOE GAYLES (tenor saxophone):

"Well, we first met him when we were in the service; that was James Moody, Dave Burns, and I. We went to hear him in Greensboro, North Carolina. They came through in Danville, Virginia, forty-eight miles from camp.

"Well, we had been following him prior to that though; it wasn't anything new. We'd heard records before we'd seen him in person. This is his first big band around 1945. His band came through and we went to see it. And we formed the nucleus of his band from 1946 on through 1950; we all stayed with him. We joined him after we got out of the service. You see, James Moody and Dave Burns lived in the East, and I'm from the West, from Denver. Dizzy needed another guy, so they recommended me. That's when I got the gig.

"It was like going back to school. In other words, a graduate course, so to speak. Because at that time they really had some great bands, but this was like graduate work. Really, I mean, with like the chord construction. It was altogether different music, and rhythmic patterns. So I found it very stimulating, very fresh.

"Playing with Diz, man, every night, you never knew what was gonna happen. Those guys were just fantastic; he was fantastic. I don't wanna give him the stereotype bit, but Diz never played the same thing twice. Don't forget now, I was with him for the longest, for about four years. And, man, this cat didn't play nothing twice; it's incredible, it's incredible. Bird's another one; Charlie was another one.

"Dizzy and his wife, Lorraine, they're sweethearts, lovely people. Don't forget, we had a hard time. Now, don't let him run it to you that everything was peaches and cream. In 1946 we had a hard time. There was a lotta rejection from people because they couldn't understand the transformation of the music. And our gigs sometimes were few and far between. But Lorraine and Diz, they managed to keep that band together—you better believe it—and were nice and helped us all out.

"It's awful hard to say why people found it so difficult to accept this music. It just seems like they couldn't grasp it. You just couldn't 'foot stomp,' so to speak. You had to get in there and learn something. Even the phrasing was different. I don't know whether you ever heard any records of Dizzy's big band. You listen to it, and it's still really ahead of time now. That music, today, is your modern music today, even the phrasing. The idioms that the musicians use today, now, are the same.

"You see, the band we had, man, was a young band at that time, and a lot of us, we'd just gotten out of college and stuff. Don't forget, man, that band was very well educated too. We didn't have any junk problem, not in our band, understand. Everybody was buddies. It was so hard, man, to find a band like that; everybody was friends. Now how do you like that? Just like today, we're all still the same buddies. After all these years we still get together and have our reunion and just laugh about old times. Everyone was wonderful; you couldn't have found a better person to work with than Diz. *Impossible*. He was fair in his dealings. We didn't have any favoritism. We didn't have a star-studded band. What we had was just a group of beautiful, ordinary musicians. Everyone just knew their instrument, but there were no stars at that time. These guys weren't stars. They didn't become stars until they went out and started making records of their own.

"Diz is probably the most dynamic force that has ever been perpetuated in the music business. The only person that I would say would be equal to him would have been Charlie Parker. That's the way I feel about Dizzy. He's one of the greatest, most dynamic personalities I've ever met.

"When we were in his band, we had a free rein. Now by this, I mean that a lotta time the sections used to create different musical passages. Whereas he would be listening for 'it,' well we made changes. Say, like, if you're playing a tune, an arrangement, night after night, night after night, right? Well, instead of going to a certain point where he thought we were going, we would do something else, altogether different from what the music called for. Now, the trumpet section, they would create something on their own, just that quickly. Then the trombones would do something, then the rhythm would do something. And, Diz used to turn around and look at us like we were crazy. You gotta understand this. Now after we got through, he'd make us all feel like we were in the fifth grade. He would take what we had done and then really just top the whole thing over, build something on that which he had never even *heard!* I'm just trying to show you the talent that this man has. Incredible! Any given night it might happen."

RAY BROWN:

"We had such fantastic, really fantastic things. I remember when Bird got out of the hospital in California. He came back East, and Dizzy's band was up at the Savoy, and he came up and sat in, and that was a fantastic night. But the biggest thing about that whole era was enthusiasm. I mean, what a lot of us lacked in musicianship and experience we made up for in enthusiasm. I mean, everybody just *wanted* to play so bad; and everybody was there early, waiting to play, you know. Come out, go to work, and stand outside on the sidewalk and wait for the guy to open the door. That kind of enthusiasm. That's the kind of job you want to get, when you can't wait to get to the bandstand, because it doesn't happen all your life.

"Oh, yeah, don't forget that sextet I told you about was very unusual. I would say out of that sextet, I was the least competent guy in the group. And they made something out of me. So that's why I think that's a fantastic sextet; everybody in there turned out to be something else.

"The big band was different. You can't get a big band like that, with the exception of maybe a couple of Ellington bands. I mean where you had a band *full* of giants. That took a lotta years. The big band had a lotta good musicians; it didn't have a lotta great musicians in it. But see, what makes a band good is that you've got one very influential and powerful leader. That's the first thing you gotta have. Then you have to have maybe three or four good soloists. Then you gotta have some workers. You can't have all chiefs; gotta be some Indians, gotta be some braves there. If you get one good lead saxophone player, and get the other four guys to follow him, you got a good section. You can get five great saxophone players, but if they ain't gonna follow the lead guy, then it doesn't mean anything. It won't sound good at all. But we had a good experienced saxophone player, a guy named Howard Johnson, who was older than the rest of us, but he was good at section work. So he had an influence on the saxophone section. The rhythm section in the original Dizzy band, which turned out to be the beginning of the MJQ [Modern Jazz Quartet], was probably the strongest section, because that section had Kenny Clarke and myself, John Collins, and John Lewis on piano, and Milt Jackson. And we made the first MJQ records, Milt and I and John Lewis and Kenny Clarke. Then Kenny went to Europe, and I left, and so they got Percy and Connie Kay. When I left Dizzy, the band was getting ready to go to Europe, and I couldn't go. I'd just gotten married to Ella Fitzgerald. At that time I was in a bit of a curl between her wanting me to travel with her as well. She wanted me to travel with the trio; she had Hank Jones playing piano. So finally I just decided that I was gonna stay in New York."

ELLA FITZGERALD (vocalist):

"I think really the first experience I had of really getting to know Dizzy was when I traveled on a tour with him. We went on a six-week tour, and we also played at some theaters together. It was a southern tour, and Ray Brown was with the band, and Bags was in the band. It was a real great tour, and we had a ball. We played Baltimore and Washington; we used to play at the theaters, what we called 'around the world.' When the band would go out to jam, I used to like to go out with Dizzy because I used to just get thrilled listening to them when he would do his bebop. That's actually the way I feel I learned how to what you call bop. It was quite an experience, and he used to always tell me, 'Come on up and do it with the fellas. . . .' That to me was my education in learning how to really bop.

"We used to do 'Ooo-Bop-Sha-Bam-a-Klook-a-Mop . . .' That's one of the first things I remember he used to do. And 'She-bop-a-da-ool-ya . . . She-bop-a-da-ool-ya-coo . . .' and that fascinated me. When I felt like I could sing that, then I felt like I was in, in. And I followed him everywhere they went. In fact he was the cause, one of the reasons I started singing 'Lady Be Good.' When they had the all-night show, 'Make Believe Ballroom,' they used to have the musicians come on and play, and Dizzy played 'Lady Be Good' with me and we jammed.

"He said, 'Come on and risk this . . .' and I did 'Lady Be Good.' Then after that, Decca had me do 'Lady Be Good' on Decca Records. A disc jockey out in Chicago played the record, and it became a big hit for me, that and 'How High the Moon.' To me it's been an education with Dizzy, and I always felt close to him, and he always called me 'Sis,' you know.

"On that southern tour, I remember that he used to always want Lorraine to make his eggs. Everywhere we'd go, he'd want Lorraine to make his eggs. No matter where we went, Lorraine had to make the eggs. At a lotta the theaters we played, my cousin and his wife used to do the cooking for everybody backstage, and everybody in the audience would be getting up because the food smell would be coming from backstage. They'd be getting the whiff. Oh, we would have some real crazy experiences, but to me it's been what you call growing up in the music, the other side of the music, and knowing that it hasn't been all easy, but worth it.

"To me he's an all-around entertainer because, you know, we used to Lindy Hop a lot. We would go into towns and go to clubs—there'd be a nightclub or somewhere to go, and the band would start playing, and we get up, and that was it! We used to take the floor over. Yeah, do the Lindy Hop because we could do it. Yeah, we danced like mad together. Dizzy was a good dancer. Both of us were good dancers. And we'd go with the old Savoy steps.

"I haven't really paid that much attention to Dizzy's voice. I only heard him sing one pretty song, the time we were in a club. I was surprised. Everybody was talking at the time, I really didn't get a chance to hear all of the song, but I was surprised because it was such a pretty tune. One of his songs that I always liked, because he used to have a fella sing it was, 'I Waited for You.' I always loved that tune."

ALICE V. WILSON:

"After John left school and went to Laurinburg, I lost touch with him. I got out of touch. And so the next time I heard anything from him, I was in Columbia, South Carolina, attending summer school. You see, I had only finished high school, and I was trying to get my college through summer school.

"Anyway, somebody said, 'Alice, you know there's a fella gonna play up at the Township Auditorium, and somebody said he's from your home. Say he's good!'

"I said, 'Who is he?'

"And they said, 'Gillespie.'

"I said, 'No!'

"And so we went, you know. And I saw a big sign out there with his name. He was gonna be there that night, and I told my roommate, 'I'm going up there to the Township Auditorium, right now, and see him!' And I went alone. She couldn't go with me. She had something to do and so I went alone to the auditorium.

"I heard the music; they were practicing, and someone was standing in the door, I guess, to keep people from coming in.

"The fellow said, 'You can't go in.'

"I say, 'Is that Gillespie in there?'

"He says, 'Yeah, but I'm sorry . . .'

"I say, 'Well, if he knows I'm out here, I can come in.' I told him who I was. And he said, 'O.K., I won't tell him you're coming.'

"He had his back to the door, because all of his men were on the stage. He was directing and showing off as usual. Ha! Ha! So I eased on up behind him, and they got kinda quiet, you know.

"Then he started, 'Man, how come y'all so . . .'

"And someone said, 'Who's that coming in there?'

"He looked back and saw me, and, boy, he picked me up. He was big, you know. He grabbed me and picked me up and whirled me around.

"They said, 'Man, well who is it? Tell us something. Don't be going on and don't tell us who it is.'

"'This is my teacher, Miss Wilson,' he said. 'From Cheraw. She's the one that taught me all the jazz I know, man. She started me off with it.'

"So I stayed a few minutes until I met them all, and he told me, 'You be sure to come back out here tonight. I'm gonna give you your money right now because we don't have any passes.' He gave me the price, gave me the money, and said, 'Whoever you want to come with you, here's the money for them because I know you can't come by yourself.' And I was right there. I was so happy.

"Well, I didn't care too much about it because it was hard for me to interpret the music. I just didn't know what it was. And I mean I couldn't understand it. You see, when I was teaching him, I always wanted a melody to be outstanding, so we'd know what we were playing. I would want harmony, but I would want the melody there too, so if you were playing 'Side by Side,' you'd know that's what it was.

"When I first heard his music, I don't remember what the first piece was, but he was rattling and going, going. I said, 'Well, what is he playing?' I didn't care too much about it because I couldn't interpret it. I didn't know. But much later, I found that what I taught him was background and led up to his playing this far-out stuff. I don't remember his word for it. But I said, 'Yeah? Well, maybe so.'

"He said, 'Well, it has helped me. That's the way it started.'

"I said, 'Well, good.' But I didn't care a thing about it because when I hear a piece, I at least wanna know what it is, and I couldn't follow the melody of his pieces when I first heard it. Course it had the beat. That's all the dancers wanted, the beat, and he had that. So all of that made him famous. Yeah, he was just getting famous."

ERNEST GILLESPIE (cousin):

"Dizzy's ten years older than I am. He lived about four blocks from where I lived and they used to practice down on the corner. When he passed my house going swimming, he used to always stop, eat a lot, and sometimes go to practice down on the corner where their drummer lived. And he was more like a big brother to me because I sort of liked to follow him around, you know, get into what he was doing, but there was that age difference.

"Well, Dizzy brought a couple of bands South, and I saw him. During the forties, when he had Milt Jackson and John Lewis and that group with him. He brought a band down to play in the tobacco warehouse; I forget the name, some kind of large building in North Carolina. And we went over; I guess the whole town went over to see him that night in Maxton, North Carolina. Maxton is the tobacco center. But it was in an auditorium that I remember. It would've been a perfect time for anybody to rob someone and tear off because everyone was out there that night. Another reason why everybody went was because another cat from Cheraw was playing in the band with him. I don't know if you know Matthew McKay or have heard of him. Well, Matthew was born in Cheraw. Matthew and James Harrington and Dizzy were the three trumpet players, and they all lived in the same block. Matthew was with him then, and Matthew was quite an accomplished player.

"The appearance was well received because everybody around there, everybody from Laurinburg and Cheraw, everybody who knew Dizzy came. And of course everyone who knew Matt McKay came. I don't know how they accepted the music. They were two home boys; people enjoyed it, you know. And I'm not sure whether they enjoyed it for the musical quality or whether it was the two hometown boys up there doing their thing. A lot of people danced, but a lot of people stood around the bandstand. They were received very well—a full house. That place was jammed, packed with people.

"Well, it was the first time he had come home, shall we say, or at least close to home, and in front of a big band. After that, I guess, during the middle 1940s, almost anybody's house that you went in had one or two records by Dizzy.

"They did not have a record store in Cheraw; they had a radio shop. This guy sold records, and I used to bug him so much about jazz, about records, he always had one or two of Dizzy's records in there but not too many. I kept asking him so much, he started buying Dizzy's records, and I would of course buy them from him every time he would get an order of jazz records for me. So I got a couple of people to put some of his records on jukeboxes around town.

"And my friends had a little social club called the Metropolitan Boppers, and everytime we went anyplace with his records on the jukebox, we played them. We had a little club, and we used to come with our little '78s, sit around and play records. We knew just about all his tunes, solos and all. A lot of young people didn't want to do anything but dance, but once they started listening to Dizzy and other jazz records, they sort of got in with it, and then their parents started listening too."

Even the folks down South had started to warm up to me by the end of 1946. We went out and made a movie called *Jivin' in Bebop*, featuring me with the band, playing all our new tunes. It swung and became quite a success. Dan Burley, the first black guy to write a book on modern jazz,† who was also a pianist, played some numbers in that movie, and our female vocalist, Alice Roberts, sang the joyful blues to end the war:

> Oh, well, oh well, I feel so fine today,
> Oh, well, oh well, I feel so fine today,
> Cause the man who sends me's coming home to stay.
> Got a man over there, and a man over here
> But my man over there
> Ooooo-ooo-ooo-ooo ba-ba-leee-bah!
> Ooooo-ooo-ooo-ooo ba-ba-leee-bah!

† Burley, Dan, *Orignal Handbook of Harlem Jive.* Jive Potentials, New York, 1944.

That man I have, he's built for speed,
Got everything that Mama needs
Ooooo-ooo-ooo-ooo ba-ba-leee-bah!
Ooooo-ooo-ooo-ooo ba-ba-leee-bah!

Kenny Hagood, "Pancho," our male vocalist, sang, "I Waited for You," and we had some comedy like:

Freddie: Hey, Diz, old man, lemme lay a question on ya'?
Diz: Shoot. . . .
Freddie: How long was Cain mad with his brother?
Diz: As long as he was Able. . . .
Freddie: You dig me, jack, you dig me. Owww!
Diz: You better dig this next number (Oop-Bop-Sha-Bam. . . .)

A couple of dancers performed an interpretation of "Night In Tunisia," and the show ended with a dialogue between Benny Carter and me, a spoof of "major" composers, like Gilbert and Sullivan. After that the band played "Things to Come," as a finale. It made a great movie. You can still see *Jivin' in Bebop;* it appears sometimes in little cinematheques.

William Alexander financed *Jivin' in Bebop.* He's a big producer now. He hired Richard Burton. We didn't get much money outta that, but it was nice to do. The film was a big success in the "colored" theaters. Black movies then didn't go in the white houses. They had a string of "colored" theaters around the U.S. then. When I came to New York, the Harlem Opera House was finished, and the Apollo Theater was in full bloom. In Philadelphia at one time they had three theaters; later on, four: the Lincoln, the Nixon Grand, Faye's Theater, and the Earle. In Baltimore, you had the Royal Theater; in Washington, the Howard; in Richmond, you had the Hippodrome. In Memphis, you had the Handy. In Atlanta, you had the Booker T.

Oh, on that southern tour in 1946, our whole troupe visited and played at Laurinburg Institute. It made me feel very proud and reminded me of how very narrowly I'd missed spending my days behind a mule.

We'd conquered the South and challenged Hollywood by the end of 1946, but I still wanted the universe.

Beboppers . . . the Cult

Around 1946, jive-ass stories about "beboppers" circulated and began popping up in the news. Generally, I felt happy for the publicity, but I found it disturbing to have modern jazz musicians and their followers characterized in a way that was often sinister and downright vicious. This image wasn't altogether the fault of the press because many followers, trying to be "in," were actually doing some of the things the press accused beboppers of—and worse. I wondered whether all the "weird" publicity actually drew some of these way-out elements to us and did the music more harm than good. Stereotypes, which exploited whatever our weaknesses might be, emerged. Suable things were said, but nothing about the good we were doing and our contributions to music.

Time magazine, March 25, 1946, remarked: "As such things usually do, it began on Manhattan's 52nd Street. A bandleader named John (Dizzy) Gillespie, looking for a way to emphasize the more beautiful notes in 'Swing,' explained: 'When you hum it, you just naturally say bebop, be-de-bop . . .'

"Today, the bigwig of bebop is a scat named Harry (the Hipster) Gibson, who in moments of supreme pianistic ecstasy throws his feet on the keyboard. No. 2 man is Bulee (Slim) Gaillard, a skyscraping zooty Negro guitarist. Gibson and Gaillard have recorded such hip numbers as 'Cement Mixer,' which has sold more than 20,000 discs in

Los Angeles alone; 'Yeproc Heresay,' 'Dreisix Cents,' and 'Who Put
the Benzedrine in Mrs. Murphy's Ovaltine?'"

The article discussed a ban on radio broadcasts of bebop records in
Los Angeles where station KMPC considered it a "degenerative influence on youth" and described how the "nightclub where Gibson and
Gaillard played" was "more crowded than ever" with teen-agers who
wanted to be bebopped. "What bebop amounts to: hot jazz overheated,
with overdone lyrics full of bawdiness, references to narcotics and
doubletalk."

Once it got inside the marketplace, our style was subverted by the
press and music industry. First, the personalities and weaknesses of the
in people started becoming more important, in the public eye, than
the music itself. Then they diluted the music. They took what were
otherwise blues and pop tunes, added "mop, mop" accents and lyrics
about abusing drugs wherever they could and called the noise that
resulted bebop. Labeled bebop like our music, this synthetic sound
was played heavily on commercial radio everywhere, giving bebop
a bad name. No matter how bad the imitation sounded, youngsters,
and people who were musically untrained liked it, and it sold well because it maintained a very danceable beat. The accusations in the
press pointed to me as one of the prime movers behind this. I
should've sued, even though the chances of winning in court were
slim. It was all bullshit.

Keeping in mind that a well-told lie usually contains a germ of
truth, let's examine the charges and see how many of those stereotypes
actually applied to me.

Lie number one was that beboppers wore wild clothes and dark
glasses at night. Watch the fashions of the forties on the late show, long
coats, almost down to your knees and full trousers. I wore drape suits
like everyone else and dressed no differently from the average leading
man of the day. It was beautiful. I became pretty dandified, I guess,
later during the bebop era when my pants were pegged slightly at the
bottom, but not unlike the modestly flared bottoms on the slacks of
the smart set today.

We had costumes for the stage—uniforms with wide lapels and belts
—given to us by a tailor in Chicago who designed them, but we didn't
wear them offstage. Later, we removed the wide lapels and sported
little tan cashmere jackets with no lapels. This was a trendsetting
innovation because it made no sense at all to pay for a wide lapel.
Esquire magazine, 1943, America's leading influence on men's fashions, considered us elegant, though bold, and printed our photographs.

Perhaps I remembered France and started wearing the beret. But I
used it as headgear I could stuff into my pocket and keep moving. I used to lose my hat a lot. I liked to wear a hat like most of the

guys then, and the hats I kept losing cost five dollars apiece. At a few recording sessions when I couldn't lay my hands on a mute, I covered the bell of the trumpet with the beret. Since I'd been designated their "leader," cats just picked up the style.

My first pair of eyeglasses, some rimless eyeglasses, came from Maurice Guilden, an optometrist at the Theresa Hotel, but they'd get broken all the time, so I picked up a pair of horn rims. I never wore glasses until 1940. As a child, I had some minor problems with vision. When I'd wake up in the morning, I couldn't open my eyelids—they'd stick together. My mother gave me a piece of cotton, someone told her that urine would help. Every time I urinated, I took a piece of cotton and dabbed my eyes with it. It cured me. I read now without glasses and only use glasses for distance. Someone coming in from the night who saw me wearing dark glasses onstage to shield my eyes from the glare of the spotlights might misinterpret their meaning. Wearing dark glasses at night could only worsen my eyesight. I never wore dark glasses at night. I had to be careful about my eyes because I needed them to read music.

Lie number two was that only beboppers wore beards, goatees, and other facial hair and adornments.

I used to shave under my lip. That spot prickled and itched with scraping. The hair growing back felt uncomfortable under my mouthpiece, so I let the hair grow into a goatee during my days with Cab Calloway. Now a trademark, that tuft of hair cushions my mouthpiece and is quite useful to me as a player; at least I've always thought it allowed me to play more effectively. Girls like my goatee too.

I used to wear a mustache, thinking you couldn't play well without one. One day I cut it off accidentally and had to play, and I've been playing without a mustache ever since. Some guy called me "weird" because he looked at me and thought he saw only half a mustache. The dark spot above my upper lip is actually a callus that formed because of my embouchure. The right side of my upper lip curls down into the mouthpiece when I form my embouchure to play.

Many modern jazz musicians wore no facial hair at all. Anyway, we weren't the only ones during those days with hair on our faces. What about Clark Gable?

Number three: that beboppers spoke mostly in slang or tried to talk like Negroes is not so untrue. We used a few "pig Latin" words like "ofay." Pig Latin as a way of speaking emerged among blacks long before our time as a secret language for keeping children and the uninitiated from listening to adult conversations. Also, blacks had a lot of words they brought with them from Africa, some of which crept over into general usage, like "yum-yum."

Most bebop language came about because some guy said something and it stuck. Another guy started using it, then another one, and before you knew it, we had a whole language. "Mezz" meant "pot," because Mezz Mezzrow was selling the best pot. When's the "eagle gonna" fly, the American eagle, meant payday. A "razor" implied the draft from a window in winter with cold air coming in, since it cut like a razor. We added some colorful and creative concepts to the English language, but I can't think of any word besides bebop that I actually invented. Daddy-O Daylie, a disc jockey in Chicago, originated much more of the hip language during our era than I did.

We didn't have to try; as black people we just naturally spoke that way. People who wished to communicate with us had to consider our manner of speech, and sometimes they adopted it. As we played with musical notes, bending them into new and different meanings that constantly changed, we played with words. Say sumpn' hip Daddy-O.*

DADDY-O DAYLIE (disc jockey):

"Well, that's like saying to a comic, 'Be funny.' You know it's been so long, and so many of the things that I used to say, I guess it's pretty much like Dizzy's solos, you hear them again on records. I just started thinking, 'People like this, and if I can do it with a certain amount of dignity, it will help me sell my product.' And my product was contemporary music. I knew that I had to expose a music that at that point had a limited audience, and if I could come up with some phrases that would cause them to say, 'Hey, did you hear Dizzy's solo?' Or when you'd get in the elevator going up in the office building, they would say, 'Did you hear what Daddy-O said?' I became an integral part of the program as a personality. So I would always try and use the bop phrases to help sell the music, to showcase modern music—modern jargon. You had, back at that time, people saying, 'Daddy-O's talking hippy-dippy talk,' and they were trying to come up with some negative vibes. But then when Arthur Godfrey started using it, a white radio personality, they accepted it. Arthur would use things that I would say, and after he put his stamp on it, they started saying Daddy-O was a great dude."

Number four: that beboppers had a penchant for loose sex and partners racially different from themselves, especially black men who desired white women, was a lie.

It's easy for a white person to become associated with jazz musi-

* See Dillard, J. L., *Black English*, Random House, New York, 1972, pp. 118–19.

cians, because most of the places we play are owned and patronized by whites. A good example is Pannonica Koenigswater, the baroness, who is the daughter of a Rothschild. She'll be noticed when she shows up in a jazz club over two or three times. Nica has helped jazz musicians, financially. She saw to it that a lotta guys who had no place to stay had a roof or put some money in their pockets. She's willing to spend a lot to help. There's not too much difference between black and white women, but you'll find that to gain a point, a white woman will do almost anything to help if it's something that she likes. There's almost nothing, if a white woman sees it's to her advantage, that she won't do because she's been taught that the world is hers to do with as she wants. This shocks the average black musician who realizes that black women wouldn't generally accept giving so much without receiving something definite in return.

A black woman might say: "I'll love him . . . but not my money." But a white woman will give anything, even her money, to show her own strength. She'll be there on the job, every night, sitting there supporting her own goodies. She'll do it for kicks, whatever is her kick. Many white women were great fans and supporters of modern jazz and brought along white males to hear our music. That's a secret of this business: Where a woman goes, the man goes.

"Where you wanna go, baby?"

"I wanna go hear Dizzy."

"O.K., that's where we go." The man may not support you, but the woman does, and he spends his money.

As a patron of the arts in this society, the white woman's role, since white males have been so preoccupied with making money, brought her into close contact with modern jazz musicians and created relationships that were often very helpful to the growth of our art. Some of these relationships became personal and even sexual but not necessarily so. Often, they were supportive friendships which the musicians and their patrons enjoyed. Personally, I haven't received much help from white female benefactors. All the help I needed, I got from my wife—an outspoken black woman, who will not let me mess with the money—to whom I've been married since 1940. Regarding friendships across racial lines, because white males would sometimes lend their personal support to our music, the bebop era, socially speaking, was a major concrete effort of progressive thinking black and white males and females to tear down and abolish the ignorance and racial barriers that were stifling the growth of any true culture in modern America.†

---

† A letter to the editor of *Time* magazine 6/4/48 stated: "Sir: do not dismiss 'bebop' so lightly (*Time*, May 17). After all jazz is the only genuine contribution to contemporary music that America can boast of. Our jazz masters are the world's

Number five: that beboppers used and abused drugs and alcohol is not completely a lie either. They used to tell jokes about it. One bebopper walked up to another and said, "Are you gonna flat your fifths tonight?"

The other one answered, "No, I'm going to drink mine." That's a typical joke about beboppers.

When I came to New York, in 1937, I didn't drink nor smoke marijuana. "You gonna be a square, muthafucka!" Charlie Shavers said and turned me on to smoking pot. Now, certainly, we were not the only ones. Some of the older musicians had been smoking reefers for forty and fifty years. Jazz musicians, the old ones and the young ones, almost all of them that I knew smoked pot, but I wouldn't call that drug abuse.

The first guy I knew to "take off" was Steve, a trumpet player with Jimmie Lunceford, a young college kid who came to New York and got hung up on dope. Everybody talked about him and said, "That guy's a dope addict! Stay away from him because he uses shit." Boy, to say that was really stupid, because how else could you help that kinda guy?

Dope, heroin abuse, really got to be a major problem during the bebop era, especially in the late forties, and a lotta guys died from it. Cats were always getting "busted" with drugs by the police, and they had a saying, "To get the best band, go to KY." That meant the "best band" was in Lexington, Kentucky, at the federal narcotics hospital. Why did it happen? The style of life moved so fast, and cats were struggling to keep up. It was wartime, everybody was uptight. They probably wanted something to take their minds off all the killing and dying and the cares of this world. The war in Vietnam most likely excited the recent upsurge of heroin abuse, together with federal narcotics control policies which, strangely, at certain points in history, encouraged narcotics abuse, especially among young blacks.‡

Everybody at one time or another smoked marijuana, and then coke became popular—I did that too; but I never had any desire to use hard drugs, a drug that would make you a slave. I always shied away from anything powerful enough to make me dependent, because realizing that everything here comes and goes, why be dependent on any

finest, which is more than I can say for our 'serious' composers. 'Bebop' is a tremendous thing—it must be heard with the brain and felt with the soul; it packs as much emotional intensity as any symphony.

"If you can discover no element of beauty or genius, I fear that you are missing one of the most exciting things that has happened in the music world in many, many years. (signed) Carleton Ryding, Detroit, Michigan."

That was really nice of him.—DG

‡ See Musto, David F. (MD) The American Disease, Origins of Narcotics Control, Yale University Press, New Haven & London, 1973.

one thing? I never even tried hard drugs. One time on Fifty-second Street a guy gave me something I took for coke and it turned out to be horse. I snorted it and puked up in the street. If I had found him, he would have suffered bodily harm, but I never saw him again.

With drugs like benzedrine, we played practical jokes. One record date for Continental, with Rubberlegs William, a blues singer, I especially remember. Somebody had this date—Clyde Hart, I believe. He got Charlie Parker, me, Oscar Pettiford, Don Byas, Trummy Young, and Specs Powell. The music didn't work up quite right at first. Now, at that time, we used to break open inhalers and put the stuff into coffee or Coca-Cola; it was a kick then. During a break at this record date, Charlie dropped some into Rubberlegs' coffee. Rubberlegs didn't drink or smoke anything. He couldn't taste it. So we went on with the record date. Rubberlegs began moaning and crying as he was singing. You should hear those records! But I wouldn't condone doing that now, Rubberlegs might've gotten sick or something. The whole point is that, like most Americans, we were really ignorant about the helpful or deleterious effects of drugs on human beings, and before we concluded anything about drugs or used them and got snagged, we should have understood what we were doing. That holds true for the individual or the society, I believe.

The drug scourge of the forties victimized black musicians first, before hitting any other large segment of the black community. But if a cat had his head together, nothing like that, requiring his own indulgence, could've stopped him. I've always believed that. I knew several guys that were real hip, musically, and hip about life who never got high. Getting high wasn't one of the prerequisites for being hip, and to say it was would be inaccurate.

BOB REDCROSS:

"About Bird and Diz and their different attitudes about drugs, I couldn't say for sure except that I do feel that Bird knew within himself that what he liked to do would eventually be one of the main reasons of his demise, his death. He always gave me the impression that he had no illusions that he would live to be an old man. We used to talk about different things. The truth of the matter is at that time, when I first met Bird, I mean, I was pretty much in the same bag he was in and into all them different things that he was doing. And we became quite a bit close on that account too, and I could understand a lotta the things about him. It's almost like a death wish, if you wanna put it that way. Anytime you indulge in something that's gonna destroy you, and then you continue to do it, it just has to be a death wish. He was a fantastic person. Diz didn't have any of that. I don't know if Dizzy knew he had a quest in life at all, something that he had to do. I just believe that his whole thing was trying to learn that horn, because he progressed and progressed and progressed over a period of years. You can go back and look. I know from the time when I first met him, 1942, 1943, up to the present, there hasn't been any stopping or hesitation of his growth. He has continued to grow, and you can't say that for musicians who've been around that long."

BUDD JOHNSON:

"Well, I'll tell ya, smoking reefers, to me, is not all that bad. I mean, I don't think it's habit forming because I have smoked reefers. The first inkling of that I got was Louis Armstrong, 'Man, Louis gets high and blows and blows!' So we all used to get high as kids. But I never saw the hard drugs. I never saw any of that. Really, I hate to say this because, I mean, I've heard on radio and television that back during World War I, it was stronger than it is out here now. I know that they had registered addicts back in those days. But I didn't know anything about hard drugs.

"And I think Charlie Parker influenced a lotta young musicians and old ones too, introduced them to a lotta hard drugs. Because they say, 'What . . . ! This guy can play like that? This stuff must do something!' And guys that had never used it started using it just for appearances. But I think it was some kind of conspiracy too that led drugs mostly into the black community. Because I mean the drug users as far back as I can remember were always white, you know, movie stars and people like that. And we never had thought about using drugs. It must be some kind of conspiracy because, I mean, you can just walk up and down in Harlem there and see it all happening right on the streets and nobody does anything about it. I believe they could stop it tomorrow if they really wanted to jump down on it.

"I remember on the Street, Fifty-second Street, when this music became very popular, they used to have two and three cops walking abreast all through that area. They didn't want these young white girls associating with the blacks, really. They used to try to give them a hard time. Rockefeller owned most of that property, and he was saying, maybe it's getting outta hand in this neighborhood. This is one of the reasons Fifty-second Street was torn down. This was supposed to be a hazardous place for society. So one way of attacking it was by saying, like, the black people are using drugs. But, I mean, we couldn't get the drugs if the white people wasn't selling any. We don't have the money to afford to buy it in quantities like that in order to distribute. All of your big distributors gotta be white. They make a big business.

"I heard on the radio a long time ago . . . the commanding officer or the chief of police saying, 'We know how it's being done, but we can't arrest these people because we don't have any evidence.' He was explaining that a lotta big billionaires, millionaires loaned money to the mob to finance drugs. Loaned them millions of dollars on a percentage. So they wasn't dealing with drugs, they were dealing with money. So they can't pin the drugs on them, he says, but we know they're loaning these different gangs and things the money to purchase the drugs. They'll loan a cat $5 million and probably get back $15 million. So actually, they really are supplying. But he says, 'We can't take that into court.'

"So the media associated drugs strongly with black people down in there, in order to finally get it broken all up. Rockefeller tore up darn near everything in there and put up office buildings, and that got rid of Fifty-second Street.

"Naturally, black musicians were very well liked by music lovers. Initially, this would draw young white couples, white girls, old white couples and what not, to hear this music. Well, this in turn would draw the pimps, because they're gonna snatch them off a broad or something. But, I mean, we never thought about that. If a cat dug a chick, it was all right; but we were down there for our music, not to pimp and not to hustle drugs. This was all naturally centered on night life. Wherever you go, you're gonna find some cats in there that's gonna try to induce you to buy drugs. Now, instead of doing that, it's happening in your elementary schools. So the musicians were just the first victims. It was all right with the movie stars, because the government would supply them with drugs. If you were a known addict, you could register and you would get drugs. I dunno, it seems like everybody wanna really find something to try to hold us back. And it got so bad that they used to stop every bus coming through the Holland Tunnel or Lincoln Tunnel, especially if they were black musicians, and search it. Looking for drugs. They really wanted to down it, you know, to down us. I might sound a little cynical about this but I know it to be true."

KENNY CLARKE:

"Well, you know, like the leather-jacket kids and the hippies, it was something to try to destroy our unity and we knew that. We were intelligent enough to realize that they were trying to tear us asunder. Trying to break up the whole movement, saying derogatory remarks and what not. Anything to disrupt what was going on, like they did with the Black Panthers. Soon as they see you—certain powers that be getting together and calling the meeting to order, then there's gonna be some kinda disruption. Some kinda way. You know all the kids were wearing horn-rimmed glasses and berets. It seemed like almost a cult. You know these are the outsiders who carry it to extremes."

Number six is really a trick: that beboppers tended to express unpatriotic attitudes regarding segregation, economic injustice, and the American way of life.

We never wished to be restricted to just an American context, for we were creators in an art form which grew from universal roots and which had proved it possessed universal appeal. Damn right! We refused to accept racism, poverty, or economic exploitation, nor would we live out uncreative humdrum lives merely for the sake of survival. But there was nothing unpatriotic about it. If America wouldn't honor its Constitution and respect us as men, we couldn't give a shit about the American way. And they made it damn near un-American to appreciate our music.

Music drew Charlie Parker and me together, but Charlie Parker used to read a lot too. As a great reader, he knew about everything, and we used to discuss politics, philosophy, and life-style. I remember him mentioning Baudelaire, I think he died of syphilis, and Charlie Parker used to talk about him all the time. Charlie was very much interested in the social order, and we'd have these long conversations about it, and music. We discussed local politics too, people like Vito Marcantonio, and what he'd tried to do for the little man in New York. We liked Marcantonio's ideas because as musicians we weren't paid well at all for what we created.

There were a bunch of musicians more socially minded, who were closely connected with the Communist Party. Those guys stayed busy anywhere labor was concerned. I never got that involved politically. I would picket, if necessary, and remember twice being on a picket line. I can't remember just what it was I was picketing for, but they had me walking around with a sign. Now, I would never cross a picket line.

Paul Robeson became the forerunner of Martin Luther King. I'll always remember Paul Robeson as a politically committed artist. A few enlightened musicians recognized the importance of Paul Robeson, amongst them Teddy Wilson, Frankie Newton, and Pete Seeger—all of them very outspoken politically. Pete Seeger is so warm, if you meet Pete Seeger, he just melts, he's so warm. He's a great man.

In my religious faith—the Baha'i faith—the Bab is the forerunner of

Baha'u'llah, the prophet. "Bab" means gate, and Paul Robeson was the "gate" to Martin Luther King. The people in power made Paul Robeson a martyr, but he didn't die immediately from his persecution. He became a martyr because if you are strangled for your principles, whether it's physical strangulation or mental strangulation or social strangulation, you suffer. The dues that Paul Robeson paid were worse than the dues Martin Luther King paid. Martin Luther only paid his life, quick, for his views, but Paul Robeson had to suffer a very long time.

When the play *Othello* opened in New York with Paul Robeson, Jose Ferrer, and Uta Hagen, I went to the theater to see it. I was sitting way up in the highest balcony. Paul Robeson's voice sounded like we were talking together in a room. That's how strong his voice was coming from the stage, three miles away. Paul Robeson, big as he was, looked about as big as a cigar from where I was sitting. But his voice was right up there next to me.

I dug Paul Robeson right away, from the first words. A lot of black people were against Paul Robeson; he was trying to help them and they were talking against him, like he was a communist. I heard him speak on many occasions and, man, talk about a speaker! He could really speak. And he was fearless! You never hear people speak out like he did with everything arrayed against you and come out like he did. Man, I'll remember Paul Robeson until I die. He was something else.

Paul Robeson became "Mr. Incorruptibility." No one could get to him because that's the rarest quality in man, incorruptibility. Nothing supercedes that because, man, there are so many ways to corrupt a personality. Paul Robeson stands as a hero of mine and he was truly the father of Malcolm X, another dynamic personality who I talked to a lot. Oh, I loved Malcolm, and you couldn't corrupt Malcolm nor Paul. We have a lot of leaders that money corrupts, and power. You give them a little money and some power, and they nut. They go nuts with it. Both Malcolm and Paul Robeson, you couldn't get to them. The people in power tried all means at their disposal to get them. So they killed Malcolm X and they destroyed Paul Robeson. But they stood up all the time. Even dying, their heads were up.

One time, on the Rudy Vallee show, I should've acted more politically. Rudy Vallee says, introducing me, "What's in the Ubangi department tonight?" I almost walked off the show. I wanted to sue him but figured there wasn't any money in it, so I just forgot about it and we played. Musicians today would never accept that, but then, somehow, the money and the chance to be heard seemed more important.

We had other quiet fighters, like Joe Louis, who was beautiful. I've known Joe Louis since way, way back when I hung out in Sugar Ray's all the time, playing checkers. Sugar Ray's a good checker player, but dig Joe Louis. He'd come down to hear me play, and people would want Joe Louis to have a ringside seat. He'd be waaay over in a corner someplace, sitting there digging the music. If you announced him, "Ladies and gentlemen, the heavyweight champion of the world, Joe Louis, is sitting over there," he'd stand up to take a bow and wave his hands one time. You look around again, he's gone. Other guys I know would want a ringside seat, want you to announce them and maybe come up on the stage. But Joe Louis was like that. He was always shy, beautiful dude. He had mother wit.

It's very good to know you're a part of something that has directly influenced your own cultural history. But where being black is concerned, it's only what I represent, not me, myself. I pay very little attention to "Dizzy Gillespie," but I'm happy to have made a contribution. To be a "hero" in the black community, all you have to do is make the white folks look up to you and recognize the fact that you've contributed to something worthwhile. Laugh, but it's the truth. Black people appreciate my playing in the same way I looked up to Paul Robeson or to Joe Louis. When Joe would knock out someone, I'd say, "Hey . . . !" and feel like I'd scored a knockout. Just because of his prowess in his field and because he's black like me.

Oh, there was a guy in Harlem, up there on the corner all the time preaching. Boy, could he talk about white people! He'd get a little soap box. I don't know his name, but everybody knew him. He wasn't dressed all fancy, or nothing, and then he had a flag, an American flag. Ha! Ha! That's how I became involved with the African movement, standing out there listening to him. An African fellow named Kingsley Azumba Mbadiwe asked me who I was and where I came from. I knew all the right answers. That was pretty hip being from South Carolina and not having been in New York too long. Our friendship grew from there; and I became attached to this African brother. One time, after the Harlem riots, 1945, Mbadiwe told me, "Man, these white people are funny here."

"Whaddayou mean . . . ?"

"Well, they told me to stay outta Harlem," he said.

"Why is that?" I asked.

"They say that it's dangerous for me up here. I might get killed."

"What'd you tell them?"

"Well, I asked them how they gonna distinguish me from anybody else up there? I look just like all the rest of them."

Heh, heh, heh. It was at that time I observed that the white people didn't like the "spooks" over here to get too close to the Africans. They didn't want us—the spooks over here—to know anything about Africa. They wanted you to just think you're somebody dangling out there, not like the white Americans who can tell you they're German or French or Italian. They didn't want us to know we have a line so

that when you'd ask us, all we could say was we were "colored." It's
strange how the white people tried to keep us separate from the Africans and from our heritage. That's why, today, you don't hear in our
music, as much as you do in other parts of the world, African heritage,
because they took our drum away from us. If you go to Brazil, to
Bahia where there is a large black population, you find a lot of African
in their music; you go to Cuba, you find they retained their heritage;
in the West Indies, you find a lot. In fact, I went to Kenya and heard
those cats play and I said, "You guys sound like you're playing calypso from the West Indies."

A guy laughed and he said to me, "Don't forget, we were first!"

But over here, they took our drums away from us, for the simple
reason of self-protection when they found out those cats could communicate four or five miles with the drums. They took our language
away from us and made us speak English. In slavery times, if they
found out that two slaves could speak the same African language, they
sold off one. As far as our heritage goes, a few words creeped in like
buckra—I used to hear my mother say, "that ole poor buckra"—buckra
meant white. But with those few exceptions when they took our
drums away, our music developed along a monorhythmic line. It
wasn't polyrhythmic like African music. I always knew rhythm or I
was interested in it, and it was this interest in rhythm that led me to
seize every opportunity to find out about these connections with
Africa and African music.

Charlie Parker and I played benefits for the African students in
New York and the African Academy of Arts and Research which was
headed by Kingsley Azumba Mbadiwe. Eventually, Mbadiwe wound
up becoming a minister of state in Nigeria under one of those re-
gimes, but over here, as head of the African Academy, he arranged for
us to play some benefit concerts at the Diplomat Hotel which
should've been recorded. Just me, Bird, and Max Roach, with African
drummers and Cuban drummers; no bass, nothing else. We also
played for a dancer they had, named Asadata Dafora.* (A-S-A-D-A-T-A
D-A-F-O-R-A—if you can say it, you can spell it.) Those concerts for
the African Academy of Arts and Research turned out to be tremendous. Through that experience, Charlie Parker and I found the connections between Afro-Cuban and African music and discovered the
identity of our music with theirs. Those concerts should definitely
have been recorded, because we had a ball, discovering our identity.

* The first African dancer to present African dance in concert form in the
United States. Dafora is called "one of the pioneer exponents of African Negro
dance and culture." Born in Sierra Leone in 1890, Mr. Dafora studied and performed as a singer at La Scala before coming in 1929 to the United States where
he died in 1965. Dafora also staged the voodoo scene in the Orson Welles production of *Macbeth*.

Within the society, we did the same thing we did with the music. First we learned the proper way and then we improvised on that. It seemed the natural thing to do because the style or mode of life among black folks went the same way as the direction of the music. Yes, sometimes the music comes first and the life-style reflects the music because music is some very strong stuff, though life in itself is bigger. Artists are always in the vanguard of social change, but we didn't go out and make speeches or say, "Let's play eight bars of protest." We just played our music and let it go at that. The music proclaimed our identity; it made every statement we truly wanted to make.

Number seven: that "beboppers" expressed a preference for religions other than Christianity may be considered only a half-truth, because most black musicians, including those from the bebop era, received their initial exposure and influence in music through the black church. And it remained with them throughout their lives. For social and religious reasons, a large number of modern jazz musicians did begin to turn toward Islam during the forties, a movement completely in line with the idea of freedom of religion.

Rudy Powell, from Edgar Hayes's band, became one of the first jazz musicians I knew to accept Islam; he became an Ahmidyah Muslim. Other musicians followed, it seemed to me, for social rather than religious reasons, if you can separate the two.

"Man, if you join the Muslim faith, you ain't colored no more, you'll be white," they'd say. "You get a new name and you don't have to be a nigger no more." So everybody started joining because they considered it a big advantage not to be black during the time of segregation. I thought of joining, but it occurred to me that a lot of them spooks were simply trying to be anything other than a spook at that time. They had no idea of black consciousness; all they were trying to do was escape the stigma of being "colored." When these cats found out that Idrees Sulieman, who joined the Muslim faith about that time, could go into these white restaurants and bring out sandwiches to the other guys because he wasn't colored—and he looked like the inside of the chimney—they started enrolling in droves.

Musicians started having it printed on their police cards where it said "race," "W" for white. Kenny Clarke had one and he showed it to me. He said, "See, nigger, I ain't no spook; I'm white, 'W.'" He changed his name to Arabic, Liaqat Ali Salaam. Another cat who had been my roommate at Laurinburg, Oliver Mesheux, got involved in an altercation about race down in Delaware. He went into this restaurant, and they said they didn't serve colored in there. So he said, "I don't blame you. But I don't have to go under the rules of colored because my name is Mustafa Dalil."

Didn't ask him no more questions. "How do you do?" the guy said.

When I first applied for my police card, I knew what the guys were doing, but not being a Muslim, I wouldn't allow the police to type anything in that spot under race. I wouldn't reply to the race question on the application blank. When the cop started to type something in there, I asked him, "What are you gonna put down there, C for me?"

"You're colored, ain't you?"

"Colored . . . ? No."

"Well, what are you, white?"

"No, don't put nothing on there," I said. "Just give me the card." They left it open. I wouldn't let them type me in W for white nor C for colored; just made them leave it blank. WC is a toilet in Europe.

As time went on, I kept considering converting to Islam but mostly because of the social reasons. I didn't know very much about the religion, but I could dig the idea that Muhammad was a prophet. I believed that, and there were very few Christians who believed that Muhammad had the word of God with him. The idea of polygamous marriage in Islam, I didn't care for too much. In our society, a man can only take care of one woman. If he does a good job of that, he'll be doing well. Polygamy had its place in the society for which it was intended, as a social custom, but social orders change and each age develops its own mores. Polygamy was acceptable during one part of our development, but most women wouldn't accept that today. People worry about all the women with no husbands, and I don't have any answer for that. Whatever happens, the question should be resolved legitimately and in the way necessary for the advancement of society.

The movement among jazz musicians toward Islam created quite a stir, especially with the surge of the Zionist movement for creation and establishment of the State of Israel. A lot of friction arose between Jews and Muslims, which took the form of a semiboycott in New York of jazz musicians with Muslim names. Maybe a Jewish guy, in a booking agency that Muslim musicians worked from, would throw work another way instead of throwing to the Muslim. Also, many of the agents couldn't pull the same tricks on Muslims that they pulled on the rest of us. The Muslims received knowledge about themselves that we didn't have and that we had no access to; so therefore they tended to act differently toward the people running the entertainment business. Much of the entertainment business was run by Jews. Generally, the Muslims fared well in spite of that, because though we had some who were Muslim in name only, others really had knowledge and were taking care of business.

Near the end of the forties, the newspapers really got worried about whether I'd convert to Islam. In 1948 *Life* magazine published a big picture story, supposedly about our music. They conned me into allowing them to photograph me down on my knees, arms outstretched, supposedly bowing to Mecca. It turned out to be a trick bag. It's one of the few things in my whole career I'm ashamed of, because I wasn't a Muslim. They tricked me into committing a sacrilege. The newspapers figured that if the "king of bebop" converted, thousands of beboppers would follow suit, and reporters questioned me about whether I planned to quit and forsake Christianity. But that lesson from *Life* taught me to leave them hanging. I told them that on my trips through the South, the members of my band were denied the right of worshiping in churches of their own faith because colored folks couldn't pray with white folks down there. "Don't say I'm forsaking Christianity," I said, "because Christianity is forsaking me—or better, people who claim to be Christian just ain't. It says in the Bible to love thy brother, but people don't practice what the Bible preaches. In Islam, there is no color line. Everybody is treated like equals."

With one reporter, since I didn't know much about the Muslim faith, I called on our saxophonist, formerly named Bill Evans, who'd recently accepted Islam to give this reporter some accurate information.

"What's your new name?" I asked him.

"Yusef Abdul Lateef," he replied. Yusef Lateef told us how a Muslim missionary, Kahlil Ahmed Nasir, had converted many modern jazz musicians in New York to Islam and how he read the Quran daily and strictly observed the prayer and dietary regulations of the religion. I told the reporter that I'd been studying the Quran myself, and although I hadn't converted yet, I knew one couldn't drink alcohol or eat pork as a Muslim. Also I said I felt quite intrigued by the beautiful sound of the word "Quran," and found it "out of this world," "way out," as we used to say. The guy went back to his paper and reported that Dizzy Gillespie and his "beboppers" were "way out" on the subject of religion. He tried to ridicule us as being too strange, weird, and exotic to merit serious attention.† Most of the Muslim guys who were sincere in the beginning went on believing and practicing the faith.

Number eight: that beboppers threatened to destroy pop, blues, and old-time music like Dixieland jazz is almost totally false.

---

† Playing on this, sometimes in Europe I'd wear a turban. People would see me on the streets and think of me as an Arab or a Hindu. They didn't know what to think, really, because I'd pretend I didn't speak English and listen to them talk about me. Sometimes Americans would think I was some kind of "Mohammedan" nobleman. You wouldn't believe some of the things they'd say in ignorance. So to know me, study me very closely; give me your attention and above all come to my concert.

It's true, melodically, harmonically, and rhythmically, we found most pop music too bland and mechanically unexciting to suit our tastes. But we didn't attempt to destroy it—we simply built on top of it by substituting our own melodies, harmonies, and rhythms over the pop music format and then improvised on that. We always substituted; that's why no one could ever charge us with stealing songs nor collect any royalties for recording material under copyright. We only utilized the pop song format as a take-off point for improvisation, which to us was much more important. Eventually, pop music survived by slowly adopting the changes we made.

Beboppers couldn't destroy the blues without seriously injuring themselves. The modern jazz musicians always remained very close to the blues musician. That was a characteristic of the bopper. He stayed in close contact with his blues counterpart. I always had good friendships with T-Bone Walker, B. B. King, Joe Turner, Cousin Joe, Muddy Waters—all those guys—because we knew where our music came from. Ain't no need of denying your father. That's a fool, and there were few fools in this movement. Technical differences existed between modern jazz and blues musicians. However, modern jazz musicians would have to know the blues.

Another story is that we looked down on guys who couldn't read. Erroll Garner couldn't read and we certainly didn't look down on him, even though he never played our type of music. A modern jazz musician wouldn't necessarily have to read well to be able to create, but you couldn't get a job unless you read music; you had to read music to get in a band.

The bopper knew the blues well. He knew Latin influence and had a built-in sense of time, allowing him to set up his phrases properly. He knew chord changes, intervals, and how to get from one key to another smoothly. He knew the music of Charlie Parker and had to be a consummate musician. In the current age of bebop, a musician would also have to know about the techniques of rock music.

Ever since the days at Minton's we had standards to measure expertise in playing our music. Some guys couldn't satisfy them. Remember Demon, who used to come to play down at Minton's; he came to play, but he never did, and he would play with anybody, even Coleman Hawkins. Demon'd get up on the stand and play choruses that wouldn't say shit, but he'd be there. We'd get so tired of seeing this muthafucka. But he'd be there, and so we let him play. Everybody had a chance to make a contribution to the music.

The squabble between the boppers and the "moldy figs," who played or listened exclusively to Dixieland jazz, arose because the older musicians insisted on attacking our music and putting it down. Ooooh, they were very much against our music, because it required more than what they were doing. They'd say, "That music ain't shit, man!" They really did, but then you noticed some of the older guys started playing our riffs, a few of them, like Henry "Red" Allen. The others remained hostile to it.

Dave Tough was playing down at Eddie Condon's once, and I went down there to see Dave because he and his wife are good friends of mine. When he looked up and saw me, he says, "You the gamest muthafucka I ever seen in my life."

"Whaddayou mean?" I said.

"Muthafucka, you liable to get lynched down in here!" he said. That was funny. I laughed my ass off. Eddie Condon's and Nick's in the Village were the strongholds of Dixieland jazz.

Louis Armstrong criticized us but not me personally, not for playing the trumpet, never. He always said bad things about the guys who copied me, but I never read where he said that I wasn't a good trumpet player, that I couldn't play my instrument. But when he started talking about bebop, "Aww, that's slop! No melody." Louis Armstrong couldn't hear what we were doing. Pops wasn't schooled enough musically to hear the changes and harmonics we played. Pops's beauty as a melodic player and a "blower" caused all of us to play the way we did, especially trumpet players, but his age wasn't equipped to go as far, musically, as we did. Chronologically, I knew that Louis Armstrong was our progenitor as King Oliver and Buddy Bolden had been his progenitors. I knew how their styles developed and had been knowing it all the time; so Louis' statements about bebop didn't bother me. I knew that I came through Roy Eldridge, a follower of Louis Armstrong. I wouldn't say anything. I wouldn't make any statements about the older guys' playing because I respected them too much.

Time 1/28/47 quoted me: "Louis Armstrong was the one who popularized the trumpet more than anyone else—he sold the trumpet to the public. He sold it, man.

"Nowadays in jazz we know more about chords, progressions—and we try to work out different rhythms and things that they didn't think about when Louis Armstrong blew. In his day all he did was play strictly from the soul, just strictly from his heart he just played. He didn't think about no chords—he didn't know nothing about no chords. Now, what we in the younger generation take from Louis Armstrong . . . is the soul."

I criticized Louis for other things, such as his "plantation image." We didn't appreciate that about Louis Armstrong, and if anybody asked me about a certain public image of him, handkerchief over his head, grinning in the face of white racism, I never hesitated to say I didn't like it. I didn't want the white man to expect me to allow the same things Louis Armstrong did. Hell, I had my own way of "Tomming." Every generation of blacks since slavery has had to develop its own way of Tomming, of accommodating itself to a basically unjust situation. Take the comedians from Step 'n Fetchit days—there are new comedians now who don't want to be bothered with "Ah yassuh, boss. . . ." But that doesn't stop them from cracking a joke about how badly they've been mistreated. Later on, I began to recognize what I had considered Pops's grinning in the face of racism as his absolute refusal to let anything, even anger about racism, steal the joy from his life and erase his fantastic smile. Coming from a younger generation, I misjudged him.

Entrenched artists, or the entrenched society, always attacks anything that's new coming in—in religion, in social upheavals, in any field. It has something to do with living and dying and the fear among the old of being replaced by the new. Louis Armstrong never played our music, but that shouldn't have kept him from feeling or understanding it. Pops thought that it was his duty to attack! The leader always attacks first; so as the leader of the old school, Pops felt that it was his duty to attack us. At least he could gain some publicity, even if he were overwhelmed musically.

"It's a buncha trash! They don't know what they're doing, them boys, running off."

Mezz Mezzrow knocked us every time he'd say something to the newspapers over in Europe about bebop. "They'd never play two notes where a hundred notes are due."

Later, when I went to Europe in 1948, they put a knife in my hand, and Mezz Mezzrow was holding his head down like I was gonna chop it off. They printed headlines: DIZZY IS GONNA CARVE MEZZ MEZZROW . . . Thank goodness this is the age of enlightenment, and we don't have to put down the new anymore; that ferocious competition between the generations has passed.

In our personal lives, Pops and I were actually very good friends. He came to my major concerts and made some nice statements about me in the press. We should've made some albums together, I thought, just to have for the people who came behind us, about twenty albums. It seemed like a good idea some years later, but Pops was so captivated by Joe Glaser, his booking agent, he said, "Speak to Papa Joe." Of course that idea fizzled because Joe Glaser who also booked me at the time didn't want anybody encroaching on Louis Armstrong. Pops really had no interest in learning any new music; he was just satisfied to do his thing. And then *Hello Dolly!* came along and catapulted him into super, super fame. Wonder if that's gonna happen to me? I wonder. Playing all these years, then all of a sudden get one number that makes a big hero out of you. History repeating itself.

Number nine: that beboppers expressed disdain for "squares" is mostly true.

A "square" and a "lame" were synonymous, and they accepted the complete life-style, including the music, dictated by the establishment. They rejected the concept of creative alternatives, and they were just the opposite of "hip," which meant "in the know," "wise," or one with "knowledge" of life and how to live.‡ Musically, a square would chew the cud. He'd spend his money at the Roseland Ballroom to hear a dance band playing standards, rather than extend his ear and spirit to take an odyssey in bebop at the Royal Roost. Oblivious to the changes which replaced old, outmoded expressions with newer, modern ones, square said "hep" rather than "hip." They were apathetic to, or actively opposed to, almost everything we stood for, like intelligence, sensitivity, creativity, change, wisdom, joy, courage, peace, togetherness, and integrity. To put them down in some small way for the sharp-cornered shape of their boxed-in personalities, what better description than "square?"

Also, in those days, there were supposedly hip guys who really were squares, pseudohip cats. How do you distinguish between the pseudo and the truly hip? Well, first, a really hip guy wouldn't have any racial prejudice, one way or the other, because he would know the hip way to live is with your brother. Every human being, unless he shows differently, is your brother.

Number ten: that beboppers put down as "commercial" people who were trying to make money is 50 per cent a lie, only half true. We all wanted to make money, preferably by playing modern jazz. We appreciated people who tried to help us—and they were very few—because we needed all the help we could get. Even during the heyday of bebop, none of us made much money. Many people who pretended to help really were there for a rip-off. New modern jazz nightclubs like the Royal Roost, which had yellow leather seats and a milk bar for teen-agers, and the Clique were opening every day, all over the country. Bebop was featured on the Great White Way, Broadway, at both the Paramount and the Strand theaters. We received a lot of publicity but very little money.

BUDD JOHNSON:

"It used to be, you had an idea, you could write it on a piece of manuscript, register it, and send it through the mail back to yourself, then you would be protected. Then they passed a new copyright law that said you cannot do that anymore. This material must be under

‡ "Hip cat" comes from Wolof, "hipicat."—A man who is aware or has his eyes open. See Dillard, p. 119.

copyright in the Library of Congress, and you receive the proper regis-
tration, and you pay a fee. A lotta guys who weren't keeping up with
what was going on would get a date, so the A & R man, or some
fellow, ofay or whatever, would say, 'O.K., gimme a riff. You know,
just make up a head. We don't need no music; we're gonna record.'

"So the cats would record, make up something. And they're actually
creating the music right on the record date. Now, when it comes out,
they wouldn't completely beat them, but usually the guy, the A & R
man, had his own publishing firm or his buddy's got one and right
away he would stick in all of this material—because you have recorded
it and you didn't have it protected—and in order for him, he says, to
save the material, he's put it in a publishing company. The publishing
company would give you one of them jive contracts, where you'd never
get no royalties on it. So this was a rip-off.

"I don't know any particular tune or anything of Dizzy's that someone has taken. I know some fellows used to run up and down that
street getting guys recording dates. Because we were all down on the
Street at the time and we were making these records and everything
was original. Especially with Dizzy and Bird. I dunno. I don't know if
they're getting any of these royalties or not."

TEDDY REIG (recording executive):

"During the war, you see, all the bands and everything were all
screwed up and there wasn't very much for anybody to do; and I
wound up working for a company called Savoy Records. I was making
records. But I never worked with Dizzy then, because I never made
friends with people like so that they should record with me because of
my friendship.

"I was in charge of artists and repertoire. And I built a very successful catalog which after thirty years has been sold for over a million and a half dollars. That was the whole legend of so-called
bop, modern music. Some Dizzy, Charlie Parker, Serge Chaloff, Allen
Eager, Don Byas, Lester Young.

"I was scuffling, dreaming, trying to be a Jewish boy who didn't
wanna be Jewish, who didn't wanna be involved with a Jewish background, with the Jewish scene, and used to come running from my
neighborhood like a thief outta west hell. I would have done anything
to get to Harlem. My mother and father, they would walk in the
house, and one would look at the other and say, 'Where is he?'

" 'With the niggers, where do you think?'

"It's the same thing. Anytime anything new comes out, and it's
above their heads and they don't understand it, they rap it and try to

get it outta the way. Anything you can't get with, you put it down. That's the American style. Very popular in America—anything you can't figure out, give up. Throw it away. Condemn it.

"Dizzy was such a warm person, like, it's so hard to pick out one time as the first time you met him. Like knowing Dizzy was just knowing him all the time. He never had any moods. He was always warm. If he liked you, you knew it, and if he didn't like you, he sure let you know it. There was nothing safe about it. He was just a happy cat, man; everybody loved him. Like you could see Dizzy playing with somebody at one o'clock in the morning, then at two-thirty in the morning up at Minton's. And then at four o'clock in the morning, you might have met him over at Monroe's. So it's kinda hard to just boil it down to one particular place. I'll tell you this, he was the vagabond. He was, always. In fact, that whole building 2040 (Seventh Avenue) all them cats in there were vagabonds: Buck Clayton, Harry Edison, Don Byas. I'm talking about musicians; I'm not talking about show people. And it was like always making the scene . . . looking to advance yourself by being seen and being around to see what was going on, to hear where you can get three dollars more so you could hurry up and get it.

"One of the funny things about Dizzy was, I was gonna record Charlie Parker, and Bud Powell was supposed to play piano. See, in those days you just didn't tell a guy, 'Like, we're gonna have a date at four o'clock,' and he'd show up. You had to go round him up, from around one o'clock on. When I finally got to where Bird was, around Dewey Square and Seventh Avenue, he had Dizzy with him. I say, 'What the hell is he doing? Where's he going? You coming down with us, John?'

"And he said something about he was gonna play piano. Seeing that Bud couldn't make it.

"Now on that date,* Dizzy was playing piano and Miles was the trumpet player, and Charlie; Charlie went through one of his things where he wasn't satisfied with his horn. So we had to stop the date and everything and I took him to Forty-eighth Street to get his horn fixed, from the studio on Fortieth Street. And by the time we'd come back, we didn't have no trumpet player. Miles was sick or something.†

"To tell the truth, 'Ko Ko' wasn't nothing but 'Cherokee,' and Charlie had took $300 for four original tunes. So when they asked for a title for the tune, I told them 'Ko Ko' to make sure Charlie didn't have to pay $75. Otherwise Lubinsky, the owner, would have had a baby. And I was recording this. Dizzy was running from the piano to the trumpet,

---

* The so-called "mystery" recording session with Charlie Parker, Miles Davis, Max Roach, Curley Russell, and me.

† No, what happened was Miles didn't know the introduction to "Ko Ko." Because we, Bird and I, had been playing "Ko Ko" together, and he didn't know the introduction.

back and forth. He took the introduction on trumpet, then he went around to the piano and if you listen, you can hear the 'choing, choing' of Dizzy letting Charlie know he got there. That's the way it always sounded to me. He went to the piano like this, 'choing, choing!'

"Well, the most exciting thing, which convinced me that this man was a genius: he went out there and made records with people that didn't even fit. And with all the cards stacked against him, he come out smelling like a rose. One of his greatest records is a thing called 'I Can't Get Started.' If you look at the personnel on that record, it makes about as much sense as a Jew in a Chinese laundry ordering minestrone soup. Excitement, Dizzy always was exciting. Everything he did was exciting.

"Dizzy's whole early record career to me was like an obstacle course. He always used to wind up with all the lemonades, and malarkeys. It seems like Dizzy deserves all the success in the world because he overcame more obstacles that were thrown in his way. Maybe they were the politics of a record company, maybe they were politics of friendship—the guy with the record company or the A & R man had a friend he had to use—all kinda reasons unbeknown to us; let's leave it at that. Whatever it was, they served no value, outside of the fact that they were there. But there were so many others that could have been on his early records if Dizzy were given more freedom. When it said 'All Star Sextet,' it never was that. It never was that. I mean they were all good players, but not the guys he could have used. And, you see, in those days, it was a different kind of a scene. For the average black musician to get a record date, he made them with a blues singer. . . .

"The ban in 1942 was caused by the welfare and the pension funds, to see that the record companies paid a sum off the top to the union; aside from the payments to the musicians from sales of records, they made contributions. And it was for this that the strike went on. And the most horrible thing about the strike: some of the most inspired Dizzy Gillespie days were never on record. It was a strike, and nobody would go in and record until this thing was straightened out. Then they had another one; there were two. Because I remember I laid Paul Williams off for a week to record 'The Hucklebuck,' because I knew that ban—they were about to come to terms, and the minute the thing was over, we wanted to run into a studio. And we recorded in a hallway because they didn't have an echo chamber. So we recorded in a hallway on Fifty-seventh Street.

"Some people never heard the band that Earl Hines had with Dizzy and Charlie Parker. There's never been a band that created such . . . it's very hard for me to describe. And the same spirit was recreated in the Eckstine band; there never was a band that created audience enthusiasm like this band did. This band could cause riots if left alone. It was the most exciting band that the world has never heard, the most exciting band that the world *never* heard, on account of the record ban.

"It all depends on what kind of a human being you were. Like a guy like me, I was for the cats. The cats were my friends. I wouldn't have made a dollar if not for the cats, so I had to be for them. And I was getting my bucks, a few dollars. In those days, if I was making thirty or forty dollars, I didn't need nothing."

People with enough bucks and foresight to invest in bebop made some money. I mean more than just a little bit. All the big money went to the guys who owned the music, not to the guys who played it. The businessmen made much more than the musicians, because without money to invest in producing their own music, and sometimes managing poorly what they earned, the modern jazz musicians fell victim to the forces of the market. Somehow, the jazz businessman always became the owner and got back more than his "fair" share, usually at the player's expense. More was stolen from us during the bebop era than in the entire history of jazz, up to that point. They stole a lot of our music, all kinds of stuff. You'd look up and see somebody else's name on your composition and say, "What'd he have to do with it?" But you couldn't do much about it. Blatant commercialism we disliked because it debased the quality of our music. Our protests against being cheated and ripped off never meant we stood against making money. The question of being politically inclined against commercialism or trying to take over anything never figured too prominently with me. The people who stole couldn't create, so I just kept interested in creating the music, mostly, and tried to make sure my works were protected.

Number eleven: that beboppers acted weird and foolish is a damned lie. They tell stories about people coming to my house at all hours of the day and night, but they didn't do it. They knew better than to ring my bell at four o'clock in the morning. Monk and Charlie Parker came up there one time and said, "I got something for you."

I say, "O.K., hand it to me through the door!" I've been married all my life and wasn't free to do all that. I could go to most of their houses, anytime, because they were always alone or had some broad. Lorraine never stood for too much fooling. My wife would never allow me to do that.

Beboppers were by no means fools. For a generation of Americans and young people around the world, who reached maturity during the 1940s, bebop symbolized a rebellion against the rigidities of the old order, an outcry for change in almost every field, especially in music. The bopper wanted to impress the world with a new stamp, the uniquely modern design of a new generation coming of age.

"To Heaven on a Mule"

      People always thought I was crazy, so I used that to my advantage to attract public attention and find the most universal audience for our music. I fell back on what I knew. While performing modern jazz, I emphasized certain inimitable parts of my own style.

      I've played with some of the best singers and some of the great comedians. Fats Waller was one of my idols. I dug the way that he was a master musician and a master pantomime artist. I patterned my career after that. It wasn't a buddy-buddy thing, but I knew Fats Waller. I loved him and he loved me, though we never did hang out together. Fats Waller influenced me not only through his music, but his whole personality, because he was funny, and then you could sit him down at the piano and close his mouth and he'd play. This niggah could eat up a piano. Everybody respected him. Art Tatum, James P. Johnson, Earl Hines—all of them respected Thomas "Fats" Waller. That's right! All you have to do is listen to "Ain't Misbehavin'" ("No one to walk with, all by myself") or "Honeysuckle Rose." Those tunes will last forever. The bridge in "Ain't Misbehavin'." Where did he get that from? Boy, I bet all the piano players, right now, love it. That change'll last. That's some hip shit. I haven't heard anything in music since that's more hip, harmonically and logically.

      Comedy is important. As a performer, when you're trying to establish audience control, the best thing is to make them laugh if you can. That relaxes you more than anything. A laugh relaxes your muscles; it relaxes muscles all over your body. When you get people relaxed, they're more receptive to what you're trying to get them to do. Sometimes, when you're laying on something over their heads, they'll go along with it if they're relaxed.

Sometimes I get up on the bandstand and say, "I'd like to introduce the men in the band . . ." and then introduce the guys to one another. There's a reason for that. I just don't come out with it to get a laugh.

See, you can do that in any country, even if they don't know how to speak English. Any language! You can say, "And now, ladies and gentlemen, I'd like to introduce the guys in the band. Mr. Jones, this is Mr. Brown . . ." I tried it in foreign countries and it works. They don't know what the hell I'm saying, but when they see those guys shaking hands, and they've heard, "introduce . . ." Man!

Song and dance is a part of me. In high school I used to sing a song called "Goin' to Heaven on a Mule." It was a big hit of the show that we did at Laurinburg Institute. Everybody remembers that now, and the old people say, "Hey, John, remember when you sang that song, 'Goin' to Heaven on a Mule'?" I don't even remember what happened, how that song goes, but I know the name of it was "Goin' to Heaven on a Mule." I sing about one new song every five years to accompany my music—tunes like "Oop-Pop-A-Dop," "Ooop-Bop-sh'-Bam," "I'm Beboppin' Too," "You Stole My Wife, You Horsethief," "Swing Low, Sweet Cadillac," "School Days," and "Something in Your Smile." I can't remember the song "Goin' to Heaven on a Mule," but I used the philosophy behind it to build my act. The "mule" is my background in black folk culture and "heaven" is where I'm at.

If I could dance to my music, it's possible. I used to dance all the time in front of the band. But it was pretty difficult, really, without that strong one-two, one-two beat. They're getting back to a more definite beat because we've figured out that our music was made primarily for dancing. Jazz was invented for people to dance to, we can't get away from that. My music calls more for listening, but it'll still make you shake your head and pat your feet. If I don't see anybody doing that in the audience, we ain't getting to them, and we're playing mostly for spirit, not for intellect.

RAY BROWN:

"We were playing in Boston one time in the ballroom, and he went out, and they announced him. He came back and we started to play, and he started doing a little dance. And when he started this dance, he tripped over one of the cymbal stands.

"And the cymbal stand fell into the drum and knocked down something else. He fell on the stage; he fell out. And so the rest of the band was a little shocked because they didn't know whether to stop or what. Fortunately, we didn't stop. We kept playing, and one of the horn players grabbed up the cymbals and helped the guy straighten up the drums; he kept playing.

"Diz got right up and kept dancing. Dizzy just kept dancing on back across the stage. I think if I had been dancing and fell out, I would've been so embarrassed, I might've run off stage for a minute to get myself together. But it didn't detour him at all.

"Then one time we were on the road down in Texas somewhere. We got a new drummer, a guy named Teddy Stewart joined the band. Teddy was not a good reader, but he could swing like a dog. While he was learning the book, I would sing the licks to him in advance of the playing, then when we got to the bar, he'd just had it, you know. And we got into about the second or third tune, and the band was swinging so hard.

"Dizzy was standing out in front of the band, and he just looked at us, he just jumped off the bandstand and ran through the audience and went outside, like fifteen or twenty minutes. So when he came back, we said, 'What happened?'

"He said, 'Man, you're swinging so much I couldn't stand it,' and he just jumped off, jumped off the stage and ran out."

ELMON WRIGHT:

"Hey, look, man, he'll crack you up. Just about everything he does will crack you up. Unless he's actually serious about something, he'll crack you up. I mean, he's a witty guy. He can be walking down the street. I don't care where he goes—it'll take Dizzy a good half an hour, or maybe a little more, to walk three blocks, and he walks fast. But everybody knows him, and he knows everybody. I don't know where this guy knows all these people from, but he always stops and talks. He don't never fluff nobody off; he always stops and talks. And then he's got a joke for everybody, understand. When you walk away, he's cracked you up. He's going three blocks, but if you're walking with him, it'll take you a while to get there. He's something else, man.

"Yeah, he is the showman. It's too bad they didn't have videotape in those days. We could have taped a lotta things. He just picks something outta the air and fan handles a thing, and it'll come out and it'll break the house up. Whereas if I picked it out, or you picked it out, or this guy over here, nothing happening. It'll go flat."

TED KELLY:

"Diz has always been a thoroughly relaxed 'for real' person. By for real, I mean there's no put-ons, man. Diz will come out, and he's straightforward with the audience. You know, he has no *prepared* patter that he has to go through, although he sometimes says things that he's said before, because he found it went over good. But that becomes a part of his act. In other words he has no real, 'I've got to do this now . . . and this is what I gotta do next,' you know.

"Once, when we were working up in the Apollo, after one of the shows, Diz said, 'Hey, fellas, why you guys so stiff, man? This is a show. Don't be sitting up there so stiff, and playing to relax people.'

"Elmon Wright was in the band, and Joe Wilder was in the band too. So next show, while Diz was out there giving his patter on the stage, from one side of the wings comes Joe Wilder with a policeman's cap and a club in his hand, clubbing behind Elmon, who's going across in front, see. He said he wanted more comedy jive going on, so these cats came out doing comedy. He kind of looked away, like, that was upstaging him a bit. So he didn't say anything that show. Next show, out comes two cats. One cat's in a wheelbarrow, the other cat's pushing the wheelbarrow. Behind that Diz says, 'All right, fellas. All right, that's enough of the comedy. Let's go on back to like you were before.' Tighten up, turn it loose, you know. But in general, man, he was very enjoyable to work with."

CECIL PAYNE (baritone saxophone):

"The first time I met Dizzy I was working with Roy Eldridge's band. He had a big band on Fifty-second Street. And that was the first time I ever played baritone. I was playing alto up to that time. Roy had needed a baritone player and I had gone home and practiced. Dizzy came down to hear Roy Eldridge, and he needed a baritone player. When he heard me playing in the band, he asked me would I play with his band, because, at that time, Bill Graham was working with him. They were so friendly, so overly friendly, Bill Graham and Moody. They were doing so much kidding around that, like, Dizzy wanted to get a baritone player that was a little bit more stable. Let's put it that way.

"So, anyway, me and Bill Graham played. I remember the first night at the Savoy. Bill Graham showed me all the parts, gave me his tie off his neck. You know, they had uniforms in those days. And up to this day, me and Bill are like the best of friends.

"My first solo playing with Dizzy was actually a blues. And when he heard me play the blues, that was it. I stayed with him almost three years. Three great years, 1947 to 1950.

"When I first went with Dizzy's band, I didn't even think that I could play the music, because the music was so . . . Nobody ever heard the way they phrased it and played it. So I was a nervous wreck. I didn't just ease on in there, man. I was actually scared to death. And then the years went by, and we all became friends, Moody, Dave Burns, Joe Gayles, and John Lewis.

"You had to really study. At that time, everybody, man, was trying to learn to play this new music that Dizzy and Bird was playing. There were so many other things we had to learn how to do. When we were rehearsing, we had to learn how to phrase the music, how to play together. Dizzy's band at that time was so tight. Like, there were fifteen, sixteen men in the band, and everybody played like one man. If anybody missed a note, man—Like, you felt bad if you missed a note during the whole evening. That's how dedicated everybody was to what was happening. Everybody just loved Dizzy; he was the whole thing. Listening to him play every night, you know. And every night, man, everybody in his band would just have to look at him, like in amazement, to see the things that he was doing then, and he's still doing now. The ways he plays, man, it's remarkable.

"The challenging thing was to be able to play like that. To be able to play what Dizzy and Bird were playing. It was difficult, to play like that, and even to think up things like that to play. Dizzy and Bird were always thinking up something original. They created the sounds and the music that goes with it. So the musicians learning to try to play then would play what they were playing. To get the different sounds, the phrasing, you have to get the fingers; the fingers and your mind have to work together. You have to think. Your mind is thinking with the horn. You can easily play what somebody else has played. You might be able to play it like them, but then, after you play the first chords, what are you gonna do? Then you have to go into your own thing. Right?

"Dizzy and Bird would be playing six or seven choruses—and every one would be different—and creating different sounds. See, Bird and Dizzy and Miles too developed to the stage where they could actually 'play.' What they were playing was free. You have groups that play 'free' music now, like the 'space' music or something like that. They're playing free. Actually, Bird and Dizzy were playing free too. In their minds, they were playing free. They didn't have any hangup about this chord or that chord. In their mind, they were playing anything they could play, freely. But they were playing correct. I mean they were playing according to what the song they were playing to implied. Now, I mean, they have musicians that get up and play, and

they play very good, soul and everything. But the reason why Bird
and Dizzy and all them excel is because they have in their mind when
they play, being free. They can hit any note and it comes out right, like
any kind of phrase, or anything, because in their mind there's no bar-
rier. And they know what they're playing. They know how the sound
should be because of playing like that all the time. They know how
one sound leads to another. They can hear anything and play it. Every
musician tries to reach that high. They're always trying to develop to
where your fingers and your mind work together. And it comes out.
Man, it's like being elevated on a different plane.

"There had to be great nights, outstanding nights, greater than
others. But I remember that he had one concert that he did with Bird,
where Bird came up and they played together. That was one of the
great things. Then there was another concert where Dizzy and Miles
got up and played together. And, the reason why I remember that, the
concert with Dizzy and Miles, was because when Miles came up to the
bandstand, we were playing a number that Miles didn't actually know.
And when Miles started taking the solo, Dizzy was calling the chords
off in his ear. And when he called the chords off, Miles was playing
them and running them all through the thing. They really knew what
they were playing. Like there is such a thing as playing and knowing
what you're playing. Plus, even up to there, anybody can actually do
that, know what you're playing and play. But the thing is to put the
feeling in, man. That's a different scene. Yeah, it was remarkable.

"Dizzy was always in a good mood. He was always scat singing or
talking; he was always funny. You see, he's an outgoing person, so he
always had something going. He's always either dancing or saying some
witty remarks. Dizzy always keeps you interested in what's going on.

"At the time we were working together, I had a lot of respect for
his musical ability and what he played. Now, over the years, we know
each other like as persons. I know he's a real sincere, dedicated person
not only to the music, but to all people. He has a deep feeling for everybody. I imagine you can tell that when he's playing; he plays and
tries to reach everybody. Everybody can actually appreciate what he's
doing."

The big band became a definite road success by 1947, but I still
hoped for a greater recognition of culture, the whole culture of our
music, and wanted a more universal appeal. By 1947, a lotta bands
had begun to imitate our style of playing. And some of them, especially the white bands like Stan Kenton's, did better in America, commercially, than we could at that time with segregation. No one could

take our style, but we had to stay in existence to keep the style alive. They had us so penned up within the concept of race that a colored big band wasn't all that economically feasible, unless you were playing and doing just what the people ordered.

I remember sometimes we'd go out . . . I'd go out with Illinois Jacquet who had seven pieces. He was playing what the people, the masses of blacks, wanted; so he hired me and my whole band; we played behind him and he became a big star. The same thing happened with Louis Jordan, a small group, five pieces, the Tympani Five. Our band got a lotta publicity, but the money didn't roll in like the publicity. We didn't play that kinda music.

BUDDY JOHNSON:

"I tell you what Diz and his band did do though. After he made his tour, we had to come around and make our tour. We made this circuit twice a year, this 'watermelon' circuit. The next time we went back to this hotel that we knew—the manager wouldn't let us in, because of what Dizzy and his band did in the hotel when they were there. They didn't want any more musicians in that hotel. The man said that people couldn't sleep because the boys ran all night long in the hallway and up to each other's rooms slamming doors and carrying on, and the girls running from room to room, ha, ha. . . . But even so, when I heard Dizzy's band play, I really got the full understanding of what he was doing that day, way back there in Paris.

"Myself, I played what I felt. . . . And what I felt was what I learned in the backwoods, out there near Darlington, South Carolina. I describe myself as a cotton picker, a plowboy, way back there, you know; sharecropping and what not. What I heard back there, I tried to bring it, bring it before them, to explain it to the people, although so many times, I guess, that idea didn't get over. I loved all types of music, always did. I like hillbilly, country-western, bebop. I like progressive music and I like 'jump' music. I love church songs. I think they have more soul than anything else that I've run into. But, uh, when I first heard bebop . . .

"Most bands in order to make it had to tour. A lot of bands, like the great Glenn Miller's band, Benny Goodman—even if it weren't one man who was backing them, it would be a corporation that would put so much money in and perfect this band before it even got out there. Then they'd buy radio time someplace. They'd put the band in some big club and broadcast over the radio. And that's hoping that the people out there would hear them. Then they would go out on tour; that's where they made the money.

"When I first heard bebop, I said it wouldn't make it down South. This was music with crazy chords. And, if you knew a little bit about music, you could really dig it. But many people didn't know music. They could tell that there was something strange going on and they loved it, you know. But as far as being the thing that would take, I couldn't play that. If I'd played it, that would have perhaps been my last tour. So bebop, when I first heard it, 'No. . . .' But, you know, then Diz got his band together, and he had such wonderful musicians there and the band played so nice, so crazy.

"But that's *his*. The music, progressive music is real baad, real nice. I'm only sorry that I was only able to make one record on a progressive side.

"You must know quite a bit to play progressive music, to play it correctly. Now, when I needed a new man in my band, they all came in with a progressive flavor. And it didn't fit the music I'd played. There was one man that did fit the band, Willie Nelson. I remember Diz coming up to the Savoy now and then to sit and listen to Willie because he was able to combine those things, the blues and the jazz flavors, to make it pretty coming around through the chords and corners, you know. Lately, I heard Dizzy play the blues and convert it into his own inimitable style."

Now, it may sound funny, but I don't consider myself a blues man. I know the blues, but Hot Lips Page is a blues man. When he plays trumpet, he plays it like a blues player would play. My music is not that deep—not as deep as his—not as deep as Hot Lips Page or Charlie Parker, because Yard knew the blues. Blues is my music, the music of my people, but I'm not what you call a "blues" player. I mean in the authentic sense of the blues. I don't want to put myself up as a blues player. I'd love to, I feel it, but I'm not. Because when I hear the blues, I hear Lips play the blues, and it's different from me. Mine ain't the real blues with toe jam between your toes, come in and bend a note around the corner. Johnny Hodges is a blues player, quiet as it's kept, from Boston, Massachusetts. He could moan a while. Moaning—all that goes with the blues. I try it. Sometimes. I play with a blues band, and I'll do pretty good, but I wouldn't be like B. B. King or "T-Bone" Walker. I wouldn't be that good. Even with Louis Armstrong, I didn't hear them bends that you can't sing. I know what it is when I hear it, but I'm not one of those players. And I hate to hear a white guy say, "I'm a blues player," because I know if I don't, and I grew up listening to that shit, right under it . . .

It's a Sad'ay night thing. Down in South Carolina, man, those cats used to come out on Saturday. Yeah, the first blues I ever heard was a guy coming uptown on Saturday with the guitars and the mouth organ, the top of a Coca-Cola bottle . . .

> No use runnin, hold out your hand
> I can get a woman anytime you can get a man
> Since you gone and left me,
> I'm sittin on top of this world.

I heard that again the other day. I heard somebody singing that, some white man singing that song, a country and western guy, singing that, and I ain't heard that since I was about ten or eleven.

Sometimes, I'll get up and sing the blues, but I don't get that thing in my voice like they do, like a Ray Charles. Ray Charles gets it in his voice, or Aretha Franklin. Ella Fitzgerald can't do it; I've never heard Ella Fitzgerald do it. Sarah Vaughan can't do it. Dinah Washington could; Little Esther; Natalie Cole's got it. Here's the sweet velvet voice of Nat Cole, and here comes his daughter, steeped in gospel. Ha! Ha! The blues. That's some funny shit. When you hear her, boy, you picture Nat singing "Nature Boy."

Well, I guess, in our music we've got different strains. I worked on developing modern jazz of a different kind, more like mixing hot peppers in a dish of black-eye peas or macaroni, rather than wrinkle steaks. That's my idea of "soul," and it's really more modern, more global. I was influenced by Latin. If you play any of my tunes in Latin countries, they understand it. I was always more of a Latin player. Charlie Parker made some records with Latin players like Machito. But mine, let's say I'm more at home with it than Charlie was. Polyrhythms exerted a major influence on me. I don't know where it comes from, because my early training was to sit and listen to music in the Sanctified church, and I've always said that spirituals were blues too. You need a psychiatrist to figure that one out.

BUDD JOHNSON:

"Dizzy had a recording date for RCA Victor with his big band. He said, 'O.K., make me an arrangement on the "St. Louis Blues."' So the cats rehearsed it. I had dissonance in it. I had everything in it, you know, moving. Dizzy liked the arrangement very much, so naturally he went to W. C. Handy and said 'Well look, man, I just recorded the "St. Louis Blues" and thank you, thank you.'

"So when the old man, Handy, heard it, he told Victor, 'Don't put that out!' He said, 'Because that's not the "St. Louis Blues."' But way later they did put it out. That was amusing to me." (Victor LJM 1009.)

For whatever it means, I got to Carnegie Hall on September 29, 1947. Billy Shaw at that time was with the Gale Agency, and he said, "We should have a concert with you and Ella Fitzgerald at Carnegie Hall." At that time they'd put packages together, and they'd always put us together with Ella.

I said, "O.K., let's go." It sold out. It was beautiful.

At that concert, Charlie Parker did something. People try to create some dissension between Charlie Parker and me. They don't know how warm a relationship we had. On the stage, after one of the numbers, Charlie Parker just walked out on the stage with one rose, one long rose—he'd probably spent his last quarter to buy it—and gave it to me. And he kissed me—on the mouth—and then walked off. I get a warm feeling every time I think about Charlie Parker.

Louis Armstrong came to that concert and stopped to visit me backstage. He said, "You're cutting the fool up there, boy. Showing your ass."

I said, "Aww, no, Pops."

Oooh, didn't we get some write-ups! Bill Gottlieb wrote prophetically on September 26, 1947 in the New York *Herald Tribune,* "No doubt about it, 'bebop' is replacing swing . . . the music in spite of its name is not nonsense. . . . Bebop is modern, progressive music, harmonically suited to the times. . . . Like other jazz forms before it, bebop, in diluted form, will eventually alter even the most commercial forms of popular music. It's begun to do so already. . . ." After that Carnegie Hall concert everybody started paying attention to the music.

LEONARD FEATHER:

"Now that I look back on it, I wonder why I had the courage to do it, because it was a risky thing to do at the time. And I put my own money into it. I don't know what it came to, maybe a couple thousand dollars, which at that time was a lot to put into a concert. There were three, all around Christmastime, and they were all at Carnegie Hall.

They were in 1947, 1948, and 1949, as I recollect. Ella was on one of them, Charlie Parker was on one. And I had some other people involved, Monte Kay and Symphony Sid; we became involved together, putting these concerts on. I think the third one, 1949, I was in the hospital after an accident. I was knocked down by a car. I didn't even attend the concert, but I was still the promoter and, luckily, it went all right.

"They did very well, surprisingly well, surprising in view of the fact that there was so much active, really nasty opposition to the music, particularly in the media. The daily press was just death on it; they didn't even acknowledge its existence. And with the exception of *Metronome,* and an occasional write-up in *Downbeat,* most of the musical press were violently opposed to it. Some very small magazines which wielded some power in jazz circles used to run whole articles attacking me and attacking bebop in general and attacking anything which was not New Orleans, which they thought was the only 'true' jazz—Bunk Johnson and them. That's what was called the 'War of the Moldy Figs.' If you look back on it, it seems ridiculous, but everybody was within two inches of fighting one another instead of trying to promote the music totally. And Dizzy and Bird were victims of that. They had to fight all through that, and he had a tremendous amount of courage for his convictions, to keep going with his beliefs and to keep doing what he wanted to do.

"Well, naturally, I was very excited by the first two concerts. Just hearing him at the head of a big band. At that time, it was a very difficult thing for him to do, economically and every other way, to be able to even lead a big band. And as he'll tell you, Billy Shaw had a tremendous loyalty and worked very hard to enable him to keep the band together. Billy was very helpful to both of us in making these concerts possible. He was very much wrapped up in the music too; he wasn't just another agent. He was a nice man.

"The two concerts: The 1947 one because it was the first that he'd ever done at Carnegie Hall and because he had the big band. And the 1948 one because Chano Pozo was there and because we presented the world premiere of 'Cubana Be' and 'Cubana Bop,' which I thought was tremendously important.

"Well, I became gradually aware of the Latin idiom when—I guess before the 1948 concert—he hired Chano Pozo in the band and he became conscious of the potential for incorporating Afro-Cuban rhythms.* And I wasn't actually aware of it. He presented it as a fait

* Actually we premiered "Cubana Be," "Cubana Bop" at the Carnegie Hall Concert, September 29, 1947. (Arco LP 8.)
After Chano Pozo joined the band, we played our first major concerts in Europe but recorded "Cubana Be," "Cubana Bop" with him on December 22, 1947. (Victor 20-3145.)

accompli, so to speak, by putting Chano Pozo in the band. Once he had done it, it seemed like a very natural thing; but just as it had been with bebop, you never envisioned it beforehand. And yet when he presented it, it seemed like, well, why hadn't somebody thought of that before? That's part of the genius of Dizzy, you know, that he had ideas that maybe somebody should've and could've thought of earlier, but nobody did."

They stuck two other feathers in my cap in 1947. *Metronome* magazine had a critic, Barry Ulanov, who was friendly to modern jazz, and they were very impressed because we'd just begun to record for Victor; we cut four tunes, among them "Oop-Pop-A-Da." (RCA 20-2480.) They named me as best trumpet of the year, and my orchestra was listed as Band of the Year in 1947. *Metronome* claimed we'd shown that "A new era in jazz began in 1947, that modern jazz had come to stay, had even come to pay." It came a few years late, but that was exciting with the Royal Roost and Bop City and everything going, really something. *Metronome* magazine and the critics thought we were the best band in the country at that time and gave us the award. I felt we deserved it. We were competing with Count Basie, Duke Ellington, Woody Herman, Lionel Hampton, Tommy Dorsey, Jimmy Dorsey, and Stan Kenton.

Cheeks

One thing about me, my physical appearance, was becoming more and more unique. My cheeks started bulging out. I didn't get any physical pain from it, but all of a sudden, I looked like a frog whenever I played. I hadn't always played like that. I remember when I didn't play like that, and it was technically incorrect for playing with a symphony orchestra; but for what I wanted, it was perfectly correct. The proper way is not to let your jaws come out, playing the trumpet; I wouldn't recommend that anyone blow his jaws out trying to play the trumpet. With your jaws out, you can be playing and not playing from your diaphragm. Of course, with your jaws down, too, you can be playing from the chest. The first important element in playing the trumpet is your diaphragm. Because you need something like a fist to push the wind up. The next thing is to have the proper embouchure, and everybody has a different embouchure; so it's the one that suits you best. When I stop the air before I hit it, before I let it go, it's like you turn on some water and hold the faucet tight so it can't get out, and all of a sudden your hand comes away from it. It's like a stream, like a firehose. That's what happens to me. My tongue stops the air. The air is there. The air is in my cheeks already and crying to get up because my diaphragm and chest are giving air to my cheeks, a little bit, not all. You don't give up all your air at one time, just what's necessary. And it's very weird, because when I get set to play, my jaws are already up and all I've got to do is move my tongue and let it loose. That might be the way to play the trumpet. Musicologists have observed African trumpeters from northern Nigeria and Chad playing the same way.

Playing like I play, you have to have perfect time because you have to let the air out at exactly the right time. I don't just pick up my horn and spit out notes. Clark Terry can do that. He can take two horns and spit out notes into each one on a different beat. I can't. I'd never be able to do that because my chops have to get set. The right side of my upper lip comes down, like, in a little twist that over the years has left a mark there. A lotta people walk up to me and say, "You got half a mustache, half a mustache, that's weird. You're a weird dude."

"Well, if you look at it properly, you'll see it's a mark, not a mustache," I say.

And they come close and look at it and say, "Yeah, it is."

"That's from the trumpet."

"From the trumpet, way up there?" they say.

Dr. Richard J. Compton of NASA wanted to x-ray my cheeks in 1969 to find out why they expand when I play the trumpet. He called my condition, "Gillespie's Pouches." I told Lorraine this and she told her friend Dewilla, "Guess what? Dizzy's gonna have a disease named after him." I missed my appointment with Dr. Compton and the true reason for my jaws expanding is still unknown.*

* Dr. Compton has speculated that these may be vestigial gills, but I prefer to let it remain a mystery.

Chano Pozo, Afro-Cuban

When I finally had the big band going strong, in the fall of 1947, I spoke to Mario Bauza again about what I'd mentioned to him back in 1938—getting a conga player—and he said, "I got just the man for you. He doesn't speak English."

"He doesn't speak English?"

"No. Come on," Mario says, "we'll go down there."

And this guy was so exciting with the instrument, I say, "Well, you don't have to speak English."

Chano Pozo was already in New York when I went down to his house on 111th Street and met him. He used to play at a place down in El Barrio. He'd dance, sing, and play; he had a spot in the show but, most of the time, he played for other dancers. Boy, he could catch them. Every time they'd move, he'd do something, a drumbeat. And he'd keep going all the time. He was playing the *quinto*. It's about two and a half feet high, and it looks like a small conga. It has a very high pitch, "a-ra-ta-ta-dah-broooo." When I first heard him down there, we talked; I mean, we didn't talk, we just looked at one another and laughed.

Chano Pozo couldn't speak a word of English, and didn't speak English up until he died except very broken English. I can understand a Puerto Rican now in spite of the accent, by the way Chano used to speak. Since he couldn't speak any English, people always asked, "Well, how do you communicate?"

"Deehee no peek pani, me no peek Angli, bo peek African," Chano would answer.

He meant something which began during slavery times. In the United States they wouldn't let us use our primary means of expression, which was the drum because we could talk with the drum, and they figured you could foment revolution with the drums. So what the hell are they gonna let you talk for? So you can talk to somebody two miles over there and say, "Let's get these muthafuckas. Get ready."

Hell, yeah, it was a foreign language to them, and they knew you could talk with it, so they said, "Look, none of that drum shit! Catch you using a drum, we'll skin your ass!"

Later on, in New Orleans, blacks could go to the opera and listen to the opera, and they let them have instruments but never the drums.

After the drums had been outlawed and taken away, our ancestors had to devise other means of expressing themselves, their emotions. So they started, like in the fields, singing and clapping their hands, and they would hit the hoe in the ground in rhythm at the same time. The rhythm was in them, but they just didn't have any means, instrumentally, to put it together so the sound could travel very far. To do that, they needed the main instrument, the rhythmmaker, the one that you play with your hands. Our ancestors still had the impulse to make polyrhythms, but basically they developed a monorhythm from that time on, and it was very easy to adapt. That was in the United States. We became monorhythmic, but the Afro-Cubans, the South Americans, and the West Indians remained polyrhythmic. They didn't give up theirs. Our beat in the United States was so basic, though, that other blacks in the hemisphere could easily hear it.

MARIO BAUZA:

"Well, I was the cause of it, that marriage, that integration. I tell you what happened. When Dizzy left Calloway, he told me he wanna do something. I said, 'Well, why don't you get on this kick?' We had this idea for a long time. We talked together in the band about it.

"So he said, 'You got the man?'

"'I got the man for you to do that gig.' So I got ahold of Chano Pozo who was a friend of mine and another bongo player, and I arranged for them to rehearse with Dizzy. And Dizzy was so enthusiastic, he kept Chano.

"Even when Dizzy organized his band with Chano and Max

Roach, the drummer used to catch hell trying to adapt. The conga used to interrupt them, you know, until they found the right kind of approach, like what we're doing now, trying to get the right kind of approach between the two countries. It's two countries, but it's the same thing. Every rhythm comes from Africa, and all blacks come from over there, regardless."

Chano was the first conga player to play with a jazz band, and he was very unusual about playing with an understanding. There were certain things about our music that he didn't understand. Take a bottle and a pen yourself. The Cubans go de-de-de, de-de. That's the clave beat. If you go against the clave, that's just like going against our one-two-three beat. Chano Pozo didn't understand that too well, and he'd play Cuban with be-be, those two extra beats. He'd be on another beat from the rest of us. I said, "Now, how am I going to explain to this guy, that he's going against the one-two-three beat?" He didn't read music, so I couldn't say come on four. He couldn't read any music, but he was a great composer. So I'd go over and whisper in his ear, because there was one number that we played called "Good Bait" that he understood perfectly. So whenever he got on that wrong beat, I'd go over and whisper in his ear, "da-da, da-da-da." He'd change immediately, because if you're doing boom-boom, and you're supposed to be doing bap on a boom-boom, that's just like beeping when you should have bopped. He'd change immediately. It was fantastic.

Chano had such a limited knowledge of our music. He was really African, you know. He probably played when he was two and a half years old or something like that. All of the Nañigo, the Santo, the Ararra, all these different sects, the African things in Cuba, he knew, and he was well versed. Another guy who's well versed in that is Mongo Santamaria, and another guy is Armando Peraza.

Chano taught us all multirhythm; we learned from the master. On the bus, he'd give me a drum, Al McKibbon a drum, and he'd take a drum. Another guy would have a cowbell, and he'd give everybody a rhythm. We'd see how all the rhythms tied into one another, and everybody was playing something different. We'd be on the road in a bus, riding down the road, and we'd sing and play all down the highway. He'd teach us some of those Cuban chants and things like that. That's how I learned to play the congas. The chants, I mix up. I don't know one from the other, really, but they're all together. You have different ones, the Nañigo, the Ararra, the Santo and several others, and they each have their own rhythm. When you say do the Nañigo, the guy goes into that specific rhythm. They're all of African derivation.

⟦⟧

AL McKIBBON (bass):

"When I joined the band in the last part of 1947 and really got to know Dizzy and his views on music, the way he felt about African influences and Afro-Cuban influences, he was kind of a revolutionary to me. That really killed me; I was very young then. He knew and still knows where it all came from you know, African and Afro-Cuban. Everything original that was being done in music was African derivative. So when he got Chano Pozo in the band, that just killed me because I was always intrigued with drums, and to hear a drum played by hand was new to me. I'm from the Midwest, and here is this guy beating this goddam drum with his hands and telling a story. And Dizzy could see him in the band, you know. I couldn't . . . I couldn't. Hell, man, to me Count Basie's rhythm section was it! Of course, Jimmy Blanton had twisted my head around sideways, but as a rhythm section, I thought Basie's was it. So, anyhow, Dizzy was always that farsighted, that he could see Chano Pozo playing in his band. And I said, 'Aww, man, what a drag.' But he came in, added another dimension, and was the first in a jazz band, you know, on conga drums. And look what's come of it.

"I learned how to play Latin music through Chano Pozo's influence; that started me because I learned a whole lot more later. But that initial thing, 'Manteca,' really opened my eyes and my mind and heart and everything. And I think I learned from Dizzy that the bass, while it can be a foundation and all that, still can be very impressive out front as a solo instrument. He also liked to hear the bass in a setting, you know, like solo arrangements. We had 'One Bass Hit,' 'Two Bass Hit,' all that. It was gorgeous, just gorgeous.

"Chano was a hoodlum. No. But in Cuba he was really a rough character. He had a bullet in him and all. He belonged to that society, Nañigo, you know. It's like being a Mason in this country except that they were very African. In fact they speak Yoruba. He used to tell me all about a lotta stuff he shouldn't have repeated."

⟦⟧

That's very interesting. When Chano came, he really opened things up. There are things that he played—he died in 1948—that I'm just beginning to understand now. Chano wasn't a writer, but stone African. He knew rhythm—rhythm from Africa. He sang a chant that was authentic on "Cubana Be" and "Cubana Bop" that was call-and-response between himself and the guys in the band. There are things he would play and sing at the same time on that, and I could never figure out where the first beat was. The downbeat, one! We really had a mutual way of working together after I learned how he heard the rhythm and could signal him to put him in the right time with the band because his beat and our beat were different. This was really the beginning of the fusion between Afro-Cuban music and jazz.

Here's an example of the difference in the music. When the Cubans came here, their music was 2/4. Our music was 3/4, 4/4, or cut time. There's a big difference. The Americans couldn't read their music too well, in 2/4 time, when the Cuban bands came up here. They couldn't read it because instead of eighth notes, there were sixteenth notes, and it looked too busy, a little too busy for them. Therefore, they wrote it like it was in 4/4 time for the benefit of these musicians up here, and they destroyed the feeling of the music. The 4/4 completely destroys the feeling of Afro-Cuban music because they're in 2/4 instead of 4/4. That was the difference and we had to become accustomed to the nuances of it.

Chano Pozo came to me when he was with the band and said, "I got an idea for a tune." "Manteca" means skin or grease in Spanish, and everybody then was saying, "Gimme some skin." That was his idea of saying, "Gimme some skin." In Spanish, skin is grease, lard, butter, whatever, so "Manteca" is something greasy. That's where the title came from. That was pretty slick. He couldn't even speak English and wrote a tune with a title that had connotations in English. When he came, he had already figured out what the bass was gonna do, how it was gonna start off, how the saxophones were gonna come in afterwards. He had that riff. He had the riffs of the trombones; he had the riffs of the trumpets.

But Chano wasn't too hip about American music. If I'd let it go like he wanted it, it would've been strictly Afro-Cuban, all the way. There wouldn't have been a bridge. I wrote the bridge. I said, "Now, wait a minute. Hold it, hold it. After that part, we need a bridge." So I started writing a bridge. I was sitting down at the piano writing the bridge, and thought I was writing an eight-bar bridge. But after eight bars, I hadn't resolved back to B-flat, so I had to keep on going and ended up writing a sixteen-bar bridge. That's how it happened. Anytime you hear something that Chano and I wrote, that we were collaborators on, I didn't just gorilla myself in it, I contributed. You see, when I use these guys from different cultures, I always try to understand their music, and then I try to put what I think should go in it. I try to add something. I just don't pick his brain. You could hear me in it; I always add something. "Manteca" was probably the largest selling record I ever had. (Victor 20-3023.)

Now, the reason you know I'm not lying is because I wrote "A Night In Tunisia" in 1942 (and before that "Pickin' The Cabbage"), where the bass player's saying "de-de-de, doom-doom, de-de-de, doom-doom" instead of saying "doom-doom-doom-doom." And the rhythm played sort of a Latin beat behind that, and it worked out very well. Later, from that came "Manteca" which was really a mixture of Afro-Cuban and jazz, and that was the first definitive breakaway from the old beat. It's dynamite. On account of Chano Pozo, the great Cuban composer and instrumentalist. Chano was really ahead of his time. Conga players now haven't really broken away from his style. They haven't yet actually broken away from what Chano Pozo was doing. They're doing different little things, yes, but the true fundamentals Chano Pozo set down.

The role of Walter Fuller in structuring, arranging, and orchestrating "Manteca" should not be overlooked, and he is properly listed as cocomposer.

◰

WALTER GILBERT FULLER:

"I think the first real Latin thing we did was 'Manteca.' And we wrote 'Manteca' in my apartment, at 94 LaSalle Street, with nobody there but Dizzy, me, Chano, and Bill Graham. Chano would sing you from thing to thing. And what broke up the night was, we asked him, 'Whaddayou want the bass to do? Whaddayou think this should be? Whaddayou want the trumpets to do?'

" 'Pee-de-do! Pee-da-do! Pee-da-do!' Chano was doing that shit.

"Finally, I told him, 'Hey, O.K., I got enough. Go ahead, I'll fix it.' Because we stayed there for about two hours with that kinda shit. As Dizzy said, Chano had some of the figures that he wanted out and out.

"We sat down at the piano then, trying to structure the thing. Dizzy sat down at the piano, 'How about this?'

"So you take the harmonies from Dizzy and say, 'We'll fix the rest of it, don't worry!'

"When Dizzy said Chano started out with the saxophones, he didn't have that shit. He didn't have none of that. He had that line; he had that melody line. And then he would say, 'Pee-do-do! Pee-de-de! Pee-de-do!' That's exactly what he said.

"Chano would have ideas for songs. To show you where that was, 'Guarachi Guaro' was another type thing that Chano was gonna do. And if you listen to 'Guarachi Guaro', it will drive you nuts because it does the same thing all over again because it just keeps going and repeats itself ad infinitum. And it never got off the ground like it should have because it wasn't structured. It wasn't structured in terms of something with form. The form was lacking."

ALBERTO SOCARRAS:

"Dizzy did something with the Cuban and the jazz music. He did something with Chano Pozo, long time ago, a number called 'Manteca,' something like that. That was very effective, see. And right after that, a whole lot of the American arrangers or orchestra leaders started having bongos, conga drums, the same rhythm that Cubans have, together with jazz. That was very effective. So for that, I credit Dizzy, I mean improvement on the rhythmically poor American music. You see, because before it was just 'one-two-three-four, one-two-three-four. . . .' Just like that. By adding the best of the conga drums and things, it added rhythmically to American music."

The collaboration on "Cubana Be" was among three of us. George Russell, who now teaches at the New England Conservatory of Music wrote the introduction, twenty-four bars, and then I wrote the first chorus, and arranged that for the band. There was another sixteen bars after the first chorus which I also wrote. In fact, I wrote one chord going from the introduction into the melody of the tune, that chord, the melody, and sixteen bars following it. Then after the sixteen bars, I played a *montuno* with Chano, just the two of us—the trumpet and the congas. Montuno is something that in English would mean *vamp;* and you play licks behind a montuno like you do on a vamp in jazz, only montuno is rhythm, not melodic like the vamp.* And then Chano took over, and he did all of the rest of the stuff by himself. A whole lot in there. Then we started singing, "Cubana Be, Cubana Bop . . . Cubana Be, Cubana Bop . . ." George Russell brought the band in, took my melody and spread it; the band came in building a figure up to my melody again, but with George's harmony which expanded on the theme. He wrote all kinds of stuff behind the melodic theme and we went out that way. Right now, that arrangement is current. George Russell is definitely a very gifted musician.

* Montuno is mostly rhythmic, and you play a solo behind it. This was not my first expression of that feeling. "Woody 'n You" had a Latin beat behind it, and so did "Night In Tunisia." Most of my tunes have got a whole lotta Latin feeling.

⛶

GEORGE RUSSELL (composer, percussion):

"Dizzy bought one arrangement from me in 1945, a thing called 'New World.' Then I became ill for sixteen months and I stayed in the hospital in the Bronx. They all came up to see me, you know. When I got out, Dizzy and I collaborated on 'Cubana Be, Cubana Bop,' that was in 1947.

"Diz had written a sketch which was mostly 'Cubana Be.' His sketch was what later turned out to be the section of the piece called 'Cubana Be' except that I wrote a long introduction to that which was at the time modal. I mean it wasn't based on any chords, which was an innovation in jazz because the modal period didn't really begin to happen until Miles popularized it in 1959. So that piece was written in 1947, and the whole concept of my introduction was modal, and then Dizzy's theme came in and we performed it. Then I wrote the second part, 'Cubana Bop.' During a bus ride to play at Symphony Hall in Boston, I heard Chano Pozo doing this Nañigo, this Cuban music that was like black mysticism. So I suggested to Dizzy at the time that at the concert that night we open the piece up and have Chano take a solo section by himself. Then we worked it out somehow so the band would come in chanting after Chano, and that was the way the piece went down. Now, actually, Dizzy and I were the writers, but when it began to get to the stage where Victor recorded it, Chano insisted that he also be listed as a composer. Well, in a sense, he's justified because his improvisations in the middle of it were his own things. They weren't written, but they were his own improvisations. So out of respect to Chano, we all agreed that he should be the third party. He was listed as one of the composers. (Victor 20-3145.)

"Diz had a very unique sense of putting chord progressions together, you know, and his theme 'Cubana Be, Cubana Bop' was really, really fabulous, amazing for that time. So really imaginative in a harmonic sense.

"Chano's concept came from Africa. When I heard it, it sounded on fire to me, the mixing of the standard American drumming together with the Afro-Cuban thing. We were striving for exactly that kind of world grasp, a kind of universality. There were all kinds of influences in that piece, but chief was the melding of the Afro-Cuban and traditional jazz. Not traditional, but the contemporary jazz drumming of the time. So the accent was on rhythm.

"The audience was in a state of shock. They didn't believe that an orchestra could really rise to that level of excitement and innovation.

"There's a funny story too. Dizzy introduced me to my first wife, and that's sorta amusing because I was taking a bath, and he just brought her right in the bathroom with me in the bathtub. This was Juanita. I was living at John Lewis' house, and he had come by to see John, but I was there and I happened to be in the bathtub. The door was open so he walked in, and he was with her. So he just brought her in and started introducing her, 'This is Juanita.' And I'm sitting totally nude in the bathtub. I didn't call her for a couple of years, but I did call her later and we got married."

You'd better believe everyone received the proper credit for these compositions because none of us was a pushover. Chano personally was a roughneck. Walter Fuller would say, "Look, the first sucker that comes in here late is gonna get a fine, a certain amount of money deducted from his pay." Now, Chano comes in late. Walter deducts it from his pay. Chano comes to me, "Deexy, what's happening, may'n? The m'hony no right; the m'hony es no right, may'n."

"What does it say, you got a slip? Well, there's a fine here."

"Tha' muthafucka took my m'hony, may'n!"

"Well, he's running it."

"You de boss. . . ."

"Yeah, I'm the boss, but that's the boss there. He's running it; he's running it." He had to pay. A lotta guys'd come to me. They'd run across some infraction, and Walter would hit them. He had to, in order to get discipline. Chano was very rough.

Chano wrote "Blangh! Blangh! Blangh!" That's the name of it, that's the clave beat. He didn't write it because he couldn't write music, but he used to hum it out. "Manteca," "Cubana Be, Cubana Bop," and "Tin Tin Deo" we did together. "Guarachi Guaro" he wrote.

Even in Cuba, Chano was known to be very high strung. He traveled with a long knife too. He got shot in Cuba. He was shot twice; the second time he didn't get up. The first time he was shot in Cuba, sometime in the early forties. He went into the publisher's office. Chano went in there with his knife and grabbed the guy and said, "I want my money, I want my royalty." He went in for his royalties, and the guy reached in his drawer and shot him. The bullet lodged near the spine and they couldn't operate because it was too close to the spine. He was pretty rough. That bullet next to his spine used to hurt him whenever the weather would get too cold. He used to sit on one half of his ass; he would be hurting on the stage. Chano had a reputation, and he got killed, later, on his reputation but not before he contributed to our music and helped to carry it, out to the world overseas.

High Seas

Our first concert tour of Europe lasted from January to March 1948, and we sailed eastward aboard the *Drottningholm,* a Swedish ship. Luckily, the worst happened first. We ran into the turbulent high seas of the North Atlantic in winter, but strangely that didn't bother me too much. A lotta good things and several bad things occurred on that trip, however, and there were different opinions among the others in the band.

▐▐

KENNY CLARKE:

"It all started on this end. We were supposed to go first class. We had first-class accommodations, going and coming. We got on the ship, and I saw a busboy whom I had made the trip with ten years earlier. So I said, 'They moved you up to first class, Hans?'

"He said, 'No, I'm still in third class.' When I found out we were in third class, that started it. You're on the ship, so how the fuck're you gonna get off. 'Put me off at the next stop!' The next stop was Gothenburg, Sweden.

"There was a storm, too, going over. I was about to go out scared like everybody else. No, we weren't really, really scared. It was just

the idea that it took us a lotta time at sea, which no one was in the
condition to endure. Another two days . . . When you figure, we're
there, they say, 'No, man, we got three more days.'"

AL McKIBBON:

"We were down in the goddamn hold. In fact it was tourist class,
you know. And when we got in the North Sea, they had to turn the
ship around backward to face the sea to keep it from capsizing. Oh, it
was frightening, man. I looked out on deck; they had it all roped off,
you know, and I just opened the door and peeked out cause they
wouldn't let you get up there. There was a big black wave, way up
over the top of the boat, man, and that water hit the deck, 'Lammm!!!'
The whole ship went sideways. I lost about fifteen pounds on the voyage. Everytime that ship would rock, I'd puke, me and Chano Pozo."

JOHN LEWIS:

"Everybody was sick, I think, except Dizzy and I. And so Dizzy
and I used to go up and eat all the breakfasts for seventeen people.
Because they couldn't eat anything, they were all sick. But Dizzy and I
ate."

DAVE BURNS:

"I remember everything about that tour, including almost getting
wasted away in the ocean. We ran into a hurricane up in the North
Atlantic. And I remember we were sitting down eating, and we all got
thrown off the table. Dizzy hit his head. He had a knot on his head
about an inch thick, and my arm was hurt. Yeah, we were sitting up
eating dinner, and all of a sudden the storm started moving in, man.
"The funny thing about that was the calm before the storm; we saw
those guys roping off the ship. So they had the head start on us—the
captains, the stewards, whatever—and they made it secure before. We
saw those guys in the daytime when it was calm. It was so beautiful
out that day. We were all up on the deck playin' shuffleboard. And
these guys started roping off everything. We said, 'Well, what in the
world are these guys doing?' They didn't tell us anything like that;
they didn't want to alarm the passengers. So about five or six hours afterward, during suppertime, round seven o'clock that night, we ran
right into it. And brother! You've never seen nothing like it. Guys
were sending home telegrams and praying. I never seen musicians
praying, standing up with their heads up in the air. You've never seen
nothing like it, man. They had to turn the ship around because the

water could've split the ship right in half, you know. We were out
there in the North Atlantic, out there in the water, and we were lucky;
we got to Sweden three days late. But when we got there, it made up
for everything. It made up for everything, when we got there."

We'd started out on the wrong foot. Being set for a concert in
Gothenburg (Göteburg), Sweden, at eight-thirty the night of January
26, our ship was due in the day before. By 10:15 P.M. on the twenty-
sixth we were still a two-minute boat ride from the shore at Gothenburg, and they had to send a tugboat out to pick us up. But plenty of
the people in the audience had waited, and we started the concert—two
and a half hours late. After the concert, we couldn't find hotel rooms for
everyone in the troupe, and some people, including my manager, Milt
Shaw, had to walk the streets all night. Gothenburg became our home
base for the month we played in Sweden, and the same problem with
hotel rooms arose every time we'd go there. We played in Stock-
holm, Örebro, Borlange, Västerås, Gävle, Storvik, Norrköping, Malmö,
Travel, and Prague in Sweden without any problems, but every time
we'd go back to Gothenburg we'd have trouble finding accommodations. I slept in the hallway of the Kung Karl Hotel in Gothenburg a
couple of nights, but for another reason.

We played in Sweden and Denmark from January 26 to February 9,
and all over that small country the Swedes really dug the music. Denmark was the greatest. We played to nine thousand people in one afternoon and evening. We did three concerts all the same day. It wasn't
just the young crowd we'd get in the States, but people from six to
sixty! We even saw old people on crutches applauding and hollering.
And the audience wouldn't stop until I put up my hand to announce
the next tune. And then they'd be so quiet you could hear a pin drop.
Musically, everything was beautiful.

KENNY CLARKE:

"One time in Sweden, I can't think of the name of the city, but
the band was swinging so hard that Dizzy jumped up on the
piano . . . !"

JOE GAYLES:

"They were more receptive in Europe than they were in America,
much more receptive, much more. It was just incredible. At that time

I would say that the music appealed much more to the white audiences than it did to the black. Now, you ask Diz, and I'm pretty sure he'd agree with that. This was the truth. The music was accepted more by whites than by our own at that time."

AL McKIBBON:

"We played Carnegie Hall just before we went to Europe, and Chubby Jackson, Woody Herman's bass player, was sitting right on the front row. He had an old-time wire recorder, you know. And we didn't give a damn if he recorded it because that thing couldn't make much of a sound. And then when we got to Sweden on the tour, the people out there said, 'Hey, listen, Chubby Jackson was just here trying to play this music that you guys are playing!' That's right. They laughed him outta the place. They told him, 'Hey, man, what are you doing? This is black music. You can't play this.' It wasn't for real, you know, and people could dig it."*

ELMON WRIGHT:

"We were treated beautifully, and it was one heck of an experience for me. The Europeans loved us. One experience made me mad, but after I dug it, I kinda understood. When we went to Europe, we started out in Sweden, and we started from the northern part of Sweden. I forget the little town, but these people, in advance, knew we were coming, you know, and they would meet us at the train station, looked like the whole town would be there. And do you know, man, they would follow us. Like we'd go to the hotel and check in, right. Do you know they'd stay outside the hotel and wait for one of us to come out, and they'd follow us all about—all over town. And it got to be a bug there for a while. But like I say, afterwards, I understood. Actually, they'd never seen black people before, but they love us, you know. Curiosity. And they'd wanna invite you to their house; they wanted you to stay. 'You spend the night with us?' Beautiful people; we had a lovely time. Especially during that time, 1948, yes, it was beautiful."

With the cold nights and warm hospitality, the reason I sometimes slept in hallways was the promoter of the tour, a crook named Harold Lundquist. Lundquist had agreed to deposit half of our money, a

* Some critics later started calling this type of reaction (from European audiences to white guys not really schooled in playing our music, but who attempted it anyway) "crow-jim," which meant the opposite of "jim-crow."

guarantee, in the bank in the United States before we left, but he hadn't done this. Since Billy Shaw handled the bookings, I didn't find out about it until we'd arrived in Europe. After we'd gotten there and were playing to packed houses, he still kept stalling with our money. Lundquist, and what he was doing with our money, became a real problem. Kenny Clarke was in the band; he was an Ahmedea Muslim, and I had a young Jewish manager, Milt Shaw. They almost came to blows. I had to step between them. I told Kenny, "No, if you hit Milt, you've got to come through me to get to Milt," because they were going to fight. There was a real big mix-up about the money, and Kenny assumed that Milt had something to do with it, but Milt didn't have anything at all to do with it. It was the Swede, Lundquist, who was absconding with the money, and Milt was in as bad a fix as we were. In a way, we'd gotten stranded, and Milt had to telephone his father, Billy Shaw, in New York to come and straighten things out. To keep Lundquist from disappearing with the money, after every concert, I slept down by his door at night. Lundquist would have to awaken me to get out of the door, until Billy Shaw could get there and extricate us from this dilemma. I didn't have to sleep there too long. Honey [Billy] Shaw came on in and got arrested in Sweden for trying to kick Lundquist in the balls. Later on Lundquist was arrested and we got some of our money.

Next, under the sponsorship of the Hot Club of Brussels, with which Lundquist was also associated, we went to Belgium. We didn't take any chances. Before we played, Milt Shaw demanded a week's salary for the band, and everyone got paid. A problem arose about who would promote the rest of the tour, and we received some quick and very welcome assistance from Charles Delaunay and the Hot Club of Paris. They eagerly accepted the opportunity to host our concerts and fortuitously became the first to turn France and the city of lights, Paris, on to bebop.

CHARLES DELAUNAY (French jazz critic):

"The first records we received in France after the liberation were those Dizzy made with Charlie Parker for Guild. I happened to receive a copy and that was a real revolution in Paris, because when I got those records, the Hot Club was a place where all the musicians and jazz fans met to hear jazz records daily and spend a few hours during the day. And when these records arrived they were the talk of the city, the very same day. So the news spread in twenty-four hours over all the music circles in Paris. And the musicians when they finished eating were all excited because they discovered something good and fantastic, and they would queue up even to listen in the small building we had on rue Chaptal. When you listen to these records nowadays they seem practically classical, and at that time it seemed completely foolish, weird, and real exciting. People were saying that 'Oh, Dizzy, he must have a special trumpet, he must have a special mouthpiece.' Everyone was wondering how the chords were built. They were discussing, at length all day long and coming to listen to these new records. Each time they were getting more excited. It was a real big first.

"The critics were pretty divided. There were those who had been living with musicians who knew—who reacted almost like musicians because the critic, after all, is just someone who comes after. He doesn't create anything. He just listens, and if he's in a proper mood to listen well, to feel what happens, he might say something interesting which the musician might not know how to say. But he knows how to make it, which is more important. Some critics who were aggressive might have reacted saying, 'Well, that's not music, it's unpleasant, and so on.' So the real world of jazz split immediately in two parts.

"It was funny. Because in those days I was still in partnership with Panassié. The trouble with Panassié: he was living down South, way down South, and he was not living with musicians. I was living with musicians, so everything new—even if I didn't notice it after a musician would play it once, after three times, I realized what was happening. I would follow. So I was more inclined to follow the musician's opinion, which was the right one. And what happened, immediately after I got those records, I wrote a letter to Panassié. I said, 'You know, I received two or three extraordinary records. I wish you could hear them.'

"The next day I received the answer, 'You have to send me those records right away. If there is someone in France who has to have those records, it's me.'

"So I said, 'Man, you should come here and find out what is happening. Because if I get rid of these records, the place would be burned in half an hour with all the musicians who are coming anytime of the day and the night to listen to these records. But I ordered three copies of each from America and as soon as I get them, I'll send one to you.'

"And in the meantime, I wrote an article for a Swiss magazine, and asked André Hodeir to write an article for my magazine. So Panassié missed the first boat. I imagine if Panassié had been in Paris with the musicians being around, with the proper mood, he would have liked bebop like I did. Unfortunately, for him . . .

"So from that time everything was in two pieces in France. There were two solid groups, each against the other one. All criticism was one way or another, but there was no possibility of appreciating both. Of course, I always liked Dixieland, New Orleans music, big band music, but those who were 100 per cent for bop and those who were 100 per cent for Dixieland were even fighting in the streets, fighting at the concerts, coming just to shout at each other's concerts. It was just insane.

"Then I was called from Brussels by the Hot Club of Brussels and told one day that there was a colored band in Antwerp stranded, coming from Scandinavia, because the manager who organized the tour in Scandinavia had stolen the money and left them, leaving the musicians without a damn cent, and the band was stuck. So I asked a guy to go to Brussels that same night and to bring the band back—dead or alive—to Paris and in the meantime we were going to start the publicity campaign with articles in the newspapers and photographs. And in twenty-four hours we launched a terrific campaign, and we held the concert two nights after. I don't know what happened, but it had such an impact. All the musicians came to listen at long last to that terrific trumpet player. Also there were those who came just to see what would happen, and all kinds of people came to fill the concert, so it was a terrific success. Moreover, the concert was supposed to start at nine, but when they came onstage it was twenty to eleven.

"Happily I had engaged a trio to start, a French trio that played King Cole music, the same numbers. They had to play for over an hour, and luckily nothing happened. You know in those days if something would fail, the people would start shouting and you never knew what to expect. But they waited for the band to arrive, and when the band got into the station they had left the tickets for the luggage, so they couldn't get their luggage right away. We had to move fast to see the customs officers, and finally we got all the instruments of the band and rushed them by bus to the concert. When the concert started everybody was completely stoned; so was I. I don't know if it was because they hadn't eaten or they were tired or what. You know sometimes something happens and you never know what or why. The band was playing with complete relaxation and the band was superb. The applauses were not that thick; they were completely in a trance as if they didn't know what was happening to them; it was something that happens to you once in a lifetime. I mean that was the impression that we got.

"A new era was being created musically. That was the impression that we got because in fact before that we knew some of the records. When I came to New York in 1946 I heard the band playing at the Apollo. I was there with Django Reinhardt and I met Dizzy then, but I didn't have the same impression as when they played in Paris at this particular concert in Salle Pleyel. And with the poor recording that was taken from that by French radio—of the three mikes only one was working, the line to the audience—they could hardly hear the band well enough. But at least we had the feeling that something was happening. (Swing M3301.) Even I, being almost familiar with the music already, maybe because I was excited and tired, could feel the coolness of the music. There was a feeling that this music had never been seen before, nowhere and by no one. I am telling you there are a lot of French people who still dream about that day. They remember whether they like it or not. Many didn't like it, but they realized what they were witnessing."

Wheew! *Sacre bleu!* They never heard nothing like that before. Not since either. We played all night without any music. We didn't have any music; the music didn't get there; we memorized the whole thing. There was just that much enthusiasm in the band. They weren't trying to memorize the parts either; they just knew it.

Paris was a little different from Scandinavia. The audiences were composed of a younger, wilder crowd, but they were ready for us. And of course I hardly knew the place, it had changed so much since I'd been there with Teddy Hill almost eleven years before. But the music had changed too, and the French loved it. We played three sold out concerts at Salle Pleyel and at the Champs Elysées Club and les Ambassadeurs. We also played one gig at the Apollo in Paris. That was funny; they had an Apollo Theater, just like in Harlem. We had Paris jumping too, just like Harlem. Then we went to Lyon and Marseilles and played a concert with Mezz Mezzrow and the Peters Sisters. That's when they printed the picture of me in the newspaper with the knife carving up Mezz Mezzrow, the dean of the "moldy figs" in France. Mezz originated the saying about us, "Them boys'll never play two notes where a hundred will do." But, as usual, he had some dynamite pot, and we had a ball playing together.

No real conflict existed between New Orleans and our music because the one came from the other, two generations removed. But while we were in Paris, the French pretended there was a big separation between modern and traditional jazz. They had a big fight in the club there one night. We were blowing in les Ambassadeurs, and two Frenchmen were sitting at the same table. All of a sudden, Lord-a mercy, they begin pounding each other. Real murder! "You call that music?" one of them said, and "Bam! Bam! Bam!" They let each other have it. Ha! Ha!

HOWARD JOHNSON:

"I remember in Paris there was a fight. . . . There were two groups, one was progressive, and one was for old-time jazz; the writers were Hugues Panassié and Charles Delaunay. We were in the Ambassadeurs cabaret, and the opening night they had a big battle up in the balcony between the two different forces; one's for pure old jazz and the other was for progressive, and they had a fight. I think we stayed there about a week. But it was interesting. It shows how enthused these people were with the music and how excited they were with their points of view."

JOHN LEWIS:

"To me it was just one really tremendous tour, probably one of the most tremendous tours. Oh, the reception was just unbelievable, finally. I'd been with Dizzy for two years, and that finalized it. So that's where his element was, there playing concerts, not playing at dances or anything like that, which he was trying to do before. Yeah, concerts for fourteen thousand people at a whack, which was enormous then. Paris was tremendous. Paris is one of the hardest cities to have a success in. If you can have a success there, you can have it anywhere. And he had an overwhelming, unbelievable success. The whole audience was awestruck by the first piece that we played in Salle Pleyel."

AL McKIBBON:

"On that 1948 tour the band was about two feet off of the ground all of the time. In fact, it was sensational. You know, I spoke to John Lewis about it in later years because he acted very strange to me on that tour. He told me he was mad because Dizzy didn't take it more seriously. He thought Dizzy was taking it lightly, and he thought that we should've been more formal because we had something that couldn't be replaced and it was entirely unique. But I didn't know he felt that way at the time. I know I thought that the goddamn music was killing me—but you know how it is when something is happening, you don't realize how really great it is. But I think had Dizzy been white—Here it is a guy comes along with a new style of playing, a new style band, a new style of dressing, a new way of talking. Now, man, suppose Stan Kenton had all those things? Dizzy would have been a rich man.

"I used to stand down sometimes near the front of the bandstand, you know. So I'd say to myself, 'Oh, this muthafucka, I'm gonna punch him right off the stand tonight,' you know, and bear down on him. The harder you play, the more he plays. After he plays a chorus, he takes a step back, you know. I used to have to push him off the bridge of the bass; his ass be sitting right on the bridge. Piping too!"

ELMON WRIGHT:

"I've got an album here right now that we didn't know the guy was making. We played in Paris, France. We played at the Apollo. They pronounce it *AP*-ollo, but it's spelled like the Apollo here. We used to do two shows a day, I believe. Anyway, there was some guy over there who was taping this, and we didn't know it. I showed it to Diz, and he didn't know it neither. The guy had waxed it up."

Commercially our tour turned out to be quite a success. This was not too long after the war, and people were paying sometimes three and four dollars apiece to see us. The promoters were grossing $15,000 on a good day. We had offers to play in Spain, Italy, and Switzerland, and they wanted us to make records over there. The French subsidiary of RCA Victor sent us a letter reminding us, as if we didn't know, that if we were allowed to record at all, it would have to be for them.

All of us picked up a little Swedish and some French, and we heard that Don Byas was speaking fluent French. Always very clever, Don was still in Spain while we stayed in France, so we didn't see him. I ran into Peanuts Holland in Scandinavia, and he liked it there so much I didn't think he'd ever come back to the States. The most impressive aspect of the tour was the way our music had taken hold among European musicians. All the young European musicians copied my records with Charlie Parker note for note. They'd paid five and ten dollars a copy for those records, and the reception we enjoyed in Europe exceeded in warmth and enthusiasm anything we'd ever experienced in the United States. Apparently the world welcomed modern music more heartily than did the people at home, at least some parts of the world.

Originally, we'd been scheduled to play in England, but the British musician's union objected to "foreigners" playing in their country, which seemed strange for a country that first got rich on "free trade." Apparently the British had become afraid of too many American musicians coming to England and taking work away from the local musicians. They had a ban on "foreign" musicians just like in New York. After they'd heard about what happened in Paris, they changed their minds and wanted us to come. The British musicians drew up a petition pleading with their union officials to waive the restriction against us so they could hear the new style of music performed in person. They particularly wanted to hear me play at least a few concerts, as one of the original creators. This was very flattering coming from the musicians themselves and could have opened the door to musical exchange among a lot of our colleagues in England and America. The union's leadership went along and withdrew its veto of our tour, but Britain's Ministry of Labour overruled them, and a situation developed where government was getting in the way of the people's progress. Who knows, considering that rock music later became one of Britain's biggest exports, the Beatles might've happened there ten years earlier. Our polyrhythmic brand of jazz with its backbeat accents was also the beginning of the trend toward rock.

The French acted more wisely and they stole Kenny Clarke from me. A Frenchman offered to set Kenny up as a teacher because the weakest thing in the bands over there was the drumming and the rhythm sections. The European musicians had started learning our music from records, and with Kenny over there in France they'd quickly learn much more. I felt sure Kenny would do very well when we left for the States and he stayed behind. The band sailed aboard a French ship, the *DeGrasse*, for the trip back to New York. Chano Pozo was suffering from a terrible backache. He, Milt Shaw, and I caught a plane and flew back home.

Groovin' High

Instead of a hero's welcome, the U.S. press, especially *Time* magazine, still railed against my music, saying it was "Screechingly loud . . . dissonant . . . and something Duke Ellington had thought better of a long time ago." Like they wanted to bring me down or just didn't want the music to change or didn't want me to change it. Maybe they didn't want *us* to change it. Because next came a bunch of silly arguments about who invented bebop. Monk, Yardbird, or me. Which one? As though all of us and others hadn't played a role. Maybe they wanted us to start fighting among ourselves.

The crowning insult came when I'd reorganized the band and played another Carnegie Hall concert in May 1948. People started asking whether my music hadn't been touched, or influenced, by the "progressive" jazz of Stan Kenton.

They tried to make Stan Kenton a "white hope," called modern jazz and my music "progressive," then tried to tell me I played progressive music. I said, "You're full of shit!" "Stan Kenton? There ain't nothing about my music that's cold, cold like his." "What?" I said, "there's not one note that I play that was influenced by anything that Stan Kenton has ever done. Not one note. Stan Kenton was the copyist."

Stan Kenton went out and got a conga drummer after he saw me with one. He hired Carlos Vidal, lured him away from Machito, and put him along with another Latin drummer, Jack Costanzo, in his

band. But Stan didn't know what to do with it. He just left it there
and they made up their own minds what to play. All this happened
after he came up to the Savoy and heard us while Chano Pozo was in
the band. Now, I don't just take what they do and leave it there. I
don't pass myself off as an expert on Latin music, but the guys who
play it respect me for knowing how to take what they do, put it in
with my music, and make it right. I never take nothing from nobody
without delivering something in return. I think when people figured
we might make a lot of money, that started the controversy about who
would get credit for creating modern jazz. My viewpoint was always
that the credit should go to the ones who developed and played it
best.

Music is a big thing. None of us can ever know it all or get to the
end. Nothing else ever stands still; why should music? I knew our music
would change and that there would be followers. Our music was
going someplace where a lot of musicians wanted to go, so a lot of
musicians followed. Check the records out—Woody Herman, Boyd
Raeburn. Once they thought I'd made an arrangement for Woody
because it sounded like one of my trumpet solos, but Ralph Burns or
somebody wrote it. Arrangers are always inspired by the chief soloists;
that's where they get their ideas about how the notes are supposed to
go and how the music should sound. Bandleaders, from Duke, Benny
Goodman on down, had to turn to modern jazz, whether they liked it
or not, just to sound up to date. After all, a new day was dawning.
All of the younger musicians wanted to play modern. What were they
going to do, hide from the sun?

AL McKIBBON:

"When Dizzy's band used to play the Savoy, Stan Kenton would come
in and bring his whole band. We didn't pay any attention, but we knew
he was there, you know. But then, later on, here he comes with Laurindo
Almeida, guitar, and Carlos Vidal, conga drums, and they started
doing the 'Peanut Vendor' and all that crap, trying to play 'Latin.' I
never heard him do 'Manteca.' Nooo, man!"

WALTER GILBERT FULLER:

"Oh, they tried to rip. Stan Kenton told Dizzy to his face in the
Savoy Ballroom, 'We can play your music better than you can.' That
was like 1947, 48, somewhere around there. We played a little battle
against Stan Kenton in the Savoy Ballroom. Stan got juiced up there

Representative Adam Clayton Powell engineered a major breakthrough;
a role for jazz in U.S. foreign relations. EBONY MAGAZINE.

Dizzy Gillespie Orchestra, 1956, in TV studio, Sao Paulo, Brazil.

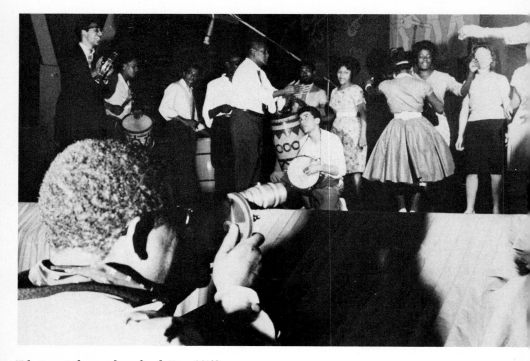

Filming at the samba school, Rio, 1956.

Blowin' with the brothers from the samba school in Rio de Janeiro, Brazil.

The band of 1956, which toured for the U. S. Department of State, performing for television in Sao Paulo, Brazil, (l to r) Walter Davis, Jr., piano; Nelson Boyd, bass; Charlie Persip, drums; Billy Mitchell, tenor; Phil Woods, alto; Jimmy Powell, alto; Benny Golson, tenor; Marty Flax, baritone. The two trumpets shown are Quincy Jones and E. V. Perry. The trombones were outta sight.

JATP on tour, 1956. UNITED PRESS INTERNATIONAL.

The Dizzy Gillespie Orchestra on tour for the U. S. Department of State in Dacca, Pakistan, 1956.

Listening to staff musicians at Radio Pakistan, Karachi, with Quincy Jones and Rod Levitt

With the Rhythm Swingette of Karachi, Pakistan.

At the park in Karachi, Pakistan, with Melba Liston and Dottie Salters, vocalist. We played for snakes!

At a party given for Danny Kaye at USIA, Ankara, Turkey, 1956.

Buying cymbals with Charlie Persip at the original Zildjan factory in Turkey.

Greeting the Sheikh of Kuwait at a party for underprivileged children in Beirut, Lebanon, with Ambassador and Mrs. Donald Heath of the U.K.

Swingin' through the Middle East, Syria, 1956; (l to r) beside me, Billy Mitchell, tenor; Joe Gordon, trumpet; Frank Rehak, trombone; Quincy Jones, trumpet; Charles Persip, drums; Carl Warwick, trumpet; and our driver, kneeling.

And riding a freight camel . . . almost came apart at the seams.

and staggered up to Dizzy and told him, 'I can play your music better than you can.'*

"What could you say? The cat was juiced. Dizzy just looked at him and said, 'Yeah . . .' and let it go. What are you gonna do, start arguing with him? He was juiced. But he was saying while he was juiced what he really meant.

"Stan really couldn't write our kind of thing.

"At that battle of the bands, both bands played 'Things Are Here.' And Stan had about thirty pieces up there, or some such shit. And we fucked them up. We wrote polyrhythms, two times going on simultaneously, and they couldn't play it. It was 3/4 and 2/2, I think, going on at the same time. That's like five different places to hit. And they had to fit that in those two measures, and they couldn't do it."

DADDY-O DAYLIE:

"I started in radio in 1948, when 78 rpm records were being sold. They had racial classifications to identify the artists at that time. To identify a black artist, they would say 'sepia' or 'race' records. And so when I started in radio, I had practically every record Diz had recorded. Anything I could find Diz on, I would buy. And I just knew that what this music needed was exposure. I believed in it. My slogan was I like what I played and played only what I liked.

"Whenever the giants came to town, Diz and Bird, playing in the little clubs that were smoke filled, piano's out of tune, it was heartbreaking to see because to me these were always superstars. And so I just knew that it needed exposure. Now, I could've made more money going another route, but I believed in this music, believed in the creators of this music, and it had something to say.

"I also discovered that because it was black music and because the stars were black and because, just through the many years of being in the business, the blacks' superstars couldn't be as easily exploited as the, for want of a better name, let's call them the 'ukey dukes,' we weren't gonna get the exposure.

"Now, the music never really became number one because the fast-buck boys could not exploit a Diz as rapidly as they could a 'ukey duke.' They could not exploit a Bird or a Duke, just because of the years that they'd been in the business. So they went and got the 'ukey duke' who knew nothing about royalties of any kind. He wanted just

* And can't even stomp off! He got on his knees to me one time though. We're playing at the Los Angeles Coliseum. One of those times he had been drinking, one of the bows he got, he bowed to me, and he got down on his knees, on the stage, and walked off. That was pretty funny.—DG

to be on the stage under the lights. He would write the tunes, they'd put it in their publishing company, and he recorded in their recording company, and they would exploit these guys to the nth degree. So they would not expose the jazz music.

"I knew immediately that I would have to take my chances, and I was fortunate enough to get Anheuser Busch as one of my clients. They said, 'O.K., we bought you,' and I had complete control. The thing that really helped was that the guys were so beautiful. Diz has the biggest heart of any guy that I've known. He would come out and go to the TB sanitariums and do a show for me, and to the prisons. We were doing that years ago, without any fanfare.

"Diz seems as though he never had that same jealousy that so many professional musicians have, that I think is based on incompetence. When a guy's extremely jealous of some other guy, you know they can't play. When they look and see another trumpet player in the audience, they think you're trying to borrow some of their solos or something. Diz was never that way. He'd get off at the Blue Note at 4:00 A.M., and there'd be two or three guys there, trumpet players. They would come and they would talk to him. Diz would get his horn out and he would sit down on the stage, at Frank Holzfeind's old Blue Note, and might just teach them for an hour and a half. Then we'd go to breakfast, and he would continue to discuss it, the technique of it. So that's Diz the man, a good, warm human being.

"I have yet to hear Diz give a poor performance, whether it was a concert at Soldier Field where we had twenty or thirty thousand people, and the PA system's cutting in and out. . . . Diz, the performer, was such a professional and such a perfectionist that he would always rise to the occasion. I don't care if the piano was out of tune. One night, he appeared at a club called the Crown Cellars that had a horrible piano. At the end of the first set, house packed, Diz had everybody giving a standing ovation which black folks don't do unless somebody prompts them. After the standing ovation, I stayed all night. And the second set, just the waitresses, myself, and about eight musicians. Diz got up there and blew, he exceeded himself in the first show, when it was packed. A lot of performers will let down if there's no one in the house, not Diz. And then a lot of performers will put out if they know it's a competitive thing, if they look out in the audience and see two or three trumpet players or some musicians or critics that they wanna impress. Diz was always, always the superperformer.

"Your 'top forties' or your 'top tens' came about because of payola. The disc jockey found that he could get a hundred dollars a week from ten record companies to play their tunes. There ain't no other way they could play it every day and have it come out to the top ten, the top fifteen, and the top twenty. Wasn't nobody gonna play Diz and Bird and Duke and Nat Cole. But the fast-buck boys were making that quick buck.

"The white fast-buck promoter wasn't about to expose this black music. If tomorrow, they took all-a the 'ukey duke' stations and said, 'We're going to play jazz, no more "ukey duke," we're gonna play jazz,' what do you think would happen?

"When you went to a concert, every one of the whites was screaming. But the fast-buck boys knew that Diz was too sophisticated. Diz had his own publishing company and was sophisticated enough to know that there were composer's royalties and then there were recording royalties, and so they couldn't just give Diz a car, a Cadillac that they leased out of his royalties. If you were a fast-buck promoter which way would you go? Merit had nothing to do with it; it was exploitation.

"Let me show you the kind of relationship Diz and I have. Diz knew I was a pipe smoker. When Diz would go somewhere abroad and see a nice pipe, he'd say, 'I bet old Dad would like this.' I have pipes here that Diz, John Lewis . . . and I have one that Louis Armstrong gave me. That's the kind of relationship that we had.

"And isn't it ironic that the top critics, who criticize jazz music, can't play it?

"I had a jazz club called the 'Gopher's Club,' people who go for jazz. And I had jazz clubs organized at about thirty-two different colleges within a radius of about three hundred miles. And I would always book talent and go and do the concerts. And one day, *Time* magazine discovered Dave Brubeck. And this is what I got from the whites who had just discovered jazz in *Time* magazine, 'Why do you send us Charlie Parker when there's Paul Desmond? Why do you play Diz, when there's Chet Baker?'"

RICHARD CARPENTER (road manager):

"Well, I never heard Diz give a bad performance because as he can tell you—it may sound funny—I didn't tolerate bad performances. And the most memorable thing about the group is that we had a system under which anybody who was late for a bus leaving—we were traveling by bus at that time—or late for a gig would get fined. We had a fund in which we would put this money to buy athletic equipment and to give parties and so on. We had it set up that everybody got fines who was late, including Dizzy Gillespie, everybody. I used to fine them $25. They got warned twice, and on the third occasion I fined them $25, and repeated offenders got fined $50. On one occasion I fined Chano Pozo $50. He said, 'Me star, me star! Me see

Dizzy.' So he saw Dizzy, and Dizzy looked at him like he was crazy. "He said, 'If Carpenter fines you, you got fined, man, that's it.'

"The audiences, or we'll say the jazz afficionados who came to hear Dizzy Gillespie didn't care too much whether it was a big band or a small group because they came to hear Diz. You know, as long as Diz appeared and he played we got an audience reaction. Many of our tours were made through the South—Georgia, Alabama, Mississippi, and places of that sort. And we did business, attracted crowds; people seemed to like it."

Touring the country, I discovered that most of the putdowns of our music came from a small elite, not the masses of people because everywhere we went large crowds flocked to hear us, even down South. So I assumed the musical ear of the country as a whole had improved. The disc jockeys like Daddy-O Daylie in Chicago helped us, and we even hired a road manager, Richard Carpenter, who took a reading of audience reaction wherever we played. For two years, from 1948 through 1949, America seemed definitely thrilled by our music; its eyes were agog and its ears wide open.

Our greatest success occurred in California. We played eight weeks out there, and the fans gave us a tremendous welcome. The tour opened with a one-week stand at the Cricket Club in Los Angeles which broke the club's attendance records. We performed in concert before three thousand people in Long Beach and then jammed for sell-out crowds in Pasadena and San Bernardino. When we got to Billy Berg's in Hollywood, it was lake "sardinia." The beboppers packed the place, and many of our old fans from the film community—Ava Gardner, Lena Horne, Howard Duff, and Mel Torme—showed up to see us and attracted more people who came to see them.

The bebopper cult had reached its zenith. I looked around, and everybody was trying to look like me. Now, why in hell did they want to do that? They even pretended to laugh like me (the newspapers said) and it was not a racial phenomenon. These were black and white people alike, by the tens of thousands, willing to stand up and testify for bebop. At the concerts, they would let the ones who wore berets, goatees, and horn-rimmed glasses sit up on the stage with the band. A lot of them were teen-aged girls who had their goatees painted on with grease paint. Visions of black panthers, they even had uniforms. Ava Gardner, I recall, didn't put on grease paint. She was such a good actress, she could make a goatee for pictures just by using her fingers. She came out two or three times a week to hear us, and I gave her one of my hats, a sailor's beret from the S.S. *Richlieu,* for being such an ardent fan and so generous with her time. Ava Gardner's from North Carolina and believed in supporting fellow Southerners, but she hated segregation and wouldn't even go home for a visit. Howard Duff was known for playing the role of Sam Spade, the famous radio private detective.

F. W. Woolworth Company in downtown Los Angeles ordered five hundred copies of "Manteca" which was already a big hit and invited me down to autograph pictures, to stimulate sales of our records and bring people into their store. One of the boppers had drawn a sketch of my face pushing through the map of the United States and they gave away these pictures with each purchase of our record. Even little children like Ellen Jenkins who was only four years old at the time came out in beret and sunglasses with her mother.

Admittedly, being the center of attraction and feeling like a young, hip black Santa Claus, I joined in all of this with great relish. Oh, I was acting crazy and went out and bought myself a pair of ostrich-leather shoes. Whenever someone would ask me about them, I'd take them off and show them.

We all went out to put on a great show. Chano Pozo used to do his water trick. He'd put a glass of water on his head, start drumming and drop his handkerchief, and, during a quick break in the drumming, kneel down on the floor, pick up the handkerchief and start drumming again, without spilling a drop of water. The fans would go wild! It was predictable in this heady atmosphere that I would become a "gopher" when *Life* magazine conned Benny Carter and me into posing for some pictures during an interview for a feature story on bebop. They made us perform a bebop greeting for them.

"Hi-ya, man!"

"Bells, man, where you been?" giving the sign of the flatted fifth, a raised open hand.

"Eel-ya-da!" We gave a three-fingered sign that we were playing triplets, ending with an elaborate handshake. That was supposed to be the bebopper's greeting, but there was no such thing in real life. It was just a bunch of horseplay that we went through so they could pretend we were something weird. We were so excited and having so much fun, we forgot to emphasize in the publicity the most important thing, the music, and we were helping to make bebop seem like just another fad, which it wasn't. That photo session in Hollywood, the part where they had me pretending to be Muslim, was something I lived to regret. That was a fiasco. The validity of the music wasn't even taken into consideration, nor the validity of the Islamic faith. They had me bowing down and all that kinda stuff. They said, "Would you like to do this?"

I said, "Yes." I went for it, like a fool. That's one of the things I'm sorry for. Duke Ellington later told me, "Birks, you should've never let them put a label, like bebop, on your music." I couldn't understand why he said that until much, much later. I was too busy partying and basking in my good fortune.

JAMES MOODY:

"We used to play places, and people used to look at us. But then I was kinda naïve myself, I didn't know what the heck was happening, you know. But now I can look back and see. I remember we played at the Pasadena Civic Auditorium, I think, and some people could get in if they wore the beret like Dizzy wore and the dark bebop glasses. And they would be sitting up on the stage with the band, stuff like that. That was outta sight to see the people and the way they were reacting to it. Lena Horne, Ava Gardner, and Howard Duff were out there. Ava Gardner was a starlet then, and we were playing the Cricket Club in Los Angeles, and Ava Gardner loved the music, Lena Horne loved it, and they'd be there every night to hear the band."

JESSE "RIP" TARRANT (trombone):

"In 1948 Diz came back from Europe, and there was an opening in the trombone section, and that's how I got the job. Oh, it was fantastic. Something I never dreamed of, it was so way out. Everything was moving so fast, playing the parts, and I had to adjust to that. Musically speaking, you had to know your horn, learn your horn, and keep up with your horn.

"Diz was a good leader, and he's a beautiful person, and I learned how to make good friends and contacts with different people. With his personality, everybody just took to him and really liked him, you know. And it stuck with me all the way, even though I'm not in music anymore. That personality is still there; it rubbed off on all of us. You got to practice a thing to keep up with it, to be sharp, to stay with it.

"I would say the best performance to my knowledge was in Chicago. We did a dance and a concert, and Diz and Bird were in front of the band. Man, that was rough, Bird and Diz. Then I remember we came right back with Diz and Miles playing with our band. But I think the one with Bird was the best I ever heard. They turned everybody on. Bird did our book with us. And then he went through things on his own with Diz, things they used to do together. But when they did them with our band . . . Boy, that band sounded beautiful that night! Teddy Stewart was the drummer. Oh, man, that was something.

I think that was Teddy's best night. Bird and Diz just looked like they just felt like doing it to each other that night, but in the sense that it wasn't no head-cutting thing; they were just showing that they were two great giants out there doing their thing. It just fractured me because I'd never been that close to Bird. Whenever it was a solo part, Bird took a sax solo, and then Diz would play his part where he'd come in with the trumpet. And there was no arrangements for Bird, he just played, maybe, where Moody would be playing, or Ernie Henry, a solo part. He just took all that, man, like it was nothing.

"Once we went to California, and we got stuck in a snowstorm, and our music got lost. I think that was in 1949, the second time we went to California; there was a terrible snowstorm, and we got stuck between Chicago and Nebraska somewhere. I think Woody Herman made a gig for us, and then we made a gig for him. And by doing that, our music and equipment got separated from us. When we got to California we didn't have any music. So that night we had to do that concert by ear. We did a concert in Frisco without any music; we had to play that book by memory. So Diz was standing there kidding us, 'Well, this is gonna separate the men from the boys.' He was so happy about it, and everybody else was all sweating and nervous. He seemed to relax us. That night was the best the band had ever sounded. He said, 'I think I'll keep the music away from you!' Oh, man, that was really something. That was swinging. He relaxed us for it. It was funny to him. I was gonna crack up, cause I knew I was gonna catch hell trying to remember the music, but it all fit right in.

"I learned how to get a little faster on my horn and get steady tone quailty and playing bebop helped my reading. Like I was a section man, I wasn't no soloist, but it helped me to play together with other fellows. You had to be together, otherwise Diz and Walter Fuller would chew you out. They were very stern, you know. I would say it was the greatest experience I've ever had in my life. I had the most fun I've had in my life. Everything was beautiful."

Coming in off the road, we'd return to New York in a blaze of glory. A lot of clubs opened between 1946–50 that featured bebop. You got clubs like the Royal Roost between Forty-seventh and Forty-eighth streets on Broadway, down in the cellar. At the Royal Roost I played . . . Fats Navarro . . . Allen Eager. It was all just one club, really. When the Royal Roost closed, the people who owned the Royal Roost bought Bop City. The Royal Roost was small and didn't hold as many people as Bop City, which was a great big place. Then from Bop City, they bought Birdland, the same people—Morris Levy, Oscar Goodstein, and the partners. Then the partners split up. Morris Levy went with Oscar Goodstein into Birdland, and Monte Kay opened up a place called the Downbeat on Fifty-fourth Street which I think Morris Levy also had something to do with because his brother and Monte Kay were the bosses there. The clubs made money, and they all became millionaires.

We musicians weren't making any large sums of money, but Morris Levy was very nice to me when I was playing in Birdland, years later, when we bought our apartment house over in Corona. Morris Levy wouldn't hire me at Birdland for about two years (during the fifties) and so I started working at Snookie's. I was living in an apartment out in Flushing, and this building was for sale in Corona. Foots Thomas, my manager at the time, negotiated a deal. Morris Levy would give me the down payment on the apartment house, and every time I worked at Birdland, so much money would be deducted outta my salary to repay the loan, without any interest. I went by Morris Levy's office one day, and he gave me a shoebox full of money. No checks, cash money. That was a friendly deal. It wasn't like a business deal because I would've had to sign papers. If I'd died, that would've been the end of his interest. So Morris Levy was a nice man; Morris Levy was very kind. If we only could have collected like that from others whose commercial success was due largely to our music, because by the end of 1948, bebop had become quite a big pop-fad phenomenon, worldwide.†

† "Bebop," said *Time* magazine, 1/3/49, "a frantic disorganized musical cult whose high priest was quid-cheeked Dizzy Gillespie, replaced Swing; the Shmoo took the place of 1947's 'Sparkle Plenty.' "

Godfather

Chano Pozo was killed in 1948. They put out a lot of stories, but I don't know exactly what happened because I wasn't there. We'd gone on tour with Ella Fitzgerald down South, and that's actually when I got my diploma from Laurinburg. We went through there, so I just took it. I said, "O.K., I'm gonna play for you all." We played at an exercise in the morning, and they held a special ceremony. Mr. McDuffy, who was still principal at the time, presented me with my diploma and my letter for football. I was very proud of that—after thirteen years, finally taking the step up from being a South Carolina high-school dropout. Mr. McDuffy said he always knew I was gonna amount to something.

Chano Pozo went back to New York because somebody stole his drums, and he got killed when he went back; we were still down there. It's said that it had to do with narcotics, that some guy had sold him some bad shit, and he went back and said, "Gimme my money," and slapped the guy.

"You better apologize," the guy said. "If you don't apologize, I'm gonna kill you."

"Apologize!" Chano said, and he cuffed the guy again. The guy went home and got his pistol and came back and shot him. Chano was still in the bar. It happened in the Rio Bar on 111th Street and Fifth Avenue in New York. That's what I heard in 1948.

There's a story that someone told me from Cuba. They have a group, a religious cult in Cuba that Chano belonged to. They had a celebration; it's like a Bar Mitzvah. At certain times, everybody'd chip in some money and nobody's supposed to touch that money. The money was supposed to be for defraying the expenses of your becoming a man, like buying food for the celebration. And they say that when Chano Pozo came to this country, he had charge of this money, and he took the people's money and brought it up here. And he died exactly one year from that time. So I said, "Wait a minute. You know, I'm from a part of the country where we've got roots. Don't be telling me no stories like that, 'cause I'm subject to believe it." Wheew!! Exactly one year to the day. When they told me that one, boy, my eyebrows went up.

Because of my relationship with Chano Pozo, I've enjoyed, ever since, a special affinity with Latin musicians. Guys would come to New York and look for me. Xavier Cugat had the most prominent of the Latin bands, but he didn't play jazz, and he didn't have any black Spanish guys in his band. You could be a nigger, but you had to be a mulatto, a mariny nigger, to play with him, and all your associations had to be away from blackness. But you had all these great Latin musicians who were black guys, like Miguelito Valdez.

It's funny how I sorta became known as a godfather of Latin musicians. Candido Camero came to New York and was looking for me. One day I was standing out in front of Birdland, and somebody said, "Hey, Diz. . . ."

When he said my name, Candido's ears perked up, and he came over to me and said, "I've been looking for you. I'm from Cuba and I play conga."

"You do?" I said. "Come on, go with me." I took him over to the Downbeat where Billy Taylor was playing with Charlie Smith, the drummer. Charlie Smith played a little conga.

I told Billy, "Let this guy, Candido, play because I play more conga than Charlie." Candido came in and he played, sat in, and he stayed there for three years.

Latin guys who played jazz never ran into any discrimination from me either because of their color. Guys who looked white like Chico O'Farrill have worked with me. Chico took parts of "Manteca" and wrote new numbers from them. The names of some of them were "Jungler" and "Contrast," but they were taken from the melody of "Manteca," the bass line. He wrote six numbers from that one tune.

I have always been interested in harmony and rhythm, especially rhythms from different ethnic backgrounds. Though not an expert at all these things, I am sophisticated enough rhythmically to recognize the basic elements. On the other hand, you find very few Latin guys who get the feeling of jazz. Their articulation is different, not loose like ours, just stiff, even the Brazilians who have terrific rhythm. That's why their music needs jazz. We can cope with their music better than they can cope with ours. I guess I shouldn't say that though, because there are a lotta jazz musicians who don't get the Latin feeling; they can hear it and play it, but they don't get the Latin feeling, musically. I guess the closest thing to my counterpart in Latin music is Mario Bauza. After him, you can forget it in terms of looking for my counterpart in understanding the two musics together. In the trumpets, Victor Paz is pretty good. He explained to me that he knew about my music for a long time down in Panama. His father is a trumpet player and used to say, "Now, you listen to this. You listen to the articulation. You listen to the rhythm of what he's playing. That makes him different from the rest of the trumpet players." I knew exactly what he was talking about because I *phrase* my notes differently from the others, and it's Latin. All these guys liked me, the Latin guys. I don't put myself up as an authority, but I'm the nearest thing to authority on Latin music in this country, including all those guys who play—like Cal Tjader, George Shearing, Herbie Mann—and stay in that groove. I don't *stay* in that groove.

One time out on the coast at the Monterey Jazz Festival, they wanted me to play and had some other guy in charge. Herbie Mann, or somebody, was supposed to be getting the Latin session together. Well, to me it seemed like one of those things where they put the white guy out in front just because he'd been playing Latin. Not only did I resent this, but the Latin guys said, "Wait a minute; what is this? How can he organize something when all he's gonna do in the organization is ask Dizzy what he should do? And then when we play it, they'll think he's the developer of it, that he got it together."

Ask Tito Puente about me, he says, "He's the father. . . ." And he's talking about straight down the middle; he ain't talking about no derivation. He says, "Well, you know, you're the foremost authority on Latin music." I don't like them to be saying that because how can I be the father when he's talking about Latin music?

I always say, "Get outta here." They respect me that much because they know that I did do my homework with Socarras and Chano Pozo. You can do a real good job of copying up to a certain point, but when it gets to the real goodies, that's your ass. I like to know about all these things; that's why I go but so far claiming to be an authority.

Tito Puente tells me, "Ahhh, the Latin master . . ."

I say, "Man, get away from that shit. I'm a country boy from Cheraw, South Carolina. I'm a master blindman playing the guitar." I know that, I know what that is, but I've been so involved with Latin music for such a long time, guys will look at me and sometimes they start speaking Spanish.

They say, "Como está usted?"

"No, wait a minute," I say. "I'm not Spanish." But I've been close to that for so long. To show you how good I am with Latin music, they had a Spanish concert recently in Madison Square Garden with Machito, Tito Puente, Ray Barretto, all the bigwigs. They invited me to perform, and the guys asked me, "Did you have rehearsal yet?"

I said, "Yeah. . . ."

"When? I didn't hear anything about it."

"Well, on the telephone," I said. I had to call up Mario Bauza on the telephone to get him ready. I said, "This is what I'm gonna do." I told him on the telephone what I would do.

Mario said, "Yeah, O.K. . . ." That's all there was to it. He never did say, "Huh . . ." He just kept counting.

My efforts to improve the vocal part of our music included bringing on such male vocalists as Johnny Hartman and, later, Joe Carroll. People seem to be able to identify more easily with songs that have lyrics that they can understand, and this would further increase the popularity of our sound. My ideal of a male vocalist for my band would be a guy who could sing like Johnny Hartman, a balladeer, and Joe Carroll, a bebop-scat singer, combined. I almost tried that for a minute, but the three of us weren't together long enough. The closest thing to it was a tune by Mary Lou Williams, who was always in the vanguard of harmony, called "In the Land of Ooo Blah Dee." I made that record and let Joe Carroll sing it with me. (Victor 20-3538.)

I've introduced many singers: Johnny Hartman, Austin Cromer, Tiny Irvin, Betty Sinclair, Alice Roberts. My favorites, not necessarily in this order, are Billie Holiday, Ella Fitzgerald, Sarah Vaughan, Carmen McRae, and Dinah Washington. That covers everything as far as I'm concerned. I like female singers more than males, but among the guys, I prefer Billy Eckstine, Arthur Prysock, Austin Cromer, and Nat Cole,—Louis Jordan, too, and Pops, Louis Armstrong. Pops's voice was lovely. He played just the way he sang. A lot of people, singers like Carmen and Sarah, think I sing pretty nice. I do one ballad that they ask for all the time. The only thing wrong with my singing is I lack the knack with words, to set words to rhythm, and make them come out correctly.

Ella, I like for her impeccable tonality and her sense of rhythm. She thinks like we do with those licks that she sings. That's from the bebop era. She listens and she does all our licks. She learned that after she got with me, going on the road.

Sarah Vaughan's a musician's singer, Sarah and Carmen McRae, with their complex harmonies. Both of them play the piano and can accompany themselves. They know all the flat fives and modern progressions and can do them vocally.

Billie Holiday was gutsy. There was nothing academic about her singing; it was just strictly from the inside of her.

Dinah sounds very warm, with a crust over the warmth to try to keep everybody out. I made her cry one time when she was with Lionel Hampton. We were down in Birdland, and I was performing. I was talking in the microphone, or something, and she was out in the audience. She was a customer, or we were working there together. I said something and she answered me, and I said something else and she said, "Tell that to Lorraine!"

I got pissed off and said, "Look, bitch, whatever we have between us, that has nothing to do with my wife who's at home minding her own business." And she cried, man. I had a lotta fun with Dinah. You could have words with Dinah because she would call you a bunch of muthafuckas in a minute, and that's the end of it. The next time, she might give you a present. Ella Fitzgerald, Sarah Vaughan, same with all of them.

I liked Dinah for the blues. Dinah reminded me of my early childhood, of the church. When I was on the road, Dinah, at one time, was married to my drummer, Teddy Stewart. And I had Johnny Hartman in the band at the time. We'd get on this bus, man, and sing spirituals, on this bus on these lonely country roads, and you would cry, it was so beautiful, man. "Nobody Knows the Trouble I've Seen," all the spirituals. Dinah knew them all, 'cause she came outta the church; Johnny Hartman, too.

JOHNNY HARTMAN (vocalist):

"Back in 1949, I was working in Atlantic City at the Club Harlem, and Dizzy came there to play a date. He came by the club and heard me sing, and then about a week later I got a telegram from him in California, asking me to join the band, and that's when I joined them. Evidently he was impressed with what he heard, you know, because he asked me to join the band and everything.

"We had different arrangers writing for me because I'm basically a ballad singer, so it didn't affect me at all working with a band that basically played bebop. But just listening and working with 'the Diz,' the kind of musician he was, was helpful to me, influencing my style a little bit—breaking and execution of different musical phrases. So he was sort of an influence. It was very beneficial for me to have been with the band for eighteen months.

"I never had played big concerts or anything before. My first date was at a tremendous concert in Pasadena, and how he helped me to pull through that was really great. He told me how to do it, the whole thing, the difference between working a concert and a nightclub, how to engage your audience. Because I had never done a concert; it was always clubs, lounges, and supper clubs. But to work a vast audience into total silence, man, was a little unnerving for a guy who'd never done it before. Dizzy was telling me just to picture and visualize a nightclub audience out there. You can't see them anyway, so you can make any picture you want, so just visualize a club and play it the same way, and it'll come across.

"His antics were something else; you never knew what he was gonna do next. In one of them, well it could have been tragic but it turned out to be very, kind of humorous. We were working the Million Dollar Theatre in Los Angeles, and one of the Mills Brothers' wives came by and she had the baby with her. And we were next door in one of those juice shops, you know those health food places where they sell fresh juices. And they had one of those old-time fans in the ceiling, like a windmill. And Dizzy took the baby up and threw it up there, and the thing just tipped the baby's head, and the Mills Brother's wife fainted out there in the middle of the floor. Yeah, we saw her laying out there on the floor, man, it was funny. But it could have been a tragic thing. Yeah, it could have been the complete opposite, but the baby wasn't hurt or anything.

"He started singing then with Joe Carroll, and you know, they're doing the shu-bob-a-dee. But his most memorable performance I can recall would be Carnegie Hall when he did the tribute to Chano Pozo. Well, he did a spiritual. I think it was 'Nobody Knows the Trouble I've Seen,' and it was just outta sight the way that he did it, you know. That was right after Chano had gotten killed."

JOE CARROLL (bebop vocalist):

"Oh, I met Diz one day when he was gonna appear at the 125th Street Apollo Theater. I approached Diz and sounded on him for a gig going into the Apollo and a big light came on in his head, you know, a big bulb. He says, 'Oh, yes, I've been hearing about you. We're rehearsing at the Apollo on Thursday; we open Friday.' He said, 'Come on down to the rehearsal,' which I did. I made the rehearsal, and just about the time that rehearsal was getting ready to break up, Dizzy took Mr. Frank Schiffman aside and spoke to him about me coming in the Apollo Theater with the band and that's how it got started.

"I would go to different clubs. I remember the Club Baby Grand when it first opened and quite a few other clubs, and I would go in and I would sing my little thing, you know, bebop. I wasn't working there but they would always bring me on stage, 'Come on and sing.' And I'd do my thing and nobody listened. But it was so beautiful after I met Diz and joined him on December 10, 1949. At that time we were appearing at the Strand Theater downtown on Broadway. From there we went on to quite a few one-nighters, college dates, so forth. Right from there I became a member of the Gillespie aggravation, or aggregation.

"Every performance Dizzy gives is a memorable thing. There is a theme a lot of the cats play now called 'Intermission Riff.' Appearing with Dizzy in Cleveland we had less than enough time for one full tune to finish out the set. And Dizzy just politely says, 'O.K., let's play this.' Years later a lot of the groups now coming up use it as a theme. Still don't really know the name of it, so I call it 'Pippin' Theme.' And that is one of the memorable themes that I can remember of Dizzy's. Another thing that I will always remember is appearing in Chicago. Louis Armstrong was appearing at the Blue Note, and Pops was ill one night. And Dizzy played our set and then he went to the Blue Note and played Pops's set, just like Pops, you know. That's what makes Dizzy. And we still call Dizzy the King of the Trumpet. Of that horn, he's the king, and as a vocalist, a bebop vocalist, because that was a new kind of vocalist too."

LEONARD FEATHER:

"It took a long time and a great deal of perseverance on Dizzy's part to get through to the public at large. I'd gotten to know him fairly well during that time and gave him a write-up in *Metronome*, in 1944. The title of the article is kind of interesting, I think —it was called 'Dizzy Gillespie: Crazy Like A Fox,' because I always had the feeling that Dizzy's name was a handicap to his serious acceptance as the important musician that he was. People really felt that that was all there was to him; he was just a dizzy personality. The people that knew him a little better realized that there was a tremendous amount of depth beneath that crazy exterior. So that was the title and some of the theme of the article. *Inside Bebop* was not published until 1949, that came quite a bit later.

"I think that some of Dizzy's antics onstage over the years have not been in the best of taste. Sometimes he steps just beyond the border of what I think is right. But that's mostly in the past and not in the present."

Things rolled along in high gear. I completed two volumes of bebop trumpet solos published by Leeds Music, for which Frank Paparelli wrote the keyboard parts, so musicians everywhere could practice what we were playing. When something is written and published it lends permanence to the record. Leonard Feather published too, with an introduction from me, a book called *Inside Bebop,* a critical discussion of our music in an entertaining but serious and scholarly way that reduced the harmful and derisive effects of faddism on modern jazz. Leonard thought, rightfully, that people were paying too much attention to the cult-behavior aspect of bebop and not enough to the importance of the music.

Headache

       The year, 1949–50, I had a beautiful band with Paul Gonsalves, John Coltrane, Jimmy Heath—oh, man, the saxophone section! Then Gerald Wilson and Melba Liston on trombone. Dave Burns, Elmon Wright, Willie Cook, and Matthew McKay, trumpets. For a while J. J. Johnson was in that band on trombone, too, and Matthew Gee, a valve trombone player. He brought a baritone horn to play in the trombone section, and it was beautiful. In the saxophones, Coltrane and Jimmy Heath played alto, Paul Gonsalves and Jesse Powell, tenor. The baritone player was either Cecil Payne or Al Gibson. In the rhythm section, John Collins, guitar; Al McKibbon, bass; Teddy Stewart or Specs Wright on drums. I remember Gerald Wilson, who is actually a trumpet player, made an arrangement on "Out of This World." I think, technically that band was the best I ever had.

    An omen of changing fortunes appeared. A car ran over me. This cat ran in the back of me and knocked me clean over the handle bars in Geneva, New York. I was working up there, and it was in the daytime. I was riding my bicycle. Boom! It's lucky I didn't fall on my head. I skewed the fall and still have the marks from it; it skinned-up my arms. We tried to get some money from the man in federal court, and all they awarded me was $1,300. I'd spent that much getting up there, taking off from jobs. That's all they awarded me in damages, even after I told them I couldn't play the high notes anymore, without getting a headache.

MELBA LISTON (trombone, arranger):

"I was studying his music and style, but I don't remember on what occasion we met physically. Because by the time you meet somebody like Diz, you feel like you know them anyway. I was into his music, so just when we saw each other, it was like we already knew each other. He knew of me. The first time I got to be around him and work with him was in 1949, but that was because I had come back East with Gerald Wilson's band, and the band disbanded. Somehow or another, I wound up in New York.

"Dizzy had the big band at what I think was Bop City, and he heard that I was in town, and there was one trombone player that he wanted to get rid of, so he immediately fired him. And I went by to visit. He says, 'Where's ya goddamned horn? Don't you see this empty chair up there? You're supposed to be working tonight.'

"I say, 'Oh, boy . . .' I didn't have my horn with me. I was on a social visit to New York, and that was the first time I worked with him, that time in New York. And I think it was in the winter. I don't even remember the exact month. I never kept a diary or anything like that. That was the bad band with Trane and Little Bird* and John Lewis and you name it. That was a terrific band. But it disbanded within four or five months or something, maybe less. I was at the tail end of that marvelous organization."

Suddenly, the fad was over, and we were stuck with the old bebop dilemma, whether jazz is primarily a music for dancing or listening. We solved it by playing the way we liked, and when I asked my wife, Lorraine, to get some audience reaction on dates when we were playing dances, she reported, "A dance band, you are not!" Dancers had to hear those four solid beats and could care less about the more esoteric aspects, the beautiful advanced harmonies and rhythms we played and our virtuosity, as long as they could dance. They didn't care whether we played a flatted fifth or a ruptured 129th. Of course, we wanted them to listen; that's one reason why we played such ear-catching solos, to let everybody know we could and how good it sounded.

* Jimmy Heath.

They'd just stand around the bandstand and gawk, so the dance-hall operators stopped sending for us. There weren't that many concert dates available, and I found myself watching what I had left dwindle. What I had left was nothing after paying off the band and the transportation bills. "Shiit . . . !"

Billy Shaw pleaded with me, "Let's try another direction."

Lorraine said, "Look, you've had it. Do you want all them raggedy-assed niggers, or do you want me? Either way . . ." So that's when the band broke up. I broke it up in 1950, in Chicago at a place on the North Side, the Silhouette Club. Everybody was sorry about that, man; cats were crying, not making any money. So was I.

But Lorraine said, "It's either me or the band," and it was the band. So for commercial reasons, at least temporarily, I had to abandon my big band which all of us who loved modern jazz knew was a great artistic success. The fad was finished, but the style stood firmly. It was there to stay.

Playin' It Cool

The bebop fad ended because the press could kill anything it created. The negative image of bebop in the press hurt the big band some, but musically it was not a creature of the press. We'd survived with a hostile press or no press at all for several years. The reasons my big band ended were mainly economic and social and sexual. Economically, there was the rising cost of paying all those musicians in a big band and their transportation to and from engagements. To survive, a big band had to travel and play one-nighters, so the costs of transportation were astronomical. Then there was collusion between some lesser bookers and the promoters. These bookers would be getting money under the table for underselling or cutting down your price, and you'd wind up paying more to get a job than you'd receive for playing it. With the end of the fad, there weren't too many jobs coming in, and I didn't have that kinda money to lay out, to pay the guys to wait for future engagements. To keep a band together, you've got to give up some money.

Some of the bebop players, it seemed, had developed into prima donnas. Playing virtuoso music went to their heads. They didn't think about showing up for gigs on time and acted as though it would be a drag if people thought a modern jazz musician liked his work. They thought it was enough for them just to blow. When you have money and can afford to play just for yourself, you can play and act any way you want, but if you plan to make a living at music, you've got to sell it. Some of them couldn't play that well. They'd play a flatted fifth in the wrong place. They'd copy our licks and just play them whenever they wanted, and most of the time they'd put them in the wrong places. That's all they knew—that's all they knew how to do—and it slowed up the public's acceptance of our music.

Socially and sexually, it was the postwar era. Most of the guys who'd come back home wanted to get next to a girl. Many, who were originally from the South and rural areas, moved to the cities still completely hooked on blues (or country and western) and they preferred the kind of music they were used to, that made it easy to dance close and screw. They weren't very interested in listening. The disc jockeys didn't play the bands, they played the singers, and a new pop fad was born out of the old rhythm and blues idiom that they called rock 'n roll. The people didn't hear any big bands, so they didn't know what it was like because these singers traveled with small accompaniment.

Our music, modern jazz, continued and grew. Miles ushered in an innovation that the press immediately smeared with the term "cool" jazz. It happened as a result of a record date that Miles played with Gerry Mulligan and Johnny Carisi who'd written some things for Miles. The record was called "Birth of the Cool" because the guys in California sort've played not hot, but "coolish." They expressed less fire than we did, played less notes, less quickly, and used more open space, and they emphasized tonal quality.

It didn't bother me because it came right out of what we'd been doing. It was just a natural progression because Miles had definitely come right out of us, and he was the leader of this new movement. So it was the same music, only cooler. I liked to fill up a bar myself—the Charlie Parker school—to take good advantage of every space that's there instead of just leaving it to go over into the next bar. Miles had wide open spaces, and the guys who followed him didn't fully take advantage of the whole space in a bar. Sometimes they would let a whole two bars go by and play one note. If you play different notes but articulate the same way another guy does, you're still in his style, even though the notes are different. Miles had a new way of approaching a given phrase, so you could say that created a style, but it was still based on bebop. A lotta guys started copying that instead of copying what we had done. I went along with it because I knew the music was in a constant state of flux and I knew it was time for a change. I never felt eclipsed by it at all because knowing what my contribution was, I knew it would pass. I was working and making just as much money as those guys, so it didn't bother me. I just went right on with what I was doing. Some disc jockeys abandoned modern jazz and turned completely to Latin.

Musically speaking, the cool period always reminded me of white people's music. There was no guts in that music, not much rhythm either. They never sweated on the stand, Lee Konitz, Lennie Tristano, and those guys. This music, jazz, is guts. You're supposed to sweat in your balls in this music. I guess the idea was not to get "savage" with it, biting, like we were. But that's jazz to me. Jazz to me is dynamic, a blockbuster. They sorta softened it up a bit, but the depth of the music didn't change. The depth. Because *we* had the depth already. You couldn't get too much deeper than Charlie Parker.

Miles wasn't cool like that anyway. Miles is from that part of St. Louis where "blues" comes from. Just part of his music is played like that, cool. They copped that part—the cool—but let the rest, the blues, go, or they missed it.

Some time later, people were talking about "third stream," and I said, "Well, there's only one river." Third stream? I was never for that. If there's only one river, and you're talking about playing on the "third stream" with Gunther Schuller and John Lewis, I was always in the mainstream. Apparently, they meant that there was one stream that dealt with European classical music, another stream—the second stream—flowed from jazz; and then they tried to create a new stream, a new tributary, called third stream. "Coolness" was supposed to be characteristic of it, too. But I'm on the main line.

WALTER GILBERT FULLER:

"Bebop didn't die. That was the main disagreement that we really had. I wanted to call it modern music; Dizzy wanted to call it bebop. It was finally named bebop.

"When they said that bebop died, it made a liar out of everybody that said it wasn't anything. That was the first thing. And that was the beginning of the age when the white record company magnates were saying that the blacks weren't doing anything. That's when you had the Gerry Mulligans learning from Charlie Parker. Those were the days when you had the Mundell Lowes talking with the guys, learning what the thing was all about, and after they all learned what it was, they began to play similar styles.

"And then came the so-called rhythm 'n blues—they were doing dances, all kinds of gyrations—Elvis Presley and that kind of thing. That's the beginning of that era. If you didn't get out there and dance, and run up and down, and get on your knees and play your horn . . .

You had all these kinds of characters out there. And if you didn't do this, then you were through. The music goes 'round and round in circles' so you had to wear all kinds of uniforms, funny hats, funny clothes. What you see today, sequins all on the clothes, if you didn't do this, you weren't in. Liberace put the candelabra on the piano. What the hell has the candelabra got to do with how he plays? That's what it was, the age of gimmickry."

MAX ROACH:

"First, I don't understand the statement about something died. To me that's always a plot. We live in a society where each year you have to have a new model car, a new model this, a new model that. This is what society is telling you, like, if they want to present a new fad, whatever was popular before, they give it a name and then they just chop it off. I never felt that the music of the forties died at all. I think the music of the forties lives and lives on more now than it did at that particular time, when it was in its embryonic stage. That was the turning point of world recognition of the virtuosity of black music in my opinion, because the people who produced and developed that —the Art Tatums, Dizzys, and the Charlie Parkers, and the Bud Powells—we haven't seen the likes of them since, and everybody is still feeding off them. So much happened in that period musically, until today everybody is feeding off of it, and the stuff that you hear that does not feed off of it pales beside it totally. John Coltrane is an extension of the whole forties thing, and all of a sudden everybody's that. McCoy Tyner, Rahsaan Roland Kirk, they are all extensions of the forties, and the reason why they are who they are today is because of the time they spent analyzing and feeding off the forties."

BUDD JOHNSON:

"Dizzy hired me for a gig; we had about five pieces—trumpet, tenor, and a rhythm section—and it was up in the Bronx, it was a little club they had opened up in the Bronx. It was Sunday afternoon, and they had also hired Miles Davis on the same job. Dizzy didn't really know this. We got to the gig and then later Miles walked into the gig. Dizzy said, 'Ahaa, this is an opportunity I have long sought,' because, now, Miles is playing real good; he'd been playing with Bird too and everything. This was back in 1949–50. It was just a little afternoon gig. I think at that time Miles was a little cocky. He was the new thing, you know. And Dizzy opened up. We opened up. And man, you never heard— All of the clowning was laid aside, and this cat just took to the business of giving Miles a lesson that he would never forget.

"When Miles came on behind Dizzy that afternoon, Miles sounded damn near like me trying to play a trumpet—Dizzy had played so much. Miles, although he played good, was nowhere near it, and Dizzy, like, every set, just bore down and played like he knew he could play, flawlessly. And he'd make these notes so high till you'd have to stop and think, 'Wait a minute. This cat hit an A natural, or this cat can hit a B-flat, man!' He does it with such ease. He may look like it's a strain with his jaws all swelling out, but he's playing with ease, you know. And like everything is falling out of this horn. He'd go up and get these notes and everything. Oh, it was pitiful. It was no contest. I was waiting to see what was gonna happen. I knew Miles was good. I knew he wasn't as good as Dizzy, but I didn't expect Dizzy to play this much.

"Symphony Sid was a broadcaster who played our music. When I first met him he was out of work, they had knocked him off the air. And he really couldn't get to his grits; he just hung around black musicians. We'd get high with him and talk shit, turn him on to a little food or something, let him 'carry the stick' in our room at the Braddock Hotel—that means sitting up sleeping in a chair or on the floor. Dizzy knew all about this because Dizzy was living at 2040 Seventh Avenue at that time. Finally, Symphony Sid started to broadcasting in Birdland, live. I was standing at the bar with Diz one night at Birdland and Symphony Sid walked by. So Dizzy stopped him. Dizzy says, 'Wait a minute.' I ain't gonna use all those words Dizzy called him at that time, but he said, 'Do you mean to tell me you can walk by me and don't speak? I oughta go upside your head.' And Diz really had him. He grabbed him, you know, he was so angry, which I could understand. Just like I told you, we sorta took care of this cat, and the minute he got on his feet, he turned left. Then after he left Birdland, he wouldn't play no more jazz. He started playing Spanish music. And all of this peeved Diz and me, and a lotta the cats—that this cat would have the gall to walk by you and not say, 'How're you doing, Diz? How you doing, Buddy?' That's all, you know, just acknowledge that he knew you and say hello. He didn't have to say I remember when you let me sleep in your room on the floor and all that. This is the thing that Dizzy was so mad about. I don't know, maybe I talked Dizzy out of going upside his head because he was really keyed off."

DR. LAWRENCE REDDICK (historian):

"I was living in New York in the 1950s, the so-called bop period, and down on Fifty-second Street, the gathering place, I first met Diz. I moved down to Atlanta very soon and he came down to give a concert there, and I wrote a special piece on Diz. I think it was titled 'Dizzy Gillespie in Atlanta' or 'Bop in Atlanta,' something like that. And he liked it so well that we became very fast friends. I liked him as a personality because it seemed to me that he had a very good perspective on the social implications of music, on top of being a very good musician. He had some of the African influences, some of the Afro-Latin-American influences—pretty strong with the Cuban, a little Brazilian. He also had the beat of the people in this country coming up the Mississippi River from New Orleans to Chicago and New York.

"He and I had a little argument, a very fine intellectual argument. Diz felt that blacks had it in the blood for their musical talent and performance. And I tried to argue that it wasn't in the blood, but it was in the culture. He said Chano Pozo couldn't speak a word of English, but as soon as he gave the downbeat, Chano picked it up and could play. So he said it must have been in the blood. I said, 'No, it wasn't in the blood,' but the traditions were similar, though the language wasn't the same. So we got that whenever he would come to Atlanta, or whenever I was in a place where he was, we would get together and talk about things.

"I liked his exuberance. In a way he has a sort of untainted sense of humor and love for life. Like myself, he's a little of a clown, he carries on. Then he will lash out in criticism. For example, we were talking about Stan Kenton once, and he pointed out to me that Stan Kenton didn't have rhythm. And then at one time, Diz was playing a solo with the background of Kenton's orchestra, and he told me afterwards that some of the men in the band said that they did better when Diz was leading them than they did with Kenton. So he was just like that. He would come out with it and he also discussed very frankly with me how many musicians, especially black musicians, are exploited by agents, and how all sorts of under-the-table deals go on, and some of the men don't get but a fraction of the money they make. So I think as a human being, Diz is very wise, full of fun, likes jokes and all that, but he can be very serious, too."

Adversity usually makes me work harder, and since at this point I had no band, no recording contract, and no definite plans for the future, I had every reason to work hard. Sometimes I'd play as a single in front of a rhythm section. For a little while at Birdland, I played with Charlie Parker in front of a string section that he'd been set up with, then he'd double and play a set with me in front of the rhythm section. I had several alternatives: to try organizing a small combo; touring with other groups as a featured artist; or fronting a woodwind en-

semble, an idea which I liked. If I had the music for a woodwind
ensemble and Yard had strings, we could pick up a rhythm section
and go on tour together. We could play concerts and clubs and pick
up woodwind and string players wherever we went. It wouldn't be
much trouble because they wouldn't have to swing. Being longhairs,
all they'd have to do would be read what was written and they could
pick it up in one rehearsal. Yard would play a set with strings, I'd play
a set with woodwinds, and we'd wind it up all together. And we'd
stress entertainment. Every time we went on stage, it would be just
like a show. We'd make people think we liked what we were doing. It
was a good idea that never materialized, because Yard and I were
with different agents, so it became difficult to create that business arrangement. Yard and I never did get together anymore as a team, but
I worked quite a bit.

Several times in those years, the early fifties, I went on tour with
Stan Kenton, as soloist. Stan paid me. He wanted to go on tour with
some extra artists he wanted to present. He contacted Billy Shaw,
hired me, then Charlie Parker, Slim Gaillard, and Erroll Garner. Each
one of us had a spot. So I did my spot; Charlie did his spot; the band
did their spot, all of us. Yard and I didn't play together; each of us
had his own music with the band. It was beautiful, you know, because
there was such a great deal of respect from the musicians in the band.
These guys had their mouths open all night, man. It was dynamite!

BUDD JOHNSON:

"A real funny thing happened when Dizzy was on tour with Stan
Kenton. Well, Kenton really wanted to try to compete with Duke
Ellington. I remember a statement a critic wrote in the paper.
He said, 'I was over in Europe, and over there it's "crow-jim."
Not "jim-crow," it's "crow-jim."' In other words the people don't like
nothing but black music over there. Like Stan Kenton had gone over
there, and Kenton, himself, tried to think he was as great as Duke
Ellington, and they pushed his stuff. They really pushed it and tried to
get it over, but it couldn't stand the test of the times. Right now,
they're trying to say, 'Well, jazz is American music, and it wasn't necessarily created by the black man.' They try to say that right now. But
I got a book on arranging that I bought quite some time ago when I
first came to New York and in it was a preface by Paul Whiteman. And
he was saying that jazz is really the black man's music, the only difference being that whites had the technical knowledge to write it down,
but blacks created the music. Well, they didn't have the technical

knowledge to write it down because black arrangers were writing for Paul Whiteman—Don Redman and Fletcher Henderson back in those days. Fred Waring and all of them had black arrangers, see. We actually taught them everything they know about the jazz scene.

"I remember when I used to play, and if they wanted anything like jazz, or Dixieland, when I was a kid, they had to hire black people because white people could only read the notes on the paper. When it came to improvising on their instruments, they couldn't get off first base, they didn't know what to do. All that came from black musicians, all of that improvisation. I even have a book on the Negro and the great musicians way back when, mentioning people like Blind Tom and the Black Swan and what they could do. They traveled all over the world doing concerts, and they got the write-ups from all of the papers, and played for kings and queens, and all of this, telling how great Blind Tom was, that there was nobody—he had no peers. There seems to be a little conspiracy; they don't want blacks to have the credit.

"Dizzy asked me to write an arrangement for him for the Kenton band. They were playing upstate somewhere, in Connecticut or something, and they had the concert that evening. I had finished the arrangement, and I went up to rehearse the band on it because Stan Kenton would accept my arrangements. I used to write for Gus Arnheim's Orchestra when he was the piano player in the band. So me and Stan were pretty tight; he was familiar with my work. The main thing was that Dizzy wanted me to write it, and so I wrote this arrangement.

"Backstage, Dizzy and I were sitting down talking and going on. Lorraine was there, and when it came time for the concert, Dizzy's still fooling around, you know. Lorraine said, 'Dizzy, if you don't get your ass up from there and get that uniform on and get on that bandstand!' So he listened to her and he did it.

"I brought Lorraine back to New York because they were going on further, and I said, 'Lorraine, why do you talk to him like that in front of all these ofays and all these people?'

"She said, 'Budd, if I don't bring this cat down an inch or two, he would be gone! He would be just off on cloud nine or something!' But the way she said it, and the way it happened, and the way he looks at her, with the expression on his face, it's so comical. 'Cause he'll look at her—never gives her any back talk—he looks at her like, 'Fool, you don't know what you're talking about.' But he don't say it, and he goes on to do what he's supposed to do. I get such a big kick out of her, just talking, but Diz is a very serious man. And he makes his job with no sweat."

Unfortunately, at that time, Yard was drinking quite a bit, and he wasn't up to his usual standard. Yard used to drink a fifth every day, man, and he'd be so juiced he couldn't play. That was at the beginning of the tour; he'd drink a fifth before he went on because he was trying to fight the other "jones" that he had. And his performance didn't come up to his own high standards. He'd be slobbering all over the horn and everything. At that time Stan Kenton had Lee Konitz, a forthright young musician, a pretty good player who went to school with Charlie Parker but wasn't blue—bluesy like him. And Lee Konitz was really playing; people would give him a big hand. So I pulled Yard off to the side, and I said, "Yard, man, you're letting your fans down and everything. Man, every time you go out there all juiced, it says nothing. You slobber all over the horn. You don't know what you can do." I say, "You play, but not up to your standards, and there's Lee Konitz, man, that guy is going out. Stan Kenton is featuring him, and he's all over the instrument. Man, you make people think . . ." He put the whiskey down immediately. That night he came out on the stage, and I was sorry that I told him because I had to follow him. Man, he ran snakes! If you can term someone a genius, Charlie Parker was a genius. If there was one, he was one. That's a story I always tell when people say Yard played better while under the influence. That's the biggest lie they ever told.

In the small bands I organized in the early 1950s, I had some younger, upcoming musicians who exemplified our style. At one time I had Coltrane, Jimmy Heath, and Percy Heath, but the first band I had for any length of time was Milt Jackson, Bill Graham, Al Jones, Wade Legge, and Lou Hackney. Joe Carroll did the bebop vocals. We had some tours in the United States—clubs like the Capitol Lounge in Chicago where we played quite a bit. Then in 1952 and 1953 we went to Europe. I had several small groups during that period which were always changing for lack of money. I just couldn't seem to make very much money during those days.

A lotta people ask me how Coltrane sounded then. Well, he was under the influence of Charlie Parker, but he still had his little thing too. He was playing alto in my big band so therefore he sounded like Charlie Parker. He and Jimmy Heath, they were the saxophone players. And then for a short time there, Coltrane had been playing with Earl Bostic, and I got him in my group when he first started playing tenor. He didn't strike me as being too far away from the way Charlie Parker had been playing. And then, later on, after he got with Miles, he started developing this other style of playing which was different. And he developed that into something really new.

It felt all right working with a small combo, but what pissed me off sometimes was when they'd put up a sign at the places where we worked—"Dizzy Gillespie and His Band." The assumption then was that I had a big band, and I had to make these people take their signs down and say, "Dizzy Gillespie and His Quintet." They'd put "Band" up there and everybody'd come expecting to see a big band. Musically, there's a difference between a small and a big band, but really it doesn't matter to me too much. Of course, when you've got a big band, you have more to work with—that's the major difference. I like a big band because it's warmer and you can get more colors with it, and more power—power when I hit down, POW! And all the different colors. But since it wasn't economically feasible, I just broke it down and went right on working. The type of band doesn't matter; you play the same type of music with a harp or a harmonica. You're what you are. People say sometimes you haven't heard me unless you've heard me with a big band, but you could say the same thing about a small band, or with strings, or with a symphony orchestra. It's not the sound, anyway, but what I do on the stage. Nothing surpasses my performances with small bands, especially with Charlie Parker. A small band doesn't forestall creativity. I'd make the route and go on tour with Jazz at the Philharmonic, alone. I'd break up the little band then, go out with JATP and make some money, then come back and organize another small band.

PERCY HEATH (bass):

"In 1950, I got the job with Dizzy. He was going out with a sextet—Specs Wright, from Philly, Coltrane, my brother Jimmy, Milt Jackson, Joe Carroll and me. Jimmy was playing alto and Trane was playing tenor. Jackson was doubling on piano and vibes.

"I had only been playing about three years, and it was school for me, as long as I stayed there. The money wasn't good enough to go out on the road so much. I had one child in 1951, and I had to cut out and try to learn some more away from Dizzy. It was school, but you gotta have a certain amount in order to absorb what's around you. You have to know quite a lot to really take advantage of the school of being in Dizzy Gillespie's band. I enjoyed every night I played with him, which is the most important thing. Because if there's happiness on the bandstand, music is being made on the bandstand. I don't care about Joe Splivik or Joe Doakes or whoever. What he says, that's his opinion.

"During that time, there were six of us in the band, and Leonard Feather came up to review a performance and never mentioned who was on bass and piano, in a sextet. Not even the name. Not even,

'Percy Heath was on bass.' And I asked him about it. I said, 'Man, how could you do that?'

"He said, 'Oh, that's a stupid mistake. I'm sorry, you know.' But there was the review of the Dizzy Gillespie Sextet and not even a mention of the bass player's name. A critic? It was years before I even wanted to speak to Leonard Feather.

"Dizzy's funny. I remember we were walking around San Francisco. We had some baskets. Somebody gave us Indian woven baskets out there on the Coast. One of them was shaped like an inverted turban, and the other one looked like a Chinese coolie hat. Dizzy and I put those baskets on with our beards and what not, and we walked into several places. And people didn't know who we were, were wondering what nationality we were, what country. We went into some French place and put people on. We really put them on. But Dizzy Gillespie is a very brilliant man, as well as a master musician, and the king of that trumpet. He says a lotta things in humor that really mean an awful lot. If you listen to Dizzy Gillespie, you'll learn an awful lot. Not only what he plays, but what he says. He tells you things, too, if you've got sense enough to listen."

MILT JACKSON:

"Every time I hear Dizzy play I think, 'He was just developing into what you heard tonight.' Simple as that—the whole thing—he's the father of everyday progressive development. That's the reason he sounds the way he does. The only reason he hasn't had a big band all these years is because of finance. If this country was anything like it should be, he'd have had a big band all these years, one of the baddest bands in the world, still. He should always have a big band, always; he should've never been without one. He's dynamic with a big band. I learned how to play good music from him, this particular kind of music, because he's the father of it, you know. We came up under that era. But I love his philosophy—his philosophy of music, and his philosophy of life, modern progressive development. I've always followed it myself, because I've always thought it's one of the most beautiful philosophies that a person could have, especially in this business."

I'm sure that Miles considered himself a leader in a new movement, within our movement, because he wasn't that far away from us to be considered "away." There was a change in the administration of the music, I guess you would call it, a change in the phrasing. The phrasing went a little differently. Phrasing changes every so often, and you can tell what age the music comes from by the way it's played. But Miles only knew what to play from what had gone on before, then he began to find his own identity. Other trumpet players following our style developed new identities, too, specifically Fats Navarro, out of whom came Clifford Brown. Fats had terrific attack, not necessarily a big sound. Fats and Miles used to copy all my licks until they got into what they were doing. Both he and Miles developed distinctive styles. From my style, Miles went this way, and Fats went the other.

In contrast to the cool school, another movement arose that was tagged "hard bop" because it reasserted the primacy of rhythm and the blues in our music and made you get funky with sweat to play it. Max Roach, Fats Navarro, Art Blakey, Horace Silver, and, later, Cannonball Adderley became the major exponents of it. Hard bop with its more earthy, churchy sound drew a lot of new black fans to our music, so both movements, it and the cool, extended the scope and popularity of modern jazz.

Dee Gee Records

One alternative to just playing it cool was to make a lotta money—make all the money. I decided it would be desirable to own a record company. I'd have the record company, compose the tunes, and be an artist on the records, the whole thing. I got together with Dave Usher, a friend of mine out in Detroit, and created Dee Gee Records. This was a great step forward, for although I was not the first black musician to produce his own records, I was the only one who had done so recently. In 1951, I was probably the only one around with the desire, the resources and the guts to try it. People said I couldn't get a recording contract, which was untrue. I just wouldn't sign. They made offers, but I wouldn't sign because I wanted to make these records for myself. I felt I could produce my own records. With the objective of building a large record company, I invested my money and talent and tried to become a musical industrialist. But later on, I signed.

We held our first recording session in Detroit, on March 1, 1951, and, man, on these records I really tried to show that good art could be popular and make money. We recorded "Tin Tin Deo" and premiered "Birks Works," a blues appropriately titled to signal the debut of a new musical industrialist. "We Love to Boogie," which added a strong West Indian flavor, featured vocals by Fred Strong and the Calypso Boys. The musicians on that set came from my small group: John Coltrane, on tenor and alto; Milt Jackson, vibraharp and piano; Kenny

Burrell, guitar; Percy Heath, bass; and Kansas Fields, drums. We came back later that year and cut some sides that had more blues and vocals on them. Joe Carroll and I sang "School Days"—people still ask for it. This tune had strong back beats for dancing and lyrics, with a special appeal to teen-agers, so we were in on fusing jazz with rock early. "Swing Low, Sweet Cadillac" was another vocal I did on those sessions, and Joe Carroll sang "Nobody Knows the Trouble I've Seen," to accent the spirituals. We did all kinds of things trying to make my music more palatable, but the bebop musicians, most of them stone broke, criticized us for it and said we'd gone commercial. They didn't even appreciate my comedy. People wanted to hear the beat and the blues, but the bebop musicians didn't like to play the blues. They were ashamed. The media had made it shameful. Blues artists at that time hardly ever played before white people, and we played mostly for white audiences. When I'd play a blues, guys would say, "Man, you're playing that?"

I'd tell them, "Man, that's my music, that's my heritage." The bebop musicians wanted to show their virtuosity. They'd play the twelve-bar outline of the blues, but they wouldn't blues it up like the older guys they considered unsophisticated. They busied themselves making changes, a thousand changes in one bar. Why make one change in a bar if you could put a thousand there? Drummers wouldn't play back beats; they all wanted to play like Max Roach. Those guys overlooked the fact that Charlie Parker personified the blues idiom. When he played the blues, he was a real blueser. You forget about changes when you play the blues, but every now and then you put a little lick in there to let 'em know, "Here's where I'm at, really." Bebop is a highly sophisticated form of music; the blues is very simple, in form.

Dave had a big idea, to take the money we made from selling my records, and plow it back into the company to record other artists. He had a date with Milt Jackson, which turned out great. Then he recorded a guy with strings and another date with somebody else, probably with strings. That's what messed it up, strings—creditors, including taxes. Dave was administering Dee Gee but he didn't know how to run the business and it got behind in taxes; that's what happened. We lost the record masters, everything, through tax liens. Dave took the blame, and the government just confiscated the masters and sold them to Savoy or some other company, probably for next to nothing. We don't own them now. We made some very good records, but we lost the record company.

DAVE USHER (former business partner):

"The guy who married my sister gave me some tickets to a performance of Dizzy Gillespie at a 'Dixieland' Jazz Concert in Detroit in
1945. He came to the Paradise Theater in Detroit which was the soul-
ville theater at that time. It used to be Orchestra Hall where I used to
go and listen to my symphonic tunes. I had a feeling for music. I had
a classical background when I was a kid. I grew up with a classical
background 'cause my mother was from Russia and so was my old
man. I'm of Russian-Jewish parentage, or better yet, Jewish-Russian
parentage. And then Orchestra Hall had a transition, and I never left
that auditorium. Did you know who the conductor of the Detroit Symphony was at Orchestra Hall that then became Paradise Theater?
Ossip Gabrilowitsch, who was the son-in-law of Mark Twain. He was
my teacher, he really was; he turned me on to the life of music."

How did you get into the record business with Dizzy?

"Well, I was a truck driver, so to stop from being a truck driver. Because my mother gave me this boss background [in music.] Anyway, I
was one of the early white boys. The greatest tribute that I ever felt,
really, as far as, like, what people felt, really, up to and from that time
on was when Roy Eldridge said to Dizzy in a hotel in Detroit: 'Damn,
Dizzy, Dave Usher sure does look like a gray.' Ha! Ha!"

What happened with Dee Gee Records?

"See this? It's a stamper to make records. One side is 'Oop Shoo Be
Do Be.' This is the way that records are made, like waffles, you know.
The batter is in the middle; you press the button. This is the thing
that does it. This is called a stamper. It's good for about 2,500 records.
These were LP's. I brought this here to put in a museum because of a
certain history. This was 'Tin Tin Deo,' 'The Champ,' 'Birks Works,'
'Lady Be Good,' 'Oop Shoo Be Do Be,' and another one, 'I'm in a
Mess. . . .' We, Dizzy and I, had an affinity for each other. I had the
potential convivialness, the verboseness, the respect, and the understanding of what he was trying to do, as an 'ofay.' And that's what it
was, remember it. You know, there's one thing I really believe in; I tell
you this very sincerely: Never should a man, woman, an indifferent
human being forget their realistic, equative beginnings. Ha, ha.

"We thought that he would be a musician who had a record company, he could say what he wanted to say. And that was essentially
it. Now we enjoyed commercial success during that period—that was
1950 through 1953. And we'd get some good meals. 'Tin Tin Deo' and
'Birks Works,' those were the things, and they just went straight

ahead. We had a very realistic feeling, but other than that . . . that's why I said that I used to listen to Ossip Gabrilowitsch in the symphony."

As a young white guy, how did your family feel about going into business with a black jazz musician?

"They didn't say too much. But I'll never forget the time that Dizzy came to watch Sugar Ray fight. My old man, my mother, and my father had this big twenty-one-inch . . . Well, it was a big TV; it was a console. It sat on the floor, had a record player, Admiral. They came to see the fight, and I didn't show up because I was with this chick, and Dizzy told them, 'Dave, ha, ha . . .' He went into the house with Dave Heard, J. C. Heard's brother, and they were watching the Sugar Ray fight. Dizzy had a Clark bar or something 'cause nobody served nothing. And Dizzy pulled out the Clark bar and said, 'Would you like some?' Ha, ha. I heard this later on; it was beautiful.

Why did Dee Gee Records fail? Why did it collapse?

"Oh, it didn't collapse. It just didn't do right because Dudley Do Rights just weren't around at that time, and they'll never be when it comes to show biz."

GEORGE WEIN (impresario):

"Well, he'd worked for me in Storyville; and of course when we did the first Newport Jazz Festival, I asked him to come up there, the very first one, in 1954. So that's how it started. I was a very young guy at that time, and at that time Dizzy was being criticized by our more pedantic and 'serious' and I'll use the word *stupid* jazz critics for being too comic on stage, not serious enough about his music. Those were the days when he was going through the rhythm and blues period, you know, because the public didn't really understand jazz that much. And so in those days he was trying to get a wider public. And so he went through a bebop rhythm and blues period with Dee Gee Records. Some of those records are now classics. In those days they were considered attempts at being commercial. And so I said to Dizzy, in my infinite wisdom of my young years, 'Dizzy, please don't clown too much on stage.' And Dizzy looked at me as if I was insane, which I must have been. And he was onstage going through this thing and playing wonderfully. And every time he'd start to get happy out there, he'd turn and see me in the wings. And he'd have a big smile on his face, and all of a sudden go 'Booh . . .' with this *big* frown, to show me that he wasn't clowning.

"And afterwards, I said here I am with an artist with a comic timing ability that rivals that of the geniuses like Charlie Chaplin in his ability to be a *funny* guy. I say that in the best sense, to be a funny guy in the best sense of all that it means to be a great clown—and I mean a great clown, not clownish. Because Dizzy is a masterful comic. And here I am, a young punk telling him not to clown. You know, these are the things you learn, and I had that opportunity to make a lotta mistakes and still survive, and, thank God, Dizzy has never held it against me too much. I think it took me about six years to get over that one with him."

Inexperience. That's why Dee Gee Records folded, but we went on to make other great records. In 1953, we recorded again for someone else, a standout performance, all unintentionally—not the performance, the record.

MAX ROACH:

"The five people that Dizzy had originally thought about in the group at the Onyx didn't really materialize until we did Jazz at Massey Hall, that album, in 1953. Some Canadians came down and they wanted that original group to play at a concert. It didn't materialize before then. Charlie Mingus was substitute bassist for Oscar Pettiford who had broken his arm playing baseball, or something like that, with Woody Herman's band.

"Well, they put us all together. We hadn't worked together recently; everybody had gone their own separate way and either had their own groups or were engaged in other things, and they pulled all of us together to do this session. Of course Mingus was new to us at that particular time, and on sessions like that you just come right in and say, 'Hey . . . !' Everybody is so happy to see each other, you don't think about what's going to happen until you get to the bandstand, and just prior to going to the bandstand, we decided what we're going to play on that particular concert. So it was pure spontaneity. That's the thing about that date. It wasn't like 'O.K., we'll rehearse two or three hours here.' We just went on the stage, and things began to happen. Mingus had been unfamiliar with the repertoire that we were playing on the East Coast because he had just come from the West Coast. In a sense he had come back and forth, but he had not played with this particular group, although we had been paying a lot of attention to him. You could tell by the way he played with us. Originally, Oscar Pettiford was supposed to be on that session. But everybody was in complete command, everybody had a wonderful time.

It was a real happy, happy day. We were very relaxed and a lot of funny things happened."

Funny is right. Do you know that Charlie Mingus, who was always being mistreated, took advantage of his position on the bandstand, tape recorded that concert, went home, and put out a record? I ain't seen no royalties until recently. I've learned to be philosophical about it. All my records are for someone else to enjoy. I just create the music and, like they preach in the blues, do my best to make advantages out of misfortune. Maybe Dee Gee Records folded because at that time they weren't ready for it. Be in the right place at the right time. The timing is of the essence.

Machinations

After my record company folded, all these bad accidents happened. My first driver's license was in New York, but they took that one because I ran over a guy. That must've happened over twenty years ago. I was working at Snookie's, and driving to work from Queens one night, I stopped for a red light around Forty-seventh Street and Northern Boulevard. A car in front of me struck out when the light turned green, and I shot off right behind him. An old man stepped in between our cars. It fucked him up. His head was bleeding, he had a hole in his head, and it was raining and very cold, too. Boy, I felt so bad. Not having seen him because he stepped out in front of me, I really hit him pretty hard. My car was a Kaiser, and it bent the car, the hood came up. He lay there, and I put my coat under his head. The rain kept coming down harder, until finally the ambulance arrived. Scared to tell anybody; trying to avoid letting Lorraine find out I had hit someone, I didn't even report it. That made me nervous, boy! In the end, we paid this old guy $5,000 over and above what the insurance company finally paid, and they took my license for not reporting it to the authorities.

Then I got hit with a couple of paternity suits. Both of them came out of Pennsylvania, but one traveled around quite a bit, from Pittsburgh. Every time I'd go to Pittsburgh, they'd arrest me and I'd be forced to make some kind of a deal. I knew that it was a game, really, really a game. This girl there, who later on I found out had several children, all by different fathers, decided to name me as the father of her latest offspring. The dude she was living with at the time put her up to it, I discovered later. He told her, "Go on and name that dude as the father." And she brought charges against me for fornication and bastardy—which means fucking and having a child. I denied the fact, but that didn't keep me from being arrested and getting in the papers. Then she moved to Toledo, Ohio, and every time I played Toledo, and in other different places, they'd arrest me. It looked like she was following me around to have me arrested. One time, in Pittsburgh, they put me in the same cell with a multiple murderer. I asked this dude, "Man, what are you in here for?"

"I offed eight people . . ." he said.

I said, "Gaaad . . . !"

When a woman brings charges against a national figure, she often doesn't have to prove the charges because you're traveling and know nothing about them and lose by default. She may be on relief, and the authorities anxious to get her off welfare want you to take the blame and pay the bill. They finally forced us to make a settlement, and, under its terms, she wasn't supposed to contact me at all anymore. Once, I went to Pittsburgh and got a note from this girl. I took it to the authorities immediately and told them, "See this note? She says she wants to see me and this girl has no authority to get in touch with me. I want to have her arrested if she shows up here." They waited for her, but she never showed up. I think she smelled a rat and knew I'd have her arrested if she tried to contact me. Nobody wants to see someone who's causing you a lot of trouble. The worst thing about it was that I was married and didn't want to embarrass my wife who couldn't help but be hurt by that kind of thing.

Another case happened in Reading, Pennsylvania, and it also received a big headline in the paper. It just happened that they brought charges in Pennsylvania, and I'd recently engaged a lawyer there. The first case had gotten out of hand by default because I was always traveling and didn't answer the court summons. The second time, we went to court.

My Philadelphia lawyer, Charlie Roisman, was a genius, a stone genius in a courtroom. He looked like Winston Churchill, always wore a flower in his lapel, with a Homburg, walked with a cane, and he gave jam sessions in Philadelphia in his apartment. He had an apartment on Sansom Street, 1526. They nicknamed him Professor Bogus. Ha! Ha! Ha! Professor Bogus and Dexter Jones were living there. Dexter Jones is the sculptor who did a bronze bust of me. He lives in Philly, and he made that big sculpture there at City Hall. Dexter Jones is a bad dude, and I've known him since he was a kid. He used to work with the sculptor Jo Davidson, and when Jo Davidson sculpted a bust, Dexter did the ears, eyes, nose—the details. Dexter works on his own now, and he's a magnificent sculptor. Charlie Roisman was a patron of the arts, when he used to have jam sessions. Dexter Jones was staying there with him. We'd get to Philly and play at his place afterward, and Charlie would cook. Charlie Roisman was a gourmet cook, a baad cook. That cat could cook and he'd even put on his chef's cap. He wrote a tune called "Professor Bogus."

> Professor Bogus went to church one day
> He put in a nickel, took a dime away.
> He crossed himself with a double cross,
> And his visit to the church wasn't a total loss,
> Bogus, Bogus, Bogus man . . .

We thought one time of a television show with me as "Professor Bogus," with rhythms and rhymes and things. "Professor Bogus" was something else.

They arrested me at the Earle Theater in Philadelphia in that paternity suit. Charlie Roisman handled the case, and we went to court and won acquittal in Reading, Pennsylvania. Roisman and I were in the elevator going up to the court, and this girl brought her little baby there. I didn't know her. She was gonna put the baby up and say the child looked like me depending on a white judge to think that all niggers looked alike. The girl said to Charlie Roisman, "Oh, you're Mr. Gillespie's lawyer. Don't you think that the child looks like her father?"

Roisman said, "Yeah, whoever he might be." Ha! Roisman wrote a poem about that case. Part of it read:

> Dizzy Gillespie one day had to go to court
> But he didn't want to take the responsibility
> If he hadn't had the sport . . .

Charlie Roisman wrote it up and after we got acquitted, he showed me this long poem. People will try to take advantage of you if they think you've got some money, and they often try it with show people who receive a lot of publicity. Sometimes they pull some shit just for the hell of it. There's always some trumpet freak if you want her. There's always a saxophone freak, who comes to see the saxophone player, who just sits there. Only the saxophone player can sleep with her. There are others who only sleep with trumpet players. They're all around if you desire that; if that's what you want, it's there. Everyone's got their admirers. I have a good wife at home.

LORRAINE GILLESPIE:

"One thing, I never ask anybody . . . you know, you're talking, and somebody says something about your husband fruiting with a chick. I don't even think about that. I feel as though if she's allowing him to make a fool of her, he's perfectly right, until he gets caught. And then, that's when he's wrong, when he gets caught. Other than that, I never thought like that, because I know musicians. I didn't like them at first, not for boyfriends, just for friends, because I know the dear boys and all about what they'll do. I really didn't care because most parents, I think, teach their girls that if your husband takes care of you and gives you respect when he's with you and has a decent place for you to stay, and you don't have any trouble, you don't have to worry about it. Because your husband can be anybody's husband after he leaves home. He doesn't have to just be yours. He can be anybody's husband out in that street. All that foolishness never worried me. 'How do you do it?' people asked. I say, 'By not thinking about it, and if I think about it, I just say to heck with it. If he doesn't get caught, good.'

"I ignore all that celebrity junk too. I 'ig' all of it because I have so much to do. I know how to do so many different things that I wouldn't even think about it. As long as Dizzy doesn't get hurt, or he's not sick or something, I don't think about that horn, that music, or him being a celebrity. Maybe if I had met him, and he already had all this . . . But when I met him, he was just as raggedy as a bowl of yat ko mein and as poor as a non-bearing beanpole. I had to scuffle to help him get this, so I don't see it like that. Some of these chicks walk in and find somebody all 'big star'; Dizzy was smaller than I was when I met him. People were calling me a fool for taking up with him. I didn't walk in on Dizzy with this. I had to help him build this, this 'empire' that he's living up on. The only part I didn't do was blow, but if I hadn't done what I did, he wouldn't have been blowing 'cause he wouldn't have had the strength to blow with. Those sisters out in the street would have messed him up. They'd have blown him all right, blown him off the map! I've got to do my part too. I don't have time to be worrying about what somebody else 'thinks.' It's easy for them to 'think' because they don't have to go through any of it, and they don't have to worry about it. It just comes out there, boom-boom. They don't worry about who's back there in the back sweeping the floor, and cleaning the garbage and all, so that can be. All they see is the smiling and Uncle Tomming and stuff. But they don't know what it takes to come to that, you know.

"When I get mad with him, Dizzy makes me happiest, everytime I see that diamond glass shining in the front door hitting the middle of his back. That's what makes me happiest. One time Dizzy bought me a fur coat, and he wouldn't tell me exactly what it cost, but I think, when I talked to the man on the phone, the man said it was $6,000, and I nearly passed out. When Dizzy walked in the door and gave me the coat, he asked me what I thought about it. I said, 'That's nice . . .' and went on working.

"I dig women's liberation, especially the part where women get tired. A man can go out on a job and say he's gonna work eight hours or twelve hours, whatever number of hours. At least he's got some hours he can look forward to and say, 'Well, I'm getting finished.' A poor lady's got to work all day and all night until she just about falls out and still there's stuff for her to start. And then you have no pay-day. And the man turns around and says, 'I'm supporting you.' Man that's for the birds. I mean, you don't work forty-eight hours a day for somebody to support you. No, no, no, no! I think it's beautiful. The part that I don't go along with is going out there driving a truck. No matter how poor I get I don't wanna be no truck driver or out there putting up signs and being a 'fireness.' Men are firemen, what are the women? Whatever she is, I don't want to be one of those.

"I can do all kinds of stitchery, and I can make this and do that, believe it, but I am nobody's cook. I'm not a for real kitchen mechanic. I'm one of those jive kitchen mechanics. I know I can't cook, because I can taste, and it never tastes like I'm trying to get it. So I have to do the best I can. Like Dizzy makes the bed up sometimes and it looks like hell, but at least he tries. That's all I can do is to try. In the first place I don't have to cook steady, everyday, like most people do. So therefore I forget. One day, after I learn how to sew, I'll learn how to cook. I can't learn how to do every damn thing. I cook. It ain't too hot, but it's cooked. See, my greens don't taste too hot because I don't put enough grease in them. They say they taste better when you put more grease in them. I say, 'Well, I'll tell you what. I'll stick with these greaseless ones, 'cause all that grease don't agree with me afterwards.' Dizzy is lucky. He's got a wife who can get full off of frankfurters and drunk off of beer. How lucky can you get?"

MARION "BOO" FRAZIER (cousin, valet):

"My father and John are cousins, so that throws me into like a second cousin situation, but the relationship was never on a cousins basis. It was more like a father-son relationship. My father died when I was at a very early age. After my father passed, I developed a strong relationship with John Birks.

"I came out of the Army in 1953, and on my way home—they discharged me in New Jersey—I stopped in New York just for a day or so. Luckily, I went by the Apollo, and he was appearing at the Apollo. I went upstairs to the dressing room, and Mrs. Gillespie was there, and I just stayed around for about two weeks or so. Then I went home to see my mother and came back to New York. That's when I started living with them.

"John's the only celebrity that I know who has never changed. He's always been the same on a day-to-day basis. I don't think he realizes that he is a celebrity and the greatness that he carries. That's what I admire about him more than anything else, his ability to just remain calm and not get excited. I don't think he knows just how talented he is. From being around him so much—I'm not talented in any way, musically, but I did learn one thing from him. Just be yourself and don't try to go out of the realm of really what you are. And Mrs. Gillespie has a lot to do with that. She preaches that to him on a day-to-day basis. He's happiest at home with Lorraine because Mrs. Gillespie is such a great person and has such a great mind, and, man, when she's not necessarily telling jokes, she can tell you things that just make you roll. It's the truth, and it's so truthful that you really just have to roll with the thing. I think he's happiest at home because Mrs. Gillespie is truly the backbone of the total situation. Without Mrs. Gillespie, I don't think things would've been as great for Mr. Gillespie this far, because she's a very strong woman and very intelligent."

CHARLES "COOKIE" COOK (friend, trumpet):

"I called them the 'Butterbeans and Susie' of the young people 'cause they had a beautiful relationship. I mean you very seldom hear about Lorraine and Dizzy when they talk about Mary Pickford and Charles Buddy Rogers. Not too much scandal, but whatever scandal Diz gets in has always been taken care of because Lorraine has always been in the background. And I think Dizzy blocks Lorraine out; he don't hear Lorraine sometimes, when she's talking. Maybe that's why they get along. Lorraine's always been a big part of Dizzy, I mean a great big thing. I'm a little partial to everything about her because if anything happens to me, God forbid, I think Dizzy and Lorraine will have to . . . they're like my family."

DEXTER JONES (friend, sculptor):

"About 1949, Charlie Roisman introduced me to Dizzy and actually brought him down to my studio which was behind Independence Hall in Philadelphia. Charlie was representing Diz in a matter, and Diz would come into town fairly frequently for that reason with Lorraine, his wife, and we started getting together. I cast up the small model of Dizzy, and we went from there to build what I think is a rather warm and lasting friendship.

"In 1950, I had moved my studio from the Independence Hall area up to Center City, and since Roisman represented a lot of jazz musicians, I became quite well acquainted with the jazz world. And so it became a meeting place. We had a piano and a set of traps there, and it became a meeting place for anybody who was in town. And so we had a few great people, and whenever Diz was there, he'd come in. At that point, we started an over life-sized bust which appeared later on the album, *The Real Thing*.

"Anyway, Roisman and I used to give sessions in my studio. We sorta shared the studio. I used it in the daytime, and he used it at night. Sometimes there were sessions in the daytime when cats weren't working, if they didn't have matinées. Sonny Stitt, J. J. Johnson, even Nat Cole used to come by. Steve Gibson and the Redcaps, oh, a lot of people. We had one session: Diz came by, and we had the police come in, even though it was not a residential area. It was right next to a firehouse, and somebody in there didn't like the idea of the 'mixed' company, I think. Somebody called the cops. It was in Center City and mainly storefronts; maybe a few odd apartments around, but nothing nearby.

"Diz handled himself very well. I remember there was some mention of him being searched which he refused. He said, 'You want to search me, you have to take me in, take me downtown.' And that stopped them because they weren't inclined to do that. It reminds me very much of the time he was playing at Convention Hall to a massive crowd. There were other people on the program of course. The police commissioner (Rizzo) decided that he had to keep what he thought were these 'immoral' sessions in check. So he sent a squad down there just before the show was to go on. Just to hold it up. And a lotta the musicians there got sorta terrified. They came up to Diz and said they wanted to search him, his trumpet case, and everything. And he says, 'You're gonna hold up all these people and take me downtown, hold up all these people?' That stopped that one. So under fire, Dizzy doesn't rattle at all. That's really good.

"Once in New York at Birdland, they had a program: Bird, with strings, Coleman Hawkins with his combo, and Diz with his combo. The three of them. What a program! He saw to it that we got a table, one of those round tables, right, practically on the stage. So our whole group was sitting there, and Dizzy was playing with his combo. And as soon as he'd finished, he came down and sat with us for a moment. The main purpose was for us to show him the photos; there were multiple views of the head which hadn't been finished yet. So he said, 'Hey,' and he grabbed them and went back up on the stage, and he showed them to Charlie Parker, and Parker was evidently high as a kite at that point, as he generally was, and he flipped out over these photos. So he sits down in something of a lull, and he stretches them out on the music stand, and he starts to riff into the photos. Really going out, talking to Diz through the horn. That was only the beginning.

"It was time for Diz to go back on, and I saw somebody hand him something as he was going on stage, and he stuck them in his outside jacket pocket, bust pocket, in which he also had a handkerchief. So he's there playing, and he goes through one long number, and he's perspiring a lot so he pulls out the handkerchief, and out comes this bundle of sticks. And they fall on the stage—right plain out to see. Anyway, I was close enough to reach out, and this drummer who was sitting right at the next table saw them too, but I was closer. I said, 'Oh, boy, you don't know who's in that audience.' So I just reached out and tapped Diz on the shoe, and he looks down. And he stepped in front of them and then gives it a kick with his heel, and they go back to the piano player. And the piano player puts his foot in front of them, and when he has a chance, he reaches over and picks them up. Somehow, they circuitously get back to Dizzy. So comes the lull, Diz says, 'Hey, come here, to Charlie and me.' So we made our way through the crowd. In the meantime, Billie Holiday was there at the bar with a bandana on her head. They'd prevailed on her to come sing. So I was in a great group. As soon as she was over, we go out in the street, having picked up a couple of other friends and we stand in Fifty-eighth Street, and Diz takes the rubber band off of these things and starts passing these sticks around. Talk about cool. A couple of these characters almost froze because police cars came by, and we're standing there, a large group to be meeting on the corner, anyway, let alone what we're doing. And we're thinking we're all gonna be locked up for those same Js that dropped on the stage. Dizzy didn't care, and he's never been busted, only for fornication and bastardy. That was a wild evening.

"Back to the studio. When we first started the larger bust, I didn't have a chair, a proper chair—a high chair—a sitter's chair. So I had a footlocker; we put a regular chair on this footlocker. The legs just fit. And I had a regular stand, a tripod; I was working on it with water clay. And Dizzy gets carried away laughing as only he can. He leaned back and it didn't quite work out right. He threw his hand out and hit the armature holding the bust, and the bust started to go over. So I had a choice of which one to grab. My impulse was . . . It was a frightening moment, see, but I was closer to the clay model, so I grabbed that. And Dizzy actually did a complete backward somersault. Then he got up and sorta just dusted himself off and put the chair back on the footlocker. That's show biz.

"An amusing thing happened when Diz played a concert at Carnegie Hall, and we had pictures of the bust blown up to full poster size to put on the outside in the cases. It had just been finished from the foundry. Dizzy wanted to get ahold of it, and I went down to the foundry and then brought it into Carnegie Hall. Then I went to see Diz; he was rehearsing backstage and the workmen were all setting up recording equipment. After rehearsals, I was talking to a group, and he said, 'Did you see that?' They took Andrew Carnegie's bust off his pedestal, and they put mine on!' This was one of the thrills of his life, I think. 'Gillespie Hall.' He got a big kick out of it."

Some time later I happened to be in Tulsa, Oklahoma, during World Series time, and there's a friend of mine from New York who's originally from Tulsa and he was visiting there at the time. He called and said, "Hey, Diz, are you looking at the World Series?" At that time the colored hotel didn't have televisions in the rooms. He said, "The World Series is on. You wanna come over? I've got a friend. This lady is a divorcée and she's got a lotta money. Come over here and have something to eat and look at the World Series."

I said, "O.K., I'm gonna bring my camera." So I took my camera and I went over there. And it was hot! You know Oklahoma can get awful hot, and so I was in my Tee shirt walking out in the yard and having lemonade, understand. So one of the neighbors saw me over there and called the policemen. We were taking pictures. You know, the girls were in bathing suits. They certainly weren't nude.

They said, "Some niggah's over there taking nude pictures of white women." Now, in the meantime, her nephew, who's about fifteen was driving the car, her car, and the police got at him. Instead of stopping, he just kept on. He was up to ninety-five, a hundred, like that. Finally, they caught him, and they asked him about it, and he made a statement that his aunt had "colored guests" in the house, that's why he was speeding.

After the game was over, I went back to the hotel, and was sitting out in front and a colored guy walked up. "You Mr. Gillespie?"

I said, "Yeah."

He showed me his badge and said, "The district attorney and the chief of police would like to speak to you down at City Hall."

"Is this an arrest?" I asked.

"No, they'd just like to speak to you."

"Well, do you mind if I go upstairs and put up my camera?"

"No, go ahead, I'll wait here for you."

I went upstairs and put up my camera and came back and went with him. When we got to police headquarters and I walked in, this cracker said, "I understand you've been taking some *pictures* today."

"Is there any law against taking photographs?"

"We want 'em."

"Well, you're the authorities," I said, "and there are ways and means of getting anything you want. There are such things as search and seizure laws, another thing such as warrants. Things like that to get what the authorities must have if they are trying to prosecute a case."

He said, "Well, we are prepared for that."

I knew they were. He probably had the warrant under his desk blotter so I said, "Look, I have nothing to hide. You may have the pictures. Send him over with me, and I can go in and pick them up."

So the colored guy and I got in the car. He said, "What's all that shit about?" He didn't even know why he was coming to get me.

I said, "Boy, you're a dumb muthafucka. They send you over to pick up somebody, and you don't even know what they're sending you for. I could have been a murderer. When you walked up to me and said, 'I'm the law,' I could have blowed your head off, and you wouldn't have known a thing."

The cat started getting mad; not with me, with the white man. He said, "You know, you're right."

"You're damned right, man. Them muthafuckas could have had you killed out here. I could have been a desperado." I went upstairs and picked out one of those little cartridges from about seventy or eighty of them up there, just reached in and grabbed one. Probably some pictures I took in Brazil. "Here, have these developed." Just laid that on them, and they cut me loose. But this colored guy was *mad* because it was dangerous sending him out like that without him knowing why. He told me later, "Man, I was so proud of you when you told them peckawoods about search and seizure laws. We don't have many of us down here that know about these things."

I said, "Yeah, I know about them. I don't wanna get beat up or nothin' like that, but I know." It's according to how you talk to people. If you speak intelligently, generally they'll treat you that way, when you know your rights. I was glad to get outta Tulsa. We only had one more day there, but there were many experiences like that, that would happen accidentally. Of course I'm much too easygoing for it to have been a conspiracy against me personally, just for blacks in general.*

---

* Monk was arrested the same week in Delaware with Nica. They impounded her Rolls-Royce, because I think someone had a little smoke in the car. But there's a big amount of jealousy involved against performers. Some white women were just dying to get near you, especially in those times when black men were very taboo. Law enforcement officers had a great deal of personal jealousy toward you. In the Tulsa case the newspapers said I'd been subpoenaed to testify in the trial of this woman for contributing to the delinquency of a minor, the woman's nephew.

Bendin' the Horn

The truth is that the shape of my horn was an accident. I could pretend that I went into the basement and thought it up, but it wasn't that way. It was an accident. Actually, I left my horn on a trumpet stand and someone kicked it over, and instead of just falling, the horn bent. I was playing at Snookie's on Forty-fifth Street, on a Monday night, January 6, 1953. I had Monday nights off, but it was my wife's birthday so we had a party and invited all the guys—Illinois Jacquet, Sarah Vaughan, Stump 'n Stumpy, and several other artists, all the people who were in show business who knew Lorraine from dancing. They were down there having a good time and the whiskey was flowing. They had a cake and drinks and everything. This guy, Henry Morgan, who had his own show in New York, invited me to come on his show and be interviewed. This was really another put-on because he wasn't really interested in music. Anyway, I went out to be interviewed; he was doing the show from a hotel around the corner. My horn was still straight when I left it on one of those little trumpet stands that sticks straight up.

When I got back to the club after making this interview, Stump 'n Stumpy had been fooling around on the bandstand, and one had pushed the other, and he'd fallen back onto my horn. Instead of the horn just falling, the bell bent. Nine hundred and ninety-nine times out of a thousand if someone fell on a horn, it would bend the valves or maybe hit and bend the valve case. The horn would be dented, and the valves would stick, but this horn bent. When I got back, the bell was sticking up in the air. Illinois Jacquet had left. He said, "I'm not going to be here when that man comes back and sees his horn sticking up at that angle. I ain't gonna be here when that crazy mutha-fucka gets back."

When I came back, it was my wife's birthday and I didn't wanna be a drag. I put the horn to my mouth and started playing it. Well, when the bell bent back, it made a smaller hole because of the dent. I couldn't get the right sound, but it was a strange sound that I got from that instrument that night. I played it, and I liked the sound. The sound had been changed and it could be played softly, very softly, not blarey. I played it like that the rest of the night, and the next day I had it straightened out again. Then I started thinking about it and said, "Wait a minute, man, that was something else." I remembered the way the sound had come from it, quicker to the ear—to my ear, the player. A forty-five-degree angle is much closer than ninety degrees. I contacted the Martin Company, and I had Lorraine, who's also an art-ist, draw me a trumpet at a forty-five-degree angle and sent it to the Martin Company. I told them, "I want a horn like this."

"You're crazy!" they said.

"O.K.," I said, "I'm crazy, but I want a horn like this." They made me a trumpet and I've been playing one like that ever since. At first they made it so the bell would screw in at forty-five degrees. Now, we've developed it to where it's all in one piece.* One of the things a horn like mine remedies is the problem of holding your instrument too far down when you're reading music. You can never hold this horn down low enough for the bell of it to be below the music stand. Also, in small clubs, you'd be playing right up on people, and a trumpet is a very forceful instrument. If it's played straight at you, it can bust someone's eardrum if you play a hard note in the upper register. My instrument, when you hit a note, Bam! You hear it right then, instead of waiting. It's only a split second, but that split second means a lot.

HAROLD "STUMPY" CROMER (comedian):

"Stump and I did comedy, singing and dancing, and the type of comedy we did was sort of like dialogue and dialect. I was like the

---

* A guy in France named DuPont invented a trumpet with a bell raised a little like mine in the 1860s. That's why I couldn't get a complete patent on my horn. He patented a horn with the bell slightly raised. It was a big one, looked like a fluegelhorn.

'proper' guy, you know. I was the 'proper' black. And that's the way we performed. We showed two sides of the 'colored' man, as they called them in those days, or the Negro. I was always the upright guy, and Stump was like the fella who was not supposed to know anything. But then he always came out with the positive or correct answers. Whatever happened in the newspaper, or on radio, that was blown up and big, we would immediately jump on it, without any rehearsals. We had what you call 'improvs,' and we'd get laughs. That's how Dizzy's trumpet got sort've smashed up. Because we were up there doing 'oo-bop-she-bop-oo-bada . . .' singing, and Stump used to do a bit. He was supposed to be giving his impression of Louis Armstrong, and I wouldn't give him a chance to get into it.

"Stump started doing his Louis Armstrong impression, with the handkerchief hanging down, and he put it down on a little stand. It stood straight up. So Stump would always push me. If anyone's seen Stump 'n Stumpy, you know he'd push me back, and as we're feinting around, he pushed me back, and bam! As the horn hit the stand, the bell bent. So we said, 'Oh, my God . . .' Stump grabbed it and played some bugle things, and some notes came out of it. 'So some air can get through,' he said.

"I said, 'Yeah, well, it'll be a lot of hot air coming out.' We threw out a whole bunch of lines which were to delight them, but then we had trepidation as to how Dizzy was gonna feel because we knew he had the balance of the evening to play. And since he was the only trumpeter, there was no other trumpet for him to get immediately.

"So when he did come back, we didn't mention that the trumpet had been turned up in the fashion that it was. And Dizzy, being such a wonderful guy and a wonderful sport, comically tried it. When it was time for him to play, he just jumped up there and he played it, and music came out. He says, 'Oh, my . . .' So we all laughed it off. He said, 'Man, you could keep on playing a trumpet like this.' And we had a whole bunch of laughs. There were a lot of lines thrown around about it, but he played it all night.

"And then we sat down real seriously, and I said, 'Well, it's quite possible . . . maybe you can introduce it to Selmer.'

"Diz said, 'I don't know.' In other words that conversation was like finished, but then I noticed later on when I saw Diz, he had his trumpet already designed and made up like that, and he was playing it on dates. Then he was invited on television shows describing the trumpet and how it came about. It was a fantastic night, and the trumpet, to me, you know, it sounded even better. He didn't get angry. Diz said, 'No, man, this is great; I can still play from it.' It might have given him the incentive to try to make it sound like a trumpet. And with ease he played it normally with his jaws, you know how he pushes his jaws out and his neckline. And he just went with ease. And the air flowed as it's supposed to go, straight out; it went up in the air, and the sound came out. So it was fantastic."

JAMES "STUMP" CROSS (comedian):

"Well, I'd been drinking. I leaned back on the stand, and as I leaned, I leaned on Dizzy's trumpet. And the bell shot up in the air, and Lorraine shouted, 'Play it! Don't do nothing, play it!'

"And I'm saying, 'How's he gonna play that thing that's bent up there?' and I'm trying to apologize to Dizzy, and she's talking about, 'Play it!' He started playing and played the most unforgettable notes you ever heard on, 'I Can't Get Started With You.' On that horn with the bell turned up, and that was a beauty.

"Diz was there. He was there. He was standing next to me. Leroy Myers, my home boy, was sitting down in front; he left me because of what I'd done. He said, 'Oh, man, you jive . . .'

"Oh, he was excited. He was excited about it in the beginning because James Moody looked at him and said, 'Man, he done bent your horn.' The horn was on a stand, and as I leaned with my left hand—I'm left-handed, and I always lean that way; I lean left-handed—I leaned on it, and the horn shot up this way. I didn't fall, just leaned back, and the horn bent in the middle; it shot up. And Lorraine called from the back and said, 'Play it!' And he played it. And you know he left me—Leroy left me; Dizzy left me. I lost friends that night. But now I got friends again. That's what happened. That's what really went on."

CHARLES COOK:

"I was there that night, but everybody was drinking. Who broke the horn? They put it on Stump. Stump's drunk, he probably don't know himself who broke it. But I know when Dizzy came back, he didn't go crazy. It's probably gonna boil down to the butler did it. Stump was there; he got accused of it, so he goes to jail for it. He was like a dog. Dizzy puts it on Stump. He laid it on him. Stump was just the outcast. The only drag was Stump. 'You done broke the man's horn.'"

Yeeeah, Man! A lotta accidents happen when you're drunk. One time I almost got killed at Snookie's. There was a guy named Chink, who's dead now. But, man, I was juiced, and he hit me. I didn't even know who hit me, but he hit me in the lip. Boy, I had a lip! I went home and my lip was hanging down. He would have walked in my face if somebody hadn't restrained him. How did it happen? I'm drunk! How the hell do I know? Down at Birdland one time, I came home all bloody. Somebody hit me in the head with a bottle. I don't know what happened then either. Being drunk you don't know what happens. They tell me, another time, somebody took a knife off of me. I used to carry a knife, and I'm juiced enough to reach in my back pocket to get my knife and cut somebody. If the guy had held his neck out there, I was so juiced, I probably couldn't have cut him. Happily, the guy took my knife and gave it to Moody. The most trouble I've ever been in is when I've had some of that juice in me. So I decided to leave it alone.

Bird and Diz

We never seriously thought about getting a group together with Charlie Parker again because Yard was a leader himself. He had his own quintet with Miles, Max, Tommy Potter, and Duke Jordan. People paint a picture of Yard as the tortured genius bedeviled by his problems with drugs and alcohol, but on the JATP tour, during the fifties, he acted like a gentleman. He made all the gigs. He didn't mess up, maybe because they treated him right for a change. Yeah, I think the cause of his problem was the way he was treated. Here's a guy with a very high sense of music, a guy who was a genius, and they treated him like a Yardbird, like he wasn't anything. I think that could have been the cause for some of his actions and his involvement with narcotics and drinking. I don't think the other view is an accurate picture of him because he was full of life, just full of life.

HAROLD "STUMPY" CROMER:

"One night we were going by Snookie's, the same crowd, Sarah, Stump, and I, we always hung out together. Charlie Parker was at Birdland. So we'd gone to see Dizzy and said, 'Hey, Man, let's go on by and see Charlie Parker between sets, O.K.?' So we walked from

Snookie's to Birdland, and Diz had taken his trumpet along. We walked on over there, and as we got downstairs little Peewee Marquette was there to greet us. Charlie Parker was leaning between the piano crease. The piano was a Baby Grand, and he was just leaning there, and another person was playing a solo, another trumpeter. And Diz said, 'Watch this . . .' and he opened up the trumpet bag and pulled it out. He put his mouthpiece in it and played some hot licks over the trumpeter who was doing something, went way up in the air, 'weee-do-be-do . . .'

"Charlie Parker went up and said, 'do-be-do-do-be-do . . .' then they went at it with fours and eights, and it was fantastic, from the door all the way up to the stage, and the people were screaming. It was a fantastic night."

MARION "BOO" FRAZIER:

"In Birdland, I'd never seen anything like it, the way their thoughts were the same, you know. Charlie Parker would end his solo on one particular note, and John would start his solo on the same note and go into something else. I've never seen anything like that. Just great! Guys try to play like that, like John and Charlie Parker. Charlie Parker was a nice man, by the way. He was really a nice person. Besides his music, what impressed me the most was his quietness. He wasn't a loud man. He was just quiet. It was funny. I had met him up at John's house one day, and I didn't know he was Charlie Parker. Then the very next day I was downtown in New York, and he walked up to me and he said, 'I'm Charlie Parker and I met you at Dizzy's house yesterday.' Boy, I was stunned. I had a friend—girl with me, you know, and she was a jazz fan—and I was really stunned. That really knocked me out, man. Then he said, 'It's good to see you again, enjoy yourself, have a nice day.'

"And I said, 'My God. Gee!' I did get a chance to meet Charlie Parker. I got a chance to know Billie Holiday and Dinah. I got a chance to meet a lot of people who were in the forties. And what people! I'm just sorry that the young kids today don't get a chance to see those entertainers because they were not only entertainers, they were true people. They were great onstage, but they were greater offstage. That was just one part of it. The people in show business today are onstage twenty-four hours. Even when they're offstage, they're onstage. There's a difference between them and the people in the forties. They really had something going, and I'm glad I had a chance to see the difference between the two."

Just before Yard died in 1955, he came up to me. Boy, I'll never forget this. I was playing at Birdland; Benny Goodman was playing at Basin Street East, down in the basement on Fifty-second Street, off Broadway. So between sets I went down there because Charlie Shavers was playing with him at the time. And I was standing outside, and some white guy asked me, "You gonna get up there and play some?"

"Play what, man? I don't play for free. . . ."

"Not even with the 'King'?" he said.

"What 'King'?" I said. "I played with all the Kings . . ." and started naming Coleman Hawkins, Benny Carter, Charlie Parker, Ben Webster, Chu Berry, Art Tatum, Earl Hines. I said, "I've been with all the kings, brother." Must have been impressive, that shut him up. And that night, Yard was in the audience, and he came over to me, and we were talking, and he said, "Save me . . ." Only that one time, just before he died. Gee, Yard was looking bad, man, fat. He walked up to me and said, "Diz, why don't you save me?"

And I saw the expression on his face. It was a pained expression on his face, and I didn't know what to say. I said, "What could I do?"

He said, "I dunno but just save me, save me, man."

I didn't know what to do. I just didn't know what to say to that man. I didn't know what to say because I already had my group, and he was just jobbing around. He wasn't doing too well. Maybe I shoulda. That woulda been the moment to get back together, I think, but I already had my group and we were on this level, and I didn't think anything of it, too much, because he'd been doing his thing. Right after that, he died. We never played together again.

It hit me pretty hard. I really took that one, but I don't feel that I let him down in any way, not necessarily. When a dude is using drugs, no one can help him. You have to have that determination to pull yourself up. Because regardless of how much someone does try to help you, if you've got in your mind to keep using, it doesn't matter. Drug addicts don't have any sense of, well, there's a guy helping me, maybe I ought to straighten up. They gotta wanna straighten up themselves. And they do it alone. There are many musicians who have kicked the habit and gone straight ahead. So I knew that you had to do it yourself. When he said, "Save me," what came to my mind was if we could get back together, we'd go someplace and have a contract for five guys, and there'd only be four of us there, just like when I took him to California and paid for six guys instead of five, figuring that sometimes he might not be there. It seemed logical to me to have someone who played a little less and was there all the time than to have this super-super-duper guy who sometimes wouldn't be there, and you'd have to go through a bunch of changes. So I didn't want to.

Probably, as soon as he died, Nica called me and said, "Yardbird just died in my apartment."

I said, "It's done . . . ?" No, I couldn't believe it, but it was the truth. That broke me up. I couldn't help it. I had to go down in the basement and cry. I didn't expect for him to die like that. It was a big shock, a great shock to me. It hit me so hard because we were so close, man. We weren't associated musically at the time, but I still had this strong feeling toward Charlie Parker and just couldn't take it when he died. It was such a big shock, I went downstairs and had my little thing, got red-eyed crying and came upstairs.

Charlie was closely associated with three women at that time. He was living with Chan and had a wife, Gerri, who was in jail in Washington. He had Doris. Everybody was wondering what to do with his compositions, so we formed a committee to try and salvage something and put it all together. There was Hazel Scott, Maely Dufty, Charlie Mingus, Mary Lou Williams, me, and a lawyer who was in charge. We started getting together discussing what to do with his body. The body was in the funeral home and they couldn't get it out. They had a big mix-up about the body and were getting ready to bury him up here, but there was some discussion about sending it to Kansas City. They didn't have any money to send it to Kansas City, and at this meeting in the lawyer's office they asked me, "What should we do?"

I said, "Well, let me call up Norman Granz." I called Norman and told him there wasn't enough money to bury Charlie, and that his mother wanted to bury him in Kansas City, and Chan wanted to bury him in New York next to his child, out on Long Island.

Norman said, "I'll tell you what. You go and find out what it is, and if his mother wants the body, just put the body on the plane and send it there, and send me the bill." So we went there—the committee—and had the body released, and we sent Norman the bill. Norman Granz paid for shipping him to Kansas City to his mother for burial. It sounded logical to me that since his wives had him all the time he was alive, after he'd died, since he predeceased his mother, he should have reverted back to her, in Kansas City. So we sent the body to Kansas City to be buried.

MARY LOU WILLIAMS:

"The world doesn't know what part Dizzy played when Charlie Parker died. If it hadn't been for him, that poor boy would probably be a cadaver or something, because nobody knew he was dead, and they were taking him to Bellevue Hospital. Dizzy got wind of it and he started to act immediately. He said, 'Charlie's dead. I gotta do something for him.' And this boy worked so damned hard. I'm telling you, it was really a shame; it kind of interfered with his work. So Lorraine thought it was best for him not to continue with it. So he brought it to me, and I got in touch with Adam Powell and Hazel Scott, and they grabbed ahold of it.

"This poor boy, Dizzy, went to Philadelphia seven o'clock at night and he did a concert there. I think he was in a nightclub. However, he raised a thousand dollars, and he came back and said, 'Now, Lou, you keep this. I don't know what to do with the money. 'Cause I know that you're honest.' He trusted me with it and he put $100 of his own money in it. He worked so damn hard, and if it hadn't been for him, we wouldn't have been able to do the concert. By the way, we raised $16,000 you know. I read a story about Charlie Parker that says it was $5,000. We raised $16,000, and everybody kept pinching off it and what not. It was at the union, and they wanted me to come down to the union and get it, and I wouldn't do it, and the money disappeared. I don't know who got ahold of it, but if it hadn't been for Dizzy, you wouldn't ever hear about Charlie Parker now. Because nobody liked Charlie Parker by that time. When I had to go to the agents to collect money—I collected quite a bit of money, maybe two or three thousand dollars—they were mad. They were calling him all kinds of dirty names, and the managers said, 'Mary, the only reason why we're giving you this money is because we believe in you, and we know you're honest and you're a nice person. But we don't give a damn about Charlie Parker.' It seems like when he died, he was just down to the lowest. Nobody liked him; he'd made a lot of enemies, you know. And so what Dizzy did helped him.

"I had just come back from Europe. I remember my brother came to me and said he saw Charlie Parker going into the Harlem Hospital. He had been sick. My brother always helped musicians, nobody knows it, and he said, 'Mary, you better do something about Charlie Parker; he's hungry, hungry and—'

"So I said, 'Well, tell him to call me.' And when he went to the baroness first and he was on his way to a job in Boston, it was two places—my house—and he stopped by the baroness', and that's when he died. He had promised to come up here; I was gonna give him some money. He looked so bad, he was so down, nobody would give him work. He had asked me to get a band with him and all that. So Dizzy did everything to help Charlie Parker. After he'd died, he said, 'Well, we can't leave him down there in Bellevue.'

"It's a shame, you better write it up right, because if it wasn't for Dizzy Gillespie, nobody would hear anymore about Charlie Parker—

did you hear me? How hard that man worked to get that guy buried.
He didn't have a quarter. And nobody's mother had anything. . . .
That poor boy stayed up from seven until seven in the morning and
raised $1,000 and gave it to the fools and the money disappeared. I
just found a receipt for the money that I turned in and showed it to
Lorraine this year. And they stole it. I can name some big-name people who took the money, went down to the union, took it, and spent it.
After we paid expenses we had $12,000 left, and that disappeared. In
this book, they said $5,000 was raised. We raised $16,000. They told
me—they called me from the union and told me to come and get that
'bad luck money.'

"I said, 'Why do you call it bad luck? I can't do that.'

"They said, 'Well, somebody has got to come and get it out,' because they'd been having a lot of trouble since they had that money
down there. So two members of the committee went down, and nobody's seen the money since. Dizzy couldn't handle it; he turned it
over to us, and we went on through with it, with Mingus, Maely
Dufty, and Hazel Scott. We did the concert. Dizzy ain't gonna say
nothing. He started the whole thing, but just let me tell it. It would be
better for me to tell the truth of it."

MAX ROACH:

"When we discussed Charlie Parker, and Dizzy's anger, or remorse
at losing Charlie Parker at such an early age, this goes beyond a personal level to the music which is what Dizzy is all about. He really is
about preserving and perpetuating black music, I mean 100 per cent,
and expanding and broadening its horizons. I know that we argue because I maintain that society is largely responsible for Bird's demise.
Dizzy maintains that Bird should've been stronger than to let them destroy him like that, at such an early age. He just discounts this society.
But you see Dizzy is a very strong person to have survived in this kind
of society with all of the pressures on him. It would be on a political
basis that we argue because I look into the society, and I say that
some of us might not have the kind of resilience and strength that
Dizzy might have and Charlie Parker was surely one of them. There
was no way that we could have saved Bird unless, perhaps, we shel-
tered him in some kind of environment that would bring him back to
himself before he got completely fed up with this situation, which is
basically what it was, and developed a kind of 'Shit, I don't give a
fuck about it anymore' attitude. Our arguments would come just on
that political level. He would be too hard on a person who didn't survive. If we do argue, I'm saying it is over losing someone as valuable

to us as Charlie Parker and why—what happened that he should die at thirty-four.

"That's how close they were and that's how much Dizzy loved Bird and how much Bird loved him. He hated the whole scene, man, but Dizzy just cannot stand weakness of any kind. And he may not project this attitude, but it is there. He just can't stand any kind of weakness, any kind at all. This leads me sometimes to believe that he will take any kind of position for his survival excepting sacrificing his own integrity. This is why I say Dizzy is a 'fox.' He is not going to sacrifice his musical integrity, but he is determined to survive out in this shit, in this maze that black folks have to do, and especially when you're dealing with black culture, because culture is such a powerful weapon. When the musicologists break down Dizzy's contribution, they are going to see the kind of intellect that prevails inside the black psyche.

"Afro-American music was here, and no one recognized it more than people like Bird and Diz. They knew that the music is here, and they would hope to add maybe a page to the history that's already been laid down by their predecessors, understand. And so that's the thing they had in common. That's how they worked. They worked hard for that. Duke Ellington had that in common with them. All the serious people also had that in common about the music, which has its own character and its own personality now. It's the child of everybody who's seriously interested in and engaged in the music.

"On the other hand the difference in the way Bird perceived himself spiritually and the way Dizzy perceived himself spiritually, I believe may be the difference. But both of them demonstrate something that I see as very important. Like Bird's statements were always that the government is responsible for the black people. He'd walk down Harlem streets and say, 'Why do you think we've got two bars on every street? Why is it that we can cop drugs anytime we want to? You can buy drugs and whiskey before you can buy milk.' That was his political and social perception of what was going on. When Bird died at thirty-four, Diz was about the same age. Diz was big too, at the same time. The spotlight was on him. So we then should perceive them positively as teaching two different lessons, actually. That shit does exist. There is a concentrated effort to destroy black folks. Billie Holiday I would give credit for that, too. Dizzy's concentrated effort is like Duke's: that you can survive that, and they epitomize that.

"Never a tragedy, that was Bird's thing—that there was no such thing as a tragedy. Bird didn't *die;* it's not a tragedy. Billie Holiday's life wasn't a tragedy. In the Western sense, it was a tragedy because they looked at it as a death, in the most materialistic way. 'Look at all the money Bird could've made. Look what he could've done for himself. He

could have had everything.' Bird stuck his fingers up his ass to the society; Lady Day did, too. Now that's integrity of another sort and
has to be perceived like that. Incidentally, this is where Dizzy and I
argue because he perceives that as a weakness. He says, 'No, that's
bullshit, man. They aren't supposed to let that shit affect them.'

"And I say, it says something, but we have to educate our people to
what it says. It's like that, man, a young Buddhist monk pouring oil on
himself and burning a match. 'Sure I got a lotta talent, and I'm not
gonna let you exploit it.'

"'Kiss my ass!' is the way Bird perceived it within himself, I believe, from just knowing him. The way Dizzy perceives it is another
way. He's gonna run like Jim Brown and shake off the tacklers, keep
on going. Now he's aware, just look at his background, he comes from
South Carolina. Life for Dizzy has never been easy. He understands
the whole game of how blacks are being ripped off by whites. So he
doesn't talk about it, but he uses music as his particular weapon. It always appears that Dizzy in fact is the most liberal person, it always
appears like that, but when you look into the music and listen to what
he is playing, he is screaming out there. The fact that he would get in
front of a big band and dance instead of standing up there with a
baton and the way he directs that band, is black. People are always
saying, 'Oh, man, that Dizzy Gillespie is a Bahai; he loves all people,'
but when you look at him culturally, he is heavily steeped in black
music, and when he makes a contribution, it's blacker than black, or
even blacker."

NORMAN GRANZ (impresario):

"I think much of the credit was given to Bird to the exclusion of
Dizzy, which I think is not only unfair, but inaccurate. Everybody
seems to think that Dizzy was 'the trumpet player' with Charlie
Parker. That's nonsense. It's true that they played together, and
maybe Bird came up with things that the public, or critics, or whatever regard as terribly important, which I do, too, but not to the exclusion of Dizzy. I think that's ridiculous. And, moreover, Dizzy had certain qualities which Bird never could have had. Dizzy, for instance, put
together an incredible big band because Dizzy's a leader, which Bird
never could've done. I hate to compare the two. I don't mean to get
into that, but Bird was totally individual, for himself and playing with
himself in the sense of a very small group. Whereas Dizzy was at
home with a small group, or a big band, but particularly with the big
band he had. That's one of the rare, rare things that happened in
music, what he put down with that band for the short time that it was
together.

"The other thing that Dizzy has done more than any musician: He's done more to investigate other rhythm patterns, particularly Brazilian and Latin American rhythms, than any jazz man has, much more. He was into it with Chano Pozo, when he did 'Manteca' in the forties. Thirty years ago, he was into that. I did some things with Machito, and then with Bird; at that time Dizzy wasn't recording for me. But Dizzy knew what was happening there and continues to; he was really the one that got away from traditional jazz patterns. Birks was an important man there, and he's had an effect on all kinds of musicians. He's one of the few leaders too that I've watched, whether it be with small or large groups, who can go over to the rhythm section and show them what he wants done. You know, he's a rounded musician. He can sit down at the piano and pick out the chords for somebody. A lot of musicians just do what *they* do.

"Another thing about Dizzy which I like is that he's adventuresome. He takes chances, and I like that. I mean, he'll try everything. And if he falls on his face, which is rare, but if he does, that's all right. Every artist has to experiment."

GEORGE WEIN:

"Dizzy, while a rebel against society, at the same time knew he had to deal with society and dealt with it well, and has continued to deal with it, and has done more for making contemporary jazz palatable. I'm not talking about the public now; I'm talking on a much higher level that the people who can hire jazz musicians can relate to. Dizzy did more to help modern jazz and contemporary music than any other person alive. Because people were afraid of it. Nightclub owners, I'm not talking about myself, although I'm involved. But Dizzy has a way of communicating with people. He still does. I don't believe in this business, but to accentuate what I'm trying to say, Dizzy's a Libra. So Libras are supposed to look at things from both sides, supposed to weigh the scales and the balance of things. Well, if you believe in that sort of thing, Dizzy does that.

"In his looking at things from both sides it was easy for him to communicate with a lot of nightclub owners that might've been turned off by Bird because of 'Bird is a junkie . . . and Bird has problems . . . Bird doesn't make time, etc.' Dizzy—don't push him around or he'll push your right back, but at the same time recognize that the guy is in business and has to run a business. He also could talk to the guy, and the guy felt that Dizzy related to his problems. And to this day, Dizzy's like that. If you call Dizzy and say, 'Diz, I got a problem,' Dizzy's listening. He doesn't shut off when you have a problem. So he understands that, give and take.

"And at the same time that Dizzy came along, musicians were going through very serious changes. Narcotics was a very big thing and a 'new' thing related to the 'new' music. A lot of people wouldn't touch it because of that. I mean our established nightclubs would not touch the new music because of the narcotics problems. To them musicians had only been drinkers or smoked pot, and it left a very heavy influence on the music scene. And it was very difficult to overcome that. If anybody did what he could do to overcome it, the single most important person was Dizzy Gillespie. He improved the acceptance of the musicians. Dizzy is very important in that respect, and he did it in a natural way. Others did it in other ways. John Lewis came along with the Modern Jazz Quartet several years later and did it on a very dignified level. But that was not as real as Dizzy's was, 'cause Dizzy never compromised. Dizzy was always Dizzy. This was just his way. And his way, people could relate to. Of the people in this business, Dizzy has as high a degree of integrity as any musician I know."

BUDD JOHNSON:

"I remember, just as clear, there was a booking agent from William Morris, Billy Shaw. When Charlie and Dizzy split up, Billy Shaw used to come around to all the guys, saying, 'Man, yeah, Dizzy's taking Charlie's style.' You know, he wanted to get the sanction of the musicians to say that Charlie Parker was the one that originated this style. And he said, 'I'm gonna take this cat and straighten him out and get him out there.' First thing he did was to give Charlie a Cadillac, the one he was gonna get rid of anyway, you know. He was trying to get his confidence and to sign him up and so he gave Charlie Parker a Cadillac. Then he got Charlie out there, and Charlie, of course, deserved everything. He deserved the name that he made, and he was fantastic. He changed all of the saxophonists' style; altos, tenors, and everybody was trying to play like Charlie. But Charlie being like what he was, like under the influence of drugs and what not, just simply . . . He got so that he wasn't dependable. He couldn't, you know. The drugs come first. So he would be late on jobs. He would do things. He would be like out of it sometimes. So these offices began to put him down, and Dizzy is going on all the time. See, Dizzy has a very wonderful wife. I gotta give her a lotta credit for holding him together. They've been together, oh, for years and years. And she's probably got one of the first dollars he made. You know, like, she's a very good woman for Dizzy. So this kept Dizzy together.

"He could have been pretty wild, but I don't think he would have ever gone into the drug situation. Like, I never did, but we've seen it; we've been around it and everything. And from me seeing what happened to people, I don't see how anybody could jump up and start to going into the mainline. Like, it's a pitiful thing. Well, anyway, this was Bird's downfall.

"Bird used to say, 'Well, Budd, I can't do nothing! I can't do nothing! I'm going up to the office and see can I get some money.' And he'd go up into the office, and they'd say, 'Well, he's in a conference now.' And Bird would sometimes sit up there for three and four hours. And then finally they'd say, 'You still here? Well, what do you want, man?'

"Bird would say, 'Well, I need some money.'

"'I'm sorry . . .' They'd give him ten or fifteen dollars. And this bugged Bird. This really bugged him. He had a lotta responsibilities."

BENNY CARTER:

"Charlie Parker was very serious, maybe even a little more serious than Dizzy. But Dizzy's seriousness was maybe a little bit deeper down because he had that humor thing. I think, probably, he's a more easy laugher than Charlie. Yeah, yeah, but I dunno what else, really."

LORRAINE GILLESPIE:

"That's the only time I've ever seen Dizzy sad. Only when his mama died and when Charlie Parker died. Oh, those were two pretty sad times. If he was sad, he didn't let nobody know. You'll never see Dizzy worried or sad. Never. He don't care. I certainly have never seen him sad except for those two times, when Charlie Parker died and when his mother died and when he had to have an operation on his eyes. He wanted to get out of the hospital. When Charlie Parker died, he didn't say nothing. He just went on downstairs to the basement, we were living in Long Island, just went down there crying. He never said a word. I knew what he was crying for."

Yard married four or five times; I only married once. I don't know. I can see the similarities much more than I can dig dissimilarities. Perhaps he wasn't as strong. He had a softer personality, and mine was pretty hard. Why did he let it get to him while I didn't let it get to me? One of the reasons is I had a wife who was with me all the time and who was a stanch defender. So I had some help. Charlie didn't have any help; you see his wives thought they were doing him a favor by letting him do whatever he wanted to, just went along with it. My wife, Lorraine, would be the first one to criticize me if I was doing something that wasn't kosher. Fortunately, with Lorraine, I had someone in my corner who'd never allow me to fling myself right into the teeth of life. So in that way, I guess, Yardbird became a martyr for our music, and I became a reformer.

School for Jazz

Not long after Charlie Parker died, our efforts to establish a proper place in U.S. society and in the world for our music began to bear fruit. We started receiving more recognition from American musicians and musicologists who'd been interested before almost exclusively in symphonic music. They could see now, after jazz and classical musicians in Europe welcomed modern jazz with such enthusiasm, how vital as a creative force it was and how essential to the development of modern music of all kinds. Starting in the summer of 1955, I began playing at the Music Inn, or Barn, and teaching at the Lenox School of Jazz in Massachusetts, where they presented a full-fledged jazz concert series. I performed at the first of these concerts held at the Music Barn in an atmosphere that was just ideal for modern jazz, where musicians didn't have to compete with customers ordering drinks and were not to be pushed around musically to satisfy commercial demands. We also lived in a perfect setting for creating music at Tanglewood, the same place where the Boston Symphony spends its summers. We stayed in Wheatleigh Hall there, and I wrote a tune with that title that summer, just named it after the building where we had our quarters. This was a great improvement on the usual nightclub scene—a 136-acre wooded estate with pine trees and lakes—a place for calm reflection where musicians and students of modern jazz could learn more about themselves and each other and create more music. During my tenure, among the faculty were John Lewis, Milt Jackson, Max Roach, and George Russell—all formerly associated with me in the big band and other musical endeavors.

There's an old saying that jazz can't be taught and the idea behind the Lenox School of Jazz was to expose young players to essential elements of jazz that were not ordinarily taught in music schools. The students could learn composition and arranging, perform in large and small ensembles, and take private lessons with leading modern jazz musicians. The curriculum featured lectures regarding the history, social, and ethnic origins of our music, and the school received the financial support of several businesses, the economic fortunes of which were closely tied to a continued tradition of quality of jazz, such as Schaefer Beer, Associated Booking Corporation, Atlantic Records, United Artists Films, BMI, the Newport Jazz Festival, Norman Granz, and Sol Hurok, international jazz impresarios. A fund-raising concert given at the end of the three-week term by students and faculty provided additional funds for scholarships. We had students at the school for jazz from every state and from Africa, Brazil, Canada, Holland, and Turkey. Realizing, as Milt Jackson said, that we couldn't teach the students "soul," we concentrated on getting each student to find himself, to set and achieve his own musical goals, using the techniques we imparted insofar as these were helpful. We had a great co-operative experience—students, faculty, and supporters—that assured the future of modern jazz would be successful because we taught at least some basic techniques of it to younger musicians from around the world. The School of Jazz at Lenox was creative and therapeutic, notably for the faculty, many of whom felt tired of the grind of being on the road, rushing from one club to another. Yard would have enjoyed it had he lived.

Changes

Things were changing during the 1950s, but you still had to fight almost every step of the way and teach people. One good example of that is Miles. He found out that he was powerful enough to demand certain things and he got them. Miles was the first one to refuse to play "forty–twenty." In the old days, you would come into a club and you would play from twenty minutes after the hour to the end of the hour, and then you would come on twenty minutes later and so on. Miles broke that up. He came to Philadelphia once and told the owner he was going to play three shows. The owner didn't want to go for it, and Miles told him, "Well, then, you ain't got no deal." Now, musicians play only two shows a night in some places. Miles did a lot for musicians.

Norman Granz always tried to get the top soloists together in a package for a Jazz at the Philharmonic tour by calling up the people who he thought were the top instrumentalists on their respective instruments and offering them a lotta money. That's how he put it together. The first JATP concert I played at was in Los Angeles in 1946 with Charlie Parker, Willie Smith, and Lester Young, but the JATP tours really began for me in the fifties after the big band. JATP wasn't much musically because Norman Granz got his nuts off by sending two or three trumpet players out there to battle one another's brains out on the stage. And he'd just sit back and laugh. He'd get Flip Phillips, Illinois Jacquet, and Lester Young, then have Roy Eldridge and me as the two trumpet players. Sometimes it was Bill Harris on trombone and J. J. Johnson, and then they'd have a drum battle with Buddy Rich and Louis Bellson. It was funny, battling all the time. Norman had a weird sense of competition. He thought that the battle would not only be on the stage, but that the guys would have a funny feeling toward one another afterward. One time we went someplace on the train, and Norman said, "O.K., Herb Ellis and Ray Brown have this berth. . . ." He and Oscar Peterson shared a berth. Ella Fitzgerald would have a berth and Ella's maid would have one.

He named all these guys, just kept naming until, finally, I asked him, "Well, what about me and Roy?"

"You all wanna stay together?" he said, thinking that in the middle of the night I would jump down on Roy and stab him in his sleep.

I said, "Man, go ahead, we'll share it."

The importance of Jazz at the Philharmonic is that it was the original "first class" treatment for jazz musicians. Norman Granz gave jazz musicians "first class" treatment. You traveled "first class," stayed in "first class" hotels, and he demanded no segregation in seating. At least twice we got in trouble, in Texas and South Carolina. Norman insisted that tickets be sold without regard to race, first come, first served, and the authorities didn't like it in Charleston, South Carolina. We had a special chartered plane. Something happened with the promoter's license because it was a mixed audience. The local officials didn't like that, and Ella Fitzgerald's maid had to take all of the money and put it down her bosom and go to the plane. We had to sneak outta there because they didn't like it.

Once in Houston, Texas, I played with Illinois Jacquet, Ella Fitzgerald, Oscar Peterson, Ray Brown, Flip Phillips, Lester Young, and Buddy Rich; and the different races of people in the audience were sitting together. Between sets, we'd be in the back, shooting dice, playing cards, or whatever, and this time in Texas, all this money was on the floor, about $185. We were shooting dice in the dressing room; the dressing room door burst open. The police came in and took us all to jail, including Ella Fitzgerald. They took us down, finger-printed us, and put us in jail. Norman put up a bond and got us out. He just wouldn't be intimidated by these people. He spent a lotta money. He sent a lawyer down there to represent us, after we'd left, to beat the case. Of course we beat it because they had no business coming in our dressing room without a warrant. They just busted in and took the money that was on the floor. Ella had on a pretty blue taffeta gown and a mink stole and she was crying. She wouldn't say anything except that she was only having a piece of pie and a cup of coffee and watching us. They asked everybody their names, and I told them my name was "Louis Armstrong." I acted pretty smart.

NORMAN GRANZ:

"Well, the whole basis for forming Jazz at the Philharmonic was initially to fight discrimination. It wasn't formed just to do jazz concerts. I mean the whole reason for JATP, basically, was to take it to places where I could break it down, break down segregation and discrimination, present good jazz and make bread for myself and for the musicians as well. I felt that it made no kind of sense to treat a musician with any kind of respect and dignity onstage and then make him go around to the back door when he's offstage. I don't understand that treatment. So wherever we went, we stayed in the best hotels. We traveled the best way because I think that's all a part of it. Because it didn't make sense for me to get a cat to work for me at Carnegie Hall, and then after work, he goes to the Alvin Hotel. That doesn't make sense. He's supposed to be treated as a great artist on and off the stage. It wasn't only antiblack discrimination, it was discrimination against musicians. You'd come to a concert hall, and they'd think you came in off the street because you weren't either a classical musician or something that they understood. And I fought for it. I don't mean to be dramatic, but I insisted that my musicians were to be treated with the same respect as Leonard Bernstein or Heifitz because they were just as good, both as men and musicians. It took a long time to convince the concert halls, even though I was paying the rent. Pretty hard to get away from those prejudices. We had bad pianos; we had bad mikes; we had bad dressing rooms. I mean there was no reason in the world, when we'd go to those drag Middle Western cities that were prejudiced, why Dizzy couldn't stay in a white hotel with me. That didn't make sense. So we always stayed in the best hotels. I mean that's part of doing a show first-class; everybody had to go first-class.

"Well, Houston is a very southern city in more ways than one. In those days, it was a very tough city and very, very prejudiced, in many ways more so than Dallas, which wasn't too far away. Because Houston was a much tougher city and a much more prejudiced city and a much more racist city, it was a difficult city to break open.

"In any case I decided to take Jazz at the Philharmonic down there. And of course the first thing I'd do was rent the auditorium myself. Then I'd hire the ticket seller to sell tickets to my concert and tell him that there was to be no segregation whatsoever. Well, that was new for Houston. I removed the signs that said 'White toilets' and 'Negro toilets.' That was new. The whole idea was to break all that shit open. And even the ticket seller who worked for me was a Texan, and I knew he didn't have eyes to do what I'd asked him to do, but he was getting paid, so he had to. Of course I'd bring in a 'mixed' show. In those days, all my shows were mixed, not on purpose, but if a cat played, I don't care if he's green, black, or whatever. It so happened, most of my cats were black, but there were some white—Gene Krupa and people like that.

"Anyway, we got down there and I wanted to be sure we wouldn't have any problems at all, so I even hired local police, white, of course, to be sure there'd be no kinda problems. And some whites came out and said, 'This is mixed with blacks, and I don't wanna sit.' They'd say, 'Could I change my seat?'

"I'd say, 'No. Here's your money back. You sit where I sit you. If you say I don't like this seat because I can't hear, fine. But don't tell me there's a cat sitting next to you, and because he's black, you don't wanna sit there. You don't wanna sit there? Here's your money back.' We did everything we could, and of course I had a strong show. People wanted to see my show. People wanna see your show, you can lay some conditions down.

"Well, the show began. We had a double-header. There were some cats standing backstage, and one of my rules was never to let anybody backstage when my show was on. These were two or three white cats, and I asked them who they were. And they showed me their badges. They were like plainclothesmen, and they said, 'We like jazz. We just wanna watch the jazz concert.'

"So I said, 'O.K., if you stand back, that'll be all right.' And I think Krupa was playing at that time. Well, Prez and Illinois Jacquet and Birks started to play dice in Ella's dressing room. I mean the way musicians would do when they were wasting time because they didn't go on for another hour. And it was like for a dollar or something, just to waste the time. Ella was eating, and the woman who dressed her was there eating with her, because we had sent out for food for these people. We didn't have time to go eat. And all of a sudden, these cats break the door down. They didn't even . . . they coulda turned the handle. These three cats who were standing there . . . They came in with flashlights and guns drawn and all that bullshit. The same guys that said to me, 'Well, we're jazz fans.' They were police, of course, and they said, 'You're all under arrest for gambling!'

"Well, Ella, first of all, was eating, and her secretary was eating, and just these three cats were playing, and it was really jive. And I ran in when I heard the commotion; and I saw one of the cats go in the bathroom, the police. And I knew what it was then. I knew he was going to try and plant some shit. That's the first thing. That's for openers. Then it's easy, you see. 'Black musicians caught . . .' good headlines. So this cat said, 'What're you doing?'

"I said, 'I'm watching you.'

"'I oughta kill you,' he said, and he took his gun out and put it in my stomach. And this is in front of everybody, in front of Ella, in front of everyone.

"I said, 'Well, man, you've got the gun. If you wanna shoot me, there's nothing I can do about it.' But he was serious. So I said, 'What are you arresting me for?'

"'Well, you're the manager of the show,' he said, 'so you're running a gambling house.' The whole thing was just jive. The thing was that in the South they didn't like the idea that we'd 'mix' everything. Because that sets a precedent. That's the thing they were bugged about 'cause if you could prove that black and white could sit next to each other, you could break up a lotta that shit down there. All they wanted to do was create an incident. I mean, if they could've gotten us on drinking backstage, anything.

"'O.K., you're all under arrest,' the cat said, 'and we're taking you all down to the station.'

"And the manager, who's one of them, a Texan, came back down, so I said, 'Look, you have a packed house out there, and you have a packed house waiting to come in,' 'cause we sold that thing out, we locked it up. I said, 'You go out there and tell the people that the concert's finished, right now, and that the people can go on home, and there's no more concert, the second show, because we've been arrested by these police. And you can settle the riot that you're gonna have on your hands.' I said, 'Now you take it from here; I'm calling the show off, right now. You do what you want.' Now, since I owned the show and rented the house, it was my bread, so he couldn't very well sue me or anything. By the same token it wouldn't look very good on his track record if the manager should suddenly have a riot.

"So he said, 'Just a minute.' And he talked to the cat in the corner, and they finally got it together. He said, 'They'll take you down, now, between concerts. Finish this one, 'cause they're gonna have to book you, but they'll get you back in time for the second concert, see.'

"Well, they took us down there, and it was a very funny thing. All the newspaper photographers were down there. And you say, 'Well, how these cats know about this?' See, all that shit had been laid out, the newspaper photographers and everything else. And they did what they do like if you're caught parking. You post a bond and then you forfeit the bond, which is in other words, a fine.

"They said, 'We're setting bail for you, each one ten dollars. And your case will be heard, like, October something.' So I put up fifty dollars bail for the five of us. Well, now they know we were leaving the next day; we're doing one-nighters. We were like in Detroit the next day. So it was just a jive way of saying, 'Now, you've got a record down here for gambling. You don't show up, you'll forfeit the bond, which means you'll be guilty and you'll lose the ten dollars.' O.K., so we went back and we did the show, and the next day I had a press conference there. And one of the newspapers—it was strange, one of the big white papers said— 'After what happened last night, they oughta give the police a medal. It should be chicken on a field of yellow.' Because he said it was bullshit, you know, what the cops did to us. Well, anyway, we left the next day. Of course the papers were all over the country then. But I tricked them. I hired the best lawyer I could and we fought the case. We beat them. We won, got the bread back, and of course then I thought we'd never go down to Houston again, but we did—we went down the next year again, and nobody touched us. It cost me a lotta bread, but I got the best lawyer in Texas. Of course we beat those cats, 'cause it was jive."

ILLINOIS JACQUET:

"I went to school in Houston and we were appearing there, Jazz at the Philharmonic, and we were to integrate the audience for the first time in Houston. So I made a lot of appearances at the colleges, the black colleges, and the high schools and what not, and I went on the radio. There were no presale tickets. You had to buy the tickets right at the door, first come, first served. So I was very much behind this because this was my hometown, and I wanted to integrate. I wanted to do something; this was in 1955. So during our performance at the Music Hall in Houston, we had police guards and everything to take care of backstage for us, uniformed patrolmen. So between shows and between appearances, we would have something to do, we'd play cards, shoot dice, have our own little private games in our dressing rooms, 'cause there was no outsiders allowed. So some plainclothes policemen, we called them 'crackers,' broke into our dressing room backstage while the show was going on. We were in Ella Fitzgerald's dressing room; we were all shooting dice, and these officers broke in the room, stopped the game, and took us all to jail. Took Dizzy, Ella Fitzgerald, and Ella's cousin, Georgia, and myself. Took us to jail and we paid a fine. We were there about half an hour. They asked Dizzy what his name was, he said, 'Louis Armstrong. . . .' They printed that. We integrated the audience for the first time in Houston, at Jazz at the Philharmonic, and it's been integrated ever since."

At San Quentin Prison with (l to r) Lalo Schifrin, Bob Cunningham, Chuck
Lampkin, and Leo Wright. Dick Gregory joined us and played bongos.

Partying with Louis Armstrong, Jimmy McPartland, and Bobby Hackett at my house in Corona, N. Y.

My brothers and sisters would come out to hear me play; (l to r) Wesley's former wife, Marie, Mattie, Wesley, Genia, and I.

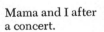
Mama and I after a concert.

About my former political aspirations . . . I dreamed
of becoming President of the United States. Vernon
Alley, bass, lent a hand to my campaign.

CHARLES STEWART.

Cover reprinted with the permission of
Downbeat. PHOTOGRAPH BY BOB SKEETZ.

Attending a Baha'i Assembly with Ruhiyah Khanum, a hand of the cause of God.

Miles dropped in one night at the Village Gate and . . .

At a session with Sonny Stitt, Max Roach, Hank Jones, John Lewis, and Percy Heath.

My hero, Paul Robeson. UNITED PRESS INTERNATIONAL.

With Chris White at Paul Robeson Award presentation.

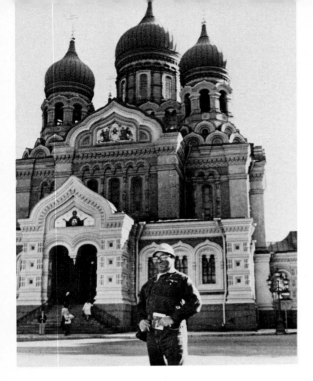

Visiting Leningrad, U.S.S.R.

My quartet performing at the Tenth Anniversary of Kenya's independence, Nairobi, Kenya, 1973.

ELLA FITZGERALD:

"Yeah, and I was the innocent one! Yeah, sitting up eating pie. He, he, he. They took us down and then when we got down there they had the nerve to ask for an autograph. That was quite an experience. That's what I mean when I say closeness. To look back and talk about things like that with someone you've known through the years. That's what you call being close."

The social ferment around this time meant now you didn't have to have an all-black band or an all-white band; you could mix up musicians, and audiences. As one of the pioneers in having white guys in my bands, with Al Haig, Stan Levey, and George Wallington, that set things partially right for me. Women players like Melba Liston and Patti Bown began asserting themselves more too.

They had only one guy then, Specs Powell at CBS; one black musician in the whole broadcasting system. We'd been shut outta that, and we had many qualified musicians. The union probably had something to do with that, by omission, because they didn't push black guys into the studios and into Broadway plays. You saw very few black guys in pit bands, though historically blacks had pioneered during the twenties in creating the concept of the Broadway musical with shows like *Shuffle Along,* and Bessie Smith had played a great role in the growth of Columbia Records and CBS, as their first major recording artist. I wasn't exactly involved in all this, being a traveling musician, and it didn't affect me as much as it did the musicians who stayed in New York. But they were definitely protesting the hiring system in music in which the leaders who contracted these jobs gave all the jobs to the white guys. The bandleaders who contracted the jobs for the Broadway shows and the networks didn't think about hiring black guys because these jobs had been traditionally reserved for whites. When I was coming up, black bands like Teddy Hill's played on the radio, but these weren't studio musicians and they had all blacks or all whites. They didn't think in terms of blacks for jobs where musicians could stay in town and work at studios: at CBS, ABC, or NBC, and do recordings. It was a big thing when Raymond Scott hired Specs Powell because they hired very few, if any, black musicians on the staffs of the major radio networks during the forties, and the same applied to television during the fifties. Now, Sammy Davis has a black musical director and Billy Taylor was musical director for David Frost. The system has been broken down to some degree and now the qualifications are musicianship. In every sphere of American life, there's a certain degree of racism, and music is no better; but on the average, I think the musical part is better than in ordinary life. If you go and see a Broadway show now, you'll see about 50 per cent blacks and whites in the orchestra, depending on the kind of show.* They don't have staff orchestras at the networks now anymore in New York City, but the musicians, the ones that play best, are on call.

Once, I went to Australia with Sarah Vaughan and Jonah Jones and was reminded of how much further we had yet to go in the struggle. When we got to the airport in Australia, who was going out when we were coming in but Paul Robeson? And he grabbed me and threw me up in the air, man. That was very nice. We were very fond of one another because I could see his uncontrollable spirit, his superdedication to ideals which he didn't vary one inch. He didn't make any kind of compromise. I think Paul Robeson was one of my favorite people in the whole world. He was in exile then.

Also, around that same time, Billie Holiday stayed at my house in California while the police were hounding her. They were looking for her, and she stayed there in the place where I was staying until a doctor could come from Los Angeles and get her and take her to a hospital for treatment. It was a long time before the police found out that drug addiction was not a crime but an illness, and that drug addicts were human beings and not lower animals. They had to be educated to accept that truth and many others.

* There were some complaints though, recently, in 1976, about the refusal to hire a sufficient number of black musicians for the Broadway revival of *Porgy and Bess.*

World Statesman

Adam Powell surprised me. I went to Washington once, in 1956, playing with a small group at the Showboat, and received a call from him saying come down to the House Office Building the next day because he had something to tell me. I arrived there and all these reporters were standing around, and then Adam made a statement: "I'm going to propose to President Eisenhower that he send this man, who's a great contributor to our music, on a State Department sponsored cultural mission to Africa, the Near East, Middle East, and Asia."

I was shocked. This was the first time I'd ever heard of it. He made the recommendation, they hired me, and I was the first one. After that, a lot of the bands went. Benny Goodman went to Russia; Duke Ellington went to Russia; Earl Hines went to Russia. Several bands went to Africa, like, Herbie Mann. It was all "mixed" to show the "democratic" spirit, but if we hadn't done well, there wouldn't have been any more bands going over.

Since I was already set to go on tour in Europe with Jazz at the Philharmonic, I got in touch with Quincy Jones, who'd helped me to organize the big bands I recorded and played with occasionally in 1954 and 1955, and told him to get the band together for me. Then I left for Europe, and they tried to get me to come back because the State Department wanted me to come to Washington and be "briefed" about what to say since we were going to the Near East and Middle East. I told Lorraine, "Tell them you can't find me. I'm in Europe, and I'll meet them in Rome," which I did. My wife took care of all the arrangements in my place. If it hadn't been for her hard work, we wouldn't have gone. Lorraine had been to the dentist, and it was wintertime, and the cold had her face all swollen, but she went through with it.

I took it as an honor, really, because they had many people they could've chosen as the first one to represent the State Department on that tour. I felt highly honored, and I liked the idea of a big band that wouldn't cost me any money. We didn't have to lay out any money to support it and didn't have to worry about jobs because all the jobs were preset. They laid it all right out in front of me, and I sort've liked the idea of representing America, but I wasn't going over to apologize for the racist policies of America. When I talked to Lorraine on the phone from Paris, she said, "Well, they want to brief you."

"Brief?" I said. "I've got three hundred years of briefing. I know what they've done to us, and I'm not gonna make any excuses. If they ask me any questions, I'm gonna answer them as honestly as I can." Over there, we really did a great job, the job we were supposed to do to try to bring the people together. I did a lot of promotional work for it, like going out into the park playing with snake charmers and giving away free concert tickets. Yeah, I was very honored to have been chosen as the first jazz musician to represent the United States on a cultural mission, and I had a good time. We had a complete "American assortment" of blacks, whites, males, females, Jews, and Gentiles in the band. Joe Gordon, Ermet Perry, Carl Warwick, and Quincy Jones, trumpets. Melba Liston, Frank Rehak, and Rod Levitt, trombones. Jimmy Powell and Phil Woods, alto saxophones; Billy Mitchell and Ernie Wilkins, tenors; Marty Flax, baritone; Walter Davis, Jr., piano; Nelson Boyd, bass; and Charlie Persip, drums. Herb Lance was our male vocalist, and Dottie Salters, our female vocalist.

HERB LANCE (vocalist):

"Dizzy's wife, Lorraine, and my wife are very good friends. The tour came up, Dizzy wasn't here. Dizzy was in Europe during that period and Quincy Jones, Melba Liston, and Ernie Wilkins got the band together. We rehearsed in New York, and we met Dizzy in Rome—we picked him up in Rome and went into the Middle East and started the tour. So really, if you know Lorraine and the relationship between Diz and Lorraine, you should definitely mention 'the Dizzy,' when Lorraine is around, and the 'other Dizzy'—a different Dizzy altogether. He was like a Sunday school teacher on that tour. See, Lorraine was there. No funny business *at all!* When we landed in Rome, Dizzy was on the ground playing 'Sweet Lorraine' on the trumpet, when we disembarked from the plane. I thought that was fabulous.

"What really killed me was playing in the remote places like Beirut, Lebanon; Damascus and Aleppo, Syria; Abadan, Iran—when we played in those type places. We flew from Karachi to Dacca, Pakistan, about an eight- or nine-hour flight. Just a remote place, but the natives were there waiting for Diz. You see the music is the same all over the world. Charlie Persip took sick from diarrhea in Karachi, and we used a native drummer to kick the big band and did a big thing. And the people just ate it up. Now you know what kind of hero that made of him. That type of thing happened, and it was fantastic! Believe me."

MELBA LISTON:

"There's those natural problems on the road, the female problems, the lodging problems, the laundry, and all those kinda things to try to keep yourself together, problems that somehow or other the guys didn't seem to have to go through. But you're on your own out there. If you're gonna be in the band, you must carry your own luggage and be self-sufficient, and the only way I could survive is that I was young and strong then, and I was self-sufficient. So when I showed them that I was not gonna be a burden to them, you know everything was cool. I think the only little doubts that the guys had was when I first came to the band. Dizzy was in Europe. Quincy Jones was the musical director and was organizing the band for Dizzy. Dizzy said, 'Get the band together, but include Melba, and Melba is to write some of the music.' So those were orders, no questioning that. But when I got to New York I heard some comments about, 'Why the hell did he send all the way to California for a bitch trombone player?'

"They didn't know me at all, but as Dizzy instructed, I arranged some things and brought them with me, 'Stella by Starlight' and 'Anitra's Dance.' I wrote the arrangement on 'Stella by Starlight' at home when Dizzy called and said, 'Well, I'm getting the big band back together and making a tour, so you write a couple of charts and bring them with you.' When we got into the initial rehearsals, and they started playing my arrangements, well, that erased all the little bullshit, you see. They say, 'Mama's all right.' Then I was 'Mama,' I wasn't bitch no more.

"Generally, people don't think of females as being able to be efficient in any endeavor. In our travels it wasn't so much that they didn't think I was capable. They wondered about the male-female relationship in the U.S. I had lots of women come to me in the Mid-

dle East tours to find out how life was over here for women and how
in the world I could be running around there traveling and single
when they were so subjected over there. And it sorta seemed to in-
spire a bunch of the sisters over there to demand a little more appreciation for their innate abilities. Whatever it was. I had many conversations with the women, especially in the Middle East in that manner.
They had things that they felt they were capable of doing and were
not permitted to do. And they wanted to know how it happened that I
could be out there doing such a thing.

"Well, I couldn't help them actually because I'd never really experienced the hard facts. . . . But Dizzy was greatly responsible for the
love and respect that I got from all the brothers. He wouldn't let anyone abuse me too much in the band. It was just like a family. In your
own household you got brothers and sisters and things be going down.
Well, that's the way bands that stay together two or three years become—like a family."

ROD LEVITT (trombone):

"For the State Department Band, in 1956, Quincy Jones got me. I
think it was my first band. I was just out of the service. I was about
twenty-five. And Quincy Jones who I played with at the University of
Washington—when I was at the University of Washington, Quincy
was in high school, so he knew me—just ran into me on the street and
said, 'You want to go to the Middle East with Dizzy Gillespie?'

"So I said, 'Sure . . .' Dizzy was an idol of mine anyway, and then
to be playing with this great band, fabulous. Oh, Jesus! To my knowledge I was the only Jew in the band at that time. There were four
whites, and everybody else was black. And at that time, there was
Egypt, and they had a lot of problems there. In 1956, they were having big problems with Israel, and there was a big war. So they were
very touchy about letting Jews in these Arabic countries when we
landed in Egypt. And we were supposed to play there, but it was canceled. We landed in Egypt, and we went into the airport for an hour.
You got a drink, a free drink, you know, so it was like a layover in
Cairo. They turned all the lights out and started showing a movie. It
was kind of a propaganda movie against Israel, you know, and here I
was sitting with Dizzy. I was kind of scared, you know. I didn't know
what was happening. And Dizzy says, laughing, 'How do you like it?'
Oh, boy, I couldn't wait to get out of there. And as a matter of fact
we had problems with a visa because there again, I put 'Jewish' down
on my visa for Pakistan, and they weren't going to let me into the next
country, which I think was Syria. The State Department resubmitted
the visa as Presbyterian or something like that. They just changed it,

you know. 'Cause they didn't really care, but technically they weren't allowing Jews in the country. But since I was under the auspices of the State Department . . . I remember Diz said, 'We may have to leave you in Pakistan, leave you in Karachi.'"

CARL WARWICK:

"Of course that was one of the highlights of my career because of the spark and everything in the band. It was sold out every place over there, countries like Pakistan; and we were surprised that those people would come out like that. We had a wonderful trumpet player on that tour, Joe Gordon. Joe turned on the band with the idea of trying to outblow Diz every night, and Diz set fire to him every night. Diz was really at his peak. He was really fired up playing in front of that big band, and that was about all that he needed, for somebody else to egg him on."

The tour became highly political. We were supposed to have opened in Bombay, India. Three or four weeks before the band left, Nehru made a statement, a non-alignment speech, in which he stated that India wasn't going to side with the United States, nor the Soviet Union, nor anybody. India had a non-alignment policy, so where did we go first? Persia [Iran]. Persia was getting arms from the United States, so instead of opening in Bombay, they canceled. I can remember the papers calling the Indians "ungrateful." We send them this, and then Nehru says he's not with us. "Ingrate." So the State Department just routed us to Iran, then to Beirut, Lebanon, because we had an American University there. From there, we flew over India to Dacca, Pakistan, because the United States was supplying Pakistan with arms. You could see the political implications and feel them. Our tour was limited to countries which had treaties with the United States or where you had U.S. military bases: Persia, Lebanon, Syria, Pakistan, Turkey, and Greece. We didn't go to any of the countries the U.S. didn't have some sort of "security" agreement with. Wherever we went, the political question was definitely involved. We opened in Abadan, Iran, and went from there to Beirut, to Damascus and Aleppo in Syria. Politics was a drag because these were such beautiful places. Beirut is like God's earth. But you name one beautiful place and ten others, just as beautiful, come to mind immediately.

In Beirut, they scheduled two concerts for us at the Dunia Theater which seated fifteen hundred people. We played twice to packed houses and they had to arrange a third performance which was also sold out. After we played (sometimes before), Marshall Stearns, a professor at Hunter College who traveled with us, would lecture on jazz at various colleges and schools.

Politics or not, for the first time that modern jazz on this scale had been presented in person to a non-Western audience, we got a magnificent reception. But it was weird. The United States guaranteed our money, but then the host country had to sell tickets and try to make up as much of that money as it could. In Pakistan, one host country, the profiteers in the country dug the way the tickets were sold. They priced the tickets so high that the little people we were trying to gain friendship with couldn't make it. In Karachi, I noticed the audience at our first performance wasn't really filled up. So I asked some of the guys around. I talked. I was trying to find out about the situation. They say, "Well, man, they just don't have the money. These are poor people. Look, people living all out in stalls with animals. Where are they gonna get five dollars to buy a ticket?"

So I asked the impresario, I say, "How many you got?" He gave away about 150 tickets. I took a whole batch of tickets, went out in the park, and gave them away. I just passed them out. We had a full house, a beautiful audience, man. After that I'd see people standing around outside trying to listen, trying to find out what's happening, so I gave away a lot of tickets in Karachi.

Someone set up a publicity event for me to go out into the park to play with a snake charmer. And on the way out there, in front of the hotel, they had an organ grinder with a monkey. And this monkey was a smart little dude, man. You stand up there and listen to the guy play the organ, and the monkey comes and jumps on you and reaches in your pocket and takes out the money. When he jumped up on Quincy Jones and went to reach into Quincy's pocket, Quincy grabbed his pocket to keep him from getting anything. This monkey slapped the shit outta Quincy! Quincy reached. I said, "Quincy, don't you cut that monkey." Quincy looked like he was ready to cut the monkey.

We went out to the park, and they had this snake charmer out there. He had two snakes. He had a little snake in a little basket, and I noticed he was very careful with that little one because it was an adder, or something like that. This little snake—if he bites you, that's the end of it. Nothing, no help, can get to you quick enough before the end. He took this little snake and dropped it out on the ground. He had a rag over his hand. And he'd show you how mean that little muthafucka was. He'd put this rag down, and this little snake—it looked like what we'd fish with down South, only about four inches long—would grab it, and he'd hold him up in the air and then put him back down into his basket. He had another big one, a long snake, musta been over fifteen feet long, but he was harmless. He wrapped this around my head and had a girl to hold it, Dottie Salters, God bless the dead. She was holding his head. In the meantime he started playing, and he opened up another basket, and a cobra just came up outta the basket. He was playing this thing and when he'd move, the cobra would move with him. And then he said, "Come on, play with me." I took my horn, I had a mute in, and I played and played along with him. Then he stopped playing and he said, "Now, move your horn from side to side," and this cobra was following my horn. Apparently, I put my horn too close to his head, and he went, "Sspeeat!!" at my horn, man. I set a world record backward broad jump. I must have jumped back fifteen feet. This was supposed to have been a "defanged" cobra, but the next day I read in the paper where a cobra, a defanged cobra, wasn't defanged and had bitten somebody and he died. I said, "Oh, my God, suppose that had been one of those that hadn't been defanged."

We heard some marvelous young musicians in Karachi. They were, like, studio musicians and all of them were soloists. They had accompaniment, and each one of them played. One guy had an instrument that looked like a violin. He held it down, and instead of putting his fingers on top, his fingers went under the strings. There was a groove in each one of his fingernails. He was an old gray-haired man, but did he play that thing. Sounded like a cello. Then they had a little sixteen-year-old flute player who was beautiful. This was in Pakistan, but they had another brother there, and this cat looked like somebody that I'd seen on the corner of 126th Street and Eighth Avenue. Hair "bad" enough to carry a nuclear weapon. It was matted, it was so nappy. And he had an instrument that he made himself, which was like a piano but the knobs came up and hit the strings. Boy, did he perform. It had a weird sound. The musicians treated us great. They played concerts for us in the studios when we went different places and they showed us things. You know, I'm always interested in the ethnic background of the music, the soulful music of a people. I learned a lot over there. I learned some scales and made some recordings with Stuff Smith using some of those scales in it that came out of Pakistan. One tune was called "Rio Pakistan." (Verve MGU 8214.) The notes I used are from the scale, but I made up the lick. I created my own lick from their scale. It's called a raga. It was very exciting and very gratifying to listen to another type of music than what I played.

A very beautiful incident occurred in Dacca, Pakistan. They gave a party for us on top of the USIS building, and they had some Pakistani dancers and players and singers to perform for us. Well, the party was going on when I left the hotel and I was supposed to go over there in this rickshaw by myself. I went outside and looked at the sky, and it was dark, man. Lorraine was sorta scared for me to go. She said, "Are you sure you're gonna go with this guy?"

I took one look at the guy, and he looked just like Jesus. I said, "If he looks that much like Jesus I've got to go with him." Ha! Ha! Ha! I said, "What can they do to me?" So I got into this rickshaw and onto this dark road. We were traveling on this dark road, and I couldn't see anything, man. But he was bicycling. It was a bicycle rickshaw, so I decided I wanted to ride the bicycle. I told him, "You sit here in the back and lemme . . ." Nobody'd ever asked him that before. He looked back at me. I said, "Yeah, I wanna ride the bicycle. You tell me where to go, and I'll ride you."

He said, "O.K. . . ." He sat back and crossed his legs, and I wailed awhile, man. For maybe a couple of miles I rode the bicycle. And then when we got near the place I took out my horn and started warming up, and a flute player on a roof started accompanying me. Boy, that was eerie, man! Oh, it was beautiful! This guy was on a roof, and I could hear. I'd play, and I heard something. I stopped and I heard the flute. I'd play a little bit more, and I'd hear the flute. And we just accompanied one another. That was beautiful. I went upstairs and told them about it at the party and played a little bit with the Pakistani guys. It felt wonderful, man; those people were very warm, and the spirituality was beautiful.

One little raggedy boy in Dacca used to sit on his heels at the stage door. They can stoop and their ass is about hitting the ground. He didn't have any money to go in and the door was cracked open. Outside of the stage entrance there were a lotta people whenever we'd come out from backstage, a lotta raggedy people with nothing back there. They were sleeping out there in the yard, and rats, big rats, were running around out there. I said, "Damn . . . !"

This little boy was a cute little kid about eleven or twelve years old and he'd sit down there and listen to us every night. When I went out one night I saw him lying down in the back there where all those rats had been running around. He had on the same clothes, still raggedy. "Oughta buy that little guy an outfit and let him clean up some," I figured. So I took a rickshaw and went back down there looking for him, and I described him to the manager of the theater. I told him I wanted to buy something for this kid. He said, "O.K., I'll have him at your hotel in the morning."

The next day this little guy was downstairs. They wouldn't let him upstairs because it seemed that sometimes these kids would spot valuables and somebody else would come and rob you. I said, "Man, they don't do nothing like that."

"Yeah, yeah, they spot for the thieves," he said.

Anyway, I came downstairs, and put some of these rupees, Pakistani

money, in my pocket, and the impresario came for me in the car.
They didn't want the little boy to ride in the car with me. So I said,
"Come here. He ain't got no room for you? Sit here, sit on my lap." So
he sat on my knee all the way. We got out and went into the shop,
and I bought him a new outfit, one of those long shirts, and a pair of
shoes. He was happy, grinning. "No, don't buy him any shoes," the
guy says, when we get back to the car.

"Whaddayou mean? He ain't got any shoes, has he?"

He said, "No. You know what he'll do. He'll sell the shoes because
nobody else will have on any shoes. So what are you gonna give him
shoes for?" I let him keep them anyway. That night when I came in
backstage, this little guy was shining. He'd taken a bath, had his hair
combed. Boy, his hair was beautiful, coal black. He was standing up
like a sentry with one hand behind him. And when I came in he
snapped to attention, clicked his heels, sharp and clean, man. That
was cute. And I didn't care whether he sold the shoes later to buy
himself some food.

People asked us a lot of questions about racism in the United States.
But they could see it wasn't as intense because *we* had white boys and
I was the leader of the band. That was strange to them because they'd
heard about blacks being lynched and burned, and here I come with
half whites and blacks and a girl playing in the band. And everybody
seemed to be getting along fine. So I didn't try to hide anything. I
said, "Yeah, there it is. We have our problems but we're still working
on it. I'm the leader of this band, and those white guys are working
for me. That's a helluva thing. A hundred years ago, our ancestors
were slaves, and today we're scuffling with this problem, but I'm sure
it's gonna be straightened out some day. I probably won't see it, completely, the eradication of racial prejudice in the United States, but it
will be eliminated." We made a lotta friends in Pakistan for the
United States, and people who were extremely poor lined up and paid
the equivalent of two and three dollars a seat to hear us. Those who
couldn't get into the theater listened to us on the radio. At first the
Pakistani audiences didn't know how to react to our music and they
just applauded politely, but by the second or third show they were
completely captivated, clapping on the right beat.

Damascus, Syria, we hit during Ramadan and our concert was just
before sunset. On the table in the back of the hall where we were
playing was this big feast waiting to be eaten to break the fast of
Ramadan. We played through our repertoire, a rapid history of jazz
and then started on the modern things. All of a sudden I looked at my
watch, and I knew it was near sundown. We had about five minutes.
I said, "I know what I'll do." We kept playing and then at exactly on
the minute, the second of sundown, I held up my hand, and boom!

We hit a big chord. And I said, "Food!" and rushed to the back, and everybody rushed back there with me. Everybody rushed back to eat right on the minute that ended Ramadan. I made a big hit with them then, because if you're not a Muslim you can get some food, but I tried to honor their custom.

In Turkey they scheduled a jam session for us to play with Turkish musicians on the embassy grounds in Ankara. That's where I first met Muraffak Fallay, the trumpet player. I gave him a horn, and he's now a close friend of mine. But when I got to the embassy, I noticed there were soldiers and a crowd, mostly kids, outside the grounds trying to get in. I went inside and jumped across a fence. They had a reviewing stand, so I climbed the fence and stood up on the reviewing stand and was signing autographs up there. The Turkish guys were playing at the time, and while signing autographs, I noticed a little kid jump across the fence inside the grounds. One of the security officers grabbed him and threw him back over. I say, "What kinda shit is that?" (to myself) and I asked someone about it.

"This is for these people," he said. I noticed the people coming in had the tickets, and they were the elite.

I said, "Man, we're not over here to play for any elites! We're over here to make friendships with the small people, those people outside the gates. I'm not gonna play unless they let those people in." The time came for me to play and I said, "I'm not playing. . . ."

They said, "What . . . ?" And boy, there was a big commotion. They went and found the ambassador. Ambassador Heath came up to me and said, "Mr. Gillespie, there's supposed to be a jam session. What's happening? Why don't you want to play?"

I told him, "You see those people out there? We're trying to gain their friendship, not these people, big shots here with the tickets, all crowded around in here."

"Yeah," he said, "but we don't have food and drinks enough for everybody."

"They're not interested in food and drinks," I said. "They're interested in joining the festivities and listening to the music. Man, I don't wanna play for these people."

He told the security guards, "Let them in. . . ." They let them in, and we had a ball. So that was a headline in the paper the next day: GILLESPIE REFUSES TO PLAY FOR THE ELITE. I played for the little people and I was a big star; I was a big hit in Ankara. It made a nice headline in the papers, and those kids went home with their stomachs full.

I never did get the Turkish feeling, musically. Turkish rhythm is funny, boy, because Turk goes, like, one-and-two-and-one-two-three-one-two-one-two, that's 11/8 time. It's like one of Dave Brubeck's things in 7/8 time. Dave Brubeck is from a classical background. They have classical music in 9/8 and 12/8, 11/8. But at that time Dave Brubeck hadn't been over there.

It was interesting when they approached the Conservatory of Music in Ankara, which really was conservative, about giving a lecture on jazz for their students, the dean refused permission because he felt the students already spent too much time with jazz. They had to hold the lecture someplace else. But the dean came to our concert and I read somewhere that he changed his mind and said, "This is wonderful music," and begged them to present a lecture on jazz at the Conservatory.

America, our government, was very much pleased with our activities because jazz was an art form the people felt, something they hadn't seen before and which many had never even heard, especially in Eastern Europe. In an interview in Yugoslavia a guy asked me questions about our music and I mentioned Armstrong in the course of the interview. They thought I was talking about a rubber company. I figured if I mentioned Louis Armstrong's name, and they didn't know who he was, then I'm really in trouble. We played a historical account of jazz from 1922 to 1956. This was some time over twenty years ago and bebop, our music, seemed pretty new to them. Just to come up to bebop then brought everything up to date. In Yugoslavia, Zagreb, and Belgrade, they clapped and hollered, but they'd be clapping their hands on one and three. Most of the ethnic people of the world clap their hands on one and three except people of African descent, they clap on two and four. Audiences in the United States still go right into clapping on one and three, but in jazz if you don't clap on two and four, you're out of it.

Already, our music had been heard in the four corners of the world. Sidney Bechet toured Russia during the czarist period, and jazz became a big thing out there. The ordinary people hadn't heard of it, but the artists had. They had a jazz band in Ankara, Turkey; and in Istanbul, a full orchestra played for us and it was very good. Jazz was a big thing in Eastern Europe. Though in a lot of the socialist countries it was forbidden to play American music, they had black market recordings that circulated among the artists. We didn't have any of those political problems because they probably considered us government workers since we were playing under the auspices of the State Department. Jazz is very big in socialist countries now, but, during the "cold war," in a lot of the countries it was forbidden to have records by jazz artists. They could have Bach and Beethoven, but they couldn't have jazz. They finally came around and got hip that jazz was something worth having.

The people in Yugoslavia seemed very enthusiastic about our music.

Even the old people loved it, like in Sweden during the forties. Our music had strong folk origins which made it fun to play and listen to. In Zagreb, they tried to jump up on the stage during the concert, and the soldiers had to push them back into their seats. After the concert they had to cordon off the stage to protect us from the crowd's unbounded enthusiasm. The mentality of jazz, its spontaneous organization, really got to them. They couldn't understand how we could seem so unorganized until we began to play. Our music really exemplifies a perfect balance between discipline and freedom.

In Eastern Europe now, you're officially sponsored by the government, and the critics write in glowing terms about the music. It's a far cry from the days when they felt that jazz was decadent and chaotic music which made the people less capable of being disciplined and therefore weak.* Jazz has taught the world a lot about the necessity for balance between the two. They gave parties and jam sessions for us in Yugoslavia that lasted all night. The Yugoslav musicians got down on their knees to us, and one lady claimed that for creating true friendship one jazz band was worth more than a hundred ambassadors. They really got the spirit.

We got a missive on the plane, saying that Greek students just threw rocks at the USIS office in Athens because of U.S. policy in Cyprus. They had a big upheaval in Cyprus. Apparently we were on the wrong side. The U.S. was on the side of the Turks because they had a base in Turkey monitoring Russia, a listening post. Naturally, since the U.S. was giving the Turks arms, the Greek people just broke out all the windows. We were on the way there, and I said, "It's too late now, man, we're on the way. Can't turn around in the middle of the air." When we got to Athens, I figured, "Well, we're gonna play anyway. We're not connected, even remotely, with politics. We're artists. We came to serve the people, not to use them." So the first show we played was a matinée for students only—the same people who'd thrown the rocks, they told us later. After the first performance I stayed backstage awhile and dried off, then I came out. When I came outside, these Greeks grabbed me and had me up in the air, on my back, up in the air. I said, "I wonder if in a moment they're gonna dash me to the ground?" As soon as I stepped outside they grabbed me and they were screaming, saying things in Greek. But I heard, "Bravo! Bravo!" And when I heard "Bravo," I knew we were a big hit in Athens. During the concert these Greek students got up and started dancing in the aisles with the policemen who were there to keep

---

* Marshall Stearns reported after lecturing at the Zagreb Conservatory of Music that the Yugoslav students and the faculty members had agreed that "jazz symbolized an element of unconscious protest which cut through the pretenses of tradition and authority. It spoke directly and truly of real life."

them from becoming unruly. The newspaper headlines said: "GREEK STUDENTS LAY DOWN ROCKS AND ROLL WITH DIZ."

Also, in Greece they had a guy named Duncan Embry who was noted for imbibement at times. As a matter of fact we called him "Drunken" Embry. He was working for the USIS there, and he scheduled an extra show for us, there at the hotel, in Greece. We were staying at the Hilton, and they wanted us to play there after we had already done a concert. I said, "No, not on your life." And that didn't go so well with him, and he sent in a bad report because we wouldn't play. Why should we do an extra show after we had already played one on the regular schedule? I wasn't gonna tell those guys to bring all that stuff up to the hotel for a drunken cocktail party. I wouldn't play and I sent in a report. I reported that "Drunken" Embry wasn't very nice and that he'd been imbibing. But that was the only untoward incident. Other than that we were having a good time. The USIS was highly visible, and when we wanted to go sightseeing they provided us with cars. They were very cordial.

E. V. PERRY (trumpet):

"I remember we went to Athens, Greece, and we had to do a concert at seven in the morning, and Dizzy astonished everyone with the performance that morning. We were on the bill with the Russian Ballet troupe, and they had the night performance, so we couldn't get the hall. They put Diz on at seven o'clock in the morning. And you would think it was eight, nine, or maybe midnight, at night, the way he performed. He gassed everyone!"

MARION "BOO" FRAZIER:

"There was a concert in Greece one Friday afternoon. There's nothing, no music, that can ever touch that. It's on a tape, and I hope that one day I can put that tape on my own record label. That's when he was at his greatest because he had an all-star band, and it was just something that you can't replace. He was just at his tops doing that. I don't remember the name of the theater, but the people were just remarkable. Just wouldn't stop the ovations. The ovations just kept coming and coming, and it was packed houses at all the concerts. It was just something about the concert in Athens with the people and the music. The music just got to the people, as simple as that."

CHARLIE PERSIP (drums):

"We were in Greece, and he picked up the mike and walked closer to the audience while he was introducing us. So there was like another step down to another small stage, another level, one step below the stage that we were on. And what he didn't know was that whole step down, that whole secondary stage, was made of papier-mâché. So when he stepped down, you know, he disappeared. And that was really funny. He didn't hurt himself, so we really laughed about it. The fall was enough to where he disappeared."

MELBA LISTON:

"I think he had a little visual problem. His peripheral vision doesn't include where his feet are. Like, he'll step off a curb or something and twist his ankle easy, because his vision doesn't seem to extend that low. And he was dancing. I think we were in Greece. We were playing a very elegant show with all these people, looked like they should've had powdered wigs on. And Dizzy wasn't about nobody being that bourgie and elegant that night. This announcer was just 'Blah-blah-blah-blah, Monsieur Deezy Gillespie.' And Dizzy ran out from the wings and jumped on the man with his legs around the man's waist and started riding him like a horse. And this very elegant dude couldn't get him off, you know. He'd bend over, and he was running, crawling back and forth across the stage. Dizzy just jumped up on him and hooked his legs around his waist and stuff, and this dude turned red and cried and everything. We laughed . . . it was beautiful. That was funny.

"At that same place or during that same tour, he was playing, and there was quite a large bandstand, and he was blowing and blowing and walking forward and fell, stepped off the stage. And there was this big pit below the stage, but it had a canvas or tarpaulin across it, but it was only a thin sheet of covering. So he disappeared under this thing and the band. . . . We just kept playing this vamp, waiting for him. And then you see the horn come up through this hole, and you see Dizzy's face talking about, 'Awww,' you know. One of them looks on it. But we were so frightened that he was hurt badly that it wasn't funny then. Well, then after he came back, we had a great big laugh. But to see him going down—the last thing you see going down is the trumpet because when you fall, you always hold your instrument up. And when he came back up, the trumpet comes first, and then he followed it, with one of them classic expressions on his face. And that was a big laugh."

It all just happened. I'd never had much interest in press agents, but I got one when I went overseas for the State Department because I figured a lotta things would happen. Lorraine collected and sent all these clippings back to Virginia Wicks, the publicity agent, who also worked for Ella Fitzgerald and Eartha Kitt. This time she was working for me and she did a helluva job of publicizing our music. We came back and played for the White House Correspondent's Dinner with James Cagney, Nat Cole, Patti Page, Jimmy Durante, and my band. We all had to go through a security check. Afterwards, President Eisenhower gave all of us plaques, and he called all the names, "Nat Cole . . ." Nat Cole came up. Then he called "Patti Page . . ." "James Cagney . . ." And then they called my name, and I didn't hear them. I'd gone somewhere investigating something. Finally, somebody told me, "Hey, man, the President called you."

I said, "Where . . . where?"

And so the President called, "Dizzy . . . Dizzy Gillespie . . . Dizzy . . . Dizzy."

I said, "Right over here, Pops." And Lukey, Patti Page's accompanist, tells that story all the time now, about me and President Eisenhower. I didn't hear him. Man, I was over there talking to Hubert Humphrey. Everybody was there—all the Supreme Court Justices, senators, and everybody.

We went into the studio and made some records for Norman Granz which really exhibited the spirit and fine musicianship of the 1956 big band. (Norgran MGN 1084.) Then we left again for another long trip. After making such a hit on the first State Department tour, it seemed just natural for us to go on another one, this time to South America.

Samba

       Samba is the bossa nova, rather the bossa nova is a watered down version of samba. Samba is the real thing. I first heard samba, live, when we toured South America. You could really learn a lot about rhythm down there, especially in Brazil. Whew! In Brazil they have a lotta brothers, Africans—and their music is African. The Brazilians reminded me of the early days of our music. I'd been into Afro-Cuban rhythm for a long time, but I wasn't hip to the rest of the rhythms of Latin America. Every now and then I listened to a little calypso, samba, and other rhythms, but, boy, it was a blockbuster when I first heard the real thing. My first exposure to samba was in the soundtrack of the film *Black Orpheus,* and when they first started getting into it, I thought, "Those are some brothers down there?" Arriving in Brazil, I found out that there were and that our music had a common bond. I really dug the connection, when they took me to Esquola de Samba, in Rio de Janeiro.

    In the samba school they had all the different rhythm instruments playing and the people were dancing. Dancing and rhythm, that's all. There were no melodic instruments. The rhythms themselves make melodies. Run you crazy. The samba school consists of rhythm sections, comprised of different instruments, like the tambourine, the cuica, and the berimbao.* The berimbao looks like a bow and arrow, and it

* Berimbao de barriga, or urucungo.

comes out from your stomach and has a gourd on it. A gourd is set on the wooden part of the bow, and the gourd is laying up against your stomach while you hold this thing that looks like a bow and arrow. You hold that with your left hand and in your right you have a little iron rod. With the rod you beat on the string, and while you beat the string with your right hand, you have a coin in your left hand that you move up and down the string making different pitches. As you're doing this, you pull the gourd in and out from your stomach, and it makes another sound. You've got the sound of the string, the sound of the gourd, and also the rhythm that you're playing, three things going for you. Really four, because there's a rattle in the gourd, too. I have a berimbao charm Norman Granz bought for me to wear around my neck.

In the samba school you also have the cuica which can sound like a woman's or a man's voice. It sounds like a voice. It's got a head and a long drum, and you stick your hand inside. Down inside, a little stick is there in the center of the drum, and you take a wet rag and go up and down the stick to make the different sounds. You mash the head of the drum with one of your fingers to make the difference in pitch. You can get a woman—a high pitch—and you can get a low, low pitch—a man. It really sounds like that too. That's the cuica. Then they have the tambourine and all kinds of different instruments including the American sock cymbal. When they put all these rhythms together, boy!

The dancers dance forever; they never stop. They go on like for ten hours, and different rhythm sections just take up from where the other one left off. There's no intermission. It's beautiful, man, and I danced and played with them. I was never in Brazil during carnival, but they put on a real carnival for me. Every region had a samba school, each with its own coat of arms. You can tell which samba school they come from by their coat of arms. There's nothing in the United States comparable to the samba school, which is really African. The only thing remotely comparable to it in the United States is the old-time revival meeting. It reminds you of the revival because they had the rhythm, the singing, the dancing, and shouting.

Down there in Brazil nobody knows what they are racially. I met the foremost Brazilian composer, Heitor Villa-Lobos. He's not real black complexioned, but who knows what. His ancestry is African, Portuguese, and Indian. Brazilians recognize racial strains, but not like in the United States. Here it's clearly racism, but down in South America, they didn't have an official policy of racism against blacks. I raised this question in Brazil while visiting the Jockey Club. Susan Hayward was there with this millionaire, Jorge Guinlé. Jorge Guinlé is a big jazz fan in South America, and he gave a party for us over at his pad. It was fabulous. He runs around with all the starlets down in Latin America. Anyway, at the Jockey Club I noticed there were very, very few people there with black faces. So I raised the question of prejudice. They denied it, "Oh, we're not prejudiced down here."

"Well, why is it out there I see—out of thousands of people—maybe ten or twenty black faces?"

He said, "No, it's not a color thing; it's economic."

I said, "Well, there it is right there, economic prejudice. You must keep all the money from the blacks then, 'cause they ain't here." Yeah, I raised that question down there, but generally on an official basis, there's no negative force holding you back because you're black. Like, a guy named Cepao, who's black, was the chief arranger at the television studio. He's there because he's qualified. If a guy is qualified down there, he can go on up. I understand they have more blacks in Bahia. We didn't get a chance to go to Bahia and missed seeing the real black part of Brazil. We saw a lot of blacks but not a heavy concentration like you'd probably see in Bahia, which is the area where most of the creativity in the arts and music comes from. I was in touch with a lot of people from Bahia, who came to my hotel, all the way from Bahia, and serenaded me. Right there in my hotel room, they danced and played for me. There were so many of them, I had two rooms full, about fifteen. The last time I was there, they did a whole show for me from the province of Bahia.

We did a session one night in the Gloria Hotel in Brazil with Cepao, which is in my collection of tapes. Cepao made an arrangement on something inspired by me and I played with it. Man, I've often thought of putting that out on a record up here. We did that before anybody even thought about making a South American jazz rhythm. This is samba. They make some terrible breaks that sound just like me and Charlie Parker. They wrote some music that sounds like the lines we played and then put some samba rhythms behind it. Cepao was the first one to do that down there, and ooooh, was he black! He's still there, in Rio, as the musical director for television there.

Brazil really broadened my scope of what music is about. It showed the oneness of music and how music from different ethnic backgrounds can be merged in complete oneness, without each losing its distinctive qualities, without losing its diversity. It taught me unity with diversity in music which the Baha'i faith teaches me about life. In the Bahai religion we don't believe in cutting loose anything good. Cut loose your heritage? Baha'is believe that you bring it in and work with others. Bring it into the whole just like a master painting. Because I'm purple and there's another cat who's orange doesn't mean that we can't come into one big compatible complementary arrangement. Just contribute from your own uniqueness, but don't get over in their groove. Stay outta theirs!

We were the first in the United States to play that music, samba, in the context of jazz. We had a lot of samba music and Stan Getz used to bug me to death trying to get some of those tunes. I meant to give them to him; it wasn't that I was trying to withhold the music, but he was here while I was there all the time. He finally got ahold of it and made a big hit with it. It doesn't matter who played it first because he did a good job on it, but the fact remains that I was the first one on the North American continent to play that kind of music. I know Latin rhythm, you see, and always put my individual stamp on the music. I don't play it just like they do. Mine goes with theirs, but isn't exactly like it because I figure you have to live a music, an ethnic music. You have to live that life to play it well, exactly like they do. In Africa they had a music for fertility, for weddings, for initiations, births and deaths, which depicts the scene in which that particular event arises, but you don't have to be a part of that to get the same feeling. Our music has influenced Brazilian music harmonically, and I can hear in the composers like Carlos Jobim that a lot of the things we played and wrote influenced them. And they influenced our playing, rhythmically. But the same thing happened to Brazilian music that happened to the Cuban music that migrated to the United States in the early twentieth century. That music was played mostly in 3/4 and 2/4, and they changed it to 4/4 to make it easier for North American musicians to play. That really messed up the Cubans' music.

South America was very picturesque. It has character; it has haunting views much like San Francisco too. Argentina struck me as being really Spanish. They're more Spanish to me than any of the other countries in South America. They concocted a press scheme in Buenos Aires to dress me up in a gaucho costume and let me ride on horseback through the streets of the city. They roped off a block on Florida Avenue, this street near the club, La Rendezvous, that was run by Oscoaldo Frisedo. He's an old tango musician and we were gonna have a session. We recorded "Capriche del Amer." It never came out here, but I made this tango record accompanied by the band that played in La Rendezvous while we stayed in Buenos Aires. It was a nice record, and later I recorded a thing called "Tangorine" to note that whole experience with the tango. (Verve 89173.)

When they gave me this gaucho costume and a horse, and I rode up the street, they taught me a couple of things to say like, "*A quin leganaste. Tomatala, swa rambute. . . .*" Now, "*A quin leganaste*" is just an expression they have down there, an idiomatic expression that defies translation. It's just a slang expression like "So what . . ." Lalo Schifrin and those who I first met on that trip to Argentina taught me that. So there was a woman out on the street who took issue about me riding up the street on this horse with a gaucho costume. Everybody else was applauding and this woman was "Aww, rahn, rahn, rahn . . ."

I said, "A quin leganaste!" And she cracked up.

On that trip to South America I also met Reverend Dr. Theodore Hesburgh, the president of Notre Dame University, while we were in Buenos Aires. He, Supreme Court Justice Harold Burton, and I were supposed to be photographed together, and they dragged me away from this recording session of tango music to pose for these pictures. Justice Burton didn't even show up. I told everybody how I'd met his boss, Chief Justice Warren, one time on an airplane and beat him in a game of chess. I caught Mr. Justice Warren in a fool's mate, just three moves, and I still have the picture of it now, hanging in my basement. So what, I figured, it only takes two to tango. That trip to South America really consolidated my position as a kind of "chief" preeminent in blending the music of the Americas. I came back with the bossa nova, showing the Brazilian influence in our music. All of this music had the same mother; the main source of inspiration is the rhythm. That makes it different from European classical music.

LALO SCHIFRIN (piano, composer, arranger):

"I met Dizzy in Argentina when he came with a big band on a State Department tour. Dizzy came with one of the best big bands in the history of jazz. I had a band in Argentina myself, and Dizzy came, and that's how we met. We played for him, after hours. One of the musicians in my band was Gato Barbieri; he was playing sax in my band. We had sixteen men, and it was quite a good band touring Latin America, the only band that played jazz. We were not playing Latin music, and the style of my band was in between Dizzy and the Basie tradition. Dizzy liked it, and when he played he offered me to come to the United States as an arranger-pianist. I didn't believe it, you know. I didn't think that he meant it. He said, 'When you come over there, look me up.'

"And I came, in 1960, but I was afraid of disappointment. Many people when they're in foreign lands say that and when you call, they say, 'Well, I don't know you.' But Dizzy meant it. Because the moment I came, I pulled myself together and lost my inhibitions and called him. He said, 'Yeah, where you been?' That's when I wrote a thing for him, 'Gillespiana Suite.' (Limelight 82022.) He commissioned me to write it and he offered me to join his quintet as a pianist, and that was the turning point. I wouldn't be here if that didn't happen. I was going to go back. I came to New York temporarily just to see what would happen. I was making much more in Argentina—you know, I was doing my own show there sponsored by Coca-Cola—than working as a sideman here. But this was the dream of my life, and I just couldn't care less about the money or anything. I decided to stay in the United States because of Dizzy.

"I was a student of his music. That's why when I joined his quintet I knew all of the compositions. By memory—I learned through records, you know—I knew all the solos by memory from the records. Dizzy was my idol, of all the jazz musicians from the history of jazz. Of course, I loved Charlie Parker, Bud Powell, but my big idol from all of them was Diz. Musically, I'm talking about, generally speaking, what Diz has is beyond. He's not just a trumpet player. There are many other trumpet players that are good, Miles Davis, Clifford Brown, but Dizzy was a fantastic trumpet player, the best of them all. His musicianship is beyond, it's probably one of the most important contributions to the American mode of music. And what makes me sad is not too many people know about it. Even the musicians don't realize that. His musicianship was beyond the playing of an instrument or making of a good solo. Sometimes, the lips can be in bad shape, but still, his musical ideas are so complete and so mature that it doesn't matter what comes out. His thoughts, his musical concepts, and his feelings make him a major musician, period. If I have to make comparisons with art in other forms, Picasso in painting. He has a sense of humor and the use of the line like Picasso does.

"By playing with him I got a better understanding of style and how to accompany. He taught me how to accompany, you know. Because in modern jazz a piano is a very difficult instrument to play accompaniment. You're midway between the bass and the soloist and you don't know what to do. You just play chords. Dizzy, for instance, would tell me when I played double, different intricate patterns very fast with many notes, just play one, wham! Then take a break and that gives a feeling of space, and at the same time I give him the freedom to choose any road he wants. There's no clash, you know. Different little things like that that sound not too important, but overall, they are. And I would say that his musicianship is contagious. So it was very beneficial for me. I learned a lot with him. But we exchanged ideas too, because since I was a student of music in general—I have a classical background—sometimes I'd bring him books of harmony of contemporary composers, I mean avant-garde composers, or Europeans, and he would like it too, and we'd sometimes incorporate some things into arrangements. It was a very nice co-operation, but in general, he was, you know, the master."

Higher than Ike

We came back to the United States and played a concert before twenty thousand people, the first New York Jazz Festival at Randalls Island, in 1956, and the band drew rave notices. It was the first time that this band had ever played before a mass audience in the United States, and everyone anticipated a great performance because of the press we'd received on the foreign tour. They turned out in droves to hear us and were absolutely thrilled by what they heard. I toured alone for a short while with Norman Granz then re-formed the band, adding Lee Morgan and Talib Dawud, on trumpet; Wynton Kelly, piano; and Paul West on bass. The tours we made in the spring of 1957 to Canada and down South to Atlanta, Georgia, succeeded musically, and really scored socially in Georgia, because this was still a mixed band with a black leader playing in Georgia where whites were still struggling to hold on to segregation. One of the reasons we'd been sent around the world was to offset reports of racial prejudice in the United States, so I figured now we had a chance to give the doctor some medicine and fight against racial prejudice and end all those reports. We opened at the black-owned Waluhaje, a beautiful new luxury apartment and entertainment complex in Atlanta, and, of course, a lot of whites there wanted to come to see us and they did, with no segregation.

BILLY MITCHELL (tenor saxophone):

"I can remember ten days in Toronto when we had so many people in the band who were so fantastic. Besides Dizzy, even—Lee Morgan, Wynton Kelly, Charlie Persip, Paul West, Benny Golson, Ernie Henry, Melba Liston. The band had so much talent in it that the fire was always going. Now, we had ten nights in Toronto where it seemed like each night the band couldn't sound any better, but every night it still sounded just a little bit better."

PAUL WEST (bass):

"It wasn't too long before 1956 that I became aware of Dizzy Gillespie and Max Roach and Kenny Clarke and Clifford Brown and all of them because my whole music discipline was in a different direction. You see, I was supposed to be the black Heifitz of the world. But anyway I had a small group, a trio, and was looking for a drummer and Charlie Persip came along, and we became quite chummy during that month that we were working. So he turned me on to Dizzy Gillespie. They had a series of three rehearsals in late September of 1956, and Charlie said that Nelson Boyd was leaving and there was a possibility that Dizzy might enjoy my playing. Dizzy said, 'O.K., bring him in and let him make the first rehearsal, and we'll check him out.' So Quincy was there rehearsing some new tunes, I think 'Jessica's Day' was being rehearsed, and Dizzy said, 'O.K., come back the second night.' I came back the second night, and while I was walking up the stairs with my bass, I heard this bass player upstairs, 'doom-doom-doom-doom-doom-doom . . .' And I was totally green. So I went out and sat with the spectators. Ha, the spectators. Come to find out, this guy was Carl Pruitt who I hadn't known. But he had a big sound, and it really frightened me to death. When Dizzy was getting ready to go into rehearsal, he noticed that I wasn't there. I wasn't at the place in the band; I was sitting up there with the spectators, scared to go up. I figured, well, I know I'm green, I don't have the talent. So then Dizzy said, 'Hey, where's the bass player, young dude? The bass player who was here last night?' And I looked young in those days. I looked like a little baby.

"I said, 'Here I am, Mr. Gillespie, sitting back here, in the back row.'

"He said, 'Naw, come up here! Didn't I tell you to come back?'

"So we both played, both Carl Pruitt and I; he was really baad. After rehearsal I said, 'Well, thanks, Dizzy, for letting me attend your rehearsal.'

"He said, 'No, you've got the gig.' That's how I met Dizzy, and from that point on he served as my mentor so far as jazz is concerned. When I went into his band I was totally green. I knew a lot about music, but I didn't know too much about jazz. I was able to read well, but he really opened my eyes up and my ears up and my soul up to what jazz was all about.

"I learned, number one, discipline, which the band taught me. And number two, I learned the differences in rhythms. Dizzy, I think, is one of the most fascinating rhythm instructors in the world. And I learned how to break down rhythm, how to count an eighth note, a quarter note, followed by a quarter note, followed by an eighth rest, followed by another eighth note tied over to the next measure. And he had a way of breaking that down, you see. And that's one of the things I learned about from Dizzy.

"In fact, the night during our first rehearsal, I didn't know 'Night In Tunisia.' I'd heard it and it so happened, the first night, Oscar Pettiford was there. I had been aware of the lines, but when you hear something and try to play it, you might play the note wrong. The basic concept of that melody might be there, but note for note, you're wrong. So I had played what I thought was correct and it wasn't correct. Oscar Pettiford was the one at the rehearsal who showed me how to play the exact line, how to finger it. And Dizzy was the one who put the rhythm in its proper perspective. In 1969, when I headed the Jazzmobile Workshop, he would always come there and meet with the whole class and break down what appeared to be complex ideas, down to very basic simple forms. So the guys would say, 'Oh, wow! That's what it's all about!' But Dizzy had the knack to do that. And more than the knack and knowledge, he had the willingness to do it. A lot of musicians don't always have that. They want to reserve and conserve what they have for their own purposes, for their own use. They're afraid to give it out.

"Lee Morgan and I joined the band at the same time, and we were the two babies in the band. We were the two youngest in the band. Lee was eighteen, and I think, at that time, I was twenty-one. This was the greatest thing that could have happened to Lee Morgan at that time, his association with Dizzy. He was the baby, and he was very cocky and very happy-go-lucky and very comical. He was almost like a baby Dizzy. When you heard Lee play that solo on 'Night In Tunisia' he was aspiring to be that kind of Dizzy, the artist, the personality. Basically, this is one of the big differences between Lee Morgan's playing, and a lot of the younger musicians, trumpet players. Lee's playing had a lot of character, a lot of personality. He wasn't trying to prove how skillful he was, how highly technical his ability was, but he used that technical ability and skill to bring out his personality, his character, and this is typical of Dizzy's playing. Dizzy is not just a technician who aspires to try to convince somebody that he is technically astute, but he uses his technical ability to bring out his personality. His playing has personality, it has character, it's not just exercises, and that's the basic difference. And this, I think, is one of the things Lee got from Dizzy as well as Brownie, whom he loved and adored. The relationship between Dizzy and Lee was one of master and student, and you can see that.

"And Dizzy never says, 'Hey, son, come here, let me teach you something.' It was never like that. He used to teach you so much but not ostentatiously. He doesn't make you aware that you're gonna get a lesson, you see. Because of his character and his personality, he's dropping stuff on you all the time, and all you have to do is be open and receive it. And that's the relationship that he had not only with Lee—especially with Lee—but with the rest of the band too. He has a way of pulling your coat to a lot of things without being overbearing with it. You don't feel somebody's trying to take you over, you see. That's his way of relating, and it's one to be admired. A lot of people who think they know a lot want to prove that they're full of knowledge and skill by trying to impose something on you. They try to impose with the conditions that you realize they're the teacher and you're the student. Dizzy never had that. He would drop a volume of material on you without you feeling that somebody's imposing on you, and there's a big difference. I think that's the ideal relationship between master and student, where you realize the amount that you're getting, but the master is not conscious of the amount that he's giving you. And that's what I appreciate about Dizzy.

"The band was at the Waluhaje in Atlanta, Georgia. This was my first road experience with Dizzy, and I'll never forget this as long as I live. This was December 26, 1956, the day after Christmas. I had just gotten married. We were playing 'Dizzy's Business,' or one of those things, and Dizzy comes in with this high, high burning note. He reared back, and reared back, and reared back to get this note, until he finally reared back to where he was sitting down on the bandstand. He reared back all the way down to a sitting position. That really cracked us up. He sat down to get that note.

"And on the same trip to Atlanta—I think we were getting ready to leave Atlanta—and Dizzy was doing some funny antics at the airport. The band was really a New York band, right, all mixed. And he did something that made the police come by. In those days, 1956, in Atlanta, Georgia, things were a little different. So the cop came over and approached Dizzy, 'Hey, what's your name? Where you from?'

"And he said, 'I'm from Cheraw, South Carolina.' The funniest thing was that Dizzy knew what the situation was, so he figured that Cheraw, South Carolina, would be an appropriate answer. The guys in the band saw what was happening and might have retreated from that area because they didn't wanna be a part of that. They said, 'I'm 'a see y'all, heah!' Nobody knew Dizzy that night."

MELBA LISTON:

"He used to frighten us. Because he would get so bold and start bitching out the white folks. And we were almost on the plane, and all these policemen came and stuff, and Dizzy was not gonna be subservient to them. All we wanted to do was get on the plane and get away. He was raising hell because they wanted him to step back and let the white folks get served at the counter first, or something. You know, little black and white shit was going on at the time. That's the band we went on the State Department tour with, and we went down South. That was a mixed band. We had Jew, we had whitey, we had brothers and sisters. He had taken us down there and we were quite bold."

Despite unprecedented success at home and abroad, in 1957 we again became the object of attacks. First, they denied us a booking at Veterans Auditorium in Los Angeles because some officials there claimed we were rock 'n roll, so we played somewhere else. Then the newspapers started churning up silly questions about whether rock 'n roll had replaced bebop. I answered them by saying that rock 'n roll was just one aspect of jazz, and that modern jazz was still right there on the scene. Rock 'n roll was a form of music older than modern jazz and had been with us for a long time. Louis Jordan had been playing it as long as I could remember, long before Elvis Presley.

The big guns attacked us. Some congressmen, Senator Ellender, from Louisiana, and Representative Rooney of Brooklyn, New York, began a big hoopla in Washington about how much money we'd made overseas. They cut the budget of the USIS by 26 per cent because they said the fees we'd been paid were "exorbitant" and a waste of the taxpayers' money. They got angry because I'd made $2,150 a week for two months, and President Eisenhower's salary was calculated at $100,000 a year, a little under $2,000 a week.* When they ques-

---

* They didn't take into account that the $7,500 per week the State Department paid had to be divided among sixteen musicians, two vocalists, and a baggage handler. The total cost of the tours only came to around $100,869. They claimed foreign ticket sales amounted to around $16,000, making the real cost somewhere

tioned me about it, I asked them how many notes could the President play at one time. I knew my horn, and they paid me what was due to an artist of my stature at that particular moment. Considering my position in the financial hierarchy of America, I got paid pretty well, but it certainly wasn't any big deal. After all we'd done to represent American culture abroad to important audiences in Europe and the 'third world,' that was the thanks we received from Congress. The State Department tried to defend the program claiming the U.S. couldn't afford to send less than the best artist on these tours, and the best required top pay. No one bothered to compare our salaries with those other American artists commanded. To send a jazz band abroad was indeed a bargain compared to certain rock 'n roll stars. Those tours abroad helped the U.S. immensely, and those guys in Washington started saying I made too much money, more than the President of the United States. Of course, I didn't have two quarters to hit together, and they were picking on me. They knew no jazz musician could make that kind of money all year.

I finally wound up getting angry about it, and told them, "Jazz is too good for Americans!" By that I meant Americans don't seem to appreciate our own native music here, as well as people do in foreign lands—in Europe, Asia, South America, and Africa. They really go wild over it; they study it, they take it more seriously. And that is still true to a large extent. Would somebody please tell me why?

---

in the neighborhood of $80,000. They didn't consider either that the normal price for the big band was $8,000–$10,000 a week.

Ancestry

Mama was fifteen when Sonny, my eldest brother who died, was born. He would've been fifty-nine years old in 1959, and they were born on the same day, so add fifty-nine and fifteen. Mama was seventy-four years old when she died. Mama had lost a lot of weight, something was wrong with her throat, and she had been sick in the hospital when I went to Europe to play a concert series. She waited until I got back from Europe to die. She was very small, and she looked up at me—boy, I can see her eyes now. When I came back and went to see her in Springfield, Massachusetts, I just went in the room, and she looked up and saw me, and man, when I think about it now, I can see her right in front of my eyes. She waited until right after I got back. She would not die—and then she was dead. All my brothers and sisters—all of them—said that Mama waited until I got back. I really went to pieces.

Russell Bennett, the mayor of Cheraw, wrote to me in 1959, saying, "Gillespie, since you've become such an international figure and all, we'd like to honor you with a celebration in your hometown. We want you to play a concert in the Armory . . ." and no blacks had ever been in the Armory. His letter coming at the height of the civil rights struggle down there sounded pretty strange, so I replied that I would let him know when I had some time. We kicked the idea around for a long time. I kept getting letters from him until, finally, he just telephoned and asked, "Come on, come on, John Birks, just when will you be free?"

"That's entirely up to you, your honor!" I told him. He laughed.

I had an engagement in Florida and then two days at the University of North Carolina in Chapel Hill. There was one day in between, so I gave him that date. When I went home they had a big parade with two high school bands (big for Cheraw) and a concert with a non-segregated audience, the first time ever in Cheraw. Mayor Bennett made a speech and said that I was an international figure and Cheraw's most-famous and most-loved native son. Around two thousand people out of a town with a population of five thousand turned out. We played at Long High School, not the Armory, but of course the tickets were sold on a first-come, first-served basis. It was all mixed up, racially, the first time in Cheraw since Reconstruction, probably the first time in South Carolina. *Ebony* covered it and took pictures, and I noticed that many of the white people were covering their faces to escape the cameras. But there was one blond white girl with her head held up high who didn't seem to care whether they took her picture or not.

ALICE V. WILSON:

"I remember that Dizzy Gillespie Day and all that. He was around at Long High School, and I went to that. All of us were kind of disappointed in the crowd, you know. Because I'll tell you, in a small place like this—well, it has improved since that time, but you know most small places—it's hard to get them to appreciate something like that, no matter who's giving it. And so we were just disgusted about it. The place should've been full because it was John, even if for no other reason, you know. But that kinda thing, you run into that anywhere, in particular small towns. The place wasn't as full as it should've been. It was a good crowd there, but I wanted it to be overflowing because it was John. The mayor who had this for John was one of the younger generation, you see. They were coming into knowing how to accept things like that, regardless of who it came from."

Before the celebration, the praises and all that, I went to visit some of the older people, and one of them was this old guy named Mr. James A. Powe, from my mother's side of the family. His grandfather,

Dr. Powe, had the most slaves of anybody in that area. It wasn't so much that I wanted to brag, nor was I holding anything against him, but more than anyone else in Cheraw, I guess I just wanted to see how he would react to my coming home a hero. He symbolized, more than anything else, the old Cheraw that had forced me to leave to find my fortune in the North. I told the cabdriver, "Pull up there, right up to the front door." The house was one of those big ones with a long, long driveway.

I went up to the door and rang the bell and Mrs. Powe came to the door. She almost fainted when she looked out and saw this black face. I started talking real fast, before she could start trying to run me away. "Mrs. Powe," I said, "my name is John Gillespie, and I am the son of Lottie Gillespie, and I'm here because they held a day of honor for me in Cheraw today. I'd like to see Mr. Powe, if you don't mind, just to say hello to him."

"Mr. Powe isn't seeing anybody," she said. "Mr. Powe is sick!"

I said, "Well, I'll only be a couple of minutes. I'd just like to say hello to him."

He'd heard my voice outside by this time, and shouted out, "Is that you, John Burch?" (Whites nor blacks could say my name correctly down there.) "Come on in here, boy, come in," he said. I went in and found that he was on crutches. "Sit down," he said. We were standing in the living room, and I was somewhat shocked because I had never seen his living room. My mother used to work for them, and the only place I'd ever seen inside his house was the kitchen. "Boy, we're mighty proud of you. You've made it, you've conducted yourself like a gentleman, and you've made us so happy and so proud," he said.

I said, "Thank you, Mr. Powe, I appreciate that."

"Another thing," he said, "your great-grandmother would have been proud of you. You didn't know her, did you? That's right, you're the youngest, aren't you?"

I told him, "Yes, sir, I've heard some things about her."

"But you didn't hear the real story about her, did you? Your great-grandmother was the daughter of a chief in Africa."

"Well, call me your majesty, then," I said.

He cracked up, went into hysterics, and after he finished laughing about three hours, he told me the rest of the story.

"My father went all the way to Charleston to buy her because he wanted her to raise the children, as a nana. They named her Nora." I knew that he was telling the truth because I had always heard my mother talk about Grand No', and I knew that Nora was my great-grandmother's name.

Grand No' had two sons, Uncle William and my grandfather, and their fathers—both of them—had been white.* She had nothing to do with, no contact at all, with the rest of the slaves on the plantation.

Grand No' was mean and "color struck." Mama used to tell stories about it. As a matter of fact, when my father first came courting my mother, Papa was very dark and had kinky hair. Grand No' took one look at him and she said, "If that black nappy-headed nigger ever comes in here again, I'm gonna put both of y'all out!" My mother persevered and she married my father in spite of it. That was the first time I'd ever heard this story. No one else in my family had ever heard it, either. But Mr. Powe told me. He must have figured that I could take it. He didn't want to give anyone else in the family any undue sense of importance or respect. After he told me, I spread it to everybody else in the family. That was nice because Mr. Powe could've just kept it a state secret until he died.

A little more about Grand No's personality also became clearer to me, not just from Mr. Powe's story but from other facts that I knew. She either had a crush on white men or was pretty attractive to them, since the fathers of both her sons had been white. That was typical of defeated royalty, sticking up under those who had the power and refusing to associate with anyone who she did not consider an equal. Being former royalty, Grand No' must have felt twice burned by slavery, and this probably accounted for her mean temperament and for the nasty way she treated Papa.

Sitting there in Mr. Powe's living room, putting two and two together, something dawned on me. If Grand No' was strictly a house slave, owned by Mr. Powe's father, who wouldn't allow for any contact between her and the black males on the plantation, then who was most likely to be the father of her children? The implications were enough to knock me off my feet, and I reared back in my seat on the sofa laughing. Savior!

* My grandfather, Paw, whose real name was Hampson, was also called "Yank" because his father was "a Yankee," we were told.

Striving

After Mama died, I knew I had to do all in my power to make my own life count, musically, and in every way possible. I started thinking a lot more about what we'd come through as a family, as a people: depression, poverty, separation, relocation, struggling and striving to survive, and creating in spite of it. A lot of black people, and certain whites too, were thinking the same way in 1959. By acting on their thoughts and feelings, they strengthened my own resolve to accept no less in my dealings than the status of a human being. This was revolutionary because it meant fighting new challenges to your humanity every day and demanded the greatest commitment of time, courage, money, and determination. Sometimes I was equal to it, sometimes I wasn't.

I wanted to fight against narcotics addiction, and on April 21, 1957, a resolution was passed by the City Council of New York appointing a committee to investigate all phases of the narcotics problem in the city, but no financial appropriation was given to the committee by the city of New York. To me it seemed clear that if the committee had no money, it couldn't do anything about the scourge of narcotics addiction. So that summer, I prevailed upon Franklin Geltman, the producer of the Randall's Island Jazz Festival, to contribute $1,000, as a part of my fee for performing at the Festival, to the committee to further its work. Geltman made the contribution in my name, and Earl

Brown, chairman of the special committee, accepted it. I considered this a personal tribute and a tribute to the memory of Charlie Parker and Billie Holiday, both of whom had been victimized by drug addiction. It wasn't much. Narcotics addiction persisted as a problem, but it was a beginning which identified jazz with life-giving rather than life-destroying forces.

Racial discrimination posed another definite threat. An incident occurred in Kansas City at a place called the Continental Hotel. They had an Olympic-sized swimming pool for their guests, but you had to go to the desk with your key to get a permit. When they gave you a permit then you could use the swimming pool. Well, I tried to get a permit, and they farted me around for days. First they told me the pool was run by an athletic club in the city which had all the say. I asked, "Well, where's the athletic club?"

They said, "We represent them," and they kept giving me the run-around which all boiled down to them not wanting to let a nigger swim in the pool. Finally, I had some friends, some white friends from Topeka, the Duffields, who were in the oil business and very dear friends of mine, come down to visit me. I told them the situation; I was trying to get into the pool.

They hollered, "What shit!" and went downstairs and asked to get in and got tickets with no trouble. They came back and gave me the tickets, and said, "O.K., you got the tickets now, so you sue the muthafuckas!"

The guy behind the desk had told Bob Duffield, "Sorta cool it with those permits because there's been a niggah trying to get in here, and we ain't 'bout to let him in that pool." Bob Duffield is a big dude, and he was getting ready to jump over the counter and throttle the guy. They had to restrain him.

Now that I had the permits, I contacted my Philadelphia lawyer, Professor Bogus. He looked it up in the book, and I called him back later and asked, "What's the chance of me owning the hotel?"

He said, "Well, the chances of your getting some money are slim. You would have to sue them under an old English common law regarding inns. Are you prepared to spend $2,500?"

I said, "Bogus, I was hurt, but I wasn't hurt that bad. It hurt my feelings, but it didn't hurt my feelings that bad." Ah! Ha! Ha! Ha!

Anyway, I sent a telegram to Robert Kennedy about it, and I think I got an answer from Robert Kennedy. The same guy who was U. S. Attorney in Kansas at the same time came by to hear me play later. But nothing happened as a result of it. I never did get into the pool. By the time all this happened, I was getting ready to leave. Even if I had gotten in, it wouldn't have proven very much. The whole thing reminded me of Louis Armstrong, back before integration. Pops could stay in the white hotels down South when the rest of us had to go to the colored places. He had to go in through the back door. Some crackers found out about this once, and they went and put a coon in Louis' room. Pops went into his room and saw this raccoon sitting up there in the middle of the bed and split. He went down to see the manager at the desk about it. "Look man," he said, "there's a coon in my room."

The manager told him, "Don't worry, sir. Just one minute, Mr. Armstrong, we'll get that nigger out of there."

Tulane University in New Orleans canceled one of my concerts because they had a state and local ordinance prohibiting blacks and whites from performing together. I had Lalo Schifrin in my band and they wanted me to substitute a black pianist for him. This happened around the same time as that Kansas City hotel incident. I told them absolutely not, and we kept the $1,000 deposit they had advanced on the date. They had the nerve to ask us to return the deposit, but my manager, Joe Glaser, and the union backed me up. We weren't about to pay any attention to a law like that. A little while later, a movement began to include non-segregation clauses in the contracts of all jazz musicians, giving the artist the right to terminate the engagement if racial segregation was required either in the audience or on the bandstand. Norman Granz became one of the leaders of that movement. A lot of jazz musicians, for economic reasons, had continued to play before segregated audiences, and one sure way to stop the whole thing was by action of the musicians themselves, especially the more prominent leaders. This movement also exposed the fact that the union itself, in 1961, still had many segregated locals, not just in the South, but in several northern cities like Philadelphia. Local union officials, black and white, often preferred segregation because it allowed them personal control over local affairs, but it wasn't doing the musicians any good. The black musicians always received the lowest paying jobs; that's what they controlled. The white locals, of course, had the greatest reason to protect economic segregation. I spoke out on this because it was no time for any "cat" to be a "Tom." However, I have to stop people, black or white, who approach me with a racist attitude about jazz because most of the people who come to see me perform are white. If it wasn't for white people, I'd starve to death. I'll never turn my back on my brothers, but neither will I turn my back on my livelihood and the people who dig my music. Too many white people like my music.

Once I performed on a show with Dinah Washington, in 1961, at the Regal Theater in Chicago, and this disc jockey, Al Benson, the foremost disc jockey in the rhythm and blues field in Chicago at the time, put the show together. I had a big band, and he allotted me about twenty minutes each show. When I'd get to "Manteca" which was about ten minutes, I'd have to go overtime. Al Benson asked me to limit myself to twenty minutes. When I went overtime again, I received a telegram from Al Benson saying that I had no regard for the wishes of the management of the theater and that my contract called for a playing to the policy of the house. He also said the telegram was the third request for me not do more than twenty minutes of entertaining on any show for the remainder of my engagement at the theater, and if any changes were to be made in the length of time I was to perform, the management would notify me of that change before each show. That's what some blacks thought about jazz. They'd give you twenty minutes with a big band after you'd already played all over the world for people who always seemed to want some more.

Crime, black on black, especially, was more than a threat to my humanity. It threatened my existence. Once, I'd just finished playing at the Sutherland Lounge in Chicago, and I was staying at a hotel on South Park. There were some guests in my room, a couple of schoolteachers trying to get me to do a benefit for a local school. And the door burst open; it wasn't locked, it was sorta cracked. These two guys came in, one with the sawed-off shotgun, the other one with a .38, and said, "This is a stick up!" I thought it was somebody kidding, and I sorta pushed the guy. "We're serious," the niggah said.

"Oh, seriously?" I said.

"Turn around!" They shouted. We went to the wall, and they took everything out of our pockets, and then they made us get into the bathroom. When they put us into the bathroom, I locked the door, and all of us got into the tub, and I started screaming my lungs out. Those guys got outta there. We were in the tub, but if we had been out in the bathroom, they coulda shot right through the door, so we got into the tub. They couldn't shoot through that brick wall. I kept screaming at the top of my voice.

We didn't lose that much money. I *never* keep any money in my room. They wanted me to call the desk and tell them to send the money I'd made at the Sutherland up to my room. I told them, "Man, that guy's not gonna come up here with any money. I have to go down there and sign to get into the safe." So they just took what we had.

One time when I was in the mountains in Denver, the most beautiful natural sight I've ever seen occurred. I looked up through the mountains, and I saw an aura. I tried to take a picture of it in color, because from the sun there was a reflection that looked like it was multicolored, and I thought that was the prettiest sight I'd ever seen. I tried to take a picture of it, but it didn't come out like I was looking at it. The camera didn't capture that, but that's what I like—all colors.

I've struggled to establish jazz as a concert music, a form of art, not just music you hear in clubs or places where they serve whiskey. I did a lot of playing along those lines in the late 1950s and early 1960s: at Circle in the Square, to show my compositions; a series of Jazz Profiles at the Museum of Modern Art in New York; at the Monterey Jazz Festival where we premiered "Perceptions," a work I commissioned by J. J. Johnson, which was the most difficult piece I'd ever played. Following that I performed "Gillespiana," which lasted forty minutes longer. When the concert was over I had to thank God for giving me the strength. The critic, Ralph Gleason, said I "blew like a man possessed or . . . blessed by an almost divine aid." To end it, we played some down-home blues. I said, "Bye," and the audience gave me a standing ovation.

Pops and I played together publicly for the first time on January 7, 1959, on the Timex All-Star Jazz Show, televised on CBS. Pops's acceptance of this engagement sort of showed he accepted the olive branch we "boppers" had held out, and it showed he recognized that there didn't have to be any competition between Dixieland and modern jazz. But to let it be known that neither of us had given up his own brand of jazz, Pops and I played "The Umbrella Man" and battled it out, "Dixieland" versus "modern." It was much more fun arguing with music than with words. (For Discriminate Collectors FDC 1017.) The whole show worked out beautifully and made it possible for more Americans than ever to hear modern jazz on a prime-time TV show and develop an understanding and appreciation of the music. That Timex show was great. Duke Ellington, Coleman Hawkins, Roy Eldridge, Gene Krupa, Jo Jones, and George Shearing also appeared.

Other concerts at the Music Barn in Lenox, Massachusetts, and at Carnegie Hall—one called "Genius at Midnight," featuring jazz and symphony brass, with four trumpets, four trombones, four French horns, one tuba, and three drummers—were memorable. I gave my first performance of "Kush" that night, an African rhythm and tone poem I'd composed. At the first all-jazz performance ever held at Lincoln Center's Philharmonic Hall we played a concert with Mary Lou Williams featuring Brazilian-influenced jazz, the bossa nova, the malakaty, and introduced another piece by Lalo Schifrin, "New Continent," which was played by a twenty-seven-piece orchestra. In the clubs, I appeared for the first time on the same bill with Monk at the Jazz Gallery; they'd had a fire the month before, and the place almost burned down. But even in clubs we featured "Gillespiana" one set each night, for forty minutes, so people who went mostly to clubs could hear good jazz in a different kind of format.

SAM JONES (bass):

"I went through three bands with Dizzy. The first one was with Wynton Kelly, Candido, Sonny Stitt, Jimmy Cobb, and myself. I stayed with Diz around three years. The second band was with Junior Mance, Les Spann, Lex Humphries, and Sonny Stitt.

"We were playing an engagement in Pittsburgh, and I remember Sonny Stitt was going through all these calisthentics with his tenor and his alto, and Dizzy was listening, and when it came time for Dizzy to play, this man played so much music on that song that when he stopped playing, the whole club stood up to give him a standing ovation. Everytime I see him right now, I say, 'Man, you know they're still applauding out in Pittsburgh.'"

JUNIOR MANCE (piano):

"I didn't want to be a bandleader until after I played with him, and aside from being the best on his instrument, I used to admire the way he had control of the audience, or how he would get control of the audience and hold it. He's got it all together."

RUDY COLLINS (drums):

"Diz is real sticky about being on time. Once he was going to play a concert down in Norfolk, Virginia. We finished at the Village Gate on a Saturday night and that Sunday we were supposed to catch an early flight to Norfolk. By the time we got off and packed up, it must've been four o'clock. I was supposed to have gotten up about six o'clock to catch the seven o'clock flight. So I should have stayed up, I guess.

"Anyway, I laid down and the phone rang. I answered and it was Dizzy. 'Wat'cha doin' answering the phone?' he said. 'You're supposed to be out here at the airport.' He was at the airport because we were supposed to catch the early flight. I forget the timing on this flight, but it was pretty early.

"I jumped in my car with my drums and drove like a maniac to get to Kennedy Airport, and as I got there I just missed the plane. I saw the plane taxiing away.

"Dizzy left a ticket at the counter for me, and they told me there was another flight out of Newark at about eight-thirty or nine. They called and got me a reservation, and I jumped back in the car and drove like a maniac over to Newark. When I got to Newark, the flight had been delayed. They delayed the flight an hour because of some kind of mechanical trouble. Then when that hour passed, they delayed it another hour. We had a two o'clock concert to make. If I had waited around for the flight, I wouldn't have been able to make the concert.

"One of the skycaps said, 'Why don't you take an air taxi?' So I went over to the phones and called the air taxi service.

"The guy said, 'Yeah, I'll take you to Norfolk. But it costs $147.' There was nothing I could do but try it. They had a Beechcraft Bonanza, just enough room in there for my drums in the back seat, the pilot, and me. After we took off and were on our way I had the pilot to radio ahead and ask them to tell Dizzy to meet me at the airport with some money, because I didn't have that much money. They called back and said, 'O.K., somebody will meet you.'

"We got there in time for the concert, but I figured, boy, Dizzy would be angry because I was late. He met me at the airport and he didn't say anything; he wasn't mad. The other guys were sorta laughing. Birks wasn't angry.

"They took me aside and said, 'Hey, man, you know what happened? Birks got the contract dates mixed up and the concert isn't until next Sunday. He went to the place where the concert was supposed to be, and instead of the concert, there was a basketball game going on.' All the cats in the band were cracking up, man. After all that running around, my heart was jumping. All I had to do was stay in bed and I woulda woke up in time for the concert. Dizzy was down there a week early. I think about that now, and laugh.

"Dizzy showed me the bossa nova rhythm, and we were one of the first bands, if not the first band, that started playing it. Later, we had a hit record, *Dizzy on the Riviera*, made from our performance at the jazz festival in Juan-les-Pins in France. (Phillips PHM 200-048.)

"We had a good band, and it wasn't just the playing. Dizzy really likes to put on a show for the people. He had a cymbal, a big garbage can top with beat-up ends and turned-up edges, and he loved the sound of that cymbal. He said Cozy Cole gave him that cymbal. It was too loud for me because all that sound would come back at me. We used to talk about it, and Dizzy would say sometimes, 'Well, all right, play my cymbal for my solo, and then for the other guy's solo, you can switch if you like.'

"One time I was coming back from Buffalo, and the cymbals got lost on the Greyhound bus. So I thought, 'Oh, oh, I'll probably lose this gig, man. Because every drummer who worked with Diz had to play on that cymbal. So we got another one, you know, but it wasn't the same as the old one. I eventually got the cymbals back, they found them. But Diz was really sorta drugged because he'd had that cymbal

a long time. They used to call it the Chinese cymbal. It was strange
playing on that at first. The old drummers used to have those cymbals,
Cozy Cole, Zutty Singleton, all the Dixieland drummers had one of
those giant cymbals. Diz was about the only dude playing modern
and using that kind of cymbal. But after that a lotta guys started using
that cymbal. Mel Lewis still uses it today. Yeah, it gets a different
sound, all right."

KENNY BARRON (piano):

"I guess one of the main things I've learned from Dizzy is, like,
being consistent. And another thing is how to use space in soloing.
Not to play everything you know all the time; save some. Breathe!
Breathe when you solo.

"We used to do a ballad, a medley of 'I Can't Get Started' and
'Round About Midnight.' Between each tune, Dizzy took a cadenza,*
alone. Once he paused to take a breath, and it was very quiet, the
mood was just so. And when he went to exhale, you know, he farted.
Loud! There was nothing you could do after that.

"Some nights at the last set, he would just play. I would get up and
he would play the last set on piano with Moody playing saxophone.
He kinda sounded like Monk and he plays very well. I think that's one
of the reasons he plays so well on the trumpet, that he plays piano.
One of the reasons that he hears the things that he hears is because he
plays piano.

"I remember one night when we were playing a concert. I think it
was somewhere in the Midwest, and it was like in a chapel. Moody
was soloing, and Dizzy was in the back shooting off firecrackers. You
know, in the church. Well, the whole band was silly. It was silly, but it
wasn't rehearsed. It was a very, very enjoyable experience. It was really very, very spontaneous. You never knew what was gonna happen."

* A passage or section of varying length in a style of brilliant improvisation,
usually inserted near or at the end of a composition where it serves as a retard-
ing element, giving the performer a chance to exhibit technical mastery.

Diz for President

One time Adam Powell came over to see me at the Embers, and of course he smoked cigars. I went over to his table at intermission, and he pulled out one of those big cigars. I said, "Wait a minute, hold it. . . ." I went and got this big lighter, about six inches high and four inches wide, picked it up and mashed it, and it lit up for him. It's a Shields, but it looks like a Zippo. That lighter had an inscription on the side: "To Dizzy Gillespie with kindest affection. From Moody and Margenia." On the other side the inscription read, "The HNIC." So when I lit the cigar, Adam laughed, man! Then he took it, and he read it. Moody was playing with me at the time, and he looked at Moody and said, "Tom . . . !"

"Turn it over, look on the other side," I said.

He says, "The HNIC, what does that mean?"

"Oh, come on Adam, you know what HNIC means," I said. A lot of people were at the table, about eight people. He asked me again so I went over and whispered in his ear, "That means 'Head Nigger In Charge!'"

"I gotta have one of them," he told me.

I said, "Well, Adam, I'll tell you what, you can get one, but you can't have those same letters because I'm the HNIC! You can be the NNIC." So I bought him one and had it inscribed, "To the NNIC which means the 'Next Nigger In Charge.'" Adam had it on his desk when I went down to Washington about a year or so later. Adam was hip, boy, but he outsmarted himself. He figured if Senator Dodd can do it, I can do it too. He thought he was 'white.' In Congress, he had some power! He thought he could do the same thing that the white man did and get away with it, but he was wrong because if you're challenging something, you have to be prepared to be challenged and be clean enough to go all the way.

That's why I thought I would run for President, to take advantage of the votes and publicity I'd receive and to promote change. It wasn't just a publicity stunt. I made campaign speeches and mobilized people. I meant to see how many votes I could get, really, and see how many people thought I'd make a good President. Anybody coulda made a better President than the ones we had in those times, dillydallying about protecting blacks in the exercise of their civil and human rights and carrying on secret wars against people around the world. One time when I ran, Goldwater was running against Johnson. History records Johnson as a pretty good President, but at that time, I didn't think there was any choice. I was the only choice for a thinking man.

The whole thing started largely as a result of the March on Washington for Jobs and Freedom in 1963 and the Newport Jazz Festival, both of which I supported.* George Wein and I appeared, just prior to the Festival and the March, on 'Youth Wants to Know,' a nationally televised interview program aimed at the young-spirited audience, and a panel of students interviewed me.

Q: Mr. Gillespie, why don't we see more Negro performers on television?

DG: I wish I could answer that question. There is discrimination there.

Q: Mr. Gillespie, in Washington, D.C., there is a special television network, so to speak, which caters to Negroes. It's made up of Negroes, it has Negro performers on it. Do you see any kind of trend toward stations which play only to Negroes?

DG: I'm for people pooling their money and buying something. I'm all for that because if they're not getting a fair shake—they are not getting a fair shake with the white ownerships—I think it's no more than right that they should have it themselves.

---

* Actually, Dizzy Gillespie for President buttons were issued by my booking agency, Associated Booking Corporation, several years before this, but only for publicity, as a gag.

Q: Mr. Gillespie, do you feel that if there is a southern filibuster on civil rights, that the Negroes are justified and should create further demonstrations?

DG: They are definitely going to. It's a definite fact that if there is a filibuster, there are going to be 200,000 or 300,000 marchers on Washington. And they will be sitting on the Senate floor and in the Senate caucus room.

Ralph Gleason's wife, Jean, felt we needed somebody as an alternative to Goldwater, so we organized a big campaign out there in California which spread across the country. We had bumper stickers and balloons. My name almost got on the ballot in California, and a lotta write-in votes were cast for me, but I can't recall how many. I just liked the idea of running for President.

On June 29, 1963, Jeannie Gleason, my chief advisor, received a telegram from Dick Gregory pledging his support: "Thanks so much for the Dizzy Gillespie campaign button. I am sure you know that Diz has my vote but I would like to make one suggestion. . . . How about Miles Davis for Secretary of State? With best wishes. Dick Gregory."

In San Francisco for my birthday, on October 21, we held a 'Dizzy for President' birthday ball at Basin Street West and invited all my California supporters to come out and bring some money. As Jon Hendricks, the campaign lyricist, put it on the invitations, RSVP (Rip Some Vonces on me, Please).

The campaign publicist was Ralph Gleason, the jazz columnist, who turned out a whole spate of articles about my better attributes such as experience in foreign affairs; and noted that people wearing buttons supporting my election were popping up all over the place at CORE rallies in Ohio, and in such cities as Paris, Chicago, New York, Philadelphia, and Los Angeles. At least one of my supporters eventually wore a campaign button to the March on Washington, which was really what motivated me to do this, and was photographed walking in the parade alongside James Baldwin. I took to wearing African garb, including my robes, fez, and shoes, around that time to emphasize that my candidacy meant a more progressive outlook toward Africa and the 'third world,' but this backfired because many people were confused about where I actually came from. They'd been just as confused when American blacks wearing African clothes would walk into still-segregated public accommodations and get served, sometimes with a smile, because the African countries were free and independent of colonial rule. Because it was wrong and presented a poor image of the U.S. overseas, I emphasized the need to eliminate racism in music, and all other fields, at my performances and lectures at various colleges.

At Raymond College, University of the Pacific, and Berkeley, the students loved it. We played a combination benefit for CORE and campaign rally outdoors in a park, in East Menlo Park, California, and I remember Moody played a duel with a freight train passing by, and won—his solo sounded so strong coming from the speakers. Jon Hendricks unveiled the lyrics of a campaign song, which he'd written, sung to the tune of "Salt Peanuts," and we performed it together.

Intro: Vote Diz, Vote Diz, Vote Diz
   Vote for Diz, Vote for Diz
   He'll show you where it is
   Vote Dizzy! Vote Dizzy!

Chorus: You want a good President who's willing to run
   Vote Dizzy! Vote Dizzy!
   You wanna make Government a barrel of fun
   Vote Dizzy! Vote Dizzy!
   Your politics oughta be a groovier thing
   Vote Dizzy! Vote Dizzy!
   So get a good President who's willing to swing
   Vote Dizzy! Vote Dizzy!

Bridge: Show the Republic where it is
   Give them a Democratic Diz, really he is

Last eight: Your political leaders spout a lot of hot air
   Vote Dizzy! Vote Dizzy!
   But Dizzy blows trumpet so you really don't care
   Vote Dizzy! Vote Dizzy!

Interlude: You oughta spend your money in a groovier way
   —Every cent
   Get that badge of the People's only candidate
   Dizzy for President!

(Lyrics by Jon Hendricks)

I thought that was cute. That was a real gas. The campaign had its humorous side. I'd announce my choices for appointments to minor posts, such as the Honorable Ross Barnett, governor of Alabama, as Chief of the USIA in the Congo, and make suggestions to the Congress and the administration. We wanted the Senate Internal Security Committee to investigate "everything under white sheets" for un-American activities, and NASA we asked to put up at least one black astronaut. I threw out trial balloons by speculating openly about changing the color of the White House and the possibility of naming Bo Diddley as Secretary of State. My fans organized the John Birks

Society and sold sweatshirts with my portrait silk-screened in front to wear as a uniform, a follow-up to the initiative of sweatshirt wearers who loved Bach and Beethoven. When asked by critics, why I, a jazz man, was running for President, I'd answer, "Because we need one."

We had a complete program and began developing a platform early on.

We also began considering solutions to real problems like finding a black astronaut because no qualified applicants were found, I intended to go to the moon myself. By early 1964, the campaign was definitely off the ground, and Jeannie Gleason had been contacted by people in twenty-five states about it. The drive began to place my name on the official ballot in California as a candidate. Members of the John Birks Society started circulating the petition: "We, the undersigned, hereby petition the Secretary of State of the State of California to place the name of John Birks 'Dizzy' Gillespie as an independent candidate for the Presidency of the United States. . . ." We decided to skip all the primaries and that I would run as a write-in candidate all the way. People all over the country and abroad loved my campaign slogan: I'm running for President "Because we need one. . . ."

I was interviewed by the *National Observer,* radio and television announcers in Washington, and had lunch with I. F. Stone. There were pressures on me to withdraw from the race after the press began to show some interest, and they found out that I was a serious candidate. Barry Goldwater, the Republican nominee, an arch conservative tried to split and draw away my support from the jazz community by naming Turk Murphy as his favorite musician. I replied, "All I can say is don't blame Turk for that. I'm glad he didn't pick me."

Reporters were curious about whether I planned to withdraw early and switch my support to President Lyndon Johnson. I had thought about that but was determined not to announce any decision until after the Democratic Convention in Atlantic City and a review of the Democrats' platform plank on civil rights. "That sounds like Governor Wallace of Alabama," Ralph Gleason said.

"Governor Wallace is a horse of a different color," I replied, adding that I was not, "a dark horse candidate." There were plans to wage a strong floor fight for my proposals on eliminating the income tax, legalizing numbers, and changing the color and/or name of the White House. I'd have my representatives at the Convention lie on the floor while blowing trumpets if necessary. In the event we did not gain our aims in this struggle, I coined a parable to describe my last-ditch position.

> I never thought the time would come when
> I'd vote for Lyndon B.
> But I'd rather burn in hell, than vote for
> Barry G.

Everyone agreed we had to look out for Dr. Strangelove.

By midway in the campaign, my standard speech was in perfect order and was reported verbatim in the press.† In this speech I disclosed my major plans for new programs and major appointments to government posts.

"When I am elected President of the United States, my first executive order will be to change the name of the White House! To the Blues House.

"Income tax must be abolished, and we plan to legalize 'numbers'— you know, the same way they brought jazz into the concert halls and made it respectable. We refuse to be influenced by the warnings of one NAACP official who claims that making this particular aspect of big business legal would upset the nation's economy disastrously.

"One of the ways we can cut down government expenditures is to disband the FBI and have the Senate Internal Security Committee investigate everything under white sheets for un-American activities. Understand, we won't take no 'sheet' off anybody!

"All U. S. Attorneys and judges in the South will be our people so we can get some redress. 'One Man-One Vote—that's our motto. We might even disenfranchise women and let them run the country. They'll do it anyhow.

"The Army and Navy will be combined so no promoter can take too big a cut off the top of the 'double-gig' setup they have now.

"The National Labor Relations Board will rule that people applying for jobs have to wear sheets over their heads so bosses won't know what they are until after they've been hired. The sheets, of course, will all be colored!

"We're going to recall every U.S. ambassador except Chester Bowles and give the assignments to jazz musicians because they really, 'know where it is.'

"The title of 'Secretary' will be replaced by the more appropriately dignified 'Minister.' Miles Davis has offered to serve as Minister of the Treasury, but I've persuaded him to head the CIA instead. Mrs. Jeannie Gleason, whose husband Ralph writes a lot, will be Ministress of the Treasury. Max Roach argued for the position of Minister of War. He said he wanted to declare it. But since we're not going to have any, I gave him some books by C. Wright Mills and convinced him to be Minister of Defense. I have Charles Mingus lined up for Minister

† See the California *Eagle*, Thursday, July 23, 1964.

of Peace because he'll take a piece of your head faster than anybody I know.

"Ray Charles will be in charge of the Library of Congress, and we have found a place for Ross Barnett—U. S. Information Officer in the Congo. We will also recommend a special act of Congress to revoke the citizenship of Governor George Wallace and deport him to Vietnam.

"Since integration will be so complete under my administration, the Muslims will be out of business, and even Malcolm X's group won't have anything to do, so rather than let all that talent go to waste, Malcolm will be appointed U. S. Attorney General, immediately. He's one cat we want on our side.

"Although Bo Diddley applied first, I told him my choice is the great Duke Ellington for Minister of State. He's a natural and can con anybody. Louis Armstrong is set for Minister of Agriculture. He knows all about raising those crops. Mary Lou Williams has already agreed to be Ambassadress to the Vatican. And, after considering the qualifications and potential of a great many candidates, I have decided that the Rabbi of Modern Jazz . . . the Maharajah of Contemporary Music . . . one of the most creative and gifted and avant-garde young men I know—Thelonious Sphere Monk—will be booked for a four-year tour as Roving Ambassador Plenipotentiary.

"There will be places in the cabinet for Peggy Lee (Ministress of Labor), Ella Fitzgerald (HEW), Carmen McRae, Benny Carter, Woody Herman, and Count Basie. They are collaborating now on the jazz curriculum to be taught to kids in every school in the country.

"The distinguished post of National Poet Laureate, a paid position, will go to Jon Hendricks who has been donating his services to our movement as a campaign lyricist.

"As Vice-President, I would like Ramona Crowell, a leader of the John Birks Society and a registered Sioux Indian."

President Johnson discovered this campaign had a very serious side when musicians picketed a fund-raising discotheque for LBJ, protesting the exclusive use of recorded music at these affairs. "Records Don't Vote," they said. One of my supporters, Bill Crow, a bassist with Gerry Mulligan, was among them and told the press that he knew it was important to stop Goldwater and would probably vote for Johnson, but he said, "In my heart, I know Diz is right."

We hammered on the issues right down to the wire, and in an interview for *Downbeat,* I stated what I believed to be the key issues: civil rights, to be gained if necessary through mass boycotts of certain products; a national lottery to remove or reduce the income tax; equality of opportunity in employment without regard to race; the diplomatic recognition of China; and an end to the war in Vietnam. In addition we pushed for a tax on jukebox operators, the proceeds to be distributed among musicians and composers, aimed at promoting the hiring of live musicians. There was a bill in Congress about it then, and I believe it's still there. I recommended more federal subsidies for the arts and pushed the creation of civil service nightclubs where musicians who'd actually be government workers could play regularly. It would lead to a great rejuvenation of jazz.

JEAN GLEASON (campaign manager):

"Well, it actually came about originally because some promotion guy had some buttons made up that said 'Dizzy Gillespie for President.' Now, who that was, I don't know; it was just for promotion purposes, right. But then we just sort of took it from there because it sounded like a great idea to us. We took off from that, but it wasn't our original idea to make up those buttons. We made many, many more of them after that; but the original buttons were made by someone who was doing promotions for him. That was the origin of it.

"My husband, who was writing a column then, wrote a column about it. He thought it was a great idea, and from then on, we just did whatever we could think of. We had more buttons made up; we had bumper stickers and sent out some publicity releases too. Then we started getting a lot of feedback from Dizzy's fans on it.

"Well, I certainly think he was of presidential caliber, but on the other hand, it was quite obvious that Dizzy was not going to give up his career in music. Not for being a politician, any more than he is now, anyway. He's always espousing what he believes in as I think he should, you know. I think it's great, but he obviously is in it only to a certain degree. There was this element of humor as there was in anything with Dizzy, but underlying it was this serious belief that he'd make a great candidate—but not as any serious belief that he was actually ever gonna run for President.

"I think that he is highly intelligent, a much more highly intelligent man than anybody that's been in the White House; also very cognizant of world problems, not just the problems of this country, but throughout the world. And he's very, very sincere. Not afraid to speak his mind at all. I don't think he ever got on the ballot, but he certainly did have write-in votes, mine among them."

I liked the idea of running for President, and it would've been nice to be elected. I'd have fought for a disarmament program and the establishment of a world government, somewhere. We've got the laws to accomplish what I want, I'd just enforce the existing laws. I would see that everyone had enough to eat and some clothes and a decent place to stay. Everybody, every citizen, is entitled to that. Education would be beautiful, free, subsidized by the government. All of it. Anytime you wanted to learn something, I'd pay you to do it. Hospitalization would also be free. The only bona-fide politician who paid any serious attention to my political ideas, which have since been in part realized, was a woman. I gave a "Dizzy Gillespie for President" button to the representative from Texas, Barbara Jordan. She wore it on the floor of the House. It's a shame she wasn't nominated for a major post in the Carter administration, like Vice-President or Attorney General. That would've been great, wouldn't it?

In the 1972 elections I started to run for the presidency a second time. I was invited to the White House for dinner and talked with President Nixon, and that's when I decided to do it. I was about to become a perennial candidate but changed my mind and withdrew from the race after consulting with my spiritual advisors. The first time, I had a real reason for running because the proceeds from the sale of buttons went to CORE, SCLC, and Dr. Martin Luther King, Jr., and I could threaten the Democrats with a loss of votes and swing them to a more reasonable position on civil rights. The second time, my ideas about politics as a whole had changed completely, and I issued the following disclaimer:

"Upon reflection, I have decided to withdraw my bid for the presidency of the United States. My real intention has not been to promote myself politically or to criticize by my candidacy the actions of anyone who holds or aspires to this high position in our government.

"Rather, I have been deeply concerned with drawing attention to the dire necessity of bringing together the peoples of the world in unity so that all wars may cease.

"I can only hope that this urgent necessity will be met soon through the efforts of all who are in positions of influence, with the support of others, like myself, working through the avenues open to their respective callings."

I issued the disclaimer because I found out it was against the principles of the Baha'i faith to run for political office. We believe that the political systems in the world that we know are finished and that there will be a new day of political activity counter to what's happening now. We think that to aspire to any political office in this age is beneath our station. Because Baha'u'llah says there will be the establishment of a true world government with representatives of all the world's people. The shibboleth of nationalism has got to fall, and politics won't work like it does today. That's why I don't have any more presidential aspirations. Faith cut my aspirations in that direction for being king of anywhere or prime minister. It was below my station to aspire to the presidency of the United States. My aspirations go higher than that. Running for President of a world government would be more in keeping with my interests.

The Cruel World

On the soundtrack of the movie *The Cool World*, in 1963, all I did was play. They hired me to play the music which was written by Mal Waldron. Mal was so nervous and everything, he was almost depending on me to get it together, to assemble the different stages of it for the film. I told him, "No, man, you get it together and you tell me what to do because this is yours, and I'll do what you want." He finally put it together, but he was pretty nervous about it. Then they wanted to make an album from the soundtrack, and I told them, "No, no. . . ." I wouldn't go for that. I would go into the studio and make an album of the music. But I wouldn't be responsible for the soundtrack of the movie; I would be responsible for the album. We added some things; the album wasn't just like the film; I put a little Gillespiana in there, you know. So that's why it came out very well, beautifully. (Phillips PHM 200-138.)

I made two other films, animated, *The Hat* and *The Hole,* in 1963, for which I was much more responsible, with John and Faith Hubley. The Hubleys have been fans of mine a long time. I met them years ago. They're followers of Paul Robeson too, and they know that I am, and we meet at different functions and things. They were in the film business, and they called me for a lot of things, various films. We have a mutual admiration society. I respect them and appreciate their creativity, and they are very good at animation. John used to work for Walt

Disney. They are wonderful people, very warm and very generous. Oh, they're so nice. They seem to see in me things that other people don't see, such as my concern for the establishment of a world order. I felt this need before I became a Baha'i, and the Hubleys always talked to me about world government and things like that. I would talk to them about how the world should be and what the ideal world would be like. They looked upon me as an authority on world order and on world law, so therefore it was natural for them to choose me for those films. Not only that, but I'm a little funny sometimes. I see funny things.

One film was commissioned by the World Law Fund of the Institute for International Order, an organization concerned with armaments control. It was completely improvised; that's what I liked about it. The Hubleys would tell you the situation. They said, "You two guys are out here and such and such a thing is happening; and you got it, now go ahead and talk."

Dudley Moore, the actor, and I made *The Hat* and I also improvised the music. In the plot, there were two opposing factions in the world; I guess it was supposed to be the socialists and the capitalists—the socialist society versus the capitalist society. It showed the nonsense and how total the illogicality of that situation is. Ooooh, that's as far as you can go. That's like the word Muhammad Ali uses, the "onliest." Yeah, somebody told me that was in the dictionary.

In *The Hat* we were two soldiers walking up this line that divided the opposing sides—border guards, one from each side. Everything else, birds and snails, even bugs cross the line between the two countries, and nobody bothers them. But one little snail comes across and goes under my feet and I stumble. And as I stumble, I lean back and my hat falls on the other side of the line. When I reach over to pick it up, this guy's got his gun pointed at me. I spend the rest of the film trying to get my hat back, with all of these reasons why I should have my hat back. And he's giving me all the reasons why I can't get it back, because we're on opposing sides.

I told him, "There was a great city on the west bank of the river Nile in Africa called Kush. Do you know what crumbled that? Kush? They weren't thinking worldly."

He said, "If I were born in B.C., I'd be thinking pretty small, I should think. When you lived in the village, you thought of the village." It's not kosher as far as he's concerned, so the argument goes on and on and on. Finally, we realize how illogical it is, get together, and walk down the line, hugging one another, walking down the line.

In *The Hole*, we were just talking about life in general down there in the hole. There are two fellas—a white guy and a black guy—working under the streets, and as the conversation drifted they talked about accidents. He said, "There are no such things as accidents," or something to that effect.

And I said, "Suppose it's an accident of people that are fat getting a heart attack?" And then that discussion developed into one about the early-warning system that the United States has with planes and submarines with nuclear weapons that are circling the globe at all times. If something happens—they see a missile or something coming towards us—they're already up in the air. They go and drop a bomb. But before they get over there, there's a little telephone connection that only the President . . .

I asked, "Well, suppose the guy who can stop the planes has a heart attack? That would be the end of the world?" Then the film showed this general walking with all these stars on him. There was a little ground mole, in the ground digging, and there was a guy sitting in an underground missile station watching a control panel. And this little ground mole bit into one of the wires, causing a short circuit. They thought it was a bomb coming this way, and they sent out these ships, these planes with nuclear warheads. There was a big holocaust. Then we talked about why, when somebody wants to own something, wants to possess something material, absolutely—like land—that's usually the cause for some shit. An actor named George Matthews and I improvised this one, and we talked about the world situation, world government, and all those things. It was very nice, and I really enjoyed it. *The Hole* won an Academy Award as the best animated short of 1963.

After becoming a Baha'i, I found out a lot about the world, but even before then I knew a lot about it, and I could make it funny. Because I'm pretty funny; sometimes I even laugh at myself. Sometimes. The newest film that I wrote the music for was another animated cartoon with a lady named Maureen Stapleton. She's some actress, and I was "Father Time" and she was "Mother Earth." It's called *Voyage to Next*.

While I was doing the soundtrack for this film, I was working at Ronnie Scott's in London. The harder I work, the better I perform because it's just like adrenalin, you know, to get in there and play. When I'm working hard I just love it and was really in good shape after three days recording the film soundtrack. Thursday and Friday of that week, Oscar Peterson and I made some recordings, using only trumpet and piano, nothing else. On the day of the record date, knowing I had to work hard because Oscar was there, I got there early, to warm up properly. Oscar came in and I was lying down in the back of the studio with my horn across my chest, snoring. It was all planned. I told them to let me know when he was coming in. Oscar said to me when he walked in the studio, "Ain't no use trying to get your rest now, brother, you're in trouble today."

I said, "Wait a minute before you go any further. I just want you to know the significance of what you see here. I have been asleep; I stayed here all night waiting for you! You better be ready!" He cracked up, and, boy, didn't we have a time those two days. But you see, Oscar had some trouble with his hands, so it takes him a little time to warm up. The first number, I said, "De-de-ah-de-de-bop-bop . . ." I told him, "You're not ready." But it was just beautiful, man. That's the way the world should be structured, I think—co-operation mixed with, never overshadowed by, competition.

Gettin' Religion

When Martin Luther King was assassinated, in 1968, they were giving a "Day" for me in Laurinburg, and I decided to drive over to Cheraw to say hello to some of my old friends. Martin Luther King got killed that day. I wasn't ready for that—not morally—I was totally unprepared. I went out to this guy's house who'd been selling whiskey since I was a little boy, for forty years, and never got busted. And I got blasted on that white lightning. They call it "creek" down home because it's cross the creek; you gotta go cross the creek to get it. My pianist, Mike Longo, my cousin, and I went out to this guy's place, and I pulled him outta the bed. I remember going into his room, and I was sitting up there talking to his wife. We were with his daughter who took us out there, and because he didn't give me the respect—I hadn't been home in a long time—to get up and sit around, I went and pulled him outta the bed. Grabbed him by his foot and pulled him; his ass hit the floor. This nigger was mad too, boy! I say, "Come on out here and gimme some of that creek."

"Oh, you don't want none of that," he says.

I said, "Go 'n get it." So he went and got a half-a-gallon jug and set it on the table. And we started drinking in the kitchen. That creek was nice, man. There was some orange juice there, and I wouldn't even drink it with any orange juice. We're drinking in the kitchen, and I was getting to feeling good.

His wife was in the dining room walking around, and we're sitting at the table. I said, "Does your wife drink?"

He said, "No, no, I ain't gonna give her none."

I said, "Why?"

"She don't know how to act."

"Maan . . ."

"No, no," he said. "She don't know how to act with that, with that 'ignunt oil' in her."

So I said, "O.K. . . ." and I started sneaking her some. She started drinking in the dining room. So about an hour or forty-five minutes later, I looked in there, and her wig was hanging down around her ear. So I got up from the table . . . I saw her. By this time, I'm crocked, boy. I say, "I'm going in the dining room and sit down for a little while." I told her, "Come on, what're you doing? As beautiful as you are, and here you just sitting . . ." and I reached my hand up to straighten out her wig.

"Dammit, what you say."

This broad attacked me, beat the dogshit outta me and bit me on the ear. Whatever I had on up top, she tore it all off. Man, I couldn't even duck. She didn't hit me in the lip, I ducked that. I had to go back to Mrs. McDuffy's—I was staying at Mrs. McDuffy's—and I had to sneak in very quietly so she wouldn't see that raggedy shirt. And this girl had bitten me, so the next day I had to take rabies shots. This broad had blue gums.

MIKE LONGO (piano):

"I think that was a Wednesday, and then we had Thursday off, and then we would go to play in Atlanta for ten days at Paschal's Motor Inn. Well, Lorraine was worried about me going down there with the band. It was during all the riots and all that stuff, and for some reason, I don't remember why, Dizzy had a pistol in his briefcase. During that time, you know, Dizzy and Moody, boy, they'd be in a nervous wreck trying to protect me all the time, because, man, we'd be playing in places. Like we played in the ghetto in Pittsburgh right there in all the trouble, and we went in there to play, like, to soothe everybody; this was during the riots.

"So we were booked at Laurinburg, and Mr. Frank McDuffy, the president of Laurinburg, and his family invited Dizzy as their houseguest, and then Moody, and Paul West, Candy Finch, and myself stayed at a motel. When we got there, they had a luncheon and a big parade in honor of 'Dizzy Gillespie Day.' In the daytime, Dizzy and I went over and played to a music class, just piano and trumpet, played for the kids. It was a really pleasant day, and then that night, we played the concert. The next night, Thursday, we've got the whole day off, we don't have to be in Atlanta till Friday. So I'm over in the motel and the phone rings and it's Dizzy. He's talking about Mr. McDuffy has loaned him his station wagon and did I want to ride over to Cheraw to see where he was born and see his relatives and all that. And I said, "Yeah, crazy." So we drove over to Cheraw, and spent the whole day hanging out, but every place we went people had some homemade wine, you know. We were in the neighborhood where Dizzy's relatives lived and his old music teacher, Mrs. Wilson. So we were hanging out all day long, but every place we went people had some homemade wine. At one place we went, the music teacher, Mrs. Wilson said something to us about Martin Luther King, and by that time, man, we were high behind that wine. So I didn't understand what she said; I don't know if Dizzy did or not. We were playing the piano, partying, and what had happened is that the assassination had occurred that same night. Dizzy decides about two o'clock in the morning that he wants to get some homemade corn whiskey.

"We go out there, man, and Dizzy woke the people up. And the man was married to a very young woman, but he was an older man, and he told Dizzy not to give his wife any of that whiskey, see. I was drinking these little paper cups full of it with orange juice, but Dizzy was drinking these water glasses full.

"Anyway, the man for some reason decided he was going to clean his pistol. And I could tell, when Dizzy would drink his face would be down a half an inch, his face would droop because he blew his cheeks out. When he really got drunk, if you ever seen a beagle . . . when he'd really get out I could tell because he'd be starting to look like a beagle.

"So, man, Dizzy tells me to come into the bathroom, and he gets in there, and now I know he's out. You think he's dizzy when he's sober, you should've seen that. He's trying to tell me to take his pistol. He said, 'Keep my pistol for me.' I remember putting his pistol in my back pocket. So, we go back out there and Dizzy pours this woman a drink, and this man is sitting there with his pistol just watching all of this. This woman started telling Dizzy something like, 'You think you're better than me just because you're Dizzy Gillespie.' And Dizzy with his beagle face just looked over, and he reached over and he pulled that woman's wig off. Boy, and that woman just went berserk. Tables were flying, chairs were flying, and she pushed Dizzy down and ripped his shirt off, his undershirt, and broke his glasses and bit him on the arm. And I had to grab Dizzy. I grabbed him by the head and went running out the screen door with his head under my arm like a hammerlock and with the pistol in my other hand shooting. I shot the pistol off so the guy would know I had a pistol too. And threw Dizzy in this station wagon, man, and cut out.

"I drove him over to his aunt's house because I remembered how to get there. When I pulled up in the yard the ladies, two ladies come running out, 'Man, you better get outta here.'

"I said, 'What's the matter?'

"They said, 'Don't you know Martin Luther King has been assassinated!'

"Dizzy is out, so I'm trying to drive back to Laurinburg now, and I don't know my way around there or anything, and he can't direct me, he's out. So we're driving along, and I said, 'No wonder all these state troopers are out.' All these sirens going, like, every two minutes there's a siren going off. Dizzy's lying on the seat, and he's got no undershirt, no shirt, and he's bleeding on the arm where he was bit. And we were running out of gas. I don't know what to do, you know, like here I'm gonna drive into this gas station and all these state troopers are there, and they might recognize that he's Dizzy Gillespie. 'Oh, Christ.' Anyway, I pulled down to the last pump and got out of the car, and the guy asks me, 'You want me to wipe the windshield?'

"I said, 'No, that's all right.'

"I revived Dizzy, and now he gets sick on his stomach, and he's throwing up all over this man's car. So now I can't take him back to Laurinburg Institute in that car. So I took Dizzy to the motel. I go to Moody's room and wake him up, say, 'Hey, Moody.'

"He says, 'What—what's the matter! What's the matter!'

"I said, 'Dizzy's out in the car, man, he's out cold and he's bleeding.'

"He said, 'What! He's bleeding! What happened?'

"So I said, 'This woman bit him, man.'

"Moody said, 'Aw, get outta here, you're crazy, man.'

"I said, 'No, I'm serious, man. A woman bit him.'

"He says, 'You gotta be putting me on. Well, what did he do?'

"I said, 'Well, he didn't do nothing,' trying to keep Moody from knowing that Dizzy'd been drinking, because the two of them kept whatever drinking they did secret from each other.

"He said, 'Aw, come on, Mickel, he musta did something.'

"I said, 'Well, he pulled this woman's wig off, man, and she bit him.'

"And Moody hit the floor. He said, 'What! He did what?' So we got Dizzy and brought him in. He was out cold, man. We put him in the bed and poured peroxide all over his bite, you know. The only plane out of there to Atlanta was nine-thirty in the morning. I went to sleep —and Dizzy was out—by the time he came to, we had missed the plane. Dizzy and I went over to a gas station and got a hose and cleaned the man's car out. There was one policeman in that town, in Laurinburg. We hired this guy to drive us. And we took the Laurinburg school bus, 'Laurinburg Blue Devils' on the side. And that's the way we went to Atlanta.

"When we got to Atlanta, we were about three hours late for the gig; we couldn't get there any quicker. When we got to Atlanta people were marching, we couldn't even get the school bus through the streets, the streets were full of people marching. When we got to Paschal's, Mr. Paschal and his brother were all out front pacing around wondering where we were because there was a whole lot of people who'd come to hear the opening night. So we come driving up in a bus with 'Laurinburg Blue Devils' on it.

"Later, on the Japanese tour, he got drunk again. The whole band except Jymie Merrit got wasted. The Japanese promoters had us booked so heavily, man. Our schedule for one day was like this: we were supposed to get up, go somewhere in the middle of Japan, I think it was Osaka, and then come back to Tokyo. And there was no plane. We were supposed to leave Osaka, catch a train, and come back to Tokyo. We had to get up at five-thirty in the morning, catch the train at six o'clock, stay on the train till noon, get off the train and go right to this hotel for a press conference at one. No time for lunch or anything. The press conference lasted a long time, and we were supposed to be back in Tokyo at the concert hall to rehearse with the Japanese orchestra till eight o'clock, at which time we put on a concert at eight-thirty with them. After the concert we were supposed to go to the Golden Ginza, this big nightclub, and play an eleven-fifteen show and then a one-fifteen show.

"When we got on the train, Moody, in the train terminal, bought five of these little splits of sake, Japanese rice wine, like the size of a 7-Up bottle. We were going to be on this train for about five hours, see. Moody handed out these things, and we hadn't had any breakfast, or anything. We were drinking this stuff like Pepsi-Cola, and playing cards as we rode along. The guy would come through the car selling sake, and Moody would buy more, one for each of us.

"We were playing cards, so it wasn't that anyone was feeling too much pain. Everybody was cool except Candy Finch. I remember Candy was nodding, man. We got to Osaka, and they rushed us from there to the hotel, with no lunch, nothing. They had the whole band sitting up there with Dizzy in the middle, looking like the Last Supper table. There were like a thousand reporters and cameramen interviewing Dizzy and asking us questions. They asked Dizzy something about jazz musicians and drugs. Dizzy was giving them an answer to the question: 'That was like a long time ago. Jazz musicians now are very straight-ahead people. That was back in the early forties when they had a few hassles with drugs.' And all the while he's saying that, Candy is nodding, boy, he's nodding. He was high from that sake. I remember cracking up. I looked over at Candy while Dizzy was talking and Candy was falling asleep.

"By the time we got to the concert hall, Moody went out in the alley. The Japanese have these little alleys with all these little stores weaving all through the streets, where they built one shop after another. Moody went out and bought two more gallons of sake, the big gallon bottles, thinking that the Japanese musicians, over twenty of them, and five of us would be partying. He had a bagful of paper cups.

"But none of the Japanese musicians wanted to drink because over there they have a tradition that nobody drinks until after a performance. And they're very strict about that. But we kept drinking this sake during rehearsal. I kept handing Dizzy up a paper cup full of sake, you know, because we all knew the music, we'd been playing it.

"All of a sudden I heard the trumpets play something really wrong. Dizzy's got ears that can hear paint dry, and he just let it go. Dizzy would never let . . . And I looked over, and there he was, the 'beagle,' with his face hanging down. His face was drooping down and he had this silly grin on his face. Everybody could play all right though, and we got through the concert, but by the time we got to the Golden Ginza . . .

"It looked like a dive because backstage was all funky, cement floors and thousands of chorus girls running around. Oliver Nelson came backstage. He and Moody were talking, and I was almost out. I found this ladder. I was looking for a place to lie down, so I climbed up this scaffold on the stage and went up above the stage and went to sleep. When it was time to start the show, they couldn't find me. Oliver Nelson had seen me go up the ladder; so when they got me down, then they couldn't find Dizzy. When they started looking for Dizzy, I went into this closet and went to sleep. And you know what woke me up! Somebody kicked me on the foot, and it was Dizzy, and he was telling me that I was in his dressing room! Get outta my dressing room! And I'm in a broom closet.

"We got out on the stage, and Diz by this time is out of it, Moody too. Dizzy starting playing the first tune and was playing the wrong notes and everything. On the second tune he decided to feature Moody. Moody was playing 'Old Folks' but he only got to about 'Everybody knows him as old folks . . .' then all of a sudden Dizzy started playing the next tune. So now Dizzy and Moody get into an argument on stage because Dizzy had come in on top of Moody's solo. The ambassador and the Emperor and all the high society of Tokyo was there.

"When Dizzy and Moody started to argue on the stage, I went and took my jacket off and laid it up on the music rack on the piano and went to sleep. That's the last thing I remember. The next thing, it was six o'clock in the morning, 'bang-bang-bang' and we had to go to do a TV show. So now, everybody's cool, and we burned on TV, we're making a film all day.

"When the intermission came, they let us go out to get a Coke, and this Japanese promoter came down the hall with these two big body-guards, yelling at me from down the hall in Japanese, motioning to me, 'Come over here, come over here.' Screaming at me in Japanese. He was angry and was pointing to headlines in the paper. I couldn't read it, but it was all about how we'd made the headlines at some big society function. It said that Dizzy couldn't play and that the piano player had gone to sleep and that the people in the audience had just gotten up and walked quietly out. I mean it was like a big scandal. And we didn't even remember it. I wondered how we'd gotten back to the hotel.

"So anyway, the promoter talked to Dizzy about this. And Dizzy can charm the pants off of anyone. About twenty minutes later, they all came out grinning and laughing. Dizzy had told them, 'Man, we didn't know sake could do that to you. We didn't have any breakfast, and you didn't give us time to eat.' Dizzy had charmed everybody. He arranged for a recording session and we agreed to go back again to the Golden Ginza. And we burned, and took care'a business. It wasn't really our fault in the sense that we didn't know you were supposed to drink sake and sip it, and they didn't give us enough time to eat. That was some wild experience."

Maybe that's the way the riots and the assassination of Brother King and, mainly, my own spiritual shortcomings at that time affected me. If something hurt or impressed me badly—or just out of plain boredom—I'd lapse into getting drunk and act extremely uncivil, until it occurred to me that I was going around the world making myself look foolish be-fore people who respected me and the music we played. Yeah, travel-ing in Japan I got drunk on sake, which I thought was some kind of Japanese tea, messed up the music in rehearsals and made an ass out of myself by getting into an argument with Moody onstage. Boy, that one was funny. The whole band got drunk on sake and went to sleep onstage. Shortly after that I stopped drinking altogether. It took me a little while to reach that conclusion.

Having attained every major goal that I'd ever really wanted, my attitude about things that were not to my liking or immediately controllable was not to give a damn.

Then this lady named Beth McKintey called me and said she would like to come over and speak to me about Charlie Parker because she read a book about him in which I'd figured very prominently. She asked, "Could I come over?" We'd have a discussion about the book.

I said, "No, madam, I don't want no strange woman coming over to my hotel, naw." This was in Milwaukee.

She said, "Well, my husband and I will be in the club tonight." So she and her husband came to the club, and they didn't say anything about the Baha'i faith, we just talked. They weren't drinking; they didn't drink, but I had four or five doubles. And it developed that she was traveling for the Baha'i faith. She had a position at that time, and sometimes we'd meet in different towns, and she'd come to visit us, and we'd talk some more about Charlie Parker. We'd talk, talk, talk, and through the conversation we started discussing my early life, and she asked me a lot about my father and my mother and all my brothers and sisters. I began to trust the lady because she didn't seem to have any ulterior motives.

And then these little pamphlets started coming. I'm a great reader, and I started reading these things. More and more these little pamphlets started showing up. And then I ran across a book called *Thief in the Night,* by Bill Sears, one of the hands of the cause of God in the Baha'i faith. It was like a detective story tracing what is supposed to happen when a new message comes from God to mankind. God doesn't pull any surprises on his people because it's hard enough for them to believe a guy when he comes up and says, "I am the manifestation of God's word." It's hard for them to accept that when they've got several versions already. He traced the history of several religions, prophecies and religions about what will come when the Christ returns. And come to find out Baha'u'llah fulfilled all these prophecies.

"He shall build his tent on Mount Carmel" is said by one of the prophets. His tent is the Baha'i Center on Mount Carmel.

"He shall come from the East. . . ." That's where Baha'u'llah came from. They speak in parables, the Holy books. They have to speak that way for men of different ages to understand what they're talking about. This *Thief in the Night* really turned me on, so I started reading.

They were in San Francisco one time while I was there. I had a day off. They called me up and got a ticket for me to take me down to Los Angeles—Beth and Nancy Jordan, another lady from the Faith who used to travel together—and they took me down to Los Angeles. Bill

Sears was down there, and I met him. I had my declaration already in
a sealed envelope, because when I read that book, I said, 'Boy, I really
wanna be something like this.' I think this is what God wants. So I
gave my declaration to make it official. I wrote this on one of the
pages of *Thief in the Night*. That's how I became a Baha'i.

Becoming a Baha'i changed my life in every way and gave me a new
concept of the relationship between God and man—between man and
his fellow man—man and his family. It's just all consuming. I became
more spiritually aware, and when you're spiritually aware, that will be
reflected in what you do. They teach you in the Baha'i faith, without
the idea of stopping you from doing things, to fill your life with doing
something that's for real, and those other things you do, that are not
for real, will fall off by themselves. I never needed to say, 'I'm gonna
stop doing this.' I just found out that there was no time for it anymore.
I started praying and reading a lot too. The writings gave me new insight on what the plan is—God's plan—for this time, the truth of the
oneness of God, the truth of the oneness of the prophets, the truth of
the oneness of mankind. That's it; that's what I learned.

There is a parallel with jazz and religion. In jazz, a messenger
comes to the music and spreads his influence to a certain point, and
then another comes and takes you further. In religion—in the spiritual
sense—God picks certain individuals from this world to lead mankind
up to a certain point of spiritual development. Other leaders come, and
they have the same Holy Spirit in their hands, so they are really one
and the same. This means that Judaism, Christianity, Islam, Buddhism,
and all the major religions are one and the same. The spiritual laws stay
right and lay right there. They never change, the spiritual laws of
Moses, Abraham, Buddha, Krishna, Zoroaster, Jesus, Muhammad—all
these people speak the same language. But the social order that goes
with it changes with all the different prophets who come. They are the
only ones who can do that.

The Guardian of my faith, the Baha'i faith, says that there has got to
be an organic change in the structure of society. An organic change
means that everything you see like it is now has got to be changed for
the peace and contentment of the world. Everything you see: the way
they're running the finances; the schools; the police department; foreign affairs—everything has got to go through an organic change to
bring about this millennium of the oneness of mankind and the peace
of the world. Racial, political—any kind of prejudice—is automatically
out. There has got to be the establishment of a universal auxiliary
language. The Baha'i have an administrative setup and at the United
Nations they consult with us to find out what Baha'u'llah said. He
said it in the nineteenth century, but that's what will be coming and

must come for a better world with peace and love and respect—regardless of who you are and where you come from.

When I encountered the Baha'i faith, it all went along with what I had always believed. I believed in the oneness of mankind. I believed we all come from the same source, that no race of people is inherently superior to any other. And they teach unity, I latched onto that. I believe that there is one God and He manifests Himself to mankind through great teachers for specific periods of time in our spiritual development, that He sends them periodically. It's like a relay runner who has a baton in his hand. You could look at the Word of God like a baton, the Holy Spirit. The runner grabs this baton and he runs and runs and runs; and while he runs that is the revelation of what's happening. When he gets to the end, he passes it on to the next guy, and he starts running with it, and that's the next religion. It's the same religion; it's just that a different prophet's running with it. He passes it to the next and the next and so on until there is peace and unity of mankind on earth as it is in Heaven.

A lotta people believe there is something "wicked" about jazz music and musicians, but I believe they are the people most "in tune" with the Universe. What is more appropriate than a musician being in tune with nature and with our Creator? The best example is the way that they perform; how do they come up with things that have never been played before? Where did they get it? They have to have some kind of divine inspiration. A lot of that negative opinion probably comes from ignorance, and then it has something to do with the early days of the music which was supposed to have been conceived in a whorehouse. I don't believe that. The jazz musicians were doing the same thing in the whorehouse as the whores, making a living. An evil society put them in there. I don't believe that jazz was conceived in a whorehouse; it's clean, the motives and everything about jazz are spotless. People who learned and created music elsewhere were simply forced to go to the whorehouse to play and earn a living.

Mahalia Jackson was friendly with a lotta jazz musicians. She was a good friend of Louis Armstrong because both of them were from New Orleans, and she had many ties with Duke Ellington and Count Basie. Her friendship with me—I don't know how she got that together. We were very close, but I don't know how she reconciled that with her beliefs about jazz music.

I tried to be courteous to her. One time I visited her in Chicago at her home, and she was telling me, "Ooh, my feet, they're hurting so bad."

I said, "Wait a minute," and called the maid and told her, "Go get me some warm water and some alcohol and some lotion." I told Mahalia, "Sit down, sit back now, just take off your shoes." And I massaged her feet for her, you know. And she laid back there, man.

She said, "Oh, man, that was nice!" I don't think anybody'd ever done that for her. Now that's an act of love because she's a brilliant person whose music eased everyone's suffering. Wait a minute! I can explain why Mahalia Jackson considered me a friend. She depended on the Spirit to guide her, and something about me that she felt, her perception of me was not wicked. Mahalia Jackson was a lady of great mother wit. So the spirit moved her and that's the way she dealt with it. And you know the gospel field is not exactly without stain. There are very few gospel singers who could cast the first stone.

I believe in this parallel between jazz and religion. Definitely! Definitely! The runners on the trumpet would be Buddy Bolden, King Oliver, Louis Armstrong, Roy Eldridge, me, Miles, and Fats Navarro, Clifford Brown, Lee Morgan, Freddie Hubbard—they're the runners. They created a distinctive style, a distinctive message to the music, and the rest of them follow that. Our Creator chooses great artists. There is no other explanation for the fact that a guy like Charlie Parker had so much talent other than the fact that he was divinely inspired. Other guys practiced just as hard as he did, so why didn't they have it? There's no other explanation. So, I just go along with, "God just gives it to you." I felt thankful, and that cured my dizziness a lot.

Dizziness

My dizziness almost took me away from here in 1973. Just what happened is missing, but apparently someone gave me something that wasn't kosher, and when I woke up I was in the hospital, dying. My heart stopped beating. I wound up in the hospital under intensive care, and when I woke up something was down in my throat; they were sticking something down in my throat to make my heart start beating again.

It must have been some kind of narcotic because I was working in a club, in the Village Vanguard, and the last thing I remember is being on the bandstand—and then the next thing in the hospital. The doctor said, "OD." Whatever I'd taken must not have been on the up and up.

I can never remember having been terrified—no instance of really being afraid of something—threatened but not afraid. That time I felt more than just threatened.

MIKE LONGO:

"I remember we went back on the stand. He hadn't been drinking in a long time, he gave up drinking, but I remember how he used to play when he had a few drinks or something, you know. At the time Alex

Blake was the bass player. He was only about twenty years old, you know. I thought it was strange; I didn't know why Dizzy started playing 'Girl of My Dreams.' You know, Alex Blake never heard it; that was about forty years before he was born. It wasn't part of our repertoire or anything, and he was playing funny; and all of a sudden I looked over at him and he was wobbling. So I got up from the piano and went over to the side, and he was behind the post so the people couldn't see him, and all of a sudden he collapsed. Dropped his horn down on the floor and fell out, you know. And I said, 'What happened to you, man?' Because before that he was wide awake, alert, and everything.

"So all Dizzy could say was 'Awww, it's beautiful,' and he fell out, you know.

"The people all left the club except Dizzy and I and this guy named Noble, and Noble told me, 'This guy gave Dizzy something, and Dizzy didn't know what it was. And he's a dirty so-and-so.'

"I said, 'Well, let's get him upstairs and get him out in the air, maybe he'll come around.' I didn't know what was wrong with him either. Noble and I carried Dizzy up, and I went back down to get his horn and his coat. When I came back upstairs from the Vanguard, Dizzy was gone, and way down the street were these two guys that gave him this shit, and they were walking off with Dizzy. So I went running after them, I said, 'Where you think you're going, man?'

"He said, 'We're taking him to the Greenwich Village Hospital.'

"I said, 'You ain't taking him no place.'

"He said, 'What do you mean?'

"I said, 'Why? Because he's Dizzy Gillespie, that's why. You ain't taking Dizzy Gillespie in some funky-ass hospital, and the next thing you know it's in the papers.' Besides that, these cats might've meant Dizzy some harm in the first place and might've taken him off to dump him someplace, you know, 'cause he was out. So I took him back to the club, and those guys split. I was trying to find somebody that could take him home. I didn't know how serious it was myself, but I knew that the thing to do was to take him home to Lorraine. So this guy in the club was a neighbor of Dizzy's, he was like a very sober gentleman and so forth, and so he promised he would take Dizzy home. Noble said he would ride with Dizzy home, so, man, I figured he was cool then.

"So he got home, and Lorraine put him in the bed, and it was about eight o'clock in the morning and my phone was ringing and it was Boo Frazier talking. 'What happened to Dizzy last night?'

"I said, 'Well, I don't know what happened, but I put him in this car and sent him home because somebody gave him something, some guy, and these people were taking him off to someplace, you know. So

I went and got him and put him in the car with his neighbor and that's the last I . . .'

"And he said, 'Well, Dizzy is on the critical list in the hospital. He was DOA at the hospital.' That was a shocker. Matter of fact, that's when I became a Baha'i. I started to pray, when they called me and said he was on the critical list and in a coma, you know."

LORRAINE GILLESPIE:

"I just happened to get up to check on him after they'd brought him home, and I'd put him to bed. I'd never seen him out like that before. When I walked in the room and looked at him, he was frothing at the mouth and having convulsions, his body was purging itself. So I called the ambulance right away and took him to the hospital. His heart had stopped and when we got him to the hospital, they had to bring him back to life on the machines. He was almost gone that time. It just so happened something told me to go in there and check on him.

"When he acts like a stupid fool, sometimes . . . gets one of his stupid spells on, it makes me sick. He does all kinds of stupid things, but it's been a long time now. I can hardly remember them. He's getting confusing here recently. Heh, heh . . . He put it on religion, but I think he's tired. I'm so glad. Better late than never. He's kinda changed a little bit now."

After that I took ten days off from work, and I thought, "There must be another reason for living. Now is the time if you're talking about a quest in life." I had to find out what that reason was and go about it better, because when you die and come back . . . I was gifted by the Supreme Being in having a unique talent for which I'm very grateful. If God gives a guy a talent, he should use it. If you don't use it, it's a sin and it'll be taken away. And if you have this talent, you must give something for it, to show appreciation. I give up many things that I like to do and can do. I sit down and write music instead of going out. That's hard work but you've got to do it or it'll be taken away. I had to make sure to safeguard the gifts I'd received, especially my talent for playing the trumpet.

How you react under pressure is important. My wife, Lorraine, under pressure, a tremendous amount of pressure, comes out smelling like a rose. There are not many, there ain't! No, no, no, no! I have been married all my life. My wife is very religious, and that has prevented me from doing things that were detrimental to me. I needed someone who was in my corner. My wife gave me that strength—like an anchor —and I was scared to do certain things. I've been a Baha'i now for only ten years, so what happened before then can be attributed to her. Lorraine is not a bender; she won't bend. She only sees things two ways, the right and the wrong way. I'm a bender, an in-betweener, but my wife is straight like an arrow. My wife is a great influence. I always say all of the nice things that you see about me, the good things, can be directly attributed to my wife because of her technique of explaining things to me. The bad things I did myself.

We have no children, but I have a poodle and his name is Maestro. He's about ten years old now. Maestro doesn't do any tricks, but he is very smart. My wife is the world's greatest housekeeper, from the beginning of housekeeping, and Maestro has only certain places that he can go in the house. I have only certain places that I can go in the house. We reserve the living room, the dining room, and a small porch room for guests. I never go in there unless I go in there to get something. I never go in there to linger. Maestro has access to the foyer, the study, the basement, and he can come into the guest room sometimes. He knows the places in the house where he's not to go. He is not allowed in the kitchen, but you have to go through the kitchen to get to the basement. One day I was washing the dishes, and Maestro was lying down at the door with his chin down on the floor. His head was in the kitchen and his body was on the outside. So I said, "I'm gonna trick him." I made like I was going down the steps into the basement, boom, boom, boom, but I was only marching in one spot. Maestro cut around there, and when he turned the corner and saw me standing there, he said, "Awww," like that and walked on back out through the kitchen. He knew he wasn't supposed to be in there; he can only walk through the kitchen going to the basement if I'm down there. So he walked back out. Whenever I leave my home more than one day, when I come back home I have to pick him up and hold him just a little while. He's so sensitive. If I pick him up and hold him just a little while and put him back down, he's up on me grabbing me to pick him up again, saying no, that ain't enough, give me some more of that loving. And I pick him up again, and I walk around with him. He's beautiful.

All the business is handled by my wife, Lorraine. She knows how to handle money, funds. She's a master of that and I'm not. I just send it there, and she takes care of it. Without her, I wouldn't have a quarter. My success as a musician may not have been as economically rewarding as I might have wished, but I understand the crux of the matter, and think it has been commensurate with my production thus far. We live in a materialistic society where you are worth what you bring in. But there are certain instances in the music business where the record company wants you for the sake of prestige, just to have your records on the shelf, not necessarily because you're sure to sell a hundred thousand dollars' worth of records right away.

The most money I've ever made at one time was a guaranteed, three-year, $100,000 contract from Mercury Records, which happened about fifteen years ago in 1963. I wouldn't take it all at one time. Quincy Jones said it was like a black snake. They sent the check to my house, and I said, "Send it right back." I had it spread out over three years, but I had it anyway. I'm a long way from being a millionaire. You've gotta have two million dollars to be a millionaire, anyway, and I'm a good distance from that plateau. I've never really wanted to be a millionaire; I just want to live like one and be able to afford what I want. My tastes don't run that high, so I am a millionaire because there are very few things I wanted and was unable to get. The simple reason for that is I don't want too much. The most expensive things I've ever purchased were a small apartment building and the house Lorraine and I live in. I'd rather stay home and not have to pack bags and be on the go all the time, but I do what's necessary to make a living. I'd like to sit on my ass, stay at home, and write music. Hell no, I don't like living outta suitcases; but there are plusses. I go to England, and Bob Farnon comes to London and says hello to me. We live in the same hotel and hang out for a couple of days. In France I visit Charles Delaunay or Moufla or Roger Guerin or Kenny Clarke, in Brussels, Carlos de Radzitzky. If I didn't travel, I wouldn't see those cats, 'cause I wouldn't travel anywhere if I weren't working—in Argentina, Rio de Janeiro, North Africa, and Kenya. Entertainment has its good points that far outweigh the drags of getting up at five o'clock in the morning to catch a plane. The main drawback is being away from your wife, but when I first got on the road, Lorraine used to go everywhere with me. Now, she doesn't like the road, so I have to go out alone, but I'll come back, right? And when I come back, I'll have another honeymoon.

After my encounter with the unknown, I looked around and saw how all these musicians had gotten wasted, and it suddenly occurred to me that I was fifty-seven years old, and I said, "Wait a minute, brother!"

Now, I take the slant board on the road with me and I work out twice a day, I try to eat the proper foods, I stay free from alcohol and drugs; I live like a married man should (which is very important, too). I have the greatest respect for the musicians and they, likewise, show me the greatest respect; I have respect for the jobs I work and if they don't show me respect, I quit and I leave it. And I hope to live to be about 160 so I can get some of that money back that I give these jive people for my social security. I hope I can just worry them, wondering, "Say, when is he going to die?" I intend to just hang on, brother.

Blowin'!!! UNITED PRESS INTERNATIONAL.

Places like the dressing room at the Lighthouse in Hermosa Beach, California, make me think . . .

With composer Cole Porter.

With Lionel Hampton, thirty years
after "Hot Mallets."

It's hard as hell to
make George Wein smile.

Just the trumpets, please.

Jazz musicians were getting together, (l to r, top to bottom) Hilton Jefferson, Benny Golson, Art Farmer, Wilbur Ware, Art Blakey, Chubby Jackson, Johnny Griffin, Dicky Wells, Buck Clayton, Taft Jordan, Zutty Singleton, Red Allen, Tyree Glenn, Miff Mole, Sonny Greer, J. C. Higginbotham, Jimmy Jones, Charles Mingus, Jo Jones, Gene Krupa, Max Kaminsky, George Wettling, Bud Freeman, Pee Wee Russell, Ernie Wilkins, Buster Bailey, Osie Johnson, Gigi Gryce, Hank Jones, Eddie Locke, Horace Silver, Lucky Roberts, Maxine Sullivan, Jimmy Rushing, Joe Thomas, Scoville Brown, Stuff Smith, Bill Crump, Coleman Hawkins, Rudy Powell, Oscar Pettiford, Sahib Shihab, Marian McPartland, Sonny Rollins, Lawrence Brown, Mary Lou Williams, Emmett Berry, Thelonious Monk, Vick Dickenson, Milt Hinton, Lester Young, Rex Stewart, J. C. Heard, Roy Eldridge, Dizzy Gillespie, Count Basie.

Trying to get into Morris Levy's pockets.

With blues singer Jimmy Rushing.

Supporting striking longshoremen in New Orleans.

At gravesite of
Charlie Parker, Kansas
City, Missouri.

My quintet by 1967; (l to r) Mike Longo, piano; Paul West, bass; Otis
Candy Finch, drums; James Moody, reeds and flute.

Receiving the Handel Medallion from Mayor John V. Lindsay of New York City; (l to r) Mayor Miller Ingraham, Cheraw, S. C., Mayor Lindsay, and John Motley.

At the Carter White House with (l to r) Sarah Vaughan, Jimmy Cobb, Mickey Roker, Benjamin Franklin Brown, President Carter, and Rodney Jones. OFFICIAL WHITE HOUSE PHOTO.

Some prerequisites for a successful jazz musician.

PAGE I

SOME of THE PREREQUISITES
FOR A SUCCESSFUL JAZZ MUSICIAN

I. Mastery of THE Instrument ___
    Important because when you think of something
To Play, you must say it quickly, because you dont have
Time to figure how ___ Chords changing so quickly.

II. Style
    which I think is THE most difficult to master
— in asmuch as there are not Too many Truly dis —
Tintive styles in all of Jazz.

III. Taste
    Is a process of elimination ___ some phrases
That you play may be Technically correct but
does not pertray the particular mood that you are
Trying For.

IV Communication
    Afer all you make your profession Jazz be-
cause first, because you love it, and secondly as
A means of Livlihood, so if there is no direct
communication with The audience for whom you
ARE playing ___ There goes your Living.

(continued)

PAGE II

V Chord progressions
    As There are rules That govern you Biologi-
cally and physically, There are rules That govern your
Taste musically. Therefore it is of prime interest
and To ones advantage to learn The key board
of the piano, as it is the basic instrument for
Western music, which Jazz is an integral part
of.

VI Rhythm
    which includes all of the other attributes
because, you may have all of these others
and dont have the rhythmic sense to put
Them Together, Then it would negate
all of your other accomplishments.

Evolutions

A student of our music, if he goes back far enough, will find out that the main source of our music is Africa. The music of the Western Hemisphere (not just our music)—the music of Cuba, the music of Brazil, the music of the West Indies, although they haven't made such a big impact on humanity as a whole, as jazz, spirituals, and blues which were created by the blacks in the United States—is primarily of African origin. The people of the calypso, the rhumba, the samba, and the rhythms of Haiti, all have something in common from the mother of their music. Rhythm. The basic rhythm because Mama Rhythm is Africa.* Africa's children in the Western Hemisphere used different means of expressing their closeness to Mama. The Brazilian Africans created the samba, the West Indians created the calypso, the Cubans created the rhumba and various other rhythms, and my own is blues, spirituals. All of them were different and showed different characteristics. Yet they're together, so it was a natural thing for me to fall under the influence of these different rhythms.

Sociologically, the reason that the blacks in the United States created the music that they did was because they didn't have the drums. The slavemasters took away the blacks' prime means of expression and

* In Africa you can go one way and hear some rhythms, then go two miles away and the cats are playing something different. They play what they live.

wouldn't let them play it, which was very smart of the slavemasters because you could talk with the drums and foment revolution and uprisings. Everybody would know what was happening, so they wouldn't let them play the drums. So the blacks devised new means of beating on tin pans and singing in the fields, and at night, they'd go way back in the woods and hold secret religious meetings by firelight and clap and stomp and sing these songs. Where they were allowed to go to church with whites, they had the amen corner, but mostly they had to meet secretly because during slavery the masters didn't want any two people on the plantation speaking the same African language. If they found out two people were from the same tribe, they'd sell off one because they wanted them to speak English so the slavemasters would know what they were talking about all the time. They couldn't have any secrets and they didn't want the Africans to practice their own religions. They wanted the Africans to accept Jesus Christ as the Son of God. Accept that but don't practice it with the slavemasters; because by the whole system of communications which the Europeans set up, the Africans were lesser, and how could you talk about brotherhood of man and hold these people in that condition of slavery? To make certain the system of slavery would stand, they created words like "blackball" and "blackmail" and the "blackest day of the year" and all these things, to put the idea in people's heads that black was something less to be desired than white. But we tricked them, we tricked the white people. We created a music that is now internationally known as having been created in the United States, and it gained acceptance and precedence over all the other music of the hemisphere and other parts of the world because of its rhythm, its harmonic variety, and, ironically enough, because of the power which the United States had to disseminate and spread it. All that work the slaves did to make the United States rich and powerful and a leader in communications made it possible to spread our music like never before, and this dissemination started way back in the nineteenth century with entertainers like "Blind Tom," who took our music overseas to Europe.

The blues are a form of our music that developed from spirituals. They changed the lyrics around and put sophisticated lyrics that talked about man and worldly life rather than just about man and God, and it started a whole new style of music that could be played and sung in worldly situations, in nightclubs and other places of entertainment. The spirituals, gospels, and the blues walk side by side; they are married. The blues came before jazz. Jazz was invented for people to dance. So when you play jazz and people don't feel like dancing or moving the feet, you're getting away from the idea of music. Never lose that feeling of somebody wanting to dance; that's one of the characteristics of our music. You wanna dance when you listen to our music because it transmits that feeling of rhythm.

Our music in the United States and the African concept of rhythm have one difference: the African is polyrhythmic, and we are basically monorhythmic. Polyrhythm is when you have four or five different musicians playing different rhythms at the same time. In jazz today, we have a sock cymbal which was brought in by Jo Jones. In my first band in South Carolina, however, one musician was playing the snare drum, another played the cymbal, and another had the bass drum with a mallet in his right hand and a wire thing in his left hand. This of course evolved into a modern drum set in which all of these functions are performed by one player.

We in the United States have a hard time understanding Afro-Cuban music and other polyrhythmic music of this hemisphere because it stays closer to Africa than we do in this country. We are more "European," more harmonically inclined, except for gospel music. Gospel music is the closest thing to African music in the United States. The fusion between African and European music actually started in the church. This evolved into ragtime, boogie woogie, rock, etc. In my present music, I keep one hand in the past and one hand in the future, in that I still retain the gospel in my playing while exploring as far as possible the marriage between African rhythm and European harmony.

Now, our music is universal. It shares the rhythmic content of African music, music of the Western Hemisphere and various lands of the East, and has merged this rhythm with European harmonies, the soul of the slaves, the blues, and the spirituals to create jazz. Boy! The new guys doing rock 'n roll today are thoroughly into gospel, and they do things with notes that you just can't write. I wish I could play like that. It was a mistake during my childhood to miss playing music in the Sanctified church, even though I used to listen, because gospel music is such a virile force and it lends itself to all kinds of improvisation. Our music is gonna be around because it ain't going nowhere but forward.

So those were some basic evolutions in the history of our music, black music, in the United States. It's just like the history in Africa that is passed down from one generation to another by the spoken word. It's the same with our music; that's why all modern musicians should get a background in old music. They don't have to play it, but they should know it. It's just like building a house. You've got to start at the bottom.

The piano is the basis of modern harmony. Now in the 1920s most of the piano players, from what the old-timers tell me, played in the vein of James P. Johnson, Scott Joplin, Eubie Blake, Jelly Roll Morton,

Fats Waller, and Willie "the Lion" Smith. They couldn't grab Art
Tatum. You speak about Art Tatum and you take a breath, then you
start speaking of other piano players. After the era of Fats Waller and
all of those great pianists, this little guy came out of Chicago, Earl
Hines. He changed the style of the piano. He's in a class with all of
those guys, and he's still around. It might be a good idea for kids to go
and listen to Earl Hines. You can find the roots of Bud Powell, Herbie
Hancock—all the guys who came after that. If it hadn't been for Earl
Hines, blazing the path for the next generation to come, it's no telling
what or how they would be playing now. To bridge the gap between
Earl Hines and the present, the bebop era, was Billy Kyle. Billy Kyle
was the idol of Bud Powell. Bud patterned himself after Billy Kyle
and he was also greatly influenced by Charlie Parker and me. He had
both of these aspects going for him and brought out a new style.
Piano players now all sound like Bud Powell. Because Bud, Oooooo, he
used to burn it! Other pianists brought specific styles to the music like
Erroll Garner who was the most sanctified pianist that we had. We
have two really good sanctified pianists, Erroll Garner and Les
McCann. They can sanctify. Give them a tambourine and let them go,
man, they are something else. Either one of those guys, give him a
tambourine, no bass, no drums, nothing else, and he'll get it. There
were individual variations, but the style of the piano—actually, the
modern piano—developed from Earl Hines.

Louis Armstrong was also a great innovator and a great bearer of a
message, and, at one time, every trumpet player in the world, everybody who wasn't in a classical band, had to be influenced by Louis
Armstrong. Louis not only influenced trumpet players, he changed the
modus operandi of music by inventing the solo. He came from King
Oliver, and then he went out, and Roy Eldridge came from Louis
Armstrong. I came from Roy Eldridge. In our music we have the same
thing happening as in my religion, the Baha'i faith. Guys come for a
specific age to be the dominant force—not the only one—but the dominant force in that era. Buddy Bolden, King Oliver—who was the messenger for that era and musicians from all over came to copy him—
Louis Armstrong, Roy Eldridge, my era, Miles Davis, Fats Navarro,
Clifford Brown, Lee Morgan. The next messengers after our era, I
think, are Ornette Coleman and John Coltrane. They brought a message to music and enriched our music by their creativity. Ornette
Coleman was versed in fundamentals because he knew all of Charlie
Parker's solos. I didn't dig Ornette Coleman at the beginning. I imagine I was just like the older guys, how they treated me when they first
listened to me. One time this lawyer brought me an album of Ornette's, a live album that he made in Town Hall, and then I listened
to what he was playing. I said, "Oh, oh," and I followed him down.

Then I started listening to him, and I said, "This guy has something." But it wasn't as strong as Charlie Parker's. It was built on Charlie Parker, but later on Coltrane developed a bigger following. He has a large number of musicians out there now.

I believe in the evolution of everything. When you look at man, himself, in a constant state of flux, we don't act in this age, like we acted twenty years ago. Fundamentally we're the same, but we've got a different way of doing it, like telling time by a computerized watch rather than by a clock face with hands and Roman numerals. The music's best for the era for which it was intended. I'm speaking of those guys who always want you to go back and get the band of 1947 and 1948. I say, "You don't want the band of 1947. Man, that doesn't suit me now."

"But man," they say, "that shit was 'baaad!'"

I say, "Yeah, it was bad in its time, but our music is moving forward now." The concerts they're having, where they go back through the music because so many people didn't hear it when it was first performed, are groovy. We need the followers to do that; the creators are supposed to step forward. That's why I can appreciate Miles. I don't care whether you like his music or not, he has stepped forward. It's up to your personal taste, but the music is there for you to taste whether you like it or not. He did have the courage to step up there.

I know about the other instruments, but I am an expert on the role of the trumpet. I know especially what the trumpet players have created in the music—Buddy Bolden to King Oliver to Louis Armstrong to Roy Eldridge and then to me. Next, Miles and Fats Navarro came to bring messages to the music, twin messages, at the same time. Each one of them was different. I know each one of them sounded like me because we played on a record together, the three of us, and I didn't know which one was playing when I listened—the Metronome All Stars date. (Victor 30-3361.) I didn't know which one of us played what solo because the three of us sounded so much alike. After that, the lineal descendancy changed. Fats was just getting ready, when he died, to break away. He could have never completely broken away from my influence, no more than I could've broken away from the influence of Roy Eldridge, or Roy from the influence of Louis Armstrong. When he died, Clifford Brown was influenced by my playing but only through what Fats had done. So that makes for a movement toward different style. Other guys came like Lee Morgan and Freddie Hubbard. I think Lee was directly influenced by my playing and Clifford Brown's, and Freddie Hubbard is a mixture of Clifford Brown and Miles. Because a style of playing is only the way you get from one note to another, since the same notes are there for everybody. How you get from one note to another is the style.

But I'm one of the old-school guys who don't care who a guy copies, just so I see a fundamental concept. If he gets a fundamental concept of the trumpet, he's got to come through me. Unless he's going to play it from another angle. If he plays it out of his mouth, he's got to come that way some time or another. What gets me is when a guy comes up, a friend of Freddie Hubbard's or a fan of Clifford Brown's or Lee Morgan's. They come to me ashamed and say, "I like Freddie Hubbard," and they give me a look. And it's the same thing as saying, "Well, I like you . . ." because the message is descended from me. The message of our music runs the same way as the message of religion. These people that come to bring messages in the different ages in the spiritual development of man are similar to the musicians, the messengers of our music who come to bring newer ages in the music.

You have a form and younger musicians who are developing all the time. The first thing you gotta have today to create good jazz is a good sense of rhythm. Without that, forget it. I don't care what notes you play, if you haven't got the rhythm to go with it, that's your ass. And to be aware of all the accents in the bar, to have a knowledgeable way with chords, the chord changes, and progressions, in our age was necessary. I don't know about the new age because they're playing scales, but whatever new comes up, it would have to be based on the old to have validity.

I've always hired musicians who were developing. When a guy argues with you, has two or three arguments with you about how the music is supposed to go, it's time for him to go out and get his, to go out and be responsible for the sound of his band. You are responsible for the sound of your group. Everybody's got to go along with you. If they wrote it or thought it up, I don't care how it is, they've got to go along with you. Because you're responsible for the sound of your band.

I was playing with a group called the Giants of Jazz—Monk, Art Blakey, Al McKibbon, Sonny Stitt, and Kai Winding. That was a good thing for the promoter when he put this together, six bandleaders instead of one for the people to come to see. All of us have bands so that's just like having six bands on the stage at one time. But no one in that group could be responsible for the sound of that group. It's all right for going around one time to get the mumps in your pockets because they're paying you well—one time and then you go out again for yourself, with your own band. But that's not good for any length of time because you fall into a groove where everybody looks at me in the band and says, "What are we gonna play?" All of them looked right at me. I can't be responsible for the sound of this group—all these bandleaders. I don't want to act like I want to be the leader of them, although all of them at one time or another have worked for me. They're now bandleaders themselves, and you don't go around telling a bandleader. The guy'll tell you, "What the fuck do you mean! What do you mean by that?" 'Cause he's a bandleader too. I didn't want to get into that.

For a guy's musical development, the same rule applies in jazz as in any other field; you collect facts, and study. You listen to Coleman Hawkins and Lester Young, two guys who played the same instrument but played it very differently. Both of them have something in common. Because both of them played the truth, your job is to find out what is the common denominator between Coleman Hawkins and Lester Young, or Lester Young and Louis Armstrong. When you find that, that's the foundation. When you play things, you assemble all this information in your mind like a computer, and you use it when it's necessary. Yeah, it is like building bricks on top of each other. You take a riff that Roy Eldridge played, and you play that riff. A lotta things happen with a specific riff, the chording behind it, and how you get from this progression to that one. And you figure the alternatives. You say, "Ah, then, you could also go here instead of going there." And when you get that far, finally you'll come up with something different. But it's the same music. It's just progressing all the time. So I never mind a guy, a trumpet player, who doesn't play like me and wants to play like Clifford Brown, because I know he's playing like me anyway.

Naturally, I know my own contribution to jazz. I know just what I created that someone else didn't, and what Monk did and what Charlie Parker did; what their main contributions have been. I was just digging and I said, "Now, let me see, what did I do that's going to be hard to get rid of?" You know the introduction that I made on "Round Midnight"? I notice sometimes when I sit down and listen and put on these guys like Nat Adderley, I notice a lot of the music is just based on that one thing. First, I did it on the end of "I Can't Get Started," and then I made that for the introduction of "Round Midnight," same thing. I've been doing it in and out of arrangements and I notice that this thing comes through to me from all this music. One guy down in South America wrote a whole symphony off that one phrase. All the guys who play "Round Midnight" use my introduction and they use my ending. So I see that when I listen to all the music that's coming out, I was the one. Take "All the Things You Are"; I heard Count Basie do an arrangement of it, and, damn, they did the same introduction that we did with Charlie Parker. It's the arrangers, the guys who write music for these things, who are influenced by certain things we play. Now, I bet you, you couldn't walk up to more

than three or four jazz musicians and ask why that introduction, and
they'd know. The first chord of "All the Things You Are" is F minor.
The chord that leads into it wasn't just something that was taken out
of the air; it's a C chord, goes right into F minor. I bet you a whole
lotta guys just play that and don't know why. I find nowadays that
musicians are not as inquisitive as they used to be. You've got to want
to know why. If you respect a guy's playing, and he does something
and you don't know why, you say, "Why did you do it?" What he does
is easy to find; you can listen to the record. Why, is what is important.
The musicians today are very quick and if they like a guy's style they'll
copy it. These modern hippies will learn a couple of riffs off a record
but they don't know what caused the guy to play them. They'll listen
to a record, and if a guy makes a mistake on the solo, they'll copy it
right off. They just figure everything he does is all right. Sometimes
you can make a whole lot of mistakes, but you know how to get out of
them. That's the fruit of knowing where you are all the time.

I've always been a Latin freak. Very early in my career, I realized that our music and that of our brothers in Latin America had
a common source. The Latin musician was fortunate in one sense. They
didn't take the drum away from him, so he was more polyrhythmic.
My conception was, "Why can't our music be more polyrhythmic?" In
1941, I wrote, "Night In Tunisia," where the bass says, "do-do-do-do-
do-do," and "daanh-da-da-da-da-da" was being played against that.
That was the sense of polyrhythm.

Yes, I use my own conception of what I hear that they do. I'm not
playing exactly like the West Indians' or Afro-Cubans' music, but mine
goes with it. I put my own personal feelings into the music of Brazil, or
wherever. You've got to be very broad nowadays—a drummer—because
the music is so closely entwined; you gotta be at home everywhere. So
rhythm's my stick. I've created a lot of harmonies that guys have used
that stuck to the music, but my real thing is rhythm. And all the drummers know it. I taught all the drummers from Max Roach, Art Blakey
on down, and they're doing things that I showed them, now. I got 6/8
time. I copied a 6/8 rhythm from Chano Pozo, and I adapted it to the
drums, and I showed it to Charlie Persip, and Charlie Persip showed it
to everybody. And now, any time they go into 6/8, they play my lick,
everybody, I don't care where you go, in Europe, everywhere, because
it was actually an authentic reproduction of what to do on the conga
drum, and I play the conga drum myself. One night the guy on the
radio played an old "Swing Low, Sweet Cadillac" of mine that I don't
even remember and the conga player . . . I was explaining to him
while the record was playing, "Now, there's the greatest in the world.
This guy has the sound of the conga drums." And come to find out, it

was I who was playing. I was so ashamed. I was saying, "Please for-give me, Chano Pozo, up there on the high concourse."

Records you can listen to and tell the stature of a musician, but with many records, not one record. You take them chronologically, and you can get a pretty good picture. Of course it's very seldom that you hear a guy who's best on records. But you can hear where his mind is go-ing. Sometimes it gets on records and then there's a masterpiece. I've never played my really best on records, and I've only played my best four or five times in my whole career. But I know records wasn't one of them—one of those times when everything was clicking. You never know when it's going to happen. The musicians I'm working with in-spire me, rhythm sections inspire me, and then soloists. My association with Charlie Parker would have to be far above anything else that I have ever done musically, in every way. Charlie Parker used to give me tremendous inspiration. He'd always play before me. We always had it arranged. Sometimes, after you play, you think, "I could have played something more effective." I listen to my records some-times, very seldom though. I only listen to them critically because after you've played it, it's all gone anyway. But even on jobs guys don't always play their best. Sometimes they will start and play all night and not strike one groove.

I'd like to be known as a major messenger to jazz rather than a leg-endary figure because sometimes legendary figures have feet made of clay, legendary figures can fade. When you're a major contributor to music, your contribution can't fade.

I'm just in a long line of contributing trumpet players to the whole picture of jazz. I look at my stature as a major contributor to the music on the same scale as that of Buddy Bolden, King Oliver, Louis Armstrong, Roy Eldridge, Miles Davis, and Clifford Brown. The mes-sage that a trumpet player brings is specific. All messengers have the same stature. The intensity of the message depends upon its reception, to whom it's going and other circumstances, so it might seem that one is brighter or stronger.

If you called me Roy Eldridge, I'd say, "Huh?" Because he brought a message and I brought one which, though equal, is not the same. Roy's message continues too, just like mine, because, you see, I'm from Roy and his message is manifested in me. There were other branches. Did you ever hear of Jabbo Smith? Well, Jabbo Smith was also from King Oliver, not necessarily from Louis Armstrong because he was a contemporary of Louis Armstrong's. They copied the same guy, and Jabbo went off on another direction. Your influence is due to how many people copy you.

Progressive jazz came after our music, bebop. But you see, you can't leave out the fundamentals like Stan Kenton did. The major fundamental of our music is rhythm, a great and definite rhythm. If you leave out these fundamentals it's just as if you took a tree with a trunk and something crept out on a limb and kept going until it fell off. That's what happened to Stan Kenton's music. It wasn't fundamentally sound, according to what we thought, whereas Miles's music is definitely an extension of our music because it's based on rhythm and also the blues.

Ray Charles and I were talking. Ray Charles was on Tom Jones's show, and Tom had a whole lot of Ray Charles's licks in his singing. Tom Jones whipped out these little idioms of Ray Charles's, but Ray reached way back in the back somewhere and came out with something that Tom Jones couldn't even identify. Given the fact of culture, and Ray Charles being the genius and the boss of that culture, he said, "Get that one. . . ."

Sometimes our music is watered down to placate the public. But if you're going to be a creator, you must be prepared to let your art speak for you. And you must be prepared to take all of the consequences of anything that might sway you from making your creation. Managers and everything will say, "We know you're creative, but the public won't take it." Sometimes I've been seduced into making records that I didn't like. But when a guy copies and is satisfied with being a copyist, the creator must go further.

About this name "jazz" and whether we should continue to use it: first, what other name are you going to give it? Jazz is all right for want of a better name. Jazz is an African word.† It doesn't detract from the importance, the seriousness, or the dignity of our music. It surely didn't bother Duke Ellington; or Louis Armstrong, they say he's a jazz artist; or Dizzy Gillespie. If the music were named anything else, I think I'd have just as much respect as I get now from my colleagues and contemporaries. I get just as much credit as I'd receive if I were playing another kind of music. I don't think it would enhance my stature at all to be known musically as something other than a jazz artist. Taste is the most important thing in music, and there are so very few who have it. You've got to know chords and have a sense of phrasing; anything that hooks us and doesn't break the continuity is good. Of course some things can be in good taste but not hooked up. I like all kinds of music and musicians, all styles of trumpet players. As for Eddie Condon and the old-timers and what they call the "real jazz," there is no real jazz—there's only good and bad. Simplicity is not enough in itself; it should be used for contrast. That goes for the "new thing" too. Anything that's played with a beat, with good taste

† From Malenke *jasi*, meaning to act out of the ordinary, thus to speed up, to excite, to act uninhibited. See Smitherman, G., *Talkin and Testifyin*, Houghton, Mifflin Co., Boston, 1977, p. 53.

and correct changes, or some sensibly patterned sounds that do not offend the ear, is good, and I don't care what name you give it.

Duke Ellington is, without a doubt, America's greatest composer. He's in a class by himself. But we have had many great composers in the United States, not only black, but white. The way composers gain influence is by people performing their music. Duke Ellington is a great composer because everybody plays his music.

In improvisation, the first thing you must have is the sight of a gifted painter. You've got to see colors and lines in music, and then you've got to be able to mix the colors and draw the lines. The better you mix colors and draw lines, the better the painting is going to be. I don't know what's gonna come into my mind when I play. Of course, you know, the way that I play, from fundamentals, I have set progressions in a specific number. But I don't know how I'm gonna enunciate on them until it comes out. Sometimes, it's surprise, surprise.

Time is really just catching up with our music, bebop. And since a music that was geared for that time has come this far, it must have been something pretty important. The role of music goes hand in hand with social reformation—the changing of society to make things right because music is a form of worship. The Guardian of the Baha'i faith has said there has got to be an "organic change" in the structure of society. Organic change means all the things we know have got to be changed around for the betterment of society as a whole. There's another great saying by our Prophet, "The earth is but one country and mankind its citizens." So I believe in that. Music must reflect society, world society, and the way the society is moving because musicians depend upon the society to sustain them; at the same time, music and musicians must help to set things right.

Honors

The past three Presidents have each invited me to the White House for dinner, and I have used these occasions to try to advance the cause of music, especially jazz. Attempting to make new friends for our music, I told Mrs. Lyndon Johnson I had a thing about her name. She said, "How is that?"

I said, "Well, your name is Lady Bird, and one of the greatest performers that we've had to come through this way was a lady named Billie Holiday. And we called her 'Lady.' And one of the greatest musicians there ever was in the world was named Charlie Parker, and we called him 'Bird.' So your name is 'Lady Bird' and you are Billie Holiday and Charlie Parker at the same time. People, when they hear your name, start thinking in terms of something very, very wonderful." That woman is something else. I really like Mrs. Johnson; she is very gracious.

She said, "You know, I never thought of that, ha, ha." She probably never heard of Charlie Parker. She probably had heard of Lady Day but never heard of Charlie Parker. But I told her that and it made her feel pretty good.

At the White House party for Duke Ellington, in 1969, I had a conversation with Richard Nixon about the possibility of my going overseas again. He said, "You've represented the United States Government several times. What do you think about your making another trip?"

I said, "I wouldn't be interested in making another trip to play *for* somebody. But I would be interested in going to play *with* somebody. That means if I go to Cuba, I have to play *with* the Cubans. If I go to Africa, I have to play *with* the Africans, using music to further the feeling of togetherness and co-operation."

With Nixon, Peggy Lee was in Washington at the time representing a group of composers. She had to make a speech about it. I wanted to speak to Nixon about something too. I was getting closer to him because he was only one seat away. They're always one person away. We couldn't be together, couldn't be sitting side by side, because there's always a woman between two men. On each side of me is a woman, and on each side of him is a woman. That's the way they have it set up in there, man-woman-man-woman, with eight at a table.

Benny Goodman was talking about the time. . . . I said, "Benny wait a minute. Lemme speak to the President about this." I said, "You're already a millionaire. I'm trying to get something." I wanted to talk to him about the jukebox industry, how they don't give us any royalties from the music played on jukeboxes. Benny Goodman was talking about his college days when Nixon used to come see him at the Trianon Ballroom.

Nixon said, "It's a shame; they should get some money for it." But I don't believe anything ever came of it. That bill is still hung up in Congress.

When I was invited to the White House by President Ford, the cab-driver took me to the wrong gate, and then he left. Yeah, I paid him and tipped him good, and he put me off at the wrong gate. And I had to walk all the way around the White House—in that park, man. And in Washington, D.C., at night, I was scared shitless I was gonna get "mugged" on the way to the White House. I had my proper credentials and I went on in.

When you go inside, they say browse around, whatever you wanna do. I went on in the Pink Room, or wherever, and looked around and didn't see anyone I knew. There were no more spooks—all white. This was for President Ford. With the other Presidents, blacks were every-where, man, with Eisenhower, Johnson, and Nixon. And every time I've been to the White House for dinner, three times, the President was sit-ting at the same table where I was sitting for dinner. I can't understand that—Presidents Johnson, Nixon, and Ford.

So I'm in there. Now, the first person I see that I know is Doris Duke, and I'm the first person she sees that she knows. And so we started talking. One time when I was in Newport, I called her house and left a message, so she came to the club where we were working. But I told her, "Boy, you're a dummy; you're a dumb bitch because you didn't invite me over to your house. I was gonna give you a piano lesson, free of charge. You couldn't get that with all of your money. With all of your bread, you couldn't buy that because it was all free. I'm leaving tomorrow, there's no time, now, so that's your ass." I told her that when she came over to the club that night.

So at the White House, she said, "Where's my lesson?"

I say, "You hafta wait in line, hafta get in line."

She says, "What number am I?"

I say, "I don't have any idea; I don't know."

And then James Earl Jones came in, and I'd never met James Earl Jones before; that was nice. Billy Taylor and his wife were there too, and that was it as far as the spooks were concerned. I figured it was good I'd accepted that invitation because it could've been my last chance to see that dude in the White House. And what happened? He's no longer in the White House. I spoke to President Ford about the Bern Treaty for composers because the United States was not a signatory of that agreement. Under the Bern Treaty, when you compose something, it's yours for your lifetime and fifty years after your death. Russia doesn't belong to it either. I asked the President, "About the Bern Agreement . . . ?"

He said, "It's way past time; a new copyright law is being worked on now." He was telling the truth. That was the difference between Nixon and Ford. Ford signed it, it went through. I believe the United States should be a signatory to the Bern Agreement because it's hard to write music. It's not hard to write, but it's hard to write anything that makes some sense. That is the only criteria of anything—it must have meaning.

I don't have much faith in jazz polls; they're just popularity. I'm a very popular person, but I don't win many polls. It's a matter of taste, I guess, the preference of the people who vote, and your popularity with them. Critics' polls I do better in than regular popular polls. I think a good example of winning a poll is to be voted in by your colleagues. Let the musicians vote and see who wins, then you sorta find a better standard. There should be a poll of musicians. The Ebony jazz poll didn't vote me into the Hall of Fame until 1977, thirty years after my major contributions were made.

In 1972, I received the Handel Medallion from the city of New York. I thought it was a great honor and really appreciated that. John Motley was the cause of it though, because he'd received the Handel Medallion. I'd been doing some work with the school kids, with the choir he directs in New York City, and they thought that because of my connection with the youth and my work with them that I deserved the Handel Medallion. Mayor Lindsay laid it on me. They invited Alice Wilson and the mayor of Cheraw, Miller Ingraham, to visit New York for the presentation of the Medallion and a special sacred concert that we did at Carnegie Hall with the All-City Choir. It was a fantastic concert and Alice Wilson and Mayor Ingraham were both very flattered and pleased by the invitation and the opportunity to see me accept that honor.

JOHN MOTLEY
(Director of Music, New York City public schools):

"Set aside the music and take Dizzy Gillespie, the man. He's one of the most generous, unselfish persons and a real gentleman that I have ever known in any field, music, or what have you. He has a thing for people that I think is purely godlike in many aspects. It's the way he deals with people, I think, that's just as important as his music. He takes time out to teach people. I mean, he has a lot of time to give most anybody. His patience and his belief in people, I think, is as great as his music. I notice the way that people come to him when he's out playing, how they just want to be near him. It's something like a shot in the arm just to be around him, not just to hear him play. And that's true! He's passed the test of a great man. Not just music. You can be in music and be the biggest scoundrel in the world. But I judge a man by his character, not by his music."

ALICE V. WILSON:

"He and Motley had this concert at Carnegie Hall in New York and they invited me to come up. I have the letter in my scrapbook where Dizzy said I was his teacher and wanted me to come up. It was supposed to be on the fifth of July. So I told my cousin, Mrs. Jackson, 'I can't go up there.'

"She said, 'Yes you can go, and you're going too!'

"I say, 'I'll go if you go with me.' They sent my plane ticket, round-trip plane ticket, she paid hers, and they had this room reserved, a double room, for us.

"The time when he presented me up on the stand in Carnegie Hall, well, I thought I'd never see it, let alone get in it, and, you know, I think that must've been about the time when I was most happy. When I went up, he told who I was, his teacher from Cheraw, something like that anyway, 'Mrs. Wilson, come up on the stage.' When I went up, he escorted me up the steps. So when I got up there, I whispered, 'I don't know what to say. What must I say?'

"He says, 'Just tell them good evening.' I did think of maybe two or three more words to say, other than that. But I think that was about the proudest moment of my life, when he introduced me that day. And he always seems so appreciative toward me—all the time. And you know that's something to be proud of. Something for me to be proud of. Later on I told him, 'Boy, you waited until I got to be an old lady, but you made me famous.'"

🔳

In 1973, I was the guest of the Kenyan Government on the auspicious occasion when they were celebrating the Tenth Anniversary of Independence. So I decided to say a speech in Swahili. I wrote out a speech in English and sent it to the Kenyan Embassy in Washington, and they translated it into Swahili for me and sent me a cassette. I put on the earphones, and I learned the speech and made it on TV, and they loved it in Kenya. The original English version is, "I want to say to all of you, the People of Kenya, that you have been my inspiration since way before Independence, and also to say that this is the culmination not only of my professional activities, but also of my human relationships, to come to Kenya to perform for you because I think of you as my people."*

Of all these honors, the one that gave me the greatest sense of pride was the Paul Robeson Award, because Paul Robeson was really my hero. Paul Robeson came at a stage in the evolution of the social order in this country, at a most opportune time, as far as he was concerned. But it was also a very opportune time on the road to the winning of our just rights. Of course they haven't been consummated yet, but on account of Paul Robeson, the struggle gained momentum which led into Martin Luther King, Malcolm X, and whoever else. Paul was an incorruptible soul. He was the biggest. He was our biggest celebrity in his time because he had so many spheres of influence: the theater, on the concert stage, and the movies, recordings, and sports. He was just number one in all of them and it was great. And he wouldn't be corrupted, wouldn't let them corrupt him. Money or nothing could corrupt Paul Robeson. That's beautiful, and I like that idea. So that really gave me great pleasure when they had a concert during the Newport Jazz Festival and presented a program of my compositions. Jazzmobile and Chris White of the Rutgers Institute of Jazz Studies sponsored it, and they gave me the Paul Robeson Award. That's the one that I'm most proud of.

* Swahili—*Ningependa Kusema Kwenu, wananchi wa Kenya, kuwu ninyi mmenitia moyo sana tokea kabla uhuru wetu, na pia ningependa kusema kowanba, kufika kwa nchini Kenya, kuwatumbuiza wananchi na kelele kikubwa sana, si katika shuguli za kazi yangu pekee pia uhusiano wa binadamu ya kuwa ninyi ni ndugu zangu.*

CHRISTOPHER WHITE
(bass, Director of the Rutgers Institute of Jazz Studies):

"The Award was intended to do several things. Number one, to commemorate the meaning and message and philosophy of some heavy warriors, like Paul Robeson. He was one of our first real warriors. And, as a matter of fact, he paid the price. I mean he was ostracized. He went the whole route as did W. E. B. Du Bois, who went that route too. They were very closely aligned, although Du Bois was thought of as an intellectual, whereas Robeson had this fiery connotation to his being—more "militant," whatever that is.

"When I perceived who these men really were and their commitment to the African continuum in this country, it became obvious to me that it was necessary to institute an award that would be given to people who, themselves, were other manifestations of the African continuum in this American milieu. Without a doubt, Dizzy, to my way of thinking, was the epitome of that, given African-American music. People point to him and Charlie Parker as being the innovators of a completely new and different style of music. And at the same time when you look at what the music is, you see that he and Bird didn't do any altering. They just brought new insight and expanded the vocabulary, expanded the whole point of view. But didn't alter the African continuum. There was still call and response in the music. There was still room for personal communication. Rhythm was really important. Discipline was a part of the music. It was an oral music, basically. Although people began to put bebop down, the idiom is reflective of black people in this country. How they talk. It's a life-style. It's all those kinds of things. So that it was only logical, only right to make that kind of award to Dizzy, 'cause like he had made a contribution to the continuum."

Being a South Carolinian by birth, I was asked by the state of South Carolina, in 1976, to come down and appear at the intermediate schools in three different cities, Columbia, Greenville, and Walterboro, sponsored by the State Arts Commission. On our second day in South Carolina we were invited to perform on the floor of the State House, during the General Session of the Legislature, where I would be asked to play one tune and also to make a speech to be inserted in the record of the Sovereign State of South Carolina. I told them that it was my greatest pleasure to come and that I had often dreamed of it and that it was the fruition of my "wildest dreams." I had wondered what I would say after growing up under a superracist state in South Carolina, so I read a prepared statement excerpted from an article in *World Order,* the Baha'i journal, called "200 Years of Imperishable Hope." The article talked about America's history, including the history of racism, and predicted that the United States would someday become a model of racial harmony. "The South will lead it on," I said because I observed how much different things were down there than when I came up. There have been massive changes. Not enough, but a lot, especially in the South. I believe that the South is going to pave the way and teach the rest of the country how to act in respecting the rights of citizens. In Boston, Massachusetts—the cradle of democracy, allegedly —they had all that trouble with the kids going to school, while in the South the schools are integrated. In my home, Cheraw, South Carolina, they have one high school, one junior high school, and one grammar school, and there ain't no more after that. The kids get along just fine. They're really showing the rest of the country the way to go. You see, the North has always had segregation. There was a time on 125th Street when a colored guy couldn't go and sit down in Blumstein's—on 125th Street. Couldn't sit down, in *Harlem!* And this hasn't been too long ago either. The North is way behind the South now. In my hometown they have a group of buildings, low-rent housing, named in my honor on a street called Dizzy Gillespie Drive. It runs around, it doesn't run straight. I'm just naming some of the advances down South because I don't see very many up North, not too many in Harlem, anyway, except Lionel Hampton Houses. And this lack of progress in social and human relationships up North seems to also hold true nowadays at the level of the national government.

In 1976, I received an invitation from the National Endowment for the Arts to serve on the "jazz, folk, ethnic section" of their musical advisory council. I accepted the invitation, but not without serious questions about officially separating musicians, not by color but by culture, into those who played European-derived symphonic music and those who didn't. Obvious, though partially hidden, economic discrimination against jazz artists is involved. The United States National Endowment for the Arts, in 1978, reportedly plans to spend $13,700,000 for music programs. Only $640,000 of this would be used to support "jazz," loosely defined. Symphony orchestras and opera, on the other hand, would receive over $10,000,000. The music has progressed beyond that now. We're playing with symphony orchestras, television, movies, clubs, concert halls. The educational system is gonna be great too. That is something I'm going to get into with Gil Fuller. We're preparing studies now with cassettes, thirty-minute lessons, teaching our music, what happened and why.

The first thing as far as the jazz artist is concerned is to complete raising the respect of the jazz musician to the level of a classical musician or concert artist. I'm gonna get into that field shortly, have all of my compositions scored for symphony orchestra and quartet, and play all over the world with it. No one is doing that as extensively as I plan on doing it, and I am qualified. I've paid my dues. That will pull our music up. That will put another notch in the triumph of our music. And the classical orchestras need it. They're in the red all the time, but when we play with one, it gets in the black.

Why doesn't America dig jazz and raise it to the proper height? I don't like to accuse America of being racist, but that doesn't take away from the fact that it is a racist country. Jazz was created by blacks in the United States and for America to truly appreciate our music and to put it on the plane that it deserves would mean elevating the creators of our music, who happen to be black—to put them on a level above the musical contribution of the white citizenry. Rhythm is the thing; we have it and that's why we prevail in the music—not just because we're black—but because of our experience. So I'm not accusing anyone of anything, just talking about the circumstances that exist. Racism has always been the drawback. America doesn't want to give blacks full credit for creating this music and for being the chief practitioners of this art. That has been the trouble. That's why rock 'n roll music didn't go too well in America until the Beatles came along. The Beatles copied our black music, and then the whites in the United States copied the Beatles. They had it all the time, right here under their noses, and wouldn't do anything about it. The United States could take a step toward leading the world in art and human relations just by accepting the gift of jazz, which has spread from its own culture all over the world.

Our music is spreading more and more. You go to places now you never heard of before. Jazz is getting bigger and bigger and bigger. Jazz artists are more well known than the politicians of the country—not just this country. So they are statesmen. They are world statesmen, these jazz artists. I said, when I heard that first they were talking about a baseball team going to Cuba from the major leagues in the United States to play against the Cubans, I could just see what would happen. When a guy, the pitcher, would throw a hard fast one up against the batter's chin to brush him back from the plate, there would be pandemonium. I said, "No, that's not the way it's supposed to be." And then I started thinking in terms of cementing relations between the U.S. and Cuba on an artistic level, of playing *with*, instead of *against*. It's a whole lotta difference in competing against and doing something in the spirit of co-operation. And that's the best way. We went to Cuba and did it, after President Carter lifted the ban on travel to that country, and it worked beautifully. Right now, I'm trying to get the United States and Cuba to co-operate in sponsoring a concert at which I would play, the proceeds of which would go toward building a school in Cuba, a living monument to Chano Pozo.

I performed at the Carter White House in November, 1977, along with Sarah Vaughan and Earl Hines. The President was very cordial and expressed great appreciation for our music. I heard he intends to raise support for our music to a level on par with music in the European classical tradition. President Carter has the makings of a great humanitarian.

That's the way I would like to be remembered, as a humanitarian, because it must be something besides music that has kept me here when all of my colleagues are dead. My main influence on whatever we'll have as a historical account must be something else because God has let me stay here this long, and most of my contemporaries—Charlie Parker, Clifford Brown, Lester Young, Bud Powell, Oscar Pettiford, Charlie Christian, Fats Navarro, Tadd Dameron—are gone. Most of them are outta here. So maybe my role in music is just a stepping-stone to a higher role. The highest role is the role in the service of humanity, and if I can make that, then I'll be happy. When I breathe the last time, it'll be a happy breath.

Selected Discography

The following records were chosen mainly for their historic value, i.e., as examples of Dizzy Gillespie's musical development and to note various Gillespie innovations which have affected the course of music, especially the jazz art form, for over forty years, a relatively long period of time, considering the age of jazz.

A few selections, particularly the classic early recordings with Charlie Parker, were included for their superb artistic qualities, most notably their brilliant creativity, which allows them to serve as hallmarks of excellence in jazz performance of whatever era.

Because Dizzy Gillespie, during the years, has also made a constant impact on society which deserved to be seen repeatedly as well as heard, a much requested item—a listing of films and video tapes featuring him—comprises a second section hereunder.

ORIGINAL LABEL	TITLE, PLACE AND DATE, PERSONNEL, AND SONGS	LMI*
Bluebird	Teddy Hill and His NBC Orchestra† New York, May 7, 1937 Dizzy Gillespie, Lester "Shad" Collins (tp); Bill Dillard (tp, vcl); Dicky Wells (tb); Russell Procope (cl, as); Howard Johnson (as); Teddy Hill, Robert Carroll (ts); Sam Allen (p); John Smith (g); Richard Fullbright (b); Bill Beason (d) San Anton (B6988)/I'm Happy Darling Dancing with You (B6989)/Yours and Mine (B7013, LPV530)/I'm Feeling Like a Million (B7013)/King Porter Stomp (B6988, LPV530)/Blue Rhythm Fantasy (B6989, LPV530)	Victor LPV530

* LMI—Latest and/or most inclusive issue(s) of songs from the matrix.
† First Gillespie performance on record.

ORIGINAL LABEL	TITLE, PLACE AND DATE, PERSONNEL, AND SONGS	LMI
Victor	Lionel Hampton and His Orchestra‡ September 11, 1939 Dizzy Gillespie (tp); Benny Carter (as); Coleman Hawkins, Ben Webster, Chu Berry (ts); Clyde Hart (p); Charlie Christian (g); Milt Hinton (b); Cozy Cole (d); Lionel Hampton (vib, vcl) When Lights Are Low (VIC26371, Smth. P11894)/One Sweet Letter from You (VIC26393)/Hot Mallets (VIC26371)/Early Session Hop (VIC26393)	Smithsonian Collection P11894
Vocalion	Cab Calloway and His Orchestra* Chicago, March 8, 1940 Dizzy Gillespie, Mario Bauza, Lamar Wright (tp); Tyree Glenn (vib, tb); Quentin Jackson, Keg Johnson (tb); Jerry Blake (cl, as); Hilton Jefferson, Andrew Brown (as); Leon "Chu" Berry, Walter (Foots) Thomas (ts); Benny Payne (p); Danny Barker (g); Milt Hinton (b); Cozy Cole (d); Cab Calloway (vcl) Pickin' The Cabbage (Vo5467, Smth. Ro04)/Chop, Chop, Charlie Chan (Vo5444)/Paradiddle (Vo5467, Smth. Ro04)/Boog It (Vo5444)	Smithsonian Collection Ro04-P13456
Esoteric (Minton's Performances)	The Men From Minton's† New York, May 1941 Dizzy Gillespie, unknown (tp); Don Byas (ts); Charlie Christian (g); Nick Fenton (b); Kenny Clarke or Harold "Doc" West (d) Up On Teddy's Hill (ES548) Above *personnel* with Leon "Chu" Berry (ts); unknown (p); minus Charlie Christian Stardust I (ES548, Smth. Ro04) Dizzy Gillespie (tp); Ken Kersey (p); Nick Fenton (b); Kenny Clarke (d) Stardust II (ES548)/Kerouac (ES548, Smth. Ro04)	Smithsonian Collection Ro04-P13456
Decca/Brunswick	Lucky Millinder and His Orchestra‡ New York, July 29, 1942 Dizzy Gillespie, William "Chiefie" Scott, Nelson Bryant (tp); George Stevenson, Joe Britton (tb); Tab Smith, Billy Bowen (as); Stafford Simon, Dave Young (ts); Ernest Purce (bar); Bill Doggett (p); Trevor Bacon	Smithsonian Collection Ro04-P13456

‡ First recorded performance by Gillespie as modern-jazz stylist.
* First recorded performance of a Gillespie composition, "Pickin' The Cabbage," and first attempt to infuse Afro-Cuban rhythmic concepts into jazz.
† First recording of early modern jazz jam sessions at Minton's Playhouse in Harlem.
‡ First recorded performance of the trumpet riff on "Little John Special" which later became the theme for the melody of "Salt Peanuts."

ORIGINAL LABEL	TITLE, PLACE AND DATE, PERSONNEL, AND SONGS	LMI
	(g, vcl); Nick Fenton (b); Panama Francis (d)	
	Are You Ready (DE18529)/Mason Flyer (BR03406)/When the Lights Go On Again (DE18496)/Little John Special (BR03406, Smth. R004)	
Home Recording Bob Redcross	Dizzy Gillespie—Charlie Parker All-Stars* Savoy Hotel, Room 305, Chicago, February 15, 1943 Dizzy Gillespie (tp); Charlie Parker (ts); Oscar Pettiford (b); Shadow Wilson (per) Sweet Georgia Brown I/Sweet Georgia Brown II	Unissued Collection of Bob Redcross
V-Disc	Duke Ellington and His Orchestra† New York, November 8, 1943 Dizzy Gillespie, Wallace Jones, Rex Stewart, Taft Jordan (tp); Joe Nanton, Juan Tizol, Lawrence Brown (tb); Jimmy Hamilton (cl, ts); Johnny Hodges (as, sop); Otto Handwick (as); Elmer Williams, Harry Carney (ts); Duke Ellington (p); Fred Guy (g); Ernest Myers (b); Sonny Greer (d); Betty Roche, Al Hibbler (vcl) Hop Skip Jump (V-Disc 355, FDC 1002)/ Boy Meets Horn (V-Disc 176)/Tea for Two/ I Don't Want Anybody at All/Baby Please Stop and Think of Me/Summertime/Sentimental Lady/Mood Indigo	For Discriminate Collectors FDC 1002
Broadcast Air Take Onyx Club	Gillespie-Pettiford Quintet, Onyx Club‡ New York, January 1944 Dizzy Gillespie (tp); Budd Johnson (ts); George Wallington (p); Oscar Pettiford (b); Max Roach (d) Night In Tunisia	Unissued Collection of Bob Redcross
Apollo	Coleman Hawkins and His Orchestra* New York, February 16, 1944 Dizzy Gillespie, Vic Coulson, Ed Vandever (tp); Leo Parker, Leonard Lowry (as); Coleman Hawkins, Don Byas, Ray Abrams (ts); Budd Johnson (bar); Clyde Hart (p); Oscar Pettiford (b); Max Roach (d) Woody 'n You (APO 751, Smth. R004)/Ba-Dee-Daht (APO 752)/Yesterdays (APO 752)/Disorder at the Border (APO 753, Smth. R004)/Feeling Zero (APO 753)/Rainbow Mist (APO 751)	Smithsonian Collection R004-P13456

* First recorded performance with Charlie Parker.
† First recorded performance with Duke Ellington Orchestra.
‡ First bebop quintet, live on New York's Fifty-second Street.
* First modern-jazz studio-recording session. First recorded performance of Gillespie's classic "Woody 'n You," played by the composer.

ORIGINAL LABEL	TITLE, PLACE AND DATE, PERSONNEL, AND SONGS	LMI
Deluxe	Billy Eckstine with the Deluxe All-Stars† New York, April 13, 1944 Dizzy Gillespie, Al Killian, Shorty McConnell, Freddie Webster (tp); Claude Jones, Howard Scott, Trummy Young (tb); Budd Johnson, Jimmy Powell (as); Wardell Gray, Thomas Crump (ts); Rudy Rutherford (bar); Clyde Hart (p); Connie Wainwright (g); Oscar Pettiford (b); Shadow Wilson (d); Billy Eckstine (vcl) I Got a Date with Rhythm (DLX1003)/I Stay in the Mood for You (DLX2000, Smth. R004)/Good Jelly Blues (DLX2000)	Smithsonian Collection R004-P13456
Deluxe	Billy Eckstine and His Orchestra‡ New York, December 5, 1944 Dizzy Gillespie, Shorty McConnell, Gail Brockman, Boonie Hazel (tp); Gerald Valentine, Taswell Baird, Howard Scott, Chips Outcalt (tb); John Jackson, Bill Frazier (as); Dexter Gordon, Gene Ammons (ts); Leo Parker (bar); John Malachi (p); Connie Wainwright (g); Tommy Potter (b); Art Blakey (d); Billy Eckstine, Sarah Vaughan (vcl) If That's the Way You Feel (DLX2001)/I Want to Talk About You (DLX2003)/Blowing the Blues Away (DLX2001, Smth. R004)/Opus X (DLX2002, Smth. R004)/I'll Wait and Pray (DLX2003, Smth. R004)/The Real Thing Happened to Me (DLX2002)	Smithsonian Collection R004-P13456
Continental	Sarah Vaughan and Her All-Stars° New York, December 31, 1944 Dizzy Gillespie (tp); Aaron Sachs (cl); Georgie Auld (ts); Leonard Feather (p); Chuck Wayne (g); Jack Lesberg (b); Morey Feld (d); Sarah Vaughan (vcl); (Gillespie doubles on piano 2, 3, 4.) Signing Off (Cont. 6024)/Interlude (Cont. 6031; Smth. R004)/No Smokes (Cont. 6061, Smth. R004)/East of the Sun (Cont. 6031)	Smithsonian Collection R004-P13456 and P13457
Manor	Dizzy Gillespie Sextet† New York, January 9, 1945 Dizzy Gillespie (tp); Trummy Young (tb); Don Byas (ts); Clyde Hart (p); Oscar Pettiford (b); Shelly Manne (d) I Can't Get Started (Manor 1042; Smth. R004, P11895)/Good Bait (Manor 1042; Smth. R004)/Salt Peanuts (Manor 5000;	Smithsonian Collection R004-P13457 and P11895

† Gillespie bop "double up" arrangement. The first ever recorded on "Good Jelly Blues," featuring Billy Eckstine, Shadow Wilson.

‡ Billy Eckstine Orchestra, the first modern jazz big band with Gillespie as soloist and musical director, features Sarah Vaughan, Art Blakey.

° First recorded performance of Gillespie "doubling" on piano.

† First Gillespie studio recording session as bandleader.

ORIGINAL LABEL	TITLE, PLACE AND DATE, PERSONNEL, AND SONGS	LMI
	Smth. R004)/Be-Bop (Manor 5000; Smth. R004)	
Guild/Musicraft	Dizzy Gillespie Sextet New York, February, March, 1945 Dizzy Gillespie (tp); Charlie Parker (as); Clyde Hart (p); Reno Palmieri (g); Slam Stewart (b); Cozy Cole (d)	Phoenix LP2 Prestige P-24030 Everest FS272 Smithsonian Collection R004-P13457
	Groovin' High (Guild 1001; Phnx. LP2; EVR FS-272; Prst. P-24030; Smth. R004-P13457)/ All the Things You Are (Mus 488; Phnx. LP2; EVR FS-272; Prst. P-24030)/Dizzy Atmosphere (Mus. 488; Phnx. LP2; EVR FS-272; Prst. P-24030)	
Guild	Dizzy Gillespie All-Star Quintet New York, May 11, 1945 Dizzy Gillespie (tp, vcl); Charlie Parker (as); Al Haig (p); Curley Russell (b); Sid Catlett (dr); Sarah Vaughan (vcl)	Phoenix LP2 Prestige P-24030 Smithsonian Collection P-11895
	Salt Peanuts (Phnx. LP2; Prst. P-24030)/ Shaw 'Nuff (Phnx. LP2, Prst. P-24030)/ Lover Man (Phnx. LP2; Prst. P-24030)/Hothouse (Phnx. LP2; Prst. P-24030)	
Savoy	Charlie Parker's Ree Boppers‡ New York, November 26, 1945 Miles Davis (tp); Charlie Parker (as); Dizzy Gillespie (p, tp); Curley Russell (b); Max Roach (d)‡ Add Argonne Thornton (Sadik Hakim) (p) on Ko Ko	Smithsonian Collection P-11895
	Billie's Bounce (1-5)/Warming Up a Riff/ Now's the Time (1-4)/Meandering/Ko Ko (1-2, Smth. P11895)	
Home Recording	Dizzy Gillespie's California Jam* Los Angeles, February 1946 Dizzy Gillespie (tp); Charlie Parker (as); Red Callender (b); unknown (p); Harold "Doc" West (d)	Collection Freddie James
	Sweet Georgia Brown/Lover Come Back to Me I/Lover Come Back to Me II	
Dial	Dizzy Gillespie Jazzmen† Los Angeles, February 7, 1946 Dizzy Gillespie (tp, vcl); Lucky Thompson (tp, vcl); Milt Jackson (vbs); Al Haig (p); Ray Brown (b); Stan Levey (d); The Three Angels (vcl)	Smithsonian Collection R004-P13457

‡ So-called "mystery" session. Mystery arose regarding who played on which tunes. Gillespie played trumpet only on the introduction to Ko Ko, and piano on all the sides.

* A little-known jam session.

† The Dizzy Gillespie Sextet, featuring Ray Brown and Milt Jackson at Billy Berg's in Los Angeles, modified by the addition of Lucky Thompson.

ORIGINAL LABEL	TITLE, PLACE AND DATE, PERSONNEL, AND SONGS	LMI
	Confirmation (Smth. R004-P13457)/Diggin' for Diz (Smth. R004-P13457)/Dynamo (A) (Smth. R004-P13457)/Dynamo (B)/When I Grow Too Old to Dream (1-2)/'Round About Midnight (Smth. R004-P13457)/ 'Round About Midnight (B)	
Paramount	Dizzy Gillespie with Johnny Richards' Orchestra‡ Los Angeles, January, February 1946	Phoenix LP-4
	Dizzy Gillespie (tp); Al Haig (p); Ray Brown (b); Roy Haynes (d) w. woodwinds; strings; French horns	
	Who/The Way You Look Tonight (Phnx. LP-4)/Why Do I Love You (Phnx. LP-4)/ All the Things You Are (Phnx. LP-4)	
Musicraft	Dizzy Gillespie Sextet* New York, May 15, 1946	Phoenix LP-2 Prestige P-24030
	Dizzy Gillespie (tp, vcl); Sonny Stitt (as); Milt Jackson (vbs); Al Haig (p); Ray Brown (b); Kenny Clarke (d); Gil Fuller (arr.); Alice Roberts (vcl)	
	One Bass Hit (Phnx. LP-2; Prst. P-24030)/ Oop Bop Sh' Bam (Phnx. LP-2; Prst. P-24030)/A Handfulla Gimme (Phnx. LP-2; Prst. P-24030)/That's Earl Brother (Phnx. LP-2; Prst. P-24030)	
Broadcasts	Dizzy Gillespie and His Orchestra† Spotlite Club, New York, May, June, 1946	Hi-Fly H-01
	Dizzy Gillespie, Dave Burns, Talib Dawud, Kinny Dorham, John Lynch, Elmon Wright (tp); Leon Comegeys, Charles Greenlea, Alton "Slim" Moore (tb); Howard Johnson, Sonny Stitt (as); Ray Abrams, Warren Luckey (ts); Leo Parker (bar); Thelonious Monk or John Lewis (p); Ray Brown (b); Kenny Clarke (d); Milt Jackson (vbs); Sarah Vaughan (vcl)	
	Unknown Title (HY H-01)/Things to Come/ One Bass Hit (HY H-01)/One Bass Hit (HY H-01)/Things to Come/I Waited For You/ Second Balcony Jump (HY H-01)/Algo Bueno/Unknown Ballad/Groovin' High (HY H-01)/The Man I Love (HY H-01)/How High the Moon/Unknown Title/Things to Come (theme) (HY H-01)/Shaw 'Nuff/I Waited for You/Our Delight (HY H-01)/ The Man I Love/Oop Bop Sh' Bam/'Round About Midnight/Ray's Idea (HY H-01)/ Cool Breeze/One Bass Hit/Things to Come/	

‡ Gillespie's trumpet first featured with "Hollywood-style" arrangements and instrumentation.

* The Gillespie Sextet modified on return to New York. First record date for Sonny Stitt.

† First recording of a full jazz orchestra led by Gillespie.

ORIGINAL LABEL	TITLE, PLACE AND DATE, PERSONNEL, AND SONGS	LMI
	I Waited for You/One Bass Hit/Don't Blame Me (HY H-01)	
	For Hecklers Only (SVY MG12110)/Smokey Hollow Jump (SVY MG12110)/Moody Speaks (SVY MG12110)/Boppin' the Blues (SVY MG12110)	
Victor	Dizzy Gillespie and His Orchestra* New York, August 22, 1947	Victor 20-2480-EPA 432
	Dizzy Gillespie (tp, vcl); Dave Burns, Elmon Wright, Matthew McKay, Ray Orr (tp); Ted Kelly, Bill Shepherd (tb); John Brown, Howard Johnson (as); George Nicholas, Joe Gayles (ts); Cecil Payne (bar); John Lewis (p); Al McKibbon (b); Kenny Clarke (d); Kenny Hagood (vcl)	Victor 20-2603-LPV 519
	Ow (Vic. 20-2480, EPA432)/Oop-Pop-A-Da (Vic. 20-2480 EPA432)/Two Bass Hit (Vic. 20-2603; LPV 519)/Stay On It (Vic. 20-2603; LPV 519)	
Black Deuce	Dizzy Gillespie's Band† Carnegie Hall, New York, September 29, 1947	Roulette RE-105
	Dizzy Gillespie (tp); Charlie Parker (as); John Lewis (p); Al McKibbon (b); Joe Harris (d)	
	A Night In Tunisia I (Rou RE-105)/A Night In Tunisia II (Rou RE-105)/ Dizzy Atmosphere (Rou RE-105)/Groovin' High I (Rou RE-105)/Groovin' High II (Rou RE-105)/ Confirmation (Rou RE-105)	
Arco	Dizzy Gillespie and His Orchestra‡ Carnegie Hall, New York, September 29, 1947	Arco LP-8
	Dizzy Gillespie, Dave Burns, Elmon Wright, Ray Orr, Matthew McKay (tp); Taswell Baird, Bill Shepherd (tb); Howard Johnson, John Brown (as); James Moody (or George Nicholas), Joe Gayles (ts); Cecil Payne (bar); Milt Jackson (vbs); John Lewis (p); Al McKibbon (b); Joe Harris (d); Kenny Hagood (vcl); and Ella Fitzgerald (vcl) on "Stairway to the Stars" and "How High the Moon"	
	Toccata for Trumpet and Orchestra/Cubana Be—Cubana Bop/Salt Peanuts/One Bass Hit/Oop-Pop-A-Da/Stairway to the Stars/How High the Moon	
Victor	Dizzy Gillespie and His Orchestra* New York, December 22, 1947	Victor 20-3186, LPV-530; 20-3023;
	Dizzy Gillespie (tp, vcl); Dave Burns, Elmon	

* Gillespie's first "bebop" vocal hit recording, "Oop-Pop-A-Da."

† Small unit in first Gillespie Carnegie Hall concert.

‡ Full jazz orchestra in first Gillespie Carnegie Hall concert, featuring Ella Fitzgerald and James Moody.

* Definitive introduction of Chano Pozo and Afro-Cuban rhythms to jazz performances of the Gillespie Orchestra.

ORIGINAL LABEL	TITLE, PLACE AND DATE, PERSONNEL, AND SONGS	LMI
	Wright, Jr., Benny Bailey (tp); Bill Shepherd, Ted Kelly (tb); Howard Johnson, John Brown (as); Joe Gayles, George Nicholas (ts); Cecil Payne (bar); John Lewis (p); Al McKibbon (b); Kenny Clarke (d); Chano Pozo (cga, vcl); Kenny Hagood (vcl)	20-3145; Victor LJM1009 Victor 20-2878
	Algo Bueno (Woody 'n You) (Vic. 20-3186, LPV-530)/Cool Breeze (Vic. 20-3023)/Cubana Be (Vic. 20-3145)/Cubana Bop (Vic. 20-3145)	
	(Same session and personnel) New York, December 30, 1947 Manteca (Vic. 20-3023)/Woody 'n You (LJM 1009)/Good Bait (Vic. 20-2878)/Ool-Ya-Koo (Vic. 20-2878)/Minor Walk (Vic. 20-3186)	
Swing	Dizzy Gillespie and His Orchestra† Salle Pleyel, Paris, France, February 28, 1948 (Same personnel as above)	Prestige 7818
	'Round About Midnight (Prst. 7818)/Algo Bueno (Prst. 7818)/I Can't Get Started (Prst. 7818)/Ool-Ya-Koo (Prst. 7818)/Afro-Cubano Suite (Prst. 7818)/Things to Come (Prst. 7818)/Oop-Pop-A-Da (Prst. 7818)/Two Bass Hit (Prst. 7818)/Good Bait (Prst. 7818)	
Gene Norman Presents	Dizzy Gillespie and His Orchestra‡ Concert, Pasadena, California, July 26, 1948 Dizzy Gillespie (tp, vcl); Dave Burns, Elmon Wright, Willie Cook (tp); Jesse Tarrant, Bill Shepherd (tb); John Brown (as, vcl); Ernie Henry (as); James Moody, Joe Gayles (ts); Cecil Payne (bar); James Forman (p); Nelson Boyd (b); Teddy Stewart (d); Chano Pozo (cga, bgo)	Gene Norman Presents S23
	Emanon (GNPS-23)/Good Bait (GNPS-23)/Manteca (GNPS-23)/One Bass Hit (GNPS-23)/Ool-Ya-Koo (GNPS-23)/'Round About Midnight (GNPS-23)/I Can't Get Started (GNPS-23)	
Broadcast	Dizzy Gillespie and His Orchestra* Royal Roost, New York, October 2, 1948 (Same personnel as above)	Bop (France) I
	Relaxin' at Camarillo (Bop-I)/Things to Come/Soulphony in Three Hearts/One Bass Hit/I Should Care/Guarachi Guaro/Oop-Pop-A-Da	

† First modern jazz concert held in Paris, France. Fantastic display of Afro-Cuban jazz innovations.
‡ Gillespie big band in California at the zenith of the "bebop" era.
* "Bebop" on Broadway. Gillespie band at the Royal Roost.

ORIGINAL LABEL	TITLE, PLACE AND DATE, PERSONNEL, AND SONGS	LMI
Broadcast	Dizzy Gillespie and His Orchestra† Royal Roost, New York, October 23, 1948 (Same personnel; add Dinah Washington, vcl) I Can't Get Started (Bop [F] 1)/More Than You Know (Bop [F] 2)/Ow/That Old Black Magic/Manteca/Emanon/Ray's Idea/ Guarachi Guaro/Confess/Stay On It/ S'Posin/Cool Breeze	Bop (France) 1 and 2
Victor	Metronome All Stars‡ New York, January 3, 1949 Dizzy Gillespie, Fats Navarro, Miles Davis (tp); J. J. Johnson, Kai Winding (tb); Buddy De Franco (cl); Charlie Parker (as); Charlie Ventura (ts); Ernie Caceres (bar); Lennie Tristano (p); Billy Bauer (g); Eddie Safran-ski (b); Shelly Manne (d) Overtime (1) (Vic 20-3361)/Overtime (2) (Vic LPT3046)/Victory Ball (1) (Vic 20-3361)/Victory Ball (2)/Victory Ball (3) (Vic LPT3046)	Victor 20-3361 Victor LPT-3046
Victor	Dizzy Gillespie and His Orchestra* New York, April 14, 1949 Dizzy Gillespie, Benny Harris, Elmon Wright, Willie Cook (tp); Andy Duryea, Sam Hurt, Jesse Tarrant (tb); John Brown, Ernie Henry (as); Yusef Lateef (Bill Evans); Joe Gayles (ts); Al Gibson (bar); James Forman (p, celeste); Al McKibbon (b); Teddy Stewart (d); Vince Guerra (cga); John Hartman, Joe Carroll (vcl) Swedish Suite (Vic 20-3457; LJM 1009)/St. Louis Blues (LJM 1009)/I Should Care (Vic 20-3457)/That Old Black Magic (Vic 20-3481)	Victor 20-3457 LJM 1009
Capitol	Dizzy Gillespie and His Orchestra† New York, November 21, 1949 Dizzy Gillespie (tp, vcl); Don Slaughter, Elmon Wright, Willie Cook (tp); Matthew Gee, Sam Hurt, Charlie Greenlea (tb); Jimmy Heath, John Coltrane (as); Jesse Powell, Paul Gonsalves (ts); Al Gibson (bar); John Acea (p); John Collins (g); Al McKibbon (b); Specs Wright (d); Tiny Irvin (vcl) Say When/Tally Ho/You Stole My Wife (Cap. M-11059)/I Can't Remember	Capitol M-11059

† Features Dinah Washington.
‡ A new "breed" of trumpets and trombonists. Features Fats Navarro, Miles Davis, J. J. Johnson, and Kai Winding.
* Features John Hartman and Joe "Bebop" Carroll.
† The Gillespie Orchestra near the time of dissolution.

ORIGINAL LABEL	TITLE, PLACE AND DATE, PERSONNEL, AND SONGS	LMI
Clef	Charlie Parker and His Orchestra New York, June 6, 1950 Dizzy Gillespie (tp); Charlie Parker (as); Thelonious Monk (p); Curley Russell (b); Buddy Rich (d) Bloomdido/An Oscar for Treadwell (1 & 2)/Mohawk (1) (Vrv VE2-2501)/Mohawk (2)/Melancholy Baby (Vrv VE2-2501)/ Leap Frog (1 & 2) (Vrv VE2-2501)/Relaxin' with Lee (1) (Vrv VE2-2501)/Relaxin' with Lee	Verve VE2-2501
Dee Gee	Dizzy Gillespie Sextet‡ Detroit, March 1, 1951 Dizzy Gillespie (tp); John Coltrane (as, ta); Milt Jackson (vbs, p); Kenny Burrell (g); Percy Heath (b); Kansas Fields (d); Fred Strong and the Calypso Boys (vcl) Love Me/We Love to Boogie (Svy SJL2209) /Tin Tin Deo (Svy SJL2209)/Birks Works (Svy SJL2209)	Savoy SJL 2209
Broadcast	Dizzy Gillespie Band* Birdland, New York, March 31, 1951 Dizzy Gillespie (tp); Charlie Parker (as); Bud Powell (p); Tommy Potter (b); Roy Haynes (d) Blue 'n Boogie (SA ERO 8035)/Anthropology (SA ERO 8035)/ 'Round About Midnight (SA ERO 8035)/A Night In Tunisia (SA ERO 8035)/Jumpin' with Symphony Sid (SA ERO 8035)	Saga (England) ERO 8035
Dee Gee	Dizzy Gillespie and His Sextet New York, October 25, 1951 Dizzy Gillespie(tp, org.); Bill Graham (as, bar); Stuff Smith (vln); Milt Jackson (p, vbs, vcl); Percy Heath (b); Al Jones (d); Joe Carroll (vcl) Caravan (Svy SJL2209)/Nobody Knows the Trouble I've Seen (Svy SJL2209)/The Bluest Blues (Svy SJL2209)/On the Sunny Side of the Street (Svy SJL2209)/Stardust (Svy SJL2209)/Time on My Hands (Svy SJL2209)	Savoy SJL2209
MGM	Dizzy Gillespie and The Cool Jazz Stars† Birdland, New York, November 24, 1952 Dizzy Gillespie (tp); Don Elliott (tp, mpn); Ray Abrams (ts); Ronnie Ball (p); Al McKibbon (b); Max Roach (d) Muskrat Ramble (MGM E3286)/Battle of the Blues (MGM E3286)/How High the Moon (MGM E3286)	MGM E 3286

‡ First session by Dee Gee Records, features John Coltrane, Kenny Burrell, and Percy Heath.
* Features Bud Powell and Roy Haynes.
† Gillespie, traditionally "hot," makes with the "cool."

ORIGINAL LABEL	TITLE, PLACE AND DATE, PERSONNEL, AND SONGS	LMI
Vogue (France)	Dizzy Gillespie Quintet‡ Salle Pleyel, Paris, February 9, 1953 Dizzy Gillespie (tp, vcl); Bill Graham (as, bar); Wade Legge (p); Lou Hackney (b); Al Jones (d); Joe Carroll (vcl)	Gene Norman Presents S9006 Roulette RE-105; 120
	Rehearsal Blues/The Champ (GNPS-9006; Rou RE-405)/Oop-Shoo-Bee-Doo (GNPS-9006; Rou RE-405)/They Can't Take That Away (GNPS-9006; Rou RE-120)/Good Bait (GNPS-9006; Rou RE-105)/On the Sunny Side of the Street (GNPS-9006)/Swing Low Sweet Cadillac (GNPS-9006; Rou RE-105)/ My Man (GNPS-9006; Rou RE-405)/The Bluest Blues (GNPS-9006; Rou RE-105)/ School Days (GNPS-9006; Rou RE-105, 120)/Birks Works (GNPS-9006; Rou RE-120)/Tin Tin Deo (GNPS-9006; Rou RE-120)/I Can't Get Started (Rou RE-120)/ Lady Be Good (Rou RE-120)	
Debut	Quintet of the Year—Jazz at Massey Hall* Toronto, May 15, 1953 Dizzy Gillespie (tp); Charlie Parker (as); Bud Powell (p); Charlie Mingus (b); Max Roach (d)	Vogue (England) LAE 12031 Saga (England) ERO 8031
	Perdido (Vg LAE 12031; SA ERO 8031)/All the Things You Are (Vg LAE 12031; SA ERO 8031)/Salt Peanuts (Vg LAE 12031; SA ERO 8031)/Wee (Vg LAE 12031; SA ERO 8031)/Hothouse (Vg LAE 12031; SA ERO 8031)/Night In Tunisia (Vg LAE 12031; SA ERO 8031)	
Broadcast	Dizzy Gillespie All-Stars† New York, June 1953 Dizzy Gillespie, unknown (maybe Miles Davis) (tp); Charlie Parker (as); Bill Graham (bar); Wade Legge (p); Lou Hackney (b); Al Jones (d); Joe Carroll (vcl)	Unissued
	The Bluest Blues/On the Sunny Side of the Street	
Clef	Jam Session‡ New York, September 2, 1953 Roy Eldridge, Dizzy Gillespie (tp); Johnny Hodges (as); Illinois Jacquet, Flip Phillips, Ben Webster (ts); Oscar Peterson (p); Ray Brown (b); Buddy Rich (d); Lionel Hampton (vbs)	Verve MGV 8094 MGV 8062
	Jam Blues (Vrv MGV 8094)/Blue Lou (Vrv MGV 8062)/Just You, Just Me (Vrv MGV 8062)/Ballad Medley (Vrv MGV 8094)	

‡ First recording of several Gillespie classics, including "Birks Works," "Tin Tin Deo," "School Days."
* The greatest jazz concert, ever.
† Last known Gillespie-Parker recording.
‡ Gillespie, in mid-career, with a company of jazz giants.

ORIGINAL LABEL	TITLE, PLACE AND DATE, PERSONNEL, AND SONGS	LMI
Norgran	Dizzy Gillespie—Stan Getz Los Angeles, December 9, 1953 Dizzy Gillespie (tp); Stan Getz (ts); Oscar Peterson (p); Herb Ellis (g); Ray Brown (b); Max Roach (d)	Verve Vrv VE2-2521
	Girl of My Dreams (Vrv VE2-2521)/It Don't Mean a Thing (Vrv VE2-2521)/Talk of the Town (Vrv VE2-2521)/Siboney I (Vrv VE2-2521)/Siboney II (Vrv VE2-2521)/Exactly Like You (Vrv VE2-2521)/I Let a Song Go Out of My Heart (Vrv VE2-2521)/Impromptu (Vrv VE2-2521)	
Norgran	Dizzy Gillespie and His Orchestra* New York, May 24, 1954 Dizzy Gillespie, Quincy Jones, Ernie Royal, Jimmy Nottingham (tp); Leon Comegeys, J. J. Johnson, George Matthews (tb); Hilton Jefferson, George Dorsey (as); Hank Mobley, Lucky Thompson (ts); Danny Bank (bar); Wade Legge (p); Lou Hackney and Robert Rodriquez (b); Charlie Persip (d); Jose Manguel (bgo); Ubaldo Nieto (timbls); Candido Camero, Ramon Santamaria (cga); Chico O'Farrill (arr)	Verve VE2-2522
	Manteca Theme (Vrv VE2-2522)/Contraste (Vrv VE2-2522)/Jungla (Vrv VE2-2522)/Rhumba Finale (Vrv VE2-2522)/6/8 (Nrgn. MGN1003)	
Norgran	Dizzy Gillespie and His Latin-American Rhythm† New York, June 3, 1954 Dizzy Gillespie (tp); Gilbert Valdez (fl); Rene Hernandez (p); Robert Rodriquez (b); Jose Manguel, Candido Camero, Ubaldo Nieto, Ralph Miranda (percs)	Verve MGV 8208
	A Night In Tunisia (Vrv MGV 8208)/Caravan (Vrv MGV 8208)/Con Alma (Vrv MGV 8208)	
Clef	Dizzy Gillespie and Roy Eldridge New York, October 29, 1954 Dizzy Gillespie, Roy Eldridge (tp); Oscar Peterson (p); Herb Ellis (g); Ray Brown (b); Louis Bellson (d)	Verve VE2-2524
	Sometimes I'm Happy (Vrv VE2-2524)/Algo Bueno (Vrv VE2-2524)/Trumpet Blues (Vrv VE2-2524)/Ballad Medley (Vrv VE2-2524)/Blue Moon (Vrv VE2-2524)/I Found a New Baby (Vrv VE2-2524)/Pretty Eyed Baby (Vrv VE2-2524)/I Can't Get Started (Vrv VE2-2524)/Limehouse Blues (Vrv VE2-2524)	

* First orchestral treatment by O'Farrill, a Latin composer/arranger, of major Gillespie rhythmic themes.
† First recording of "Con Alma."

ORIGINAL LABEL	TITLE, PLACE AND DATE, PERSONNEL, AND SONGS	LMI
Norgran	Dizzy Gillespie and His Orchestra‡ New York, May 18, 19, June 6, 1956 Dizzy Gillespie (tp, vcl); Joe Gordon, Ernest Perry, Carl Warwick, Quincy Jones (tp); Melba Liston, Frank Rehak, Rod Levitt (tb); Jimmy Powell, Phil Woods (as); Bill Mitchell, Ernie Wilkins (ts); Marty Flax (bar); Walter Davis, Jr. (p); Nelson Boyd (b); Charlie Persip (d)	Norgran MGV 1084 Verve MGV 8017
	Dizzy's Business (Nrg MGV 1084)/Night In Tunisia (Nrg MGV 1084)/Jessica's Day (Nrg MGV 1084)/Tour de Force (Nrg MGV 1084)/I Can't Get Started (Nrg MGV 1084)/ Stella by Starlight (Nrg MGV 1084)/ Doodlin' (Nrg MGV 1084)/Hey Pete (Vrv MGV 8017)/The Champ (Nrg MGV 1084)/ Yesterdays (Vrv MGV 8017)/Tin Tin Deo (Vrv MGV 8017)/Groovin' for Nat (Vrv MGV 8017)/My Reverie (Nrg MGV 1084)/ Dizzy's Blues (Nrg MGV 1084)/Annie's Dance (Vrv MGV 8017)/Cool Breeze (Vrv MGV 8017)/School Days (Vrv MGV 8017)	
Verve	Dizzy Gillespie's All-Stars (For Musicians Only) Los Angeles, October 16, 1956 Dizzy Gillespie (tp); Sonny Stitt (as); Stan Getz (ts); John Lewis (p); Herb Ellis (g); Ray Brown (b); Stan Levey (d)	Verve VE2-2521
	BeBop (Vrv VE2-2521)/Wee (Vrv VE2-2521)/Dark Eyes (Vrv VE2-2521)/Lover Come Back to Me (Vrv VE2-2521)	
Verve	Dizzy Gillespie and His Orchestra* New York, March 23, April 17, 18, 1957 Dizzy Gillespie (tp, vcl); Lee Morgan, Ernest Perry, Carl Warwick, Talib Dawud (tp); Melba Liston, Al Grey, Rod Levitt (tb); Jimmy Powell, Ernie Henry (as); Billy Mitchell, Benny Golson (ts); Billy Root (bar); Wynton Kelly (p); Paul West (b); Charlie Persip (d); Austin Cromer (vcl)	Verve MGV 8222
	Jordu (Vrv MGV 8222)/Birks Works (MGV 8222)/Umbrella Man (Vrv MGV 8222)/ Autumn Leaves (MGV 8222)/Tangorine (Vrv MGV 8222)/Over the Rainbow (Vrv MGV 8222)/Yo No Quiore Bailar (Vrv MGV 8222)/If You Could See Me Now (Vrv MGV 8222)/Left-Hand Corner (Vrv MGV 8222)/ Whisper Not (Vrv MGV 8222)/Stablemates (Vrv MGV 8222)/That's All (Vrv MGV 8222)/Groovin' High (Vrv MGV 8222)/ Mayflower Rock (Vrv 89173)	

‡ First jazz orchestra assembled for U. S. Department of State tour of Africa, the Middle and Near East, Asia, and Eastern Europe; recorded following the tours.
* Gillespie orchestra featuring Lee Morgan.

ORIGINAL LABEL	TITLE, PLACE AND DATE, PERSONNEL, AND SONGS	LMI
Verve	Dizzy Gillespie—Stuff Smith† New York, April 17, 1957 Dizzy Gillespie (tp); Stuff Smith (vln); Wynton Kelly (p); Paul West (b); J. C. Heard (d); The Gordon Family (vcl) Rio Pakistan (Vrv MGV 8214)/Paper Moon (Vrv MGV 8214)/Purple Sounds (Vrv MGV 8214)/Russian Lullaby (Vrv MGV 8214)/Lady Be Good (Vrv MGV 8214)	Verve MGV 8214
Verve	Dizzy Gillespie and His Orchestra‡ Newport Jazz Festival, Rhode Island, July 6, 1957 Dizzy Gillespie (tp, vcl); Lee Morgan, Ernest Perry, Carl Warwick, Talib Dawud (tp); Melba Liston, Al Grey, Ray Connor (tb); Jimmy Powell, Ernie Henry (as); Billy Mitchell, Benny Golson (ts); Pee Wee Moore (bar); Wynton Kelly (p); Paul West (b); Charlie Persip (d); Austin Cromer (vcl); Mary Lou Williams (p); (substitutes on Zodiac Suite and Carioca) Dizzy's Blues (Vrv MGV 8242)/Doodlin' (Vrv MGV 8242)/School Days (Vrv MGV 8242)/I Remember Clifford (Vrv MGV 8242)/Cool Breeze (Vrv MGV 8242)/Manteca (Vrv MGV 8242)/Night In Tunisia (Vrv MGV 8244)/Zodiac Suite (Vrv VE2-2514)/Carioca (Vrv VE2-2514)/Over the Rainbow/You'll Be Sorry	Verve MGV 8242 MGV 8244 VE2-2514
Verve	Dizzy Gillespie with Sonny Stitt and Sonny Rollins New York, December 11, 1957 Dizzy Gillespie (tp); Sonny Stitt (as, ts); Ray Bryant (p); Tom Bryant (b); Charlie Persip (d) Wheatleigh Hall (Vrv MGV 8260)/Sumpin' (Vrv VE2-2505)/Con Alma (Vrv VE2-2505)/Haute Mon' (Vrv VE2-2505)	Verve MGV 8260 VE2-2505
Verve	Dizzy Gillespie with Sonny Stitt and Sonny Rollins New York, December 19, 1957 Dizzy Gillespie (tp); Sonny Stitt (as); Sonny Rollins (ts); Ray Bryant (p); Tom Bryant (b); Charlie Persip (d) The Eternal Triangle (Vrv MGV 8262)/On the Sunny Side of the Street (Vrv MGV 8262)/After Hours (Vrv MGV 8262)/I Know That You Know (Vrv MGV 8262)	Verve MGV 8262
For Discriminate Collectors	Timex Jazz Show* New York, January 7, 1959 Features Dizzy Gillespie, Louis Armstrong (tp, vcl)	For Discriminate Collectors FDC-1017

† Dizzy develops and adapts Asian- and Middle Eastern-inspired harmonic devices to jazz.
‡ Marks return of Mary Lou Williams to jazz scene as a performer.
* Dizzy's only recorded performance with Louis Armstrong.

ORIGINAL LABEL	TITLE, PLACE AND DATE, PERSONNEL, AND SONGS	LMI
	Umbrella Man (FDC-1017)	
Verve	Katie Bell Nubin with Dizzy Gillespie and His Orchestra† New York, 1960 Dizzy Gillespie (tp); Leo Wright (as); Julian Nance, Sister Rosetta Tharpe (p); Les Spann (g); Art Davis (b); Lex Humphries (d); Katie Bell Nubin (vcl)	Verve MGV 3004
	Virgin Mary (Vrv MGV 3004)/Miami Storm (Vrv MGV 3004)/Pressin' On (Vrv MGV 3004)/When the Bridegroom Comes (Vrv MGV 3004)/Angels Watchin' Over Me (Vrv MGV 3004)/Where's Adam? (Vrv MGV 3004)/Come Over Here (Vrv MGV 3004)/I Shall Not Be Moved (Vrv MGV 3004)/Sad to Think of My Savior (Vrv MGV 3004)	
Verve	Dizzy Gillespie Quintet Concert, Museum of Modern Art, New York, February 9, 1961 Dizzy Gillespie (tp, vcl); Leo Wright (as, fl); Lalo Schifrin (p); Bob Cunningham (b); Chuck Lampkin (d); Candido Camero (cga)	Verve V-8401
	Kush (Vrv V-8401)/Salt Peanuts (Vrv V-8401)/A Night In Tunisia (Vrv V-8401)/The Mooche (Vrv V-8401)/I Can't Get Started/Groovin' High/Hothouse/Confirmation/Manteca/I Remember Clifford	
Philips	The Dizzy Gillespie Quintet‡ New York, May 1962 Dizzy Gillespie (tp); Leo Wright (as, fl); Lalo Schifrin (p); Chris White (b); Rudy White (d); Charlie Ventura (on Chega de Saudade II) (bs); Jose Paula (g, tamb.); Carmen Costa (cabassa)	Philips PHM 200-048 PHM 200-070
	Pau de Arara (Ph PHM 200-048)/Desafinado (Ph PHM 200-048)/Chega de Saudade I (Ph PHM 200-048)/Chega de Saudade II (Ph PHM 200-070)/Taboo (Ph PHM 200-070)/Long Long Summer (Ph PHM 200-048) I Waited for You (Ph PHM 200-048)/Morning of the Carnival (Ph PHM 200-070)/Pergunte Ao Joao (Ph PHM 200-070)	
Philips	Dizzy on the Riviera Jazz Festival, Juan les Pins, France, July 24, 1962 Dizzy Gillespie (tp); Leo Wright (fl, as); Lalo Schifrin (p); Elec Bacsik (g); Chris White (b); Rudy Collins (d); Pepito Riestria (percs.)	Philips PHM 200-048 PHM 200-070
	Here It Is (Ph PHM 200-048)/Chega de Saudade I (Ph PHM 200-048)/Olé (Ph	

† Afro-American spirituals and gospel music.
‡ First studio recording of "bossa nova" in the United States.

ORIGINAL LABEL	TITLE, PLACE AND DATE, PERSONNEL, AND SONGS	LMI

40076)/One Note Samba (Ph PHM 200-070)/
For the Gypsies (Ph PHM 200-048)

Limelight   Dizzy Gillespie and His Orchestra* Los   Mercury
      Angeles, September 1962   EMS2-410
      Dizzy Gillespie, Al Porcino, Ray Triscari, Stu
      Williamson, Conte Candoli (tp); Frank Ros-
      solino, Mike Barone, Bob Edmundson, Kenny
      Shroyer (tb); Ches Thompson, Steward
      Rensey, Luis Kent (frh); Red Callender (tu);
      Phil Woods, Charlie Kennedy (as); James
      Moody, Bill Perkins (ts); Bill Hood (bar);
      Lalo Schifrin (p); Al Hendrickson (g);
      Buddy Clark, Chris White (b); Mel Lewis,
      Rudy Collins (d); Emil Richards, Larry
      Bunker, Francisco Aquabella (percs); Benny
      Carter (conductor)

      The Conquerors (Mer EMS2-410)/The
      Sword (Mer EMS2-410)/The Chains (Mer
      EMS2-410)/Chorale (Mer EMS2-410)/The
      Legend of Atlantis (Mer EMS2-410)/The
      Empire (Mer EMS2-410)

Philips   The Dizzy Gillespie Quintet† New York, Philips
      April 23, 24, 25, 1963   PHM 200-091
      Dizzy Gillespie (tp); James Moody (as, ts, Mercury
      fl); Kenny Barron (p); Chris White (b);   EMS2-410
      Rudy Collins (d)

      Bebop (Ph PHM 200-091)/Good Bait (Ph
      PHM 200-091)/Early Morning Blues (Ph
      40124[?])/I Can't Get Started/'Round Mid-
      night (Ph PHM 200-091)/Dizzy Atmosphere
      (Ph PHM 200-091)/The Cup Bearers (Mer
      EMS2-410)/The Day After (Mer EMS2-410)/
      November Afternoon (Mer EMS2-410)/This
      Lovely Evening (Ph PHM 200-091)

Philips   Dizzy Gillespie and Les Doubles Six‡ Paris, Philips
      France, June/July, 1963   PHM 200-106
      Dizzy Gillespie (tp); Bud Powell (p); Pierre
      Michelot (b); Kenny Clarke (d); Les Dou-
      bles Six (Mimi Perrin, Claudine Berge, Chris-
      tiana Legrand, Ward Single, Robert Smart,
      Jean-Claude Brodin, Eddy Louis (vcl)

      One Bass Hit (PHM 200-106)/Two Bass
      Hit (PHM 200-106)/Emanon (PHM 200-
      106)/Blue 'n Boogie (PHM 200-106)/The
      Champ (PHM 200-106)/Tin Tin Deo (PHM
      200-106)/Groovin' High (PHM 200-106)/
      Ow (PHM 200-106)/Hothouse (PHM 200-
      106)/Anthropology (PHM 200-106)

* Features Lalo Schifrin's compositions for Gillespie.
† Features Tom McIntosh's compositions for Gillespie.
‡ Last commercial recording with Bud Powell. Features unique "bop" chorale.

ORIGINAL LABEL	TITLE, PLACE AND DATE, PERSONNEL, AND SONGS	LMI
Philips	The Dizzy Gillespie Sextet* New York, April 21, 22, 23, 1964 Dizzy Gillespie (tp); James Moody (fl, ts); Kenny Barron (p); Chris White (b); Rudy Collins (d)	Mercury EMS2-410
	Bonnie's Blues (EMS2-410)/Coney Island (EMS2-410)/Theme from the Cool World (EMS2-410)/Duke's Fantasy (EMS2-410)/ Street Music (EMS2-410)/The Pushers (EMS2-410)/Enter Priest (EMS2-410)/ Duke's Last Soliloquy (EMS2-410)/Duke's Awakening (EMS2-410)/Coolie (EMS2-410)/ Duke on the Run (EMS2-410)	
Limelight	Dizzy Gillespie Quintet (Jambo Caribe)† Chicago, November 4, 1964 Dizzy Gillespie (tp); James Moody (fl, ts); Kenny Barron (p); Chris White (b); Rudy Collins (d)	Limelight LM 82007
	Barbados Carnival (LM 82007)/And Then She Stopped (LM 82007)/Trinidad Hello (LM 82007)/Jambo (LM 82007)/Poor Joe (LM 82007)/Fiesta Mo-Jo (LM 82007)/ Trinidad Goodbye (LM 82007)/Don't Try to Keep Up with the Joneses (LM 82007)/ Fickle Finger of Fate (LM 82007)	
Solid State	Jazz On a Sunday Afternoon‡ Village Vanguard, New York, October 6, 1967 Dizzy Gillespie (tp); Garett Brown (tb); Pepper Adams (bars); Chick Corea (p); Richard Davis (b); Elvin Jones (2-4); Mel Lewis (d)	Solid State SS 18027 SS 18034 SS 18028
	Lullaby of the Leaves (SS 18027)/Blues for Max (SS 18034)/Lover Come Back to Me (SS 18027)/Dizzy's Blues (SS 18034)/Sweet Georgia Brown (SS 18028)/On the Trail (SS 18028)/Tour de Force (SS 18028)	
SABA	Dizzy Gillespie Reunion Big Band Berlin, Germany, Fall 1968 Dizzy Gillespie, Victor Paz, Jimmy Owens, Dizzy Reece, Stu Hamer (tp); Curtis Fuller, Tom McIntosh, Ted Kelly (tb); Chris Woods (as); James Moody (ts, fl); Paul Jeffrey (ts); Sahib Shihab, Cecil Payne (bars); Mike Longo (p); Paul West (b); Candy Finch (d)	SABA MPS 15-207
	Things to Come (MPS 15-207)/One Bass Hit (MPS 15-207)/Frisco (MPS 15-207)/ Con Alma (MPS 15-207)/Things Are Here (MPS 15-207)/Theme (Birks Works) (MPS 15-207)	

* Features Mal Waldron's compositions for Gillespie's performance on the soundtrack of the film, *The Cool World.*

† Features West Indian-inspired compositions.

‡ Features unusual instrumentation including Ray Nance (vln) and several innovative "postbop" stylists.

ORIGINAL LABEL	TITLE, PLACE AND DATE, PERSONNEL, AND SONGS	LMI
Perception	The Real Thing* Englewood, N.J., December 1969 and January 1970 Dizzy Gillespie (tp, vcl); Mike Longo (p); James Moody (ts) (tracks 1, 6, 7, 9, 10); Eric Gayle (tracks 1, 6, 7, 10), or George Davis (g); Paul West (tracks 1, 7, 10), Chuck Rainey (6) or Phil Upchurch (6) (b); Nate Edmonds (org, 6); Candy Finch (tracks 1, 7, 10), Bernard Purdie (6) or David Lee (d) N'Bani (PLP-2)/Matrix (PLP-2)/Alligator (PLP-2)/Closer (vcl. PLP-2)/Closer (inst. PLP-2)/Soul Kiss (PLP-2)/High On a Cloud (PLP-2)/Summertime (PLP-2)/Let Me Outta' Here (PLP-2)/Ding-A-Ling (PLP-2)	Perception PLP-2
Perception	A Portrait of Jenny (Djenne)† Englewood Cliffs, N.J., January 1971 Dizzy Gillespie (tp); Mike Longo (p); George Davis (g); Andrew Gonzalez (b); Nicholas Marrero (timbls); Carlos Valdez, Jerry Gonzalez (cga) Olinga (PLP-13)/Diddy Wah Diddy (PLP-13)/Me 'n Them (PLP-13)/Timet (PLP-13)	Perception PLP-13
Perception	Giants‡ Concert, Overseas Press Club, New York, January 31, 1971 Dizzy Gillespie, Bobby Hackett (tp); Mary Lou Williams (p); George Duvivier (b); Grady Tate (d) Love for Sale (PLP-19)/Autumn Leaves (PLP-19)/Caravan (PLP-19)/Jitterbug Waltz (PLP-19)/Willow Weep for Me (PLP-19)/Birks Works (PLP-19)/My Man (PLP-19)	Perception PLP-19
Mainstream	Dizzy Gillespie/Mitchell—Ruff Duo New York, 1971 Dizzy Gillespie (tp); Willie Ruff (frh, b); Duke Mitchell (p) Con Alma (MRL 325)/Dartmouth Duet (MRL 325)/Woody 'n You (MRL 325)/Blues People (MRL 325)/Bella Bella (MRL 325)	Mainstream MRL 325
Prestige	The Giant* Paris, France, April 1973 Dizzy Gillespie (tp); Johnny Griffin (ts) (tracks 1, 3, 4, 8); Kenny Drew (p); Niels Henning, Orstad Pedersen (b); Kenny Clarke (d); Humberto Canto (cga) Manteca (Prs 24047)/Alone Together (Prs 24047)/Brother K (Prs 24047)/Wheatleigh	Prestige 24047

* Jazz "rock," spiritually tinged, new Gillespie riffs.
† Forever modern, Gillespie having influenced the emergence of rock, now exhibits a rock influence.
‡ Just what the title implies.
* Most recent recording with forty-year colleague, drummer, Kenny Clarke.

ORIGINAL LABEL	TITLE, PLACE AND DATE, PERSONNEL, AND SONGS	LMI
	Hall (Prs 24047)/Stella by Starlight (Prs 24047)/I Waited for You (Prs 24047)/ Fiesta Mo-Jo (Prs 24047)/Serenity (Prs 24047)	
Unissued	Dizzy Gillespie Sacred Concert with John Motley and N. Y. C. All-City Concert Choir† Carnegie Hall, New York, July 5, 1974 Dizzy Gillespie (tp); Mike Longo (p); Al Gafa (g); Earl May (b); Mickey Roker (d); John Motley, conductor Olinga/Manteca/The Brother K/(choir only, Way Up in Beulah Land)	Unissued Collection of John Motley
Pablo	Dizzy Gillespie's Big 4‡ Los Angeles, September 19, 1974 Dizzy Gillespie (tp); Ray Brown (b); Joe Pass (g); Mickey Roker (d) Tanga (2310-719)/Hurry Home (2310-719)/ Russian Lullaby (2310-719)/Be Bop (2310-719)/Birks Works (2310-719)/September Song (2310-719)/Jitterbug Waltz (2310-719)	Pablo 2310-719
Pablo	Oscar Peterson and Dizzy Gillespie* London, England, November 28, 29, 1974 Oscar Peterson (p); Dizzy Gillespie (tp) Caravan (2310-740)/Mozambique (2310-740)/Autumn Leaves (2310-740)/Close Your Eyes (2310-740)/Blues for Bird (2310-740)/Dizzy Atmosphere (2310-740)/Alone Together (2310-740)/Con Alma (2310-740)	Pablo 2310-740
Pablo	Dizzy Gillespie y Machito: Afro-Cuban Jazz Moods† New York, June 4, 5, 1975 Dizzy Gillespie (tp, soloist); Victor Paz, Raul Gonzalez, Ramon Gonzalez, Jr., Manny Duran (tp, flgh); Barry Morrow, Jack Jeffers (side 2), Lewis Kahn, Jerry Chamberlain (tb); Mario Bauza (as, cl); Mauricio Smith (as, fl, pic); Jose Madera, Sr. (ts, cl, side 2); Mario Rivera (ts, fl, side 1); Brooks Tillotson, Don Corrado (frh, side 1); Bob Stewart (btu); Carlos Castillo, (fnb); Jorge Datto, Julito Collazo, R. Hernandez (Af. dr); Frank "Machito" Grillo (mar, clus); Mario Grillo (bgs, cbl); Pepin Pepin (cga); Jose Madera, Jr. (tmb, cabassa); Mickey Roker (d) Oro Incensio y Mirra (2310-771)/Ca lido-scopico (2310-771)/Pensativo (2310-771)/ Exuberante (2310-771)	Pablo 2310-771

† Tape recording of concert performance, with choir from New York City Public Schools.

‡ Shows Gillespie, an elder modernist's still high standard of skill and artistry.

* Grammy Award, 1975. Best jazz recording.

† Gillespie remains in close and fruitful collaboration with Afro-Cuban and Latin jazz musicians.

ORIGINAL LABEL	TITLE, PLACE AND DATE, PERSONNEL, AND SONGS	LMI
Pablo	Dizzy's Party‡ Los Angeles, September 15, 16, 1976 Dizzy Gillespie (tp); Ray Pizzi (ts, sps, fl); Rodney Jones (g); Benjamin Franklin Brown (fnb); Mickey Roker (d); Paulinho da Costa (percs) Dizzy's Party (2310-784)/Shim-Sham Shimmy on the St. Louis Blues (2310-784)/ Harlem Samba (2310-784)/Land of Milk and Honey (2310-784)	Pablo 2310-784
Pablo	Carter, Gillespie Inc.: Benny Carter and Dizzy Gillespie* Los Angeles, April 27, 1976 Benny Carter (as); Dizzy Gillespie (tp); Joe Pass (g); Tommy Flanagan (p); Mickey Roker (d, vcl); Al McKibbon (b) Sweet and Lovely (2310-784)/Broadway (2310-784)/The Courtship (2310-784)/ Constantinople (2310-781)/Nobody Knows the Trouble I've Seen (2310-781)/Night In Tunisia (2310-784)	Pablo 2310-784
Pablo	Free Ride† Dizzy Gillespie, composed and arranged by Lalo Schifrin Hollywood, January 31–February 1, 2, 1977 Dizzy Gillespie (solo, tp); Lalo Schifrin (col, arr, elec. keyboards); Oscar Brashear, Jack H. Laubach (tp); Lew McCreary (tb); James Horn (as, fl); Ernest Watts (ts); Jerome Richardson (fl); Ray Parker, Jr., Lee Ritenour, Wa Wa Watson (elec. g); Wilton L. Felder (b); Paulinho da Costa (percs); Sonny Burke (fndr, Rhodes, p) Unicorn (2310-794)/Free Ride (2310-794)/ Incantation (2310-794)/Wrong Number (2310-794)/Fire Dance (2310-794)/Ozone Madness (2310-794)/Love Poem for Donna (2310-794)/The Last Stroke of Midnight (2310-794)	Pablo 2310-794
Pablo	Dizzy Gillespie Jam—Montreux '77‡ Festival, Montreux, Switzerland, July 14, 1977 Dizzy Gillespie, Jon Faddis (tp); Milt Jackson (vib); Monty Alexander (p); Ray Brown (b); Jimmie Smith (d) Girl of My Dreams (2308-211)/Get Happy (2308-211)/Medley: Once in a While (2308-211)/But Beautiful (2308-211)/Here's That Rainy Day (2308-211)/The Champ (2308-211)	Pablo 2308-211

‡ Gillespie deeply into rock, with younger sidemen.
* Renewed association between two grand masters of jazz.
† Schifrin's slow-rock arrangement on Unicorn created a near-hit.
‡ Gillespie's first commercial recording with Jon Faddis, trumpet prodigy-protégé.

ORIGINAL LABEL	TITLE, PLACE AND DATE, PERSONNEL, AND SONGS	LMI
Unissued	Dizzy in Cuba* Concert Teatro Mella, Havana, Cuba, April, 1977 Dizzy Gillespie (tp); Rodney Jones (g); Benjamin Franklin Brown (b); Mickey Roker (d); Joe Ham (tmb); with Iraquires Orchestra featuring Paquito (as); Arturo Sandoval (tp) Swing Low, Sweet Cadillac/A Night In Tunisia/Olinga/Oop-Pop-A-Da/Manteca	Unissued Collection of Al Fraser

* First Gillespie concert in Cuba. Features superheated Afro-Cuban rhythm.

FILMOGRAPHY

f—film   v—videotape
a—appearance   r—recorded music on sound track
p—musical performance   n—narration

1942   *Case of the Blues* (fp), with Maxine Sullivan and Benny Carter
1947   *Jivin' in Bebop* (fap), featuring Benny Carter, James Moody, Dan Burley,
        and Dizzy Gillespie Orchestra
1948   *Gulf Road Show* (vap), starring Bob Smith
1949   *The Three Flames Show* (vap)
1952   *Stage Entrance* (vap), with Charlie Parker, Dick Hyman, Sandy Block, and
        Charlie Smith
1954   *Tonight Show* (vap, 12/23), starring Johnny Carson
1955   *Tonight Show* (vap, 3/30), starring Johnny Carson
        Tonight Show (vap, 9/9), starring Johnny Carson
1956   *A Date with Dizzy* (fap), with Sahib Shihab, Wade Legge, Nelson Boyd,
        and Charlie Persip
        Tonight Show (vap, 1/7), starring Johnny Carson
        Tonight Show (vap, 6/1), starring Johnny Carson
        Person to Person (va, 6/29), with Edward R. Murrow
        Today Show (vap, 5/26)
        Tonight Show (vap, 11/23), starring Johnny Carson
1957   *This Is New York* (vap)
1958   *Les Tricheurs* (fr, France)
1959   *Timex All-Star Jazz Show* (vap), with Louis Armstrong, Junior Mance, Les
        Spann, Sam Jones, and Lex Humphries
        Newport Jazz Festival (vap/CBS)
1961   *Ed Sullivan Show* (vap), with Leo Wright, Lalo Schifrin, Bob Cunningham,
        and Chuck Lampkin
1962   *The Lively Ones* (vap/NBC)
        De Werkelijkeid van Karel Appel (fp, Netherlands), music partly by Dizzy
        Gillespie
        The Hole (fpn), animated cartoon, features music and dialogue by Dizzy
        Gillespie
1963   *Tonight Show* (vap, 6/13), starring Johnny Carson
        The Cool World (fp), music by Mal Waldron played by Dizzy Gillespie
        Orchestra
        Youth Wants to Know (fa), youths interview Dizzy Gillespie and George
        Wein
1964   *Jazz Casual* (fap), with Leo Wright, Lalo Schifrin, Chuck Lampkin, and
        Robert Cunningham, features interview with Dizzy Gillespie by Ralph
        Gleason
        Dizzy Gillespie (fap), with James Moody, Kenny Barron, Chris White, and
        Rudy Collins at the Lighthouse, Hermosa Beach, California
        Today Show (vap, 8/4)
        The Hat (fpn), animated cartoon with music and dialogue improvised by
        Dizzy Gillespie
        Jazz All the Way (fa, Great Britain)
1966   *Duke Ellington—I Love You Madly* (fa)
        Tonight Show (ap, 5/5), starring Johnny Carson

1967   *Monterey Jazz Festival* (fap), with Carmen McRae
       It Don't Mean a Thing (fp), animated cartoon, Denmark
1968   *Bell Telephone Hour: Jazz the Intimate Art* (vap), with Louis Armstrong,
         Dave Brubeck, and Charles Lloyd
       Contemporary Memorial (nap/CBS)
       Tonight Show (vap, 7/26), starring Johnny Carson
       Monterey Jazz (fap), with James Moody, Rudy Collins, Michael Longo, and
         Christopher White
1969   *Duke Ellington at the White House* (fa)
       Al Hirt Show (vap)
1970   *Tonight Show* (vap, 2/19), starring Johnny Carson
       Merv Griffin Show (vap, 4/24)
       Al Hirt Show (vap, 5/9)
       Tonight Show (vap, 11/10), starring Johnny Carson
       Legacy of the Drum (fap), with Duke Mitchell and Willie Ruff
1971   *4th Bill Cosby Special* (vap)
       Til the Butcher Cuts Him Down (fap), at a New Orleans jazz festival
       Just Dizzy (vap/NJPT), featuring Milt Jackson, James Moody, Hank Jones,
         Sam Jones, and Mickey Roker
1972   *Timex All-Star Swing Festival* (vap)
       Jazz Is Our Religion (vap, Great Britain)
       Jazz the American Art Form (vap/WABC)
1973   *Singer Bowl Renamed* (fap/WNGT), with others on occasion of Singer
         Bowl, Louis Armstrong Stadium
       Dizzy in Brazil (fap), with Al Gafa, Michael Longo, Earl May, and Mickey
         Roker
1974   *Voyage to Next* (fp), animated cartoon; music composed and performed by
         Dizzy Gillespie
1975   *Newport Jazz Festival* (fap/ABC), with Sonny Stitt and Art Blakey
       Profile: Dizzy Gillespie (vap/SC-ETV), first music teacher Mrs. Alice Wil-
         son and childhood friend and pianist Bernis Tillman
1976   *In Performance at Wolf Trap* (vap/WTOP), with Billy Eckstine and Earl
         "Fatha" Hines
       Second Chance Sea (fp), animated cartoon, trumpet solo
       The Rompin', Stompin', Hot and Heavy, Cool and Groovy All-Star Jazz Show
         (vap/CBS), with Count Basie, Lionel Hampton, Max Roach, Stan Getz,
         Herbie Hancock, and Joe Williams
       Everybody Rides the Carousel (fp), animated cartoon, trumpet solo
       Like It Is (vap/WABC), with Michael Longo, Al Gafa, Benjamin Brown,
         and Mickey Roker. Features interview with Dizzy Gillespie regarding his
         views on U.S. Bicentennial and South Africa
       Soundstage: Dizzy Gillespie's Be Bop Reunion (vap), with Kenny Clarke,
         Al Haig, Milt Jackson, Ray Brown, James Moody, Sarah Vaughan, and
         Joe Carroll
1977   *Tonight Show* (vap, 12/27), starring Johnny Carson
       Whither Whether (fn), animated cartoon, voice only
1978   *Like It Is* (va/WABC), panel discussion with Reggie Workman, Bobbie
         Humphrey, and Gil Scott Heron
       Big Band Bash (vap/WNET)
       Soundstage: David Amram and His Friends (vap/WTTW)

HONORS AND AWARDS

Esquire Magazine New Star Award—1944
Metronome Magazine Jazz Polls
  Best Trumpet, 1947
  Best Trumpet, 1948
  Band of the Year, 1948
  Best Trumpet, 1949
  Second Place Band of the Year, 1949
  Best Trumpet, 1950
  Second Place Best Trumpet, 1951
  Second Place Best Trumpet, 1952
  Second Place Best Trumpet, 1953
  Second Place Best Trumpet, 1954
  Second Place Best Trumpet, 1955
  Best Trumpet, 1956
  Third Place Best Trumpet, 1957
  Third Place Best Trumpet, 1958
  Second Place Best Trumpet, 1959
  Second Place Best Trumpet, 1960
Jazz Hot Magazine Poll (France and Western Europe)
  Second Place Best Trumpet, 1948 (First Place, Louis Armstrong, 1948–53)
  Second Place Best Trumpet, 1949
  Second Place Best Trumpet, 1950
  Second Place Best Trumpet, 1951
  Second Place Best Trumpet, 1952
  Second Place Best Trumpet, 1953
  Best Trumpet, 1954
  Best Trumpet, 1955
  Best Trumpet, 1956
  Second Place Best Trumpet, 1957 (First Place, Miles Davis 1957–68. Damn!)
  Second Place Best Trumpet, 1958
  Second Place Best Trumpet, 1959
  Second Place Best Trumpet, 1960
  Second Place Best Trumpet, 1961
  Second Place Best Trumpet, 1962
  Second Place Best Trumpet, 1963
  Second Place Best Trumpet, 1964
  Second Place Best Trumpet, 1965
  Second Place Best Trumpet, 1966
  Second Place Best Trumpet, 1967
  Second Place Best Trumpet, 1968

Downbeat Magazine Jazz Polls
  Best Trumpet, 1956
  Best Trumpet, Readers' Poll, 1959
  Ninth Member Music Hall of Fame, Readers of *Downbeat,* 1960
  Best Trumpet, International Jazz Critics Poll, 1960
  Best Trumpet, International Jazz Critics Poll, 1961
  Best Trumpet, International Jazz Critics Poll, 1962
  Best Trumpet, International Jazz Critics Poll, 1963
  Best Trumpet, International Jazz Critics Poll, 1971
  Best Trumpet, International Jazz Critics Poll, 1972
  Best Trumpet, International Jazz Critics Poll, 1973
  Best Trumpet, International Jazz Critics Poll, 1974
  Best Trumpet, International Jazz Critics Poll, 1975
  Best Trumpet, International Jazz Critics Poll, 1976
Playboy Magazine Jazz Polls
  Third Trumpet, 1957; Readers' Poll
  Third Trumpet, 1958; Readers' Poll
  Fourth Trumpet, 1959; Readers' Poll
  Third Trumpet, 1960; Readers' Poll
  Third Trumpet, 1961; Readers' Poll
  Second Trumpet, 1962; Readers' Poll
  Second Trumpet, 1963; Readers' Poll
  Third Trumpet, 1964; Readers' Poll
  Fourth Trumpet, 1965; Readers' Poll
  Third Trumpet, 1966; Readers' Poll
  Fourth Trumpet, 1967; Readers' Poll
  Winner Best Trumpet; Musicians' Poll, 1960–71
Jazzmobile Award—July 28, 1967
Key to the City, Laurinburg, N. C., 1967
National Academy of Recording Arts and Sciences, Nomination for the Best Jazz
  Performance by a Group, *Giants* Album, 1971
National Academy of Recording Arts and Sciences, Nomination for the Best Jazz
  Performance by a Soloist, "Portrait of Jenny," 1971
Handel Medallion, City of New York, July 4, 1972
Richmond College, Staten Island Music Workshop, November 8, 1972
Paul Robeson Award, Rutgers University Institute of Jazz Studies, 1972
Branford College, Yale University, Duke Ellington Fellow, October 14, 1972
Manhattan School of Music, Contemporary Jazz Ensemble Workshop, May 16, 1973
The National Association of Jazz Educators, Quinnipac College Jazz Festival, 1974
Quinnipac College, 7th Annual Jazz Festival, 1974
Monterey Jazz Festival, April 21, 1974
Key to the City of Hamden, Connecticut, April 24, 1974
WRVR Jazz Radio, September 13, 1975
Citation Mayor of the City of New York, Abraham D. Beame, September 13, 1975
National Academy of Recording Arts and Sciences, Grammy Award, Best Jazz Per-
  formance, *Oscar Peterson and Dizzy Gillespie,* 1975
Grand Master Award, Jazz Heritage Society, October 3, 1976
Citation, Joint Session of the South Carolina Legislature, March 9, 1976
National Academy of Recording Arts and Sciences, Dizzy Gillespie and Machito,
  Nomination Best Jazz Performance by a Big Band, *Afro-Cuban Jazz Moods,* 1976
Ruffin High School Band, Ruffin, South Carolina, March 10, 1976
Tau Nu Chapter, Omega Psi Phi Fraternity, Inc., Fort Wayne, Indiana, 1976
National Music Award, The Music Industry, 1976
Jazzmobile Incorporated, Grand Master of Jazz Award, August 26, 1976

WRVR on sixtieth birthday, October 21, 1977

Jazz Showcase and Joe Segal, October 21, 1977

Students, Faculty, and Staff, Cheyney State College, October 21, 1977

Mather House, Harvard University, Honorary Associate, April 1977

City of Washington, D.C., Anacostia Neighborhood Museum, Distinguished Service Award

Key to the City, Telluride, Colorado

Key to the City, Annapolis, Maryland

Bill Sears Heavenly Horn Award, Winner (Runner up, Angel Gabriel)

Music Educators National Conference

Honorary Degrees: Ph.D. Rutgers University, 1972
              Ph.D. Chicago Conservatory of Music, 1978

INDEX

ABOUT THE COAUTHOR

Al Fraser (Wilmot Alfred Fraser), a native of Charleston, South Carolina, is Associate Professor of African-American Studies at Cheyney State College, Pennsylvania. He is the son of Wilmot J. and Mary Young Fraser of Charleston. A long-time friend and former next door neighbor of Dizzy and Lorraine Gillespie, he has served as a United Nations press officer and a program officer at the African-American Institute where he edited the magazine *Baobab*. He is a graduate of Howard University and the School of Advanced International Studies of the Johns Hopkins University.

His other published works include (under the pseudonym B. Poyas) *Les Noirs aux États-Unis Pour Lecteurs Africains,* a history of African-Americans for French-speaking African readers, coauthored with J.-P. N'Diaye and Joachim Bassene; articles in *Révolution* and *L'Express;* and feature stories, distributed by International Feature Service, which have been reprinted by newspapers around the world. His poetry has appeared in *Dasein, Burning Spear, Black Fire, Drumvoices,* and *Colloquy.*

Author and publisher with Joan Ramsey of *Rhythm and Reading,* a method for teaching language skills through popular music, he has completed an unpublished novella for young readers, *Ace Carrier's Dream,* and has appeared as a guest of anthropologist Colin Turnbull in the NBC television series "Man in Africa," produced by the American Museum of Natural History. His current projects include writing a docudrama for film and television on the life and career of Dizzy Gillespie and pursuing a doctoral degree in folklore at the University of Pennsylvania.

S781.57   G42   266-84

Gillespie

TO BE, OR NOT ... TO BOP - MEMOIRS

DATE DUE

S781.57   G42   266-84

Gillespie

TO BE, OR NOT ... TO BOP - MEMOIRS

                                    14/95

DATE DUE	BORROWER'S NAME
JE 0 4 '90	BEKAH ZUERCHER